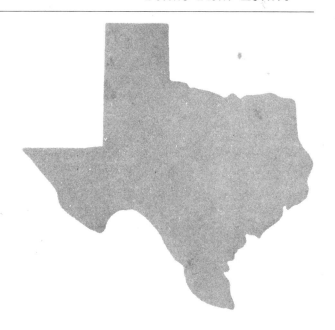

CHARLES J. JACOBUS

BRUCE HARWOOD

Texas Real Estate

FOURTH EDITION

A Reston Book
PRENTICE-HALL, INC.
Englewood Cliffs, New Jersey 07632

Library of Congress Cataloging-in-Publication Data

JACOBUS, CHARLES J.
  Texas real estate.

  "A Reston book."
  Includes index.
    1. Real estate business—Law and legislation—
Texas.   2. Vendors and purchasers—Texas.   3. Real
property—Texas.   4. Real estate business—Texas.
I. Harwood, Bruce M. (date).   II. Title.
KFT1482.R4J32 1987   346.76404'37   87–2328
ISBN 0–13–912213–3   347.6406437

Cover photo: *Courtesy of the San Jacinto Museum of History Association,*
  Houston Texas
Cover design: *Diane Saxe*
Manufacturing buyer: *Carol Bystrom/Margaret Rizzi*

Texas Real Estate, fourth edition
CHARLES J. JACOBUS & BRUCE HARWOOD

A Reston Book
Published by Prentice-Hall, Inc.
A Division of Simon & Schuster
Englewood Cliffs, New Jersey 07632

Printed in the United States of America

10 9 8 7 6 5 4 3 2 1

ISBN 0-13-912213-3 01

PRENTICE-HALL INTERNATIONAL (UK) LIMITED, *London*
PRENTICE-HALL OF AUSTRALIA PTY. LIMITED, *Sydney*
PRENTICE-HALL CANADA INC., *Toronto*
PRENTICE-HALL HISPANOAMERICANA, S.A., *Mexico*
PRENTICE-HALL OF INDIA PRIVATE LIMITED, *New Delhi*
PRENTICE-HALL OF JAPAN, INC., *Tokyo*
PRENTICE-HALL OF SOUTHEAST ASIA PTE. LTD., *Singapore*
EDITORA PRENTICE-HALL DO BRASIL, LTDA., *Rio de Janeiro*

*This book is dedicated
to the memory of Dr. Bruce Harwood
and his commitment to excellence
in real estate education.*

CONTENTS

APPENDICES

LIST OF ILLUSTRATIONS & TABLES

PREFACE

It is becoming more and more apparent that the state of Texas is on the forefront of real estate law and practice. Texas currently has the highest educational requirements for real estate licensees. The Texas Real Estate Research Center, located in College Station, Texas, is the premier real estate research facility in the country. The State Bar of Texas is widely acknowledged as one of the leading bar associations in the country for real estate research and education. There are many excellent resources to draw upon, and this new fourth edition is a primary beneficiary of Texas's efforts to pursue excellence in real estate education. Updating this edition—with the new Texas statutes, new Real Estate Commission forms, and other pertinent changes currently emerging in the licensee's day-to-day business practice—makes one realize how fast these changes occur and how beneficial they have been for Texans.

The subject of real estate has never been as simple as some have tried to make it. Authoritative national textbooks, while functional and complete, have tended to neglect local trends and practices of the business, and include topics not applicable to the local areas. This text was organized to be authoritative yet functionally adapted for the Texas real estate practitioner and student. Without additional supplements, it is intended to facilitate your learning of Texas real estate, along with national trends, in a single integrated volume.

An effort has also been made to cover most substantive Texas topics in such depth that this book can be used for future reference as well as for an introduction to other in-depth considerations of Texas real estate. Reproduction of the Texas Real Estate Licensing Act and the required promulgated forms have been included. The official regulations are detailed and voluminous. They are readily available, complete and in a convenient booklet, from the Texas Real Estate Commission at P.O. Box 12188, Capital Station, Austin, Texas 78711. As a first assignment, you should write for the booklet and get to know it well.

A SPECIAL NOTE
TO READERS

The authors anticipate that as many women as men will read this book. However, it would make the sentences in this book harder to read if "he and she" and "his and her" were used on every possible occasion. Therefore, when you read, "he," "his," or "him" in this book, please note that they are being used in their grammatical sense and refer to women as well as men.

*   *   *

This publication is designed to provide accurate and authoritative information in regard to the subject matter covered. It is sold with the understanding that the publisher is not engaged in rendering legal, accounting, or other professional service. If legal advice or other expert assistance is required, the services of a competent professional should be sought.

From a Declaration of Principles jointly
adapted by a Committee of the American Bar
Association and a Committee of Publishers and Associations

ACKNOWLEDGMENTS

Special thanks to the following people for their assistance in preparing this book: Mark Moseley, Richard Chumbley, Carroll Gentry, Robert Goforth, Jim Howze, Cheryl E. Nance, Tina L. Tussay, Rita Vitale, Sharon Teusink, Ralph Tamper, Paul Metzger, Lee Stringfellow, Dean Stout, Alicia Smith, Ken Combs, Betty Barrett, Gerry Irby, Katherine Tyra, Wayne Landin, Dorothy Turner, and Bob Lewis.

C.J.J.

Introduction to Real Estate

Welcome!

Real estate is an exciting business. But it is also a demanding one since it requires that one know the ethical and business principles fundamental to the successful selling and buying of real property. There are some who say that the only way to learn these principles is by experience. That can be extremely time-consuming and costly, no matter how good a teacher experience is. A more logical approach is to learn a substantial portion of this complicated body of knowledge from experts already at work in the field. Then personal experience can be acquired. With that combination in mind, this book has been written to provide you with an understanding of the basic principles and business fundamentals of real estate. Emphasis is placed on an easily readable presentation that combines explanations of "how" things are done in real estate with "why" they are done.

HOW TO READ THIS BOOK

At the beginning of each chapter (2 through 23) there is a list of the new "Key Terms" that you will learn, along with brief definitions. Read these before starting your work in each chapter. In the body of each chapter these terms, along with other terms important to real estate, are set in **boldface type** and given an in-depth discussion. At the end of each chapter is a vocabulary review plus questions and problems. These are designed to help you test yourself on your comprehension of the material in the chapter you've just read. The answers are given in Appendix H in the back of the book.

A combined index-glossary is also in the back of this book. This approach was taken to help reinforce your familiarity with the language of real estate. When you use this index-glossary, you will receive a short definition followed by a page reference for more detailed discussion.

A unique feature of this book is its simplified documents. *1*

Deeds, mortgages and title policies, for example, are usually written in legal language and small type that defies comprehension by anyone except a lawyer. In the chapters ahead, you will find simplified versions of these documents, written in plain English and set in standard size type. The benefit to you is that you will come away with an understanding as to what is actually inside these important real estate documents. A number of sample documents printed by the State Bar of Texas are also included.

Another special feature of this book is the wide margin on each page. Besides its eye appeal, it is helpful for locating subject headings, and it provides a handy place for your study notes.

Persons who wish to make a career in real estate may want additional questions, problems and situations in order to test and improve their grasp of the subject. An accompanying workbook by Paul Metzger, Bruce Harwood, and John T. Ellis is designed to fill that need. It is available from bookstores and the publisher of this book and is called *Texas Real Estate Resource Book*.

TRANSACTION OVERVIEW

Figure 1:1 provides a visual summary of the real estate transaction cycle. It is included here to give you an overview of the different steps involved in the sale of real property and to show how the steps are related to each other. The chapter where each step is discussed is also shown. Whether your point of view is that of a real estate agent, owner, buyer, or seller, you will find the chapters which follow to be informative and valuable.

Chapter Organization

Great care has been taken in organizing this text so as to carefully build your knowledge of real estate. For example, land description methods and rights and interests in land are necessary to sales contracts, abstracts, deeds, mortgages and listings and therefore are discussed early in the text.

In Chapter 2, you will find such topics as metes and bounds and tract maps. You will also find a discussion of what is real estate and what is not, and how land is physically and economically different from other commodities. Having described real estate, the next logical step is to look at the

AN OVERVIEW OF A REAL ESTATE TRANSACTION

Figure 1:1

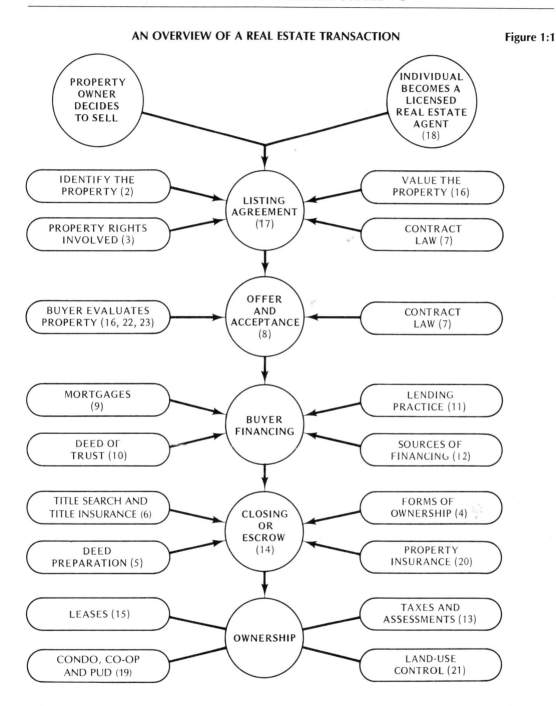

NOTE: Numbers in parentheses refer to Chapter Numbers.

various rights and interests that exist in a given parcel of land. In Chapter 3 you will see that there is much more to ownership of land than meets the eye! In Chapter 4 we look at how a given right or interest in land can be held by an individual, by two or more persons, or by a business entity. Included in this chapter are discussions of joint tenancy, tenancy in common, and community property.

Chapters 5 and 6 deal with the process by which the ownership of real estate is transferred from one person to another. In particular, Chapter 5 discusses deeds and wills, and Chapter 6 deals with how a person gives evidence to the world that he possesses a given right or interest in land. Abstracts and title insurance are among the topics included.

In Chapters 7 and 8, we turn to contract law and its application to offers and acceptances. Because so much of what takes place in real estate is in the form of contracts, you will want to have a solid understanding of what makes a contract legally binding, and what doesn't.

Chapters 9 through 12 are devoted to real estate finance. In Chapter 9, mortgages and the laws regarding their use are explained. Chapter 10 covers the deed of trust and is intended for readers in those states, including Texas, where the deed of trust is used in place of a mortgage. Amortized loans, points, FHA and VA programs, loan application, and mortgage insurance are discussed in Chapter 11. Mortgage lenders, the secondary mortgage market, due-on-sale clauses, adjustable rate mortgages, and financing alternatives are covered in Chapter 12.

In Chapter 13, we see how property taxes and assessments are calculated; and Chapter 14 explains title closing and escrow. Chapter 15 deals with leasing real estate and includes a sample lease document with discussion. Chapter 16 explores the language, principles, and techniques of real estate appraisal.

In Chapter 17 we examine the relationship between real estate agents, buyers, and sellers. Special emphasis is placed on the duties and obligations of the broker to his clients and on fair housing laws. The chapter following that deals with real estate license law requirements, how a salesperson goes about choosing a broker to affiliate with, and with professional ethics.

The remaining chapters of this book deal with a number of individual and specialized real estate topics. Chapter 19 explores the condominium, cooperative, and planned unit development forms of real estate ownership. Included is a look at how they are created and the various rights and interests in land that are created by them. In Chapter 20 we take a brief and informative look at property insurance. As an owner of real property, you should know how to insure against financial loss due to property damage and public liability.

Zoning, land planning and deed restrictions are covered in Chapter 21. These are important topics because any limitations on a landowner's right to develop and use his land can have a substantial effect on the value of his property. Chapter 22 explores several pertinent and timely relationships between the value of real estate and the condition of the United States economy. The final chapter, Chapter 23, is an introduction to the opportunities available to you as a real estate investor. Topics include tax shelter, equity build-up, what to buy and when to buy.

Following the final chapter are several appendices which you will find useful. There are construction illustrations to help acquaint you with construction terminology. There are appendices with the Texas Real Estate License Act, Texas Standard Contract Forms, and the Texas Canons of Professional Conduct. Lastly, you will find a short real estate math review section, measurement conversion tables, and the answers to the quizzes and problems found at the end of Chapter 2 through 23.

CAREER OPPORTUNITIES

The contents and organization of this book are designed for persons who are interested in real estate because they now own or plan to own real estate, and for persons interested in real estate as a career. It is to those who are considering real estate as a profession that the balance of this chapter is devoted.

Most persons who think of real estate from the career standpoint see only the real estate agent who specializes in selling homes. This is quite natural as home selling is the most visible segment of the real estate industry. Selling residential real estate is how most people enter the real estate business, and where most practicing real estate licensees make their living. Residential sales experience is a good way to find out whether real estate sales appeals to you, and whether residential property is the type of property in which you wish to specialize.

RESIDENTIAL BROKERAGE

Residential brokerage requires a broad knowledge of the community and its neighborhoods, finance, real estate law, economics, and the money market. Working hours will often include nights and weekends as these times are usually most convenient to buyers and sellers. A residential agent must also supply and drive his or her own automobile—one that is suitable for taking clients to see property.

In only a few real estate offices are new residential salespersons given a minimum guaranteed salary or a draw against future commissions. Therefore, a newcomer should have enough capital to survive until the first commissions are earned—and that can take four to six months. Additionally, the salesperson must be capable of developing and handling a personal budget that will withstand the feast and famine cycles that can occur in real estate selling.

A person who is adept at people relations, who can identify clients' buying motives, and who can find property to fit, will probably be quite successful in this business.

COMMERCIAL BROKERAGE

Commercial brokers specialize in income-producing properties such as apartment and office buildings, retail stores, and warehouses. In this specialty, the salesperson is primarily selling monetary benefits. These benefits are the income, appreciation, mortgage reduction and tax shelter that a property can reasonably be expected to produce.

To be successful in commercial brokerage, one must be very competent in mathematics, know how to finance transactions, and keep abreast of current tax laws. One must also have a sense for what makes a good investment, what makes an investment salable, and what the growth possibilities are in the neighborhood where a property is located.

Commission income from commercial brokerage is likely to be less frequent, but in larger amounts compared to residential brokerage. The time required to break into the business is longer, but once in the business, agent turnover is low. The working hours of a commercial broker are much closer to regular business hours than for those in residential selling.

Industrial brokers specialize in finding suitable land and buildings for industrial concerns. This includes leasing and developing industrial property as well as listing and selling it. An industrial broker must be familiar with industry requirements such as proximity to raw materials, water and power, labor supplies, and transportation. He must also know about local building, zoning, and tax laws as they pertain to possible sites, and about the schools, housing, cultural and recreational facilities that would be used by future employees of the plant.

Commissions are irregular, but usually substantial. Working hours are regular business hours and one's sales efforts are primarily aimed at locating facts and figures and presenting them to clients in an orderly fashion. Industrial clients are usually sophisticated business people. Gaining entry to an industrial brokerage and acquiring a client list can be slow.

INDUSTRIAL BROKERAGE

With the rapid disappearance of the family farm, the farm broker's role is changing. Today he must be equally capable of handling the 160-acre spread of farmer Jones and the 10,000-acre operation owned by an agribusiness corporation. College training in agriculture is an advantage and on-the-job training is a must. Knowledge of soil types, seeds, fertilizers, production methods, new machinery, government subsidies, and tax laws are vital to success. Farm brokerage offers as many opportunities to earn commissions and fees from leasing and property management as from listing and selling property.

FARM BROKERAGE

For an investment property, the property manager's job is to supervise every aspect of a property's operation so as to produce the highest possible financial return over the longest period of time. The manager's tasks include renting, tenant relations, building repair and maintenance, accounting, advertising and supervision of personnel and tradesmen.

The current boom in condominiums has resulted in a growing demand for property managers to maintain them. In addition, large businesses that own property for their own

PROPERTY MANAGEMENT

use hire property managers. Property managers are usually paid a salary, and if the property is a rental, a bonus for keeping the building fully occupied. To be successful, a property manager should be at ease with tenants, a public relations expert, handy with tools, a good bookkeeper, and knowledgeable about laws applicable to rental units.

APARTMENT LOCATORS   In recent years, the service of helping tenants find rental units and helping landlords find tenants has become increasingly popular. This is normally a free service to the public. Locators are paid commissions by management companies and owners of apartment projects for finding qualified tenants. A locating agent must have an in-depth knowledge of the apartment complexes in the community and their requirements for tenants. The locating business has expanded in the last few years to include the leasing of condominiums, townhouses and single-family homes.

An offshoot of apartment locators are roommate locators. These are especially popular in cities with substantial numbers of single persons. Roommate locators are central places where persons looking for other persons who are willing to share living space can meet. The locator service maintains files on persons with space to share (such as the second bedroom in a two-bedroom apartment) and those looking for space. The files will contain information on location, rent, male or female, smoking or nonsmoking, etc. Most roommate and tenant locator services have been started by individual entrepreneurs and are not affiliated with real estate offices. In Texas, a real estate license is required to operate as an apartment locator or a roommate locator.

REAL ESTATE APPRAISING   The job of the real estate appraiser is to gather and evaluate all available facts affecting a property's value. Appraisal is a real estate career opportunity that demands a special set of skills of its own. The job requires practical experience, technical education and good judgment. If you have an analytical mind and like to collect and interpret data, you might consider becoming a real estate appraiser. The job combines office work and field work, and the income of an expert appraiser can match that of a top real estate salesperson. One can be an independent appraiser, or there are numerous opportunities to work as a salaried appraiser for local tax authorities or lending institutions.

GOVERNMENT SERVICE

Approximately one-third of the land in the United States is government owned. This includes vacant and forested lands, office buildings, museums, parks, zoos, schools, hospitals, public housing, libraries, fire and police stations, roads and highways, subways, airports and courthouses. All of these are real estate and all of these require government employees who can negotiate purchases and sales, appraise, finance, manage, plan and develop. Cities, counties and state governments all have extensive real estate holdings. At the federal level, the Forest Service, Park Service, Department of Agriculture, Army Corps of Engineers, Bureau of Land Management, and General Services Administration are all major landholders. In addition to outright real estate ownership, government agencies such as the Federal Housing Administration, Veterans Administration, and Federal Home Loan Bank employ thousands of real estate specialists to keep their real estate lending programs operating smoothly.

LAND DEVELOPMENT

Most new houses in the United States are built by developers who in turn sell them to homeowners and investors. Some houses are built by small-scale developers who produce only a few a year. Others are part of 400-house subdivisions and 40-story condominiums that are developed and constructed by large corporations that have their own planning, appraising, financing, construction, and marketing personnel. There is equal opportunity for success in development whether you build 4 houses a year or work for a firm that builds 400 a year.

URBAN PLANNING

Urban planners work with local governments and civic groups for the purpose of anticipating future growth and landuse changes. The urban planner makes recommendations for new streets, highways, sewer and water lines, schools, parks and libraries. The current emphasis on environmental protection and controlled growth has made urban planning one of real estate's most rapidly expanding specialties. An urban planning job is usually a salaried position and does not emphasize sales ability.

MORTGAGE FINANCING   Specialists in mortgage financing have a dual role: (1) to find economically sound properties for lenders, and (2) to locate money for borrowers. A mortgage specialist can work independently, receiving a fee from the borrower for locating a lender, or as a salaried employee of a lending institution. The commission paid to a mortgage specialist on a multi-million dollar loan can be quite substantial.

SECURITIES AND SYNDICATIONS   Limited partnerships and other forms of real estate syndications that combine the investment capital of a number of investors to buy large properties have become popular over the past 25 years. The investment opportunities and professional management offered by syndications are eagerly sought after by people with money to invest in real estate. As a result, there are a number of job opportunities connected with the creation, promotion and management of real estate syndications.

COUNSELING   Real estate counseling involves giving others advice about real estate for a fee. A counselor must have a very broad knowledge of real estate—including financing, appraising, brokerage, management, development, construction, investing, leasing, zoning, taxes, title, economics and law. To remain in business as a counselor, one must develop a good track record of successful suggestions and advice.

RESEARCH AND EDUCATION   A person interested in real estate research can concentrate on solutions to applied questions such as improved construction materials and management methods or to economic questions such as "What is the demand for homes going to be next year in this community (state, country)?"

Opportunities abound in real estate education. Nearly all states require the completion of specified real estate courses before a real estate license can be issued. A growing number of states also require continued education for license renewal. As a result, persons with experience in the industry and an ability to effectively teach the subject are much sought after as instructors.

One of the advantages of the free-enterprise system is that you can choose to become a full-time investor solely for yourself. There are a substantial number of people who have quit their jobs to work full time with their investment properties and who have done quite well at it. A popular and successful route for many has been to purchase, inexpensively and with a low down payment, a small apartment building that has not been well maintained, but is in a good neighborhood. The property is then thoroughly reconditioned and rents are raised. This process increases the value of the property. The increase is parlayed into a larger building—often through a tax-deferred exchange—and the process is repeated. Alternatively, the investor can increase the mortgage loan on the building and take the cash he receives as a "salary" for himself or use it as a down payment on another not-too-well maintained apartment building in a good neighborhood.

Other individual investors have done well financially by searching newspaper ads and regularly visiting real estate brokerage offices looking for underpriced properties which can be sold at a mark-up. A variation of this is to write to out-of-town property owners in a given neighborhood to see if any wish to sell at a bargain price. Another approach is to become a small-scale developer and contractor. (No license is needed if you work with your own property.) Through your own personal efforts you create value in your projects and then hold them as investments. One should be cautioned, however, that there are very few legitimate "get rich quick" schemes in the real estate business.

FULL-TIME INVESTOR

Property owners dealing with their own property are not required to hold a real estate license. However, any person who for compensation or the promise of compensation lists or offers to list, sells or offers to sell, buys or offers to buy, negotiates or offers to negotiate either directly or indirectly for the purpose of bringing about a sale, purchase or option to purchase, exchange, auction, lease, or rental of real estate,

LICENSE REQUIREMENTS

or any interest in real estate, is required to hold a valid real estate license. Texas also requires persons offering their services as real estate appraisers and property managers to hold real estate licenses.

If your real esate plans are such that you may need a license, you should turn to Chapter 18 and read the material on real estate licensing.

ADDITIONAL READINGS

In Search of Excellence by **Thomas Peters** and **Robert Waterman, Jr**. (Harper and Row, 1982, 360 pages). Valuable and interesting reading for anyone planning to go into business, including real estate, and be successful.

The Language of Real Estate, 2nd ed. by **John W. Reilly**. (Real Estate Education Co., 1982, 630 pages). This single-volume reference book contains over 2,200 of the most frequently encountered real estate terms. Includes basic definitions, examples and cross references.

Real Estate Programs. (National Association of Realtors, 1984, 318 pages). This is a guide to real estate courses offered at universities, colleges and junior colleges in the United States. Includes school names and addresses, course titles, scholarship availability, degrees offered and program goals (license preparation, continuing education, general education, professional training, theory, analysis, etc.). Updated periodically.

"A Self-Evaluation Quiz" by **Ron Riggins**. (Real Estate Today, Nov/Dec 84, page 28). Article and three-page quiz to help determine your potential for success in real estate. Looks at competence, professionalism, determination and attitude.

Texas Real Estate Resource Book by **Paul Metzger, Bruce Harwood,** and **John Ellis.** (Prentice-Hall, 1987, 360 pages). Contains over 1,400 practice questions with answers. Keyed to the chapters in the book you are now reading.

Nature and Description of Real Estate

Base line: an east-west or geographer's line selected as a basic reference in the rectangular survey system

Fixture: an object that has been attached to land so as to become real estate

Improvements: any form of land development, such as buildings, roads, fences, pipelines, etc.

Meridian: a north-south line running from the starting point as the correlated base line, used as references in mapping land

Metes and bounds: a method of land description that identifies a parcel by specifying its shape and boundaries

Monument: an iron pipe, stone, tree or other fixed point used in making a survey

Personal property: a right or interest in things of a temporary or movable nature; anything not classed as real property

Real estate: any land and its improvements in a physical sense as well as the rights to own or use both

Recorded plat: a subdivision map filed in the county recorder's office that shows the location and boundaries of individual parcels of land

Riparian right: the right of a landowner whose land borders a river or stream to use and enjoy that water

What is real estate? **Real estate** or **real property** is land and the improvements made to land, and the rights to use them. Let us begin in this chapter by looking more closely at what is meant by land and improvements. Then in the next chapter we shall focus our attention on the various rights one may possess in land and improvements.

LAND

Often we think of land as only the surface of the earth. But, it is substantially more than that. As Figure 2:1 illustrates, land starts at the center of the earth, passes through the earth's surface, and continues on into space. An understanding of this concept is important because, given a particular parcel of land, it is possible for one person to own the rights to use its surface **(surface rights),** another to own the rights to drill or dig below its surface **(subsurface rights),** and still

Figure 2:1

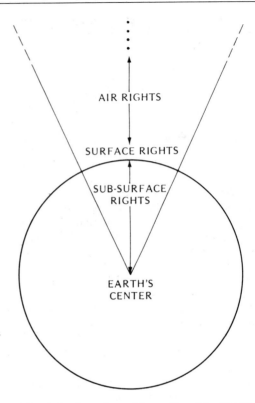

AIR RIGHTS

SURFACE RIGHTS

SUB-SURFACE
RIGHTS

EARTH'S
CENTER

Land includes the surface of the earth and the sky above
and everything to the center of the earth.

another to own the rights to use the airspace above it **(air rights).**

IMPROVEMENTS

Anything affixed to land with the intent of being permanent is considered to be part of the land and therefore real estate. Thus houses, schools, factories, barns, fences, roads, pipelines and landscaping are real estate. As a group, these are referred to as **improvements** because they improve or develop land.

Being able to identify what is real estate and what is not is important. For example, in conveying ownership to a house, only the lot is described in the deed. It is not necessary to describe the dwelling unit itself, or the landscaping, driveways, sidewalks, wiring or plumbing. Items that are not a part of the land, such as tables, chairs, beds, desks, automobiles, farm machinery, and the like, are classified as **personal**

property; if the right to use them is to be transferred to the buyer, there must be a separate **bill of sale** in addition to the deed.

When an object that was once personal property is attached to land (or a building thereon) so as to become real estate, it is called a **fixture.** As a rule, a fixture is the property of the landowner and when the land is conveyed to a new owner, it is automatically included with the land.

FIXTURES

Whether or not an object becomes real estate depends on whether the object was affixed or installed with the apparent intent of permanently improving the land. In Texas, the determination of what constitutes a fixture has primarily revolved around three criteria:

Tests of a Fixture

1. Method of annexation to the real estate;
2. Fitness or adaptation to a particular use of the premises;
3. The intention of the parties.

The first test, **method of annexation,** refers to how the object is attached to the land. Ordinarily, when an object which was once personal property is attached to land by virtue of its being imbedded in the land or affixed to the land by means of cement, nails, bolts, etc., it becomes a fixture. To illustrate, when asphalt and concrete for driveways and sidewalks are still on the delivery truck, they are movable and therefore personal property. But once they are poured into place, the asphalt and concrete become part of the land. Similarly, lumber, wiring, pipes, doors, toilets, sinks, water heaters, furnaces and other construction materials change from personal property to real estate when they become part of a building. Items brought into the house that do not become permanently affixed to the land remain personal property; for example, furniture, clothing, cooking utensils, radios and television sets.

Annexation

Historically, the manner of attachment was the only method of classifying an object as personal property or real estate, but as time progressed, this test alone was no longer adequate. For example, how would you classify storm win-

Adaptation

dows, which for a few months of the year are temporarily clipped or hung in position? For the answer, we must apply a second test: **How is the article adapted** to the building? If the storm windows were custom cut for the windows in the building, they are automatically included in the purchase or rental of the building. Storm windows of a general design and suitable for use on other buildings are personal property and are not automatically included with the building. Note the difference: in the first case, the storm windows are specifically adapted to the building; in the second case, they are not.

Intention   Of the three tests, preeminence is given to the question of intention of the parties. **Intention** is inferred from the nature of the article, the relationship and situation of the parties involved, the policy of the law, the mode of annexation, and the purpose or use for which the annexation is made. So intention, in its broadest sense, includes the other two criteria.

Prior Liens Against   In addition to the misunderstandings that often arise be-
Fixtures   tween buyer and seller in determining the intention of the parties regarding fixtures, there are also priorities given in the law which create a priority interest in fixtures if that interest is timely and properly recorded. If the interest is of record, the buyer may find that an important fixture may have prior claims by a supplier or vendor that gives the purchaser an inferior priority in the event of nonpayment or subsequent default by the seller. For instance, if a homeowner purchased a central air conditioning unit from an air conditioning contractor, the air conditioning contractor would probably record and properly file a chattel mortgage to reflect his interest in the air conditioning system until it is fully paid for. The air conditioning system once affixed to the real estate is a part of that real estate. However, Texas statute gives that air conditioning contractor, as a materialman and supplier, the right to remove that air conditioner in the event it is not paid for. Therefore, even a subsequent purchaser may discover that the air conditioner can be removed after he takes possession of the premises.

Normally, when a tenant makes permanent additions to the property that he is renting, the additions belong to the landlord when the lease or rental agreement expires. However, this can work a particular hardship on tenants operating a trade or business. For example, a supermarket moves into a rented building, then buys and bolts to the floor various **trade fixtures** such as display shelves, meat and dairy coolers, frozenfood counters, and checkout stands. When the supermarket later moves out, do these items, by virtue of their attachment, become the property of the building owner? Modern courts rule that tenant-owned trade fixtures do not become the property of the landlord. However, for the tenant to keep the trade fixtures, they must be removed before the expiration of the lease and without seriously damaging the building.

Trade Fixtures

Trees, cultivated perennial plants, and uncultivated vegetation of any sort are classed as **fructus naturales** and are considered part of the land. Annual cultivated crops are called **fructus industriales** or **emblements** and most courts of law regard them as personal property even though they are attached to the soil.

Ownership of Plants, Trees, and Crops

The ownership of land that borders on a river or stream carries with it the right to use that water in common with the other landowners whose land borders on the same watercourse. This is known as a **riparian right.** The landowner does not have absolute ownership of the water that flows through or past his land, but he may use it in a reasonable manner. Where land borders on a lake or sea, it is said to carry **littoral rights** rather than riparian rights. Littoral rights allow a landowner to use and enjoy the water touching his land provided he does not alter the water's position by artificial means.

Ownership of land normally includes the right to drill for and remove water found below the surface. Where water is not confined to a defined underground waterway, it is known as **percolating water.** When speaking of underground water, the term **water table** refers to the upper limit of percolating water below the earth's surface. It is also called the

WATER RIGHTS

groundwater level. This may be only a few feet below the surface or hundreds of feet down.

Texas Department of Water Resources

The laws of the State of Texas with respect to water rights are contained in the State's Water Code. The agency of the state given primary responsibility for implementing the provisions of the Constitution and laws of the State of Texas is the Texas Department of Water Resources. This agency is responsible for carrying out legislative, executive, and judicial functions provided under the Texas Water Code, delegated to it by the Constitution and other laws of the State of Texas. The legislative functions of the Department of Water Resources are vested in the Texas Water Development Board. The Texas Department of Water Resources was created for the purpose of assigning the duties and responsibilities and functions of the Texas Water Quality Board and the Texas Water Rights Commission to the new department. Other than reorganization of the State's water agencies, there was no substantive change in the State's water laws.

Water Development Board

The Texas Water Development Board is composed of six members who are appointed by the Governor with the advice and consent of the state Senate. The board establishes and approves all general policies of the Department of Water Resources.

Water Rights Commission

The Texas Water Commission is the agency of the state which exercises the judicial functions of the department. The commission is composed of three members who are appointed by the Governor with the advice and consent of the Senate and each must be from a different section of the state. They hold staggered terms for six years and no person may serve more than two six-year terms. This agency has the function of holding hearings to authorize the issuing of permits and judicial review. Any person affected by a ruling, order, decision or other act of the department may file a petition to review, set aside, modify or suspend the act of the department.

Ownership of Waterways

The Texas Water Code specifies that the water of the ordinary flow, underflow and tides of every flowing river,

natural stream, and lake, and of every bay or arm of the
Gulf of Mexico, and the storm water, flood water, and rain
water, of every river, natural stream, canyon, ravine, depression, and watershed in the State is the property of the State.

Water imported from any source outside the boundaries
of the State for use in the State and which is transported
through the beds and banks of any applicable stream within
the State or by utilizing any facilities owned or operated by
the State is the property of the State. The State may authorize
the use of state water which may be acquired by appropriation
in the manner provided for by statute. Once the permit has
been obtained from the Department of Water Resources, the
right to use the state water under that permit is limited not
only to the amount specifically appropriated, but also to the
amount which can be beneficially used for the purposes specified in the appropriation. All water not used within the specified limits is not considered as having been appropriated.
So if one doesn't use his appropriation, it may be limited or
prohibited in future years.

Texas also reserves, under the Open Beaches Act, the
free and unrestricted right of ingress or egress to and from
the state-owned beaches on the shore of the Gulf of Mexico.
This area extends from the line of mean low tide to the line
of vegetation bordering on the Gulf of Mexico.

Conflicting Claims

If the appropriation has been given to two conflicting
claimants, the first in time is first in right. The only exception
to the doctrine of appropriation by the Department of Water
Resources is that any city or town can make further appropriations of the water for domestic or municipal use without
paying for the water. When a person uses water under the
terms of a certified filing or permit for a period of three years,
he acquires title to his appropriation against any other claimant of the water. Conversely, if any lawful appropriation or
use of state water is willfully abandoned during the three
years, the right to use the water is forfeited and the water
is again subject to appropriation. All persons having an appropriation by the State must file by March 1 of each and every
year a written report to the Department on forms prescribed
by the Department or be subject to a statutory penalty.

State Rights   The Code basically vests water rights in the State. It does not recognize any riparian rights in the owner of any land the title to which passed out of the State of Texas after July 1, 1895. Current owners who can trace their riparian rights to a date prior to that date may still claim them.

State Water Agencies   There are other state agencies which are concerned with specific requirements for water use and water development. They include Water Control and Improvement Districts, Underground Water Conservation Districts, Fresh Water Supply Districts, Municipal Utility Districts, Water Improvement Districts, Drainage Districts, Levee Improvement Districts, and Navigation Districts. There have recently been established Subsidence Districts which affect control and permit procedures for development along the Texas coastal areas. There is a very good chance that if any development is to take place, one or several of the preceding districts or agencies will significantly affect the proposed project.

REALTY, REAL PROPERTY, AND PERSONALTY   **Realty** refers to land and buildings and other improvements from a physical standpoint; **real property** refers to the right to own land and improvements; and **real estate** refers to land and improvements and the rights to own or use them. As a practical matter, however, these three terms are used interchangeably in everyday usage. A similar situation also exists with regard to the terms personal property and personalty. **Personal property** refers to ownership rights to intangibles and to items of a temporary or movable nature, whereas **personalty** refers to the physical object itself. Again, in everyday usage both the object and the right to own it are known as "property." In this book, we shall follow everyday usage because it is standard in the real estate industry and because most people are already familiar with it.

LAND DESCRIPTIONS   There are six commonly used methods of describing the location of land: (1) informal reference, (2) metes and bounds, (3) rectangular survey system, (4) recorded plat, (5) assessor parcel number, and (6) reference to documents other than maps. We shall look at each in detail.

Street numbers and place names are informal references: the house located at 7216 Maple Street; the apartment identified as Apartment 101, 875 First Street; the office identified as Suite 222, 3570 Oakview Boulevard; or the ranch known as the Rocking K Ranch—in each case followed by the city (or county) and state where it is located—are informal references. The advantage of an informal reference is that it is easily understood. The disadvantage from a real estate standpoint is that it is not a precise method of land description: a street number or place name does not provide the boundaries of the land at that location, and these numbers and names change over the years. Consequently, in real estate the use of informal references is limited to situations in which convenience is more important than precision. Thus, in a rental contract, Apartment 101, 875 First Street, City and State, is sufficient for a tenant to find the apartment unit. The apartment need not be described by one of the following more formal land descriptions.

INFORMAL REFERENCES

A **metes and bounds** land description is one which identifies a parcel by specifying its shape and boundaries. Early land descriptions in America depended on convenient natural or man-made objects. A stream might serve to mark one side of a parcel, an old oak tree to mark a corner, a road another side, a pile of rocks a second corner, a fence another side, and so forth. This method was handy, but it had two major drawbacks: there might not be a convenient corner or boundary marker where one was needed, and over time, oak trees died, stone heaps were moved, streams and rivers changed course, stumps rotted, fences were removed, and unused roads became overgrown with vegetation. The following description in the Hartford, Connecticut, probate court records for 1812 illustrates what is sometimes encountered:

METES AND BOUNDS

> Commencing at a heap of stone about a stone's throw from a certain small clump of alders, near a brook running down off from a rather high part of said ridge; thence, by a straight line to a certain marked white birch tree, about two or three times as far from a jog in a fence going around a ledge nearby; thence by another straight line in a different direction, around said ledge and the

Great Swamp, so called; thence, in line of said lot in part and in part by another piece of fence which joins on to said line, and by an extension of the general run of said fence to a heap of stone near a surface rock; thence, as aforesaid, to the "Horn," so called, and passing around the same as aforesaid, as far as the "Great Bend," so called, and from thence to a squarish sort of a jog in another fence, and so on to a marked black oak tree with stones piled around it; thence, by another straight line in about a contrary direction and somewhere about parallel with the line around by the ledge and the Great Swamp, to a stake and stone bounds not far off from the old Indian trail; thence, by another straight line on a course diagonally parallel, or nearly so, with "Fox Hollow Run," so called, to a certain marked red cedar tree out on a sandy sort of a plain; thence, by another straight line, in a different direction, to a certain marked yellow oak tree on the off side of a knoll with a flat stone laid against it, thence, after turning around in another direction, and by a sloping straight line to a certain heap of stone which is, by pacing, just 18 rods and about one half a rod more from the stump of the big hemlock tree where Philo Blake killed the bear; thence, to the corner begun at by two straight lines of about equal length, which are to be run by some skilled and competent surveyor, so as to include the area and acreage as herein before set forth.*

Permanent Monuments   The drawbacks of the above outmoded method of land description are resolved by setting a permanent man-made **monument** at one corner of the parcel, and then describing the parcel in terms of distance and direction from that point. From the monument, the surveyor runs the parcel's outside lines by compass and distance so as to take in the land area being described. Distances are measured in feet, usually to the nearest tenth or one-hundredth of a foot. Direction is shown in degrees, minutes and seconds. There are 360 degrees (°) in a circle, 60 minutes (') in each degree and 60 seconds (") in each minute. The abbreviation 29°14'52" would be read as 29 degrees, 14 minutes, and 52 seconds. Figure 2:2 illustrates a modern metes and bounds land description.

---

* F. H. Moffit and Harry Bouchard, *Surveying,* 6th ed. (New York: Harper and Row, 1975). By permission.

DESCRIBING LAND BY METES AND BOUNDS   **Figure 2:2**

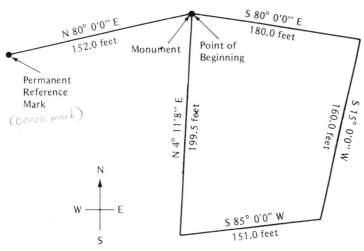

At the corner where the survey begins, a monument in the form of an iron pipe or bar 1 to 2 inches in diameter is driven into the ground. Alternatively, concrete or stone monuments are sometimes used. To guard against the possibility that the monument might later be destroyed or removed, it is referenced by means of a **connection line** to a nearby **permanent reference mark** established by a government survey agency. The corner where the parcel survey begins is called the **point of beginning** or **point of commencement.** From this point in Figure 2:2, we travel clockwise along the parcel's perimeter, reaching the next corner by going in the direction 80 degrees east of south for a distance of 180 feet. We then travel in a direction 15 degrees west of south for 160 feet, thence 85 degrees west of south for 151 feet, and thence 4 degrees, 11 minutes and 18 seconds east of north for 199.5 feet back to the point of beginning. In mapping shorthand, this parcel would be described by first identifying the monument, then the county and state within which it lies, and "thence S80°0'0"E, 180.0'; thence S15°0'0"W, 160.0'; thence S85°0'0"W, 151.0'; thence N4°11'18"E, 199.5' back to the p.o.b." It is customary to describe a parcel as if traveling clockwise around it.

Compass Directions   The compass illustrated in Figure 2:3 A shows how the direction of travel along each side of the parcel in Figure 2:2 is determined. Note that the same line can be labeled two ways depending on which direction you are traveling. To illustrate, look at the line from *P* to *Q*. If you are traveling toward *P* on the line, you are going N45°W. But, if you are traveling toward point *Q* on the line, you are going S45°E.

Curved boundary lines are produced by using arcs of a circle. The length of the arc is labeled *L* or *A*; the radius of the circle producing the arc is labeled *R*. The symbol △ (delta) indicates the angle used to produce the arc (see Figure 2:3 B). Where an arc connects to a straight boundary or another arc the connection is indicated by the symbol —●— or the symbol —○—.

Figure 2:3   **METES AND BOUNDS MAPPING**

(A) NAMING DIRECTIONS FOR
A METES AND BOUNDS SURVEY   (B) MAPPING A CURVE

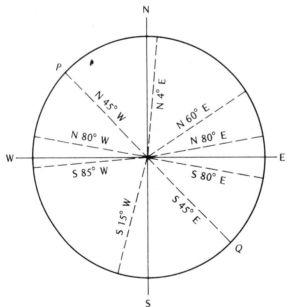

A = Length of the arc. (Some maps use the letter 'L'')
R = Radius of the circle necessary to make the required arc (shown here by the broken lines)
△ = Angle necessary to make the arc, i.e., the angle between the broken lines

Moving in a clockwise direction from the point of beginning, set the center of a circle compass (like the one shown above) on each corner of the parcel to find the direction of travel to the next corner. (*Note:* Minutes and seconds have been omitted above for clarity).

Bench marks are commonly used as permanent reference markers. A bench mark is a fixed marker of known location and elevation. It may be as simple as an iron post or as elaborate as an engraved 3¾" brass disc set into concrete. The mark is usually set in place by a government survey team from the U.S. Geological Survey (USGS) or the U.S. Coast and Geodetic Survey (USCGS). Bench marks are referenced to each other by distance and direction. The advantages of this type of reference point, compared to trees, rocks, and the like, are permanence and accuracy to within a fraction of an inch. Additionally, even though it is possible to destroy a reference point or monument, it can be replaced in its exact former position because the location of each is related to other reference points.

It is also possible to describe a parcel using metes and bounds when there is no physical monument set in the ground. This is done by identifying a corner of a parcel of land by using the rectangular survey system or a recorded plat map, and then using that corner as a reference point to begin a metes and bounds description. As long as the starting place for a metes and bounds description can be accurately located by future surveyors, it will serve the purpose.

The **rectangular survey system** was authorized by Congress in May 1785 in order to systematically divide the land north and west of the Ohio River into six-mile squares, now called congressional townships. It was also designed to provide a faster and simpler method than metes and bounds for describing land in newly annexed territories and states. Rather than using physical monuments, the rectangular survey system, also known as the **government survey** or **U.S. public lands survey,** is based on the system of mapping lines first imagined by ancient geographers and navigators. These are the east-west **latitude** lines and the north-south **longitude** lines that encircle the earth, as illustrated in Figure 2:4.

Certain longitude lines were selected to act as **principal meridians.** For each of these an intercepting latitude line was selected as a **base line.** Every 24 miles north and south of a base line, **correction lines** or **standard parallels** were established. Every 24 miles east and west of a principal merid-

*RECTANGULAR
SURVEY SYSTEM*

Figure 2:4   **SELECTED LATITUDE AND LONGITUDE LINES SERVE AS**
                                  BASE LINES AND MERIDIANS

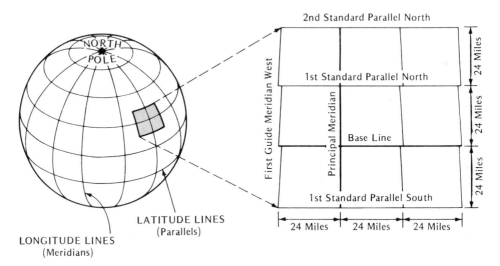

ian, **guide meridians** were established to run from one standard parallel to the next. These are needed because the earth is a sphere, not a flat surface. As one travels north in the United States, longitude (meridian) lines come closer together; that is, they converge toward the pole. Figure 2:4 shows how guide meridians and correction lines adjust for this problem. Each 24 by 24 mile area created by the guide meridians and correction lines is called a **check.**

There are 36 principal meridians and their intersecting base lines in the U.S. public land survey system. Figure 2:5 shows the states in which this system is used and the land area for which each principal meridian and base line act as a reference. For example, the Sixth Principal Meridian is the reference point for land surveys in Kansas, Nebraska, and portions of Colorado, Wyoming, and South Dakota. In addition to the U.S. public land survey system, a portion of western Kentucky was surveyed into townships by a special state survey. Also, the state of Ohio contains eight public lands surveys that are rectangular in design, but which use state boundaries and major rivers rather than latitude and longitude as reference lines.

THE PUBLIC LAND SURVEY SYSTEM OF THE UNITED STATES   Figure 2:5

Figure 2:6 shows how land is referenced to a principal   *Range*
meridian and base line. Every 6 miles east and west of each
principal meridian, parallel survey lines are drawn. The resulting 6-mile-wide columns are called **ranges** and are numbered
consecutively east and west of the principal meridian. For
example, the first range west is called Range 1 West and
abbreviated R1W. The next range west is R2W, and so forth.
The fourth range east is R4E.

Every six miles north and south of a base line, township   *Township*
lines are drawn. They intersect with the range lines and produce 6- by 6-mile mapped squares called **townships** (not to
be confused with the word township as applied to political
subdivisions). Each tier or row of townships thus created is
numbered with respect to the base line. Townships lying in
the first tier north of a base line all carry the designation

Figure 2:6   **IDENTIFYING TOWNSHIP AND SECTIONS**

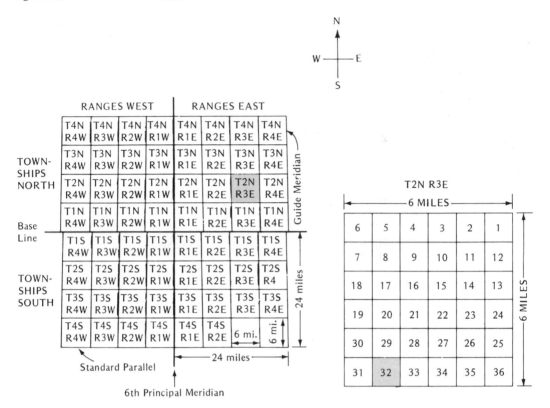

IDENTIFYING TOWNSHIPS   TOWNSHIP DIVIDED INTO SECTIONS

Township 1 North, abbreviated T1N. Townships lying in the first tier south of the base line are all designated T1S, and in the second tier south, T2S. By adding a range reference, an individual township can be identified. Thus, T2S, R2W would identify the township lying in the second tier south of the base line and the second range west of the principal meridian. T14N, R52W would be a township 14 tiers north of the base line and 52 ranges west of the principal meridian.

Section   Each 36-square-mile township is divided into 36 one-square-mile units called **sections.** When one flies over farming areas, particularly in the Midwest, the checkerboard pattern of farms and roads that follow section boundaries can be seen. Sections are numbered 1 through 36, starting in the upper-right corner of the township. With this numbering system, any two sections with consecutive numbers share a common boundary. The section numbering system is illustrated in the right half of Figure 2:6 where the shaded section is described as Section 32, T2N, R3E, 6th Principal Meridian.

Each square-mile **section** contains 640 acres, and each **acre** contains 43,560 square feet. Any parcel of land smaller than a full 640-acre section is identified by its position in the section. This is done by dividing the section into quarters and halves as shown in Figure 2:7. For example, the shaded parcel shown at Ⓐ is described by dividing the section into quarters and then dividing the southwest quarter into quarters. Parcel Ⓐ is described as the NW¼ of the SW¼ of Section 32, T2N, R3E, 6th P.M. Additionally, it is customary to name the county and state in which the land lies. How much land does the NW¼ of the SW¼ of a section contain? A section contains 640 acres; therefore, a quarter-section contains 160 acres. Dividing a quarter-section again into quarters results in four 40-acre parcels. Thus, the northwest quarter of the southwest quarter contains 40 acres.

Acre

The rectangular survey system is not limited to parcels of 40 or more acres. To demonstrate this point, the SE¼ of section 32 is exploded in the right half of Figure 2:7. Parcel Ⓑ is described as the SE¼ of the SE¼ of the SE¼ of the SE¼ of section 32 and contains 2½ acres. Parcel Ⓒ is described as the west 15 acres of the NW¼ of the SE¼ of section 32. Parcel Ⓓ would be described in metes and bounds using the northeast corner of the SE¼ of section 32 as the starting point.

Not all sections contain exactly 640 acres. Some are smaller because the earth's longitude lines converge toward the North Pole. Also, a section may be larger or smaller than 640 acres due to historical accommodations or survey errors dating back a hundred years or more. For the same reasons, not all townships contain exactly 36 square miles.

In terms of surface area, more land in the United States is described by the rectangular survey system than by any other survey method. But in terms of number of properties, the recorded plat is the most important survey method.

Figure 2:7   **SUBDIVIDING A SECTION**

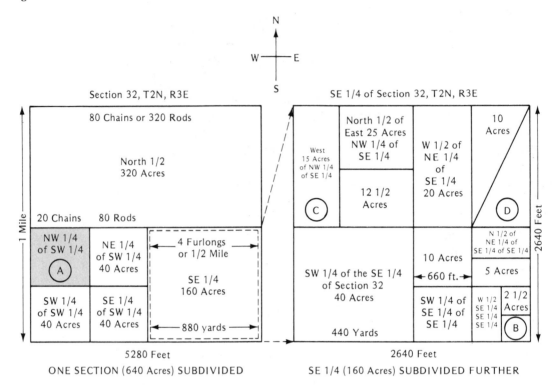

ONE SECTION (640 Acres) SUBDIVIDED   SE 1/4 (160 Acres) SUBDIVIDED FURTHER

As shown on the map in Figure 2:5, Texas does not use the rectangular survey system for surface estates. While this system of legal descriptions is very functional, Texas has not seen fit to adopt it. Note, however, that information pertaining to it has particular application for Texas real estate practitioners who work in other states where this system is more common.

RECORDED PLAT   When a tract of land is ready for subdividing into lots for homes and businesses, reference by **recorded plat** provides the simplest and most convenient method of land description. A **plat** is a map that shows the location and boundaries of individual properties. Also known as the **lot–block–tract system, recorded map,** or **recorded survey,** this method of land description is based on the filing of a surveyor's plat in the public recorder's office of the county where the land is located.

Figure 2:8 illustrates a plat. Notice that a metes and bounds survey has been made and a map prepared to show in detail the boundaries of each parcel of land. Each parcel is then assigned a lot number. Each block in the tract is given a block number, and the tract itself is given a name or number. A plat showing all the blocks in the tract is delivered to the county recorder's office, where it is placed in **map books** or **survey books,** along with plats of other subdivisions in the county.

LAND DESCRIPTION BY RECORDED PLAT   **Figure 2:8**

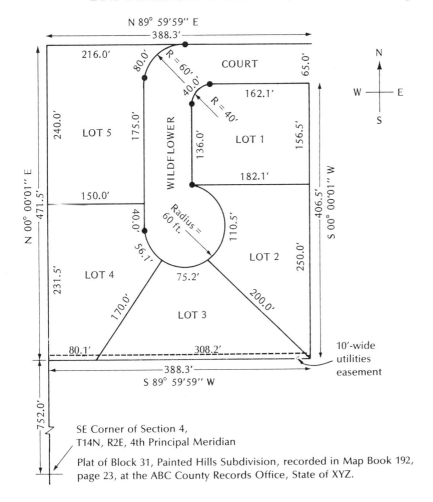

SE Corner of Section 4,
T14N, R2E, 4th Principal Meridian

Plat of Block 31, Painted Hills Subdivision, recorded in Map Book 192, page 23, at the ABC County Records Office, State of XYZ.

Each plat is given a book and page reference number, and all map books are available for public inspection. From that point on, it is no longer necessary to give a lengthy metes and bounds description to describe a parcel. Instead, one need only provide the lot and block number, tract name, map book reference, county, and state. To find the location and dimensions of a recorded lot in Texas, one simply looks at the map book at the county clerk's office.

Note that the plat in Figure 2:8 combines both of the land descriptions just discussed. The boundaries of the numbered lots are in metes and bounds. These, in turn, are referenced to a section corner in the rectangular survey system.

APPRAISAL DISTRICT'S PARCEL NUMBER

In many Texas counties, the appraisal district assigns a **parcel number** to each parcel of land in the county. The primary purpose is to aid in the assessment of property for tax collection purposes. However, these parcel numbers are public information and real estate brokers, appraisers, and investors can and do use them extensively to assist in identifying real properties.

The method used in Texas is to divide the county into map books. Each book is given a number and covers a given portion of the county. Depending on the size of the county and the number of separate parcels of land in the county, the number of map books necessary to cover a county can range from less than a dozen to several hundred. On each page of the map book are parcel maps, each with its own number. For subdivided lots, these maps are based on the plats submitted by the subdivider to the county clerk's office when the subdivision was made. For unsubdivided land, the appraisal district prepares its own maps.

Each parcel of land on the map is assigned a parcel number by the appraisal district. The appraisal district's parcel number may or may not be the same as the lot number assigned by the subdivider. To reduce confusion, the parcel number is either circled or underlined. Figure 2:9 illustrates a page out of an appraisal district's map book.

The appraisal district's maps are open to viewing by the public at the appraisal district's office. In many counties, pri-

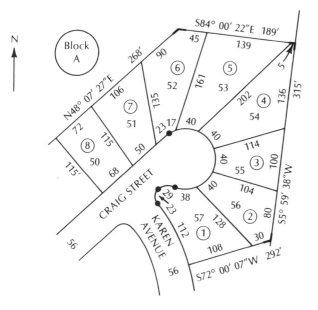

Assessor's Map
Book 34
Page 18

Assessor Parcel Numbers
shown in circles

Lots 50 through 57 of
Tract 2118, filed in
Recorded Maps, Book 63,
page 39.

The tax assessor assigns every parcel of land in the county its own parcel number. For example, the westernmost parcel (Lot 50) in the map would carry the number 34-18-8, meaning Book 34, Page 18, Parcel 8.

vate firms reproduce the maps and rolls and make them available to real estate brokers, appraisers, lenders, etc., for a fee.

Before leaving the topic of the appraisal district's maps, a word of caution is in order. These maps should not be relied upon as the final authority for the legal description of a parcel. That can come only from a title search that will include looking at the current deed to the property and the recorded copy of the subdivider's plat. Note also that the appraisal district's parcel number is never used as a legal description in a deed.

REFERENCE TO DOCUMENTS OTHER THAN MAPS

Land can also be described by referring to another publicly recorded document, such as a deed or a mortgage, that contains a full legal description of the parcel in question. For example, suppose that several years ago Baker received a deed from Adams which contained a long and complicated metes and bounds description. Baker recorded the deed in the public records office, where a photocopy was placed in Book 1089, page 456. If Baker later wants to deed the same land to Cooper, Baker can describe the parcel in his deed to Cooper by saying, "all the land described in the deed from Adams to Baker recorded in Book 1089, page 456, county of ABC, state of XYZ, at the public recorder's office for said county and state." Since these books are open to the public, Cooper (or anyone else) could go to Book 1089, page 456 and find a detailed description of the parcel's boundaries.

The key test of a land description is: "Can another person, reading what I have written or drawn, understand my description and go out and locate the boundaries of the parcel?"

VERTICAL LAND DESCRIPTION   In addition to surface land descriptions, land may also be described in terms of vertical measurements. This type of measurement is necessary when air rights or subsurface rights need to be described.

A point, line, or surface from which a distance, vertical height, or depth is measured is called a **datum.** The most commonly used datum plane in the United States is mean sea level, although a number of cities have established other data surfaces for use in local surveys. Starting from a datum, **bench marks** are set at calculated intervals by government survey teams; thus, a surveyor need not travel to the original datum to determine an elevation. These same bench marks are used as reference points for metes and bounds surveys.

In selling or leasing subsurface drilling or mineral rights, the chosen datum is often the surface of the parcel. For example, an oil lease may permit the extraction of oil and gas from a depth greater than 500 feet beneath the surface of a parcel of land. (Subsurface rights are discussed more in the next chapter.)

An **air lot** (a space over a given parcel of land) is described by identifying both the parcel of land beneath the air lot and the elevation of the air lot above the parcel (see Figure 2:10 A). Multi-story condominiums use this system of land description.

Contour maps (topographic maps) indicate elevations. On these maps, **contour lines** connect all points having the same elevation. The purpose is to show hills and valleys,

AIR LOT AND CONTOUR LINES   **Figure 2:10**

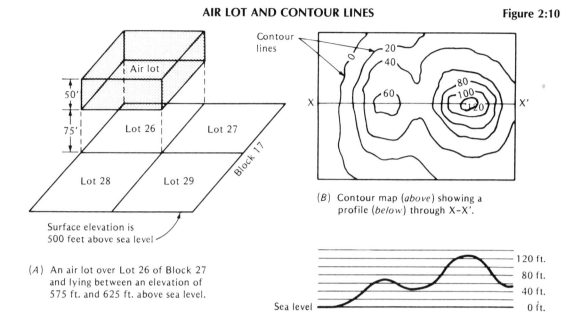

(A) An air lot over Lot 26 of Block 27
and lying between an elevation of
575 ft. and 625 ft. above sea level.

(B) Contour map (*above*) showing a
profile (*below*) through X–X'.

slopes, and water runoff. If the land is to be developed, the map shows where soil will have to be moved to provide level building lots. Figure 2:10 B illustrates how vertical distances are shown using contour lines.

The physical characteristics of land are immobility, indestructibility, and nonhomogeneity. This combination of characteristics makes land different from other commodities and directly and indirectly influences man's use of it.

PHYSICAL
CHARACTERISTICS
OF LAND

A parcel of land cannot be moved. It is true that soil, sand, gravel, and minerals can be moved by the action of nature (erosion) or man (digging); however, the parcel itself still retains its same geographical position on the globe. Because land is **immobile,** a person must go to the land; it cannot be brought to him. When land is sold, the seller cannot physically deliver his land to the buyer. Instead, the seller gives the buyer a document called a deed that transfers to the buyer the right to go onto that land and use it. Because land is immobile, real estate offices nearly always limit their

Immobility

sales activities to nearby properties. Even so, a great deal of a salesperson's effort is used in traveling to show properties to clients. Immobility also creates a need for property-management firms, because, unless an owner of rental property lives on the property or nearby, neither land nor buildings can be efficiently managed.

Indestructibility   Land is **indestructible,** that is, durable. For example, today one can travel to the Middle East and walk on the same land that was walked on in Biblical days, and most of the land that we use in the United States today is the same land used by the American Indians a thousand years ago.

The characteristic of physical durability encourages many people to buy land as an investment because they feel that paper money, stocks and bonds, and other commodities may come and go, but land will always be here. Although this is true in a physical sense, whether a given parcel has and will have economic value depends on one's ability to protect his ownership and on subsequent demand for that land by other persons. In other words, physical durability must not be confused with economic durability.

Nonhomogeneity   The fact that no two parcels of land are exactly alike because no two parcels can occupy the same position on the globe is known as **nonhomogeneity** (heterogeneity). Courts of law recognize this characteristic of land and consequently treat land as a **nonfungible** (pronounced non·fun'je' ble) commodity; that is, nonsubstitutable. Thus, in a contract involving the sale or rental of land (and any improvements to that land), the courts can be called upon to enforce specific performance of the contract. For example, in a contract to sell a home, if the buyer carries out his obligations and the seller fails to convey ownership to the buyer, a court of law will force the seller to convey ownership of *that* specific home to the buyer. The court will not require the buyer to accept a substitute home. This is different from a homogeneous or **fungible** commodity which is freely substitutable in carrying out a contract. For example, one bushel of No. 1 grade winter wheat can be freely replaced by another bushel of the same grade, and one share of United States Steel common stock can be substituted for another as all are identical.

Although land is nonhomogeneous, there can still be a high degree of physical and economic similarity. For example, in a city block containing 20 house lots of identical size and shape, there will be a high degree of similarity even though the lots are still nonhomogeneous. Finding similar properties is, in fact, the basis for the market-comparison approach to appraising real estate.

The dividing line between the physical and economic characteristics of land is sometimes difficult to define, because the physical aspects of land greatly influence man's economic behavior toward land. However, four economic characteristics are generally recognized: scarcity, modification, permanence of investment (fixity), and area preference (situs, pronounced sĭ'tus).

ECONOMIC CHARACTERISTICS OF LAND

The shortage of land in a given geographical area where there is great demand for land is referred to as **scarcity.** It is a man-made characteristic. For example, land is scarce in Dallas and Houston, because a relatively large number of people want to use a relatively small area of land. Yet outside of Texas cities there is plenty of uncrowded land available for purchase at very reasonable prices.

Scarcity

Land scarcity is also influenced by man's ability to use land more efficiently. To illustrate, in agricultural areas, production per acre of land has more than doubled for many crops since 1940. This is not due to any change in the land, but is the result of improved fertilizers and irrigation systems, better seeds and modern crop management. Likewise, in urban areas, an acre of land that once provided space for five houses can be converted to high-rise apartments to provide homes for 100 or more families.

Thus, although there is a limited physical amount of land on the earth's surface, scarcity is chiefly a function of demand for land in a given geographical area and the ability of man to make land more productive. The persistent notion that all land is scarce has led to periodic land sale booms in undeveloped areas, which can be followed by a collapse in land prices when it becomes apparent that that particular land is not economically scarce.

Modification   Land use and value are greatly influenced by **modification,** that is, improvements made by man to surrounding parcels of land. For example, the construction of an airport will increase the usefulness and value of land parallel to runways but have a negative effect on the use and value of land at the ends of runways because of noise from landings and takeoffs. Similarly, land subject to flooding will become more useful and valuable if government-sponsored flood control dams are built upriver.

One of the most widely publicized cases of land modification occurred near Orlando, Florida, when Disney World was constructed. Nearby land previously used for agricultural purposes suddenly became useful as motel, gas station, restaurant, house, and apartment sites and increased rapidly in value.

Fixity   The fact that land and buildings and other improvements to land require long periods of time to pay for themselves is referred to as **fixity** or **investment permanence.** For example, it may take 20 or 30 years for the income generated by an apartment or office building to repay the cost of the land and building plus interest on the money borrowed to make the purchase. Consequently, real estate investment and land use decisions must consider not only how the land will be used next month or next year, but also the usefulness of the improvements 20 years from now. There is no economic logic in spending money to purchase land and improvements that will require 20 to 30 years to pay for themselves, if their usefulness is expected to last only 5 years.

Fixity also reflects the fact that land cannot be moved from its present location to another location where it will be more valuable. With very few exceptions, improvements to land are also fixed. Even with a house, the cost of moving it, plus building a foundation at the new site, can easily exceed the value of the house after the move. Thus, when an investment is made in real estate, it is regarded as a **fixed** or **sunk cost.**

Situs or **location preference** refers to location from an economic rather than a geographic standpoint. It has often been said that the single most important word in real estate is "location." What this means is the preference of people for a given area. For a residential area, these preferences are the result of *natural* factors, such as weather, air quality, scenic views, and closeness to natural recreation areas, and *man-made* factors, such as job opportunities, transportation facilities, shopping, and schools. For an industrial area, situs depends on such things as an available labor market, adequate supplies of water and electricity, nearby rail lines, and highway access. In farming areas, situs includes soil and weather conditions, water and labor availability, and transportation facilities.

Situs

Situs is the reason that house lots on street corners sell for more than identical-sized lots not on corners. This reflects a preference for open space. The same is true in apartments; corner units usually rent for more than similar-sized noncorner units. In a high-rise apartment building, units on the top floors, if they offer a view, command higher prices than identical units on lower floors. On a street lined with stores, the side of the street that is shaded in the afternoon will attract more shoppers than the unshaded side. Consequently, buildings on the shaded side will generate more sales and as a result be worth more.

It is important to realize that, since situs is a function of people's preferences and preferences can change with time, situs can also change. For example, the freeway and expressway construction boom, that started up in the 1950s, and accelerated during the 1960s, increased the preference for suburban areas. This resulted in declining property values in inner city areas and increasing land values in the suburbs. Today, people are starting to show a preference for living closer to the centers of cities, due to transportation convenience and proximity to work.

VOCABULARY REVIEW

Match terms **a–r** *with statements* **1–18.**

a. *Acre*
b. *Base line*
c. *Contour lines*
d. *Datum*
e. *Emblements*
f. *Fixity*
g. *Fixture*
h. *Government survey*
i. *Lot-block-tract*

j. *Meridian*
k. *Metes and bounds*
l. *Monument*
m. *Quarter-section*
n. *Riparian rights*
o. *Section*
p. *Subsurface rights*
q. *Township*
r. *Water table*

1. An object that has been attached to so as to become real estate land.
2. Contains 36 sections of land.
3. The depth below the surface at which water-saturated soil can be found.
4. A survey line running east and west from which townships are measured off at six-mile intervals.
5. Contains 640 acres of land.
6. The right of a landowner to use water flowing through his land.
7. An iron pipe or other object set in the ground to establish land boundaries.
8. A survey line that runs north and south in the rectangular survey system.
9. Annual crops produced by man.
10. A horizontal plane from which height and depth are measured.
11. Refers to the permanence of real estate investments.
12. A system of land description that identifies a parcel by specifying its shape and boundaries.
13. A land survey system based on recognized latitude and longitude lines.
14. Includes the right to mine minerals and drill for oil.
15. Lines on a map that connect points having the same elevation.
16. Land description by reference to a recorded map.
17. 43,560 square feet.
18. Contains 160 acres of land.

QUESTIONS AND PROBLEMS

1. Is the land upon which you make your residence described by metes and bounds, lot-block-tract, or the rectangular survey system?
2. On a sheet of paper sketch the following parcels of land in Section 6, T1N, R3E: (a) the NW¼; (b) the SW¼ of the SW¼; (c) the W½ of the SE¼; (d) the N17 acres of the E½ of the NE¼; (e) the SE¼ of the SE¼ of the SE¼ of the NE¼.
3. How many acres are there in each parcel described in number 2?

4. Describe the parcels labeled A, B, C, D, and E in the section shown in the margin.

5. Using an ordinary compass and ruler, sketch the following parcel of land: "Beginning at monument M, thence due east for 40 feet, thence south 45° east for 14.1 feet, thence due south for 40 feet, thence north 45° west for 70.7 feet back to the point of beginning."

6. If a landowner owns from the center of the earth to the limits of the sky, are aircraft that pass overhead trespassers?

7. Would you classify the key to the door of a building as personal property or real property?

8. With regard to your own residence, itemize what you consider to be real property and what you consider to be personal property.

9. With regard to riparian rights, does your state follow the doctrine of prior appropriation or the right to a reasonable share?

10. What effects do you think changes in the location of the magnetic north pole would have on surveys over a long period of time? How would earthquakes affect bench marks?

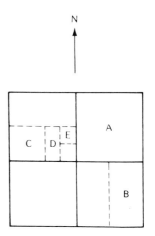

"Boundary Disputes: Is the Broker on the Line?" by **Jeffrey Krivis.** (*First Tuesday,* Sept 84, p. 19). Article points out the broker and seller can be liable if there were misleading statements or concealments.

"Land for All: A History of U.S. Real Estate to 1900" by **John McMahan.** (*Real Estate Review,* Winter 76, p. 78). A fascinating four-part history of American real estate speculation and development before the year 1900.

Real Estate Law, 8th ed. by **Robert Kratovil** and **Raymond Werner.** (Prentice-Hall, 1983, 650 pages). Chapter 2 discusses land and its elements, Chapter 3 is on fixtures and Chapter 5 deals with land descriptions.

Real Estate Quick and Easy by **Roy Maloney.** (Dropzone Press, 1983, 336 pages). A guide to real estate purchase and ownership. Profusely illustrated to help the reader see the points being made.

Real Estate Securities and Syndication Picture Dictionary by **Edward** and **Darlene Hooper.** (Hooper, 1984, 336 pages). Contains 1,008 cartoon-illustrated real estate and real estate syndication terms. Both entertaining and educational as the cartoons reinforce the definitions.

Surveying: Principles and Applications by **Barry Kavanagh** and **Glenn Bird.** (Reston, 1984, 640 pages). Two-part text covers both introductory and advanced surveying. Includes latest in instrumentation and computation systems.

Texas Real Estate Law, 4th ed. by **Charles J. Jacobus.** (Reston, 1985, 560 pages). Provides up-to-date explanations of law pertinent to the daily operation of a real estate brokerage office in Texas. Chapter 2 discusses legal descriptions; Chapter 4 discusses fixtures.

ADDITIONAL READINGS

Rights and Interests in Land

KEY TERMS

Chattel: an article of personal property

Easement: the right or privilege one party has to use land belonging to another for a special purpose not inconsistent with the owner's use of the land

Eminent domain: the right of government to take privately held land for public use, provided fair compensation is paid

Encroachment: the unauthorized intrusion of a building or other improvement onto another person's land

Encumbrance: any impediment to a clear title, such as a lien, lease, or easement

Fee simple: extensive interest (ownership) one can hold in land; often called the complete bundle of rights; an absolute estate

Homestead protection: state laws that protect against the forced sale of a person's home

Lien: a hold or claim which one person has on the property of another to secure payment of a debt or other obligation

Title: the right to or ownership of something; also the evidence of ownership such as a deed or bill of sale

FEUDAL AND ALLODIAL SYSTEMS

Early man was nomadic and had no concept of real estate. Roaming bands followed game and the seasons, and did not claim the exclusive right to use a given area. When man began to cultivate crops and domesticate animals, the concept of an exclusive right to the use of land became important. This right was claimed for the tribe as a whole, and each family in the tribe was given the right to the exclusive use of a portion of the tribe's land. In turn, each family was obligated to aid in defending the tribe's claim against other tribes.

Feudal System

As time passed, individual tribes allied with each other for mutual protection; eventually these alliances resulted in political states. In the process, land ownership went to the head of the state, usually a king. The king, in turn, gave the right (called a feud) to use large tracts of land to select individuals, called lords. The lords did not receive ownership.

They were tenants of the king, and were required to serve and pay duties to the king and to help fight the king's wars. It was customary for the lords to remain tenants for life, subject, of course, to the defeat of their king by another king. This system, wherein all land ownership rested in the name of the king, became known as the **feudal system.**

The lords gave their subjects the right to use small tracts of land. For this, the subjects owed their lord a share of their crops and their allegiance in time of war. The subjects (vassals) were, in effect, tenants of the lord and subtenants of the king. Like the lord, the vassal could not sell his rights nor pass them to his heirs.

Allodial System   The first major change in the feudal system occurred in 1285 when King Edward I of England gave his lords the right to pass their tenancy rights to their heirs. Subsequently, tenant vassals were permitted to convey their tenancy rights to others. By the year 1650, the feudal system had come to an end in England; in France it ended with the French Revolution in 1789. In its place arose the **allodial system** of land ownership under which individuals were given the right to own land. Initially, lords became owners and the peasants remained tenants of the lord. As time passed, the peasants became landowners either by purchase or by gift from the lord.

When the first European explorers reached North American shores, they claimed the land in the name of the king or queen whom they represented. When the first settlers later came to America from England, they claimed the land in the name of their mother country. However, since the feudal system had been abolished in the meantime, the king of England granted the settlers private ownership of the land upon which they settled, while retaining the claim of ownership to the unsettled lands.

Claims by the king of England to land in the 13 colonies were ended with the American Revolution. Subsequently, the U.S. government acquired the ownership right to additional lands by treaty, wars, and purchase, resulting in the borders of the United States as we know them today. The United States adopted the allodial system of ownership, and not only permits but encourages its citizens to own land within its borders.

Under the feudal system, the king was responsible for organizing defense against invaders, making decisions on land use, providing services such as roads and bridges, and the general administration of the land and his subjects. An important aspect of the transition from feudal to allodial ownership was that the need for these services did not end. Consequently, even though ownership could now be held by private citizens, it became necessary for the government to retain the rights of taxation, eminent domain, police power, and escheat. Let us look at each of these more closely.

GOVERNMENT RIGHTS IN LAND

Under the feudal system, governments financed themselves by requiring lords and vassals to share a portion of the benefits they received from the use of the king's lands. With the change to private ownership, the need to finance governments did not end. Thus, the government retained the right to collect **property taxes** from landowners. Before the advent of income taxes, taxes levied against land were the main source of government revenues. Taxing land was a logical method of raising revenue for two reasons: (1) until the Industrial Revolution, which started in the mid-eighteenth century, land and agriculture were the primary sources of income; the more land one owned, the wealthier one was considered to be and therefore the better able to pay taxes to support the government; (2) land is impossible to hide, making it easily identifiable for taxation. This is not true of other valuables such as gold or money.

Property Taxes

The real property tax has endured over the centuries, and today it is still a major source of government revenue. The major change in real estate taxation is that initially it was used to support all levels of government, including defense. Today, defense is supported by the income tax, and real estate taxes are sources of city, county, and, in some places, state revenues. At state and local government levels, the real property tax provides money for such things as schools, fire and police protection, parks, and libraries. To encourage property owners to pay their taxes in full and on time, the right of taxation also enables the government to seize ownership of real estate upon which taxes are delinquent and to sell the property to recover the unpaid taxes.

Eminent Domain   The right of government to take ownership of privately held real estate regardless of the owner's wishes is called **eminent domain.** Land for schools, freeways, streets, parks, urban renewal, public housing, public parking, and other social and public purposes is obtained this way. Quasi-public organizations, such as utility companies and railroads, are also permitted to obtain land needed for utility lines, pipes, and tracks by state law. The legal proceeding involved in eminent domain is a **condemnation proceeding,** and the property owner must be paid the fair market value of the property taken from him. The actual condemnation is usually preceded by negotiations between the property owner and an agent of the public body wanting to acquire ownership. If the agent and the property owner can arrive at a mutually acceptable price, the property is purchased outright. If an agreement cannot be reached, a formal proceeding in eminent domain is filed against the property owner in a court of law. The court hears expert opinions from appraisers brought by both parties, and then sets the price the property owner must accept in return for the loss of ownership.

When only a portion of a parcel of land is being taken, **severance damages** may be awarded in addition to payment for land actually being taken. For example, if a new highway requires a 40-acre strip of land through the middle of a 160-acre farm, the farm owner will not only be paid for the 40 acres; he will also receive severance damages to compensate for the fact that his farm will be more difficult to work because it is no longer in one piece.

An **inverse condemnation** is a proceeding brought about by a property owner demanding that his land be purchased from him. In a number of cities, homeowners at the end of airport runways have forced airport authorities to buy their homes because of the deafening noise of jet aircraft during takeoffs. Damage awards may also be made when land itself is not taken but its usefulness is reduced because of a nearby condemnation. These are **consequential damages,** and might be awarded, for instance, when land is taken for a sewage treatment plant, and privately owned land downwind from the plant suffers a loss in value owing to the prevalence of foul odors.

The right of government to enact laws and enforce them for the order, safety, health, morals, and general welfare of the public is called **police power.** Examples of police power applied to real estate are zoning laws, planning laws, building, health and fire codes, and rent control. A key difference between police power and eminent domain is that, although police power restricts how real estate may be used, there is no legally recognized "taking" of property. Consequently, there is no payment to an owner who suffers a loss of value through the exercise of police power. A government may not utilize police power in an offhand or capricious manner; any law that restricts how an owner may use his real estate must be deemed in the public interest and applied evenhandedly to be valid. The breaking of a law based upon police power results in either a civil or criminal penalty rather than in the seizing of real estate, as in the case of unpaid property taxes. Of the various rights government holds in land, police power has the most impact on land value.

Police Power

When a person dies and leaves no heirs and no instructions as to how to dispose of his real and personal property, or when property is abandoned, the ownership of that property reverts to the state. This reversion to the state is called **escheat** from the Anglo-French word meaning to fall back. Escheat solves the problem of property becoming ownerless.

Escheat

It cannot be overemphasized that, to have real estate, there must be a system or means of protecting rightful claims to the use of land and the improvements thereon. In the United States, the federal government is given the task of organizing a defense system to prevent confiscation of those rights by a foreign power. The federal government, in combination with state and local governments, also establishes laws and courts within the country to protect the ownership rights of one citizen in relation to another citizen. Whereas armed

PROTECTING OWNERSHIP

forces protect against a foreign takeover from outside, written deeds, public records, contracts, and other documents have replaced the need for brute force to prove and protect ownership of real estate within the country.

FEE SIMPLE   The concept of real estate ownership can be more easily understood when viewed as a collection or bundle of rights. Under the allodial system, the rights of taxation, eminent domain, police power, and escheat are retained by the government. The remaining bundle of rights, called **fee simple,** is available for private ownership. The fee simple bundle of rights can be held by a person and his heirs forever, or until his government can no longer protect those rights. Figure 3:1 illustrates the fee simple bundle of rights concept.

The term **estate** refers to one's legal interest or rights in land. A fee simple is the largest estate one can hold in land. Most real estate sales are for the fee simple estate. When a person says he or she "owns" or has "title" to real estate, it is usually the fee simple estate that is being discussed. The word **title** refers to the right or ownership of something. All other lesser estates in land, such as life estates and lease-holds, are created from the fee estate.

Real estate is concerned with the "sticks" in the bundle: how many there are, how useful they are, and who possesses the sticks not in the bundle. With that in mind, let us describe what happens when sticks are removed from the bundle.

Figure 3:1   **THE FEE SIMPLE BUNDLE OF RIGHTS**

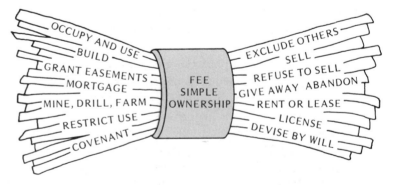

Real estate ownership is, in actuality, the ownership of rights to land.
The largest bundle available for private ownership is called "fee simple".

Whenever a stick is removed from the fee simple bundle, it creates an impediment to the free and clear ownership and use of that property. These impediments to title are called encumbrances. An **encumbrance** is defined as any claim, right, lien, estate, or liability that limits the fee simple title to property. An encumbrance is, in effect, a stick that has been removed from the bundle. Commonly found encumbrances are easements, encroachments, deed restrictions, liens, leases and air and subsurface rights. In addition, qualified fee estates are encumbered estates, as are life estates.

ENCUMBRANCES

The party holding a stick from someone else's fee simple bundle is said to hold a claim to or a right or interest in that land. In other words, what is one person's encumbrance is another person's right or interest or claim. For example, a lease is an encumbrance from the standpoint of the fee simple owner. But from the tenant's standpoint, it is an interest in land that gives the tenant the right to the exclusive use of land and buildings. A mortgage is an encumbrance from the fee owner's viewpoint, but a right to foreclose from the lender's viewpoint. A property that is encumbered with a lease and a mortgage is called "a fee simple subject to a lease and a mortgage." Figure 3:2 illustrates how a fee simple bundle shrinks as rights are removed from it. Meanwhile, let us turn our attention to a discussion of individual sticks found in the fee simple bundle.

An **easement** is a right or privilege one party has to the use of land of another for a special purpose consistent with the general use of the land. The landowner is not dispossessed from his land, but rather coexists side by side with the holder of the easement. Examples of easements are those given to telephone and electric companies to erect poles and run lines over private property, easements given to people to drive or walk across someone else's land, and easements given to gas and water companies to run pipelines to serve their customers. Figure 3:3 illustrates several examples of easements.

EASEMENTS

The usual procedure in creating an easement is for the landowner to use a written document to specifically grant an easement to someone else or to reserve an easement to himself in the deed when he sells the property. A land devel-

Figure 3:2   REMOVING STICKS FROM THE FEE SIMPLE BUNDLE

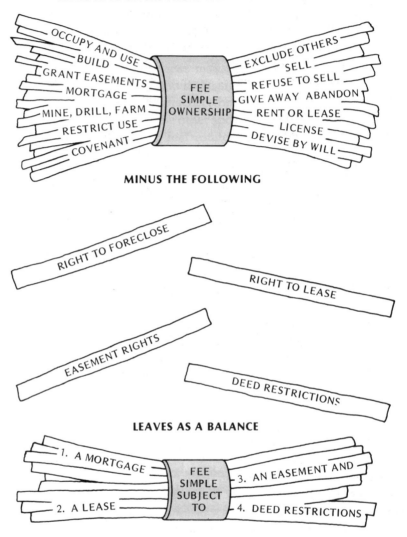

Note that the fee simple bundle shrinks as an owner voluntarily removes rights from it.

oper may reserve easements for utility lines and then grant them to the utility companies that will service the lots.

It is also possible for an easement to arise without a written document. For example, a parcel of land fronts on a road and the owner sells the back half of the parcel. If the only

COMMONLY FOUND EASEMENTS   **Figure 3:3**

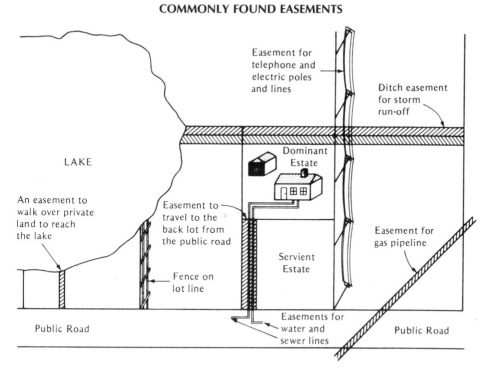

access to the back half is by crossing over the front half, even if the seller did not expressly grant an easement, the law may protect the buyer's right to travel over the front half to get to his land. This may create an **easement by implication.** Another method of acquiring an easement without a written document is by constant use, or **easement by prescription:** if a person acts as though he owns an easement long enough, he will have a legally recognized easement. Persons using a private road without permission for a long enough period of time can acquire a legally recognized easement by this method.

In Figure 3:3, the driveway from the road to the back lot is called an **easement appurtenant.** This driveway is automatically included with the back lot whenever the back lot is sold or otherwise conveyed. This is so because this easement is physically and legally connected (appurtenant) to the back lot which is the dominant estate. Please note that just as

Easement Appurtenant

the back lot benefits from this easement, the front lot is burdened by it. Whenever the front lot is sold or otherwise conveyed, the new owners must continue to respect the easement to the back lot. The owner of the front lot owns all the front lot, but cannot put a fence across the easement, or plant trees on it or grow a garden on it or otherwise hamper access to the back lot. The front lot, being burdened by the easement, is called the **servient estate** and the back lot, which benefits from the easement, is called the **dominant estate.**

Easement In Gross

An **easement in gross** is given to a person or business, and a subsequent sale of the land does not usually affect ownership of the easement. It benefits the user only, and is an encumbrance to the fee estate (no benefit to the contiguous land owner). Therefore, there is neither a dominant or a servient estate. Telephone, electricity, and gas line easements are examples of easements in gross. The holder of a commercial easement usually has the right to sell, assign, or devise it. However, easements in gross for personal use are not transferable and terminate with the death of the person holding the easement. An example of a personal easement in gross would be a landowner giving a friend an easement to travel over his land to reach a choice fishing area.

Party Wall Easement

Party wall easements exist when a single wall straddles the lot line that separates two parcels of land. The wall may be either a fence or the wall of a building. In either case, each lot owner owns that portion of the wall on his land, plus an easement in the other half of the wall for physical support. Party walls are common where stores and office buildings are built right up to the lot line. Such a wall can present an interesting problem when the owner of one lot wants to demolish his building. Since the wall provides support for the building next door, it is usually his responsibility to either leave the wall or provide special supports for the adjacent building during demolition and until another building is constructed on the lot.

Easement Termination

Easements may be terminated when the purpose for the easement no longer exists (for example, a public road is built

1. Purpose for its existence ends
2.

adjacent to the back half of the lot mentioned earlier), or when the dominant and servient estates are combined with the intent of extinguishing the easement, or by release from the owner of the dominant estate to the servient estate, or by lack of use.

ENCROACHMENTS

The unauthorized intrusion of a building or other improvement onto another person's land is called an **encroachment.** A tree that overhangs into a neighbor's yard, or a building or eave of a roof that crosses a property line are examples of encroachments. The owner of the property being encroached upon has the right to force the removal of the encroachment. Failure to do so may eventually injure his title and make his land more difficult to sell. Ultimately, inaction may result in the encroaching neighbor claiming a legal right to continue his use. Figure 3:4 illustrates several commonly found encroachments.

DEED RESTRICTIONS

Private agreements that govern the use of land are known as **deed restrictions** or **deed covenants.** For example, a land subdivider can require that persons who purchase lots from

COMMONLY FOUND ENCROACHMENTS   **Figure 3:4**

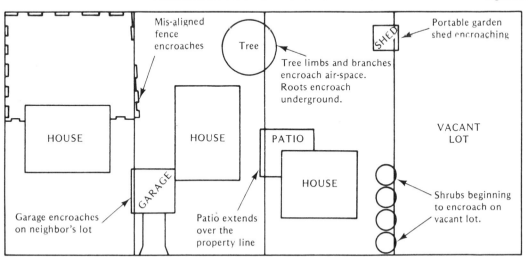

Most commonly found encroachments are not intentional but are due to poor or nonexistent planning. For example, a weekend garden shed, fence, or patio project is built without surveying to find the lot line, or a tree or bush grows so large it encroaches upon a neighbor's land.

him build only single-family homes containing 1,200 square feet or more. The purpose would be to protect those who have already built houses from an erosion in property value due to the construction of nearby buildings not compatible with the neighborhood. Where scenic views are important, deed restrictions may limit the height of buildings and trees to 15 feet. A buyer would still obtain fee simple ownership, but at the same time would voluntarily give up some of his rights to do as he pleases. As a buyer, he is said to receive a fee simple title subject to deed restrictions. The right to enforce the restrictions is usually given by the developer to the subdivision's homeowner association. Violation of a deed restriction can result in a civil court action brought by other property owners who are bound by the same deed restriction.

LIENS

A hold or claim that one person has on the property of another to secure payment of a debt or other obligation is called a **lien.** Common examples are property tax liens, mechanic's liens, judgment liens, and mortgage liens. From the standpoint of the property owner, a lien is an encumbrance on his title. Note that a lien does not transfer title to property. The debtor retains title until the lien is foreclosed. When there is more than one lien against a property, the lien which was recorded first usually has the highest priority in the event of foreclosure. Property tax liens are, however, always superior to other liens.

Property Tax Lien

A **property tax lien** results from the right of government to collect taxes from property owners. At the beginning of each tax year, a tax lien is placed on taxable property. It is removed if the property taxes are paid. If they are not paid, the lien gives the state the right to force the sale of the property in order to collect the unpaid taxes.

Mechanic's Lien

Mechanic's lien laws give anyone who has furnished labor or materials for the improvement of land the right to place a lien against that land if payment has not been received. A sale of the property can then be forced to recover the money owed. To be entitled to a mechanic's lien, the work or materials must have been provided under contract with the property owner or his representative. For example, if a landowner hires a contractor to build a house or add a room to his existing house, and then fails to pay the contractor, the contractor may file a mechanic's lien against the land and its improvements. Furthermore, if the landowner pays the contractor, but the contractor does not pay his subcontractors, the subcontractors are entitled to file a mechanic's lien against the property. In this situation, the owner may have to pay twice.

The legal theory behind mechanic's lien rights is that the labor and materials supplied enhance the value of the property. Therefore the property should be security for payment. If the property owner does not pay voluntarily, the lien can be enforced with a court supervised foreclosure sale. To be valid, a mechanic's lien must be recorded in the county clerk's office within the time limits set by state law.

Judgment liens arise from lawsuits for which money damages are awarded. The law permits a hold to be placed against the real and personal property of the debtor until the judgment is paid. Usually the lien created by the judgment covers only property in the county where the judgment was awarded. However, the creditor can extend the lien to property in other counties by filing an **abstract of judgment** in each of those counties. If the debtor does not repay the lien voluntarily, and the property is not the debtor's homestead (or is in excess of allowable homestead limits) the creditor can ask the court to issue a **writ of execution** that directs the county sheriff to seize and sell a sufficient amount of the debtor's property to pay the debt and expenses of the sale. If a writ of execution is not issued, the creditor must renew the abstract of judgment every ten years or it will expire and be of no further effect.

Judgment Lien

A **mortgage lien** is a pledge of property by its owner to secure the repayment of a debt. In contrast to a property tax lien which is imposed by law, a mortgage lien is a voluntary lien created by the property owner. In contrast to a judgment lien which applies to all the debtor's property, a mortgage lien covers only the specific property that its owner elects to pledge. If the debt secured by the mortgage lien is not

Mortgage Lien

repaid, the creditor can foreclose and sell the pledged property. If this is insufficient to repay the debt, some states allow the creditor to petition the court for a judgment lien for the balance due. (Mortgage law is covered in more detail in Chapter 9.)

Voluntary and Involuntary Liens

A **voluntary lien** is a lien created by the property owner. A mortgage lien is an example of a voluntary lien; the owner voluntarily creates a lien against his/her own property in order to borrow money. An **involuntary lien** is one that is created by operation of law, against the wishes of the owner. Examples are property tax liens and judgment liens.

Specific and General Liens

A **specific lien** is a lien on a specific property. A property tax lien is a specific lien because it is a lien against a specific property and no other. Thus, if a person owns five parcels of land scattered throughout a given county and fails to pay the taxes on one of those parcels, the county can force the sale of just that one parcel; the others cannot be touched. Mortgages and mechanic's liens are also specific liens in that they apply to only the property receiving the materials or labor. In contrast, a **general lien** is a lien on all the property of a person in a given jurisdiction. For example, a judgment lien is a lien on all the debtor's property in the county or counties where the judgment has been filed. Federal tax liens are also general liens.

QUALIFIED FEE ESTATES

A **qualified fee estate** is a fee estate that is subject to certain limitations imposed by the person creating the estate. Qualified fee estates fall into three categories: determinable, condition subsequent, and condition precedent. They will be discussed only briefly as they are rather uncommon.

A **fee on conditional limitation,** also called a **fee simple determinable estate,** results when the estate created is limited by the happening of a certain event. For example, Mr. Smith donates a parcel of land to a church so long as the land is used for religious purposes. The key words are "so long as." So long as the land is used for religious purposes the church has all the rights of fee simple ownership. But, if some other use is made of the land, it reverts to the grantor

(Mr. Smith) or someone else named by Mr. Smith (called a **remainderman**). Note that the termination of the estate is automatic if the land is used contrary to the limitation stated in the deed.

A **fee simple subject to condition subsequent** is similar to a determinable fee except that it gives the grantor the right to terminate the estate rather than wait for it to terminate automatically. Continuing the above example, Mr. Smith would have the right to reenter the property and take it back if it was no longer being used for religious purposes.

With a **fee simple upon condition precedent,** title will not take effect until a condition is performed. For example, Mr. Smith could deed his land to a church with the condition that the deed will not take effect until a religious sanctuary is built.

Occasionally qualified fees have been used by land developers in lieu of deed restrictions or zoning. For example, the buyer has fee title so long as he uses the land for a single-family residence. In another example, a land developer might use a condition precedent to encourage lot purchasers to build promptly. This would enhance the value of his unsold lots. From the standpoint of the property owner, a qualification is an encumbrance to his title.

A **life estate** conveys an estate for the duration of someone's life. The duration of the estate can be tied to the land of the **life tenant** (the person holding the life estate) or to a third party. In addition, someone must be named to acquire the estate upon its termination. The following example will illustrate the life estate concept. Suppose you have an aunt who needs financial assistance and you have decided to grant her, for the rest of her life, a house to live in. When you create the life estate, she becomes the life tenant. Additionally, you must decide who gets the house upon her death. If you want it back, you would want a **reversionary interest** for yourself. This way the house reverts to you, or if you predecease her, to your heirs. If you want the house to go to someone else, your son or daughter for example, you could name him or her as the **remainderman.** Alternatively, you could name a friend, relative, or charity as the remainderman.

LIFE ESTATES

While your aunt is alive, the remainderman is said to hold a **remainder interest** in the house. When she dies, that interest changes to a fee simple estate.

A life estate does not have to be based on the lifespan of the life tenant. It can be based upon the lifespan of a third party in which case it is called a life estate **pur autre vie,** i.e., for the life of another. Continuing the above example, suppose that you know your rich uncle is naming your aunt to receive a substantial portion of his wealth upon his death. If this would adequately take care of her future financial needs, you could grant your aunt a life estate until your uncle dies. Sometimes a life estate is used to avoid the time and expense of probating a will and to reduce estate taxes. For example, an aging father could deed his real estate to his children but retain a life estate for himself.

Prohibition of Waste

Since a life estate arrangement is temporary, the life tenant must not commit **waste** by destroying or harming the property. Furthermore, the life tenant is required to keep the property in reasonable repair and to pay any property taxes, assessments, and interest on debt secured by the property. During the tenancy, the life tenant is entitled to the use and/ or income generated by the property, and may sell, lease, rent, or mortgage his or her interest. Note, however, that it is impossible for the life tenant to sell, lease, or mortgage any greater interest than the life tenant holds.

STATUTORY ESTATES

Statutory estates are created by state law. They include **dower,** which gives a wife rights in her husband's real property; **curtesy,** which gives a husband rights in his wife's real property; and **community property** that gives each spouse a one-half interest in marital property. Additionally there are **homesteads** which are designed to protect the family's home from certain debts and, upon the death of one spouse, provide the other with a home for life. In Texas there is homestead protection and community property, but no dower or curtesy.

Dower

Historically, **dower** came from old English common law, in which the marriage ceremony was viewed as merging the wife's legal existence into that of her husband's. From this viewpoint, property bought during marriage belongs to the husband, with both husband and wife sharing the use of it. As a counterbalance, the dower right recognizes the wife's efforts in marriage and grants her legal ownership to one-third (in some states one-half) of the family's real property for the rest of her life. This prevents the husband from convey-ing ownership of the family's real estate without the wife's permission and protects her even if she is left out of her husband's will.

Because the wife's dower right does not ripen into actual ownership until her husband's death, her right is described as being **inchoate** until then. Once she obtains her life estate, she can sell, give, rent, or mortgage it, as described previously. Recognizing the impractical nature of an undivided life estate and the need for equal rights between husband and wife, some states award the wife an undivided fee simple estate rather than a life estate.

In real estate sales, the effect of dower laws is that, when a husband and wife sell their property, the wife must relin-quish her dower rights. This is usually accomplished by the wife signing the deed with her husband or by signing a sepa-rate quit claim deed. If she does not relinquish her dower rights, the buyer (or even a future buyer) may find that, upon the husband's death, the wife may return to legally claim an undivided ownership in the property. This is an important reason why, if you are buying real estate, you should have the property's ownership researched by a compe-tent abstractor and have the title you receive insured by a title insurance company. Because the wife's dower right is inchoate while her husband is alive, she cannot sell it or otherwise part with it except when they mutually sell family real estate.

Curtesy

Roughly the opposite of dower, **curtesy** gives the husband benefits in his deceased wife's property as long as he lives. However, unlike dower, the wife can defeat those rights in her will. Furthermore, state law may require the couple to have had a child in order for the husband to qualify for curtesy. In some states, husbands are given dower rights rather than curtesy. States with statutory dower and curtesy rights are shown in Table 3:1.

Community Property   Eight states (Arizona, California, Idaho, Louisiana, Nevada, New Mexico, Texas, and Washington) subscribe to the legal theory that during marriage, each spouse has an equal

Table 3:1   DOWER, CURTESY, AND HOMESTEAD PROTECTION BY STATE

	Dower Right for Wife	Curtesy or Dower Right for Husband	Homestead Protection		Dower Right for Wife	Curtesy or Dower Right for Husband	Homestead Protection
Alabama	×		×	Missouri			×
Alaska			×	Montana			×
Arizona			×	Nebraska			×
Arkansas	×	×	×	Nevada			×
California			×	New Hampshire			×
Colorado			×	New Jersey	×	×	
Connecticut				New Mexico			×
				New York			×
Delaware				North Carolina			×
District of Columbia	×	×		North Dakota			×
Florida			×	Ohio	×	×	×
				Oklahoma			×
Georgia			×	Oregon			×
Hawaii	×	×		Pennsylvania			
Idaho			×	Rhode Island			
Illinois			×	South Carolina			×
Indiana			×	South Dakota			×
Iowa			×				
Kansas	×	×	×	Tennessee			×
Kentucky			×	Texas			×
Louisiana			×	Utah		×	×
Maine			×	Vermont	×	×	×
Maryland	×	×		Virginia	×	×	×
Massachusetts			×	Washington	×	×	×
Michigan			×	West Virginia			×
Minnesota			×	Wisconsin			×
Mississippi			×	Wyoming			×

interest in all property acquired by their joint efforts during the marriage. This jointly produced property is called **community property.** Upon the death of one spouse, one-half of the community property passes to his or her heirs. The other one-half is retained by the surviving spouse. When community property is sold or mortgaged, both spouses should sign the document. Community property rights arise upon marriage (either formal or common law) and terminate upon divorce or death. Community property is discussed at greater length in Chapter 4.

Forty-two of the fifty states (see Table 3:1) have passed **homestead laws,** usually with two purposes in mind: (1) to provide some legal protection for the homestead claimants from debts and judgments against them that might result in the forced sale and loss of the home, and (2) to provide a home for a widow, and sometimes a widower, for life. Homestead laws also restrict one spouse from acting without the other when conveying the homestead or using it as collateral for a loan. Dower, curtesy, and community property rights are automatic in those states that have them. In some states, the homestead right may require that a written declaration be recorded in the public records. This is not required in Texas, however. Additionally, the "homestead" exemption from forced sale should not be confused with the "homestead exemption" which Texas grants to homeowners in order to reduce their property taxes.

Homestead Protection

In Texas the homestead right is constitutional and, as a constitutional right, cannot be waived through any contractual agreement or change in state law. Basically, homestead rights are expressed as exemptions from forced sale. All rights vested under the homestead laws are rights secure in the homestead claimant. The independence and security of a home may be enjoyed without the danger of its loss or harassment by reason of the improvidence or misfortune of a head, or *any member* of, the family. That is, the homestead claimant cannot be deprived of his homestead by creditors in the normal course of business. Therefore, a homeowner could own a very expensive house, which falls within the homestead exemption lim-

TEXAS HOMESTEAD RIGHTS

its, and *no creditor,* regardless of the amount of the debt, could force the homeowner to sell his home to satisfy the debt, except under certain constitutionally specified circumstances.

Article 16, Section 50 of the Texas Constitution specifically states that the homestead of a family, or a single adult person, is protected from forced sale for payment of all debts, with three exceptions: (1) purchase money mortgages, which secure the payment of the purchase price of the house, (2) taxes, and (3) mechanics' and materialmen's liens levied because of constructing improvements to the homestead, *if* the improvements were contracted for in writing and signed by the husband and wife before any work was performed in constructing said improvements. In addition, the homestead may not be conveyed without the consent of the spouse if the homestead claimant is married. Single adult persons obtained homestead rights as a result of constitutional amendment which became effective November 6, 1973.

Protection is Automatic   There is no official document one must sign to create homestead rights. The fact that the realty is in the possession of the owner and that the owner resides upon it as his principal residence makes it the homestead of the family in law and in fact. Additionally, even if the homestead is not occupied by the owner, the intent of making it the owner's homestead, accompanied by circumstances manifesting said intention, is enough to vest the homestead character of the property and make the exemption rights applicable to it. There must be a declaration of homestead, however, in order to get the benefit of certain tax exemptions provided for under state and county taxing authorities. However, this declaration is *not* required to create homestead rights. Note that in both situations only one property (the principal residence) can be claimed as a homestead.

Once the homestead rights have vested in a certain piece of real property, it maintains its homestead character during the entire life of the occupant and loses its homestead character only by (1) death, (2) abandonment, or (3) alienation (subsequent sale).

While death and alienation are self-explanatory, abandonment is a fact question. Abandonment of a homestead property cannot be accomplished by mere intention. There must be a discontinuance of use of the property coupled with an intention not to use it again as a home before it will constitute abandonment.

Homestead Limitations

There are limits established as to the homestead, however, depending on the type of homestead exemption one wishes to claim. The Constitution of Texas states that a **rural homestead** consists of not more than 200 acres of land, which may be in one or more parcels, with the improvements thereon. If more than 200 acres is owned, the owner may designate which 200 acres constitutes his homestead, so long as the designated 200 acres do contain the owner's home. A state statute limits the **single homestead** to only 100 acres. An **urban homestead** is a homestead in a city, town, or village, and can consist of a lot or lots amounting to not more than one acre of land, together with any improvement on the land. The homestead, too, can consist of both a business and residential homestead, provided that the amount of both homestead claims does not exceed one acre. The value of the improvements have no bearing whatsoever in the evaluation of the homestead. The temporary renting of a homestead shall not change the character of the homestead when no other homestead has been acquired, and even if another house had been acquired, there must have been sufficient abandonment of the previous homestead before the homestead rights vest in the newly acquired home. These homestead rights, being constitutional, can only be changed by constitutional amendment, ratified by the voters of the State of Texas.

FREEHOLD ESTATES

1. Actual ownership
2. Unpredictable duration

Examples:
Fee estates
Life estates
Statutory estates

In a carryover from the old English court system, estates in land are classified as either **freehold estates** or **leasehold estates.** The main difference is that freehold estate cases are tried under real property laws whereas leasehold (also called non-freehold or less-than-freehold) estates are tried under personal property laws.

The two distinguishing features of a freehold estate are (1) there must be actual ownership of the land, and (2) the estate must be of unpredictable duration. Fee estates, life estates, and estates created by statute are freehold estates. The distinguishing features of a leasehold estate are (1) although there is possession of the land, there is no ownership, and (2) the estate is of definite duration.

LEASEHOLD ESTATES

1. No ownership
2. Definite duration

As previously noted, the user of a property need not be its owner. Under a leasehold estate, the user is called the **lessee** or **tenant,** and the person from whom he leases is the **lessor** or **landlord.** As long as the tenant has a valid lease, abides by it, and pays the rent on time, the owner, even though he owns the property, cannot occupy it until the lease has expired. During the lease period, the freehold estate owner is said to hold a **reversionary interest.** This is his right to recover possession at the end of the lease period. Meanwhile, the lease is an encumbrance against the property.

There are four categories of leasehold estates: estate for years, periodic estate, estate at will, and tenancy at sufferance. Note that in this chapter, we will be examining leases primarily from the standpoint of estates in land. Leases as financing tools are discussed in Chapter 12 and lease contracts are covered in Chapter 15.

Estate for Years

1. Specific starting & ending time
2. No automatic renewal

Also called a tenancy for years, the **estate for years** is somewhat misleadingly named as it implies that a lease for a number of years has been created. Actually, the key criterion is that the lease have a specific starting time and a specific ending time. It can be for any length of time, ranging from less than a day to many years. An estate for years does not automatically renew itself. Neither the landlord nor the tenant must act to terminate it, as the lease agreement itself specifies a termination date.

Usually the lessor is the freehold estate owner. However, the lessor could be a lessee himself. To illustrate, a fee owner leases his property to a lessee, who in turn leases his right to still another person. By doing this, the first lessee has become a **sublessor** and is said to hold a **sublease.** The person who leases from him is a **sublessee.** It is important to realize that in no case can a sublessee acquire from the lessee any more rights than the lessee has under his lease. Thus, if a lessee has a 5-year lease with 3 years remaining, he can sublease to a sublessee only the remaining 3 years or a portion of that.

Also called an estate from year-to-year or a periodic ten-ancy, a **periodic estate** has an original lease period with fixed length; when it runs out, unless the tenant or his landlord acts to terminate it, renewal is automatic for another like period of time. A month-to-month apartment rental is an example of this arrangement. To avoid last minute confusion, rental agreements usually require that advance notice be given if either the landlord or the tenant wishes to terminate the tenancy.

Periodic Estate

1. Original lease period of fixed length
2. Automatic renewal

Also called a tenancy at will, an **estate at will** is a landlord-tenant relationship with all the normal rights and duties of a lessor-lessee relationship, except that the estate may be termi-nated by either the lessor or the lessee at anytime. However, most states recognize the inconvenience a literal interpretation of "anytime" can cause and require that reasonable advance notice be given.

Estate at Will

1. Terminated at will of either party

A **tenancy at sufferance** occurs when a tenant stays be-yond his legal tenancy without the consent of the landlord. In other words, the tenant wrongfully holds the property against the owner's wishes. In a tenancy at sufferance, the tenant is commonly called a **holdover tenant,** although once he stays beyond his legal tenancy he is not actually a tenant in the normal landlord-tenant sense. The landlord is entitled to evict him and recover possession of the property, provided the landlord does so in a timely manner. A tenant at sufferance differs from a trespasser only in that his original entry was rightful. If during the holdover period the tenant pays and the landlord accepts rent, the tenancy at sufferance changes to a periodic estate.

Tenancy at Sufferance

Figure 3:5 provides an overview of the various rights and interests in land that are discussed in this chapter and the previous chapter. This chart is designed to give you an overall perspective of what the term real estate includes.

Overview

A **license** is not a right or an estate in land, but a personal privilege given to someone to use land. It is nonassignable and can be canceled by the person who issues it. A license

LICENSE

Figure 3:5   **RIGHTS AND INTERESTS IN LAND**

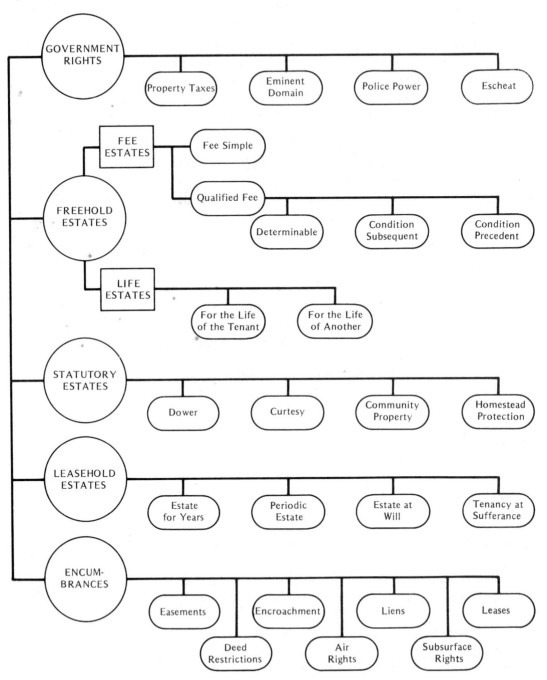

to park is typically what an automobile parking lot operator provides for persons parking in his lot. The contract creating the license is usually written on the stub that the lot attendant gives the driver, or it is posted on a sign on the lot. Tickets to theaters and sporting events also fall into this category. Because it is merely a personal privilege, a license is not an encumbrance against land.

A chattel is an article of personal property. Chattels are divided into two categories: chattels personal and chattels real. Examples of **chattels personal** are automobiles, clothes, food, and furniture. **Chattels real** are interests in real estate that remain personal property; for example, a contract for the purchase of real estate or a lease. In the United States, chattels are governed by personal property laws. Freehold estates are governed by real property laws.

CHATTELS

Let us conclude this chapter by combining what has been discussed in Chapter 2 regarding the physical nature of land with what has been covered in this chapter regarding estates and rights in land. The results, diagrammed in Figure 3:6, show why real estate is both complicated and exciting at the same time. A single parcel of land can be divided into subsurface, surface, and air-space components, and each of these carries its own fee simple bundle of rights, which can be divided into the various estates and rights discussed in this chapter.

PICTORIAL SUMMARY

To more clearly convey this idea, let us turn our attention to Figure 3:6. In parcel A, the fee landowner has leased the bulk of his surface and air rights, plus the right to draw water from his wells, to a farmer for the production of crops and livestock. This leaves the fee owner with the right to lease or sell subterranean rights for mineral, oil, and gas extraction. With a single parcel of land, the fee owner has created two estates, one for farming and another for oil and gas production. With the minor exception of the placement of the well platforms, pumps, and pipes, neither use interferes with the other and both bring income to the landowner. The farmer, in turn, can personally utilize the leasehold estate he possesses or he can sublease it to another farmer. The

Figure 3:6   **CROSS SECTION OF ESTATES AND RIGHTS IN LAND**

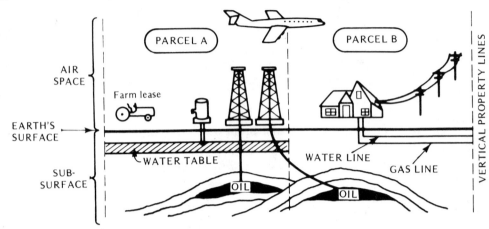

oil company, if it has leased its rights, can sublease them; if it has purchased them, it can sell or lease them. A variation would be for an oil company to buy the land in fee, conduct its drilling operations, and lease the remainder to a farmer. In the public interest, the government has claimed the right to allow aircraft to fly over the land. Although technically a landowner owns from the center of the earth out to the heavens, the right given aircraft to fly overhead creates a practial limit on that ownership.

Subsurface Rights

Dominant estate in Texas

In Texas, oil and mineral rights are subsurface estates in real estate and occupy a unique position. Once the subsurface rights have been leased or conveyed, there is an immediate conflict of rights as to surface control. The subsurface mineral owner has the dominant estate in Texas; that is, an owner of mineral rights has the right, unless otherwise specified, to reasonably enter upon any property to extract the minerals to which he holds a fee or leasehold estate. A mineral owner or lessee may waive these rights by relinquishing surface control of the property so that the surface estate owner can develop his property without worry of interference from the subsurface interest below.

Any rights to the subsurface oil, gas, or minerals are always subject to prior notices of record, local land use legislation and regulation, and any other prior existing interests which may affect the surface estate as well as the subsurface estate. Therefore, one could assume that any oil, gas, or mineral rights acquired after the property has been deed restricted would be subject to those deed restrictions, and any oil, gas, and mineral rights owned within a municipality that has an ordinance against drilling would probably not be allowed to drill without a special permit from the city's governing body.

While the oil or minerals in the ground are considered real property, once they are extracted from the ground they become personalty. Texas courts have recently held that once oil and minerals are extracted from the ground and then later injected into the ground for storage purposes, the oil and minerals still maintain their character as personal property and do not revert to real estate.

It is important for a developer in Texas to recognize that even though he has built on a parcel of land, the mineral estate owner has the right to extract his mineral interests, regardless of the nuisance or inconvenience to the subsequent property owner. This may create a serious problem in subdivision property or fully developed property where the mineral rights have not been waived or surface control has not been relinquished by the mineral estate owner.

VOCABULARY REVIEW

*Match terms **a–t** with statements **1–20.***

a. *Allodial*	**k.** *Estate for years*
b. *Bundle of rights*	**l.** *Holdover tenant*
c. *Chattel*	**m.** *Inverse condemnation*
d. *Curtesy*	**n.** *Lessee*
e. *Dower*	**o.** *Lessor*
f. *Easement*	**p.** *Lien*
g. *Eminent domain*	**q.** *Periodic tenancy*
h. *Encroachment*	**r.** *Police power*
i. *Escheat*	**s.** *Reversionary interest*
j. *Estate*	**t.** *Waste*

1. A lease with a specific starting and ending date and no automatic renewal provision.
2. A charge or hold against property to use it as security for a debt.
3. A leasehold estate that automatically renews itself unless canceled.
4. An article of personal property.

5. The unauthorized intrusion of a building or other improvement upon the land of another.
6. A tenant who wrongfully remains in possession of leased property after his lease expires.
7. The right of government to take property from private owners, who in turn must be compensated.
8. A real property ownership system that allows land to be owned by individuals.
9. The right of government to enact laws and enforce them for the order, safety, health, morals, and general welfare of the public.
10. A lawsuit by a property owner demanding that a public agency purchase his property.
11. The abuse or destructive use of property.
12. Real estate ownership viewed as a collection of many rights.
13. The reversion of property to the state when the owner dies without leaving a will or heirs.
14. The extent of interest which a person has in real property. Also used to describe all the real and personal property owned by a person.
15. One who holds title and leases out his property; the landlord.
16. One who holds the right to use property but does not own it; the tenant.
17. The right that a wife has in her husband's estate at his death.
18. The right that a husband has in his wife's estate at her death.
19. A right or privilege one party has in the use of land belonging to another.
20. The right to the future enjoyment of property presently in the possession of another.

QUESTIONS AND
PROBLEMS

1. Distinguish between freehold and leasehold estates in land.
2. Under what conditions is it possible for an easement to be created without their being specific mention of it in writing?
3. What steps have been taken by the Texas state legislature to recognize the legal equality of married women in real estate ownership?
4. Why are dower, curtesy, and homestead protection sometimes referred to as statutory estates?
5. From the standpoint of possession, what is the key difference between an easement and a lease?
6. What is an encumbrance? Give three examples.
7. In your community, name specific examples of the application of police power to the rights of landowners.
8. How much protection does the Texas homestead law offer and what must a person do to qualify?
9. Technically speaking, a 99-year lease on a parcel of land is personal property. However, from a practical standpoint, the exclusive right

to use a parcel of land for such a long period of time seems more like real property. Do the laws of your state treat a 99-year lease as real or personal property?

The Allen and Wolfe Illustrated Dictionary of Real Estate by **Robert Allen** and **Thomas Wolfe.** (Wiley, 1983, 266 pages). Defines over 3,000 terms from real estate and allied fields. Includes maps, charts, graphs and tables.

Hidden Fortunes by **Albert Lowrey.** (Simon and Schuster, 1983, 368 pages). This is an entry-level real estate investment book covering such topics as how to borrow, how to buy, buying at foreclosure sales, auctions, price versus terms, sharing ownership and syndication.

How to Survive While Realestating by **Marvin Myers** and **Alison Myers.** (M&M Productions, 1985, 63 pages). Contains 55 humorous cartoons about real estate that both teach and entertain.

Land Rush by **Mark Stevens.** (McGraw-Hill, 1984, 290 pages). An entertaining visit into the world of powerful and well-connected real estate brokers and developers both residential and commercial.

Real Estate Law by **Marianne Jennings.** (Kent, 1985, 657 pages). Chapters 2 through 6 deal with rights and interests in real estate. Includes freehold, nonfreehold, easements, subsurface rights and fixtures. Court cases used as examples.

The Smart Investors Guide to Real Estate, 3rd ed. by **Robert Bruss.** (Crown, 1984, 270 pages). Emphasis is on the do-it-yourself investor with a small amount to invest. Author is a nationally syndicated real estate columnist.

Texas Real Estate Law, 4th ed. by **Charles J. Jacobus.** (Reston, 1985, 560 pages). Chapter 2 explains estates in land.

ADDITIONAL READINGS

Forms of Ownership

KEY TERMS

Association: a not-for-profit organization that can own property and transact business in its own name

Community property: property co-ownership wherein husband and wife are treated as equal partners with each owning a one-half interest

Estate in severalty: owned by one person; sole ownership

Financial liability: the amount of money one can lose; one's risk exposure

Joint tenancy: a form of property co-ownership that features the right of survivorship

Joint venture: an association of two or more persons or firms in order to carry out a single business project

Right of survivorship: a feature of joint tenancy whereby the surviving joint tenants automatically acquire all the right, title and interest of the deceased joint tenant

Tenants in common: shared ownership of a single property among two or more persons; interests need not be equal and no right of survivorship exists

Undivided interest: ownership by two or more persons that gives each the right to use the entire property

In Chapter 2 we looked at land from a physical standpoint: the size and shape of a parcel, where it is located and what was affixed to it. In Chapter 3 we explored various legal rights and interests that can be held in land. In this chapter, we shall look at how a given right or interest in land can be held by one or more individuals.

SOLE OWNERSHIP

When title to property is held by one person, it is called an **estate in severalty** or **sole ownership.** Although the word "severalty" seems to imply that several persons own a single property, the correct meaning can be easily remembered by thinking of "severed" (separated) ownership. Sole ownership is available to single and married persons. However, in the case of married persons, most states require one spouse to waive community property, dower, or curtesy rights in writing. Businesses usually hold title to property in severalty. It *73* is from the estate in severalty that all other tenancies are carved.

The major advantage of sole ownership for an individual is flexibility. As a sole owner you can make all the decisions regarding a property without having to get the agreement of co-owners. You can decide what property or properties to buy, when to buy, and how much to offer. You can decide whether to pay all cash or to seek a loan by using the property as collateral. Once bought, you control (within the bounds of the law) how the property will be used, how much will be charged if it is rented, and how it will be managed. If you decide to sell, you alone decide when to offer the property for sale and at what price and terms.

But freedom and responsibility go together. For example, if you purchase a rental property you must determine the prevailing rents, find tenants, prepare contracts, collect the rent, and keep the property in repair; or you must hire and pay someone else to manage the property. Another deterrent to sole ownership is the high entry cost. This form of real estate ownership is not possible for someone with only a few hundred dollars to invest.

TENANTS IN COMMON

1. Undivided interest in whole property (w/ separate legal title)

2. No right of survivorship

When two or more persons wish to share the ownership of a single property, they may do so as **tenants in common.** As tenants in common, each owns an **undivided interest** in the whole property. This means that each owner has a right to possession of the entire property. None can exclude the others nor claim any specific portion for himself. In a tenancy in common, these interests need not be the same size, and each owner can independently sell, mortgage, give away, or devise his individual interest. This independence is possible because each tenant in common has a separate legal title to his undivided interest.

Suppose that you invest $20,000 along with two of your friends, who invest $30,000 and $50,000, respectively; together you buy 100 acres of land as tenants in common. Presuming that everyone's ownership interest is proportional to his or her cash investment, you will hold a 20% interest in the entire 100 acres and your two friends will hold 30% and 50%. You cannot pick out 20 acres and exclude the other co-owners from them, nor can you pick out 20 acres and say, "These are mine and I'm going to sell them"; nor can they do that to you. You do, however, have the legal right to sell or otherwise dispose of your 20% interest (or a portion of it) without the permission of your two friends. Your friends have the same right. If one of you sells, the purchaser becomes a new tenant in common with the remaining co-owners.

Wording of the Conveyance

As a rule, a tenancy in common is indicated by naming the co-owners in the conveyance and adding the words "as tenants in common." For example, a deed might read, "Samuel Smith, John Jones, and Robert Miller, as tenants in common." If nothing is said regarding the size of each co-owner's interest in the property, the law presumes that all interests are equal. Therfore, if the co-owners intend their interests to be unequal, the size of each co-owner's undivided interest must be stated as a percent or a fraction such as 60% and 40% or one-third and two-thirds.

In Texas, if two or more persons are named as owners, and there is no specific indication as to how they are taking title, they are presumed to be tenants in common. Thus, if a deed is made out to "Donna Adams and Barbara Kelly," the law would consider them to be tenants in common, each holding an undivided one-half interest in the property. An important exception to this presumption is when the co-owners are married to each other. In this case, they may be automatically considered to be taking ownership as community property.

No Right of Survivorship

When a tenancy in common exists, if a co-owner dies his interest passes to his heirs or devisees, who then become tenants in common with the remaining co-owners. There is no **right of survivorship;** that is, the remaining co-owners do not acquire the deceased's interest unless they are named in the deceased's last will and testament to do so. When a creditor has a claim on a co-owner's interest and forces its sale to satisfy the debt, the new buyer becomes a tenant in common with the remaining co-owners. If one co-owner wants to sell (or give away) only a portion of his undivided interest, he may; the new owner becomes a tenant in common with the other co-owners.

Any income generated by the property belongs to the tenants in common in proportion to the size of their interests. Similarly, each co-owner is responsible for paying his proportionate share of property taxes, repairs, upkeep, and so on, plus interest and debt repayment, if any. If any co-owner fails to contribute his proportionate share, the other co-owners can pay on his behalf and then sue him for that amount. If co-owners find that they cannot agree as to how the property is to be run and cannot agree on a plan for dividing or selling it, it is possible to request a court-ordered partition. A **partition** divides the property into distinct portions so that each person can hold his proportionate interest in severalty. If this is physically impossible, such as when three co-owners each have a one-third interest in a house, the court will order the property sold and the proceeds divided among the co-owners.

The major advantage of tenancy in common is that it allows two or more persons to achieve goals that one person could not accomplish alone. However, prospective co-owners should give advance thought to what they will do (short of going to court) if (1) a co-owner fails to pay his share of ownership expenses, (2) differences arise regarding how the property is to be operated, (3) agreement cannot be reached as to when to sell, for how much, and on what terms, and (4) what happens if a co-owner dies and those who inherit his interest have little in common with the surviving co-owners. The counsel of an attorney experienced in property ownership can be very helpful when considering the co-ownership of property.

JOINT TENANCY

Another form of multiple-person ownership is **joint tenancy**. The most distinguishing characteristic of joint tenancy is the right of survivorship. Upon the death of a joint tenant, his interest does not descend to his heirs or pass by his will. Rather, the entire ownership remains in the surviving joint tenant(s). In other words, there is just one less owner.

Four Unities

To create a joint tenancy, **four unities** must be present. They are the unities of time, title, interest, and possession.

[handwritten marginal notes:]
Unity of:
1. Time
2. Title
3. Interest
4. Possession

Right of survivorship
Not allowed with community property
Can defeat dower or curtesy rights

Unity of time means that each joint tenant must acquire his or her ownership interest at the same moment. Once a joint tenancy is formed, it is not possible to add new joint tenants later unless an entirely new joint tenancy is formed among the existing co-owners and the new co-owner. To illustrate, suppose that *A, B,* and *C* own a parcel of land as joint tenants. If *A* sells his interest to *D* then *B, C,* and *D* must sign documents to create a new joint tenancy among them. If this is not done, *D* automatically becomes a tenant in common with *B* and *C* who, between themselves, remain joint tenants. *D* will then own an undivided one-third interest in common with *B* and *C* who will own an undivided two-thirds interest as joint tenants.

Unity of title means that the joint tenants acquire their interests from the same source; i.e., the same deed or will. (Some states allow a property owner to create a valid joint tenancy by conveying to himself, or herself, and another without going through a third party.)

Unity of interest means that the joint tenants own one interest together and each joint tenant has exactly the same right in that interest. (This, by the way, is the foundation upon which the survivorship feature rests.) If the joint tenants list individual interests, they lack unity of interest and will be treated as tenants in common. Unity of interest also means that, if one joint tenant holds a fee simple interest in the property, the others cannot hold anything but a fee simple interest.

Unity of possession means that the joint tenants must enjoy the same undivided possession of the whole property. All joint tenants have the use of the entire property, and no individual owns a particular portion of it. By way of contrast, unity of possession is the only unity essential to a tenancy in common.

Texas requires that the joint tenancy be expressly agreed to in writing by the parties involved. Any automatic presumption of joint tenancy has been abolished by statute.

The feature of joint tenancy ownership that is most widely recognized is its **right of survivorship.** Upon the death of a joint tenant, that interest in the property is extinguished. In

Right of Survivorship

a two-person joint tenancy, when one person dies, the other immediately becomes the sole owner. With more than two persons as joint tenants, when one dies the remaining joint tenants are automatically left as owners. Ultimately, the last survivor becomes the sole owner. The legal philosophy is that the joint tenants constitute a single owning unit. The death of one joint tenant does not destroy that unit—it only reduces the number of persons owning the unit. For the public record, a copy of the death certificate and an affidavit of death of the joint tenant is recorded in the county where the property is located. The property must also be released from any estate tax liens.

It is the right of survivorship that has made joint tenancy a popular form of ownership among married couples in other states. Married couples often want the surviving spouse to have sole ownership of the marital property. Any property held in joint tenancy goes to the surviving spouse without the delay of probate and usually with less legal expense. Community property (discussed later in this chapter) may not be held in joint tenancy.

''Poor Man's Will''   Because of the survivorship feature, joint tenancy has loosely been labeled a "poor man's will." However, it should not replace a properly drawn will as it affects only that property held in joint tenancy. Moreover, a will can be changed if the persons named therein are no longer in one's favor. But once a joint tenancy is formed, title is permanently conveyed and there is no further opportunity for change, unless the joint tenancy is terminated. A joint tenant cannot name someone in his will to receive his joint tenant interest because his interest ends upon his death. One should also be aware of the possibility that ownership in joint tenancy may result in additional estate taxes.

Another important aspect of joint tenancy ownership is that it can be used to defeat dower or curtesy rights. If a married man forms a joint tenancy with someone other than his wife (such as a business partner) and then dies, his wife has no dower rights in that joint tenancy. As a result, courts have begun to look with disfavor upon the right of survivorship. Louisiana, Ohio, and Oregon either do not recognize joint tenancy or have abolished it.* Of the remaining, 47 states and the District of Columbia recognize joint tenancy ownership, but 14 have abolished the automatic presumption of survivorship (see Table 4:1). In those 14 states, if the right of survivorship is desired in a joint tenancy, it must be clearly stated in the conveyance. For example, a deed might read, "Karen Carson and Judith Johnson, as joint tenants with the right of survivorship and not as tenants in common." Even in those states not requiring it, this wording is often used to ensure that the right of survivorship is intended. In community property states, one spouse cannot take community funds and establish a valid joint tenancy with a third party.

There is a popular misconception that a debtor can protect himself from creditors' claims by taking title to property as a joint tenant. It is true that in a joint tenancy, the surviving joint tenant(s) acquire(s) the property free and clear of any liens against the deceased. However, this can happen only if the debtor dies before the creditor seizes the debtor's interest.

Only a human being can be a joint tenant. A corporation cannot be a joint tenant. This is because a corporation is an artificial legal being and can exist in perpetuity; i.e., never die. Joint tenancy ownership is not limited to the ownership of land: any estate in land and any chattel interest may be held in joint tenancy.

Tenancy by the entirety (also called tenancy by the entireties) is a form of joint tenancy specifically for married persons. To the four unities of a joint tenancy is added a fifth: **unity of person.** The basis for this is the legal premise that a husband and wife are an indivisible legal unit. Two key characteristics of a tenancy by the entirety are (1) the surviving spouse becomes the sole owner of the property upon the death of

TENANCY BY THE ENTIRETY

Joint tenancy for married couples.

Not recognized in Texas

---

* In Ohio and Oregon other means are available to achieve rights of survivorship between nonmarried persons. When two or more persons own property together in Louisiana, it is termed an "ownership in indivision" or a "joint ownership." Louisiana law is based on old French civil law.

Table 4:1 **CONCURRENT OWNERSHIP BY STATES**

	Tenancy in Common	Joint Tenancy	Tenancy by the Entirety	Community Property
Alabama	X	X		
Alaska	X	X	X	
Arizona	X	X		X
Arkansas	X	X	X	
California	X	X		X
Colorado	X	X		
Connecticut	X	X		
Delaware	X	X	X	
District of Columbia	X	X	X	
Florida	X	X	X	
Georgia	X	X		
Hawaii	X	X	X	
Idaho	X	X		X
Illinois	X	X		
Indiana	X	X	X	
Iowa	X	X		
Kansas	X	X		
Kentucky	X	X	X	
Louisiana				X
Maine	X	X		
Maryland	X	X	X	
Massachusetts	X	X	X	
Michigan	X	X	X	
Minnesota	X	X		
Mississippi	X	X	X	

	Tenancy in Common	Joint Tenancy	Tenancy by the Entirety	Community Property
Missouri	X	X	X	
Montana	X	X		
Nebraska	X	X		
Nevada	X	X		X
New Hampshire	X	X		
New Jersey	X	X	X	
New Mexico	X	X		X
New York	X	X	X	
North Carolina	X	X	X	
North Dakota	X	X		
Ohio	X		X	
Oklahoma	X	X	X	
Oregon	X		X	
Pennsylvania	X	X	X	
Rhode Island	X	X	X	
South Carolina	X	X		
South Dakota	X	X		
Tennessee	X	X	X	
Texas	X	X		X
Utah	X	X	X	
Vermont	X	X	X	
Virginia	X	X	X	
Washington	X	X		X
West Virginia	X	X	X	
Wisconsin	X	X		
Wyoming	X	X	X	

the other, and (2) neither spouse has a disposable interest in the property during the lifetime of the other. Thus, while both are alive and married to each other, both signatures are necessary to convey title to the property. With respect to the first characteristic, tenancy by the entirety is similar to joint tenancy because both feature the right of survivorship. They are quite different, however, with respect to the second characteristic. A joint tenancy can be terminated by one tenant's conveyance of his or her interest, but a tenancy by the entirety can be terminated only by joint action of husband and wife. Since Texas has community property laws, tenancy by the entireties is not recognized in this state.

States that recognize tenancy by the entirety are listed in Table 4:1. Some of these states automatically assume that a tenancy by the entirety is created when married persons buy real estate. However, it is best to use a phrase such as "John and Mary Smith, husband and wife as tenants by the entirety with the right of survivorship" on deeds and other conveyances. This avoids later questions as to whether their intention might have been to create a joint tenancy or a tenancy in common.

COMMUNITY PROPERTY

Due largely to its Spanish heritage, Texas has adopted community property laws which vest particular rights in property as a result of the marital community. Table 4:1 identifies the eight community property states. The laws of each community property state vary slightly, but the underlying concept is that the husband and wife contribute jointly and equally to their marriage and thus should share equally in any property purchased during marriage. Whereas English law is based on the merging of husband and wife upon marriage, community property law treats husband and wife as equal partners, with each owning an undivided one-half interest.

Community Property, Separate Property

Community property rights do not come into effect until there is a marriage and, similarly, end with the dissolution of that marriage. The law in Texas presumes that all property acquired after marriage is **community property.**

Property that is not community property is referred to as **separate property.** Article XVI, Section 15, of the Texas Constitution constitutionally defines separate property as property acquired prior to marriage (even if the owner subsequently marries, the real estate remains separate property) and property acquired by gift, devise, or descent after marriage. In addition, spouses can agree in writing, before or during marriage, that property can be separate rather than community. Courts have held that property purchased after marriage with separate funds can also be construed as separate property. However, rents and revenues from separate property are construed to be community property, unless the spouses agree otherwise.

Community property cannot be generally conveyed without both spouses' signatures. There are statutes that will allow property under the sole management and control of one spouse to be sold without the signature of the other spouse. As a good business practice, however, the wise real estate agent should obtain the other spouse's signature on any pertinent documents for real estate believed to be community property.

The major advantage of the community property system is found in its philosophy: it treats the spouses as equal partners in property acquired through their mutual efforts during marriage. Even if the wife elects to be a full-time homemaker and all the money brought into the household is the result of her husband's job (or vice versa), the law treats them as equal co-owners in any property bought with that money. This is true even if only one spouse is named as the owner.

In the event of divorce, if the parting couple cannot amicably decide how to divide their community property, the courts will usually do so. If the courts do not, the ex-spouses will become tenants in common with each other. If it later becomes necessary, either can file suit for partition.

PARTNERSHIP

A **partnership** exists when two or more persons, as partners, unite their property, labor, and skill as a business to share the profits created by it. The agreement between the partners may be oral or written. The partners may hold the partnership property either in their own names (as tenants in common or as joint tenants) or in the name of the partnership (which would hold title in severalty). For convenience, especially in a large partnership, the partners may designate two or three of their group to make contracts and sign documents on behalf of the entire partnership. There are two types of partnerships: general partnerships made up entirely of general partners and limited partnerships composed of general and limited partners.

General Partnership

The **general partnership** is an outgrowth of common law. However, to introduce clarity and uniformity into general partnership laws across the United States, 48 states and the District of Columbia have adopted the **Uniform Partnership Act** either in total or with local modifications. (The two exceptions are Georgia and Louisiana.) Briefly, the highlights of the Act are that (1) title to partnership property may be held in the partnership's name, (2) each partner has an equal right of possession of partnership property—but only for partnership purposes, (3) upon the death of one partner his rights in the partnership property vest in the surviving partners—but the decedent's estate must be reimbursed for the value of his interest in the partnership, (4) a partner's right to specific partnership property is not subject to dower or curtesy, and (5) partnership property can only be attached by creditors for debts of the partnership, not for debts of a partner.

As a form of property ownership, the partnership is a method of combining the capital and expertise of two or more persons. It is equally important to note that the profits and losses of the partnership are taxable directly to each individual partner in proportion to his or her interest in the partnership. Although the partnership files a tax return, it is only for informational purposes. The partnership itself does not pay taxes. Negative aspects of this form of ownership center around financial liability, illiquidity, and in some cases, management.

Financial liability means each partner is personally responsible for all the debts of the partnership. Thus, each general partner can lose not only what he has invested in the partnership, but more, up to the full extent of his personal financial worth. If one partner makes a commitment on behalf of the partnership, all partners are responsible for making good on that commitment. If the partnership is sued, each partner is fully responsible. **Illiquidity** refers to the possibility that it may be very difficult to sell one's partnership interest on short notice in order to raise cash. **Management** means that each general partner is expected to take an active part in the operation of the partnership.

The nature of the Texas community property laws has generally dictated that a partnership has three distinct interests, and are set out by the Texas partnership statutes. They are as follows:

Texas Partnership Statutes

1. A partner's right to specific Partnership property (such as desks, typewriters, machinery, etc.), which is *not* community property;
2. A partner's interest in the Partnership (usually determined by a dollar amount), which *may be* community property;
3. A partner's right to Management in the Partnership, which is *not* community property.

Limited Partnership

Because of unlimited financial liability and management responsibility an alternative partnership form, the **limited partnership,** has developed. Forty-nine states, plus the District of Columbia, had adopted the **Uniform Limited Partnership Act.** (The exception is Louisiana, which has its own general and limited partnership laws.) This act recognizes the legality of limited partnerships and requires that a limited partnership be formed by a written document.

A limited partnership is composed of general and limited partners. The general partners organize and operate the partnership, contribute some capital, and agree to accept the full financial liability of the partnership. The **limited partners** provide the bulk of the investment capital, have little say in the day-to-day management of the partnership, share in the profits and losses, and contract with their general partners to limit the financial liability of each limited partner to the amount he or she invests. Additionally, a well-written partnership agreement will allow for the continuity of the partnership in the event of the death of either a general or limited partner.

The advantages of limited liability, minimum management responsibility, and direct pass-through of profits and losses for taxation purposes have made this form of ownership popular. However, being free of management responsibility is only advantageous to the investors if the general partners are capable and honest. If they are not, the only control open to the limited partners is to vote to replace the general partners.

Before investing in a limited partnership, one should investigate the past record of the general partners, for this is usually a good indication of how the new partnership will be managed. The investigation should include their previous investments, talking to past investors, and checking court records for any legal complaints brought against them. Additionally, the prospective partner should be prepared to stay in for the duration of the partnership as the resale market for limited partnership interests is small.

A **joint venture** is an association of two or more persons or firms to carry out a single business project. A joint venture is similar to a partnership and is treated as a partnership for tax purposes. However, whereas a general partner can bind his partnership to a contract, a joint venturer cannot bind the other joint venturers to a contract for anything outside the scope of that single business project. Examples of joint ventures in real estate are the purchase of land by two or more persons with the intent of grading it and selling it as lots, the association of a landowner and builder to build and sell, and the association of a lender and builder to purchase land and develop buildings on it to sell to investors. Each member of the joint venture makes a contribution in the form of capital or talent, and all have a strong incentive to make the joint venture succeed. If more than one project is undertaken, the relationship becomes a partnership rather than a joint venture.

JOINT VENTURE

To carry out a single business project

A **syndication** (or **syndicate**) is not a form of ownership; rather, it refers to individuals or firms combining to pursue an investment enterprise too large for any of them to undertake individually. The form of ownership might be a tenancy in common, joint tenancy, general or limited partnership, land trust, or a corporation. Applied to real estate investing, the term "syndicate" usually refers to a limited partnership in which the limited partners provide the investment capital and the general partners provide the organizational talent and ongoing management services. The general partners receive compensation for purchasing, managing, and reselling the properties. The limited partners receive both a return of and a return on their investment if the syndicate is successful. Most states require that real estate syndicates be registered with the state before they can be sold to investors. Federal registration may also be necessary. Registration does not re-

SYNDICATION

lieve an interested investor from investigating carefully and seeking experienced legal direction.

CORPORATIONS   Each state has passed laws to permit groups of people to create **corporations** that can buy, sell, own, and operate in the name of the corporation. The corporation, in turn, is owned by stockholders, who possess shares of stock as evidence of their ownership.

Texas, by statute, gives corporations the right to acquire, purchase, and sell real property. To effect a conveyance, the conveying instrument must be signed by the corporation's president, vice president, or attorney-in-fact and be accompanied by a resolution by the Board of Directors of the corporation. A sale, mortgage, or pledge of substantially all the assets of the corporation must have approval of a majority of the shareholders.

Because the corporation is an entity (or legal being) in the eyes of the law, the corporation must pay income taxes on its profits. What remains after taxes can be used to pay dividends to the stockholders, who in turn pay personal income taxes on their dividend income. This double taxation of profits is the most important negative factor in the corporate form of ownership. On the positive side, the entity aspect shields the investor from unlimited liability. Even if the corporation falls on the hardest of financial times and owes more than it owns, the worst that can happen to the stockholder is that the value of his stock will drop to zero. Another advantage is that shares of stock are much more liquid than any previously discussed form of real estate ownership, even sole ownership. Stockbrokers and stock exchanges who specialize in the purchase and sale of corporate stock, usually complete a sale in a week or less. Furthermore, shares of stock in most corporations sell for less than $100, thus enabling an investor to operate with small amounts of capital. In a corporation, the stockholders elect a board of directors, who in turn hire the management needed to run the day-to-day operations of the company. As a practical matter, however, unless a person is a major shareholder in a corporation, he will have little control over management. His alternative is to buy stock in firms where he likes the management and sell where he does not.

Several large real estate corporations are traded on the New York Stock Exchange, and the corporation is a popular method of organization for real estate brokers and developers. Nevertheless, most real estate investors shun corporations because of the double taxation feature and because the tax benefits of owning real estate are trapped inside the corporation.

S Corporations

In 1958, the Internal Revenue Code first allowed stockholders to organize **Subchapter S** corporations which provided the liability protection of a corporation with the profit-and-loss pass-through of a partnership. Although the initial 10 stockholder maximum was a drawback, the real problem for real estate investors was that no more than 20% of a Subchapter S's gross receipts could come from passive income. And rent is passive income. In October of 1982, Congress revised the rules and eliminated the passive income restriction, increased the maximum number of shareholders to 35 and changed the name to **S Corporations.** (Regular corporations are now called C Corporations.) The advantages of S corporations were further enhanced by the new Internal Revenue Code of 1986 which reduced the top personal tax rate below the top rate on corporations.

An **association** is an organization that can own property and transact business in its own name. Several examples of associations are the homeowner associations found in condominiums and planned unit developments. There are also professional associations organized for business purposes, such as doctors associations and architects associations. If properly incorporated, an association will shield its members from personal liability in the event of lawsuits against the association.

ASSOCIATIONS

The idea of creating a trust that in turn carries out the investment objectives of its investors is not new. What has changed is that in 1961 Congress passed a law allowing trusts

REAL ESTATE INVESTMENT TRUSTS

Pools money of many persons for real estate purchases.

Investors = beneficiaries who purchase beneficial interests.

Avoids double taxation

that specialize in real estate investments to avoid double taxation by following strict rules. Texas has also passed a REIT act that sets forth state guidelines and requirements. These **real estate investment trusts (REITS)** pool the money of many investors for the purchase of real estate, much as mutual funds do with stocks and bonds. Investors in a REIT are called **beneficiaries** and they purchase **beneficial interests** somewhat similar to shares of corporate stock. The trust officers, with the aid of paid advisors, buy, sell, mortgage, and operate real estate investments on behalf of the beneficiaries. If a REIT confines its activities to real estate investments, and if the REIT has at least 100 beneficiaries and distributes at least 95% of its net income every year, the Internal Revenue Service will collect tax on the distributed income only once—at the beneficiaries' level. Failure to follow the rules results in double taxation.

The REIT is an attempt to combine the advantages of the corporate form of ownership with single taxation status. Like stock, the beneficial interests are freely transferable and usually sell for $100 each or less, a distinct advantage for the investor with a small amount of money to invest in real estate. Beneficial interests in the larger REITs are sold on a national basis, thus enabling a REIT to have thousands of beneficiaries and millions of dollars of capital for real estate purchases.

INTER VIVOS AND TESTAMENTARY TRUSTS

In all states, the trust form of ownership can be used to provide for the well-being of another person. Basically, this is an arrangement whereby title to real and/or personal property is transferred by its owner (the **trustor**) to a trustee. The **trustee** holds title and manages the property for the benefit of another (the **beneficiary**) in accordance with instructions given by the trustor. Two popular forms are the inter vivos trust, also called a living trust, and the testamentary trust.

An **inter vivos trust** takes effect during the life of its creator. For example, you can transfer property to a trustee with instructions that it be managed and that income from the trust assets be paid to your children, spouse, relatives, or a charity.

A **testamentary trust** takes effect after death. For example, you could place instructions in your will that upon your death, your property is to be placed into a trust. You can name whomever you want as trustee (a bank or trust company or friend, for example) and whom you want as beneficiaries. You can also give instructions as to how the assets are to be managed and how much (and how often) to pay the beneficiaries. Because trusts provide property management and financial control as well as a number of tax and estate planning advantages, this form of property ownership is growing in popularity.

In several states an owner of real estate may create a trust wherein he is both the trustor and the beneficiary. Called a **land trust,** the landowner conveys his real property to a trustee, who in turn manages the property according to the beneficiary's (owner's) instructions. Since the beneficial interest created by the trust is considered personal property, the land trust effectively converts real property to personal property. Originally, the land trust gained popularity because true ownership could be cloaked in secrecy behind the name of a bank's trust department. Today, however, its popularity is mainly because it is a useful vehicle for group ownership and may not be subject to legal attachment like real property which is held in the name of the beneficiary. Land trusts are commonly used in Texas although there is no specific statutory authority for their existence.

LAND TRUSTS

Owner conveys property to trustee. In effect, converts real property to personal property

Owner is both trustee and beneficiary.

Useful vehicle for group ownership

The purpose of this chapter has been to acquaint you with the fundamental aspects of the most commonly used forms of real estate ownership in the United States. You undoubtedly saw instances where you could apply these. Unfortunately, it is not possible in a real estate principles book to discuss each detail of each state's law (many of which change frequently), nor to take into consideration the specific characteristics of a particular transaction. In applying the principles in this book to a particular transaction, you should add competent legal advice regarding your state's legal interpretation of these principles.

CAVEAT

Figure 4:1   **METHODS OF HOLDING TITLE**

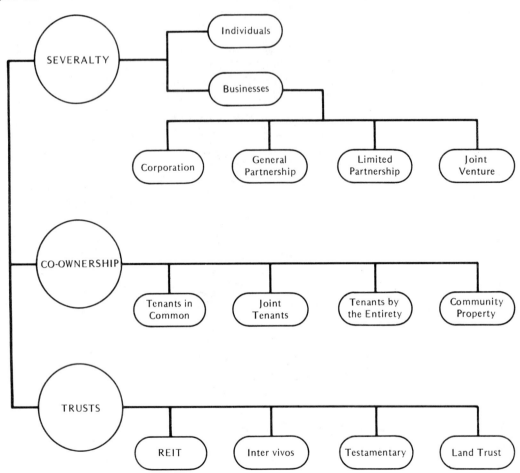

A visual summary of the various methods of holding
title to real estate discussed in this chapter.

VOCABULARY   *Match terms* **a–q** *with statements* **1–17.**
REVIEW
   8 **a.** *Community property*   *11* **g.** *Limited partner*
   1 **b.** *Estate in severalty*   *17* **h.** *Partition*
 16 **c.** *Financial liability*   *14* **i.** *Real estate investment trust*
 10 **d.** *General partnership*   *4* **j.** *Right of survivorship*
   5 **e.** *Joint tenancy*   *13* **k.** *Separate property*
 12 **f.** *Joint venture*   *15* **l.** *Syndication*

9 **m.** *Tenancy by the entirety*   6 **p.** *Unity of interest*
3 **n.** *Tenants in common*   7 **q.** *Unity of time*
2 **o.** *Undivided interest*

1. Owned by one person only. Sole ownership.
2. Each owner has a right to use the entire property.
3. Undivided ownership by two or more persons without right of survivorship; interests need not be equal.
4. The remaining co-owners automatically acquire the deceased's undivided interest.
5. A form of co-ownership in which the most widely recognized feature is the right of survivorship.
6. All co-owners have an identical interest in the property. A requirement for joint tenancy.
7. All co-owners acquired their ownership interests at the same time. A requirement for joint tenancy.
8. Spouses are treated as equal partners with each owning an undivided one-half interest. French and Spanish law origin.
9. An English law form of ownership reserved for married persons. Right of survivorship exists and neither spouse has a disposable interest during the lifetime of the other.
10. Each partner is fully liable for all the debts and obligations of the partnership.
11. A member of a limited partnership whose financial liability is limited to the amount invested.
12. Two or more persons joining together on a single project as partners.
13. Property acquired before marriage in a community property state.
14. A type of mutual fund for real estate investment and ownership wherein a trustee holds property for the benefit of the beneficiaries.
15. A general term that refers to a group of persons who organize to pool their money.
16. Refers to the amount of money a person can lose.
17. To divide jointly held property so that each owner can hold a sole ownership.

QUESTIONS AND PROBLEMS

1. What is the key advantage of sole ownership? What is the major disadvantage?
2. Explain what is meant by the term "undivided interest" as it applies to joint ownership of real estate.
3. Name the four unities of a joint tenancy. What does each mean to the property owner?
4. What does the term "right of survivorship" mean in real estate ownership?
5. Suppose that a deed was made out to "John and Mary Smith, husband and wife" with no mention as to how they were taking

title. Which would Texas law assume: joint tenancy, tenancy in common, tenancy by the entirety, or community property?

6. Does Texas permit the right of survivorship among persons who are not married?

7. If a deed is made out to three women as follows, "Susan Miller, Rhoda Wells, and Angela Lincoln," with no mention as to the form of ownership or the interest held by each, what can we presume regarding the form of ownership and the size of each woman's ownership interest?

8. In a community property state, if a deed names only the husband (or the wife) as the owner, can we assume that only that person's signature is necessary to convey title? Why or why not?

9. List two ways in which a general partnership differs from a limited partnership.

10. What advantages does a real estate investment trust offer a person who wants to invest in real estate?

ADDITIONAL READINGS

Martindale-Hubble Law Dictionary. (Martindale-Hubble, 1986, 4,500 pages). Contains summaries of law, including real estate, for each state and several foreign countries. Excellent reference material. Published annually.

Origins of the Common Law by **Arthur Hogue.** (Indiana University Press, 1966, 276 pages). Provides a fascinating historical review of the origins of common law in England and how it transplanted to the United States.

"Real Estate Partnerships: Can They Weather the Storm?" (*Changing Times,* April 1985, p. 48). Article points out that high fees and commissions, pricey properties and tougher tax laws are reducing yields from publicly offered real estate partnerships. This magazine regularly offers very readable and practical articles on real estate ownership.

Texas Real Estate Law, 4th ed. by **Charles J. Jacobus.** (Reston, 1985, 560 pages). See Chapter 3 on forms of ownership in Texas.

You and the Law, rev. ed. (Pleasantville, N.Y.: Reader's Digest Association, 1979, 863 pages). Presents in nontechnical language one's legal rights and obligations under the law. Contains sections on contract law, landlord-tenant law, home purchase, mortgages, real estate taxes, and rights and interests of spouses. Charts show how laws vary from state to state.

The Wonderful World of Real Estate by **Emmanuel Halper.** (Warren, Gorham and Lamont, 1975, 203 pages). A delightful and highly readable collection of 17 timeless real estate stories designed to educate and entertain.

*   *   *

The following periodicals may also be of interest to you: *Real Estate Securities Journal, Real Estate Syndication Digest, Realty Stock Review and REIT Review.*

Adverse possession: acquisition of real property through prolonged and unauthorized occupation of another's land

Bargain and sale deed: a deed that contains no covenants, but does imply the grantor owns the property being conveyed by the deed

Cloud on the title: any claim, lien or encumbrance that impairs title to property

Color of title: some plausible, but not completely clear-cut indication of ownership rights

Consideration: anything of value given to induce another to enter into a contract

Covenant: a written agreement or promise

Deed: a written document that when properly executed and delivered conveys title to land

Grantee: the person named in a deed who acquires ownership

Grantor: the person named in a deed who conveys ownership

Quitclaim deed: a legal instrument used to convey whatever title the grantor has; it contains no covenants, warranties, nor implication of the grantor's ownership

Warranty: an assurance or guarantee that something is true as stated

KEY TERMS

The previous three chapters emphasized how real estate is described, the rights and interests available for ownership, and how title can be held. In this chapter we shall discuss how ownership of real estate is conveyed from one owner to another. We begin with the voluntary conveyance of real estate by deed, and then continue with conveyance after death, and conveyance by occupancy, accession, public grant, dedication, and forfeiture.

A **deed** is a written legal document by which ownership of real property is conveyed from one party to another. Deeds were not always used to transfer real estate. In early England, when land was sold its title was conveyed by inviting the purchaser onto the land. In the presence of witnesses, the seller picked up a clod of earth and handed it to the purchaser. Simultaneously, the seller stated that he was delivering ownership of the land to the purchaser. In times when land sales

DEEDS
Convey title to land
must be in writing & signed

were rare, because ownership usually passed from generation to generation, and when witnesses seldom moved from the towns or farms where they were born, this method worked well. However, as transactions became more common and people more mobile, this method of title transfer became less reliable. Furthermore, it was susceptible to fraud if enough people could be bribed or forced to make false statements. In 1677, England passed a law known as the **Statute of Frauds.** This law, subsequently adopted by each of the American states, requires that transfers of real estate ownership be in writing and signed in order to be enforceable in a court of law. Thus, the need for a deed was created.

ESSENTIAL ELEMENTS OF A DEED

1. Identifiable grantor & grantee
2. Consideration
3. Words of conveyance
4. Legal description
5. Signature of grantor
6. Delivery & acceptance

What makes a written document a deed? What special phrases, statements and actions are necessary to convey the ownership rights one has in land and buildings? First, a deed must identify the **grantor,** who is the person giving up ownership, and the **grantee,** the person who is acquiring that ownership. The actual act of conveying ownership is known as a **grant.** To be legally enforceable, the grantor must be of legal age (18 years in Texas) and of sound mind.

Second, the deed must state that **consideration** was given by the grantee to the grantor. In Texas it is common to use the phrase, "For ten dollars ($10.00) and other good and valuable consideration," or the phrase, "For valuable consideration." These meet the legal requirement that consideration be shown, but retain privacy regarding the exact amount paid. If the conveyance is a gift, the phrase, "For natural love and affection," may be used, provided the gift is not for the purpose of defrauding the grantor's creditors.

Third, the deed must contain **words of conveyance.** With these words the grantor clearly states that he is making a grant of real property to the grantee, and identifies the quantity of the estate being granted. Usually, this is the fee simple estate, but it may also be a lesser estate (such as a life estate) or an easement.

A land **description** that cannot possibly be misunderstood is the fourth requirement. Acceptable legal descriptions are made by the metes and bounds method, by the government survey system, by recorded plat, or by reference to another recorded document that in turn uses one of these methods. Street names and numbers are not used as they do not identify the exact boundaries of the land and because street names and numbers can and do change over time. Appraisal district parcel numbers are subject to change, and not used either. If the deed conveys only an easement or air right, the deed states that fact along with the legal description of the land. The key point is that a deed must clearly specify what the grantor is granting to the grantee.

Fifth, the grantor must execute the deed by signing it. Eight states also require that the grantor's signature be witnessed and that the witnesses sign the deed. If the grantor is unable to write his name, he may make a mark, usually an X, in the presence of witnesses. They in turn print his name next to the X and sign as witnesses. If the grantor is a corporation, the corporation's seal may be affixed to the deed and an officer of the corporation with the proper authority signs the deed.

Figure 5:1 illustrates the essential elements that combine to form a deed. Notice that the example includes an identification of the grantor and grantee, fulfills the requirement for consideration, has words of conveyance, a legal description of the land involved, and the grantor's signature. The words of conveyance are "grant" and the phrase, "to have and to hold forever," says that the grantor is conveying all future benefits, not just a life estate or a tenancy for years. Ordinarily, the grantee does not sign the deed.

As a sixth and final requirement, there must also be **delivery and acceptance.** Although a deed may be completed and signed, it does not transfer title to the grantee until the grantor

---

Figure 5:1

Witnesseth, ___John Stanley___ , *grantor, for valuable consideration given by* ___Robert Brenner___ , *grantee, does hereby grant unto the grantee, his heirs and assigns to have and to hold forever, the following described land: [insert legal description here].*

_____*John Stanley*_____
Grantor's signature

voluntarily delivers it to the grantee and the grantee willingly accepts it. At that moment title passes.

Under Texas law, if a deed has been recorded it is presumed that a proper delivery has been effected. Delivery of the deed into escrow without recordation may also constitute delivery. When a deed has been irrevocably delivered into escrow, and the condition of the escrow is thereafter performed, title is said to have passed from the Seller when the deed is deposited into escrow. This is sometimes referred to as the **Relation Back Doctrine,** which effects a full and valid delivery for the grantor. For instance, when a grantor delivers title into escrow, but dies before closing of escrow, the conveyance would still be accomplished.

COVENANTS AND WARRANTIES

Although legally adequate, a deed meeting the preceding requirements can still leave a very important question unanswered in the grantee's mind: "Does the grantor possess all the right, title, and interest he is purporting to convey by this deed?" As a protective measure, the grantee can ask the grantor to include certain covenants and warranties in the deed. These are written promises by the grantor that the condition of title is as stated in the deed together with the grantor's guarantee that if title is not as stated he will compensate the grantee for any loss suffered.

Texas law generally recognizes two basic warranties. One warranty is called the **covenant of seizin,** which means that the grantor has not previously conveyed the same estate or any right, title, or interest therein to a person other than the grantee named in the deed. The second warranty is called a **covenant against encumbrances.** This warrants that the estate passed is free from encumbrances other than those therein specified at the time of the execution of the deed. These warranties basically provide that in the event there is a third-party claimant at some later date claiming title to the property, the grantee has the right to recover against the grantor any damages that he may suffer as a result of the failure of the warranties of the grantor in his general warranty deed.

Date and Acknowledgment

Although it is customary to show on the deed the date it was executed by the grantor, it is not essential to the deed's validity. Remember that title passes upon **delivery** of the deed to the grantee, and that this may not necessarily be the date it was signed.

It is standard practice to have the grantor appear before a notary public or other public officer and formally declare that he signed the deed as a voluntary act. This is known as an **acknowledgment.** An acknowledgment is not necessary in Texas to make the deed a valid conveyance. However, without the acknowledgment, the deed is binding only between the parties to the instrument. To protect against third-party claimants, the deed must be recorded in the county clerk's office in the county courthouse in the county in which the land is located. Acknowledgments and the importance of recording deeds will be covered in more detail in Chapter 6. Meanwhile, let us turn our attention to examples of the most commonly used deeds in Texas.

GENERAL WARRANTY DEED

Figure 5:2 illustrates a typical Texas general warranty deed. The name of the deed is shown in ①, although this usually has no effect if the deed is in fact something other than a general warranty deed. An introduction to the deed is usually combined with the location of the property as shown in ②. This is usually the recording jurisdiction; i.e., the county where the property is located. The designation of the grantors, as shown in ③ and ④, generally shows the marital status of the grantor(s). This helps keep the chain of title intact in the event there are any conflicts or discrepancies regarding the grantor and grantee in future conveyances. The residence of the grantors, although not a legal requirement for deeds, is shown at ⑤. Consideration, a requirement for deeds generally, although it need not be valuable consideration, is shown at ⑥. Consideration is usually stated as "$10.00 and other good and valuable consideration" to show that consideration was in fact paid, but to keep the actual amount of the transaction out of the public record. The granting clause is shown in ⑦. The use of the word "grant" or "convey" in Texas implies general warranty covenants, and unless otherwise stated, Texas law presumes fee simple title. The names of the grantees are shown in ⑧ and their residence in ⑨. If a deed does not have a grantee, it is void because no effective

Figure 5:2   **NOTICE**   Prepared by the State Bar of Texas for use by Lawyers only.
To select the proper form, fill in blank spaces, strike out form provisions or insert special terms constitutes the practice of law. No "standard form" can meet all requirements.

WARRANTY DEED (1)

THE STATE OF TEXAS   (2)   } KNOW ALL MEN BY THESE PRESENTS:

COUNTY OF HARRIS

(3)   (4)

That I. M. Seller and wife Happy Seller

of the County of Harris   (5)   and State of Texas   for and in

(6) consideration of the sum of TEN AND NO/100----------($10.00)-------------DOLLARS

and other valuable consideration to the undersigned paid by the grantee s   herein named, the receipt of

which is hereby acknowledged,

(7)

have GRANTED, SOLD AND CONVEYED, and by these presents do GRANT, SELL AND CONVEY unto

N. Debted and wife, May B. Debted (8)

of the County of Harris   (9)   and State of Texas   , all of

the following described real property in Harris   County, Texas, to-wit:

(10)   Lot 1, Block 1, Shakey Acres Subdivision,
Harris County, Texas, as shown of record
at Volume 7, Page 3, of the Map Records
of Harris County, Texas.

(11)   TO HAVE AND TO HOLD the above described premises, together with all and singular the rights and

appurtenances thereto in anywise belonging, unto the said grantee s ,   their   heirs and assigns

forever; and   we   do hereby bind ourselves, our   heirs, executors and administrators to

(12) WARRANT AND FOREVER DEFEND all and singular the said premises unto the said grantee s, their

heirs and assigns, against every person whomsoever lawfully claiming or to claim the same or any part thereof.

(13)   EXECUTED   this   28th   day of   February   , A. D. 19 xx

I. M. Seller ....

(14)

Happy Seller ....

Acknowledgment
THE STATE OF TEXAS   }
COUNTY OF Harris   }

Before me, the undersigned authority, on this day personally appeared

I. M. Seller and Happy Seller

known to me to be the person s   whose name s are   subscribed to the foregoing instrument, and acknowledged to me

that   they   executed the same for the purposes and consideration therein expressed.

Given under my hand and seal of office on this the   28th   day of February   , A. D. 19 xx

Rose Bloom ....

(SEAL)

Notary Public in and for   Harris   County, Texas.

conveyance took place. A legal description, a requirement for all deeds, is shown at ⑩. The habendum and warranty clauses, which defines the obligations of the grantor with respect to the warranties are shown at ⑪ and ⑫. Although not legally required, the deed is generally dated, as shown in ⑬. The important date is not the date of the deed but the date the deed was recorded. The Texas Recording Act provides that priority interests are determined by the first to record, therefore the date of conveyance is not technically as important as the recording date. The final requirement for a deed is that it have the signature of the grantor(s), which are shown at ⑭. Although not required to convey property, an acknowledgment of the grantors' signatures before a notary public is usually attached so that the deed can be recorded. Texas does not require a seal in order to make the deed valid. However, the acknowledgment must have a seal to be effective.

The exact style or form of a deed is not critical as long as it contains all the essentials clearly stated and in conformity with state law. For example, one commonly used warranty deed format begins with the words "Know all men by these presents," is written in the first person, and has the date at the end. Although a person may prepare his own deed, the writing of deeds should be left to experts in the field. In fact, some states permit only attorneys to write deeds for other persons. Even the preparation of preprinted deeds from stationery stores and title companies should be left to knowledgeable persons. Preprinted deeds contain several pitfalls for the unwary. First, the form may have been prepared and printed in another state and, as a result, may not meet the laws of your state. Second, if the blanks are incorrectly filled in, the deed will not be legally recognized. This is a particularly difficult problem when neither the grantor nor grantee realizes it until several years after the deed's delivery. Third, the use of a form deed presumes that the grantor's situation can be fitted to the form and that the grantor will be knowledgeable enough to select the correct form.

In a **special warranty deed,** the grantor covenants and warrants the property's title only against defects occurring

SPECIAL WARRANTY DEED

Used by trustees & executors

during the grantor's ownership and not against defects existing before that time. The special warranty deed is typically
used by executors and trustees who convey on behalf of an
estate or principal because the executor or trustee has no
authority to warrant and defend the acts of previous holders
of title. The grantee can protect against the gap in warranty
by purchasing title insurance. The special warranty deed is
also known in some states as a bargain and sale deed with
a covenant against the grantor's acts.

BARGAIN AND
SALE DEED

No covenants

Grantor purports
to own property

Passes "after-acquired
title"

The basic **bargain and sale deed** contains no covenants,
and only the minimum essentials of a deed (see Figure 5:3).
It has a date, identifies the grantor and grantee, recites consideration, describes the property, contains words of conveyance, and has the grantor's signature. But lacking covenants,
what assurance does the grantee have that he is acquiring
title to anything? Actually, none. In this deed the grantor
purports to own the property described in the deed, and
that he is granting it to the grantee. Logically, then, a grantee
will much prefer a warranty deed over a bargain and sale
deed, or require title insurance.

QUITCLAIM DEED

No covenants

No implication of
ownership

Renounces any right or
interest grantor may
have in the property

Used to clear cloud on
title.

Standard format for
granting an easement.

Does not pass after-
acquired title

A **quitclaim deed** has no covenants or warranties (see
Figure 5:4). Moreover, the grantor makes no statement, nor
does he even imply that he owns the property he is quitclaim-
ing to the grantee. Whatever rights the grantor possesses at
the time the deed is delivered are conveyed to the grantee.
If the grantor has no interest, right, or title to the property
described in the deed, none is conveyed to the grantee. However, if the grantor possesses fee simple title, fee simple title
will be conveyed to the grantee.

The critical wording in a quitclaim deed is the grantor's
statement that he "does hereby quitclaim." The word **quitclaim** means to renounce all possession, right, or interest.
If the grantor subsequently acquires any right or interest in
the property, he is not obligated to convey it to the grantee.

At first glance it may seem strange that such a deed should
even exist, but it does serve a very useful purpose. Situations
often arise in real estate transactions when a person claims
to have a partial or incomplete right or interest in a parcel

BARGAIN AND SALE DEED

Figure 5:3

STATE OF TEXAS   )
)   KNOW ALL MEN BY THESE
COUNTY OF HARRIS)   PRESENTS:

THAT WE,   I. M. SELLER   and wife,   MAY B.
SELLER,   of the County of Harris and State of Texas, for and in
consideration of the sum of   TEN AND NO/100 DOLLARS
($10.00)   and other good and valuable consideration in hand
paid by the grantees herein named, the receipt and sufficiency
of which is hereby acknowledged, have granted, sold and
conveyed, and by these presents do grant, sell and convey unto
    WILL B. DEBTED   and wife,   N. DEBTED,   of the
County of Harris and State of Texas, the following described
real property situated in Harris County, Texas, to wit:

> Lot 1, Block 1, Shakey Acres Subdivision, Harris
> County, Texas, as shown of record at Volume
> 7, Page 3 of the Map Records of Harris County,
> Texas.

TO HAVE AND TO HOLD the above described property
and premises unto the said Grantees, their heirs and assigns
forever. This conveyance is made without warranty, express or
implied.

EXECUTED this   28th   day of   February,
19xx.

_____
I. M. Seller
I. M. Seller

_____
May B. Seller
May B. Seller

of land. Such a right or interest, known as a **cloud on the
title,** may have been due to an inheritance, a dower, curtesy,
or community property right, or to a mortgage or right of
redemption due to a court-ordered foreclosure sale. By releasing that claim to the fee simple owner through the use of a
quitclaim deed, the cloud on the fee owner's title is removed.

Figure 5:4

QUITCLAIM DEED
Prepared by the State Bar of Texas for use by Lawyers Only

THE STATE OF TEXAS   }

COUNTY OF HARRIS   }   KNOW ALL MEN BY THESE PRESENTS:

That I. M. Seller and wife Happy Seller

of the County of   Harris   , State of   Texas   , for and

in consideration of the sum of TEN AND NO/100---------- ($10.00) ------------DOLLARS

in hand paid by the grantee S herein named, the receipt of which is hereby acknowledged, have QUIT-

CLAIMED, and by these presents do QUITCLAIM unto N. Debted and wife, May B. Debted

of the

County of   Harris   , State of Texas   , all of their right,

title and interest in and to the following described real property situated in   Harris   County,

Texas, to-wit: Lot 1, Block 1, Shakey Acres Subdivision, Harris County,
Texas, as shown of record at Volume 7, Page 3, of the Map
Records of Harris County, Texas.

TO HAVE AND TO HOLD all of   our   right, title and interest in and to the above described property

and premises unto the said grantee S , their heirs and assigns forever, so that neither   we   nor

our   heirs, legal representatives or assigns shall have, claim or demand any right or title to the

aforesaid property, premises or appurtenances or any part thereof.

EXECUTED this   28th   day of   February   , A. D. 19 XX .

Happy Seller   *I. M. Seller*
Happy Seller   I. M. Seller

THE STATE OF TEXAS   }
COUNTY OF HARRIS   }

Before me, the undersigned authority, on this day personally appeared
I. M. Seller and Happy Seller

known to me to be the person S whose name S are subscribed to the foregoing instrument, and acknowledged to me that
t he y executed the same for the purposes and consideration therein expressed.

Given under my hand and seal of office on this the   28th   day of February   , A. D. 19 XX .

Rose Bloom
(SEAL)   Notary Public in and for   Harris   County, Texas.

A quitclaim deed is also the standard deed format for granting an easement.

The basic bargain and sale deed contains no covenants of warranty. It does purport to pass an interest in real estate but with no warranties. It is superior to the quitclaim deed in that it passes **"after-acquired title."** While generally considered a legal technicality, the after-acquired title doctrine generally states that if a grantor conveys an interest in property which he does not own at the time of the conveyance, and if the grantor ever acquires that property subsequent to his initial conveyance, title automatically passes to the initial grantee. A quitclaim deed contains no warranties; the grantor does not claim to own an interest in property. A quitclaim deed is merely a relinquishment of all right, title, and interest that the grantor *may* have. Because of the loose wording of the quitclaim deed, it does not pass after-acquired title. Therefore, for most real estate situations a bargin and sale deed is preferred to a quitclaim deed.

After-Acquired Title

A **gift deed** is created by simply replacing the recitation or money and other valuable consideration with the statement, "in consideration of his [her, their] natural love and affection." This phrase may be used in a warranty, special warranty, or grant deed. However, it is most often used in quitclaim or bargain and sale deeds as these permit the grantor to avoid committing himself to any warranties regarding the property.

OTHER TYPES OF DEEDS

A **guardian's deed** is used to convey a minor's interest in real property. It contains only one covenant, that the guardian and minor have not encumbered the property. The deed must state the legal authority (usually a court order) that permits the guardian to convey the minor's property.

A **sheriff's deed** or **trustee's deed in foreclosure** is issued to the new buyer when a person's real estate is sold as the result of a mortgage or other court-ordered foreclosure sale. The deed should state the source of the sheriff's or referee's authority and the amount of consideration paid. Such a deed conveys only the foreclosed party's title, and, at the most, carries only one covenant: that the sheriff or referee has not damaged the property's title.

A **correction deed,** also called a deed of confirmation, is used to correct an error in a previously executed and delivered deed. For example, a name may have been misspelled or an error found in the property description. A **tax deed** is used to convey title to property that has been sold by the state or local government because of the non-payment of real property taxes.

CONVEYANCE
AFTER DEATH

If a person dies without leaving a last will and testament (or leaves one that is subsequently ruled void by the courts because it was improperly prepared), he is said to have died **intestate,** which means without a testament. When this happens, state law directs how the deceased's assets shall be distributed. This is known as **title by descent** or **intestate succession.**

Under Texas law, when a person dies, whether testate or intestate, his real or personal property passes immediately upon his death to his heirs or to his beneficiaries, subject to the payments of any debts, except those which are exempted by law. The surviving spouse and children are usually the dominant recipients of the deceased's assets. If there is no spouse or children, the deceased's grandchildren receive the next share. If there are no lineal descendants, the deceased's parents, brothers and sisters, and their children receive the next largest share. These are known as the deceased's **heirs.** The amount each heir receives, if anything, depends on state law and on how many persons with superior positions in the succession are alive. If no heirs can be found, the deceased's property escheats (reverts) to the state.

Testate, Intestate

A person who dies and leaves a valid will is said to have died **testate,** which means that he died leaving a testament telling how his property shall be distributed. The person who made the will, now deceased, is known as the **testator** (male) or **testatrix** (female). In the will, the testator names the persons or organizations who are to receive his real and personal property after he dies. Real property that is willed is known as a **devise** and the recipient, a **devisee.** Personal property that is willed is known as a **bequest** or **legacy,** and the recipient, a **legatee.** The will usually names an **executor** (male) or **executrix** (female) to carry out its instructions. If one is not named, the court will appoint an **administrator** (male) or **administratrix** (female).

Notice an important difference between the transfer of real estate ownership by deed and by will: once a deed is made and delivered, the ownership transfer is permanent, the grantor cannot change his mind and take back the property. With respect to a will, the devisees, although named, have no rights to the testator's property until the testator dies. Until that time the testator can change his mind and his will.

Upon death, the deceased's will must be filed with a court having power to admit and certify wills called a **probate court** in Texas. In lesser populated Texas counties, the county court performs this function. This court determines if the will meets all the requirements of law: in particular, that it is genuine, properly signed and witnessed, and that the testator was of sound mind when he made it. At this time anyone may step forward and contest the validity of the will. If the court finds the will to be valid, the executor is permitted to carry out its terms. If the testator owned real property, its ownership is conveyed using an **executor's deed** prepared and signed by the executor. The executor's deed is used both to transfer title to a devisee and to sell real property to raise cash. The executor's deed is usually a special warranty deed.

Probate Court
(County court in rural areas)

Because the deceased is not present to protect his assets, state laws attempt to ensure that fair market value is received for the deceased's real estate by requiring court approval of proposed sales, and in some cases by sponsoring open bidding in the courtroom. To protect his interests, a purchaser should ascertain that the executor has the authority to convey title.

For a will to be valid, and subsequently bind the executor to carry out the instructions, it must meet specific legal requirements. All states recognize the **formal** or **witnessed** will, a written document prepared, in most cases, by an attorney. The testator must declare it to be his will and sign it in the

Protecting the Deceased's Intentions

presence of two witnesses, who, at the testator's request and in his presence, sign the will as witnesses. A formal will prepared by an attorney is the preferred method, as the will then conforms explicitly to the law. This greatly reduces the likelihood of its being contested after the testator's death. Additionally, an attorney may offer valuable advice on how to word the will to reduce inheritance taxes.

Holographic Wills   **Holographic wills** are wills that are entirely handwritten, dated, and signed by the testator; but there are no witnesses. Nineteen states, including Texas, recognize holographic wills as legally binding. Persons selecting this form of will generally do so because it saves the time and expense of seeking professional legal aid, and because it is entirely private. Besides the fact that holographic wills are considered to have no effect in 31 states, they often result in much legal argument in states that do accept them. This can occur when the testator is not fully aware of the law as it pertains to the making of wills. Many otherwise happy families have been torn apart by dissension when a relative dies and the will is opened— only to find that there is a question as to whether or not it was properly prepared and hence valid. Unfortunately, what follows is not what the deceased intended; those who would receive more from intestate succession will contest that the will be declared void and of no effect. Those with more to gain if the will stands as written will muster legal forces to argue for its acceptance by the probate court.

Oral Will   A nuncupative will is an oral will made at the time of the last sickness of the deceased while at his home, or where he has resided for ten days or more preceding the date of the will. If the value of the property distributed under a nuncupative will exceeds $30.00, it must be proved by three credible witnesses that the testator called upon a person to take notice of his testimony that this was his last will and testament prior to his death. An oral will can only be used to dispose of personal property. Any real estate belonging to the deceased would be disposed of by intestate succession.

Codicil   A **codicil** is a written supplement or amendment made to a previously existing will. It is used to change some aspect of the will or to add a new instruction, without the work of rewriting the entire will. The codicil must be dated, signed, and witnessed in the same manner as the original will. The only valid way to change a will is with a codicil or by writing a complete new will. The law does not recognize cross-outs, notations, or other alterations made on the will itself.

Through the unauthorized occupation of another person's land for a long enough period of time, it is possible under certain conditions to acquire ownership by **adverse posses-sion.** The historical roots of adverse possession go back many centuries to a time before written deeds were used as evidence of ownership. At that time, in the absence of any claims to the contrary, a person who occupied a parcel of land was presumed to be its owner. Today, adverse possession is, in effect, a statute of limitations that bars a legal owner from claiming title to land when he has done nothing to oust an adverse occupant during the statutory period. From the adverse occupant's standpoint, adverse possession is a method of acquiring title by possessing land for a specified period of time under certain conditions.

ADVERSE POSSESSION

Courts of law are quite demanding of proof before they will issue a decree in favor of a person claiming title by virtue of adverse possession. The claimant must have maintained actual, visible, continuous, hostile, exclusive, and notorious possession, and be publicly claiming ownership to the property. These requirements mean that the claimant's use must have been visible and obvious to the legal owner, continuous and not just occasional, and exclusive enough to give notice of the claimant's individual claim. Furthermore, the use must have been without permission and the claimant must have acted as though he were the owner, even in the presence of the actual owner. Finally, the adverse claimant must be able to prove that he has met these requirements for a period ranging from 3 to 30 years, as shown in Table 5:1.

Adverse possession is statutorily defined in Texas and consists of four types: 3-year, 5-year, 10-year, and 25-year adverse possession.

Under the **3-year possession** statute, the possessor must claim title to the property under "some title" or "color of

Table 5:1   ADVERSE POSSESSION: NUMBER OF YEARS OF OCCUPANCY REQUIRED TO CLAIM TITLE*

State	Adverse Occupant Lacks Color of Title & Does Not Pay the Property Taxes	Adverse Occupant Has Color of Title &/or Pays the Property Taxes	State	Adverse Occupant Lacks Color of Title & Does Not Pay the Property Taxes	Adverse Occupant Has Color of Title &/or Pays the Property Taxes
Alabama	20	3–10	Missouri	10	10
Alaska	10	7	Montana		5
Arizona	10	3	Nebraska	10	10
Arkansas	15	2–7	Nevada		5
California		5	New Hampshire	20	20
Colorado	18	7	New Jersey	30–60	20–30
Connecticut	15	15	New Mexico	10	10
Delaware	20	20	New York	10	10
District of Columbia	15	15	North Carolina	20–30	7–21
Florida		7	North Dakota	20	10
Georgia	20	7	Ohio	21	21
Hawaii	20	20	Oklahoma	15	15
Idaho	5	5	Oregon	10	10
Illinois	20	7	Pennsylvania	21	21
Indiana		10	Rhode Island	10	10
Iowa	10	10	South Carolina	10–20	10
Kansas	15	15	South Dakota	20	10
Kentucky	15	7	Tennessee	20	7
Louisiana	30	10	Texas	10–25	3–5
Maine	20	20	Utah		7
Maryland	20	20	Vermont	15	15
Massachusetts	20	20	Virginia	15	15
Michigan	15	5–10	Washington	10	7
Minnesota	15	15	West Virginia	10	10
Mississippi	10	10	Wisconsin	20	10
			Wyoming	10	10

* As may be seen, in a substantial number of states, the waiting period for title by adverse possession is shortened if the adverse occupant has color of title and/or pays the property taxes. In California, Florida, Indiana, Montana, Nevada, and Utah, the property taxes must be paid to obtain the title. Generally speaking, adverse possession does not work against minors and other legal incompetents. However, when the owner becomes legally competent, the adverse possession must be broken within the time limit set by each state's law (the range is one to 10 years). In the states of Louisiana, Oklahoma, and Tennessee, adverse possession is referred to as title by prescription.

title," which might even be "irregular." (One or more of the documents of title in the chain of title may be missing.)

Title means a regular chain of transfers from or under the sovereignty of the soil. **Color of title** means a consecutive chain of transfers down to such person in possession, which may be irregular, as long as said defect does not extend to or include the want of intrinsic fairness or honesty.

The **5-year adverse possession** statute requires that the adverse claimant have peaceable and adverse possession of the property, cultivating, using, enjoying, and paying taxes on it, and claiming under a deed or deeds duly registered.

The **10-year adverse possession** statute requires that the adverse claimant have peaceable and adverse possession of the property, cultivating, using, and enjoying the same, and has a restriction of 160 acres unless the property has been fenced off, and unless the claimant has some memorandum of title which fixes the boundaries of the property. The memorandum of title as used in the 10-year statute does not require a deed, but merely a memorandum of title.

The **25-year adverse possession** statute requires peaceable and adverse possession of the real estate for a period of 25 years under a claim of right in good faith under any instrument purporting to convey same which has been recorded in the records of the county in which the real estate is located. This type of adverse possession is valid against minors and incompetents.

It is important to realize that any adverse possession in Texas under a fraudulent claim or under a forged document does not comply with the adverse possession requirements as set out by statute. Also, it is easy to understand why the owner of a large ranch would "ride the range" to maintain his fence and boundaries against poachers or other adverse claimants to either maintain his own title or perfect his own adverse possession interest.

In accumulating the required number of years, an adverse   *Tacking on*
claimant may **tack on** his period of possession to that of a prior adverse occupant. This could be done through the purchase of that right. The current adverse occupant could in

turn sell his claim to a still later adverse occupant until enough years were accumulated to present a claim in court.

Although the concept of adverse possession often creates the mental picture of a trespasser moving onto someone else's land and living there long enough to acquire title in fee, this is not the usual application. More often, adverse possession is used to extinguish weak or questionable claims to title. For example, if a person buys property at a tax sale, takes possession, and pays the property taxes each year afterward, adverse possession laws act to cut off claims to title by the previous owner. Another source of successful adverse possession claims may arise from encroachments. If a building extends over a property line and nothing is said about it for a long enough period of time, the building might constitute a valid adverse possession claim.

EASEMENT BY PRESCRIPTION

By prolonged adverse use
Only applies to public roads
in Texas

An easement can also be acquired by prolonged adverse use. This is known as acquiring an **easement by prescription.** Like adverse possession, the laws are strict: the usage must be openly visible, continuous and exclusive, as well as hostile and adverse to the owner. Additionally the use must have occurred over a period of 10 years in Texas. All these facts must be proved in a court of law before the court will issue the claimant a document legally recognizing his ownership of the easement. As an easement is a right to use land for a specific purpose, and not ownership of the land itself, Texas courts do not require the payment of property taxes to acquire a prescriptive easement.

As may be seen from the foregoing discussion, a landowner must be given obvious notification *at the location* of his land that someone is attempting to claim ownership or an easement. Since an adverse claim must be continuous and hostile, an owner can break it by ejecting the trespassers or by preventing them from trespassing, or by simply giving them permission to be there. Any of these actions would demonstrate the landowner's superior title. Owners of stores and office buildings with private sidewalks or streets used by the public can take action to break any possible claims to a public easement by either periodically barricading the sidewalk or street or by posting signs giving permission to pass. These signs are often seen in the form of brass plaques embedded in the sidewalk or street. In certain states, a land-owner may record with the public records office a **notice of consent.** This is evidence that subsequent uses of his land for the purposes stated in the notice are permissive and not adverse. The notice may be later revoked by recording a **notice of revocation.** There is no authority in Texas creating ease-ments by prescription to the public, except for public roads. Federal, state, and local governments protect themselves against adverse claims to their lands by passing laws making themselves immune from adverse possession claims.

The extent of one's ownership of land can be altered by the process of **accession.** This can result from natural or man-made causes. With regard to natural causes, the owner of land fronting on a lake, river, or ocean may acquire additional land due to the gradual accumulation of rock, sand, and soil. This process is called **accretion** and the results are referred to as alluvion and reliction. **Alluvion** is the increase of land that results when waterborne soil is gradually deposited to produce firm dry ground. **Reliction** (or dereliction) results when a lake, sea or river permanently recedes, exposing dry land. When land is rapidly washed away by the action of water, it is known as **avulsion.** Man-made accession occurs when man attaches personal property to land. For example, when lumber, nails, and cement are used to build a house, they alter the extent of one's land ownership.

OWNERSHIP BY
ACCESSION (Natural or man-made)

1. Accretion
   a. Alluvion - deposits of waterborne soil produce firm dry ground
   b. Reliction - body of water permanently recedes
2. Avulsion - land washed away by action of water

A transfer of land by a government body to a private individual is called a **public grant** or **patent.** The Homestead Act passed by the U.S. Congress in 1862 permits persons wishing to settle on otherwise unappropriated federal land to acquire fee simple ownership by paying a small filing charge and occupying and cultivating the land for 5 years. Similarly, for only a few dollars, a person may file a mining claim to federal land for the purpose of extracting whatever valuable minerals he can find. To retain the claim, a certain amount of work must be performed on the land each year. Otherwise, the government will consider the claim abandoned and an-other person may claim it. If the claim is worked long enough,

PUBLIC GRANT
OF LAND
Transfer by govt. to individual

a public grant can be sought and fee simple title obtained. In 1976, the U.S. government ended the homesteading program in all states except Alaska.

DEDICATION OF LAND   When an owner makes a voluntary gift of his land to the public, it is known as **dedication.** To illustrate, a land developer buys a large parcel of vacant land and develops it into streets and lots. The lots are sold to private buyers, but what about the streets? In all probability they will be dedicated to the town, city, or county. By doing this, the developer, and later the lot buyers, will not have to pay taxes on the streets, and the public will be responsible for maintaining them. The fastest way to accomplish the transfer is by either statutory dedication or dedication by deed. In **statutory dedication,** the developer prepares a map showing the streets, has the map approved by local government officials, and then records it as a public document. In **dedication by deed** the developer prepares a deed that identifies the streets and grants them to the city.

Common law dedication takes place when a landowner, by his acts or words, shows that he intends part of his land to be dedicated even though he has never officially made a written dedication. For example, a landowner may encourage the public to travel on his roads in an attempt to convince a local road department to take over maintenance.

REVERSION   **Reversion** can occur when a deed contains a condition or limitation. For example, a grantor states in his deed that the land conveyed may be used for residential purposes only. If the grantee constructs commercial buildings, the grantor can reacquire title on the grounds that the grantee forfeited his interest by not using the land for the required purpose. Similarly, a deed may prohibit certain uses of land. If the land is used for a prohibited purpose, the grantor can claim forfeiture has occurred.

ALIENATION   A change in ownership of any kind is known as an **alienation.** In addition to the forms of alienation discussed in this chapter, alienation can result from court action in connection with escheat, eminent domain, partition, foreclosure, execution sales, quiet title suits, and marriage. These topics are discussed in other chapters.

Match terms **a–t** with statements **1–20**.

VOCABULARY REVIEW

a. *Adverse possession*	**k.** *Easement by prescription*
b. *Alluvion*	**l.** *Grantee*
c. *Bargain and sale deed*	**m.** *Grantor*
d. *Cloud on the title*	**n.** *Holographic will*
e. *Codicil*	**o.** *Intestate*
f. *Color of title*	**p.** *Land patent*
g. *Consideration*	**q.** *Probate*
h. *Covenants and warranties*	**r.** *Quitclaim deed*
i. *Dedication*	**s.** *Statute of Frauds*
j. *Deed*	**t.** *Warranty deed*

J **1.** A written document that, when properly executed and delivered, conveys title to land.

S **2.** Requires that transfers of real estate be in writing to be enforceable.

M **3.** Person named in a deed who conveys ownership.

L **4.** Person named in a deed who acquires ownership.

G **5.** Anything of value given to produce a contract. It may be personal or real property, or love and affection.

H **6.** Promises and guarantees found in a deed.

D **7.** Any claim, lien, or encumbrance that impairs title to property.

T **8.** A deed that contains the covenants of seizin, quiet enjoyment, encumbrances, further assurance, and warranty forever.

C **9.** A deed that contains no covenants; it only implies that the grantor owns the property described in the deed.

R **10.** A deed with no covenants and no implication that the grantor owns the property he is deeding to the grantee.

O **11.** To die without a last will and testament.

N **12.** A will written entirely in one's own handwriting and signed but not witnessed.

Q **13.** The process of verifying the legality of a will and carrying out its instructions.

E **14.** A supplement or amendment to a previous will.

A **15.** Acquisition of real property through prolonged and unauthorized occupation.

F **16.** Some plausible, but not completely clear-cut, indication of ownership rights.

K **17.** Acquisition of an easement by prolonged use.

B **18.** Waterborne soil deposited to produce firm, dry ground.

P **19.** A document for conveying government land in fee to settlers and miners.

I **20.** Private land voluntarily conveyed to the government.

QUESTIONS AND PROBLEMS

1. Is it possible to convey fee title to land even though it does not contain the word "deed"? If so, why?

2. In the process of conveying real property from one person to another, at what instant in time does title actually pass from the grantor to the grantee?

3. What legal protections does a full covenant and warranty deed offer a grantee?

4. As a real estate purchaser, which deed would you prefer to receive: warranty, special warranty, bargain and sale? Why?

5. Does Texas require a seal on deeds?

6. What are the hazards of preparing your own deeds?

7. Name five examples of title clouds.

8. What is meant by the term "intestate succession"?

9. With regard to probate, what is the key difference between an executor and an administrator?

10. Does Texas consider holographic wills to be legal? How many witnesses are required for a formal will?

11. Can a person who has rented the same building for 30 years claim ownership by virtue of adverse possession? Why or why not?

12. Cite examples from your own community or state where land ownership has been altered by alluvion, reliction, or avulsion.

ADDITIONAL READINGS

New Encyclopedia of Real Estate Forms by **Jerome Gross.** (Prentice-Hall, 1983, 701 pages). Chapter 10 contains examples of deeds, including warranty deed, grant deed, special warranty deed, quitclaim deed, executor's deed, life estate deed, correction deed, cession deed, and referee deed.

Mastering Real Estate Mathematics, 4th ed. by **William Ventolo, Jr., and Wellington Allaway.** (Real Estate Education Co., 1984, 368 pages). A self-instruction book for percentages, fractions and decimals as they apply to commissions, interest, appraisal, leases, loan points, taxes, proration, and price problems.

Plan Your Estate, 4th ed. by **Denis Clifford.** (Nolo Press, 1986, 242 pages). Explains wills, probate avoidance, trusts, and taxes. Most bookstores carry a variety of books on this subject.

Real Estate Math Made Easy—A Step-by-Step Self Instructional Approach, 2d. ed. by **Ordway, Ordway and Tosh.** (Reston Publishing Co., 1986, 352 pages). A math book designed to supplement real estate principles. Addresses math anxiety.

Rental Homes: The Tax Shelter that Works and Grows for You by **Vincent Zucchero.** (Reston, 1983, 188 pages). Takes the reader step-by-step through an achievable rental home program from start to finish.

Texas Real Estate Law, 4th ed. by **Charles J. Jacobus.** (Reston, 1985, 560 pages). Provides up-to-date explanations of Texas law. Chapters 8 and 9 provide detailed information on voluntary and involuntary means of transferring land titles in Texas.

"Why Real Estate Projects Fail" by **James Boykin.** (Real Estate Review, Spring 85, p. 88). Article points out the importance of feasibility studies before developing land and notes there may be pressure on the feasibility firm to produce positive findings so they will receive the architectural or engineering contract.

Recordation, Abstracts, and Title Insurance

Abstract: a summary of all recorded documents affecting title to a given parcel of land

Acknowledgment: a formal declaration by a person signing a document that he or she, in fact, did sign that document

Actual notice: knowledge gained from what one has seen, heard, read, or observed

Chain of title: the linkage of property ownership that connects the present owner to the original source of title

Constructive notice: notice given by the public records and by visible possession, and the legal presumption that all persons are thereby notified

Marketable title: title that is free from reasonable doubt as to who the owner is

Mechanic's lien: a lien placed against real property by any unpaid workman or supplier who has done work or furnished building materials

Quiet title suit: court ordered hearings held to determine land ownership

Title insurance: an insurance policy against defects in title not listed in the title report or abstract

Torrens system: a state-sponsored method of registering land titles

KEY TERMS

In this chapter we shall focus on (1) the need for a method of determining real property ownership, (2) the process by which current and past ownership is determined from public records, (3) the availability of insurance against errors made in determining ownership, (4) the Torrens system of land title registration, and (5) the Uniform Marketable Title Act.

Until the enactment of the Statute of Frauds in England in 1677, determining who owned a parcel of land was primarily a matter of observing who was in physical possession. A landowner gave notice to the world of his claim to ownership by visibly occupying his land. After 1677 written deeds were required to show transfers of ownership. The problem then became one of finding the person holding the most current deed to the land. This was easy if the deedholder

NEED FOR PUBLIC RECORDS

117

also occupied the land, but was more difficult if he did not. The solution was to create a government-sponsored public recording service where a person could record his deed. These records would then be open free of charge to anyone. In this fashion, an owner could post notice to all that he claimed ownership of a parcel of land.

Constructive Notice

Since 1677 two ways have evolved for a person to give notice of a claim or right to land. One is by recording documents in the public records that give written notice to that effect. The other is by visibly occupying or otherwise visibly making use of the land. At the same time the law holds the world at large responsible for looking at the public records and looking at the land for this notice of right or claim. This is called **constructive notice.** Constructive notice charges the public with the responsibility of looking in the public records and at the property itself so as to have knowledge of all who are claiming a right or interest.

Actual Notice

Actual notice is knowledge that one has actually gained based on what he has seen, heard, read, or observed. For example, if you read a deed from Jones to Smith, you have actual notice of the deed and Smith's claim to the property. If you go to the property and you see someone in possession, you have actual notice of his/her claim to be there.

Actual notice also includes notice the law presumes you to have where circumstances, appearances, or rumors warrant further inquiry. For example, suppose you are considering the purchase of vacant acreage and upon inspecting it see a dirt road cutting across the land that is not mentioned in the public records. The law expects you to make further inquiry. The road may be a legal easement across the property. Another example is that anytime you buy rental property, you are expected to make inquiry as to the rights of the occupants. They may hold substantial rights you would not know about without asking them.

Remember that anyone claiming an interest or right is expected to make it known either by recorded claim or visible use of the property. Anyone acquiring a right or interest is expected to look in the public records and go to the property to make a visual inspection for claims and inquire as to the extent of those claims.

All states have passed **recording acts** to provide for the recording of every instrument (i.e., document) by which an estate, interest, or right in land is created, transferred, or encumbered. In Texas, each county has a County Clerk's Office. Located at the seat of county government, each county clerk's office will record documents submitted to it that pertain to real property in that county. Thus a deed to property in Tarrant County is recorded with the county clerk in Tarrant County. Similarly, anyone seeking information regarding ownership of land in Tarrant County would go to the clerk's office in Tarrant County. The recording process itself involves photocopying the documents and filing them for future reference.

To encourage people to use public recording facilities, laws in each state decree that (1) a deed, mortgage, or other instrument affecting real estate is not effective as far as subsequent purchasers and lenders are concerned if it is not recorded, and (2) prospective purchasers, mortgage lenders, and the public at large are presumed notified when a document is recorded. Figure 6:1 illustrates the concept of public recording.

Recording Acts

To illustrate the effect of constructive and actual notice laws, suppose that Brown offers to sell his land to Carver. Carver then inspects both the land and the public records and finds Brown to be the owner. Satisfied as to Brown's ownership, Carver pays Brown and receives a deed in return. Suppose that Carver does not occupy the land, but he does record his deed with the public recorder's office in the county where the land is located. If Brown now approaches Dawson and attempts to sell the same land, Dawson will find, upon visiting the public records office, that Brown has already conveyed title to Carver.

But what if Dawson assumes that Brown is telling the truth and does not trouble himself to inspect the land or the records? Even though Dawson pays for the land and receives a deed from Brown, the law will not regard Dawson

*Example of
Notice Laws*

Figure 6:1

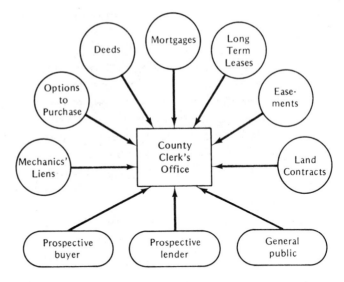

The County Clerk's office serves as a central information station for changes in rights, estates, and interests in land.

as the owner, even if Dawson records his deed. When Dawson discovers that Carver is the true owner, the only recourse open to Dawson is to sue Brown for the return of his money, presuming he can still locate Brown.

What would the result be if Carver did not record the deed he received and did not occupy the land? If Dawson became interested in buying the land and inspected the public records, he would find Brown to be the owner of the record. Upon inspecting the land, Dawson would find no notice of Carver's ownership either. Having satisfied the law and himself regarding the land's ownership, Dawson would pay Brown and receive a deed to the land. If Dawson records his deed before Carver does, the law will consider Dawson to be the new owner. At this point, the only recourse open to Carver is to try to get his money back from Brown. Even if Carver later records his deed and claims that the date on his deed is earlier than the date on Dawson's deed, it is of no avail. Priority is established by the date of recording, not by the date written on the deed. Failure to record does not invalidate the deed itself; it is still binding between the parties who made it. But it is not valid with respect to the rest of the world.

If Carver does not record the deed he receives, but does occupy the land, the law holds Dawson responsible for visiting the land and asking Carver what his rights are. At that point Dawson would learn of Brown's deed to Carver. Anytime a person buys property knowing that it has been sold before to another and the deed has not been recorded, he will not receive good title.

Although recording acts permit the recording of any estate, right, or interest in land, many lesser rights are rarely recorded because of the cost and effort involved. Month-to-month rentals and leases for a year or less fall into this category. Consequently, only an on-site inspection would reveal their existence, or the existence of any developing adverse possession or prescriptive easement claim.

With respect to actual and constructive notice, we can draw two important conclusions. First, a prospective purchaser (or lessee or lender) is presumed by law to have inspected both the land itself and the public records to determine the present rights and interests of others. Second, upon receiving a deed, mortgage, or other document relating to an estate, right, or interest in land, one should have it *immediately* recorded in the county in which the land is located.

Texas requires that a document be **acknowledged** before it is eligible to be recorded, or will permit **proper witnessing** as a substitute.

To effect a proper witnessing, the witness must personally appear before some officer authorized to take acknowledgments (notary public) and state under oath that (1) he saw the person execute the instrument and that said person executed the instrument for the purposes and consideration therein stated; and (2) that he signed the instrument as a witness at the request of the person who executed such instrument.

The objective of these requirements is to make certain that the person who signs the document is the same person named in the document and that the signing was a free and voluntary act. This is done to ensure the accuracy of the

REQUIREMENTS FOR RECORDING

public records and to eliminate the possibility of forgery and fraud. To illustrate, suppose that you own 50 acres of vacant land and someone is intent on stealing it from you. Since the physical removal of your land is an impossibility, an attempt could be made to change the public records. A deed would be typed and the forger would sign your name to it. If he were successful in recording the deed, and then attempted to sell the land, the buyer would, upon searching the records, find a deed conveying the land from you to the forger. A visual inspection of the vacant 50 acres would not show you in actual possession. Although innocent of any wrongdoing and buying in good faith, the buyer would be left with only a worthless piece of paper, as there was no intent on your part to convey title to him.

Acknowledgment

An **acknowledgment** is a formal declaration by a person signing a document that he or she, in fact, did sign the document. Persons authorized to take acknowledgments include notaries public, recording office clerks, commissioners of deeds, judges of courts of record, justices of the peace, and certain others as authorized by state law. Commissioned military officers are authorized to take the acknowledgments of persons in the military; foreign ministers and consular agents can take acknowledgments abroad. In Texas a notary public can take an acknowledgment anywhere in the state. If an acknowledgment is taken outside the state where the document will be recorded, either the recording county must already recognize the out-of-state official's authority or the out-of-state official must provide certification that he or she is qualified to take acknowledgments. The official seal of the notary on the acknowledgment normally fulfills this requirement.

The acknowledgment illustrated in Figure 6:2 is typical of those used by an individual in Texas. A short form acknowledgment, shown in Figure 6:3, is also used in Texas. Notice that the person signing the document must personally appear before the notary, and that the notary states that he or she knows that person to be the person described in the document. If they are strangers, the notary will require proof of identity. The person executing the document states that he

Figure 6:2

ACKNOWLEDGMENT FOR AN INDIVIDUAL

THE STATE OF TEXAS
COUNTY OF _____   ss

   Before me, the undersigned authority, on this day personally appeared _____ *, known to me to be the person whose name is subscribed to the foregoing instrument and acknowledged to me that he executed the same for the purpose and consideration therein expressed.*
   Given under my hand and seal of office this _____ *day of* _____ *, A.D., 19* _____ .

                    _____
                    Notary Public in and for _____
                    County, Texas

or she acknowledges executing the document by signing it in the presence of the notary. Note that it is the signer who does the acknowledging, not the notary. At the completion of the signing, a notation of the event is supposed to be made in a permanent record book kept by the notary.

PUBLIC RECORDS ORGANIZATION

Each document brought to a public recorder's office for recordation is photocopied and then returned to its owner. The photocopy is arranged in chronological order with photocopies of other documents and bound into a book. These books (often referred to by the Latin name for book, **liber**) are placed in chronological order on shelves that are open

Figure 6:3

SHORT FORM ACKNOWLEDGMENT

STATE OF TEXAS
COUNTY OF _____   ss
   This instrument was acknowledged before me on (date) by (name or names of person or persons acknowledging).
                    (Signature of officer) _____
                    (Title of officer) _____
                    My commission expires: _____

to the public for inspection. When the word liber is used, pages within the book are called **folios.** Otherwise, these are simply called **book and page.**

Filing incoming documents in chronological order makes sense for the recorder's office, but it does not provide an easy means for a person to locate all the documents relevant to a given parcel of land. To illustrate, suppose that you are planning to purchase a parcel of land and want to make certain that the person selling it is the legally recognized owner. Without an index to guide you, you would have to inspect every document in every volume, starting with the most recent book, until you located the current owner's deed. In a heavily populated county, your search might require you to look through hundreds of books, each containing up to 1,000 pages of documents. Consequently, recording offices have developed systems of indexing called grantor and grantee indexes.

In addition to the book and page records which are used in most counties in Texas, the legislature has specifically enacted legislation which provides for the microfilming of records by counties. Rather than record them under mortgage records, deed records, or other similar records, all records relating to or affecting real property are recorded under the heading of "Official Public Records of Real Property." Then, instead of getting a volume and page number, the document is given a Clerk's File Number and a Film Code Number. Texas has also provided for a *fixture* recording system for property which is personalty but is to become attached to realty. These are commonly termed **UCC liens** or **chattel mortgage liens** (UCC liens are liens which attach pursuant to the provisions of the Uniform Commercial Code, which Texas has adopted as the Texas Business and Commerce Code). As discussed in the fixture portion of this text, there are certain criteria under which the lien created by a supplier of certain fixtures may be even superior to that of a first lien deed of trust. Therefore it is important that the fixture records be searched as well as the lis pendens records, judgment rolls, and mechanics' liens filings in those counties that have those extra records.

Of the two indexing systems, the **tract index** is the simplest to use. In it, one page is allocated to either a single parcel of land or to a group of parcels, called a tract. On that page you will find a reference to all the recorded deeds, mortgages, and other documents at the recorder's office that relate to that parcel. Each reference gives the book and page where the original document is recorded. Title companies organize their records this way. The county clerks in Texas do not.

Tract Indexes

Title companies use; county clerks do not.

Grantors and grantee indexes are alphabetical indexes and are usually bound in book form. There are several variations in use in the United States, but the basic principle is the same. For each calendar year, the **grantor index** lists in alphabetical order all grantors named in the documents recorded that year. Next to each grantor's name is the name of the grantee named in the document, the book and page where a photocopy of the document can be found, and a few words describing the document. The **grantee index** is arranged by grantee names and gives the name of the grantor and the location and description of the document. This type of indexing system is required for county clerk's offices in Texas.

Grantor and
Grantee Indexes

A **chain of title** shows the linkage of property ownership that connects the present owner to the original source of title. In most cases it starts with the original sale or grant of the land from the government to a private citizen. It is used to prove how title came to be **vested** in (i.e., possessed by) the current owner. Figure 6:4 illustrates the chain-of-title concept.

CHAIN OF TITLE

Sometimes, while tracing (running) a chain of title back through time, an apparent break or dead end will occur. This can happen because the grantor is an administrator, executor, sheriff, or judge, or because the owner died or because a mortgage against the land was foreclosed. To regain the title sequence, one must search outside the recorder's office by checking probate court records in the case of a death, or by checking civil court actions in the case of a foreclosure.

Figure 6:4

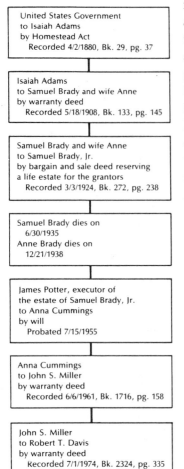

United States Government
to Isaiah Adams
by Homestead Act
    Recorded 4/2/1880, Bk. 29, pg. 37

Isaiah Adams
to Samuel Brady and wife Anne
by warranty deed
    Recorded 5/18/1908, Bk. 133, pg. 145

Samuel Brady and wife Anne
to Samuel Brady, Jr.
by bargain and sale deed reserving
a life estate for the grantors
    Recorded 3/3/1924, Bk. 272, pg. 238

Samuel Brady dies on
6/30/1935
Anne Brady dies on
12/21/1938

James Potter, executor of
the estate of Samuel Brady, Jr.
to Anna Cummings
by will
    Probated 7/15/1955

Anna Cummings
to John S. Miller
by warranty deed
    Recorded 6/6/1961, Bk. 1716, pg. 158

John S. Miller
to Robert T. Davis
by warranty deed
    Recorded 7/1/1974, Bk. 2324, pg. 335

In addition to looking for grantors and grantees, a search must be made for any outstanding mortgages, judgments, actions pending, liens, and unpaid taxes that may affect the title. In Texas, mortgages are placed in the general grantor and grantee indexes, listing the borrower (mortgagor) as the grantor and the lender (mortgagee) as the grantee. The process involves looking for the name of the property owner in each annual **mortgagor index** published while he owned the land. If a mortgage is found, a further check will reveal whether or not it has been satisfied and released. If it has been released, the recorder's office will have noted on the margin of the recorded mortgage the book and page where the release is located. When one knows the lender's name, the mortgage location and its subsequent release can also be found by searching the **mortgagee index.**

Public records must also be checked to learn if any lawsuits have resulted in judgments against recent owners, or if any lawsuits are pending that might later affect title. This information is found, respectively, on the **judgment rolls** and in the **lis pendens index** at the office of the county clerk. The term "lis pendens" is Latin for pending lawsuits. A separate search must also be made for **mechanics' liens** against the property that may have been filed by unpaid workmen and material suppliers. This step should also include an on-site inspection of the land for any recent construction activity or material deliveries. A visit must also be made to the local tax assessor's office to check the tax rolls for unpaid property taxes. This does not exhaust all possible places that must be visited to do a thorough title search. A title searcher may also find himself researching birth, marriage, divorce, and adoption records, probate records, military files, and federal tax liens in an effort to identify all the parties with an interest or potential interest in a given parcel of land and its improvements.

ABSTRACT OF TITLE

Although it is useful for the real estate practitioner to be able to find a name or document in the public records, full-scale title searching should be left to professionals. In a sparsely populated county, title searching is usually done on a part-time basis by an attorney. In more heavily populated counties, a full-time **abstractor** (also spelled **abstracter**) will search the records. These persons are experts in the field of title search, and for a fee they will prepare an abstract of title for a parcel of land.

An **abstract of title** is a complete historical summary of all recorded documents affecting the title of a property. It recites all recorded grants and conveyances as well as identifies and summarizes recorded easements, mortgages, wills, tax liens, judgments, pending lawsuits, marriages, divorces, etc., that might affect title. The abstract also includes a list of the public records searched, and not searched, in preparing the abstract.

The abstract is next sent to an attorney. Based on his knowledge of law and the abstract he is reading, he renders an **opinion** as to who the fee owner is and names anyone else he feels has a legitimate right or interest in the property. Generally speaking, the seller usually pays the cost of updating the abstract, and the buyer pays his attorney to give the opinion.

Despite the diligent efforts of conveyancers, abstracters, and attorneys to give as accurate a picture of land ownership as possible, there is no guarantee that the finished abstract, or its certification, is completely accurate. Persons preparing abstracts and opinions are liable for mistakes due to their own negligence, and they can be sued if that negligence results in a loss to a client. But what if a recorded deed in the title chain is a forgery? Or what if a married person represented himself on a deed as a single person, thus resulting in unextinguished dower rights? Or what if a deed was executed by a minor or an otherwise legally incompetent person? Or what if a document was misfiled, or there were undisclosed heirs, or a missing will later came to light, or there was confusion because of similar names on documents? These situations can result in substantial losses to a property owner, yet the fault may not lie with the conveyancer, abstracter, or attorney. The solution has been the organization of private companies to sell insurance against losses arising from title defects such as these as well as from errors in title examination.

TITLE INSURANCE

Efforts to insure titles date back to the last century and were primarily organized by and for the benefit of attorneys who wanted protection from errors that they might make in the interpretation of abstracts. As time passed, **title insurance** became available to anyone wishing to purchase it. The basic principle of title insurance is similar to any form of insurance: many persons pay a small amount into an insurance pool that is then available if any one of them should suffer a loss.

Title Commitment

When a title company receives a request for a title insurance policy, the first step is an examination of the public records. This is done either by an independent abstracter or attorney, or by an employee of the title company. A company attorney then reviews the findings and renders an opinion as to who the fee owner is and lists anyone else he feels has a legitimate right or interest in the property such as a mortgage lender or easement holder. This information is typed up and becomes the **title commitment,** which obligates the title insurance company to issue a policy of title when curative requirements, if any, have been satisfied. An example of a title commitment is illustrated in plain language in Figure 6:5. The State Board of Insurance in Texas publishes standard forms for commitments whose use is required by all title companies in Texas. They are much longer and in much greater detail than the sample one shown.

Notice how a title commitment differs from an abstract of title. Whereas an abstract is a summary of all recorded events that have affected the title to a given parcel of land, a title commitment is more like a snapshot that shows the condition of title at a specific moment in time. A title commitment does not tell who the previous owners were; it only tells who the current owner is. A title commitment does not list all mortgage loans ever made against the land, but only those that have not been removed.

Texas Title Policy

The standard Texas title insurance policy form provides insurance coverage for loss of title. It must be issued on a form promulgated by the State Board of Insurance. Ordinarily it contains the following exceptions from coverage:

Figure 6:5

TITLE COMMITMENT

The following is a report of the title to the land described in your application for a policy of title insurance.

LAND DESCRIPTION: Lot 17, Block M, Atwater's Addition, Jefferson County, State of _____ .

DATE AND TIME OF SEARCH: March 3, 19xx at 9:00am

PROPOSED INSURED: Barbara Baker, a single woman

ESTATE OR INTEREST: Fee simple

EXCEPTIONS:

1. *A lien in favor of Jefferson County for property taxes, in the amount of $645.00, due on or before April 30, 19xx.*

2. *A mortgage in favor of the First National Bank in the amount of $30,000.00, recorded June 2, 1974, in Book 2975, Page 245 of the Official County Records.*

3. *An easement in favor of the Southern Telephone Company along the eastern five feet of said land for telephone poles and conduits. Recorded on June 15, 1946, in Book 1210, Page 113 of the Official County Records.*

4. *An easement in favor of Coastal States Gas and Electric Company along the north ten feet of said land for underground pipes. Recorded on June 16, 1946, in Book 1210, Page 137 of the Official County Records.*

1. Restrictive covenants affecting the land described or referred to above
   (This normally refers to any deed restrictions or covenants which may have been reserved by a prior deed holder, such as those used for land-use control. If there are none "none of record" is written after this exception, to effectively delete the provision.)

2. Any discrepancies, conflicts, or shortages in area or boundary lines, or any encroachments, or any overlapping of improvements
   (This exception to the title policy may be amended to read "shortages in area" upon request and payment of an additional fee.)

3. Taxes for the current year and subsequent years, and for subsequent years due to changes in usage or ownership
(The title policy only warrants that taxes due prior to the closing have been paid and are up to date.)
4. Rights of parties in possession
(The Texas law still puts the burden on the purchaser to inspect the premises prior to the closing. Actual notice of parties in possession is equivalent to the constructive notice provided by recording.)

Policy Premium

In Texas, it is customary for the seller to pay the cost of both the title search and the insurance. However, this is negotiable between the buyer and the seller. When a property is sold, it is insured for an amount equal to the purchase price. This insurance remains effective as long as the buyer (owner) or his heirs have an interest in the property.

The insurance premium consists of a single payment. Title policy rates are set by the Texas Board of Insurance and are the same for all title companies. Each time the property is sold, a new policy must be purchased. The old policy cannot be assigned to the new owner.

Mortgagee's Policy

Thus far our discussion of title insurance has centered on what is called an **owner's policy.** Title insurance companies also offer what is called a **mortgagee's policy.** This protects a lender who has taken real estate as collateral for a loan. There are three significant differences between an owner's and a mortgagee's policy. First, the owner's policy is good for the full amount of coverage stated on the policy for as long as the insured or his heirs have an interest in the property. In contrast, the mortgagee's policy protects only for the amount owed on the mortgage loan. Thus, the coverage on a mortgagee's policy declines and finally terminates when the loan is fully repaid. The second difference is that the mortgagee's policy does not make exceptions for claims to ownership that could have been determined by physically inspecting the property. The third difference is that the mortgagee's title policy provides coverage to subsequent holders of the same mortgage loan.

The cost of a mortgagee's policy (also known as a lender's policy or loan policy) is similar to an owner's policy. Although the insurance company takes added risks by eliminating some exceptions found in the owner's policy, this is balanced by the fact that the liability decreases as the loan is repaid. When an owner's and a mortgagee's policy are purchased at the same time, as in the case of a sale with new financing, the combined cost is only a few dollars more than the cost of the owner's policy alone. The mortgagee's policy covers only title problems. It does not insure that the loan will be repaid by the borrower.

When an insured defect arises, the title insurance company reserves the right to either pay the loss or fight the claim in court. If it elects to fight, any legal costs the company incurs are in addition to the amount of coverage stated in the policy. If a loss is paid, the amount of coverage is reduced by that amount and any unused coverage is still in effect. If the company pays a loss, it acquires the right to collect from the party who caused the loss. In Texas, the title company is only liable for a proportionate amount of the title which fails. If 100% of the title fails, coverage is limited to the face value of the policy.

Claims for Losses

In comparing title insurance to other forms of insurance (e.g., life, fire, automobile), note that title insurance protects against something that has already happened but has not been discovered. A forged deed may result in a disagreement over ownership: the forgery is a fact of history, the insurance is in the event of its discovery. But in some cases the problem will never be discovered. For example, heirs may be totally unaware of their property rights and fail to timely claim them. If they never claim them, the rights extinguish themselves by limitations, and the intervening property owners will have been unaffected.

Only a small part of the premiums collected by title insurance companies are used to pay claims, largely because they take great pains to maintain on their own premises complete copies of the public records for each county in which they do business. These are called **title plants;** in many cases they are actually more complete and better organized than those available at the public recorder's office. The philosophy is that the better the quality of the title search, the fewer the claims that must be paid.

The Growth of Title Insurance

The title insurance business has mushroomed due to three important reasons. First, in a warranty deed, the grantor makes several strongly worded covenants. As you will recall, the grantor covenants that he is the owner, that there are no encumbrances except as stated in the deed and that the grantor will warrant and forever defend the premises. Thus, signing a warranty deed places a great obligation on the grantor. By purchasing title insurance and using only a special warranty, the grantor can transfer a significant portion of that obligation to an insurance company.

Second, a grantee is also motivated to have title insurance. Even with a warranty deed, there is always the lingering question of whether or not the seller would be financially capable of making good on his covenants and warranties. They are useless if one cannot enforce them.

Third, the broad use of title insurance has made mortgage lending more attractive and borrowing a little easier and cheaper for real property owners. This is because title insurance has removed the risk of loss due to defective titles while insuring the lender's lien priority. Secondary market purchasers of loans such as FNMA and FHLMC (Chapter 12) require title insurance on any loan they purchase.

QUIET TITLE SUIT

When a title defect (or **title cloud**) must be removed, it is logical to remove it by using the path of least resistance. For example, if an abstract or title report shows unpaid property taxes, the buyer may require the seller to pay them in full before the deal is completed. Similarly, a distant relative with ownership rights might be willing, upon negotiation, to quitclaim them for a price.

Sometimes a stronger means is necessary to remove title defects. For example, the distant relative may refuse to negotiate, or the lender may refuse to remove a mortgage lien despite pleas from the borrower that it has been paid. The solution is a **quiet title suit** (also called a quiet title action). In Texas, a property owner can ask the courts to hold hearings on the ownership of his land. At these hearings anyone claiming to have an interest or right to the land in question may present verbal or written evidence of that claim. A judge, acting on the evidence presented and the laws of his state, rules on the validity of each claim. The result is to legally recognize those with a genuine right or interest and to "quiet" those without a genuine interest.

THE TORRENS SYSTEM

Over a century ago, Sir Richard Torrens, a British administrator in Australia, devised an improved system of identifying land ownership. He was impressed by the relative simplicity of the British system of sailing-ship registration. The government maintained an official ships' registry that listed on a single page a ship's name, its owner, and any liens or encumbrances against it. Torrens felt land titles might be registered in a similar manner. The system he designed, known as the **Torrens system** of land title registration, starts with a landowner's application for registration and the preparation of an abstract. This is followed by a quiet title suit at which all parties named in the abstract and anyone else claiming a right or interest to the land in question may attend and be heard.

Torrens Certificate
of Title

Based on the outcome of the suit, a government-appointed **registrar of titles** prepares a **certificate of title.** This certificate names the legally recognized fee owner and lists any legally recognized exceptions to that ownership, such as mortgages, easements, long-term leases, or life estates. The registrar keeps the original certificate of title and issues a duplicate to the fee owner. (Although they sound similar, a Torrens certificate of title is not the same as an attorney's certificate of title. The former shows ownership and claims against that ownership as established by a court of law. The latter is strictly an opinion of the condition of title.)

Once a title is registered, any subsequent liens or encumbrances against it must be entered on the registrar's copy of the certificate of title in order to give constructive notice. When a lien or encumbrance is removed, its notation on the certificate is canceled. In this manner, the entire concept of constructive notice for a given parcel of land is reduced to a single-page document open to public view at the registrar's office. This, Torrens argued, would make the whole process of title transfer much simpler and cheaper.

When registered land is conveyed, the grantor gives the grantee a deed. The grantee takes the deed to the registrar of titles, who actually transfers the title by canceling the grantor's certificate and issuing a new certificate in the name of the grantee. The deed, though delivered, does not actually transfer title in a Torrens jurisdiction. Any liens or other encumbrances not removed at the same time are carried over from the old to the new certificate. The deed and certificate are kept by the registrar; the grantee receives a duplicate of the certificate. If the conveyance is accompanied by a new mortgage, it is noted on the new certificate, and a copy of the mortgage is retained by the registrar. Except for the quiet title suit aspect, the concept of land title registration is quite similar to that used in the United States for registering ownership of motor vehicles.

Adoption   In the United States, the first state to have a land registration act was Illinois in 1895. Other states slowly followed, but often their laws were vague and cumbersome to the point of being useless. At one point, 20 states had land title registration acts, but since then 9 states have replaced their acts and only 11 remain. They are Hawaii, Illinois, Massachusetts, Minnesota, New York, Colorado, Georgia, North Carolina, Ohio, Virginia, and Washington.

In all 11 states the Torrens title system co-exists with the regular recording procedures described earlier in this chapter. Thus it is possible for a house on one side of a street to be Torrens registered and a house across the street to be recorded the regular way. Also, it may be customary to use Torrens in just certain areas of the state. In Illinois, use has been concentrated in Cook County (the Chicago area); in Minnesota, in the Minneapolis area; in Massachusetts, the Boston area; and in New York, Suffolk County (eastern Long Island). In Hawaii, Torrens is used statewide, but primarily by large landowners and subdivision developers who want to clear up complex title problems. In the remaining 6 states the public has made relatively little use of land title registration. This limited adoption of Torrens is due, among other things, to the promotion, wide-spread availability and lower short-run cost of title insurance. (The quiet title suit can be costly.) Note too that although a state-run insurance fund is usually available to cover registration errors, some lenders do not feel this is adequate protection and require title insurance.

At least 10 states (but not Texas) have a **Marketable Title Act.** This is *not* a system of title registration. Rather, it is legislation aimed at making abstracts easier to prepare and less prone to error. This is done by cutting off claims to rights or interests in land that have been inactive for longer than the act's statutory period. In Connecticut, Michigan, Utah, Vermont, and Wisconsin, this is 40 years. Thus, in these states, a person who has an unbroken chain of title with no defects for at least 40 years is regarded by the law as having marketable title. Any defects more than 40 years old are outlawed. The result is to concentrate the title search process on the immediate past 40 years. Thus, abstracts can be produced with less effort and expense, and the chance for an error either by the abstracter or in the documents themselves is greatly reduced. This is particularly true in view of the fact that record-keeping procedures in the past were not as sophisticated as they are today.

The philosophy of a marketable title act is that a person has 40 years to come forward and make his claim known; if he does not, then he apparently does not consider it worth pursuing. As protection for a person actively pursuing a claim that is about to become more than 40 years old, the claim can be renewed for another 40 years by again recording notice of the claim in the public records. In certain situations, a title must be searched back more than 40 years (e.g., when there is a lease of more than 40-year duration or when no document affecting ownership has been recorded in over 40 years). In Nebraska the statutory period is 22 years; in Florida, North Carolina, and Oklahoma it is 30 years; in Indiana, 50 years.

Marketable title acts do not eliminate the need for legal notice nor do they eliminate the role of adverse possession.

MARKETABLE TITLE ACTS

VOCABULARY REVIEW

Match terms **a–q** *with statements* **1–17.**

a. Abstract
b. Acknowledgment
c. Actual notice
d. Chain of title
e. Constructive notice
f. Grantor index
g. Lis pendens index
h. Marketable title
i. Marketable title acts

j. Mechanic's lien
k. Mortgagee's title policy
l. Notary public
m. Owner's title policy
n. Public recorder's office
o. Quiet title suit
p. Title report
q. Torrens system

c **1.** Knowledge gained from what one has seen, heard, read, or observed.

e **2.** Notice given by means of a document placed into the public records.

b **3.** A formal declaration, made in the presence of a notary public or other authorized individual, by a person affirming that he or she signed a document.

l **4.** A person authorized to take acknowledgments.

n **5.** A place where a person can inform the world as to his land ownership by recording his deed.

f **6.** A book at the public recorder's office that lists grantors alphabetically by name.

d **7.** The linkage of ownership that connects the present owner to the original source of title.

g **8.** A publicly available index whereby a person can learn of any pending lawsuits that may affect title.

j **9.** A lien placed against real property by unpaid workmen and material suppliers.

a **10.** A complete summary of all recorded documents affecting title to a given parcel of land.

m **11.** Insurance to protect a property owner against monetary loss if his title is found to be imperfect.

p **12.** A report made by a title insurance company showing current title condition.

k **13.** A title policy written to protect a real estate lender.

h **14.** Title that is free from reasonable doubt as to who the owner is.

o **15.** Court-ordered hearings held to determine land ownership.

i **16.** Laws that automatically cut off inactive claims to rights or interest in land.

q **17.** A method of registering land titles that is similar to that of automobile ownership registration.

1. Explain in your own words the concepts of actual and constructive notice and the roles that they play in real estate ownership.
2. Where is the public recorder's office for your community located?
3. How much does your public recorder's office charge to record a deed? A mortgage? What requirements must a document meet before it will be accepted for recording?
4. What is the purpose of grantor and grantee indexes?
5. Why is it important that a title search be carried out in more places than just the county recorder's office?
6. What is the difference between a certificate of title issued by an attorney and a Torrens certificate of title?
7. How does a title report differ from an abstract?
8. What is the purpose of title insurance?
9. Thorsen sells his house to Williams. Williams moves in but for some reason does not record his deed. Thorsen discovers this and sells the house to an out-of-state investor who orders a title search, purchases an owner's title policy, and records his deed. Thorsen then disappears with the money he received from both sales. Who is the loser when this scheme is discovered: Williams, the out-of-state investor, or the title company? Why?
10. If you are located near the public recorder's office for your county, examine the records for a parcel of land (such as your home) and trace its ownership back through three owners.

QUESTIONS AND PROBLEMS

Real Estate Counseling by **James Boykin.** (Prentice-Hall, 1984, 288 pages). Written for those who plan to offer real estate counseling services and those who plan to use those services. Nineteen professional counselors offer advice on real estate analysis and decision making.

The Texas Homebuyer's Manual, published by the State Bar of Texas 1985 (56 pages). A manual intended to assist persons buying a home in Texas for the first time, discussing the various legal and other consideration involved in real estate transactions.

Texas Real Estate Law, 4th ed. by **Charles J. Jacobus.** (Reston, 1985, 560 pages). Provides up-to-date explanations of law pertinent to the daily operation of a real estate brokerage office in Texas. See Chapter 10 on recordation of documents in Texas and Chapter 13 deals with title assurance.

Title Insurance. Most title insurance companies have booklets explaining title insurance they give free to anyone who asks.

"Title Insurance and the Lender" by **Robert Bates.** (Guarantor, July/Aug 83, p. 8). Article points out how title insurance has helped make possible a large and efficient mortgage lending industry in the United States.

ADDITIONAL READINGS

"What's Covered in a Title Policy" by **Frederick Romanski.** (*Real Estate Today,* July/Aug 83, p. 43). Also in the same issue "What You Should Know About Title Insurance" and "Title Insurance: Buyer Security." These three articles explain the need for title insurance with eye-opening cases histories of title problems.

*   *   *

The following periodicals may also be of interest to you: *Lawyers Title News, MGIC Newsletter, National Property Law Digest, Your Public Lands* and *Title News.*

Contract Law

Breach of contract: failure without legal excuse to perform as required by a contract

Competent parties: persons considered legally capable of entering into a binding contract

Contract: a legally enforceable agreement to do (or not to do) a particular thing

Duress: the application of force to obtain an agreement

Fraud: an act intended to deceive for the purpose of inducing another to give up something of value

Liquidated damages: an amount of money specified in a contract as compensation to be paid if the contract is not satisfactorily completed

Minor, Infant: a person under the age of legal competence; in most states, under 18 years

Specific performance: contract performance according to the precise terms agreed upon

Void contract: a contract that has no binding effect on the parties who made it

Voidable contract: a contract that binds one party but gives the other the right to withdraw

A **contract** is a legally enforceable agreement to do (or not to do) a specific thing. In this chapter we shall see how a contract is created and what makes it legally binding. Topics covered include offer and acceptance, fraud, mistake, lawful objective, consideration, performance, and breach of contract. In Chapter 8 we will turn our attention to the purchase contract, trade agreeement, and installment contract as they relate to the buying and selling of real estate.

HOW A CONTRACT IS CREATED

A contract may be either expressed or implied. An **expressed contract** occurs when the parties to the contract declare their intentions either orally or in writing. (The word **party** [plural, **parties**] is a legal term that refers to a person or group involved in a legal proceeding.) A lease or rental agreement, for example, is an expressed contract. The lessor (landlord) expresses his intent to permit the lessee (tenant) to use the premises, and the lessee agrees to pay the rent. A contract to purchase real estate is also an expressed contract.

implied: actions

An **implied contract** is created by neither words nor writing but rather by actions of the parties indicating that they intend to create a contract. For example, when you step into a taxicab, you imply that you will pay the fare. The cab driver, by allowing you in the cab, implies that he will take you where you want to go. The same thing occurs at a restaurant. The presence of tables, silverware, menus, waiters, and waitresses implies that you will be served food. When you order, you imply that you are going to pay when the bill is presented.

Bilateral Contract

promise for promise

A contract may be either bilateral or unilateral. A **bilateral contract** results when a promise is exchanged for a promise. In the typical real estate sale, the buyer promises to pay the agreed price, and the seller promises to deliver title to the buyer. In a lease contract the lessor promises the use of the premises to the lessee and the lessee promises to pay rent in return. A bilateral contract is basically an "I will do this *and* you will do that" arrangement.

Unilateral Contract

(if)
promise for performance

A **unilateral contract** results when a promise is exchanged for performance. For instance, during a campaign to get more listings, a real estate office manager announces to the firm's sales staff that an extra $100 bonus will be paid for each salable new listing. No promises or agreements are necessary from the salespersons. However, each time a salesperson performs by bringing in a salable listing, he or she is entitled to the promised $100 bonus. An option to purchase is a unilateral contract until it is exercised, at which time it becomes a bilateral contract. A unilateral contract is basically an "I will do this *if* you will do that" arrangement.

Forbearance

not to act

Most contract agreements are based on promises by the parties involved to act in some manner (pay money, provide services, or deliver title). However, a contract can contain a promise to **forbear** (not to act) by one or more of its parties. For example, a lender may agree not to foreclose on a delinquent mortgage loan if the borrower agrees to a new payment schedule.

Legal [Effect]

A contract can be construed by the courts to be valid, void, or unenforceable.

A **valid contract** is one that meets all the requirements
of law. It is binding upon its parties and legally enforceable
in a court of law. A **void contract** has no legal effect and, in
fact, is not a contract at all. Even though the parties may
have gone through the motions of attempting to make a contract, no legal rights are created and any party thereto may
ignore it at his pleasure. A **voidable contract** binds one party
but not the other. An **unenforceable contract** is one that may
have been valid, but its enforcement is now barred by the
statute of limitations or the doctrine of laches. Let us now
turn our attention to the requirements of a valid contract.

For a contract to be **legally valid,** and hence binding   *ESSENTIALS OF A*
and enforceable, the following five requirements must be   *VALID CONTRACT*
met:

1. Legally competent parties. 18yrs, sane, capable of understanding transaction
2. Mutual agreement. willingness, no fraud, misrepresentation, mistake; offer & acceptance; freely given
3. Lawful objective.
4. Consideration or cause. Promise to do something, money, property, personal services, forbearance, love and affection
5. Contract in writing when required by law. Required for real estate

If these conditions are met, any party to the contract may,
if the need arises, call upon a court of law to either enforce
the contract as written or award money damages for nonper-
formance. In reality, a properly written contract seldom ends
in court because each party knows it will be enforced as
written. It is the poorly written and unenforceable contract
that ends in court. A judge must then decide if a contract
actually exists and the obligations of each party. It is much
better if the contract is correctly prepared in the first place.
Let's look more closely at the five requirements of an enforceable contract.

For a contract to be legally enforceable, all parties entering   *COMPETENT PARTIES*
into it must be legally competent. In deciding competency,
the law provides a mixture of objective and subjective standards. The most objective standard is that of age. A person
must reach the age of *majority* to be legally capable of entering
into a contract. **Minors** do not have contractual capability.
Until the voting age in national elections was reduced from
21 to 18 years by Congress, persons were considered to be

minor by most states until the age of 21. Since then most state legislatures (including Texas) have lowered the age for entering into legally binding contracts to 18 years. The purpose of majority laws is to protect minors (also known as "infants" in legal terminology) from entering into contracts that they may not be old enough to understand. Depending on the circumstances, a contract entered into by a minor may be void or voidable. For example, the adult might be bound but the minor could withdraw. If a contract with a minor is required, it is still possible to obtain a binding contract by working through the minor's legal guardian.

Persons of unsound mind who have been declared incompetent by a judge may not make a valid contract, and any attempt to do so results in a void contract. The solution is to contract through the person appointed to act on behalf of the incompetent. If a person has not been judged legally incompetent but nonetheless appears incapable of understanding the transaction in question, he has no legal power to contract. In some states persons convicted of felonies may not enter into valid contracts without the prior approval of the parole board.

Regarding intoxicated persons, if there was a deliberate attempt to intoxicate a person for the purpose of approving a contract, the intoxicated person, upon sobering up, can call upon the courts to void the contract. If the contracting party was voluntarily drunk to the point of incompetence, when he is sober he may ratify or deny the contract if he does so promptly. However, some courts look at the matter strictly from the standpoint of whether the intoxicated person had the capability of formulating the intent to enter into a contract. Obviously, there are some fine and subjective distinctions among these three categories, and a judge may interpret them differently than the parties to the contract. Most other mind altering drugs are dealt with in the same manner as alcohol.

Power of Attorney   An individual can give another person the power to act on his behalf: for example to buy or sell land, or to sign lease documents. This is called a **power of attorney.** The person holding the power of attorney is called an **attorney-**

in-fact. With regard to real estate, a power of attorney must be stated in writing because the real estate documents to be signed must be in writing. Any document signed with a power of attorney should be executed as follows: "Paul Jones, principal, by Samuel Smith, agent, his attorney-in-fact." If the agent has power to convey title to land, then the document granting him power of attorney should be acknowledged by the principal and recorded. The agent is legally competent to the extent of the powers granted to him by the principal as long as the principal remains alive. The power of attorney can, of course, be terminated by the principal at any time. A recorded notice of revocation is needed to revoke a recorded power of attorney.

Corporations are considered legally competent parties. However, the individual contracting on behalf of the corporation must have authority from the board of directors. Some states also require that the corporate seal be affixed to contracts, although Texas does not. A partnership can contract either in the name of the partnership or in the name of any of its general partners. Executors and administrators can legally contract on behalf of trusts and estates, provided that they have proper authorization.

Corporations

The requirement of **mutual agreement** (also called **mutual consent,** or **mutual assent,** or **meeting of the minds**) means that there must be agreement to the provisions of the contract by the parties involved. In other words, there must be a mutual willingness to enter into a contract. The existence of mutual agreement is evidenced by the words and acts of the parties indicating that there is a valid offer and an unqualified acceptance. In addition, there must be no fraud, misrepresentation, or mistake, and the agreement must be genuine and freely given. Let us consider each of these points in more detail.

MUTUAL AGREEMENT

Offer and acceptance requires that one party (the **offeror**) make an offer to another party (the **offeree**). The offeree must then communicate to the offeror that he accepts. The means of communication may be spoken or written or an action

Offer and Acceptance

that implies acceptance. To illustrate, suppose that you own an apartment and want to rent it. You tell a prospective tenant that he can rent it for $350 per month beginning today, and inform him of the house rules, when the rent is due, how much the deposit is, and under what conditions it will be returned. This is the offer, and you, the offeror, have just communicated it to the offeree. One requirement of a valid contract is that the offer be specific in its terms. Mutual agreement cannot exist if the terms of the offer are vague or undisclosed and/or the offer does not clearly state the obligations of each party involved. If you were to say to a prospective tenant, "Do you want to rent this apartment?" without stating the price, and the prospective tenant said "Yes," the law would not consider this to be a contract.

Counteroffer   Upon receiving an offer, the offeree has three options: to agree to it, to reject it, or to make a counteroffer. If he agrees, he must agree to every item in the offer. An offer is considered by law to be rejected if the offeree either rejects it outright or makes a change in the terms. If he makes any changes, it is a **counteroffer** and, although it would appear the offeree is only amending the offer before he will accept it, in reality the offeree has rejected it and is making an offer of his own. This now makes him the offeror. To illustrate, suppose that the prospective tenant for your apartment states that he would like to rent the apartment on the terms you offered, but instead of paying $350 per month, he wants to pay $330 per month. This is a rejection of your offer and the making of a counteroffer. You now have the right to accept or reject his offer. If you counter at $340 per month, this rejects his offer and you are again the offeror. If $340 is agreeable with the offeree, he must communicate his acceptance to you. In this case, a spoken, "Yes, I'll take it" would be legally adequate.

If the offeree does not wish to accept the offer nor make a counteroffer, how is the offer terminated? Certainly he can simply say "No." However, if he says nothing, the passage of time can also terminate the offer. This can happen in two ways. The offeror can state how long the offer is to remain open; for example, "You have until 8:00 P.M. tonight to decide if you want the apartment." If nothing is heard by 8:00 P.M., the offer terminates. When nothing is said as to how long the offer is to remain open, the courts will permit a reasonable amount of time, depending on the situation. To illustrate, it is reasonable to presume that if the prospective tenant left without accepting your offer or arranging for time to think about it, your offer terminates with his departure. This frees you to look for another tenant and make another offer without still being committed to the first offeree. When the offer is for the purchase of real estate and no termination date is given, law courts have ruled that a reasonable period of time might be several days or a week.

The best policy is to state the length of time an offer is open to avoid the problem of receiving two acceptances. Selecting a time period depends on the amount of time the offeror feels the offeree needs to decide and the length of time the offeror is willing to tie up his property.

Mutual agreement requires that there be no fraud, mis-   *Fraud*
representation, or mistake in the contract if it is to be valid. A **fraud** is an act intended to deceive for the purpose of inducing another to part with something of value. It can be as blatant as knowingly telling a lie or making a promise with no intention of performance. For example, you are showing your apartment and a prospective tenant asks if there is frequent bus service nearby. There isn't, but you say, "Yes," as you sense this is important and you want to rent the apartment. The prospective tenant, relying on this information from you, rents the apartment and moves in. The next day he calls and says that there is no public transportation and he wants to break the rental agreement immediately. Because mutual agreement was lacking, the tenant can **rescind** (cancel) the contract and get his money back.

Fraud can also result from failing to disclose important information, thereby inducing someone to accept an offer. For example, the day you show your apartment to a prospective tenant the weather is dry. But you know that during every rainstorm the tenant's automobile parking stall becomes a lake of water 6 inches deep. This would qualify as a fraud if the prospective tenant was not made aware of it before agreeing to the rental contract. Once again, the law will permit the aggrieved party to rescind the contract. However, the tenant does not have to rescind the contract. If he likes the other features of the apartment enough, he can elect to live with the flooded parking stall.

If a real estate agent commits a fraud to make a sale and the deceived party later rescinds the sales contract, not only is the commission lost, but explanations will be necessary to the other parties of the contract. Moreover, state license laws provide a suspension or revocation of a real estate license for fraudulent acts.

Innocent
Misrepresentation

Innocent misrepresentation differs from fraud (intentional misrepresentation) in that the party providing the wrong information is not doing so to deceive another for the purpose of reaching an agreement. To illustrate, suppose that over the past year you have observed that city buses stop near your apartment building. If you tell a prospective tenant that there is bus service, only to learn the day after the tenant moves in that service stopped last week, this is innocent misrepresentation. Although there was no dishonesty involved, the tenant still has the right to rescind the contract. If performance has not begun on the contract (in this case the tenant has not moved in), the injured party may give notice that he **disaffirms** (revokes) the contract. However, if the tenant wants to break the contract, he must do so in a timely manner; otherwise the law will presume that the situation is satisfactory to the tenant.

Mistake

1. Ambiguity in negotiations
2. Mistake of material fact

Mistake as applied in contract law has a very narrow meaning. It does not include innocent misrepresentation nor does it include ignorance, inability, or poor judgment. If a person enters into a contract that he later regrets because he did not investigate it thoroughly enough, or because it did not turn out to be beneficial, the law will not grant relief to him on the grounds of mistake, even though he may now consider it was a "mistake" to have made the contract in the first place. Mistake as used in contract law arises from ambiguity in negotiations and mistake of material fact. For example, you offer to sell your mountain cabin to an acquaintance. He has never seen your cabin, and you give him instructions on how to get there to look at it. He returns and accepts your offer, however, he made a wrong turn and the cabin he looked at was not your cabin. A week later he discovers his error. The law considers this ambiguity in negotiations. In this case the buyer, in his mind, was purchasing a different cabin than the seller was selling; therefore, there is no mutual agreement and any contract signed is void.

To illustrate a mistake of fact, suppose that you show your apartment to a prospective tenant and tell him that he must let you know by tomorrow if he wants to rent it. The next day he visits you and together you enter into a rental contract. Although neither of you is aware of it, there has just been a serious fire in the apartment. Since a fire-gutted apartment is not what the two of you had in mind when the rental contract was signed, there is no mutual agreement.

Occasionally, "mistake of law" will be claimed as grounds for relief from a contract. However, mistake as to one's legal rights in a contract is not generally accepted by courts of law unless it is coupled with a mistake of fact. Ignorance of the law is not considered a mistake.

Mutual agreement also requires that the parties express **contractual intent.** This means that their intention is to be bound by the agreement, thus precluding jokes or jests from becoming valid contracts.

Contractual Intent

The last requirement of mutual agreement is that the offer and acceptance be genuine and freely given. **Duress** (use of force), **menace** (threat of violence), or **undue influence** (unfair advantage) cannot be used to obtain agreement. The law permits a contract made under any of these conditions to be revoked by the aggrieved party.

Duress

To be enforceable, a contract cannot call for performing an illegal act. This is because a court of law cannot be called upon to enforce a contract that requires that a law be broken. Such a contract is void, or if already in operation, it is unenforceable in a court of law. For example, a debt contract requiring interest rates in excess of those allowed by state law

LAWFUL OBJECTIVE

would be void. If the borrower had started repaying the debt and then later stopped, the lender would not be able to look to the courts to enforce collection of the balance. Contracts contrary to good morals and general public policy are also unenforceable.

CONSIDERATION

1. Valuable
2. Good — love & affection

For an agreement to be enforceable it must be supported by **consideration.** Money is usually thought of as meeting this requirement. Yet in the vast majority of contracts, the consideration requirement is met by a promise for a promise. For example, in selling real estate the promise of a purchaser to buy and the promise of an owner to sell constitute sufficient consideration to support their agreement. No deposit money is necessary.

The purpose of requiring consideration is to demonstrate that a bargain has been struck between the parties to the contract. The size, quantity, nature, or amount of what is being exchanged is irrelevant as long as it is present. Consideration can be a promise to do something, money, property, or personal services. For example, there can be an exchange of a promise for a promise, money for a promise, money for property, goods for services, etc. Forbearance also qualifies as consideration.

In a typical offer to purchase a home, the consideration is the mutual exchange of promises by the buyer and seller to obligate themselves to do something they were not previously required to do. In other words, the seller agrees to sell on the terms agreed and the buyer agrees to buy the property on those same terms. The earnest money the buyer may put down is not the consideration necessary to make the contract valid. Rather, earnest money is a tangible indication of the buyer's intent and may become a source of compensation (damages) to the seller in the event the buyer does not carry out his promises.

In a deed, which is evidence of a contract, the consideration requirement is usually met with a statement such as "For ten dollars and other good and valuable consideration." In a lease, the periodic payment of rent is the consideration for the use of the premises.

A contract fails to be legally binding if consideration is lacking from any party to the contract. The legal philosophy is that a person cannot promise to do something of value for someone else without receiving in turn some form of consideration. Stated another way, each party must give up something; i.e., each must suffer a detriment. For example, if I promise to give you my car, the consideration requirement is not met because you promise nothing in return. But if I promise to give you my car when you quit smoking, that meets the consideration requirement.

As a group, money, plus promises, property, legal rights, services, and forbearance are classified as **valuable consideration,** if they are worth money. There is one exception to the requirement that each party must provide valuable consideration. That is the case of a gift. If a person wishes to give something of value to a friend or loved one, courts have ruled that ''love and affection'' will meet the consideration requirement. Although this is not valuable consideration, it is nonetheless **good consideration** as such fulfills the legal requirement that consideration be present. The law generally will not inquire as to the adequacy of the consideration unless there is evidence of fraud, mistake, duress, threat, or undue influence. For instance, if a man gave away his property or sold it very cheaply to keep it from his creditors, the creditors could ask the courts to set aside those transfers.

If the word consideration continues to be confusing to you, it is because the word has three meanings in real estate. The first is consideration from the standpoint of a legal requirement for a valid contract. You may wish to think of this form of consideration as **legal consideration** or **cause.** The second meaning is money. For example, the consideration upon which deed stamps are charges is the amount of money exchanged in the transaction. The third meaning is acknowledgment. Thus the phrase ''in consideration of ten dollars'' means ''in acknowledgment of'' or ''in receipt of.''

In each state there is a law that is commonly known as a **statute of frauds.** The purpose of such laws is to prevent frauds by requiring that all contracts for the sale of land, or

CONTRACT IN WRITING

Offers, acceptances, binders, land contracts, deeds, escrows, options to purchase, mortgages, trust deeds, leases more than one year, listing contracts an interest in land, be in writing and signed in order to be enforceable in a court of law. This includes such things as offers, acceptances, binders, land contracts, deeds, escrows, and options to purchase. Mortgages and trust deeds (and their accompanying bonds and notes) and leases whose obligations cannot be completed within one year must be in writing to be enforceable. In addition, most states have adopted the **Uniform Commercial Code** that requires, among other things, that the sale of property with a value in excess of $500 be in writing. Most states also require that real estate listing contracts be expressed in writing.

The purpose of requiring that a contract be written and signed is to prevent perjury and fraudulent attempts to seek legal enforcement of a contract that never existed. It is not necessary that a contract be a single formal document. It can consist of a series of signed letters or memorandums as long as the essentials of a valid contract are present. Note that the requirement for a written contract relates only to the enforceability of the contract. Thus if Mr. Cheddar orally agrees to sell his land to Mr. Cheese and they carry out the deal, neither can come back after the contract was performed and ask a court to rescind the deal because the agreement to sell was oral.

The most common real estate contract that does not need to be in writing to be enforceable is a month-to-month rental agreement that can be terminated by either landlord or tenant on 1-month notice. Nonetheless, most are in writing, because people tend to forget oral promises. While the unhappy party can go to court, the judge may have a difficult time determining what oral promises were made, particularly if there were not witnesses other than the parties to the agreement. Hence, it is advisable to put all important contracts in writing and for each party to recognize the agreement by signing it. It is also customary to date written contracts, although most can be enforced without showing the date the agreement was reached.

A written contract will supersede an oral one. Thus, if two parties orally promise one thing and then write and sign something else, the written contract will prevail. This has been the basis for many complaints against overzealous real estate agents who make oral promises that do not appear anywhere in the written contract.

Under certain circumstances the **parol evidence rule** permits oral evidence to complete an otherwise incomplete or ambiguous written contract. However, the application of this rule is quite narrow. If a contract is complete and clear in its intent, the courts presume that what the parties put into writing is what they agreed upon.

Parol Evidence Rule

Most contracts are discharged by being fully performed by the contracting parties in accordance with the contract terms. However, alternatives are open to the parties of the contract. One is to sell or otherwise **assign** the contract to another party. Unless prohibited by the contract, rights, benefits, and obligations under a contract can be assigned to someone else. The original party to the contract, however, still remains ultimately liable for its performance. Note, too, that an assignment is a contract in itself and must meet all the essential contract requirements to be enforceable. A common example of an assignment occurs when a lessee wants to move out and sells his lease to another party. When a contract creates a personal obligation, such as a listing agreement with a broker, an assignment may not be made.

PERFORMANCE AND DISCHARGE OF CONTRACTS

Full performance
Assignments or sale
Novation
Objective becomes legally impossible
Mutual agreement
Death (if substitution not possible)
Damage to premises unless minor & repaired by seller)

A contract can also be performed by **novation.** Novation is the substitution of a new contract between the same or new parties. For example, novation occurs when a buyer assumes a seller's loan, *and* the lender releases the seller from the loan contract. With novation the departing party is released from the obligation to complete the contract.

Novation
Substitution of a new contract

If the objective of a contract becomes legally impossible to accomplish, the law will consider the contract discharged. For example, a new legislative statute may forbid what the contract originally intended. If the parties mutually agree to cancel their contract before it is executed, this too is a form of discharge. For instance, you sign a 5-year lease to pay $500 per month for an office. Three years later you find a better location and want to move. Meanwhile, rents for similar offices in your building have increased to $575 per month.

Under these conditions the landlord might want to cancel your lease.

If one of the contracting parties dies, a contract is considered discharged if it calls for some specific act that only the dead person could have performed. For example, if you hired a free-lance gardener to tend your landscaping and he died, the contract would be discharged. However, if your contract is with a firm that employs other gardeners who can do the job, the contract would still be valid. Damage to the premises may also discharge the agreement. As a case in point, it is common in real estate sales contracts to provide that the contract is deemed canceled if the property is destroyed or substantially damaged before title passes. However, if the damage is minor and promptly repaired by the seller, the contract would still be valid.

If nothing is said in the contract about damage to the premises, then the general rule in Texas is that if neither possession nor title has passed and there is material destruction to the property, the seller cannot enforce the contract and the purchaser is entitled to his money back. If damage is minor and promptly repaired by the seller, the contract would still be enforceable. If either title or possession has passed and destruction occurs, the purchaser is not relieved of his duty to pay the price, nor is he entitled to a refund of money already paid.

BREACH OF CONTRACT

Alternatives:
(1) *Accept partial performance*
(2) *Rescind unilaterally*
(3) *Sue for specific performance*
(4) *Sue for money damages*
(5) *Accept liquidated money damages*
(6) *Mutually rescind*

When one party fails to perform as required by a contract and the law does not recognize the reason for failure to be a valid excuse, there is a **breach of contract.** The wronged or innocent party has six alternatives: (1) accept partial performance, (2) rescind the contract unilaterally, (3) sue for specific performance, (4) sue for money damages, (5) accept liquidated money damages, or (6) mutually rescind the contract. Let us consider each of these.

Partial Performance

Partial performance may be acceptable to the innocent party because there may not be a great deal at stake or because the innocent party feels that the time and effort to sue would not be worth the rewards. Suppose that you contracted with a roofing repairman to fix your roof for $400. When he was finished you paid him. A week later you discover a spot that he had agreed to fix, but missed. After many futile phone calls, you accept the breach and consider the contract discharged, because it is easier to fix the spot yourself than to keep pursuing the repairman.

Under certain circumstances, the innocent party can **unilaterally rescind** a contract. That is, the innocent party can take the position that if the other party is not going to perform his obligations, then the innocent party will not either. An example would be a rent strike in retaliation to a landlord who fails to keep the premises habitable. Unilateral rescission should be resorted to only after consulting an attorney.

Unilateral Rescission

The innocent party may sue in a court of equity to force the breaching party to carry out the remainder of the contract according to the precise terms, price, and conditions agreed upon. For example, you make an offer to purchase a parcel of land and the seller accepts. A written contract is prepared and signed by both of you. If you carry out all your obligations under the contract, but the seller changes his mind and refuses to deliver title to you, you may bring a lawsuit against the seller for **specific performance.** In reviewing your suit, the court will determine if the contract is valid and legal, if you have carried out your duties under the contract, and if the contract is just and reasonable. If you win your lawsuit, the court will force the seller to deliver title to you as specified in the contract.

Specific Performance

If the damages to the innocent party can be reasonably expressed in terms of money, the innocent party can sue for **money damages.** For example, you rent an apartment to a tenant. As part of the rental contract you furnish the refrigerator and freezer unit. While the tenant is on vacation, the unit breaks down and $200 worth of frozen meat and other perishables spoil. Since your obligation under the contract is to provide the tenant with a working refrigerator-freezer, the tenant can sue you for $200 in money damages. He can also recover interest on the money awarded to him from the day of the loss to the day you reimburse him.

Money Damages

Comparison of Remedies

Note the difference between suing for money damages and suing for specific performance. When money can be used to restore one's position (such as the tenant who can buy $200 worth of fresh food), a suit for money damages is appropriate. In situations where money cannot provide an adequate remedy, and this is often the case in real estate because no two properties are exactly alike, specific performance is appropriate. Notice, too, that the mere existence of the legal rights of the wronged party is often enough to gain cooperation. In the case of the spoiled food, you would give the tenant the value of the lost food before spending time and money in court to hear a judge tell you to do the same thing. A threat of a lawsuit will often bring the desired results if the defendant knows that the law will side with the wronged party. The cases that do go to court are usually those in which the identity of the wronged party and/or the extent of the damages is not clear.

Liquidated Damages

The parties to a contract may decide in advance the amount of damages to be paid in the event either party breaches the contract. An example is an offer to purchase real estate that includes a statement to the effect that, once the seller accepts the offer, if the buyer fails to complete the purchase, the seller may keep the buyer's deposit (earnest money) as **liquidated damages.** If a broker is involved, the seller and broker usually agree to divide the damages, thus compensating the seller for damages and the broker for time and effort. Another case of liquidated damages occurs when a builder promises to finish a building by a certain date or pay the party that hired him a certain number of dollars per day until it is completed. This impresses upon the builder the need for prompt completion and compensates the property owner for losses due to the delay.

Mutual Rescission

Specific performance, money damages, and liquidated damages are all designed to aid the innocent party in the event of a breach of contract. However, as a practical matter the time and cost of pursuing a remedy in a court of law may sometimes exceed the benefits to be derived. Moreover, there is the possibility the judge for your case may not agree with your point of view. Therefore, even though you are the innocent party and you feel you have a legitimate case that can be pursued in the courts, you may find it more practical to agree with the other party (or parties) to simply cancel (i.e., rescind or annul) the contract. To properly protect everyone involved, the agreement to cancel must be in writing and signed by the parties to the original contract. Properly executed, mutual rescission relieves the parties to the contract from their obligations to each other.

An alternative to mutual rescission is novation. As noted earlier, this is the substitution of a new contract for an existing one. Novation provides a middle ground between suing and rescinding. Thus the breaching party may be willing to complete the contract provided the innocent party will voluntarily make certain changes in it. If this is acceptable, the changes should be put into writing (or the contract redrafted) and then signed by the parties involved.

The **statute of limitations** limits by law the amount of time a wronged party has to seek the aid of a court in obtaining justice. The aggrieved party must start legal proceedings within a certain period of time or the courts will not help him. The amount of time varies from state to state and by type of legal action involved. Texas recognizes a four-year limit on written contracts and a two-year limit on oral contracts.

STATUTE OF LIMITATIONS

Written – 4 years
Oral – 2 years

As was pointed out at the beginning of this chapter, one can incur contractual obligations by implication as well as by oral or written contracts. Home builders and real estate agents provide two timely examples. For many years, if a homeowner discovered poor design or workmanship after he had bought a new home, it was his problem. The philosophy was **caveat emptor,** let the buyer beware *before* he buys. Today, courts of law find that in building a home and offering it for sale, the builder simultaneously implies that it is fit for living. Thus, if a builder installs a toilet in a bathroom, the implication is that it will work. In fact, Texas law now requires builders to guarantee their work for one year.

IMPLIED OBLIGATIONS

Similarly, real estate agent trade organizations, such as the National Association of Realtors and state and local realtor associations, are constantly working to elevate the status of real estate brokers and salesmen to that of competent professionals in the public's mind. But as professional status is gained, there is an implied obligation to dispense professional-quality service. Thus, an individual agent will find himself not only responsible for acting in accordance with written laws, but will also be held responsible for being competent and knowledgeable in his field. Once recognized as a professional by the public, the real estate agent will not be able to plead ignorance.

In view of the present trend towards consumer protection, it appears that the concept of "Let the buyer beware" is being replaced with "Let the agent beware."

VOCABULARY REVIEW

*Match terms **a–q** with statements **1–17**.*

12 **a.** Assign	5 **j.** Minor	
14 **b.** Breach	13 **k.** Money damages	
4 **c.** Competent party	7 **l.** Offeror	
1 **d.** Contract	9 **m.** Rescind	
8 **e.** Counteroffer	15 **n.** Specific performance	
10 **f.** Duress	17 **o.** Statute of limitations	
11 **g.** Forbear	2 **p.** Unilateral contract	
3 **h.** Fraud	6 **q.** Void contract	
16 **i.** Liquidated damages		

d **1.** A legally enforceable agreement to do (or not to do) something.

p **2.** A contract in which one party makes a promise or begins performance without first receiving any promise to perform from the other.

h **3.** An act intended to deceive for the purpose of inducing another to part with something of value.

c **4.** A person who is considered legally capable of entering into a contract.

j **5.** A person who is not old enough to enter into legally binding contracts.

q **6.** A contract that is not legally binding on any of the parties that made it.

l **7.** The party who makes an offer.

e **8.** An offer made in response to an offer.

m. **9.** To cancel a contract and restore the parties involved to their respective positions before the contract was made.

f. **10.** Use of force to obtain contract agreement.

g. **11.** Not to act.

a. **12.** To transfer one's rights in a contract to another person.

k. **13.** Damages that can be measured in and compensated by money.

b. **14.** Failure, without legal excuse, to perform any promise called for in a contract.

n. **15.** Contract performance according to the precise terms agreed upon.

i. **16.** A sum of money called for in a contract that is to be paid if the contract is breached.

o. **17.** Law that sets forth the period of time within which a lawsuit must be filed.

QUESTIONS AND PROBLEMS

1. What is the difference between an expressed contract and an implied contract? Give an example of each.
2. Name the five requirements of a legally valid contract.
3. What is the difference between a void contract and a voidable contract?
4. Give four examples of persons not considered legally competent to enter into contracts.
5. How can an offer be terminated prior to its acceptance?
6. What does the word "mistake" mean when applied to contract law?
7. Why must consideration be present for a legally binding contract to exist? Give examples of three types of consideration.
8. If a contract is legally unenforceable, are the parties to the contract stopped from performing it? Why or why not?
9. If a breach of contract occurs, what alternatives are open to the parties to the contract?
10. Assume that a breach of contract has occurred and the wronged party intends to file a lawsuit over the matter. What factors would he consider in deciding whether to sue for money damages or for specific performance?

ADDITIONAL READINGS

"The Business of Writing" by **Douglas Mueller.** (*Real Estate Today,* Nov/Dec 84, p. 34). Article explains techniques of clear writing for the real estate business. Including explanation of the Fog Index and how to apply it to your writing. Emphasizes the need to express, not impress, when writing.

Homeowners Checklist by **Robert DeHeer.** (Lord Publishing, 1980, 80 pages). Contains numerous checklists, with extra copies, to be used when choosing a house or condominium. The *Homeowners Book* by the same author and publisher deals with the selection, purchase, financing, taxes, insurance, maintenance, insulation, safety and resale of a home.

Real Estate Law by **Marjanne Jennings.** (Kent, 1985, 657 pages). Emphasizes real estate law application and how legal problems can be solved. Narrative style followed by numerous court cases to illustrate the points made. Chapter 9 deals with conveyancing and Chapter 11 with purchase contracts.

Real Estate Principles and Practices, 10th ed. by **Alfred Ring** and **Jerome Dasso.** (Prentice-Hall, 1985, 650 pages). A decision-making and analysis approach to real estate from the point of view of the investor. Book covers ownership rights, conveying those rights, financing, markets, investment, ownership and management.

Texas Real Estate Law, 4th ed. by **Charles J. Jacobus.** (Reston, 1985, 560 pages). Provides up-to-date explanations of laws in Texas. See Chapter 7 on Contracts.

Texas Real Estate Law: Contracts, by **G. E. Irby** and **Darol L. Graham, Ph.D.** (Texas Association of Realtors, 1984, 173 pages). Provides basic information on the law of contracts with examples.

*   *   *

The following periodicals may also be of interest to you: *Real Estate Law Journal, Real Estate Law Report, Real Estate Letter, Real Estate Magazine, Real Estate Newsletter* and *Strategic Real Estate.*

8

Real Estate Sales Contracts

KEY TERMS

"As is": said of property offered for sale in its present condition with no guaranty or warranty of quality provided by the seller

Counteroffer: an offer made in response to an offer

Default: failure to perform a legal duty; such as failure to carry out the terms of a contract

Deposit receipt: a receipt given for a deposit that accompanies an offer to purchase; also refers to a purchase contract that included a deposit receipt

Earnest money deposit: money that accompanies an offer to purchase as evidence of good faith

Equitable title: the right to demand that title be conveyed upon payment of the purchase price

Installment contract: a method of selling and financing property whereby the seller retains title but the buyer takes possession while he makes his payments

"Lease-option": allows the tenant to buy the property at present price and terms for a given period of time

Right of first refusal: the right to match or better an offer before the property is sold to someone else

"Time is of the essence": a phrase that means that the time limits of a contract must be faithfully observed or the contract is voidable

KEY TERMS

The present chapter focuses on contracts used to initiate the sale of real estate. Chiefly we will look at the purchase contract, the installment contract and the lease with option to buy. There will also be a brief discussion of right of first refusal and exchange.

What is the purpose of a real estate sales contract? If a buyer and a seller agree on a price, why can't the buyer hand the seller the necessary money and the seller simultaneously hand the buyer a deed? The main reason is that the buyer needs time to ascertain that the seller is, in fact, legally capable of conveying title. To protect himself, the buyer will enter into a written and signed contract with the seller, promising that the purchase price will be paid only after

PURPOSE OF SALES CONTRACTS
Buyer needs time

159

title has been searched and found to be in satisfactory condition. The seller in turn promises to deliver a deed to the buyer when the buyer has paid his money. This exchange of promises forms the legal consideration of the contract. A contract also gives the buyer time to arrange financing and to specify how such matters as taxes, mortgage debts, existing leases, and fire insurance on the property will be discharged.

A properly prepared contract commits each party to its terms. Once a sales contract is in writing and signed, the seller cannot suddenly change his mind and sell his property to another person. He is obligated to convey title to the buyer when the buyer has performed everything required of him by the contract. Likewise, the buyer must carry out his promises, including paying for the property, provided the seller has done everything required by the contract.

EARNEST MONEY CONTRACTS

1. Written
2. Signed
3. Evidence of intent to convey
4. Identifiable grantor and grantee
5. Identifiable subject matter to be conveyed

The purchase contract, or as it is commonly called in Texas, the **earnest money contract,** must basically satisfy five requirements in Texas in order for it to be upheld as an enforceable agreement:

1. It must be in writing;
2. The instrument must be signed by the parties sought to be charged therewith;
3. There must be evidence of an intent to convey an interest at sometime in the future;
4. There must be an identifiable grantor and grantee;
5. The subject matter to be conveyed must be identifiable.

For general information purposes, it is also recognized in this state that there is such a thing as an **oral earnest money contract.** However, this is very rare.

All real estate licensees are required to use, when appropriate, one of the standard contract forms and applicable addendums in all real estate transactions. The forms are promulgated by the Texas Real Estate Commission. Copies of two of these TREC contracts are shown in this chapter and others are in Appendix C. If the property sold borders the Gulf of Mexico an additional addendum must also be used. A copy of this form is also included in Appendix C. If one of the promulgated forms is not used, the licensee is required to use either a form prepared by an attorney at law licensed in this state, or forms prepared by the owner, or forms prepared by an attorney and required by the property owner.

Conventional Loan Contract

The Real Estate Commission promulgated two earnest money contract forms in 1985, replacing the previously promulgated forms and substantially changing some of the promulgated addendums. One of the new purchase contracts, known as the One- to Four-Family Earnest Money Contract (Resale) etc. (TREC 20–0) is reprinted here as Figure 8:1 and begins at ① and ② by identifying the buyer and seller by name. This is followed by proper legal description to be filled in at ③ and ④, a place for the address of the property. The cash down payment, payable at closing, is to be filled in at ⑤ with the amount of the note to be filled in at ⑥. In Paragraph 3, line C of the contract there is a provision for the total sum, or total selling price, to be filled in at ⑦.

Paragraph 4 describes the various types of financing that can be used with this form. There are five alternatives (A through E), which can be selected by checking the appropriate box, and filling in the corresponding blanks. The ALL CASH box (A) is self-explanatory, shown at ⑧. The ASSUMPTION provision, (B), provides for assuming the first lien note to the proper payee, shown at ⑨, and installment amounts, shown at ⑩. The contract further provides for assumption of the second lien note, if any, with provisions to fill in the payee and installment amount at ⑪ and ⑫, respectively. The principal balances of the notes are to be filled in at ⑬, as applicable to the particular transaction. Note that the following paragraph provides for the principal balances to vary as much as $350.00. If the variation is greater, either party may terminate the contract. Guidelines for the buyer's assumption terms are outlined in ⑭ and ⑮.

If THIRD PARTY FINANCING (C) is involved, provisions for the first lien note are provided at ⑯, and the second lien note, if any, provided at ⑰. The TEXAS VETERAN'S HOUSING ASSISTANCE PROGRAM LOAN terms (D), if applicable, are shown at ⑱.

Figure 8:1

02-08-85

ONE TO FOUR FAMILY RESIDENTIAL EARNEST MONEY CONTRACT (RESALE)
ALL CASH, ASSUMPTION, THIRD PARTY CONVENTIONAL OR OWNER FINANCED

PROMULGATED BY TEXAS REAL ESTATE COMMISSION

NOTICE: Not For Use For Condominium Transactions

1. PARTIES: ①_____(Seller) agrees to

   sell and convey to ②_____(Buyer) and Buyer

   agrees to buy from Seller the property described below.

2. PROPERTY: Lot ③_____, Block _____, _____

   Addition, City of _____, _____, County, Texas, known as

   ④_____(Address); or as described on attached exhibit, together with the following items,
   if any: curtains and rods, draperies and rods, valances, blinds, window shades, screens, shutters, awnings, wall-to-wall carpeting, mirrors fixed in place, ceiling
   fans, attic fans, mail boxes, television antennas, permanently installed heating and air conditioning units and equipment, built-in security and fire detection
   equipment, lighting and plumbing fixtures, water softener, trash compactor, garage door openers with controls, shrubbery and all other property owned by Seller
   and attached to the above described real property. All property sold by this contract is called the "Property".

3. CONTRACT SALES PRICE:
   A. Cash payable at closing .... $ ⑤_____
   B. Sum of all financing described in Paragraph 4 below .... $ ⑥_____
   C. Sales Price (Sum of A and B) .... $ ⑦_____

4. FINANCING: (Check applicable boxes below)
   ⑧ ☐ A. ALL CASH: This is an all cash sale; no financing is involved.
   ☐ B. ASSUMPTION:
      (1) Buyer's assumption of the unpaid principal balance of a first lien promissory note payable to ⑨_____
          in present monthly installments of $ ⑩_____, including principal, interest and any reserve deposits, with Buyer's first installment payment
          being payable on the first installment payment date after closing, the assumed principal balance of which at closing will be $_____.
      (2) Buyer's assumption of the unpaid principal balance of a second lien promissory note payable to ⑪_____
          in present monthly installments of $ ⑫_____, including principal, interest and any reserve deposits, with Buyer's first installment payment
          being payable on the first installment payment date after closing, the assumed principal balance of which at closing will be $ ⑬_____.
      Buyer's assumption of an existing note includes all obligations imposed by the deed of trust securing the note.

      If the total principal balance of all assumed loans varies in an amount greater than $350.00 at closing either party may terminate this contract and the Earnest
      Money shall be refunded to Buyer. If the noteholder on assumption (a) requires Buyer to pay an assumption fee in excess of $ ⑭_____ in
      B(1) above or $_____ in B(2) above and Seller declines to pay such excess or (b) raises the existing interest rate above ⑮____%
      in B(1) above or _____% in B(2) above, Buyer may terminate this contract and the Earnest Money shall be refunded to Buyer. The cash payable at
      closing shall be adjusted by the amount of any variance in the loan balance(s) shown above.
      NOTICE TO BUYER: Monthly payments, interest rates or other terms of some loans may be adjusted after closing. Before signing the contract, examine the
      notes and deeds of trust to determine the possibility of future adjustments.

   ☐ C. THIRD PARTY FINANCED:
      ☐ 1. A third party first lien note of $ ⑯_____, due in full in _____year(s), payable in initial monthly payments of principal
           and interest not exceeding $_____ for the first _____year(s) of the loan.
      ☐ 2. A third party second lien note of $ ⑰_____, due in full in _____year(s), payable in initial monthly payments of principal
           and interest not exceeding $_____ for the first _____year(s) of the loan.
      NOTICE TO PARTIES: Before signing this contract Buyer is advised to determine the financing options from lenders. Certain loans have variable rates of
      interest, some have monthly payments which may not be sufficient to pay the accruing interest, and some have interest rate "buydowns" which reduce the
      rate of interest for part or all of the loan term at the expense of one or more of the parties to the contract.

   ☐ D. TEXAS VETERANS' HOUSING ASSISTANCE PROGRAM LOAN:
      This contract is also subject to approval for Buyer of a Texas Veterans' Housing Assistance Program Loan (the Program Loan) in an amount of
      $ ⑱_____ for a period of at least _____ years at the interest rate established by the Texas Veterans' Land Board at the time
      of closing.

   ☐ E. SELLER FINANCED: A promissory note from Buyer to Seller in the amount of $ ⑲_____, bearing ⑳____% interest per annum,
      and payable:

      ☐ 1. In one payment due _____after the date of the note with interest payable _____.
      ☐ 2. In installments of $_____ [ ] including interest [ ] plus interest beginning _____

186

TREC NO. 20-0

Figure 8:1 *continued*

One To Four Family Residential Earnest Money Contract — Page Two   02-08-85

    after the date of the note and continuing at _____intervals thereafter for _____year(s) when the entire balance of the note shall be due and payable.

☐ 3. Interest only in _____installments for the first _____year(s) and thereafter in installments of $_____
    [ ] including interest [ ] plus interest beginning _____after the date of the note and continuing at _____
    intervals thereafter for _____year(s) when the entire balance of the note is due and payable.

☐ 4. This contract is subject to Buyer furnishing Seller evidence of good credit within _____days from the effective date of this contract. If notice of disapproval of Buyer's credit is not given within five (5) days thereafter, Seller shall be deemed to have approved Buyer's credit. Buyer hereby authorizes Buyer's credit report to be furnished to Seller.
    Any Seller financed note may be prepaid in whole or in part at any time without penalty. The lien securing payment of such note will be inferior to any lien securing any loan assumed or given in connection with third party financing. If an Owner's Policy of Title Insurance is furnished, Buyer shall furnish Seller with a Mortgagee's Title Policy.

Buyer shall apply for all third party financing or noteholder's approval of Buyer for assumption and waiver of the right to accelerate the note within ____㉑____ days from the effective date of this contract and shall make every reasonable effort to obtain the same. Such financing or assumption shall have been approved when Buyer has satisfied all of lender's financial conditions, e.g., sale of other property, requirement of co-signer or financial verifications. If such financing or noteholder's approval and waiver is not obtained within ____㉒____days from the effective date hereof, this contract shall terminate and the Earnest Money shall be refunded to Buyer.

5. EARNEST MONEY: $____㉓_____ is herewith tendered by Buyer and is to be deposited as Earnest Money with
_____㉔_____, at _____(Address),
as Escrow Agent, upon execution of the contract by both parties. ☐ Additional Earnest Money of $____㉕____ shall be deposited by Buyer with the Escrow Agent on or before _____, 19___.

6. TITLE: Seller shall furnish to Buyer at Seller's expense either:
☐ A. Owner's Policy of Title Insurance (the Title Policy) issued by _____
    in the amount of the Sales Price and dated at or after closing; OR

☐ B. Abstracts of Title certified by an abstract company (1) from the sovereignty to the effective date of this contract (Complete Abstract) and (2) supplemented to the Closing Date (Supplemental Abstract).
NOTICE TO SELLER AND BUYER: AS REQUIRED BY LAW, Broker advises Buyer that Buyer should have an Abstract covering the Property examined by an attorney of Buyer's selection, or Buyer should be furnished with or obtain a Title Policy. If a Title Policy is to be obtained, Buyer should obtain a Commitment for Title Insurance (the Commitment) which should be examined by an attorney of Buyer's choice at or prior to closing. If the Property is situated in a Utility District, Section 50.301 Texas Water Code requires the Buyer to sign and acknowledge the statutory notice from Seller relating to the tax rate and bonded indebtedness of the District.

7. PROPERTY CONDITION: (Check A or B)
☐ A. Buyer accepts the Property in its present condition, subject only to any lender required repairs and_____

☐ B. Buyer requires inspections and repairs required by any lender and the Property Condition Addendum attached hereto.
On Seller's receipt of all loan approvals and inspection reports, Seller shall commence repairs and termite treatment required of Seller by the contract, any lender and the Property Condition Addendum, if any, and complete such repairs prior to closing. Seller's responsibility for the repairs, termite treatment and repairs to termite damage shall not exceed $____㉖_____. If Seller fails to complete such repairs, Buyer may do so and Seller shall be liable up to the amount specified and the same paid from the proceeds of the sale. If the repair costs will exceed the stated amount and Seller refuses to pay such excess, Buyer may (1) pay the additional cost or (2) accept the Property with the limited repairs unless such repairs are required by lender or (3) Buyer may terminate this contract and the Earnest Money shall be refunded to Buyer. Buyer shall make his election within three (3) days after Seller notifies Buyer of Seller's refusal to pay such excess. Failure of Buyer to make such election within the time provided shall be deemed to be Buyer's election to accept the Property with the limited repairs, and the sale shall be closed as scheduled; however, if lender required repairs prohibit Buyer's acceptance with the limited repairs, this contract shall terminate and Earnest Money shall be refunded to Buyer.

If the repair costs will exceed five (5) percent of the Sales Price of the Property and Seller agrees to pay the cost of such repairs, Buyer shall have the option of closing the sale with the completed repairs, or terminating the sale and the Earnest Money shall be refunded to Buyer. Buyer shall make this election within three (3) days after Seller notifies Buyer of Seller's willingness to pay the cost of such repairs that exceed five (5) percent of the Sales Price. Failure of Buyer to make such election within the time provided shall be deemed to be Buyer's election to close the sale with the completed repairs.

Broker(s) and sales associates have no responsibility or liability for inspections or repairs made pursuant to this contract.

8. BROKER'S FEE: _____. Listing Broker, and any Co-Broker represent Seller unless otherwise specified herein. Seller agrees to pay Listing Broker the fee specified by separate agreement between Listing Broker and Seller. Escrow Agent is authorized and directed to pay Listing Broker said fee from the sale proceeds.

9. CLOSING: The closing of the sale shall be on or before ____㉗_____, 19___, or within seven (7) days after objections to title have been cured, whichever date is later (the Closing Date); however, if financing or assumption approval has been obtained pursuant to Paragraph 4, the Closing Date shall be extended daily up to fifteen (15) days if necessary to complete loan requirements. If either party fails to close this sale by the Closing Date, the non-defaulting party shall be entitled to exercise the remedies contained in Paragraph 16 immediately and without notice.

10. POSSESSION: The possession of the Property shall be delivered to Buyer on ____㉘_____in its

Figure 8:1 *continued*

One To Four Family Residential Earnest Money Contract concerning _____ Page Three   02-08-85
                                                                    (Address of Property)

present or required improved condition, ordinary wear and tear excepted. Any possession by Buyer prior to or Seller after closing that is not authorized by the Buyer's Temporary Residential Lease or Seller's Temporary Residential Lease Forms promulgated by the Texas Real Estate Commission shall establish a landlord-tenant at sufferance relationship between the parties.

11. SPECIAL PROVISIONS: (Insert factual statements and business details applicable to this sale.)

12. SALES EXPENSES TO BE PAID IN CASH AT OR PRIOR TO CLOSING:
   A. Loan appraisal fees shall be paid by _____ (29) _____
   B. The total of the loan discount and any buydown fees shall not exceed $ _____ (30) _____of which Buyer shall pay the first $ _____
      and Seller shall pay the remainder.
   C. Seller's Expenses: Prepayment penalties on any existing loans paid at closing, plus cost of releasing such loans and recording releases; tax statements; ½ of any escrow fee; preparation of deed; preparation and recording of any deed of trust to secure assumption; any Texas Veterans' Housing Assistance Program Participation Fee; other expenses stipulated to be paid by Seller under other provisions of this contract.

   D. Buyer's Expenses: Application, origination and commitment fees; private mortgage insurance premiums and any loan assumption fee; expenses incident to new loan(s) (e.g., preparation of any note, deed of trust and other loan documents, survey, recording fees, copies of restrictions and easements, Mortgagee's Title Policies, credit reports, photos); ½ of any escrow fee; any required premiums for flood and hazard insurance; any required reserve deposits for insurance premiums, ad valorem taxes and special governmental assessments; interest on all monthly installment payment notes from date of disbursements to one (1) month prior to dates of first monthly payments; expenses stipulated to be paid by Buyer under other provisions of this contract and any customary Texas Veterans' Housing Assistance Program Loan costs for Buyer.
   E. If any sales expenses exceed the maximum amount herein stipulated to be paid by either party, either party may terminate this contract unless the other party agrees to pay such excess.

13. PRORATIONS: Taxes, flood and hazard insurance (at Buyer's option), rents, maintenance fees, interest on any assumed loan and any prepaid unearned mortgage insurance premium which has not been financed as part of any assumed loan and which is refundable in whole or in part at a later date shall be prorated through the Closing Date. If Buyer elects to continue Seller's insurance policy, it shall be transferred at closing.

14. TITLE APPROVAL:
   A. If abstract is furnished, Seller shall deliver Complete Abstract to Buyer within twenty (20) days from the effective date hereof. Buyer shall have twenty (20) days from date of receipt of Complete Abstract to deliver a copy of the examining attorney's title opinion to Seller, stating any objections to title, and only objections so stated shall be considered.
   B. If Title Policy is furnished, the Title Policy shall guarantee Buyer's title to be good and indefeasible subject only to (1) restrictive covenants affecting the Property (2) any discrepancies, conflicts or shortages in area or boundary lines, or any encroachments, or any overlapping of improvements (3) taxes for the current and subsequent years and subsequent assessments for prior years due to a change in land usage or ownership (4) existing building and zoning ordinances (5) rights of parties in possession (6) liens created or assumed as security for the sale consideration (7) utility easements common to the platted subdivision of which this Property is a part and (8) reservations or other exceptions permitted by the terms of this contract. Exceptions permitted in the Deed and zoning ordinances shall not be valid objections to title. If the Title Policy will be subject to exceptions other than those recited above in sub-paragraphs (1) through (7) inclusive, Seller shall deliver to Buyer the Commitment and legible copies of any documents creating such exceptions that are not recited in sub-paragraphs (1) through (7) above at least five (5) days prior to closing. If Buyer has objection to any such previously undisclosed exceptions, Buyer shall have five (5) days after receipt of such Commitment and copies to make written objections to Seller. If no Title Commitment is provided to Buyer at or prior to closing, it will be conclusively presumed that Seller represented at closing that the Title Policy would not be subject to exceptions other than those recited above in sub-paragraphs (1) through (7).
   C. In either instance if title objections are raised, Seller shall have fifteen (15) days from the date such objections are disclosed to cure the same, and the Closing Date shall be extended accordingly. If the objections are not satisfied by the extended closing date, this contract shall terminate and the Earnest Money shall be refunded to Buyer, unless Buyer elects to waive the unsatisfied objections and complete the purchase.
   D. Seller shall furnish tax statements showing no delinquent taxes, a Supplemental Abstract when applicable, showing no additional title exceptions and a General Warranty Deed conveying title subject only to liens securing payment of debt created or assumed as part of the consideration, taxes for the current year, restrictive covenants and utility easements common to the platted subdivision of which the Property is a part and reservations and conditions permitted by this contract or otherwise acceptable to Buyer. Each note shall be secured by vendor's and deed of trust liens. A vendor's lien and deed of trust to secure any assumption shall be required, which shall automatically be released on execution and delivery of a release by noteholder. If Seller is released from liability on any assumed note, the vendor's lien and deed of trust to secure assumption shall not be required. In case of dispute as to the form of the Deed, note(s), deed of trust or deed of trust to secure assumption, forms prepared by the State Bar of Texas shall be used.

15. CASUALTY LOSS: If any part of Property is damaged or destroyed by fire or other casualty loss, Seller shall restore the same to its previous condition as soon as reasonably possible, but in any event by Closing Date. If Seller is unable to do so without fault, Buyer may terminate this contract and the Earnest Money shall be refunded to Buyer.

16. DEFAULT: If Buyer fails to comply herewith, Seller may either (a) enforce specific performance and seek such other relief as may be provided by law or (b) terminate this contract and receive the Earnest Money as liquidated damages. If Seller is unable without fault, within the time herein required, to (a) make any non-casualty repairs or (b) deliver the Commitment or (c) deliver the Complete Abstract, Buyer may either terminate this contract and receive the Earnest Money

186

as the sole remedy or extend the time for performance up to fifteen (15) days and the Closing Date shall be extended pursuant to other provisions of this contract. If Seller fails to comply herewith for any other reason, Buyer may either (a) enforce specific performance hereof and seek such other relief as may be provided by law or (b) terminate this contract and receive the Earnest Money, thereby releasing Seller from this contract.

17. ATTORNEY'S FEES: Any signatory to this contract, Broker or Escrow Agent who is the prevailing party in any legal proceeding brought under or with relation to this contract or transaction shall be additionally entitled to recover court costs and reasonable attorney fees from the non-prevailing party.

18. ESCROW: The Earnest Money is deposited with Escrow Agent with the understanding that Escrow Agent (a) is not a party to this contract and does not assume or have any liability for performance or non-performance of any signatory (b) has the right to require from all signatories a written release of liability of the Escrow Agent which authorizes the disbursement of the Earnest Money (c) is not liable for interest or other charge on the funds held and (d) is not liable for any losses of escrow funds caused by the failure of any banking institution in which such funds have been deposited, unless such banking institution is acting as Escrow Agent. If any signatory unreasonably fails to deliver promptly the documents described in (b) above, then such signatory shall be liable to the other signatories as provided in Paragraph 17. At closing, the Earnest Money shall be applied first to any cash down payment required, then to Buyer's closing costs and any excess refunded to Buyer. Any refund or payment of the Earnest Money under this contract shall be reduced by the amount of any actual expenses incurred on behalf of the party receiving the Earnest Money, and Escrow Agent will pay the same to the creditors entitled thereto.

19. REPRESENTATIONS: Seller represents that as of the Closing Date (a) there will be no unrecorded liens, assessments or Uniform Commercial Code Security Interests against any of the Property which will not be satisfied out of the Sales Price, unless securing payment of any loans assumed by Buyer and (b) assumed loan(s) will be without default. If any representation in this contract is untrue on the Closing Date, this contract may be terminated by Buyer and the Earnest Money shall be refunded to Buyer. All representations contained in this contract shall survive closing.

20. AGREEMENT OF PARTIES: This contract contains the entire agreement of the parties and cannot be changed except by their written agreement. Texas Real Estate Commission promulgated addenda which are a part of this contract are (list): _____

21. NOTICES: All notices shall be in writing and effective when delivered at the addresses shown below.

22. CONSULT YOUR ATTORNEY: The Broker cannot give you legal advice. This is intended to be a legally binding contract. READ IT CAREFULLY. Federal law may impose certain duties upon Brokers or Signatories to this contract when any of the signatories is a foreign party, or when any of the signatories receives certain amounts of U.S. currency in connection with a real estate closing. If you do not understand the effect of any part of this contract, consult your attorney BEFORE signing.

SELLER'S ATTORNEY: _____③①_____	BUYER'S ATTORNEY: _____③②_____

EXECUTED in multiple originals effective the _____ day of _____, 19_____. **(BROKER: FILL IN THE DATE OF FINAL ACCEPTANCE.)**

Buyer	Seller
Buyer	Seller
Buyer's Address	Seller's Address
Phone No.	Phone No.

AGREEMENT BETWEEN BROKERS

Listing Broker agrees to pay _____, Co-Broker, a fee of _____ of the total sales price when the Broker's fee described in Paragraph 8 is received. Escrow Agent is authorized and directed to pay Co-Broker from Listing Broker's fee at closing.

Co-Broker License No.	Listing Broker License No.
By _____	By _____
Co-Broker's Address Phone No.	Listing Broker's Address Phone No.

EARNEST MONEY RECEIPT

Receipt of $_____ Earnest Money is acknowledged in the form of _____

Figure 8:1 *continued*

Escrow Agent: _____   By: _____

Date _____, 19____

> The form of this contract has been approved by the Texas Real Estate Commission. Such approval relates to this contract form only. No representation is made as to the legal validity or adequacy of any provision in any specific transaction. It is not suitable for complex transactions. Extensive riders or additions are not to be used. (02-85) TREC NO. 20-0. This form replaces TREC NOS. 1-1, 4-0 and 6-0.

If the property is to be SELLER FINANCED (E), four different alternatives are provided. The basic terms of amount and interest rate are specified at ⑲ and ⑳, respectively. The various terms are next set out in 1 through 4 of E in Paragraph 4. Note also that the seller has five (5) days to disapprove buyer's credit. Otherwise, it is deemed approved. Time constraints are also put on the buyer at ㉑ and ㉒. Note that ALL of the lender's financial requirements must be satisfied before the loan or assumption is considered to be approved.

In Paragraph 5 the EARNEST MONEY amount is set out at ㉓, with the depository, usually a title company, shown at ㉔. A provision for additional earnest money, if any, is shown at ㉕.

The first provision for TITLE is set out in Paragraph 6, advising the buyer (as required by the License Act) to have an attorney of his choice examine the abstract of title, or that a policy of title insurance should be obtained. If the property is located in a utility district, both parties agree to execute the statutorily required notice of this act.

The PROPERTY CONDITION provision gives the buyer two alternatives. He may accept the property in its present condition with limited repairs, or he may require the extensive inspections provided in the Property Condition Addendum (Figure 8:2, discussed later in this chapter). Note that there is a dollar limit provided for seller repairs at ㉖. A key provision of this paragraph provides that if the repairs cannot be made as required and within the limits set out, the buyer has three specific choices, which must be made within three days. This gives the seller some comfort that the deal is still intact if he receives no objections within the time limit. Note also that if the repairs are expensive, the seller has a decision to make! A helpful, and hopefully enforceable, waiver of responsibility is provided for the broker and sales associates.

Paragraph 8, although titled Broker's Fee, provides only that the listing broker is to be identified. The amount of his compensation is specified in the listing agreement and is not a part of this contract between the buyer and seller. A correct, but sometimes controversial, clause provides that both brokers represent the seller. This has been long-standing Texas law (absent a contrary agreement between the parties, which is also provided for), and the contract simply makes this clear to the parties.

Provisions and deadlines for closing are set forth at ㉗. Possession date for the buyer is stated at ㉘. This is generally "at closing" or perhaps "upon funding."

A Special Provisions section is provided at Paragraph 11 of the Earnest Money Contract. This particular Earnest Money Contract has very little need for special provisions, except for specifying certain exceptions to the fixtures which the purchaser may expect to be conveyed with the house, because of the all-encompassing type of language set out in Paragraph 2 of the contract.

Paragraph 12 deals with various expenses the buyer and seller will be expected to pay at or prior to closing. Responsibility for loan appraisal fees is shown at ㉙. (These are generally paid by the party obtaining the loan.) Seller's expenses, which may include the dollar amount for points or commitment fees or discount fees to enable purchaser to secure his loan, are set out at ㉚, along with certain other expenses that are incidental to selling. Note that if the costs are *less* than expected, the seller gets the benefit of the reduced cost.

Paragraphs 13 through 20 are very specific and explanatory provisions that are generally standard to all earnest money contracts. Items generally prorated are taxes, insurance, and rents. Paragraph 14 (Title Approval) carefully and clearly sets out what exceptions there may be to title. There are also additional provisions for loss (damage or destruction) of the real estate, penalties in the event of default of buyer or seller, and explanations as to escrow and representations.

Paragraph 20 sets out addenda to be attached, if any. The last provision in the earnest money contract, Paragraph 22, is the provision which suggests to the purchaser and seller that if they need some legal advice, they should consult an attorney. Those names are inserted at ③ and ㉜.

The brokers' commission agreement is now *after* the contractual agreement between the seller and buyer. It is a separate agreement, *negotiated* between the brokers.

Acceptance

For an offer to become binding, the seller must accept everything in it. The rejection of even the smallest portion of the offer is a rejection of the entire offer. If the seller wishes to reject the offer but keep negotiations alive, he can make a counteroffer. This is a written offer to sell to the buyer at a new price and with terms that are closer to the buyer's offer than the seller's original asking price and terms. The agent prepares the counteroffer by either filling out a fresh purchase contract identical in all ways to the buyer's offer except for these changes, or by writing on the back of the offer (or on another sheet of paper) that the seller offers to sell at the terms the buyer had offered except for the stated changes. The counteroffer is then dated and signed by the seller. A time limit may be given to the buyer to accept. The seller keeps a copy, and the counteroffer is delivered to the buyer for his decision. If the counteroffer is acceptable to the buyer, he signs and dates it, and the contract is complete. Another commonly used, but less desirable practice is to take the buyer's offer, cross out each item unacceptable to the seller, and write above or below it what the seller will accept. Each change is then initialed by the seller and buyer. If the offer is rejected, it is good practice to have the seller write the word "rejected" on the offer followed by his signature.

Federal Clauses

In two instances, the government requires that specific clauses be included in real estate sales contracts. First, an **amendatory language** clause must be included whenever a sales contract is signed by a purchaser prior to the receipt of an FHA Appraised Value or a VA Certificate of Reasonable Value on the property. The purpose is to assure that the purchaser may terminate the contract without loss when it appears that the agreed purchase price may be significantly above appraised value. The specific clauses, which must be used verbatim, are contained in the TREC promulgated form for FHA insured or VA guaranteed financing (TREC No. 21–0). Second, the Federal Trade Commission (FTC) requires that builders and sellers of new houses must include **insulation disclosures** in all earnest money contracts. Disclosures, which may be based upon manufacturer claims, must cite the type, thickness, and R-value of the insulation installed in the home. These disclosures are contained in the TREC promulgated New Home Insulation Addendum (TREC No. 13–0).

Negotiation

One of the most important principles of real estate contracts in general is that everything is negotiable and nearly everything has a price. In preparing or analyzing any contract, consider what the advantages and disadvantages of each condition are to each party to the contract. A solid contract results when the buyer and seller each feel that they have gained more than they have given up. The prime example is the sales price of the property itself. The seller prefers the money over the property, while the buyer prefers the property over the money. Each small negotiable item in the purchase contract has its price too. For example, the seller may agree to include the refrigerator for $200 more. Equally important in negotiating is the relative bargaining power of the buyer and seller. If the seller is confident he will have plenty of buyers at his asking price, he can elect to refuse offers for less money, and reject those with numerous conditions or insufficient earnest money. However, if the owner is anxious to sell and has received only one offer in several months, he may be quite willing to accept a lower price and numerous conditions.

PROPERTY CONDITION ADDENDUM

The **Property Condition Addendum** (revised 02/85; TREC 2–2) published by the Texas Real Estate Commission is shown in Figure 8:2. It is intended to be attached to the foregoing contract by specifying the applicable property at ①.

If the parties agree, provisions for termite inspection can be checked at ②. Note that the buyer may require it, at buyer's

Figure 8:2

PROPERTY CONDITION ADDENDUM

02-08-85

PROMULGATED BY TEXAS REAL ESTATE COMMISSION

ADDENDUM TO EARNEST MONEY CONTRACT BETWEEN THE UNDERSIGNED PARTIES CONCERNING THE PROPERTY AT _____①_____

(Street Address and City)

CHECK APPLICABLE BOXES:

☐ A. TERMITES: Buyer, at Buyer's expense (except at Seller's expense in VA transactions), may have the Property inspected by a Structural Pest Control Business Licensee to determine whether or not there is visible evidence of active termite infestation or visible termite damage to the improvements. If termite treatment

② or repairs are required, Buyer will furnish a written report to Seller from such Licensee within _____days from the effective date of this Contract, but no treatment or repairs will be required for fences, trees or shrubs. Buyer's failure to furnish such report to Seller within the time specified shall constitute a waiver of Buyer's right to any treatment and repairs.

☐ B. INSPECTIONS: Buyer, at Buyer's expense, may have any of the items designated below inspected by inspectors of Buyer's choice. Repairs will only be required of items designated by this Contract for inspection and reported to be in need of immediate repair or which are not performing the function for which intended.

③ Failure of Buyer to furnish written inspection reports and to designate the repairs to which Buyer is entitled by this Contract within the times specified below shall be deemed a waiver of Buyer's repair rights.

STRUCTURAL: Buyer requires inspections of the following: (check applicable boxes)

☐ foundation, ☐ roof, ☐ load bearing walls, ☐ ceilings, ☐ basement, ☐ water penetration, ☐ fireplace and chimney, ☐ floors,

☐ and _____④_____

Within _____days from the effective date of this Contract, Buyer will furnish Seller written inspection reports with a designation of repairs if repairs are required.

EQUIPMENT AND SYSTEMS: Buyer requires inspections of the following: (check applicable boxes)

☐ plumbing system (including any water heater, wells and septic system), ☐ electrical system, ☐ all heating and cooling units and systems,
☐ any built-in range, oven, dishwasher, disposer, exhaust fans, trash compactor, ☐ swimming pool and related mechanical equipment, ☐ sprinkler systems,
☐ gas lines (inspection by private inspector) ☐ gas lines (inspection by gas supplier) ☐ and _____⑤_____

Within _____days from the effective date of this Contract, Buyer will furnish Seller written inspection reports with a designation of repairs if repairs are required.

☐ C. OTHER REPAIRS: Seller shall make the following repairs in addition to those required above: _____⑥_____

All inspections shall be by persons who regularly provide such service and who are either registered as inspectors with the Texas Real Estate Commission or otherwise permitted by law to perform inspections. Repairs shall be by trained and qualified persons who are, whenever possible, manufacturer-approved service persons and who are licensed or bonded whenever such license or bond is required by law. Seller shall permit access to the Property at any reasonable time for inspection or repairs and for reinspection after repairs have been completed. Seller shall be responsible for termite treatment and repairs to termite damage, repairs to items specifically designated above for inspection, and repairs specifically described in Paragraph C, subject to the provisions of Paragraph 7 of this Contract. Broker and sales associates shall not be liable or responsible for any inspections or repairs pursuant to this Contract and Addendum. ⑦

_____   _____
SELLER   BUYER

_____   _____
SELLER   BUYER

> The Form of this Addendum has been approved by the Texas Real Estate Commission for use only with similarly approved or promulgated forms of contracts. No representation is made as to the legal validity or adequacy of any provision in any specific transactions. (Rev. 02-85) TREC No. 2-2. This form replaces TREC No. 2-1.
>
> **177**

expense. This attempts to eliminate seller and broker responsibility. In Texas, particularly along the Gulf Coast, it is advisable for the buyer to obtain this certification. As stated in the form, the inspection certificate should be no more than 30 days old.

If applicable and the parties agree, provisions for property condition can be checked at ③. Items to be inspected are further specified in ④ and ⑤, as well as additional repairs in ⑥. The additional repairs may include, but are not limited to repainting, glass repair, and carpeting repairs.

In an effort to protect the broker and sales associates, a disclaimer is added near the bottom of the form at ⑦. Due to the expansion of the Real Estate License Act, and provisions of the Deceptive Trade Practices Act, this disclaimer should never, by itself, be relied upon by the licensee to relieve him of any liability.

The use of the foregoing contracts will benefit the licensee in his normal residential real estate transactions. Most of the technical legal questions concerning title, default, escrow, and closing guarantees, as well as representations and warranties of buyer and seller are contained as a matter of form in these forms. All the licensee has to do is fill in the blanks. Most clients who are parties to a residential earnest money contract find it easy to understand a fill-in-the-blank type form.

Licensee Benefits

It should be well understood by all real estate brokers and salesmen that they are not permitted to practice law. This is specifically prohibited under Section 16 of the Texas Real Estate Licensing Act, but the nature of the real estate business has led to some confusion and dissension between lawyers and real estate licensees. For instance, it is common practice for real estate agents to fill in the blanks of an earnest money contract, yet not fill in the blanks of a deed. To clarify this matter, there is an Attorney General's opinion that was issued in 1972 which explained that real estate agents, under law, do not have the right to fill in the blanks of an earnest money contract. However, the opinion went on to say that if the Texas Real Estate Commission wished to require the

Practicing Law

use of a standard form for certain types of transactions, that such forms could be sanctioned by the Texas Real Estate Commission for use by real estate brokers and salesmen. This enables brokers and salesmen to fill in the blanks of earnest money contracts without violating Section 16 of the revised Texas Real Estate Licensing Act.

INSTALLMENT CONTRACTS

Installment contract = land contract = conditional sales contract = contract for deed = agreement of sale

Buyer holds equitable title until deed is delivered.

An **installment contract,** also known as a **land contract, conditional sales contract, contract for deed,** or **agreement of sale** combines features from a sales contract, deed, and a mortgage. It is used to sell property in situations where the seller does not wish to convey title until all, or at least a substantial portion, of the purchase price is paid by the buyer. This is different from the purchase contract shown in Figure 8:1 wherein the buyer receives possession and a deed at the closing. With an installment contract, the buyer is given possession and the right to use the property upon signing the contract, but he does not acquire title. Instead, he receives a contract promising that a deed will be delivered at a later date. During the period between signing the contract and the seller delivering the deed, the buyer is said to hold **equitable title** to the property. That is, he has the exclusive right to acquire the title, along with possession of the property. This equitable title can even be sold, usually by the first buyer who can assign his interest on the contract to the second buyer.

A common use of the installment contract occurs when the buyer does not have the full purchase price in cash or he cannot borrow it from a lender. Under these conditions, the seller must be willing to accept a down payment plus monthly payments until the property is paid for. The seller can either deliver a deed to the buyer at closing and simultaneously have the buyer pledge the property as collateral for the balance due (a mortgage) or the seller can agree to deliver title only after the buyer has completed his payments (an installment contract).

Delivering title after payment is advantageous to the seller because if the buyer fails to make his payments, the title to the property is still in the name of the seller. This avoids the time and costs consumed by foreclosure, a requirement if title has already been conveyed to the buyer.

Figure 8:3 is a simplified illustration of an installment contract. In paragraph ① the buyer and seller are identified, the purchase price is given and dated, and the amount and terms of the balance due are stated. The buyer is sometimes referred to as the **vendee** and the seller as the **vendor.** In paragraph ②, the seller promises to deliver a deed to the buyer when the buyer has made all the payments stated in paragraph ①. Paragraph ② also describes the property. Paragraph ③ deals with the possibility that the buyer may fail to make the required payments or fail to abide by the other contract terms. The strong wording in this paragraph is typical of the installment contract, particularly when it is utilized to sell vacant land. If you read paragraph ③ carefully, you will see that, in the event of the buyer's default, the seller can retain all payments made *and* retake possession of the property. This is the feature that makes the installment contract popular with sellers.

Sample Contract

Paragraph ④ deals with property taxes. In this example, the buyer agrees to pay them. Sometimes the seller will agree to pay the property taxes until a deed is delivered to the buyer. This is not an act of kindness but protection for the seller. The seller does not want to risk the possibility of the buyer's failure to pay the taxes, thus giving the county tax collector the right to take the property.

In paragraph ⑤, the seller sets construction restrictions. The object is to prevent unsightly structures from being built that would have a negative impact on surrounding property values. This enhances the buyer's resale value; for the seller, it means that the property is more valuable if the buyer defaults.

Repossession

In agreement with the provisions in paragraph ③, paragraph ⑥ provides the seller with a means of smooth recovery of possession and ownership in the event of default by the buyer. If the buyer records his contract with the public recorder, he serves notice that he has an interest in the property. This creates a cloud on the seller's title. If the buyer were to default, the effort necessary to remove this cloud would be inconsistent with the seller's objective of easy recovery. Also, such a cloud makes it more difficult for the seller to borrow against the property. However, a nonrecording provi-

Figure 8:3

INSTALLMENT CONTRACT

① *RECEIVED this* __15th__ *day of* __October, 19xx__ , *from* __Cliff Fisher and wife Sandy__ *(hereafter called the "buyer") of* __7778 Spinner Street, Bridgetown, Anystate__ *the sum of $* __200.00__ *as down payment toward the sales price of $* __10,000.00__ . *The balance of $* __9,800.00__ *is to be paid in equal monthly installments of $* __98.00__ *until paid in full. The monthly payment includes principal and interest of* __10__ *% per annum on the unpaid balance. Payments are to be made on the first of each month to the Sunrise Lakes Land Company (hereafter called the "seller").*

② *BE IT AGREED: if the buyer makes the payments and performs the agreements stated in this contract, the seller agrees to convey to the buyer in fee simple, clear of all encumbrances whatsoever, by special warranty deed, Lot #* __17__ , *Block* __B-1__ , *Sunrise Lakes Tract, situated and recorded in the County of Sunrise, State of Anywhere.*

③ *IF THE BUYER fails to make any of the payments herein designated or fails to perform any of the other agreements made herein, this contract shall be terminated and the buyer shall forfeit all payments made on this contract. Such payments will be retained by the seller as accumulated rent on the property described above, and the seller shall have the right to reenter and take possession of the premises.*

④ *THE BUYER AGREES to pay all property taxes subsequent to the year* __19xx__ .

⑤ *CONSTRUCTION shall be limited to residences built with new materials. Structures must be located at least twenty feet from the front lot line and five feet from the other lot lines. Shacks or unsightly structures are not permitted.*

⑥ *THE BUYER AND SELLER agree that this contract, or any assignment thereof, is not to be recorded without the permission of the seller. To do so shall result in any exist-*

Figure 8:3 *continued*

*ing balance on this contract becoming due and payable imme-
diately.*

⑦ *THE BUYER AND SELLER agree that prompt payment
is an essential part of this contract and that this contract is binding
upon their assigns, heirs, executors, and administrators.*

⑧ *THE BUYER HAS the right to examine the master
abstract.*

BUYER[s] ⑨	SELLER
Cliff Fisher	*Salem Bigland*
Sandy Fisher	Salem Bigland President, Sunrise Lakes Land Company

sion is definitely not to the advantage of the buyer, as anyone
inspecting the public records would not find a record of the
buyer's interest. The seller would still be shown as the owner.
In view of this, some states outlaw these clauses, but Texas
does not.

While repossession and forfeiture in the default of the
installment land contract is the same in Texas as it is in most
other states, it is important to recognize that the Recording
Act in Texas provides that virtually any acknowledged instrument may be recorded. While there may be a prohibition
against recording the land contract itself or of any assignment
thereof (provisions which may be legally questionable), it is
possible to lease the property, sublet the property, or create
some other kind of material interest in the property that can
be recorded. The constructive notice will then be effective
to show that there is other interest in the property besides
that of the owner.

Paragraph ⑦ reemphasizes that payments must be made
promptly and adds that the terms of the contract are binding
on anyone to whom the buyer may sell or assign the contract.
In the illustrated contract, the buyer does not receive a title
report or title insurance for his individual lot when he signs
the contract. However, at ⑧, he is invited to see the abstract;
presumably it shows the seller as the owner of the land.
The balance of the contract, ⑨, is for the signatures of the
buyer and seller and, when required, witnesses or a notary.

Consumer Criticism   The installment contract has received much consumer criticism because its wording so strongly favors the seller. In numerous instances, buyers, although they have paid a substantial portion of the purchase price, have lost the property and their money due to one or two late payments. Strictly interpreted, that is what the contract says; if the buyer signs it, presumably he agrees. However, the courts and legislatures in several states have found this too harsh.

Texas has provided some statutory relief to this harsh remedy of automatic forfeiture in the installment land contract. The statutes are as follows:

SUBCHAPTER D. EXECUTORY CONTRACT FOR CONVEYANCE

§ 5.061.   Avoidance of Forfeiture and Acceleration

A seller may enforce a forfeiture of interest and the acceleration of the indebtedness of a purchaser in default under an executory contract for conveyance of real property used or to be used as the purchaser's residence only after notifying the purchaser of the seller's intent to enforce the forfeiture and acceleration and the expiration of the following periods:

(1) if the purchaser has paid less than 10 percent of the purchase price, 15 days after the date notice is given;

(2) if the purchaser has paid 10 percent or more but less than 20 percent of the purchase price, 30 days after the date notice is given; and

(3) if the purchaser has paid 20 percent or more of the purchase price, 60 days after the date notice is given.

§ 5.062.   Notice

(a) Notice under Section 5.061 of this code must be in writing. If the notice is mailed, it must be by registered or certified mail. The notice must be conspicuous and printed in 10-point boldface type or uppercase typewritten letters, and must include the statement:

N O T I C E

YOU ARE LATE IN MAKING YOUR PAYMENT UNDER THE CON-
TRACT TO BUY YOUR HOME. UNLESS YOU MAKE THE PAYMENT
BY (date) THE SELLER HAS THE RIGHT TO TAKE POSSESSION
OF YOUR HOME AND TO KEEP ALL PAYMENTS YOU HAVE MADE
TO DATE.

(b) Notice by mail is given when it is mailed to the purchaser's residence or place of business. Notice by other writing is given when it is delivered to the purchaser at the purchaser's residence or place of business.

§ 5.063. Right to Cure Default

Notwithstanding an agreement to the contrary, a purchaser in default under an executory contract for the conveyance of real property used or to be used as the purchaser's residence may, at any time before expiration of the applicable period provided by Section 5.061 of this code, avoid forfeiture of interest and acceleration of indebtedness by complying with the terms of the contract up to the date of compliance.

These statutes strongly restrict the legal title holder's right of forfeiture and acceleration, and the buyer cannot be summarily evicted without the specified notices.

Another key weak point in the installment sale contract *Other Pitfalls* is that the seller does not deed ownership to the buyer until some later date. Thus, a buyer might make payments for several years only to find that the seller cannot deliver title as promised. At that point, unless the seller is willing to give the buyer a refund, the buyer's only recourse is to sue the seller for specific performance or money damages. However, a lawsuit works only if the buyer has the time and money to pursue the matter, if the suit is successful, and if the seller has the money to pay the judgment.

If an installment contract is used for the purchase of real estate, it should be done with the help of legal counsel to make certain that it provides adequate safeguards for the buyer as well as the seller. In Chapter 11, the installment contract is discussed as a tool to finance the sale of improved property when other sources of financing are not available.

LEASE WITH OPTION
TO BUY

An option contract is an agreement to keep an offer open for a fixed period of time. This is often done by a seller who gives a buyer an option to buy property for a fixed period of time and for a fixed price. One of the most popular option contracts in real estate is the **lease with option to buy.** Often simply referred to as a **"lease-option,"** it allows the tenant to buy the property at a present price and terms during the option period. For a residential property, the lease is typically for one year and the option to buy must be exercised during that time.

In this lease-option contract, all the normal provisions of a lease are present, such as those shown in Figure 15:1. The terms of the option to purchase are also present, stating that the tenant has the right to exercise the option to buy, provided the tenant notifies the landlord in writing of that intent during the option period. All terms of the option to buy must be negotiated and in writing when the lease is signed. Both the tenant and landlord must sign the lease. If the tenant wants to buy during the option period, the tenant notifies the landlord in accordance with the terms of the contract that as the tenant he wishes to exercise the option to buy. Together they (landlord and tenant) proceed to carry out the purchase as in a normal sale.

If the tenant does not exercise the option within the option period, the option expires and the purchase contract is null and void. If the lease also expires at the end of the option period the tenant must either arrange with the landlord to continue renting or move out. Alternatively, they can negotiate a new purchase contract or a new lease-option contract.

Popularity during
"Soft Markets"

Lease-options are particularly popular in soft real estate markets where a home seller is having difficulty finding a buyer. One solution is to lower the asking price and/or make the financing terms more attractive. However, the seller may wish to hold out in hopes that prices will rise within a year. Meantime the seller needs someone to occupy the property and provide some income.

The lease-option is attractive to a tenant because the tenant has a place to rent plus the option of buying for the price in the purchase contract anytime during the option period. In other words, the tenant can wait a year and see if he likes the property and if values rise to or above the price in the purchase contract. If the tenant does not like the property and/or the property does not rise in value, the tenant is under no obligation to buy. Once the lease expires, the tenant is under no obligation to continuing renting either.

To encourage a tenant to exercise the option to buy, the contract may allow the tenant to apply part or all of the rent paid to the purchase price. In fact, quite a bit of flexibility and negotiation can be exercised in a lease-option. For example, take a house that would rent for $750 per month and sell for $100,000 on the open market. Suppose the seller wants $110,000 and won't come down to the market price. Meanwhile the house is vacant and there are mortgage payments to be made. The homeowner could offer a one-year lease-option with a rental charge of $750 each month and an exercise price of $110,000. Within a year, $110,000 may look good to the tenant, especially if the market value of the property has risen significantly above $110,000. The tenant can exercise the option or, if not prohibited by the contract, can sell it to someone who intends to exercise it. The owner receives $10,000.00 more for the property than was possible the previous year, and the tenant has the benefit of any value increase above that.

Examples of Useful Lease-Options

Continuing the above example, what if the property rises to $105,000 in value? There is no economic incentive for the tenant to exercise the option at $110,000. The tenant can simply disregard the option and make an offer of $105,000 to the landlord. The landlord's choice is to sell at that price or continue renting the house, perhaps with another one-year lease-option.

The landlord could also charge the tenant extra for the privilege of having the option, but it must make economic sense to a tenant. Suppose in the above example the purchase price is set at the current market value: i.e., $100,000. This would be valuable and benefit the tenant. The landlord could charge an up-front cash fee for the option and/or charge above-market rent. The amounts would depend on market expectations regarding the value of this house a year from now.

There is nothing special about one-year option periods although it is a very popular length of time. The landlord and tenant can agree to a three-month, or six-month or nine-month option if it fits their needs, and the lease can run longer than the option period. Options for longer than one year are generally reserved for commercial properties. For example, a person just starting out in business, or perhaps expanding, wants to buy a building but needs a year or two to see how successful the business will be and how much space it will need.

Potential Problem Areas   Be aware that lease-options may create income tax consequences that require professional tax counseling. Legal advice is also recommended in preparing and reviewing the lease-option papers. There are no TREC forms for lease options, so Texas laws require that either the owner or his attorney prepare such an instrument. The entire deal (lease and option contract) must be clearly set out from the beginning. One cannot wait until the option is exercised to define the purchase terms or even material parts of it. Some licensees have attempted to achieve the same goal by using the TREC promulgated Earnest Money Contract coupled with the Buyer's Temporary Residential Lease form. Even though these are promulgated forms, they have the potential for conflict and shouldn't be used except with a great deal of caution. An option to buy is an example of a unilateral contract. When it is exercised it becomes a bilateral purchase contract. The person giving the option is called the **optionor** (the landlord in a lease-option). The person receiving the option is the **optionee** (the tenant in a lease-option). The owner should be cautioned to make the period between the exercise of the option and the purchase very short (15 to 30 days). Once the option is exercised, the landlord-tenant relationship terminates and rental payments are no longer due, unless the contract provides otherwise. You will see how an option can be used by a home builder to buy land in Chapter 12 and how options can be used to renew leases in Chapter 15.

Sometimes a tenant will agree to rent a property only if given an opportunity to purchase it before someone else does. In other words, the tenant is saying, "Mr. Owner, if you get a valid offer from someone else to purchase this property, show it to me and give me an opportunity to match the offer." This is called a **right of first refusal.** If someone presents the owner with a valid offer, the owner must show that offer to the tenant before accepting it. If the tenant decides not to match it, the owner is free to accept it.

A right of first refusal protects a tenant from having the property sold out from under him when, in fact, if the tenant knew about the offer he would have been willing to match it. The owner usually does not care who buys, as long as the price and terms are the same. Therefore, an owner may agree to include a right of first refusal clause in a rental contract for little or no additional charge if the tenant requests it.

RIGHT OF FIRST REFUSAL

Most real estate transactions involve the exchange of real estate for monetary consideration. However, among sophisticated real estate investors, exchanging real property for real property has become popular for two important reasons. First, real estate trades can be accomplished without large amounts of cash by trading a property you presently own for one you want. This sidesteps the intermediate step of converting real estate to cash and then converting cash back to real estate. Second, by using an exchange, you can dispose of one property and acquire another without paying income taxes on the profit in the first property at the time of the transaction. As a result, the phrase "tax-free exchange" is often used when talking about trading.

To illustrate, suppose that you own, as an investment, an apartment building. The value on your accounting books is $150,000, but its market value today is $250,000. If you sell for cash, you will have to pay income taxes on the difference between the value of the property on your accounting books and the amount you receive for it. If instead of selling for cash, you find another building that you want and can arrange a trade, then for income tax purposes the new building acquires the accounting book value of the old and no income taxes are due at the time of the trade. Taxes will be due,

EXCHANGE AGREEMENTS

however, if and when you finally sell rather than trade. Owner-occupied dwellings are treated differently. The Internal Revenue Service permits a homeowner to sell and still postpone paying taxes on the gain provided another home of equal or greater value is purchased within 24 months.

Trading Up   Real estate exchanges need not involve properties of equal value. For example, if you own a small office building worth $100,000 that is free of debt, you could trade it for a building worth $500,000 that has $400,000 of mortgage debt against it. Alternatively, if the building you wanted was priced at $600,000 with $400,000 in debt against it, you could offer your building plus $100,000 in cash.

When a simple two-way trade does not leave each party satisfied, exchanges involving several parties can be arranged. In the four-way trade shown in part A of Figure 8:4, Fisher would like to own Garcia's property but cannot arrange a trade because Garcia does not want Fisher's property. Fisher then looks for a property Garcia would like to own. He finds one that belongs to Hayden. However, Hayden does not want Fisher's property, and the search must continue to find someone who will take Fisher's property and who has something acceptable to Hayden. Ingram fills this gap, and the four-way trade is possible. Fisher gets Garcia's property, who in turn gets Hayden's property, who in turn acquires Ingram's property, who in turn takes Fisher's property.*

In part B of Figure 8:4, a combination trade and cash sale is shown. Nelson wants Mitchell's property and is willing to pay cash for it. Mitchell refuses to sell for cash because of the income taxes he would have to pay; he will only trade. Owens has a property for sale that Mitchell would like to have. To make the deal, Nelson buys it and gives it to Mitchell, receiving Mitchell's property in return. The combination trade and cash sale has become very popular in recent years among sophisticated real estate investors. Correctly applied in an

---

* Although recent tax developments indicate a "wheel" type exchange can be carried out tax-free exactly as shown in Figure 8:4A, a few tax experts feel that they are on safer ground by working the trade as a series of two-party exchanges.

POSSIBLE TRADING COMBINATIONS   **Figure 8:4**

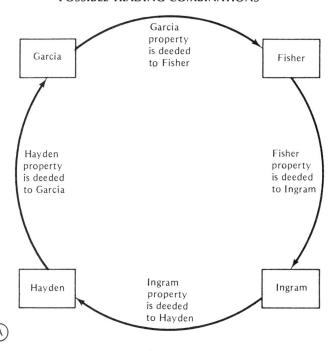

Garcia property is deeded to Fisher

Hayden property is deeded to Garcia

Fisher property is deeded to Ingram

Ingram property is deeded to Hayden

Garcia

Fisher

Hayden

Ingram

(A)

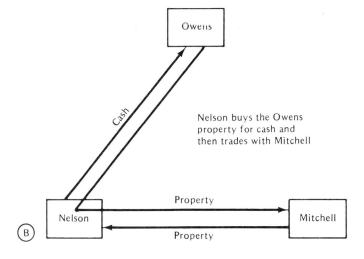

Owens

Nelson buys the Owens property for cash and then trades with Mitchell

Cash

Property

Property

Nelson

Mitchell

(B)

appreciating real estate market, an investor can pyramid his or her wealth with it.

Although trading is a complicated business, it is also very lucrative for real estate agents. Whereas an ordinary sale results in one brokerage commission, a two-party exchange results in two commissions, and a four-party exchange, in four commissions.

DELAYED EXCHANGES   The Internal Revenue Code allows nonsimultaneous exchanges to be tax-deferred under certain circumstances. Such an exchange, commonly called a **delayed exchange,** occurs when property is exchanged for a right to receive property at a future date. It is a helpful technique when one party is willing to exchange out of a property but has not yet chosen a property to exchange into. Meanwhile the other parties to the exchange are ready and want to close. The delayed exchange allows the closing to take place by giving the party that has not chosen a property the right to designate a property and take title after the closing. The 1984 act specifically allows this provided (1) the designated property is identified within 45 days of the original closing, (2) the title to the designated property is acquired within 180 days of the original closing date, and (3) the designated property is received before the designating party's tax return is due. If these rules are not met the transaction will be treated as a sale for the designating party, not an exchange.

Typical Trade Contract   Space does not permit a detailed review of a trade contract. However, very briefly, a typical trade contract identifies the traders involved and their respective properties; names the type of deed and quality of title that will be conveyed; names the real estate brokers involved and how much they are to be paid; discusses prorations, personal property, rights of tenants, and damage to the property; provides a receipt for the deposit that each trader makes; requires each trader to provide an abstract of title; and sets forth the consequences of defaulting on the contract. If the same broker represents more than one trader, he must disclose this to each trader whom he represents.

*Match terms **a–k** with statements **1–11**.*

4. **a.** *"As is"*
7. **b.** *Bill of sale*
6. **c.** *Closing date*
3. **d.** *Deposit*
5. **e.** *Dry rot*
9. **f.** *Installment sale contract*

10. **g.** *Nonrecording provision*
2. **h.** *Property condition addendum*
1. **i.** *Purchase contract*
8. **j.** *"Time is of the essence"*
11. **k.** *Vendee*

1. A written and signed agreement specifying the terms at which a buyer will purchase and an owner will sell.
2. Contains provisions for termite inspection, and inspection of structural items and equipment systems.
3. Money that accompanies an offer to purchase as evidence of good faith; also called earnest money.
4. Property offered for sale in its present condition with no guarantee or warranty of quality provided by the seller.
5. Rotted wood; usually the result of alternative soaking and drying over a long period of time.
6. The day on which the buyer pays his money and the seller delivers title.
7. Written evidence of the sale of personal property.
8. A phrase meaning that all parties to a contract are expected to perform on time as a condition of the contract.
9. Also known as a conditional sales contract, land contract, contract for deed, or agreement of sale.
10. A clause in a land contract that requires immediate payment of the entire balance still owing if the contract is recorded.
11. The buyer under a contract for deed.

1. Why is it necessary to include the extra step of preparing and signing a purchase contract when it would seem much easier if the buyer simply paid the seller the purchase price and the seller handed the buyer a deed?
2. Why is it preferable to prepare a purchase contract that contains all the terms and conditions of sale at the outset rather than to leave some items to be "ironed out" later?
3. What are the advantages and the disadvantages of using preprinted real estate purchase contract forms?
4. Is it legal for a seller to accept an offer that is not accompanied by a deposit? Why or why not?
5. If a purchase contract for real property describes the land, is it also necessary to mention the fixtures? Why or why not?
6. How will the relative bargaining strengths and weaknesses of the buyer and seller affect the contract negotiation process?

7. Under an installment contract, what is the advantage to the seller if he does not have to deliver title to the buyer until all required payments are made?
8. What position does Texas take toward payment forfeiture and nonrecording clauses in land contracts?
9. What are the advantages of trading real estate rather than selling it? What do you consider the disadvantages to be?

ADDITIONAL
READINGS

"Buyer's Personal Inspection" by **Shari Lynn Anderson.** (*First Tuesday,* Jan 85, p. 21). Article explains broker's duty of disclosure and includes a sample property inspection agreement form.

"Option to Buy as a Counter Offer" by **Matt Collette.** (*First Tuesday,* July 84, p. 20). Article suggests sellers may wish to counter with an option to buy when a buyer makes an offer that is laden with contingencies.

Profits from Small-Town Property by **James Koch.** (Van Nostrand Reinhold, 1984, 293 pages). Cites Census study that shows greater growth in rural counties than urban counties for the first time since 1820. Explains the how and where of small-town investing.

Successful Real Estate Negotiation Strategy by **Herbert Holtje** and **Donald Christman.** (Wiley, 1982, 190 pages). A how-to book on behavioral psychology and how this can be applied to real estate sales and negotiations.

Texas Earnest Money Contracts, 2d. ed. by **G. E. Irby** and **Darol L. Graham, Ph.D.** (TREC Association of Realtors, 1985, 209 pages). A step by step analysis of the Real Estate Commission forms along with information for the practitioner.

Texas Real Estate Law, 4th ed. by **Charles J. Jacobus.** (Reston, 1985, 560 pages). Provides up-to-date explanations of law pertinent to the daily operation of a real estate brokerage office in Texas. See Chapter 7 on Contracts.

The Guidebook for Completing TREC Contract Forms by **Lynn Puruis.** (171 pages). A guidebook to help Texas licensees learn how to fill out the various Real Estate Commission promulgated forms.

The Texas Homebuyer's Manual, published by the State Bar of Texas 1985 (56 pages). A manual intended to assist persons buying a home in Texas for the first time, discussing the various legal and other consideration involved in real estate transactions.

The Tax Shelter of Real Estate by **Dave Diegelman.** (Real Estate Education Co., 1984, 401 pages). Book teaches exchanging, syndicating, managing and negotiating and how to use tax shelters.

*   *   *

The following periodicals may also be of interest to you: *Real Estate Professional, Real Estate Quarterly, Real Estate Review* and *Real Estate Secrets.*

Mortgage Theory and Law

Accleration clause: allows the lender to demand immediate payment of the balance owed
Deficiency judgment: a judgment against a borrower if the sale of pledged property at foreclosure does not bring in enough to pay the balance owed
Foreclosure: the procedure for taking over a pledged property and selling it to satisfy an unpaid debt
Hypothecate: to pledge property to secure a debt but without giving up possession of it
Junior mortgage: any mortgage on a property that is subordinate in priority to the first mortgage
Mortgage: a pledge of property to secure the repayment of a debt
Mortgagee: the party receiving the mortgage; the lender
Mortgagor: the person who gives a mortgage pledging his property; the borrower
Power of sale: allows a mortgagee to conduct a foreclosure sale without first going to court
Subordination: voluntary acceptance of a lower mortgage priority than one would otherwise be entitled to

A mortgage is a pledge of property to secure the repayment of a debt. If the debt is not repaid as agreed between the lender and borrower, the lender can force the sale of the pledged property and apply the proceeds to repayment of the debt. To better understand present-day mortgage laws, it is helpful to first look at their history.

EARLY MORTGAGES

The concept of pledging property as collateral for a loan is not new. According to historians, the mortgage was in use when the pharaohs ruled Egypt and during the time of the Roman Empire. According to Roman laws, loans could be secured by mortgages on either personal or real property. In the early years of the Empire, nonpayment of a mortgage loan entitled the lender to make the borrower his slave. In the year 326 B.C. Roman law was modified to allow the debtor his freedom while working off his debt. Later, Roman law was again changed, this time to permit an unpaid debt to be satisfied by the sale of the mortgaged property.

Hypothecation   Mortgages were also an important part of English law and, as a result of the English colonization of America, ultimately were incorporated into the laws of each state. In England, the concept of pledging real estate by temporarily conveying its title to a lender as security for a debt was in regular use by the eleventh century. However, the Christian church at that time did not allow its members to charge interest. Because of this, the Christian lender took possession of the mortgaged property and collected the rents it produced instead of charging interest.

In contrast, Jewish lenders in England charged interest and left the borrower in possession. It was not until the fourteenth century that charging interest, rather than taking possession, became universal. Leaving the borrower in possession of the pledged property is known as **hypothecation.** The borrower conveys his title to the lender, but he still has the use of the property. This conveyance of title in the mortgage agreement is conditional. The mortgage states that, if the debt it secures is paid on time, the mortgage is defeated and title returns to the borrower. This was and still is known as a **defeasance clause.**

LIEN THEORY VERSUS   Although the United States inherited the whole of Eng-
TITLE THEORY   land's mortgage law, it began to be modified following independence. In 1791 in South Carolina, lawmakers asked the question, "Should a mortgage actually convey title to the lender subject only to the borrower's default? Or does the mortgage, despite its wording, simply create a lien with a right to acquire title only after proper foreclosure?" Their decision was that a mortgage is a lien rather than a conveyance, and South Carolina became the first **lien theory** state in regard to mortgages. Today, 33 states have adopted this viewpoint.*

---

* Alaska, Arizona, California, Colorado, Delaware, Florida, Georgia, Hawaii, Idaho, Illinois, Indiana, Iowa, Kansas, Kentucky, Louisiana, Michigan, Minnesota, Missouri, Montana, Nebraska, Nevada, New Mexico, New York, North Dakota, Oklahoma, Oregon, South Carolina, South Dakota, Texas, Utah, Washington, Wisconsin, and Wyoming.

Fifteen jurisdictions adhere to the older idea that a mortgage is a conveyance of title subject to defeat when the debt it secures is paid. They are classified as **title theory** states.† Three states are classified as **intermediate theory** states because they take a position midway between the lien and title theories.‡ In the intermediate states, title does not pass to the lender with the mortgage, but only upon default. In real estate practice, as long as default does not occur the differences among the three theories are more technical than real.

PLEDGE METHODS

A person can pledge his real estate as collateral for a loan by using any of four methods: the regular mortgage, the equitable mortgage, the deed as security, and the deed of trust.

Regular Mortgage

Borrower conveys title to lender

The **standard** or **regular mortgage** is the mortgage handed down from England and the one commonly found and used in the United States today. In it, the borrower conveys his title to the lender as security for his debt. The mortgage also contains a statement that it will become void if the debt it secures is paid in full and on time. In title theory states, the conveyance feature of the mortgage stands. In lien theory states, such a mortgage is considered to be only a lien against the borrower's property despite its wording.

Equitable Mortgage

Considered same as regular mortgage although it doesn't follow same form.

An **equitable mortgage** is a written agreement that, although it does not follow the form of a regular mortgage, is considered by the courts to be one. For example, Black sells his land to Green, with Green paying part of the price now in cash and promising to pay the balance later. Normally, Black would ask Green to execute a regular mortgage as security for the balance due. However, instead of doing this, Black makes a note of the balance due him on the deed before handing it to Green. The laws of most states would regard this notation as an equitable mortgage. For all intents and

† Alabama, Arkansas, Connecticut, Maine, Maryland, Massachusetts, New Hampshire, North Carolina, Pennsylvania, Rhode Island, Tennessee, Vermont, Virginia, West Virginia, and the District of Columbia.

‡ Mississippi, New Jersey, and Ohio.

purposes, it is a mortgage, although not specifically called one. Another example of an equitable mortgage can arise from the money deposit accompanying an offer to purchase property. If the seller refuses the offer and refuses to return the deposit, the courts will hold that the purchaser has an equitable mortgage in the amount of the deposit against the seller's property.

Deed as Security

Borrower conveys Bargain and sale or warranty deed as security

Occasionally, a borrower will give a bargain and sale or warranty **deed as security** of a loan. On the face of it, the lender (grantee) would appear to be able to do whatever he pleases since he has the title. However, if the borrower can prove that the deed was, in fact, security for a loan, the lender must foreclose as with a regular mortgage if the borrower fails to repay. If the loan is repaid in full and on time, the borrower can force the lender to convey the land back to him. Like the equitable mortgage, a deed used as security is treated according to its intent, not its label.

Deed of Trust

Borrower conveys deed to trustee

Whereas a mortgage is a two-party arrangement with a borrower and a lender, the **trust deed,** also known as a **deed of trust,** is a three-party arrangement consisting of the borrower (the trustor), the lender (the beneficiary), and a neutral third party (a trustee). The key aspect of this system is that the borrower executes a deed to the trustee rather than to the lender. If the borrower pays the debt in full and on time, the trustee reconveys title back to the borrower. If the borrower defaults on the loan, the lender asks the trustee to sell the property to pay off the debt. In Texas, debts are most often secured by trust deeds. Trust deeds are covered in more detail in Chapter 10.

Chattel Mortgage

A mortgage used to pledge personal property as security for a debt.

A mortgage can also be used to pledge personal property as security for a debt. This is a **chattel mortgage.** The word chattel is a legal term for personal property and derives from the Old English word for cattle. As with real property mortgages, a chattel mortgage permits the borrower to use his mortgaged personal property as long as the loan payments are made. If the borrower defaults, the lender is permitted to take possession and sell the mortgaged goods. In Texas, the use of chattel mortgages is usually in the form of financing statements and security agreements as provided for in the Texas Business and Commerce Code.

Two documents are involved in a standard mortgage loan, a promissory note and the mortgage itself; both are contracts. The **promissory note** establishes who the borrower and lender are, the amount of the debt, the terms of repayment, and the interest rate. A sample promissory note, usually referred to simply as a **note,** or a real estate lien note, is shown in Figure 9:1. Some states use a **bond** to accomplish the same purpose as the promissory note. What is said there regarding promissory notes also applies to bonds.

To be valid as evidence of debt, a note must (1) be in writing, (2) be between a borrower and lender who both have contractual capacity, (3) state the borrower's promise to pay a certain sum of money, (4) show the terms of payment, (5) be signed by the borrower, and (6) be voluntarily delivered by the borrower and accepted by the lender. If the note is secured by a mortgage or deed of trust or a vendor's lien, it must say so. Otherwise, it is solely a personal obligation of the borrower. Although interest is not required to make the note valid, most loans do carry an interest charge; when they do, the rate of interest must be stated in the note. Finally, in some states it is necessary for the borrower's signature on the note to be acknowledged and/or witnessed.

Referring to Figure 9:1, number ① identifies the document as a real estate lien note and ② gives the location and date of the note's execution (signing). At ③, the borrower states that he has received something of value and in turn promises to pay the debt described in the note. Typically, the "value received" is a loan of money in the amount described in the note; it could, however, be services or goods or anything else of value.

The section of the note at ④ identifies to whom the obligation is owed, sometimes referred to as the **obligee,** and where the payments are to be sent.

The **principal** or amount of the obligation, $83,000, is shown at ⑤. Number ⑥ gives the rate of interest on the debt and the date from which it will be charged. The amount

PROMISSORY NOTE

To be valid evidence of debt:
1. In writing
2. Between parties with contractual capacity
3. State promise to pay a certain amount
4. Show terms of payment
5. Be signed by borrower
6. Be voluntarily delivered by borrower and accepted by lender
* 7. State interest rate if any
* 8. must state if secured by mortgage or deed of trust

Obligor–Obligee
maker – lender

The Principal

Figure 9:1

REAL ESTATE LIEN NOTE ⑴
Prepared by the State Bar of Texas for use by Lawyers only

$ 83,000.00   Houston , Texas,   February 1, 19xx ⑵

⑶ For value received, I, We, or either of us, as principals, promise to pay to the order of
Friendly Lender Savings and Loan Association ⑷

in the City of ..Houston,   Harris ......County, Texas, the sum of
⑸ Eighty-three thousand and no/100---------------------- Dollars ($ 83,000.00),
in legal and lawful money of the United States of America, with interest thereon from date hereof until
maturity at the rate of eleven and one-half ⑹ per cent (11½ %) per annum; the interest payable
monthly   ; matured unpaid principal and interest shall bear interest at the rate of ten per
cent (10%) per annum from date of maturity until paid.

This note is due and payable as follows, to-wit: In equal monthly installments of eight
⑺ hundred twenty-one and 95/100 dollars ($821.95), or more, ⑽
including interest. The first such installment shall be due and payable
on the first day of ⑻ March, 19xx, and the like installments shall be
due and payable on the same day of each succeeding month thereafter
until fully paid. ⑼ This note may be prepaid in whole or in part at
any time without penalty. ⑾ Each installment shall be applied first to
the payment of accrued interest due on the unpaid principle balance and
the remainder of each installment shall be applied to the reduction of
unpaid principle.

⑿ It is expressly provided that upon default in the punctual payment of this note or any part thereof, principal
or interest, as the same shall become due and payable, the entire indebtedness secured by the hereinafter
mentioned lien shall be matured, at the option of the holder; and in the event default is made in the prompt
payment of this note when due or declared due, and the same is placed in the hands of an attorney for collection, or suit is brought on same, or the same is collected through Probate, Bankruptcy or other judicial proceedings, then the makers agree and promise to pay ten per cent (10%) additional on the amount of principal
and interest then owing, as attorney's fees. ⒀

Each maker, surety and endorser of this note expressly waives all notices, demands for payment, presentations for payment, notices of intention to accelerate the maturity, protest and notice of protest, as to this note
and as to each, every and all installments hereof.

Payment hereof is secured by a Deed of Trust of even date herewith, executed by
the Makers hereof to Charles J. Jacobus, Trustee, upon the following
⒁ described real property: Lot 1, Block 1, Shakey Acres Subdivision,
Harris County, Texas, as shown of record at Volume 7, Page 3, of the
Map Records of Harris County, Texas.

N. Debted _____   ⒂   May B. Debted _____
N. Debted   May B. Debted

of the periodic payment at ⑺ is calculated from the loan
tables like those discussed in Chapter 11. In this case, $821.95
each month for 30 years will return the lender's $83,000 plus
interest at the rate of 11½% per year on the unpaid portion
of the principal. Number ⑻ outlines when payments will
begin and when subsequent payments will be due. In this

example, they are due on the first day of each month until the full $83,000 and interest have been paid. The clause at ⑨ is a **prepayment privilege** for the borrower. It allows the borrower to pay more than the required $821.95 per month and to pay the loan off early without penalty. Without this very important privilege, the note requires the borrower to pay $821.95 per month, no more and no less, until the $83,000 plus interest has been paid. On some note forms (look back at ⑦) the prepayment privilege is created by inserting the words "or more" after the word "dollars" as shown at ⑩. The "or more" can be any amount from $821.95 up to and including the entire balance remaining.

The clause at ⑪ states that, whenever a payment is made, any interest due on the loan is first deducted, and then the remainder is applied to reducing the loan balance. Also, if interest is not paid, it too will earn interest at the same rate as the principal, in this example 11½% per year. The provision at ⑫ allows the lender to demand immediate payment of the entire balance remaining on the note if the borrower misses any of the individual payments. This is called an **acceleration clause,** as it "speeds up" the remaining payments due on the note, and makes them due immediately. Without this clause, the lender can only foreclose on the payments that have come due and not been paid. In this example, that could take as long as 30 years. This clause also has a certain psychological value: knowing that the lender has the option of calling the entire loan balance due upon default makes the borrower think twice about being late with his payments.

Acceleration Clause

At ⑬, the borrower agrees to pay any collection costs incurred by the lender if the borrower falls behind in his payments. At ⑭, the promissory note is tied to the mortgage or deed of trust that secures it, making it a secured loan. Without this reference, it would be like a personal loan. At ⑮, the borrower signs the note. A person who signs a note is sometimes referred to as a **maker** of the note. If two or more persons sign the note, it is common to include a statement in the note that the borrowers are "jointly and severally liable" for all provisions in the note. Thus, the terms of the note and the obligations it creates are enforceable upon the

Signature

makers as a group and upon each maker individually. This is done at ③. If the borrower is married, lenders generally require both husband and wife to sign. An acknowledgment is not required, as it is the mortgage rather than the note that is recorded in the public records.

THE MORTGAGE
INSTRUMENT

The mortgage is a separate agreement from the promissory note. Whereas the note is evidence of a debt and a promise to pay, the mortgage pledges collateral that the lender can sell if the note is not paid. The sample mortgage in Figure 9:2 illustrates in simplified language the key provisions most commonly found in real estate mortgages used in the United States. Let's look at these provisions.

The mortgage begins at ① with the date of its making and the names of the parties involved. In mortgage agreements, the person or party who pledges his property and gives the mortgage is the **mortgagor.** The person or party who receives the mortgage (the lender) is the **mortgagee.** For the reader's convenience, we shall refer to the mortgagor as the borrower and the mortgagee as the lender.

At ②, the debt for which this mortgage acts as security is identified. This mortgage does not act as security for any other debts of the borrower. The key wording in the mortgage occurs at ③, where the borrower conveys to the lender the property described at ④. The pledged property is most often the property that the borrower purchased with the loan money, but this is not a requirement. The mortgaged property need only be something of sufficient value in the eyes of the lender; it could just as easily be some other property the borrower owns. At ⑤, the borrower states that the pledged property is his and that he will defend its ownership. The lender will, of course, verify this with a title search before making the loan.

As you may have already noticed, the wording of ③, ④, and ⑤ is strikingly similar to that found in a warranty deed. In states that take the title theory position toward mortgages, this wording is interpreted to mean that the borrower is deeding his property to the lender. In lien theory states, this wording gives only a lien right to the lender, and the borrower (mortgagor) retains title. In either case, the borrower

Figure 9:2

MORTGAGE

①*THIS MORTGAGE is made this* ___31st___ *day of* ___March, 19xx,___ *between* ___Hap P. Toborrow___ *hereinafter called the Mortgagor, and* ___Pennywise Mortgage Company___ *hereinafter called the Mortgagee.*

②*WHEREAS, the Mortgagor is indebted to the Mortgagee in the principal sum of* ___Eighty thousand and no/100- - -___ *Dollars, payable* ___$720.00, including 9% interest per annum, on the first day of each month starting May, 19xx, and continuing until paid___ *, as evidenced by the Mortgagor's note of the same date as this mortgage, hereinafter called the Note.*

③*TO SECURE the Mortgage the repayment of the indebtedness evidenced by said Note, with interest thereon, the Mortgagor does hereby mortgage, grant, and convey to the Mortgagee the following described property in the County of* ___Travis___ *, State of* ___Texas___ *.*

④*Lot 39, Block 17, Harrison's Subdivision, as shown on Page 19 of Map Book 25, filed with the County Recorder of said County and State.*

⑤*FURTHERMORE, the Mortgagor fully warrants the title to said land and will defend the same against the lawful claims of all persons.*

⑥*IF THE MORTGAGOR, his heirs, legal representatives, or assigns pay unto the Mortgagee, his legal representatives or assigns, mortgage and estate created hereby shall cease and be null and void.*

⑦*UNTIL SAID NOTE is fully paid:*

⑧*A. The Mortgagor agrees to pay all taxes on said land.*

⑨*B. The Mortgagor agrees not to remove or demolish buildings or other improvements on the mortgaged land without the approval of the lender.*

Figure 9:2 *continued*

⑩C. *The Mortgagor agrees to carry adequate insurance to protect the lender in the event of damage or destruction of the mortgaged property.*

⑪D. *The Mortgagor agrees to keep the mortgaged property in good repair and not permit waste or deterioration.*

IT IS FURTHER AGREED THAT:

⑫E. *The Mortgagee shall have the right to inspect the mortgaged property as may be necessary for the security of the Note.*

⑬F. *If the Mortgagor does not abide by this mortgage or the accompanying Note, the Mortgagee may declare the entire unpaid balance on the Note immediately due and payable.*

⑭G. *If the Mortgagor sells or otherwise conveys title to the mortgaged property, the Mortgagee may declare the entire unpaid balance on the Note immediately due and payable.*

⑮H. *If all or part of the mortgaged property is taken by action of eminent domain, any sums of money received shall be applied to the Note.*

⑯*IN WITNESS WHEREOF, the Mortgagor has executed this mortgage.*

⑰	[this space for witnesses and/or acknowledgment if required by state law]	*Hap P. Toborrow* (SEAL)
		Mortgagor

is allowed to remain in physical possession of the mortgaged property as long as he abides by the terms of the note and mortgage.

Provisions for the defeat of the mortgage are given at ⑥. The key words here state that the "mortgage and estate created hereby shall cease and be null and void" when the note is paid in full. This is the **defeasance clause.**

After ⑦, there is a list of covenants (promises) that the borrower makes to the lender. They are the covenants of taxes, removal, insurance, and repair (8 through 11). These covenants protect the security for the loan.

In the **covenant to pay taxes** at ⑧, the borrower agrees to pay the taxes on the mortgaged property even though the title may be technically with the lender. This is important to the lender, because if the taxes are not paid on time they become a lien on the property that is superior to the lender's mortgage.

In the **covenant against removal** at ⑨, the borrower promises not to remove or demolish buildings or other improvements. To do so may reduce the value of the property as security for the lender.

The **covenant of insurance** at ⑩ requires the borrower to carry adequate insurance against damage or destruction of the mortgaged property. This protects the value of the collateral for the loan, for without insurance, if buildings or other improvements on the mortgaged property are damaged or destroyed, the value of the property might fall below the amount owed on the debt. With insurance, the buildings can be repaired or replaced, thus restoring the value of the collateral.

The **covenant of good repair** at ⑪, also referred to as the covenant of preservation and maintenance, requires the borrower to keep the mortgaged property in good condition. The clause at ⑫ gives the lender the right to inspect the property to make sure that it is being kept in good repair and has not been damaged or demolished.

If the borrower breaks any of the mortgage covenants or note agreements, the lender wants the right to terminate the loan. Thus, an **acceleration clause** at ⑬ is included to permit the lender to demand the balance be paid in full immediately. If the borrower cannot pay, foreclosure takes place and the property is sold.

When used in a mortgage, an **alienation clause** (also called a **due-on-sale clause**) gives the lender the right to call the entire loan balance due if the mortgaged property is sold or otherwise conveyed (alienated) by the borrower. An example

Covenants

Alienation Clause
(due-on-sale clause)

is shown at ⑭. The purpose of an alienation clause is two-fold. If the mortgaged property is put up for sale and a buyer proposes to assume the existing loan, the lender can refuse to accept that buyer as a substitute borrower if the buyer's credit is not good. But, more importantly, lenders have been using it as an opportunity to eliminate old loans with low rates of interest. Responding to complaints by consumers, seventeen states have taken the attitude that due-on-sale clauses cannot be enforced in order to raise interest rates. However, the U.S. Supreme Court has ruled that a due-on-sale clause can be enforced by the lender in most circumstances. (The due-on-sale issue, from both the borrower's and lender's perspectives is discussed more in Chapter 12.) Texas courts have tended to uphold due-on-sale clauses.

Condemnation Clause

Number ⑮ is a **condemnation clause.** If all or part of the property is taken by action of eminent domain, any money so received is used to reduce the balance owing on the note.

At ⑯, the mortgagor states that he has made this mortgage. Actually, the execution statement is more a formality than a requirement; the mortgagor's signature alone indicates his execution of the mortgage and agreement to its provisions. At ⑰, the mortgage is acknowledged and/or witnessed as required by state law for placement in the public records. Like deeds, mortgages must be recorded if they are to be effective against any subsequent purchaser, mortgagee, or lessee. The reason the mortgage is recorded, but not the promissory note, is that the mortgage deals with rights and interests in real property, whereas the note represents a personal obligation.

MORTGAGE
SATISFACTION

By far, most mortgage loans are paid in full either on or ahead of schedule. When the loan is paid, the standard practice is for the lender to cancel the promissory note and to issue to the borrower a document called a **release** of the mortgage. Issued by the lender, this document states that the promissory note or bond has been paid in full and the accompanying mortgage may be discharged from the public records. It is extremely important that this document be promptly recorded by the public recorder in the same county

Release should be recorded immediately!

where the mortgage is recorded. Otherwise, the records will continue to indicate that the property is mortgaged. When a release is recorded, a recording office employee often makes a note of its book and page location on the margin of the recorded mortgage. This is done solely to assist title searchers. The release itself is filed in the county records just as any other document is.

Occasionally, the situation arises wherein the borrower wants the lender to release a portion of the mortgaged property from the mortgage after part of the loan has been repaid. This is known as asking for a **partial release.** For example, a land developer purchases 40 acres of land for a total price of $500,000 and finances his purchase with $100,000 in cash plus a mortgage and note for $400,000 to the seller. In the mortgage agreement he might ask that the seller release 10 acres free and clear of the mortgage encumbrance for each $100,000 paid against the loan.

Partial Release

If an existing mortgage on a property does not contain a due-on-sale clause the seller can pass the benefits of that financing along to the buyer. (This is popular when the existing loan carries a lower rate of interest than currently available on new loans.) One method of doing this is for the buyer to purchase the property **subject to the existing loan.** In the purchase contract the buyer states that he is aware of the existence of the loan and the mortgage that secures it, but takes no personal liability for it. Although the buyer may pay the remaining loan payments as they come due, the seller continues to be personally liable to the lender for the loan. As long as the buyer faithfully continues to make the loan payments, which he would normally do as long as the property is worth more than the debts against it, this arrangement presents no problem to the seller. However, if the buyer stops making payments before the loan is fully paid, even though it may be years later, in most states the lender can require the seller to pay the balance due plus interest. This is true even though the seller thought he was free of the loan because he sold the property.

"SUBJECT TO" CLAUSE

Seller remains responsible

ASSUMPTION OF
THE LOAN

Buyer assumes responsibility,
but seller also remains
responsible

The seller is on safer ground if he requires the buyer to **assume the loan.** Under this arrangement, the buyer promises in writing to the seller that he will pay the loan, thus personally obligating himself. In the event of default on the loan or a breach of the mortgage agreement, the lender will first expect the buyer to remedy the problem. If the buyer does not pay, the lender will look to the seller, because the seller's name is still on the original promissory note.

NOVATION

The safest arrangement for the seller is to ask the lender to **substitute** the buyer's liability for his. This releases the seller from the personal obligation created by his promissory note, and the lender can now require only the buyer to repay the loan. The seller is also on safe ground if the mortgage agreement or state law prohibits deficiency judgments, a topic that will be explained later in this chapter.

When a buyer is to continue making payments on an existing loan, he will want to know exactly how much is still owing. An **estoppel certificate** (also called a **mortgagee's information letter**) is prepared by the lender to show how much of the loan remains to be paid. If a recorded mortgage states that it secures a loan for $35,000, but the borrower has reduced the amount owed to $25,000, the certificate of reduction will show that $25,000 remains to be paid. This is also used when the holder of a mortgage loan sells it to another investor. In it, the borrower is asked to verify the amount still owed and the rate of interest.

DEBT PRIORITIES

The same property can usually be pledged as collateral for more than one mortgage. This presents no problems to the lenders involved as long as the borrower makes the required payments on each note secured by the property. The difficulty arises when a default occurs on one or more of the loans, and the price the property brings at its foreclosure sale does not cover all the loans against it. As a result, a priority system is necessary. The debt with the highest priority is satisfied first from the foreclosure sale proceeds, and then the next highest priority debt is satisfied, then the next, until either the foreclosure sale proceeds are exhausted or all debts secured by the property are satisfied.

In the vast majority of foreclosures, the sale proceeds are not sufficient to pay all the outstanding debt against the property; thus, it becomes extremely important that a lender know his priority position before making a loan. Unless there is a compelling reason otherwise, a lender will want to be in the most senior position possible. This is normally accomplished by being the first lender to record a mortgage against a property that is otherwise free and clear of mortgage debt; this lender is said to hold a **first lien mortgage** on the property. If the same property is later used to secure another note before the first is fully satisfied, the new mortgage is a **second lien mortgage,** and so on. The first mortgage is also known as the **senior mortgage.** Any mortgage with a lower priority is a **junior mortgage.** As time passes and higher priority mortgages are satisfied, the lower priority mortgages move up in priority. Thus, if a property is secured by a first and a second mortgage and the first is paid off, the second becomes a first mortgage. Note that nothing is stamped or written on a mortgage document to indicate whether it is a first or second or third mortgage, etc. That priority can only be determined by searching the public records for mortgages recorded against the property that have not been released.

First Lien Mortgage

Sometimes a lender will voluntarily take a lower priority position than he would otherwise be entitled to by virtue of his recording date. This is known as **subordination** and it allows a junior loan to move up in priority. For example, the holder of a first mortgage can volunteer to become a second mortgagee and allow the second mortgage to move into the first position. Although it seems irrational that a lender would actually volunteer to lower his priority position, it is sometimes done by landowners to encourage developers to buy their land.

Subordination

An interesting situation regarding priority occurs when chattels are bought on credit and then affixed to land that is already mortgaged. If the chattels are not paid for, can the chattel lienholder come onto the land and remove them? If there is default on the mortgage loan against the land, are the chattels sold as fixtures? The solution is for the chattel

Chattel Liens

lienholder to record a **chattel mortgage** or a **financing statement.** This protects his interest even though the chattel becomes a fixture when it is affixed to land.

THE FORECLOSURE
PROCESS

Although relatively few mortgages are foreclosed, it is important to have a basic understanding of what happens when foreclosure takes place. First, knowledge of what causes foreclosure can help in avoiding it; and, second, if foreclosure does occur, one should know the rights of the parties involved.

Although noncompliance with any part of the mortgage agreement by the borrower can result in the lender calling the entire balance immediately due, in most cases foreclosure occurs because the note is not being repaid on time. When a borrower is behind in his payments, the loan is said to be **delinquent** or **nonconforming.** At this stage, rather than presume foreclosure is automatically the next step, the borrower and lender usually meet and attempt to work out an alternative payment program. Contrary to early motion picture plots in which lenders seem anxious to foreclose their mortgages, today's lender considers foreclosure to be the last resort. This is because the foreclosure process is time consuming, expensive, and unprofitable. The lender would much rather have the borrower make regular payments. Consequently, if a borrower is behind in his loan payments, the lender prefers to arrange a new, stretched-out, payment schedule rather than immediately to declare the acceleration clause in effect and move toward foreclosing the borrower's rights to the property.

If a borrower realizes that stretching out payments is not going to solve his financial problem, instead of presuming foreclosure to be inevitable, he can seek a buyer for the property who can make the payments. More than any other reason, this is why relatively few real estate mortgages are foreclosed. The borrower, realizing he is in, or is about to be in, financial trouble, sells his property. It is only when the borrower cannot find a buyer and when the lender sees no further sense in stretching the payments that the acceleration clause is invoked and the path toward foreclosure taken. Let's look at a summary of the foreclosure process for a standard mortgage. (See Chapter 10 for deed of trust foreclosures.)

Basically there are two foreclosure routes: judicial and nonjudicial. **Judicial foreclosure** means taking the matter to a court of law in the form of a lawsuit that asks the judge to foreclose (cut off) the borrower. A **nonjudicial foreclosure** does not go to court and is not heard by a judge. It is conducted by the lender (or by a trustee) in accordance with provisions in the mortgage and in accordance with state law pertaining to nonjudicial foreclosures. Comparing the two, a judicial foreclosure is more costly and more time-consuming, but it does carry the approval of a court of law and it may give the lender rights to collect the full amount of the loan if the property sells for less than the amount owed. It is also the preferred method when the foreclosure case is complicated and involves many parties and interests. The nonjudicial route is usually faster, simpler, and cheaper, and it is preferred by lenders when the case is simple and straightforward. Let's now look at foreclosure methods for standard mortgages. (Deed of trust foreclosures will be discussed separately in Chapter 10.)

Foreclosure Routes

The judicial foreclosure process begins with a title search. Next, the lender files a **lawsuit** naming as defendants the borrower and anyone who acquired a right or interest in the property after the lender recorded his mortgage. In the lawsuit the lender identifies the debt and the mortgage securing it, and states that it is in default. The lender then asks the court for a judgment directing that (1) the defendants' interests in the property be cut off in order to return the condition of title to what it was when the loan was made, (2) the property be sold at a public auction, and (3) the lender's claim be paid from the sale proceeds.

JUDICIAL FORECLOSURE

A copy of the complaint along with a summons is delivered to the defendants. This officially notifies them of the pending legal action against their interests. A junior mortgage holder who has been named as a defendant has basically two choices; he will choose the one that he feels will leave him less worse off. One choice is to allow the foreclosure to proceed and file his own **surplus money action.** By doing this, he hopes that the property will sell at the foreclosure

Surplus Money Action

sale for enough money to pay all claims senior to him as well as his own claim against the borrower. The other choice is to halt the foreclosure process by making the delinquent payments on behalf of the borrower and then adding them to the amount the borrower owes him. To do this, the junior mortgage holder must use cash out of his own pocket and decide whether this is a case of "good money chasing bad." It is true that he can add these sums to the amount owed him, but he must also consider whether he will have any better luck being paid than did the holder of the senior mortgage.

Notice of Lis Pendens   At the same time that the lawsuit to foreclose is filed with the court, a **notice of lis pendens** is filed with the county recorder's office where the property is located. This notice informs the public that a legal action for disputed title is pending against the property. If the borrower attempts to sell the property at this time, the prospective buyer, upon making his title search, would learn of the pending litigation. He can still proceed to purchase the property if he wants, but he is now informed that he is buying under the cloud of an unsettled lawsuit.

Public Auction   The borrower, or any other defendant named in the lawsuit, may now reply to the suit by presenting his side of the issue to the court judge. If no reply is made, or if the issues raised by the reply are found in favor of the lender, the judge will order that the interests of the borrower and other defendants in the property be foreclosed (terminated) and the property sold. The sale is usually a **public auction.** The objective is to obtain the best possible price for the property by inviting competitive bidding and conducting the sale in full view of the public. To announce the sale, the judge orders a notice to be posted on the courthouse door and advertised in local newspapers.

Equity of Redemption   The sale is conducted by the **county sheriff** or by a **referee** or **master** appointed by the judge. At the sale, which is held at either the property or at the courthouse, the lender and all parties interested in purchasing the property are present.

If the borrower should suddenly locate sufficient funds to pay the judgment against him, he can, up to the minute the property goes on sale, step forward and redeem his property. This privilege to redeem property anytime between the first sign of delinquency and the moment of foreclosure sale is the borrower's **equity of redemption.** If no redemption is made, the bidding begins. Anyone with adequate funds can bid. Typically, a cash deposit of 10 percent of the successful bid must be made at the sale, with the balance of the bid price due upon closing, usually 30 days later.

While the lender and borrower hope that someone at the auction will bid more than the amount owed on the defaulted loan, the probability is not high. If the borrower was unable to find a buyer at a price equal to or higher than the loan balance, the best cash bid will probably be less than the balance owed. If this happens, the lender usually enters a bid of his own. The lender is in a unique position as he can "bid his loan." That is, he can bid up to the amount owed him without having to pay cash. All other bidders must pay cash, as the purpose of the sale is to obtain cash to pay the defaulted loan. In the event the borrower bids at the sale and is successful in buying back his property, the junior liens against the property are not eliminated. Note however, that no matter who the successful bidder is, the foreclosure does not cut off property tax liens against the property. They remain.

This procedure is similar to the out of court, nonjudicial foreclosures used in Texas pursuant to the deed of trust form except that they require cash payment, in full, at the sale.

If the property sells for more than the claims against it, including any junior mortgage holders, the borrower receives the excess. For example, if a property with $50,000 in claims against it sells for $55,000, the borrower will receive the $5,000 difference, less unpaid property taxes and expenses of the sale. However, if the highest bid in only $40,000, how is the $10,000 deficiency treated? The laws of the various states differ on this question. Most allow the lender to request a **deficiency judgment** for the $10,000, with which the lender can proceed against the borrower's other unsecured assets.

Deficiency Judgment

In other words, the borrower is still personally obligated to the lender for $10,000 and the lender is entitled to collect it. This may require the borrower to sell other assets.

Several states (for example, California, Montana, North Dakota, and North Carolina) have outlawed deficiency judgments in most foreclosure situations so that a lender cannot reach beyond the pledged property for debt satisfaction. In these states the lender would have to stand the $10,000 deficiency loss. Also, there can be no deficiency judgment in a strict foreclosure case. In many states where deficiency judgments are permitted, if the property sells for an obviously depressed price at its foreclosure sale, a deficiency judgment may be allowed only for the difference between the court's estimate of the property's fair market value and the amount still owing against it. Texas has no restrictions on a creditor's right to a deficiency judgment.

In states that allow deficiency judgments, if the borrower is in a strong enough bargaining position, he can place language in the promissory note to the effect that the note is "without recourse." This generally prohibits the lender from seeking a deficiency judgment.

In states that do not give a foreclosed borrower a redemption period, the purchaser at the foreclosure sale receives a **sheriff's deed.** This is usually a special warranty deed that conveys the title the borrower had at the time the foreclosed mortgage was originally made. The purchaser may take immediate possession and the court will assist him in removing anyone in possession who was cut off in the foreclosure proceedings.

Texas does not allow a foreclosed mortgagor the right to redeem his property after the foreclosure sale has taken place. An installment land contract holder does, however, have this right.

NONJUDICIAL
FORECLOSURE

Forty-two states, including Texas, permit the use of **power of sale,** also known as **sale by advertisement,** as a means of simplifying and shortening the foreclosure proceeding itself. If it is necessary to foreclose, this clause in the mortgage gives the lender the power to conduct the foreclosure and sell the mortgaged property without taking the issue to court. States that permit the use of the power of sale require a waiting period between default and the sale. This is the borrower's equity of redemption. The property is then advertised and sold at an auction held by the lender and open to the public. The precise procedures the lender must follow are set by state statutes. After the auction, the borrower can still redeem the property if his state offers statutory redemption. The deed the purchaser receives is prepared and signed by the lender. A lender foreclosing under power of sale cannot award himself a deficiency judgment. If there is a deficiency as a result of the sale, and the lender wants a deficiency judgment, the lender must go to court for it. A major weak point with power of sale is that in many states junior claimants need not be personally notified of a pending sale. Thus, conceivably, a junior claimant could have his rights cut off without being aware of it. Texas procedure for non-judicial foreclosure is discussed in greater detail in Chapter 10, *Deed of Trust.*

DEED IN LIEU OF FORECLOSURE

To avoid the hassle of foreclosure proceedings, a borrower may voluntarily deed his property to the lender. In turn, the borrower should demand cancellation of the unpaid debt and a letter to that effect from the lender. This method relieves the lender of foreclosing and waiting out any required redemption periods, but it also presents the lender with a sensitive situation. With the borrower in financial distress and about to be foreclosed, it is quite easy for the lender to take advantage of the borrower. As a result, courts of law will usually side with the borrower if he complains of any unfair dealings. Thus, the lender must be prepared to prove conclusively that the borrower received a fair deal by deeding his property voluntarily to the lender in return for cancellation of his debt. If the property is worth more than the balance due on the debt, the lender must pay the borrower the difference in cash. A deed in lieu of foreclosure is a voluntary act by both borrower and lender; if either feels he will fare better in regular foreclosure proceedings, he need not agree to it. Note also that a deed in lieu of foreclosure will not cut off the rights of junior mortgage holders.

VOCABULARY REVIEW

Match terms **a-t** *with statements* **1–20.**

9. **a.** *Alienation clause*
13. **b.** *Assumption*
6. **c.** *Chattel mortgage*
10. **d.** *Covenant of insurance*
2. **e.** *Defeasance ~~judgment~~ clause*
18. **f.** *Deficiency judgment*
5. **g.** *Equitable mortgage*
3. **h.** *Equity of redemption*
4. **i.** *Foreclosure suit*
15. **j.** *Junior mortgage*

1. **k.** *Mortgage*
8. **l.** *Mortgagor*
16. **m.** *Nonconforming*
12. **n.** *Partial release*
17. **o.** *Power of sale*
7. **p.** *Promissory note*
11. **q.** *Satisfaction*
19. **r.** *Statutory redemption*
14. **s.** *Subject to*
20. **t.** *Subordination*

1. A pledge of property to secure the repayment of a debt.
2. A clause in a mortgage stating that the mortgage is defeated if the borrower repays the accompanying note on time.
3. The borrower's right, prior to the day of foreclosure, to repay the balance due on a delinquent loan.
4. A lawsuit filed by a lender that asks a court to set a time limit on how long a borrower has to redeem his property.
5. An agreement that is considered to be a mortgage in its intent even though it may not follow the usual mortgage wording.
6. A pledge of personal property as security for a promissory note.
7. The evidence of debt; contains amount owed, interest rate, repayment schedule, and a promise to repay.
8. One who gives a mortgage pledging his property; the borrower.
9. A clause in a mortgage that permits the lender to demand full payment of the loan if the property changes ownership. Also called a due-on-sale clause.
10. A clause in a mortgage whereby the mortgagor agrees to keep mortgaged property adequately insured against destruction.
11. Discharge of a mortgage upon payment of the debt owed.
12. Release of a portion of a property from a mortgage.
13. The buyer personally obligates himself to repay an existing mortgage loan as a condition of the sale.
14. The buyer of an already mortgaged property makes the payments but does not take personal responsibility for the loan.
15. Any mortgage lower than a first mortgage in priority.
16. A loan on which the borrower is behind in his payments.
17. A clause in a mortgage that gives the mortgagee the right to conduct a foreclosure sale without first going to court.
18. A judgment against a borrower if the sale of pledged property at foreclosure does not bring in enough to pay the balance owing.
19. The right of a borrower, after a foreclosure sale, to reclaim his property by repaying his defaulted loan.
20. Voluntary acceptance of a lower mortgage priority position than one would otherwise be entitled to.

1. Is a prepayment privilege to the advantage of the borrower or the lender?
2. What are the legal differences between lien theory and title theory?
3. How does strict foreclosure differ from foreclosure by sale? Which system does Texas use?
4. A large apartment complex serves as security for a first, a second, and a third mortgage. Which of these are considered junior mortgage(s)? Senior mortgage(s)?
5. Describe the procedure in your county that is used in foreclosing delinquent real estate loans.
6. What do the laws of your state allow real estate borrowers in the way of equitable and statutory redemption?
7. Do the laws of Texas allow a delinquent borrower adequate opportunity to recover his mortgaged real estate? Do you advocate more or less borrower protection than is presently available?
8. In a promissory note, who is the obligor? Who is the obligee?
9. Why does a mortgage lender insist on including covenants pertaining to insurance, property taxes and removal, in the mortgage?
10. What roles do a certificate of reduction and an estoppel certificate play in mortgage lending?

Analyzing Real Estate Decisions Using Lotus 1–2–3 by **Austin Jaffee.** (Reston, 1985, 288 pages). Includes introduction, explanation and application of Lotus 1–2–3 to real estate lending, leverage, taxes, brokerage, risk and appraisal problems. Includes templates for creating spreadsheets. This book is also available in a VisiCalc edition.

Basic Real Estate Finance and Investments by **Donald Epley** and **James Millar.** (Wiley, 1984, 656 pages). Book takes a decision-making perspective. Includes souces of mortgage money, mortgage documents, alternative financing methods, leverage, capitalization rates, value and risk.

Introduction to Real Estate Law, 2nd ed. by **Charles Coit.** (Real Estate Education Co., 1985, 330 pages). Nontechnical style addresses legal issues important to real estate including trust accounts, timesharing, fiduciary duty of the broker, title insurance, etc.

Real Estate Finance by **Jerome Dasso** and **Gerald Kuhn.** (Prentice-Hall, 1983, 464 pages). Provides a comprehensive and practical overview of law, instruments, terminology, institutions and calculations pertinent to real estate finance.

Residential Mortgage Lending by **Marshall Dennis.** (Reston, 1985, 400 pages). Written for students and professionals. Includes mortgage lending techniques, procedures, laws and history. Has case studies of actual mortgage transactions.

Texas Real Estate Law, 4th ed. by **Charles J. Jacobus.** (Reston, 1985, 560 pages). Provides up-to-date explanations of law pertinent to the daily operation of a real estate brokerage office in Texas. See Chapter 11 on mortgage law in Texas.

Deed of Trust

Assignment of rents clause: wording that establishes the right to collect the rents from a property in the event the borrower does not repay the note
Beneficiary: one for whose benefit a trust is created; the lender in a deed of trust arrangement
Deed of trust: a document that conveys title to a neutral third party trustee as security for a debt
Naked title: title that lacks the rights and privileges usually associated with ownership
Reconveyance: the return to the borrower of legal title to his property upon repayment of the debt against it
Release deed: a document used to reconvey title from the trustee back to the property owner once the debt has been paid
Trustee: one who holds property in trust for another
Trustor: one who creates a trust; the borrower in a deed of trust arrangement

The basic purpose of a Texas **deed of trust,** also referred to as a **trust deed** is the same as a mortgage. Real property is used as security for a debt; if the debt is not repaid, the property is sold and the proceeds are applied to the balance owed. The main legal difference between a deed of trust and a mortgage is diagrammed in Figure 10:1.

Figure 10:1 shows that when a debt is secured by a mortgage the borrower delivers his promissory note and mortgage to the lender, who keeps them until the debt is paid. But when a note is secured by a deed of trust, three parties are involved: the borrower (the **trustor** or **grantor**), the lender (the **beneficiary**), and a neutral third party (the **trustee**). The lender makes a loan to the borrower, and the borrower gives the lender a promissory note (like the one shown in Chapter 9) and a deed of trust. In the deed of trust document, the borrower conveys title to the trustee, to be held in trust until the note is paid in full. The deed of trust is recorded in the county where the property is located and then is usually given to the lender for safekeeping. A variation used in other

PARTIES TO A DEED OF TRUST

Figure 10:1   **COMPARING A MORTGAGE WITH A DEED OF TRUST**

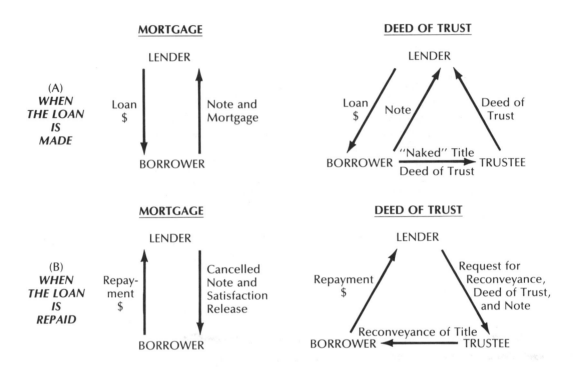

areas of the country is to deliver the recorded deed of trust to the trustee to be held in a long-term escrow until the note is paid in full. Anyone searching the title records on the borrower's property would find the deed of trust conveying title to the trustee. This would alert the title searcher to the existence of a debt against the property.

In Texas the title granted to the **trustee** is only a conditional conveyance. The title held by the trustee is limited only to what is necessary to carry out his duty as trustee when requested to do so by the **beneficiary (lender)** under the beneficiary's rights as set out in the deed of trust.

When the note is paid in full, the lender cancels the note and issues the **grantor (borrower)** a **release of lien,** which is recorded in the county records to indicate a full discharge of the previously recorded deed of trust lien. Depending on the terms of the deed of trust instrument, the conveyance to the trustee may become void and of no further force and effect.

If a borrower defaults under a deed of trust, the beneficiary (lender) generally instructs the trustee to post the notice of foreclosure at the courthouse and to hold a public sale of the property according to the requirements of the deed of trust and in accordance with Texas statutes. The deed of trust generally specifies this procedure in its **power of sale** provision, and the borrower agrees to this provision upon signing the deed of trust.

In Texas an individual is ordinarily named as a trustee in the deed of trust instrument. He may be the attorney who draws the papers for the lender, or some other agent of the lender. There is normally a provision that allows the lender to appoint a substitute trustee in the event of death or refusal to act by the named trustee. The trustee is supposed to be an impartial third party, although the beneficiary may himself act as trustee. But, because the power of sale remedy is so strict, the instrument and authority of the trustee thereunder is strictly construed to avoid irregularities in the sale. If a person acts as both the trustee and beneficiary, the court may find a conflict of interest or lack of impartiality.

SAMPLE DEED OF TRUST

Figure 10:2 is an example of a deed of trust form prepared by the State Bar of Texas, with several additional clauses included for educational purposes only. The Texas Real Estate Commission (TREC) requires that its promulgated forms be used in the event there is a dispute involving the kind of form used. Other deed of trust forms have provisions which may vary. This example shows the agreement between borrower and lender and states the responsibilities of the trustee. Beginning at ①, the document is identified as a deed of trust. This is followed by the identification of the grantor (borrower) at ②. His county of residence, the amount of consideration, and conveyance of the trustee are shown at ③, and the property is legally described at ④. At ⑤ and ⑥ are the habendum and warranty clauses where the borrower states that he will defend the title against claims of others. It is interesting to note that, up to this point, the deed of trust closely resembles the standard warranty deed form.

Figure 10:2   Prepared by the State Bar of Texas for use by lawyers only. Revised 1-1-76.
Revised as to interest and to include grantee's address (art. 6626, RCS) 1-1-82.
Revised as to sale on default (§ 51.002, Prop. Code) 10-83.

①DEED OF TRUST

THE STATE OF TEXAS   }   KNOW ALL MEN BY THESE PRESENTS:
COUNTY OF HARRIS   }

That ② N. DEBTED AND WIFE, MAY B. DEBTED

of __HARRIS__ County, Texas, hereinafter called Grantors (whether one or more) for the purpose of securing the indebtedness hereinafter described, and in consideration of the sum of TEN DOLLARS ($10.00) to us in hand paid by the Trustee hereinafter named, the receipt of which is hereby acknowledged, and for the further consideration of the uses, purposes and trusts hereinafter set forth, have granted, sold and conveyed, and by these presents do grant, sell and convey unto __CHARLES J.__ ③ JACOBUS __, Trustee, of __HARRIS__ County, Texas, and his substitutes or successors, all of the following described property situated in __HARRIS__ County, Texas, to-wit:

④ Lot 1, Block 1, Shakey Acres Subdivision, Harris County, Texas,
as shown of record at Volume 7, Page 3, of the Map Records of
Harris County, Texas

⑤ TO HAVE AND TO HOLD the above described ⑥ property, together with the rights, privileges and appurtenances thereto belonging unto the said Trustee, and to his substitutes or successors forever. And Grantors do hereby bind themselves, their heirs, executors, administrators and assigns to warrant and forever defend the said premises unto the said Trustee, his substitutes or successors and assigns forever, against the claim, or claims, of all persons claiming or to claim the same or any part thereof.

⑦ This conveyance, however, is made in TRUST to secure payment of __one__ promissory note _____ of even date herewith in the principal sum of ⑧ EIGHTY-THREE THOUSAND AND NO/100ths------------------
--Dollars ($ 83,000.00)

executed by Grantors, payable to the order of __FRIENDLY LENDER SAVINGS AND LOAN ASSOCIATION__

in the City of __Houston__   __Harris__ County, Texas, as follow, to-wit:

AS THEREIN PROVIDED,

bearing interest as therein stipulated, providing for acceleration of maturity and for Attorney's fees;

(9) Should Grantors do and perform all of the covenants and agreements herein contained, and make prompt payment of said indebtedness as the same shall become due and payable, then this conveyance shall become null and void and of no further force and effect, and shall be released at the expense of Grantors, by the holder thereof, hereinafter called Beneficiary (whether one or more).

Grantors covenant and agree as follows:

That they are lawfully seized of said property, and have the right to convey the same; that said property is free from all liens and encumbrances, except as herein provided.

(11) To protect the title and possession of said property and to pay when due all taxes and assessments now existing or hereafter levied or assessed upon said property, or the interest therein created by this Deed of Trust, and to preserve and maintain the lien hereby created as a first and prior lien on said property including any improvements hereafter made a part of the realty.

(12) To keep the improvements on said property in good repair and condition, and not to permit or commit any waste thereof; to keep said buildings occupied so as not to impair the insurance carried thereon.

To insure and keep insured all improvements now or hereafter created upon said property against loss or damage by fire and wind-storm, and any other hazard or hazards as may be reasonably required from time to time by Beneficiary during the term of the indebtedness hereby secured, to the extent of the original amount of the indebtedness hereby secured, or to the extent of the full insurable value of said improvements, whichever is the lesser, in such form and with such Insurance Company or Companies as may be approved by Beneficiary, and to deliver to Beneficiary the policies of such insurance having attached to said policies such mortgage indemnity clause as Beneficiary shall direct; to deliver renewals of such policies to Beneficiary at least ten (10) days before any such insurance policies shall expire; any proceeds which Beneficiary may receive under any such policy, or policies, may be applied by Beneficiary, at his option, to reduce the indebtedness hereby secured, whether then matured or to mature in the future, and in such manner as Beneficiary may elect, or Beneficiary may permit Grantors to use said proceeds to repair or replace all improvements damaged or destroyed and covered by said policy.

(13) That in the event Grantors shall fail to keep the improvements on the property hereby conveyed in good repair and condition, or to pay promptly when due all taxes and assessments, as aforesaid, or to preserve the prior lien of this Deed of Trust on said property, or to keep the buildings and improvements insured, as aforesaid, or to deliver the policy, or policies, of insurance or the renewal thereof to Beneficiary, as aforesaid, then Beneficiary may, at his option, but without being required to do so, make such repairs, pay such taxes and assessments, purchase any tax title thereon, remove any prior liens, and prosecute or defend any suits in relation to the preservation of the prior lien of this Deed of Trust on said property, or insure and keep insured the improvements thereon in an amount not to exceed that above stipulated; that any sums which may be so paid out by Beneficiary and all sums paid for insurance premiums, as aforesaid, including the costs, expenses and Attorney's fees paid in any suit affecting said property when necessary to protect the lien hereof shall bear interest from the dates of such payments at the rate stated in said note and shall be paid by Grantors to Beneficiary upon demand, at the same place at which said note is payable, and shall be deemed a part of the debt hereby secured and recoverable as such in all respects.

(10) That in the event of default in the payment of any installment, principal or interest, of the note hereby secured, in accordance with the terms thereof, or of a breach of any of the covenants herein contained to be performed by Grantors, then and in any of such events Beneficiary may elect, Grantors hereby expressly waiving presentment and demand for payment, to declare the entire principal indebtedness hereby secured with all interest accrued thereon and all other sums hereby secured immediately due and payable, and in the event of default in the payment of said indebtedness when due or declared due, it shall thereupon, or at any time thereafter, be the duty of the Trustee, or his successor or substitute as hereinafter provided, at the request of Beneficiary (which request is hereby conclusively presumed), to enforce this trust; and after advertising the time, place and terms of the sale of the above described and conveyed property, then subject to the lien hereof, and mailing and filing notices as required by section 51.002, Texas Property Code, as then amended (successor to article 3810, Texas Revised Civil Statutes), and otherwise complying with that statute, the Trustee shall sell the above described property, then subject to the lien hereof, at public auction in accordance with such notices on the first Tuesday in any month between the hours of ten o'clock A.M. and four o'clock P.M., to the highest bidder for cash, selling all of the property as an entirety or in such parcels as the Trustee acting may elect, and make due conveyance to the Purchaser or Purchasers, with general warranty binding Grantors, their heirs and assigns; and out of the money arising from such sale, the Trustee acting shall pay first, all the expenses of advertising the sale and making the conveyance, including a commission of five percent (5%) to himself, which commission shall be due and owing in addition to the Attorney's fees provided for in said note, and then to Beneficiary the full amount of principal, interest, Attorney's fees and other charges due and unpaid on said note and all other indebtedness secured hereby, rendering the balance of the sales price, if any, to Grantors, their heirs or assigns; and the recitals in the conveyance to the Purchaser or Purchasers shall be full and conclusive evidence of the truth of the matters therein stated, and all prerequisites to said sale shall be presumed to have been performed, and such sale and conveyance shall be conclusive against Grantors, their heirs and assigns.

It is agreed that in the event a foreclosure hereunder should be commenced by the Trustee, or his substitute or successor, Beneficiary may at any time before the sale of said property direct the said Trustee to abandon the sale, and may then institute suit for the collection of said note, and for the foreclosure of this Deed of Trust lien; it is further agreed that if Beneficiary should institute a suit for the collection thereof, and for a foreclosure of this Deed of Trust lien, that he may at any time before the entry of a final judgment in said suit dismiss the same, and require the Trustee, his substitute or successor to sell the property in accordance with the provisions of this Deed of Trust.

Beneficiary, if he is the highest bidder, shall have the right to purchase at any sale of the property, and to have the amount for which such property is sold credited on the debt then owing.

(14) Beneficiary in any event is hereby authorized to appoint a substitute trustee, or a successor trustee, to act instead of the Trustee named herein without other formality than the designation in writing of a substitute or successor trustee; and the authority hereby conferred shall extend to the appointment of other successor and substitute trustees successively until the indebtedness hereby secured has been paid in full, or until said property is sold hereunder, and each substitute and successor trustee shall succeed to all of the rights and powers of the original trustee named herein.

Figure 10:2 *continued*

In the event any sale is made of the above described property, or any portion thereof, under the terms of this Deed of Trust, Grantors, their heirs and assigns, shall forthwith upon the making of such sale surrender and deliver possession of the property so sold to the Purchaser at such sale, and in the event of their failure to do so they shall thereupon from and after the making of such sale be and continue as tenants at will of such Purchaser, and in the event of their failure to surrender possession of said property upon demand, the Purchaser, his heirs or assigns, shall be entitled to institute and maintain an action for forcible detainer of said property in the Justice of the Peace Court in the Justice Precinct in which such property, or any part thereof, is situated.

It is agreed that the lien hereby created shall take precedence over and be a prior lien to any other lien of any character whether vendor's, materialmen's or mechanic's lien hereafter created on the above described property, and in the event the proceeds of the indebtedness secured hereby as set forth herein are used to pay off and satisfy any liens heretofore existing on said property, then Beneficiary is, and shall be, subrogated to all of the rights, liens and remedies of the holders of the indebtedness so paid.

It is further agreed that if Grantors, their heirs or assigns, while the owner of the hereinabove described property, should commit an act of bankruptcy, or authorize the filing of a voluntary petition in bankruptcy, or should an act of bankruptcy be committed and involuntary proceedings instituted or threatened, or should the property hereinabove described be taken over by a Receiver for Grantors, their heirs or assigns, the note hereinabove described shall, at the option of Beneficiary, immediately become due and payable, and the acting Trustee may then proceed to sell the same under the provisions of this Deed of Trust.

As further security for the payment   the hereinabove described indebtedness, Grantors hereby transfer, assign, and convey unto Beneficiary all rents issuing or to hereafter issue from said real property, and in the event of any default in the payment of said note or hereunder, Beneficiary, his agent or representative, is hereby authorized, at his option, to collect said rents, or if such property is vacant to rent the same and collect the rents, and apply the same, less the reasonable costs and expenses of collection thereof, to the payment of said indebtedness, whether then matured or to mature in the future, and in such manner as Beneficiary may elect. The collection of said rents by Beneficiary shall not constitute a waiver of his right to accelerate the maturity of said indebtedness nor of his right to proceed with the enforcement of this Deed of Trust.

It is agreed that an extension, or extensions, may be made of the time of payment of all, or any part, of the indebtedness secured hereby, and that any part of the above described real property may be released from this lien without altering or affecting the priority of the lien created by this Deed of Trust in favor of any junior encumbrancer, mortgagee or purchaser, or any person acquiring an interest in the property hereby conveyed, or any part thereof; it being the intention of the parties hereto to preserve this lien on the property herein described and all improvements thereon, and that may be hereafter constructed thereon, first and superior to any liens that may be placed thereon, or that may be fixed, given or imposed by law thereon after the execution of this instrument notwithstanding any such extension of the time of payment, or the release of a portion of said property from this lien.

In the event any portion of the indebtedness hereinabove described cannot be lawfully secured by this Deed of Trust lien on said real property, it is agreed that the first payments made on said indebtedness shall be applied to the discharge of that portion of said indebtedness.

⑮ Beneficiary shall be entitled to receive any and all sums which may become payable to Grantors for the condemnation of the hereinabove described real property, or any part thereof, for public or quasi-public use, or by virtue of private sale in lieu thereof, and any sums which may be awarded or become payable to Grantors for damages caused by public works or construction on or near the said property. All such sums are hereby assigned to Beneficiary, who may, after deducting therefrom all expenses actually incurred, including attorney's fees, release same to Grantors or apply the same to the reduction of the indebtedness hereby secured, whether then matured or to mature in the future, or on any money obligation hereunder, as and in such manner as Beneficiary may elect. Beneficiary shall not be, in any event or circumstances, liable or responsible for failure to collect, or exercise diligence in the collection of, any such sums.

Nothing herein or in said note contained shall ever entitle Beneficiary, upon the arising of any contingency whatsoever, to receive or collect interest in excess of the highest rate allowed by the laws of the State of Texas on the principal indebtedness hereby secured or on any money obligation hereunder and in no event shall Grantors be obligated to pay interest thereon in excess of such rate.

If this Deed of Trust is executed by only one person or by a corporation the plural reference to Grantors shall be held to include the singular, and all of the covenants and agreements herein undertaken to be performed by and the rights conferred upon the respective Grantors named herein, shall be binding upon and inure to the benefit of not only said parties respectively but also their respective heirs, executors, administrators, grantees, successors and assigns.

Grantors expressly represent that this Deed of Trust and the Note hereby secured are given for the following purpose, to-wit:

```
     The Note secured hereby represents funds advanced by the Friendly
Lender Savings and Loan Association at the special instance and request
of the Grantors and used in payment of the purchase price of the herein-
above described property, and Grantors hereby expressly confess, recognize
and acknowledge a vendor's lien on said property as security therefore.
```

EXECUTED this   First   day of   February   A. D. 19 xx

_____   _____
N. Debted   May B. Debted

Mailing address of trustee: Mailing address of each beneficiary: **Figure 10:2** *continued*

Name: Charles J. Jacobus   Name: Friendly Lender Savings and
Address: 10 Lovers Lane   Address: Loan Association
          Sweetwater, Texas   10 Lenders Lane
                                                         Houston, Texas

                                             Name:
                                             Address:

(Acknowledgment)

STATE OF TEXAS
COUNTY OF HARRIS

    This instrument was acknowledged before me on the   first   day of   February   , 19 **XX** ,
by N. Debted and May B. Debted

                                      Rose Bloom
                                      Notary Public, State of Texas
                                      Notary's name (printed):

                                      Notary's commission expires: 30 June, xx

(Acknowledgment)

STATE OF TEXAS
COUNTY OF

    This instrument was acknowledged before me on the   day of   , 19   ,
by

                                      Notary Public, State of Texas
                                      Notary's name (printed):

                                      Notary's commission expires:

(Corporate Acknowledgment)

STATE OF TEXAS
COUNTY OF

    This instrument was acknowledged before me on the   day of   , 19   ,
by
of
a   corporation, on behalf of said corporation.

                                      Notary Public, State of Texas
                                      Notary's name (printed):

                                      Notary's commission expires:

AFTER RECORDING RETURN TO: PREPARED IN THE LAW OFFICE OF:

This similarity ends, however, at ⑦, where it is clearly stated that the conveyance is made *in* TRUST, to secure the payment of the promissory note, described at ⑧. Payoff of the note, release obligations of the beneficiary, and nullity of the trust conveyance, are shown at ⑨.

While the obligations and covenants of any one deed of trust can vary, the other provision necessary to complete the standard Texas deed of trust form is the **Power of Sale** clause shown at ⑬. Note that in the power of sale clause, and upon default by the grantor, the trustee acts at the request of the beneficiary to enforce the provisions of the trust to sell the therein described property at public auction.

There are other obligations of the deed of trust which are considered standard and may be summarized as follows:

1. Payment of taxes and maintenance of the lien provisions of the mortgage, at ⑪;
2. Covenant against waste, at ⑫;
3. Maintenance of adequate insurance, at ⑬;
4. Appointment of substitute trustee, at ⑭;
5. Beneficiary's right to condemnation proceeds and other awards of the subject property, at ⑮.

DEED OF TRUST TO SECURE ASSUMPTION

In the event the grantor under a deed of trust wants to sell his property and allow the purchaser to assume the obligations of that deed of trust, the TREC promulgated forms require that the proposed purchaser execute a deed of trust in favor of the grantor to secure the assumption. An example of a deed of trust to secure an assumption is shown in Figure 10:3. In this instrument, we will assume that the parties, N. Debted and wife May B. Debted, have conveyed their property to Chuck Roast and wife Berna. The only significant difference between Figure 10:3 and Figure 10:2 is the obligation secured. Instead of securing a real estate lien note, Figure 10:3 secures the assumption of an existing note. The grantors, Mr. and Mrs. Debted, become the beneficiaries under this Deed of Trust to Secure Assumption.

There has been little Texas law to date regarding the use of the Deed of Trust to Secure Assumption form. In practice, if the purchaser defaults, the sellers probably are unaware of it. However, since the Texas statutes for foreclosures under a deed of trust specify that "each debtor" must

Figure 10:3

Prepared by the State Bar of Texas for use by lawyers only. Revised 1-1-76.
Revised to include grantee's address 1-1-82.
Revised as to sale on default (§ 51.002, Prop. Code) 10-83.
Revised to change Trustee's fee to 5% 8-84.

DEED OF TRUST TO SECURE ASSUMPTION

(WHERE BENEFICIARY IS LIABLE ON NOTE ASSUMED)

THE STATE OF TEXAS   }   KNOW ALL MEN BY THESE PRESENTS:
COUNTY OF   HARRIS

That   CHUCK ROAST and wife BERNA ROAST

of __Harris_____ County, Texas, hereinafter called Grantors (whether one or more) for the purpose of securing the indebtedness hereinafter described, and in consideration of the sum of TEN DOLLARS ($10.00) to us in hand paid by the Trustee hereinafter named, the receipt of which is hereby acknowledged, and for the further consideration of the uses, purposes and trusts hereinafter set forth, have granted, sold and conveyed, and by these presents do grant, sell and convey unto __Charles J._____ __Jacobus_____, Trustee, of __Harris_____ County, Texas, and his substitutes or successors, all of the following described property situated in ___ __Harris_____ County, Texas, to-wit:

> Lot 1, Block 1, Shakey Acres Subdivision, Harris County, Texas, as shown of record at Volume 7, Page 3, of the Map Records of Harris County, Texas.

TO HAVE AND TO HOLD the above described property, together with the rights, privileges and appurtenances thereto belonging, unto the said Trustee and to his substitutes or successors forever. And Grantors named herein do hereby bind themselves, their heirs, executors, administrators and assigns to warrant and forever defend the said premises unto the said Trustee, his substitutes or successors and assigns forever, against the claim, or claims, of all persons claiming or to claim the same or any part thereof.

This conveyance, however, is made in TRUST for the following purposes:
WHEREAS, __N. Debted and wife, May B. Debted_____

hereinafter called Beneficiary, by deed of even date herewith conveyed the herein described property to Grantors named herein, who, as part of the consideration therefor assumed and promised to pay, according to the terms thereof, all principal and interest remaining unpaid upon that one certain promissory note in the original principal sum of $ __83,000.00_____, dated __February 1, 19xx_____, executed by __N. Debted and wife, May B. Debted__

and payable to order of __Friendly Lender Savings and Loan Association_____

Figure 10:3 *continued*

which said note is secured by a Deed of Trust recorded in Volume ___666___, Page ___444___,
___Deed of Trust___ Records of ___Harris___ County,
Texas, the obligations and covenants of the grantors named in said Deed of Trust were also assumed by Grantors named herein, and in said Deed the superior title and a vendor's lien were expressly reserved and retained by Beneficiary until said indebtedness and obligations so assumed are fully paid and satisfied, and should Grantors do and perform all of the obligations and covenants so assumed and make prompt payment of the indebtedness evidenced by said note so assumed as the same shall become due and payable, then this conveyance shall become null and void and of no further force and effect, it being agreed that a release of such indebtedness so assumed and of the liens securing the same by the legal owner and holder thereof prior to the advancement and payment thereon by Beneficiary of any sum or sums required to cure any default, shall be sufficient to release the lien created by this instrument as well as said vendor's lien so retained, without the joinder of Beneficiary. Unless, prior to the filing of a release of the indebtedness so assumed and of the liens securing the same in the office of the County Clerk of the County where said real property is situated, Beneficiary shall have filed in the office of the County Clerk of said County a sworn statement duly acknowledged and containing a legal description of the real property hereinbefore described and setting forth any and all sums that Beneficiary may have so advanced and paid, it shall be conclusively presumed that no sum or sums have been advanced and paid thereon by Beneficiary.

Grantors agree that in the event of default in the payment of any installment, principal or interest, of the note so assumed by Grantors, or in the event of default in the payment of said note when due or declared due, or of a breach of any of the obligations or covenants contained in the Deed of Trust securing said note so assumed, Beneficiary may, at his option, advance and pay such sum or sums as may be required to cure any such default, and that any and all such sums so advanced and paid by Beneficiary to cure such default shall be paid by

Grantors to Beneficiary at ___Piggy National Bank___

___, in the City of___Houston___, ___Harris___
County, Texas, within five (5) days after the date of such payment, without notice or demand, which are expressly waived.

Grantors covenant to pay promptly to Beneficiary, without notice or demand, within the time and as provided in the foregoing paragraph, any and all sums that may, under the provisions of the foregoing paragraph, be due Beneficiary.

In the event of a breach of the foregoing covenant, it shall thereupon, or at any time thereafter, be the duty of the Trustee, or his successor or substitute as hereinafter provided, at the request of Beneficiary (which request is hereby conclusively presumed), to enforce this Trust, and after advertising the time, place and terms of sale of the above described and conveyed property, then subject to the lien hereof, and mailing and filing notices as required by section 51.002, Texas Property Code, as then amended (successor to article 3810, Texas Revised Civil Statutes), and otherwise complying with that statute, the Trustee shall sell the above described property, then subject to the lien hereof, at public auction in accordance with such notices on the first Tuesday in any month between the hours of ten o'clock A.M. and four o'clock P.M., to the highest bidder for cash, and make due conveyance to the Purchaser or Purchasers, with general warranty binding Grantors, their heirs and assigns; and out of the money arising from such sale the Trustee shall pay, first, all expenses of advertising the sale and making the conveyance, including a commission of 5% to himself and, second, to Beneficiary the full amount of all sums so advanced and paid and that are then owing to Beneficiary under the provisions hereof, rendering the balance of the sales price, if any, to the person or persons legally entitled thereto; and the recitals in the conveyance to the Purchaser or Purchasers shall be full and conclusive evidence of the truth of the matters therein stated, and all prerequisites to said sale shall be presumed to have been performed, and such sale and conveyance shall be conclusive against Grantors, their heirs and assigns; said sale and deed to be made subject to the then unpaid part of the indebtedness so assumed by Grantors and the lien or liens securing the same, and it is agreed that such sale shall not in any manner affect any indebtedness which may thereafter become due and owing to Beneficiary under the covenants and provisions of this Deed of Trust, it being agreed that this Deed of Trust and all rights of Beneficiary shall be and remain in full force and effect so long as the obligations and indebtedness so assumed by Grantors or any part thereof remains unsatisfied or unpaid; that a sale by the Trustee or Substitute Trustee hereunder shall not exhaust the right of the Trustee or Substitute Trustee in event of any subsequent default hereunder, and at the request of Beneficiary, to thereafter enforce this trust and make sale of said property as herein provided.

Beneficiary, if he is the highest bidder, shall have the right to purchase at any sale of the property, and to have the amount for which such property is sold credited on the total sums owed Beneficiary.

Beneficiary in any event is hereby authorized to appoint a substitute trustee, or a successor trustee, to act instead of the Trustee named herein without other formality than the designation in writing of a substitute or successor trustee; and the authority hereby conferred shall extend to the appointment of other successor and substitute trustees successively until the full and final payment and satisfaction of the indebtedness and obligations so assumed by Grantors, and each substitute and successor trustee shall succeed to all of the rights and powers of the original Trustee named herein.

The term "Grantors" used in this instrument shall also include any and all successors in interest of Grantors to all or any part of the herein described and conveyed property as well as any and all purchasers thereof at any sale made hereunder by the Trustee or Substitute Trustee, and the provisions of this Deed of Trust shall be covenants running with the land.

If this Deed of Trust is or becomes binding upon one person or upon a corporation, the plural reference to Grantors shall be held to include the singular and all of the agreements and covenants herein undertaken to be performed by and the rights conferred upon Grantors, shall be binding upon and inure to the benefit of not only Grantors respectively but also their respective heirs, executors, administrators, grantees, successors and assigns.

It is expressly stipulated that the liability of Grantors to Beneficiary, arising by virtue of the assumption by Grantors of the payment of the note herein described and of the obligations of the Deed of Trust securing said note, as well as the liability to Beneficiary of any and all persons hereafter assuming payment of said note and performance of the obligations of said Deed of Trust, shall in no wise be discharged or released by this instrument or by the exercise by Beneficiary of the rights and remedies herein provided for, it being agreed that this instrument and all rights and remedies herein accorded Beneficiary are cumulative of any and all other rights and remedies existing at law.

Figure 10:3 *continued*

Grantors expressly represent that any indebtedness becoming due and payable under and by virtue of the terms and provisions of this Deed of Trust is in part payment of the purchase price of the herein described and conveyed property and that this Deed of Trust is cumulative and in addition to the Vendor's Lien expressly retained in deed of even date herewith executed by Beneficiary to Grantors, and it is expressly agreed that Beneficiary may foreclose under either or both of said liens as Beneficiary may elect, without waiving the other, said deed hereinbefore mentioned, together with its record, being here referred to and made a part of this instrument.

In the event any sale is made of the above described property, or any portion thereof, under the terms of this Deed of Trust, Grantors, their heirs and assigns, shall forthwith upon the making of such sale surrender and deliver possession of the property so sold to the Purchaser at such sale, and in the event of their failure to do so they shall thereupon from and after the making of such sale be and continue as tenants at will of such Purchaser, and in the event of their failure to surrender possession of said property upon demand, the Purchaser, his heirs or assigns, shall be entitled to institute and maintain an action for forcible detainer of said property in the Justice of the Peace Court in the Justice Precinct in which such property, or any part thereof, is situated.

EXECUTED this First   day of   February   , A.D. 19 xx

Ernest Byer   Patsy Byer
Ernest Byer   Patsy Byer

Mailing address of trustee: Mailing address of each beneficiary:

Name: Charles J. Jacobus   Name: Piggy National Bank
Address: 10 Lovers Lane   Address: 10 Loan Heights
          Sweetwater, Texas   Houston, Texas

                                                     Name:
                                                     Address:

(Acknowledgment)

STATE OF TEXAS
COUNTY OF HARRIS

       This instrument was acknowledged before me on the   first   day of February   , 19 xx .
by   Ernest Byer and Patsy Byer

                                                     Rose Bloom
                                                     Notary Public, State of Texas
                                                     Notary's name (printed):

                                                     Notary's commission expires: 30 June, 19xx

Figure 10:3 *continued*

(Acknowledgment)

STATE OF TEXAS
COUNTY OF   }

    This instrument was acknowledged before me on the   day of   , 19
by   .

Notary Public, State of Texas
Notary's name (printed):

Notary's commission expires:

(Acknowledgment)

STATE OF TEXAS
COUNTY OF   }

    This instrument was acknowledged before me on the   day of   , 19   ,
by   .

Notary Public, State of Texas
Notary's name (printed):

Notary's commission expires:

(Corporate Acknowledgment)

STATE OF TEXAS
COUNTY OF   }

    This instrument was acknowledged before me on the   day of   , 19   ,
by   ,
of   ,
a   corporation, on behalf of said corporation.

Notary Public, State of Texas
Notary's name (printed):

Notary's commission expires:

AFTER RECORDING RETURN TO: PREPARED IN THE LAW OFFICE OF:

Piggy National Bank   Charles J. Jacobus
10 Loan Heights   10 Lovers Lane
Houston, Texas   Sweetwater, Texas

receive written notice of the proposed sale, it is assumed that the sellers, who are the original debtors on the deed of trust and promissory note, would be given notice of such sale. This would give them the right to pay the obligation or buy the property at the foreclosure sale.

At best, the Assumption form purports to give the seller of the property some tangible equity in the property. Note the paragraph specifying default in the payment of the note being assumed. The seller (the beneficiary) may, at his option, advance and pay the sums required to cure any such default. The grantors (purchasers of the property) must reimburse the beneficiaries (sellers of the property) within five days. If this is not done, the beneficiaries may exercise their right to foreclose under the power of sale clause.

The Deed of Trust to Secure Assumption form is intended to be used in conjunction with an assumption deed. An assumption deed is similar to other deeds, except that for consideration it specifies that the grantee is to assume the obligations of the note and deed of trust signed by the grantor.

FORECLOSURE PROCESS

The foreclosure process, as set out in the power of sale provision, is pursuant to statutory guidelines that provide for executions by sales under a deed of trust. To be enforceable, the power of sale provisions cannot be in violation of state law.

Texas law states that upon default, sale of real estate under the power conferred by the deed of trust shall be made in the county in which the real estate is located. When the real estate is situated in more than one county, the sale may be held in any of these counties, as long as all notices specify in which county the real estate will be sold. Notice of the proposed sale shall be given by posting written notice of the sale at least 21 days preceding the date of the sale. The notice must be posted at the courthouse door (and most courthouses provide a bulletin board located in close proximity to the courthouse door). If the real estate is situated in more than one county, the notice is to be posted at the courthouse door of each county in which the real estate is located, and filed in the office of the County Clerk. The lender must also serve written notice of the proposed sale at least 21 days preceding the date of the sale (by certified mail) on each debtor obligated to pay such debt, according to the records of the lender or note holder. Service of the notice is considered complete upon deposit of the notice in the United States Mail in a properly addressed post-paid wrapper. The sale is held open to the public between the hours of 10 a.m. and 4 p.m. on the first Tuesday of any month.

As a practical matter, the mortgagee generally gives the trustee a Request to Act (Figure 10:4), and the trustee posts the notice (Figure 10:5) on the courthouse door 21 days prior to the first Tuesday of the following month in which said sale is to take place and file a copy of the notice in the county clerk's office. Then, on the day and time specified by statute, a public auction is held at the courthouse door. If there are no other bidders, the sale is normally made to a representative of the mortgage company or the note holder. Upon finalization of the sale and execution of the trustee's deed, the trustee executes an affidavit that such notice was properly carried out in compliance with state law. By execution of the deed and signing of this affidavit, the law presumes that the sale was carried out correctly.

Redemption   As discussed in the previous Chapter, some states provide an equity of redemption to redeem the property prior to sale and reinstate the borrower's right to continue to make payments. In Texas, however, once the note has been accelerated in the event of default and notice is posted for the foreclosure sale, the only equity of redemption that the debtor has is to pay the full amount owing, or to buy the property at the foreclosure. There is also no statutory **right of redemption** in Texas to reinstate the deed of trust after the foreclosure sale has taken place. The net effect of this is that once the note has been accelerated, the mortgagor has no rights except that of paying the full amount of the note due in cash at or before the foreclosure sale, unless otherwise agreed to by the mortgagee.

Prior to the passage of the 1976 law, pursuant to deed of trust foreclosures, there was no requirement that notice be sent to the mortgagor, and the mortgages with power of sale were consistently upheld as being private and enforceable contracts between the parties. The power of sale provision

FRIENDLY LENDER SAVINGS and LOAN   **Figure 10:4**

000 Sunrise Valley / Anywhere, Texas 00091

REQUEST TO ACT

Mr. Charles J. Jacobus
P. O. Box 1000000
Houston, Texas 77001

RE: Deed of Trust, dated February 1, 19xx,
executed by N. Debted and wife, May B.
Debted, to Charles J. Jacobus,
Trustee, recorded in Volume 666 ,
page   444 , Deed of Trust Records of
Harris County, Texas.

Dear Sir:

    Default has occurred in the payment of the indebtedness described in and secured by the above mentioned Deed of Trust and by reason thereof said entire indebtedness is now past due and unpaid.

    The undersigned, being the holder of said indebtedness and lien, hereby request you, Charles J. Jacobus, as Trustee, to sell the property in said Deed of Trust described and as provided therein, in order to satisfy said indebtedness.

    Please furnish the undersigned several signed copies of the Notice of the Trustee's Sale so that notice thereof can be served by certified mail at least twenty-one (21) days preceding the date of sale on each debtor obligated to pay such indebtedness according to the records of the undersigned and as required by law.

FRIENDLY LENDER SAVINGS AND LOAN

BY: *Mort Gage*
                          President

Figure 10:5

NOTICE OF TRUSTEE'S SALE

Pursuant to authority conferred upon me by that certain Deed of Trust executed by N. Debted and wife, May B. Debted, of Harris County, Texas, dated February 1, 19xx, and duly recorded in Volume ___666___, on page ___444___ of the Deed of Trust Records of Harris County, Texas, I will as Trustee under said Deed of Trust, in order to satisfy the indebtedness secured thereby and at the request of the holder of said indebtedness, default having been made in the payment thereof, sell on Tuesday, April 4, 19xx, at public auction to the highest bidder for cash before the courthouse door of Harris County, Texas, in Houston, Texas, between the hours of ten o'clock A.M. and four o'clock P.M. of that day, the following described property, to-wit:

> *Lot 1, Block 1, Shakey Acres Subdivision, Harris County, Texas, as shown of record at Volume 7, Page 3 of the Map Records of Harris County, Texas.*

EXECUTED this 4th day fo March, 19xx

Charles J. Jacobus
_____
Charles J. Jacobus, Trustee

of a deed of trust has consistently been upheld to be constitutional, even before the statute was changed to require that notice be sent to the mortgagor. However, it is important to take into consideration that because the state allows this type of foreclosure, lenders are more ready to make loans and provide money for mortgages, knowing that in the event of default their remedy is reasonably swift and inexpensive. One consistently finds in states that do not allow a quick and swift remedy to foreclosure proceedings that loan procedures and credit searches become much more intense, to allow the mortgagee to minimize the risk of making a real estate loan. This, coupled with the fact that most mortgagees do not want to foreclose on property, means that mortgagees will generally give the mortgagor an agreed time to redeem, rather than immediately foreclose. The lender is in the business of making money on house payments, not in foreclosing and becoming a homeowner. A consistent string of foreclosures puts the lender into the real estate business, and most mortgagees wish to remain solely in the lending business.

JURISDICTIONS USING DEEDS OF TRUST

The deed of trust is customarily used as the primary security instrument in Alaska, Arizona, California, Colorado, the District of Columbia, Idaho, Maryland, Mississippi, Missouri, North Carolina, Oregon, Tennessee, Texas, Virginia, and West Virginia. They are also used to a certain extent in Alabama, Delaware, Hawaii, Illinois, Montana, Nevada, New Mexico, Utah, Washington, and a few other states. The extent of their use in a state is governed by that state's attitude toward conveyance of title to the trustee, power of sale, and statutory redemption privileges. Many states not listed here allow the use of a deed of trust, but consider it to be a lien. As such it is treated no differently than a mortgage with a power of sale clause.

A few states recognize some, but not all, of the provisions of a deed of trust. For example, a state may allow a power of sale clause in a deed of trust, but not in a regular mortgage. Or it may rule that a foreclosed mortgage must have a statutory redemption period while a deed of trust does not. In those states that allow all the provisions of a deed of trust to function without hindrance, the deed of trust has flourished. In Texas, for example, where it is well established legally that a deed of trust does convey title to the trustee upon default, that the trustee has the power of sale, and that there is no statutory redemption deed of trust recordings far outnumber regular mortgages.

ADVANTAGES OF THE DEED OF TRUST

The popularity of the deed of trust can be traced to the following attributes: (1) if a borrower defaults, the lender can take possession of the pledged property to protect it and collect the rents; (2) the time between default and foreclosure is relatively short, on the order of 30 to 180 days; (3) the foreclosure process under the power of sale provision is far less expensive and complex than a court-ordered foreclosure; and (4) once the foreclosure sale takes place, there is no statutory redemption. These are primarily advantages to the lender, but such advantages have attracted lenders and made real estate loans easier for borrowers to obtain and less expensive. Some states prohibit deficiency judgments against borrowers when a deed of trust is used.

Property can be purchased "subject to" an existing deed of trust or it can be "assumed," just as with a regular mortgage. Debt priorities are established as for mortgages: there are first and second, senior and junior trust deeds. Deeds of trust can be subordinated and partial releases are possible.

VOCABULARY REVIEW

Match terms **a-d** *with statements* **1–4.**

a. *Beneficiary*
b. *Deed of trust*
c. *Grantor*
d. *Trustee*

1. A document that conveys legal title to a neutral third party as security for a loan.
2. One who creates a trust; the borrower under a deed of trust.
3. The lender.
4. One who holds property in trust for another.

QUESTIONS AND PROBLEMS

1. How does a deed of trust differ from a mortgage?
2. Does possession of a deed of trust give the trustee any rights of entry or use of the property in question as long as the promissory note is not in default? Explain.
3. What role does a release of lien play?
4. What is the purpose of a power of sale clause in a deed of trust?
5. Explain the purpose of an assignment of rents clause.
6. What is the most common mortgage form in Texas?

ADDITIONAL READINGS

Essentials of Real Estate Investment, 3rd ed. by **David Sirota.** (Real Estate Education Co., 1983, 366 pages). Part I of this book deals with the concepts of real estate investment while Part II deals with application. Book covers investing in land, residential and commercial properties, retail stores and industrial property.

Modern Real Estate, 2nd ed. by **Charles Wurtzebach** and **Mike Miles.** (Wiley, 1984, 625 pages). Provides an analytical decision-making approach to real estate. Includes financing, law, construction, taxation, management, development and marketing.

Real Estate Finance and Investment Tables by **Jack Friedman** and **Peggy Pearson.** (Reston, 1983, 522 pages). Contains tables for loan payments, remaining balance, effective yields at discount, wrap-around loan yields, prorations, discount percentages, etc.

Reference Book. (California Department of Real Estate, 1986, 840 pages). Includes a section on trust deeds, trust deed forms, default and foreclosure, and trust deeds compared to mortgages.

Texas Real Estate Law, 4th ed. by **Charles J. Jacobus.** (Reston, 1985, 560 pages). Provides up-to-date explanations of law pertinent to the daily operation of a real estate brokerage office in Texas. See Chapter 11 on deeds of trust.

*   *   *

The Texas Homebuyer's Manual, published by the State Bar of Texas 1985 (56 pages). A manual intended to assist persons buying a home in Texas for the first time, discussing the various legal and other considerations involved in real estate transactions.

Amortized loan: a loan requiring periodic payments that include both interest and partial repayment of principal.

Balloon loan: any loan in which the final payment is larger than the preceding payments

Conventional loans: real estate loans that are not insured by the FHA or guaranteed by the VA

Equity: the market value of a property less the debt against it

Impound or reserve account: an account into which the lender places monthly tax and insurance payments; also called an **escrow account**

Loan-to-value ratio: a percentage reflecting what a lender will lend divided by the market value of the property

Maturity: the end of the life of a loan

PITI payment: a loan payment that combines principal, interest, taxes, and insurance

Point: one percent of the loan amount

Principal: the balance owing on a loan

Section 203(b): FHA's popular mortgage insurance program for houses

Truth in Lending Act: a federal law that requires certain disclosures when extending or advertising credit

KEY TERMS

Whereas Chapters 9 and 10 dealt with the legal aspects of notes, mortgages, and trust deeds, Chapters 11 and 12 will deal with the money aspects of these instruments. We will begin in Chapter 11 with term loans, amortized loans, balloon loans, partially amortized loans, loan-to-value, and equity. This will be followed by the functions and importance of the FHA and VA, private mortgage insurance, loan points, and Truth In Lending. The last topic in Chapter 11 will be a helpful and informative description of the loan application and approval process you (or your buyer) will experience when applying for a real estate loan. In Chapter 12, we will look at sources and types of financing. This will include information on where to find mortgage loan money, where mortgage lenders obtain their money, and various types of financing instruments such as the adjustable rate mortgage, equity mortgage, seller financing, wraparound mortgage and so forth. Note that from here on whatever is said about mortgages applies equally to trust deeds.

TERM LOANS

A loan that requires only interest payments until the last day of its life, at which time the full amount borrowed is due, is called a **term loan** (or straight loan). Until 1930, the term loan was the standard method of financing real estate in the United States. These loans were typically made for a period of 3 to 5 years. The borrower signed a note or bond agreeing (1) to pay the lender interest on the loan every 6 months, and (2) to repay the entire amount of the loan upon **maturity;** that is, at the end of the life of the loan. As security, the borrower mortgaged his property to the lender.

Loan Renewal

In practice, most real estate term loans were not paid off when they matured. Instead, the borrower asked the lender, typically a bank, to renew the loan for another 3 to 5 years. The major flaw in this approach to lending was that the borrower might never own the property free and clear of debt. This left the borrower continuously at the mercy of the lender for renewals. As long as the lender was not pressed for funds, the borrower's renewal request was granted. However, if the lender was short of funds, no renewal was granted and the borrower was expected to pay in full.

The inability of lenders to renew term loans caused hardship to hundreds of thousands of property owners during the Great Depression that began in 1930 and lasted most of the decade. Banks were unable to accommodate requests for loan renewals and at the same time satisfy unemployed depositors who needed to withdraw their savings to live. As a result, owners of homes, farms, office buildings, factories and vacant land lost their property as foreclosures reached into the millions. The market was so glutted with properties being offered for sale to satisfy unpaid mortgage loans that real estate prices fell at a sickening pace.

AMORTIZED LOANS

In 1933, a congressionally legislated Home Owner's Loan Corporation (HOLC) was created to assist financially distressed homeowners by acquiring mortgages that were about to be foreclosed. The HOLC then offered monthly repayment plans tailored to fit the homeowner's budget that would repay the loan in full by its maturity date without the need for a balloon payment. The HOLC was terminated in 1951 after rescuing more than 1 million mortgages in its 18-year life. However, the use of this stretched-out payment plan, known as an **amortized loan,** took hold in American real estate, and today it is the accepted method of loan repayment.

The amortized loan requires regular equal payments during the life of the loan, of sufficient size and number to pay all interest due on the loan and reduce the amount owed to zero by the loan's maturity date. Figure 11:1 illustrates the contrast between an amortized and a term loan. Part A of Figure 11:1 shows a 6-year, $1,000 term loan with interest of $90 due each year of its life. At the end of the sixth year the entire **principal** (the amount owed) is due in one lump sum payment along with the final interest payment. In part B of Figure 11:1, the same $1,000 loan is fully amortized by making six equal annual payments of $222.92. From the borrower's standpoint, $222.92 once each year is easier to budget than $90 for 5 years and $1,090 in the sixth year.

Furthermore, the amortized loan shown in part B actually costs the borrower less than the term loan. The total payments made under the term loan are $90 + $90 + $90 + $90 +

Repayment Methods

REPAYING A 6-YEAR $1,000 LOAN   **Figure 11:1**

Carrying 9% Interest per Year

(A) Total payments = $1,540.00   (B) Total payments = $1,337.52

$90 + $1,090 = $1,540. Amortizing the same loan requires total payments of 6 × $222.92 = $1,337.52. The difference is due to the fact that under the amortized loan the borrower begins to pay back part of the $1,000 principal with his first payment. In the first year, $90 of the $222.92 payment goes to interest and the remaining $132.92 reduces the principal owed. Thus, the borrower starts the second year owing only $867.08. At 9% interest per year, the interest on $867.08 is $78.04; therefore, when the borrower makes his second payment of $222.92, only $78.04 goes to interest. The remaining $144.88 is applied to reduce the loan balance, and the borrower starts the third year owing $722.20. Figure 11:2 charts this repayment program. Notice that the balance owed drops faster as the loan becomes older; that is, as it matures.

Monthly Payments   As you have just seen, calculating the payments on a term loan is relatively simple compared to calculating amortized loan payments. As a result, **amortization tables** are published and used throughout the real estate industry. Table 11:1 shows the monthly payments per $1,000 of loan for interest rates from 5% to 25% for periods ranging from 5 to 40 years. (Amortization tables are also published for quarterly, semiannual and annual payments.) When you use an amorti-

Figure 11:2   **REPAYING A 6-YEAR $1,000 AMORTIZED LOAN**

Carrying 9% Interest per Year

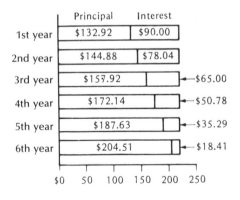

(A) Allocation of each annual
payment to principal and interest

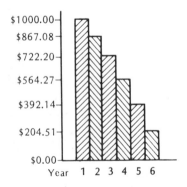

(B) Balance owed during each
year of the loan.

zation table, notice that there are five variables: (1) frequency of payment, (2) interest rate, (3) maturity, (4) amount of the loan, and (5) amount of the periodic payment. If you know any four of these, you can obtain the fifth variable from the tables. For example, suppose that you want to know the monthly payment necessary to amortize a $60,000 loan over 30 years at 10½% interest. The first step is to look in Table 11:1 for the 10½% line. Then locate the 30-year column. Where they cross, you will find the necessary monthly payment per $1,000: $9.15. Next, multiply $9.15 by 60 to get the monthly payment for a $60,000 loan: $549. If the loan is to be $67,500, then multiply $9.15 by 67.5 to get the monthly payment: $617.63.

Continuing the above example, suppose we reduce the repayment period to 15 years. First look for the 10½% line, then go over to the 15-year column. The number there is $11.06. Next, multiply $11.06 by 60 to get the monthly payment for a $60,000 loan: $663.60. If the loan is to be $67,500, then multiply $11.06 by 67.5 to get the monthly payment: $746.55.

Loan Size

Amortization tables can also be used to determine the amount of loan a borrower can support if you know how much the borrower has available to spend each month on loan payments. Suppose that a prospective home buyer can afford monthly principal and interest payments of $650 and lenders are making 30-year loans at 10%. How large a loan can this buyer afford? In Table 11:1 find where the 10% line and the 30-year column meet. You will see 8.78 there. This means that every $8.78 of monthly payment will support $1,000 of loan. To find how many thousands of dollars $650 per month will support, just divide $650 by $8.78. The answer is 74.031 thousands or $74,031. By adding the buyer's down payment, you know what price property the buyer can afford to purchase. If interest rates are 7½%, the number from the table is 7.00 and the loan amount if $92,857. (You can begin to see why the level of interest rates is so important to real estate prices.)

As you have noticed, everything in Table 11:1 is on a monthly payment per thousand basis. With a full book of

Table 11:1   **AMORTIZATION TABLE OF**
A MONTHLY PAYMENT PER $1,000 OF LOAN

Interest Rate per year	Life of the Loan							
	5 years	10 years	15 years	20 years	25 years	30 years	35 years	40 years
5%	$18.88	$10.61	$ 7.91	$ 6.60	$ 5.85	$ 5.37	$ 5.05	$ 4.83
5½	19.11	10.86	8.18	6.88	6.15	5.68	5.38	5.16
6	19.34	11.11	8.44	7.17	6.45	6.00	5.71	5.51
6½	19.57	11.36	8.72	7.46	6.76	6.32	6.05	5.86
7	19.81	11.62	8.99	7.76	7.07	6.66	6.39	6.22
7½	20.04	11.88	9.28	8.06	7.39	7.00	6.75	6.59
8	20.28	12.14	9.56	8.37	7.72	7.34	7.11	6.96
8½	20.52	12.40	9.85	8.68	8.06	7.69	7.47	7.34
9	20.76	12.67	10.15	9.00	8.40	8.05	7.84	7.72
9½	21.01	12.94	10.45	9.33	8.74	8.41	8.22	8.11
10	21.25	13.22	10.75	9.66	9.09	8.78	8.60	8.50
10½	21.50	13.50	11.06	9.99	9.45	9.15	8.99	8.89
11	21.75	13.78	11.37	10.33	9.81	9.53	9.37	9.29
11½	22.00	14.06	11.69	10.67	10.17	9.91	9.77	9.69
12	22.25	14.35	12.01	11.02	10.54	10.29	10.16	10.09
12½	22.50	14.64	12.33	11.37	10.91	10.68	10.56	10.49
13	22.76	14.94	12.66	11.72	11.28	11.07	10.96	10.90
13½	23.01	15.23	12.99	12.08	11.66	11.46	11.36	11.31
14	23.27	15.53	13.32	12.44	12.04	11.85	11.76	11.72
14½	23.53	15.83	13.66	12.80	12.43	12.25	12.17	12.13
15	23.79	16.14	14.00	13.17	12.81	12.65	12.57	12.54

amortization tables rather than one page, it is possible to look up monthly payments for loans from $100 to $100,000, to determine loan maturities for each year from 1 to 40 years, and to calculate many more interest rates. Amortization books are available from most local bookstores.

Change in Maturity Date   An amortization table also shows the impact on the size of the monthly payment when the life of a loan is extended. For example, at 11% interest, a 10-year loan requires a monthly payment of $13.78 per thousand of loan. Increasing the life of the loan to 20 years drops the monthly payment to $10.33 per $1,000. Extending the loan payback to 30 years reduces the monthly payment to $9.53 per thousand. The smaller monthly payment is why 30 years is a popular loan with borrowers. Note, however, that going beyond 30 years does not significantly reduce the monthly payment. Going from 30 to 35 years reduces the monthly payment by only 16¢ per thousand but adds 5 years of monthly payments. Extending the payback period from 35 to 40 years reduces the monthly payment by just 8¢ per $1,000 ($4 per month on a $50,000 loan) and adds another 60 months of payments at $464.50 per month. As a practical matter, amortized real estate loans are seldom made for more than 30 years.

BUDGET MORTGAGE

The **budget mortgage** takes the amortized loan one step further. In addition to collecting the monthly principal and interest payment (often called P + I), the lender collects one-twelfth of the estimated cost of the annual property taxes and hazard insurance on the mortgaged property. The money for tax and insurance payments is placed in an **impound account** (also called an **escrow** or **reserve account**). When taxes and insurance payments are due, the lender pays them. Thus, the lender makes certain that the value of the mortgaged property will not be undermined by unpaid property taxes or by uninsured fire or weather damage. This form of mortgage also helps the borrower to budget for property taxes and insurance on a monthly basis. To illustrate, if insurance is $240 per year and property taxes are $1,800 per year, the lender collects an additional $20 and $150 each month along with the regular principal and interest payments. This combined principal, interest, taxes, and insurance payment is often referred to as a PITI payment.

BALLOON LOAN

A **balloon loan** is any loan which has a final payment larger than any of the previous payments on the loan. The final payment is called a **balloon payment.** The term loan described at the beginning of this chapter is a type of balloon loan. Partially amortized loans, discussed next, are also a type of balloon loan. In the tight money market of 1979–82, the use of balloon loans increased considerably. Balloon loans with maturities as short as 3 to 5 years were commonplace. This arrangement gives the buyer (borrower) 3 to 5 years to find cheaper and longer-term financing elsewhere. If such financing does not materialize and the loan is not repaid on time, the lender has the right to foreclose. The alternative is for the lender and borrower to agree to an extension of the loan, usually at prevailing interest rates.

PARTIALLY AMORTIZED LOAN

When the repayment schedule of a loan calls for a series of amortized payments followed by a balloon payment at maturity, it is called a **partially amortized loan.** For example, a lender might agree to a 30-year amortization schedule with a provision that at the end of the tenth year all the remaining principal be paid in a single balloon payment. The advantage to the borrower is that for 10 years the monthly payments will be smaller than if the loan was completely amortized in 10 years. (You can verify this in Table 11:1.) However, the disadvantage is that the balloon payment due at the end of the tenth year might be the borrower's financial downfall. Just how large that balloon payment will be can be determined in advance by using a **loan balance table** (also called a **remaining balance table**). Presuming an interest rate of 11½% and a 30-year loan, at the end of 10 years the loan balance table in Table 11:2 shows that for each $1,000 originally loaned, $929 would still be owed. If the original loan was for $100,000, at the end of 10 years 100 × $929 = $92,900 would be due as one payment. This qualifies it as a balloon loan.

As you can see from this example, when an amortized loan has a long maturity, relatively little of the debt is paid off during the initial years of the loan's life. Nearly all the early payments go for interest, so that little remains for principal reduction. For example, Table 11:2 shows that even after 16 years of payments on a 30-year, 11½% loan, 82½% of the loan is still unpaid. Not until this loan is about 6 years from maturity will half of it have been repaid.

EARLIER PAYOFF

During the late 1970s when inflation rates exceeded interest rates, the popular philosophy was to borrow as much as possible for as long as possible. Then in the early 1980s inflation rates dropped below interest rates and the opposite philosophy became attractive to many borrowers. This was especially true for those who had borrowed (or were contemplating borrowing) at double-digit interest rates. Let us use as an example an $80,000 loan at 11½% interest. If the loan has a maturity of 30 years, from Table 11:1 we can determine

Table 11:2　　　　　　BALANCE OWING ON A $1,000 AMORTIZED LOAN

9½% Annual Interest							11½% Annual Interest						
Age of Loan (years)	Original Life (years)						Age of Loan (years)	Original Life (years)					
	10	15	20	25	30	35		10	15	20	25	30	35
2	$868	$934	$963	$978	$987	$992	2	$880	$944	$971	$984	$991	$995
4	708	853	918	952	971	983	4	729	873	935	965	981	989
6	515	756	864	921	953	971	6	539	784	889	940	967	982
8	282	639	799	883	930	957	8	300	672	831	909	950	972
10		497	720	837	902	940	10		531	759	870	929	960
12		326	625	781	869	920	12		354	667	821	902	945
14		119	510	714	828	896	14		132	553	759	868	926
16			371	633	780	866	16			409	682	825	903
18			203	535	721	830	18			228	585	772	873
20				416	650	787	20				462	704	836
22				273	564	735	22				308	620	789
24				100	460	671	24				115	513	729
26					335	595	26					380	655
28					183	503	28					211	561
30						391	30						444
32						256	32						296
34						94	34						110

the monthly payments to be $792.80. (Follow this example on your own.)

Suppose the maturity of the above loan is charged from 30 to 15 years. Looking at Table 11:1, the monthly payments will now be $935.20. This is $142.40 more per month, but the loan is fully paid in 15 years, not 30 years. The total amount of interest paid on the 15-year loan is (15 × 12 × $935.20) − $80,000 = $88,336. The total amount of interest paid on the 30-year loan is (30 × 12 × $792.80) − $80,000 = $205,408. Thus, for an extra $142.40 per month for 180 months (which amounts to $25,632) the borrower saves the difference between $205,408 and $88,336 (which is $117,072). Many borrowers consider this a very good return on their money. (It is, in fact, an 11½% compounded rate of return.) Lenders are more receptive to making fixed-rate loans for 15 years than for 30 years. This is because the lender is locked into the loan for 15 years, not 30 years. As a result, a lender is usually willing to offer a 15-year loan at a lower rate of interest

15-Year Loan

than a 30-year loan. In view of these benefits to borrower and lender alike, the 15-year loan is becoming a popular home financing tool.

Biweekly Payments   A small but growing number of lenders offer a biweekly repayment plan. The loan is amortized as if it were going to last 30 years. But instead of paying once a month, the borrower makes one-half the monthly payment every two weeks. This may not sound like much difference but the results are eye-opening. Assume you borrow $100,000 at 13% interest, paying (see Table 11:1) $1,107 per month. You will retire the loan in 30 years at a cost of $298,520 in interest. If you decide to pay half of $1,107 every two weeks, the loan will be fully paid in just 18 years and will have cost you $160,023 in interest. This happens because biweekly compounding works in your favor and because you make 26 half-size payments a year, not 24.

Existing Loans   For borrowers with existing loans who want to celebrate with an early mortgage burning, this is done by simply adding a few dollars each month to the required monthly payment. This can be particularly beneficial for persons who borrowed at rates of 13%, 14% and 15% or more. In effect, whatever extra amount is added to the monthly payment will "earn" interest at the loan's interest rate. Thus, if a loan has a 14% rate, early payments "earn" at 14%. If the borrower has no alternative places to invest that will yield 14%, then a few additional dollars each month will work miracles. For example, a 30-year $100,000 loan at 14% interest requires monthly payments (see Table 11:1) of $1,185. Voluntarily adding an extra $19 per month will reduce the maturity (payoff) date from 30 years to 25 years (see Table 11:1 again). If an extra $40 is added to the $19, the maturity date shrinks to 20 years. In other words, an extra $59 per month eliminates 10 years of payments.

You may be wondering why borrowers have not thought of this before. There are two key reasons. First, there was a time in 1979 when inflation was 18% per year and 14% to borrow looked cheap by comparison. Second, when interest rates are around 6% and 7% (as they were in the 1960 decade), the mathematics of early payoff is not as impressive.

When interest rates fall it may be advantageous for a mortgage borrower to **refinance;** i.e., obtain a new loan to replace the old one. For example, between March 1985 and March 1986, interest rates for residential loans dropped from 13% to 9½%. Thus, refinancing would allow a person who had borrowed at 13% per year to replace the old loan with one costing 9½% per year. There are, however, certain costs to refinancing and the existing loan must allow early repayment. If you are considering refinancing, the first step is to read the existing loan agreement to see if it can be repaid early; generally speaking, most can. The next step is to compare the cost of refinancing with the benefits. The cost will be a loan origination fee typically amounting to $150 to $300 per every $10,000 borrowed (1 ½ to 3 points), plus charges for a new appraisal, a new title insurance policy (although a credit may be allowed for the old mortgagee's title premium), a new credit check, escrow fees, prepayment penalties, and legal fees. The benefit will be the lower rate of interest on the new loan. If the difference in monthly mortgage payments is large enough for a long enough period of time, it's worth it to spend the money to refinance.

REFINANCING

If you are considering refinancing, there are three basic questions to ask: (1) Is the difference between what you are now paying and what you could pay at least 2% per year? (2) Do you plan to stay in your home for at least another 2 to 5 years? (3) Do you have the money to pay the refinancing costs? Gaining a 1% lower interest rate is rarely worth the cost, but there may be other reasons such as changing the maturity date or switching from an adjustable rate mortgage to a fixed rate mortgage or vice versa. Note that if you sell your home in the not-too-distant future and the buyer obtains new financing, you may not have had time to recover your refinancing costs.

As a final thought, you should know that the cost of refinancing may not require cash from your pocket if you add these additional loan costs to the then existing principal balance to create a new loan amount. This can be done if the property appraises high enough and you have the monthly income to qualify. Although there are some technicalities involving homestead laws in Texas, most lenders will allow these fees to be added to the original principal balance.

LOAN-TO-VALUE RATIO

The relationship between the amount of money a lender is willing to loan and the lender's estimate of the market value of the property that will serve as security is called the **loan-to-value ratio** (often abbreviated **L/V ratio**). For example, a prospective home buyer wants to purchase a house priced at $80,000. A local lender appraises the house, finds it has a market value of $80,000, and agrees to make an 80% L/V loan. This means that the lender will loan up to 80% of the $80,000 and the buyer must provide at least 20% in cash. In dollars, the lender will loan up to $64,000 and the buyer must make a cash down payment of at least $16,000. If the lender appraises the home for more than $80,000 the loan will still be $64,000. If the appraisal is for less than $80,000 the loan will be 80% of the appraised value, and the buyer must pay the balance in cash. The rule is that price or value, whichever is lower, is applied to the L/V ratio. This rule exists to prevent the lender from overlending on a property just because the borrower overpaid for it.

EQUITY

The difference between the market value of a property and the debt owed against it is called the owner's **equity.** On a newly purchased $80,000 home with a $16,000 cash down payment, the buyer's equity is $16,000. As the value of the property rises or falls and as the mortgage loan is paid down, equity changes. For example, if the value of the home rises to $90,000 and the loan is paid down to $62,000 the owner's equity will be $28,000. If the owner completely repays the loan so that there is no debt against the home, the owner's equity is equal to the market value of the property.

LOAN POINTS

Probably no single term in real estate finance causes as much confusion and consternation as the word **points.** In finance, the word **point** means one percent of the loan amount. Thus, on a $60,000 loan, one point is $600. On a $40,000 loan, three points is $1,200. On a $100,000 loan, eight points is $8,000.

The use of points in real estate mortgage finance can be split into two categories: (1) loan origination fees expressed in terms of points, and (2) the use of points to change the effective yield of a mortgage loan to a lender. Let's look at these two uses in more detail.

Origination Fee

When a borrower asks for a mortgage loan, the lender incurs a number of expenses, including such things as the time its loan officer spends interviewing the borrower, office overhead, the purchase and review of credit reports on the borrower, an on-site appraisal of the property to be mortgaged, title searches and review, legal and recording fees and so on. For these, some lenders make an itemized billing, charging so many dollars for the appraisal, credit report, title search and so on. The total becomes the **loan origination fee,** which the borrower pays to get his loan. Other lenders do not make an itemized bill, but instead simply state the origination fee in terms of a percentage of the loan amount, for example, one point. Thus, a lender quoting a loan origination fee of one point is saying that, for a $65,000 loan, its fee to originate the loan will be $650.

Discount Points

Points charged to raise the lender's monetary return on a loan are known as **discount points**. A simplified example will illustrate their use and effect. If you are a lender and agree to make a term loan of $100 to a borrower for 1 year at 10% interest, you would normally expect to give the borrower $100 now (disregard loan origination fees for a moment), and 1 year later the borrower would give you $110. In percentage terms, the **effective yield** on your loan is 10% per annum (year) because you received $10 for your 1-year, $100 loan. Now suppose that, instead of handing the borrower $100, you handed him $99 but still required him to repay $100 plus $10 in interest at the end of the year. This is a discount of one point ($1 in this case), and the borrower paid it out of his loan funds. The effect of this financial maneuver is to raise the effective yield (yield to maturity) to you without raising the interest rate itself. Therefore, if you loan out $99 and receive $110 at the end of the year, you effectively have a return of $11 for a $99 loan. This gives you an effective yield of $11 + $99 or 11.1%, rather than 10%.

Calculating the effective yield on a discounted 20- or 30-year mortgage loan is more difficult because the amount owed drops over the life of the loan, and because the majority are paid in full ahead of schedule due to refinancing. Computers and calculators usually make these calculations; however, a useful rule of thumb states that on the typical home loan each point of discount raises the effective yield by ⅛ of 1%. Thus, four discount points would raise the effective yield by approximately ½ of 1% and eight points would raise it by 1%. Discount points are most often charged during periods of **tight money,** that is, when mortgage money is in short supply. During periods of **loose money,** when lenders have adequate funds to lend and are actively seeking borrowers, discount points disappear.

FHA INSURANCE PROGRAMS

The Great Depression caused a major change in the attitude of the federal government toward home financing in the United States. In 1934, one year after the Home Owners Loan Corporation was established, Congress passed the National Housing Act. The act's most far-reaching provision was to establish the Federal Housing Administration (FHA) for the purpose of encouraging new construction as a means of creating jobs. To accomplish this goal, the FHA offered to insure lenders against losses due to nonrepayment when they made loans on both new and existing homes. In turn, the lender had to grant 20-year fully amortized loans with loan-to-value ratios of 80% rather than the 3- to 5-year, 50% to 60% term loans common up to that time.

The FHA did its best to keep from becoming a burden to the American taxpayer. When a prospective borrower approached a lender for an FHA-secured home loan, the FHA reviewed the borrower's income, expenses, assets, and debts. The objective was to determine if there was adequate room in the borrower's budget for the proposed loan payments. The FHA also sent inspectors to the property to make certain that it was of acceptable construction quality and to determine its fair market value. To offset losses that would still inevitably occur, the FHA charged the borrower an annual insurance fee of approximately ½ of 1% of the balance owed on his loan. The FHA was immensely successful in its task. Not only did it create construction jobs, but it raised the level of housing quality in the nation and, in a pleasant surprise to taxpayers, actually returned annual profits to the U.S. Treasury. In response to its success, in 1946 Congress changed its status from temporary to permanent.

The FHA has had a marked influence on lending policies in the real estate industry. Foremost among these is the widespread acceptance of the high loan-to-value, fully amortized loan. In the 1930s, lenders required FHA insurance before making 80% L/V loans. By the 1960s, lenders were readily making 80% L/V loans without FHA insurance. Meanwhile, the FHA insurance program was working so well that the FHA raised the portion it was willing to insure. By 1985, the FHA offered to insure a lender for 97% of the first $50,000 of appraised value and 95% above that to a maximum loan of $67,500 to $90,000. To illustrate, on a $60,000 home the FHA would insure 97% of the first $50,000 and 95% of the remaining $10,000, for a total of $58,000. This means a cash down payment of only $2,000 for the buyer. The borrower is not permitted to use a second mortgage to raise this $2,000. The FHA requires some down payment; otherwise, it is too easy for the borrower to walk away from the debt and leave the FHA to pay the lender's insurance claim. Please be aware that the maximum amount the FHA will insure varies from city to city and is changed from time to time by the FHA.

Current FHA Coverage

Besides allowing a low down payment, FHA loans are popular because they are 30-year, fixed-rate loans that can be assumed without an increase in interest. Moreover, FHA loans can be repaid early without a prepayment penalty. Thus, in a period of rising interest rates, a seller can pass along the benefits of an existing low-interest rate loan to the buyer. This means the seller can get more money for the property than if the buyer had to completely refinance at a higher rate of interest. If interest rates in the open market fall below the rate on the FHA loan, the borrower can get a new loan and repay the FHA loan ahead of schedule without penalty.

Assumability

The major disadvantage of an FHA loan is the low loan limit. The FHA's mission is to serve buyers with limited funds who are looking for modestly priced housing. It is possible to get an FHA loan on a more expensive home, but the buyer must make such a large down payment that an FHA loan becomes impractical. You will, however, find existing FHA loans on more expensive homes in the resale market. This is because the loan was written 10 or 20 years ago and the value of the home has risen from modest to expensive since then. Nonetheless, these homes are often eagerly sought by buyers because the existing FHA loan is assumable and may carry an interest rate several percentage points below current market rates. Furthermore, a second mortgage can be used to finance the difference between the existing FHA loan and the buyer's down payment.

Mortgage Insurance

From 1934 until September 1, 1983, the FHA charged an annual insurance premium of approximately ½ of 1% of the balance owing on the loan. This was added to the interest rate and collected each month as part of the borrower's regular monthly payment. Thus, an FHA loan made at 10% interest actually cost approximately 10½% per year once the FHA insurance premium was added. Loans made prior to that date still carry the annual charge.

Effective September 1, 1983, the FHA changed to a one-time lump-sum **mortgage insurance premium** (MIP) that is paid when the loan is made. The amount of the MIP is 3.8% of the loan amount and can be paid in cash or added to the amount borrowed. If borrowed, it can be over and above the FHA ceiling. Thus, if the ceiling is $90,000 and the loan requested is $90,000, the MIP will be $3,420 and the total amount financed will be $93,420. The $93,420 becomes the principal amount of the loan and an amortization table is used to find the monthly payment. If the loan is fully repaid within 11 years, the borrower is entitled to a refund of part of the MIP. After 11 years, there may be a partial refund depending on loan loss experience for the pool of loans that contains the borrower's particular loan. Borrowers under the old annual system may also be entitled to refunds on insurance premiums collected in excess of actual operating experience. In fact, the FHA has several tens of millions of dollars to refund but cannot locate the borrowers on these long-since repaid loans. (FHA borrowers who have repaid in full can contact the FHA to learn if they have a refund coming.)

Another major change in the way the FHA has done business occurred on November 30, 1983. Effective that date, interest rates on FHA loans were freed from government control. Prior to that date the FHA attempted to hold down interest rates by setting ceilings on how much a lender could charge. Whereas this might be a reasonably workable approach in times of stable interest rates, it created nightmares for buyers, sellers, lenders and real estate agents when interest rates spurted upward in the 1970s and early 1980s. What happened was that a seller would put his (or her) home on the market. A buyer would see it and make an acceptable offer subject to obtaining an FHA loan. The FHA would appraise the property, evaluate the borrower and agree to insure a loan. The FHA limited the number of points a borrower could pay to 1 point for existing homes and 2½ points for homes under construction. These were usually consumed by loan origination costs. The FHA required the seller to pay any additional points.

Interest Rate Ceilings

With only two exceptions since 1950, the FHA ceiling was below the prevailing rates on **conventional loans;** i.e., loans not insured by the FHA or guaranteed by the Veterans Administration (VA). When the FHA ceiling was below the market rate on conventional loans, lenders would not make FHA loans unless they were paid discount points. For example, if the open market rate was 12½% and the FHA ceiling was 12%, it was necessary to offer the lender enough discount points to raise the effective yield of the 12% FHA loan to 12½%. This amounted to 4 points. But since the buyer was limited to 1 point and that was used for origination costs, the 4 points came from the seller's pocket. Suppose the loan amount was $60,000. This amounted to $2,400 in points the seller would have to pay so the buyer could enjoy the privilege of obtaining a loan with an interest rate ½ of 1% below the market.

By placing yourself in the seller's position, you can see the situation this creates. A buyer making an offer under

Seller's Position

the above conditions is in effect asking you to take a $2,400 cut in price. If you were planning on reducing your price $2,400 anyway, you would accept the offer. However, if you felt you could readily sell at your price to a buyer not requiring seller's points, you would refuse the offer. The alternative is to price the property high enough to allow for anticipated points. However, this is an effective solution only if your price does not exceed the FHA appraisal or VA certificate of reasonable value. If it does, the FHA or VA buyer is either prohibited from buying or must make a larger cash down payment.

Buyers, sellers, lenders and real estate agents can learn to live with the above conditions if interest rates remain fairly stable. But such a system is difficult at best when interest rates change rapidly and/or FHA ceilings change between the date the purchase contract was signed and the day the deed is delivered. Horror stories abound of times when a seller agreed to an FHA sale when the number of points required of the seller was 4 at the time the purchase contract was signed and 8 to 12 by the time the deed was to be delivered. (This would be caused by a market rise without a ceiling increase.) Buyers, meanwhile, would secretly hope the ceiling would not be raised before the closing day.

Floating Interest Rates

Fixed-rate FHA loans are now negotiable and float with the market, and the seller now has a choice in how many points to contribute toward the borrower's loan. This can be none, some or all the points, and the seller can even pay the borrower's MIP. Typical purchase contract language is, "The seller will pay X points and the buyer will pay not more than Y points and the agreed upon interest rate is Z%." Thus, "X" is the contribution the seller will make, and the seller is protected from having to pay more. The buyer will pay any additional points, but not more than "Y" points. Beyond that, the buyer can cancel the purchase contract. That would happen if the market rates rose quickly while the rate at "Z" is fixed.

Other FHA Programs

Thus far, we have been concentrating on the FHA's most popular program—mortgage insurance on single-family houses. The FHA's authority to offer this is found in **Section 203(b)** of Title II of the National Housing Act. These loans are commonly referred to as "Section 203b" loans. However, the FHA administers a number of other real estate mortgage insurance programs and several of the better known will be mentioned now.

Under **Section 203(k)** the FHA insures mortgage loans made to finance home improvements. Under **Section 234** the FHA insures loans on condominium units in a manner similar to Section 203(b). **Section 213** insures loans for cooperative housing projects. **Section 235** offers a single-family residence loan subsidy program.

Under **Section 245** the FHA will insure a graduated payment mortgage (GPM). This loan format allows the borrower to make smaller payments initially and to increase payment size gradually over time. The idea is to parallel the borrower's rising earning capacity. (GPMs will receive more coverage in Chapter 12.) The FHA also insures adjustable rate mortgage loans with a program started in mid-1984. These are available to owner-occupants under Section 203(b) and 203(k) and carry an interest rate tied to one-year U.S. Treasury securities. The rate can be adjusted up or down by not more than 1% annually or 5% over the life of the loan. Negative amortization—the addition of unpaid interest to the principal balance—is prohibited. (Adjustable loans will also receive more attention in Chapter 12.)

Loan Qualification

Before leaving the topic of the FHA it is interesting to note that much of what we take for granted as standard loan practice today was the result of FHA innovation years ago. As already noted, standard real estate loan practice called for short-term renewable loans before 1934. Then the FHA boldly offered 20-year amortized loans. Once these were shown to be successful investments for lenders, loans without FHA insurance were made for 20 years. Later, when the FHA successfully went to 30 years, non-FHA-insured loans followed. The FHA also established loan application review techniques that have been widely accepted and copied throughout the real estate industry. The biggest step in this direction was to analyze a borrower's loan application in terms of his earning power. Prior to 1934, emphasis had been placed on how large the borrower's assets were, a measurement that tended to exclude all but the already financially well-to-do from home ownership. Since 1934, the emphasis has shifted primarily to the borrower's ability to meet monthly PITI payments. The rule of thumb today is that no more than 38% of a person's before-tax monthly income should go to the repayment of fixed monthly obligations, including monthly PITI payments.

Construction Regulations   Since its inception, the FHA has imposed its own minimum construction requirements. Often this was essential where local building codes did not exist or were weaker than the FHA wanted. Before issuing a loan, particularly on new construction, the FHA would impose minimum requirements as to the quantity and quality of building materials to be used. Lot size, street access, landscaping, siting and general house design also were required to fit within broad FHA guidelines. During construction, an FHA inspector would come to the property several times to check if work was being done correctly.

The reason for such care in building standards was the FHA recognized that if a building is defective either from a design or construction standpoint, the borrower is more likely to default on the loan and create an insurance claim against the FHA. Furthermore, the same defects will lower the price the property will bring at its foreclosure sale, thus increasing losses to the FHA. Because building codes are now becoming stricter and more standardized in states, counties and cities, the FHA anticipates eliminating its own minimum property standards.

As we leave the FHA and go to the Veterans Administration, keep in mind that the FHA is not a lender. The FHA is an insurance agency. The loan itself is obtained from a savings and loan, mortgage company, bank or similar lender. In addition to principal and interest payments, the lender collects an insurance premium from the borrower which is forwarded to the FHA. The FHA, in turn, guarantees repayment of the loan to the lender. This arrangement makes lenders much more willing to loan to buyers who are putting only 3% to 5% cash down. Thus, when you hear the phrase "FHA loan" in real estate circles, know that it is an FHA-*insured* loan, not a loan from the FHA.

To show its appreciation to servicemen returning from World War II, in 1944 Congress passed far-reaching legislation to aid veterans in education, hospitalization, employment training and housing. In housing, the popularly named G.I. Bill of Rights empowered the comptroller general of the United States to guarantee the repayment of a portion of first mortgage real estate loans made to veterans. For this guarantee, no fee would be charged to the veteran. Rather, the government itself would stand the losses. The original 1944 law provided that lenders would be guaranteed against losses up to 50% of the amount of the loan, but in no case more than $2,000.

VETERANS ADMINISTRATION

The objective was to make it possible for a veteran to buy a home with no cash down payment. Thus, on a house offered for sale at $5,000 (houses were much cheaper in 1944) this guarantee enabled a veteran to borrow the entire $5,000. From the lender's standpoint, having the top $2,000 of the loan guaranteed by the U.S. government offered the same asset protection as a $2,000 cash down payment. If the veteran defaulted and the property went into foreclosure, the lender had to net less than $3,000 before suffering a loss.

No Down Payment

In 1945, Congress increased the guarantee amount to $4,000 and 60% of the loan and turned the entire operation over to the Veterans Administration (VA). The VA was quick to honor claims, and the program rapidly became popular with lenders. Furthermore, the veterans turned out to be excellent credit risks, bettering, in fact, the good record of FHA-insured homeowners. (The FHA recognizes this and gives higher insurance limits to FHA borrowers who have served in the Armed Forces.) The program blossomed, and to date over 10 million home loans have been guaranteed by the VA, over two-thirds of them with no down payment.

To keep up with the increased cost of homes, the guarantee has been increased several times and in early 1986 was at $27,500. Generally, a $27,500 guarantee means a veteran can purchase up to a $110,000 home with no down payment, provided, of course, that the veteran has enough income to support the monthly PITI payments. Some lenders will go higher if the borrower makes a down payment. Also, the guarantee amount and rules are subject to change by Congress and the VA.

In the original G.I. Bill of 1944, eligibility was limited to World War II veterans. However, subsequent legislation has broadened eligibility to include any veteran who served for a period of at least 90 days in the armed forces of the United States, or an ally, between September 16, 1940, and July 25, 1947, or between June 27, 1950, and January 31, 1955. Any veteran of the United States who has served at least 181 days of continuous active duty since January 31, 1955, to the present is also eligible. If service was during the Viet Nam conflict period (August 5, 1964 to May 7, 1975) 90 days is sufficient to qualify. The veteran's discharge must be on conditions other than dishonorable and the guarantee entitlement is good until used. If not remarried, the spouse of a veteran who died as a result of service can also obtain a housing guarantee. Active duty personnel can also qualify. Shorter active duty periods are allowed for service-connected disabilities.

VA Certificates   To determine benefits, a veteran should make application to the Veterans Administration for a **certificate of eligibility.** This shows if the veteran is qualified and the amount of guarantee available. It is also one of the documents necessary to obtain a VA-guaranteed loan.

The VA works diligently to protect veterans and reduce foreclosure losses. When a veteran applies for a VA guarantee, the property is appraised and the VA issues a **certificate of reasonable value.** Often abbreviated **CRV,** it informs the veteran of the appraised value of the property and the maximum VA guaranteed loan a private lender may make. Similarly, the VA establishes income guidelines to make certain that the veteran can comfortably meet the proposed loan payments. Also, the veteran must agree to occupy the property.

The VA will guarantee fixed-rate loans for as long as 30 years on homes, and there is no prepayment penalty if the borrower wishes to pay sooner. Moreover, there is no due-on-sale clause that requires the loan to be repaid if the property is sold. The VA will guarantee loans for the purchase of townhouses and condominiums, to build or improve a home, and to buy a mobile home as a residence. A veteran wishing to refinance his existing home or farm can obtain a VA-guaranteed loan provided there is existing debt that will be repaid. The VA will also make direct loans to veterans if there are no private lending institutions nearby.

No matter what loan guarantee program is elected, the veteran should know that in the event of default and subsequent foreclosure he is required to eventually make good any losses suffered by the VA on his loan. (This is not the case with FHA-insured loans. There the borrower pays for protection against foreclosure losses that may result from his loan.) Even if the veteran sells the property and the buyer assumes the VA loan, the veteran is still financially responsible if the buyer later defaults. To avoid this, the veteran must arrange with the VA to be released from liability.

Financial Liability

A veteran is permitted a full new guarantee entitlement if complete repayment of a previous VA-guaranteed loan has been made. If a veteran has sold and let the buyer assume his VA loan, the balance of the entitlement is still available. For example, if a veteran has used $15,000 of his (her) entitlement to date, the difference between $15,000 and the current VA guarantee amount is still available for use.

From its inception until October 1, 1982, the VA made loan guarantees on behalf of veterans without a charge. Then starting on that date a ½ of 1% fee was charged at the time of loan funding. In 1984, this **funding fee** was raised to 1% of the loan amount. A major reason has been loan losses. Until the beginning of the 1980 decade, increasing real estate prices coupled with good repayment records of veterans enabled the VA to avoid any sizable losses. But that has changed, and by mid-1985 the VA had thousands of homes that it had to take from lenders because veterans had stopped making payments. The VA has been selling these through price reductions and attractive financing to anyone willing to buy

Funding Fee

who can make the payments. (The FHA also offers foreclosed properties for sale.)

As of early 1986, the VA still set interest rate ceilings on the loans it will guarantee. This is nearly the same system as the FHA used until November 30, 1983, at which time the FHA switched to floating rates. If floating rates work well for the FHA, the VA will probably adopt the idea.

As Congress frequently changes eligibility and benefits, a person contemplating a VA or FHA loan should make inquiry to the field offices of these two agencies and to mortgage lenders to ascertain the current status and details of the law, as well as the availability of loan money. Field offices also have information on foreclosed properties that are for sale. Additionally, one should query lenders as to the availability of state veteran benefits. A number of states offer special advantages, including mortgage loan assistance, to residents who have served in the armed forces.

PRIVATE MORTGAGE INSURANCE

In 1957, the Mortgage Guaranty Insurance Corporation (MGIC) was formed in Milwaukee, Wisconsin, as a privately owned business venture to insure home mortgage loans. Demand was slow but steady for the first 10 years but then grew rapidly and today there are over a dozen private mortgage insurance companies. Like FHA insurance, the object of **private mortgage insurance (PMI)** is to insure lenders against foreclosure losses. But unlike the FHA, PMI insures only the top 20% to 25% of a loan, not the whole loan. This allows a lender to make 90% and 95% L/V loans with about the same exposure to foreclosure losses as a 70% to 75% L/V loan. The borrower, meanwhile, can purchase a home with a cash down payment of either 10% or 5% rather than the 20% to 30% down required by lenders when mortgage insurance is not purchased. For this privilege the borrower pays a PMI fee of 1% or less when the loan is made plus an annual fee of a fraction of 1%. When the loan is partially repaid (for example, to a 70% L/V), the premiums and coverage can be terminated. PMI is also available on apartment buildings, offices, stores, warehouses and leaseholds but at higher rates than on homes.

Private mortgage insurers work to keep their losses to a minimum by first approving the lenders with whom they will do business. Particular emphasis is placed on the lender's operating policy, appraisal procedure and degree of government regulation. Once approved, a lender simply sends the borrower's loan application, credit report and property appraisal to the insurer. Based on these documents, the insurer either agrees or refuses to issue a policy. Although the insurer relies on the appraisal prepared by the lender, on a random basis the insurer sends its own appraiser to verify the quality of the information being submitted. When an insured loan goes into default, the insurer has the option of either buying the property from the lender for the balance due or letting the lender foreclose and then paying the lender's losses up to the amount of the insurance. As a rule, insurers take the first option because it is more popular with the lenders and it leaves the lender with immediate cash to re-lend. The insurer is then responsible for foreclosing.

Approval Procedure

The **Farmer's Home Administration (FmHA)** is a federal agency under the U.S. Department of Agriculture. Like the FHA, it came into existence due to the financial crises of the 1930s. The FmHA offers programs to help purchase or operate farms. The FmHA will either guarantee a portion of a loan made by a private lender or it will make the loan itself. FmHA loans can also be used to help finance the purchase of homes in rural areas.

FARMER'S HOME ADMINISTRATION

The **Federal Consumer Credit Protection Act,** popularly known as the **Truth in Lending Act,** went into effect in 1969. The act, implemented by Federal Reserve Board **Regulation Z,** requires that a borrower be clearly shown how much he is paying for credit in both dollar terms and percentage terms before committing to the loan. The borrower is also given the right to rescind (cancel) the transaction in certain instances. The act came into being because it was not uncommon to see loans advertised for rates lower than the borrower actually wound up paying. Once put into use, several weaknesses and ambiguities of the act and Regulation Z became

TRUTH IN LENDING ACT

apparent. Thus, the **Truth in Lending Simplification and Reform Act** (TILSRA) was passed by Congress and became effective October 1, 1982. Concurrently, the Federal Reserve Board issued a **Revised Regulation Z** (RRZ) which details rules and regulations for TILSRA. For purposes of discussion we will refer to all of this as the Truth in Lending Act, or TIL for short.

Advertising
Whether you are a real estate agent or a property owner acting on your own behalf, TIL rules affect you when you advertise just about anything (including real estate) and include financing terms in the ad. If an advertisement contains any one of the TIL list of financing terms (called **trigger terms** and explained below), the ad must also include other required information. For example, an advertisement that reads: "Bargain! Bargain! Bargain! New 3-bedroom townhouses only $499 per month" may or may not be a bargain depending on other financing information missing from the ad.

Trigger Terms
If an ad contains any of the following trigger terms, five specific disclosures must be included in the ad. Here are the trigger terms: the amount of down payment (for example, only 5% down, 10% down, $4,995 down, 95% financing); the amount of any payment (for example, monthly payments only $499, buy for less than $650 a month, payments only 1% per month); the number of payments (for example, only 36 monthly payments and you own it, all paid up in 10 annual payments); the period of repayment (for example, 30-year financing, owner will carry for five years, 10-year second available); and the dollar amount of any finance charge (finance this for only $999) or the statement that there is no charge for credit (pay no interest for three years).

If any of the above trigger terms is used, then the following five disclosures must appear in the ad. They are (1) the cash price or the amount of the loan; (2) the amount of down payment or a statement that none is required; (3) the number, amount and frequency of repayments; (4) the annual percentage rate; and (5) the deferred payment price or total payments. Item 5 is not a requirement in the case of the sale of a dwelling or a loan secured by a first lien on the dwelling that is being purchased.

The **annual percentage rate** (APR) combines the interest rate with the other costs of the loan into a single figure that shows the true annual cost of borrowing. This is one of the most helpful features of the law as it gives the prospective borrower a standardized yardstick by which to compare financing from different sources.

Annual Percentage Rate (APR)

If the annual percentage rate being offered is subject to increase after the transaction takes place (such as with an adjustable rate mortgage), that fact must be stated. For example, "12% annual percentage rate subject to increase after settlement." If the loan has interest rate changes that will follow a predetermined schedule, those terms must be stated. For example, "8% first year, 10% second year, 12% third year, 14% remainder of loan, 13.5% annual percentage rate."

If you wish to say something about financing and avoid triggering full disclosure, you may use general statements. The following would be acceptable: "assumable loan," "financing available," "owner will carry," "terms to fit your budget," "easy monthly payments," or "FHA and VA financing available."

If you are in the business of making loans, the Truth in Lending Act requires you to make 18 disclosures to your borrower. Of these, the four that must be most prominently displayed on the papers the borrower signs are (1) the amount financed, (2) the finance charge, (3) the annual percentage rate and (4) the total payments.

Lending Disclosures

The **amount financed** is the amount of credit provided to the borrower. The **finance charge** is the total dollar amount the credit will cost the borrower over the life of the loan. This includes such things as interest, borrower-paid discount points, loan fees, loan finder's fees, loan service fees, required life insurance, and mortgage guarantee premiums. On a long-term mortgage loan, the total finance charge can easily exceed the amount of money being borrowed. For example, the total amount of interest on a 9%, 30-year, $60,000 loan is $113,880.

The annual percentage rate was just described. The **total payments** is the amount in dollars the borrower will have paid after making all the payments as scheduled. In the previous 9%, 30-year loan it would be the interest of $113,880 plus the principal of $60,000 for a total of $173,880.

The other 14 disclosures that a lender must make are as follows: (1) the identity of the lender; (2) the payment schedule; (3) prepayment penalties and rebates; (4) late payment charges; (5) any insurance required; (6) any filing fees; (7) any collateral required; (8) any required deposits; (9) whether the loan can be assumed; (10) the demand feature, if the note has one; (11) the total sales price of the item being purchased if the seller is also the creditor; (12) any adjustable rate features of the loan; (13) an itemization of the amount financed; and (14) a reference to any terms not shown on the disclosure statement but which are shown on the loan contract.

These disclosures must be delivered or mailed to the credit applicant within three business days after the creditor receives the applicant's written request for credit. The applicant must have this information before the transaction can take place; e.g., before the closing can take place.

Who Must Comply?   Any person or firm that regularly extends consumer credit subject to a finance charge (such as interest) or payable by written agreement in more than four installments must comply with the lending disclosures. This includes banks, savings and loans, credit unions, finance companies, etc., and private individuals who extend credit more than five times a year.

Whoever is named on the note as the creditor must make the lending disclosures even if the note is to be resold. A key difference between the old and the new TIL acts is that the new TIL act does not include mortgage brokers or real estate agents as creditors just because they broker a deal containing financing. This is because they do not appear as creditors on the note. But if a broker takes back a note for part of the commission on a deal, that is the extension of credit and the 18 lending disclosures must be made.

Exempt Transactions   Certain transactions are exempt from the lending disclosure requirement. The first exemption is for credit extended primarily for business, commercial, or agricultural purposes. This exemption includes dwelling units purchased for rental purposes (unless the property contains four units or less and the owner occupies one of them, in which case special rules apply).

The second exemption applies to credit over $25,000 secured by personal property unless the property is the principal residence of the borrower. For example, a mobile home that secures a loan over $25,000 qualifies under this exemption if it is used as a vacation home. But it is not exempt if it is used as a principal residence.

If the Federal Trade Commission (FTC) determines that an advertiser has broken the law, the FTC can order the advertiser to cease from further violations. Each violation of that order can result in a $10,000 civil penalty each day the violation continues.   *Failure to Disclose*

Failure to properly disclose when credit is extended can result in a penalty of twice the amount of the finance charge with a minimum of $100 and a maximum of $1,000 plus court costs, attorney fees, and actual damages. In addition the FTC can add a fine of up to $5,000 and/or one year imprisonment. If the required disclosures are not made or the borrower is not given the required 3 days to cancel (see below), the borrower can cancel the transaction at any time within 3 years following the date of the transaction. In that event the creditor must return all money paid by the borrower, and the borrower returns the property to the creditor.

A borrower has a limited right to rescind (cancel) a credit transaction. The borrower has 3 business days (counting Saturdays) to back out after signing the loan papers. This aspect of the law was inserted primarily to protect a homeowner from unscrupulous sellers of home improvements and appliances where the credit to purchase is secured by a lien on the home. Vacant lots for sale on credit to buyers who expect to use them for principal residences are also subject to cancellation privileges.   *Right to Cancel*

The right to rescind does not apply to credit used for the acquisition or initial construction of one's principal dwelling.

Summary　　　Truth In Lending regulations are complex and only the highlights have been presented here. If you are involved in transactions that require disclosure, you should seek more information from your local real estate board, lender, attorney or the FTC. Note that the whole topic of truth in lending deals only with disclosure—who must disclose, in what types of situations, what must be disclosed, etc. Truth In Lending legislation does not set the price a lender can charge for a loan. That is determined by supply and demand for funds in the marketplace and, to a lesser degree, by usury laws.

LOAN APPLICATION AND APPROVAL　　　When a mortgage lender reviews a real estate loan application, the primary concern for both applicant and lender is to approve loan requests that show a high probability of being repaid in full and on time, and to disapprove requests that are likely to result in default and eventual foreclosure. How is this decision made? Figure 11:3 summarizes the key items that a loan officer considers when making a decision regarding a loan request. Let us review these items and observe how they affect the acceptability of a loan to a lender.

In section ①, the lender begins the loan analysis procedure by looking at the property and the proposed financing. Using the property address and legal description, an appraiser is assigned to prepare an appraisal of the property and a title search is ordered. These steps are taken to determine the fair market value of the property and the condition of title. In the event of default, this is the collateral the lender must fall back upon to recover the loan. If the loan request is in connection with a purchase, rather than the refinancing of an existing property, the lender will know the purchase price. As a rule, loans are made on the basis of the appraised value or purchase price, whichever is lower. If the appraised value is lower than the purchase price, the usual procedure is to require the buyer to make a larger cash down payment. The lender does not want to overlend simply because the buyer overpaid for the property.

Continuing in section ①, the year the home was built is requested in order to give the lender some indication of the age of the structure. Note however, chronological age is only part of the loan decision because age must be considered in light of the upkeep and repair of the structure and its construction quality. "No. Units" refers to the number of dwelling units in the structure. For a single-family house this would be 1. For **a duplex,** it's 2; **a triplex,** 3; and **a fourplex,** 4. In a convention that has its roots in FHA history, residential structures containing 1, 2, 3, or 4 units are processed as residential properties. Structures of 5 or more dwelling units are processed as income properties, a topic you will learn more about in Chapter 16 under "Income Approach."

In the past, it was not uncommon for lenders to refuse to make loans in certain neighborhoods regardless of the quality of the structure or the ability of the borrower to repay. This was known as **redlining,** and it effectively shut off mortgage loans in many older or so-called "bad risk" neighborhoods across the country. Today a lender cannot refuse to make a loan simply because of the age or location of a property, or because of neighborhood income level, or because of the racial, ethnic or religious composition of the neighborhood.

Redlining

A lender can refuse to lend on a structure intended for demolition, a property in a known geological hazard area, a single-family dwelling in an area devoted to industrial or commercial use or upon a property that is in violation of zoning laws, deed covenants, conditions or restrictions, or significant health, safety or building codes.

The lender next looks at the amount of down payment the borrower proposes to make, the size of the loan being requested and the amount of other financing the borrower plans to use. This information is then converted into loan-to-value ratios. As a rule, the larger the down payment, the safer the loan is for the lender. On an uninsured loan, the ideal loan-to-value (L/V) ratio for a lender on owner-occupied residential property is 70% or less. This means the value of the property would have to fall more than 30% before the debt owed would exceed the property's value, thus encouraging the borrower to stop making loan payments.

Loan-to-Value Ratios

Loan-to-value ratios from 70% through 80% are considered acceptable but do expose the lender to more risk. Lenders sometimes compensate by charging slightly higher interest

Figure 11:3

RESIDENTIAL MORTGAGE LOAN ANALYSIS

① Property address _____
Legal description _____
Appraised value $ _____ Purchase price $ _____ Year Built _____ No. Units _____
Down payment $ _____ Total cash required for settlement $ _____
Amount of this mortgage loan $ _____ Other financing $ _____
Loan-to-value ratio: This mortgage loan _____ % All financing for the property _____ %
Source of settlement funds? _____
Purpose of loan? _____ Occupancy of property? _____
Attitude of borrower _____

② Borrower

Name _____
Age _____ Marital status _____ School years _____
Present address _____ Years _____ Own _____ Rent _____
Former address _____ Years _____ Own _____ Rent _____
Dependents other than co-borrower _____
Number _____ Ages _____
Employer _____
Years with current employer _____ Years this line of work _____
Position/Title _____
Type of business _____
Self-employed? _____
Previous employer _____
Position _____ Years _____

③ Co-Borrower

Name _____
Age _____ Marital status _____ School years _____
Present address _____ Years _____ Own _____ Rent _____
Former address _____ Years _____ Own _____ Rent _____
Dependents other than co-borrower _____
Number _____ Ages _____
Employer _____
Years with current employer _____ Years this line of work _____
Position/Title _____
Type of business _____
Self-employed? _____
Previous employer _____
Position _____ Years _____

262

④ Gross Monthly Income

	Borrower	Co-borrower
Base income	$ _____	$ _____
Overtime	_____	_____
Bonuses	_____	_____
Commissions	_____	_____
Interest/Dividends	_____	_____
Rental income	_____	_____
Social Security	_____	_____
Retirement income	_____	_____
Other	_____	_____
Total	$ _____	$ _____

⑤ Monthly Housing Expense

	Previous	Proposed
Rent	$ _____	$ _____
First loan (P + 1)	_____	_____
Other loans (P + 1)	_____	_____
Mortgage insurance	_____	_____
Hazard insurance	_____	_____
Real estate taxes	_____	_____
Assessments	_____	_____
Owners' Assn.	_____	_____
Utilities	_____	_____
Total	$ _____	$ _____

Ratio of monthly housing expense to gross monthly income _____ % ⑥

⑦ Assets

Cash toward purchase	$ _____
Checking and savings	_____
Stocks and bonds	_____
Life insurance cash value	_____
(Face amount $ _____)	
Sub-total liquid assets	$ _____
Real estate owned	_____
Retirement fund	_____
Net worth of business	_____
Automobiles	_____
Furniture	_____
Other assets	_____
Total Assets	$ _____

⑧ Liabilities

	Mo. Pymt/Mos.	Balance
Installment debts	$ _____ / _____	$ _____
	_____ / _____	_____
	_____ / _____	_____
Auto loan	_____ / _____	_____
Real estate loans	_____ / _____	_____
Other debts	_____ / _____	_____
	_____ / _____	_____
Alimony/Child support	_____ / _____	_____
Total Mo. Payments	$ _____	
Total Debts		$ _____

Net Worth: Total assets minus total debts equals $ _____ ⑨

⑩ List credit references _____

Have you declared bankruptcy in the last 7 years? _____ Any pending lawsuits? _____

Any outstanding judgments? _____ Have you ever had property foreclosed upon? _____

Is either applicant a co-maker or endorse on any other loans? _____

263

rates. Loan-to-value ratios above 80% present even more risk of default to the lender, and the lender will either increase the interest rate charged on these loans or require that an outside insurer, such as the FHA or a private mortgage insurer, be supplied by the borrower.

Settlement Funds   Next in section ①, the lender wants to know if the borrower has adequate funds for settlement. Are these funds presently in a checking or savings account, or are they coming from the sale of the borrower's present property? In the latter case, the lender knows the present loan is contingent on closing that escrow. If the down payment and settlement funds are to be borrowed, then the lender will want to be extra cautious as experience has shown that the less money a borrower personally puts into a purchase, the higher the probability of default and foreclosure.

Purpose of Loan   The lender is also interested in the proposed use of the property. Lenders feel most comfortable when a loan is for the purchase or improvement of a property the loan applicant will actually occupy. This is because owner-occupants usually have pride-of-ownership in maintaining their property and even during bad economic conditions will continue to make the monthly payments. An owner-occupant also realizes that losing the home still means paying for shelter elsewhere. It is standard practice for lenders to ask loan applicants to sign a statement stating whether or not they intend to occupy the property.

If the loan applicant intends to purchase a dwelling to rent out as an investment, the lender will be more cautious. This is because during periods of high vacancy, the property may not generate enough income to meet the loan payments. At that point, a strapped-for-cash borrower is likely to default. Note too, that lenders generally avoid loans secured by purely speculative real estate. If the value of the property drops below the amount owed, the borrower may see no further logic in making the loan payments.

Lastly in this section, the lender assesses the borrower's attitude toward the proposed loan. A casual attitude, such as "I'm buying because real estate always goes up," or an applicant who does not appear to understand the obligation being undertaken would bring a low rating here. Much more welcome is the applicant who shows a mature attitude and understanding of the loan obligation and who exhibits a strong and logical desire for ownership.

In sections ② and ③ the lender begins an analysis of the borrower, and if there is one, the co-borrower. At one time, age, sex and marital status played an important role in the lender's decision to lend or not to lend. Often the young and the old had trouble getting loans, as did women and persons who were single, divorced or widowed. Today, the Federal Equal Credit Opportunity Act prohibits discrimination based on age, sex, race and marital status. Lenders are no longer permitted to discount income earned by women from part-time jobs or because the woman is of child-bearing age. If the applicant chooses to disclose it, alimony, separate maintenance and child support must be counted in full. Young adults and single persons cannot be turned down because the lender feels they have not "put down roots." Seniors cannot be turned down as long as life expectancy exceeds the early risk period of the loan and collateral is adequate. In other words, the emphasis in borrower analysis is now focused on job stability, income adequacy, net worth and credit rating.

Borrower Analysis

Thus in sections ② and ③ we see questions directed at how long the applicants have held their present jobs and the stability of those jobs themselves. An applicant who possesses marketable job skills and has been regularly employed with a stable employer is considered the ideal risk. Persons whose income can rise and fall erratically, such as commissioned salespersons, present greater risks. Persons whose skills (or lack of skills) or lack of job seniority result in frequent unemployment are more likely to have difficulty repaying a loan. In these sections the lender also inquires as to the number of dependents the applicant must support out of his or her income. This information provides some insight as to how much will be left for monthly house payments.

In section ④ the lender looks at the amount and sources of the applicants' income. Quantity alone is not enough for loan approval since the income sources must be stable too.

Monthly Income

Thus a lender will look carefully at overtime, bonus and commission income in order to estimate the levels at which these may be expected to continue. Interest, dividend and rental income is considered in light of the stability of their sources also. Income from social security and retirement pensions is entered and added to the totals for the applicants. Alimony, child support and separate maintenance payments received need not be revealed. However, such sums must be listed in order to be considered as a basis for repaying the loan.

In section ⑤ the lender compares what the applicants have been paying for housing with what they will be paying if the loan is approved. Included in the proposed housing expense total are principal, interest, taxes and insurance along with any assessments or homeowner association dues (such as in a condominium). Some lenders add the monthly cost of utilities to this list.

At ⑥, proposed monthly housing expense is compared to gross monthly income. A general rule of thumb is that monthly housing expense (PITI) should not exceed 25% to 30% of gross monthly income. A second guideline is that total fixed monthly expenses should not exceed 33% to 38% of income. This includes housing payments plus automobile payments, installment loan payments, alimony, child support and investments with negative cash flows. These are general guidelines, but lenders recognize that food, health care, clothing, transportation, entertainment and income taxes must also come from the applicants' income.

Assets and Liabilities   In section ⑦ the lender is interested in the applicants' sources of funds for closing and whether, once the loan is granted, the applicants have assets to fall back upon in the event of an income decrease (a job lay-off) or unexpected expenses (hospital bills). Of particular interest is the portion of those assets that are in cash or are readily convertible into cash in a few days. These are called **liquid assets.** If income drops, they are much more useful in meeting living expenses and loan payments than assets that may require months to sell and convert to cash; that is, assets which are **illiquid.**

Note in section ⑦ that two values are shown for life insurance. **Cash value** is the amount of money the policyholder would receive if the policy were surrendered to the insurance company or, alternatively, the amount the policy-holder could borrow against the policy. **Face amount** is the amount that would be paid in the event of the insured's death. Lenders feel most comfortable if the face amount of the policy equals or exceeds the amount of the proposed loan. Obviously a borrower's death is not anticipated before the loan is repaid, but lenders recognize that its possibility increases the probability of default. The likelihood of foreclosure is lessened considerably if the survivors receive life insurance benefits.

In section ⑧, the lender is interested in the applicants' existing debts and liabilities for two reasons. First, these items will compete each month against housing expenses for available monthly income. Thus high monthly payments in this section may reduce the size of the loan the lender calculates that the applicants will be able to repay. The presence of monthly liabilities is not all negative: it can also show the lender that the applicants are capable of repaying their debts. Second, the applicants' total debts are subtracted from their total assets to obtain their **net worth,** reported at ⑨. If the result is negative (more owed than owned) the loan request will probably be turned down as too risky. In contrast, a substantial net worth can often offset weaknesses elsewhere in the application, such as too little monthly income in relation to monthly housing expense or an income that can rise and fall erratically.

References, etc. At number ⑩, lenders ask for credit references as an indicator of the future. Applicants with no previous credit experience will have more weight placed on income and employment history. Applicants with a history of collections, adverse judgments, foreclosure or bankruptcy will have to convince the lender that this loan will be repaid on time. Additionally, the applicants may be considered poorer risks if they have guaranteed the repayment of someone else's debt by acting as a co-maker or endorser.

Credit Report As part of the loan application, the lender will order a **credit report** on the applicant(s). The applicant is asked to authorize this and to pay for the report. This provides the lender with an independent means of checking the applicant's credit history. A credit report that shows active use of credit with a good repayment record and no derogatory information is most desirable. The applicant will be asked by the lender to explain any negative information. Because it is possible for inaccurate or untrue information in a credit report to unfairly damage a person's credit reputation, Congress passed the **Fair Credit Reporting Act.** This act gives an individual the right to inspect his or her file at a credit bureau, correct any errors and make explanatory statements to supplement the file.

OVERVIEW

In this chapter you received a good grounding in the mechanics of term loans, amortized loans, balloon loans, partially amortized loans, loan-to-value and equity. Also, you learned something about the functions and importance of the FHA, the VA, private mortgage insurance, loan points and Truth In Lending legislation. Lastly you saw a sample of the type of information a lender requests and considers before granting a real estate loan. In the next chapter you will learn about real estate lenders from whom you can borrow and where those lenders get their money. You will also read about financing techniques that are popular in the United States today.

VOCABULARY REVIEW

Match terms **a-x** *with statements* **1–24.**

10	**a.** Amortized loan	15	**m.** Maturity
9	**b.** Annual percentage rate	18	**n.** Mortgage insurance
11	**c.** Balloon payment	20	**o.** Origination fee
8	**d.** Conventional loan	16	**p.** Partially amortized loan
6	**e.** CRV	3	**q.** PITI
12	**f.** Equity	7	**r.** Point
23	**g.** FmHA	1	**s.** Principal
14	**h.** Illiquid assets	22	**t.** Redlining
4	**i.** Impound account	19	**u.** Section 203(b)
24	**j.** Liquid assets	2	**v.** Term loan
17	**k.** Loan balance table	13	**w.** Truth In Lending
5	**l.** L/V ratio	21	**x.** Trigger term

1. Balance owing on a loan.
2. A loan that requires the borrower to pay interest only until maturity, at which time the full amount of the loan must be repaid.

3. Refers to a monthly loan payment that includes principal, interest, property taxes, and property insurance.

4. An escrow or reserve account into which the lender places the borrower's monthly tax and insurance payments.

5. The amount a lender will loan on a property divided by the valuation the lender places on the property.

6. A document issued by the Veterans Administration showing the VA's estimate of a property's value.

7. One hundredth of the total amount; 1% of a loan.

8. A real estate loan made without FHA insurance or a VA guarantee.

9. A uniform measure of the annual cost of credit.

10. A loan requiring periodic payments that include both interest and principal.

11. A payment that is larger than any of the previous payments.

12. The market value of a property less the debt against it.

13. A federal law that requires certain disclosures when extending or advertising credit.

14. Assets that may require months to sell and convert to cash.

15. The end of the life of a loan.

16. A loan with a series of amortized payments followed by a balloon payment at maturity.

17. Shows the principal still owing during the life of a loan.

18. Purchased and paid for by the borrower to protect the lender in the event of the borrower's default.

19. FHA's popular mortgage insurance program for houses.

20. The fee charged by a lender to make a loan.

21. Credit information used in advertising that requires additional credit disclosures.

22. Refusal to make a real estate loan based solely on the location of the property.

23. A federal agency under the U.S. Department of Agriculture that will help purchase and operate farms and finance homes in rural areas.

24. Assets that are in cash or are readily convertible to cash in a few days.

QUESTIONS AND PROBLEMS

1. What is the major risk that the borrower takes when he agrees to a loan with a balloon payment?

2. Explain how an amortized loan works.

3. Using Table 11:1, calculate the monthly payment necessary to completely amortize a $65,000, 30-year loan at 11½% interest.

4. A prospective home buyer has a $10,000 down payment and can afford $800 per month for principal and interest payments. If 30-year, 11% amortized loans are available, what price home can the buyer afford?

5. Same problem as in number 4 except that the interest rate has dropped to 9%. What price home can the buyer afford now?

6. Using Table 11:2, calculate the balance still owed on a $90,000, 9½% interest, 30-year amortized loan that is 10 years old.
7. Explain the purpose and operation of the FHA 203(b) home mortgage insurance program.
8. What advantage does the Veterans Administration offer veterans who wish to purchase a home?
9. Explain "points" and their application to real estate lending.
10. What is the basic purpose of the Truth in Lending Act?
11. Why is the monthly income of a loan applicant more important to a lender than the sheer size of the applicant's assets?

ADDITIONAL READINGS

The Complete Real Estate Math Book, rev. ed. by **Margie Sussex** and **John Stapleton.** (Prentice-Hall, 1983, 320 pages). Book provides tools and techniques to pass the math portion of real estate licensing exams in all 50 states.

Computers for Real Estate by **Peter Luedtke** and **Rainer Luedtke.** (Harcourt Brace Jovanovich, 1984, 138 pages). Explains benefits of computer systems in real estate and how to choose the right equipment and successfully put it to use.

Monthly Interest Amortization Tables. (Contemporary Books, 1984, 283 pages). Tables cover interest rates from 5% to 28.75%, amounts from $50 to $160,000 and terms up to 40 years. Remaining balance and proration tables are also provided.

Mortgage Lending: Fundamentals and Practices by **Marshall Dennis.** (Reston, 1983, 349 pages). Book includes loan standards and approval, federal regulations, mortgage law, FHA, VA, private mortgage insurance, loan closing and income property financing. Also included are three residential loan case studies.

"Watching the Fed Watch the Aggregates" by **Daniel Blumberg.** (*Real Estate Review,* Spring 85, p. 80). Describes how the Federal Reserve Bank works and shows that to forecast interest rates, watch the monetary variables that the Fed tries to influence and observe whether the Fed currently favors high employment, stable prices, steady growth or stable dollar exchange value.

Sources and Types of Financing

Adjustable rate mortgage: a mortgage on which the interest rate rises and falls with changes in prevailing interest rates

Alienation clause: requires immediate repayment of the loan if ownership transfers; also called a due-on-sale clause

Equity sharing: an arrangement whereby a party providing financing gets a portion of the ownership

Fannie Mae: a real estate industry nickname for the Federal National Mortgage Association

Mortgage company: a firm that makes mortgage loans and then sells them to investors

Option: a right, for a given period of time, to buy, sell or lease property at specified price and terms

Secondary mortgage market: a market where mortgage loans can be sold to investors

Seller financing: a note accepted by a seller instead of cash

Usury: charging a rate of interest higher than that permitted by law

Wraparound mortgage: a mortgage that encompasses any existing mortgages and is subordinate to them

This chapter will (1) identify various mortgage lenders (the primary market), (2) describe where these lenders get much of their money (the secondary market), and (3) explain mortgage loan instruments and financing techniques currently in use in the United States. Many people consider financing to be the most important of all real estate topics because without financing real estate profits and commissions would be difficult to achieve.

PRIMARY MARKET

The **primary market** (also called the **primary mortgage market**) is where lenders originate loans; i.e., where lenders make funds available to borrowers. Examples are savings and loans (S&Ls), commercial banks, mutual savings banks and mortgage companies. The primary market is what the borrower sees as the source of mortgage loan money. It's the institution with which the borrower has direct and personal contact. It's the place where the loan application is taken, the place where the loan officer interviews the loan applicant, the place where the loan check comes from, and the place to which loan payments are sent by the borrower.

Most borrowers assume that the loan they receive comes from depositors who visit the same bank or S&L to leave their excess funds. This is partly true. But this by itself would be an inadequate source of loan funds in today's market. Thus, primary lenders often sell their loans in what is called the secondary market. Insurance companies, pension funds and individual investors as well as other primary lenders with excess deposits buy these loans for cash. This makes available to a primary lender more money that, in turn, can be loaned to borrowers. The secondary market is so huge that it rivals the entire U.S. corporate bond market in size of annual offerings. We will return to the secondary market later in this chapter. Meanwhile, let us discuss the various lenders a borrower will encounter when looking for a real estate loan.

SAVINGS AND LOAN
ASSOCIATIONS

As a group, the nation's 4,000 **savings and loan associations** are the foremost money lenders for residential real estate. Historically, their origin can be traced to early building societies in England and Germany and to the first American building society, the Oxford Provident Building Association, started in 1831 in Pennsylvania. These early building societies were cooperatives whose savers were also borrowers. Over time, the emergence of two distinct groups led to the savings and loan associations of today: those who wanted to save and those who wanted to borrow. Today, savings and loan associations (S&Ls) offer interest bearing passbook accounts that allow savers to make deposits at any time and in any amount; and withdrawals, for all practical purposes, are available on demand.

Disintermediation

Savings and loans also offer **certificates of deposit (CDs)** at rates higher than passbook rates in order to attract depositors. This is necessary to compete with higher yields offered by U.S. Treasury bills, notes and bonds and to prevent disintermediation. **Disintermediation** results when depositors take money out of their savings accounts and invest directly in government securities, corporate bonds and money market funds. A major problem, and one that nearly brought the S&L industry to its knees in the late 1970s and early 1980s, was that S&Ls traditionally relied heavily upon short-term deposits from savers and then loaned that money on long-term (often 30-year) loans to borrowers. When interest rates rose sharply in the 1970s, S&Ls either had to raise the interest paid to their depositors or watch depositors withdraw their savings and take the money elsewhere for higher returns. Meanwhile, the S&Ls were holding long-term, fixed-rate mortgage loans, and with interest rates rising, borrowers were not anxious to repay those loans early.

Today, S&Ls are aggressively stretching out their deposit accounts by offering higher rates on longer-term (often 5- and 10-year) certificates of deposit. S&Ls are also aggressively enforcing due-on-sale clauses in existing mortgage loans, and are encouraging new mortgage loan borrowers to take adjustable rate loans. These actions will help S&Ls to more closely match the rates they must pay depositors with the rates they receive on loans.

COMMERCIAL BANKS

The nation's 15,000 **commercial banks** store far more of the country's money than the S&Ls. However, only one bank dollar in six goes to real estate lending. As a result, in total number of dollars, commercial banks rank second behind S&Ls in importance in real estate lending. Of the loans made by banks on real estate, the tendency is to emphasize short-term maturities since the bulk of a bank's deposit money comes from demand deposits (checking accounts) and a much smaller portion from savings and time deposits. Consequently, banks are particularly active in making loans to finance real estate construction as these loans have maturities of 6 months to 3 years. Some banks offer real estate loans up to 30 years. However, a bank will usually sell loans with long maturities rather than keep them in its investment portfolio.

MUTUAL SAVINGS BANKS

Important contributors to real estate credit in several states are the nation's 400 **mutual savings banks.** Started in Philadelphia in 1816 and in Boston in 1817, mutual savings banks are found primarily in the northeastern United States, where they compete aggressively for the savings dollar. The states of Massachusetts, New York, and Connecticut account for 75% of the nation's total. As the word "mutual" implies, the depositors are the owners, and the "interest" they receive is the result of the bank's success or failure in lending. Mutual savings banks offer accounts similar to those offered by S&Ls. To protect depositors, laws require mutual savings banks to place deposits in high-quality investments, including sound real estate mortgage loans.

LIFE INSURANCE COMPANIES

As a group, the nation's 2,200 **life insurance companies** have long been active investors in real estate as developers, owners and long-term lenders. Their source of money is the premiums paid by policyholders. These premiums are invested and ultimately returned to the policyholders. Because premiums are collected in regular amounts on regular dates and because policy payoffs can be calculated from actuarial tables, life insurers are in ideal positions to commit money to long-term investments. Life insurance companies channel their funds primarily into government and corporate bonds and real estate. The dollars allocated to real estate go to buy land and buildings, which are leased to users, and to make loans on commercial, industrial and residential property. Generally, life insurers specialize in large-scale investments such as shopping centers, office and apartment buildings, and million-dollar blocks of home loans purchased in the secondary mortgage market.

Repayment terms on loans made by insurance companies for shopping centers, office buildings and apartment complexes sometimes call for interest and a percentage of any profits from rentals over a certain level. This **participation** feature, or "piece of the action," is intended to provide the insurance company with more inflation protection than a fixed rate of interest.

MORTGAGE COMPANIES

A **mortgage company** makes a mortgage loan and then sells it to a long-term investor. The process begins with locating borrowers, qualifying them, preparing the necessary loan papers, and finally making the loans. Once a loan is made, it is sold for cash on the secondary market. The mortgage company will usually continue to **service the loan,** that is, collect the monthly payments and handle such matters as insurance and property tax impounds, delinquencies, early payoffs and mortgage releases.

Mortgage companies, also known as **mortgage bankers,** vary in size from one or two persons to several dozen. As a rule, they are locally oriented, finding and making loans within 25 or 50 miles of their offices. This gives them a feel for their market, greatly aids in identifying sound loans, and makes loan servicing much easier. For their efforts, mortgage bankers typically receive 1% to 3% of the amount of the loan when it is originated, and from ¼ to ½ of 1% of the outstanding balance each year thereafter for servicing. Mortgage banking, as this business is called, is not limited to mortgage companies. Commercial banks, savings and loan associations, and mutual savings banks in active real estate areas often originate more real estate loans than they can hold themselves, and these are sold on the secondary market. Mortgage companies often do a large amount of their business in FHA and VA loans.

Texas has made its own loan programs available for veterans and low- to middle-income borrowers. All of them have had a very beneficial impact on the Texas housing industry and deserve more detailed discussion.

TEXAS LOAN PROGRAMS

The Texas Veterans Land Board has made a program available by which an eligible veteran may buy land from the Veterans Land Board by a contract of sale (installment land contract or contract for deed, see Chapter 8) at very favorable interest rates which are determined by the Texas Veterans Land Board. The contract can not exceed forty (40) years and the purchase price of the property can not exceed $20,000.00. There must be a minimum down payment of five percent (5%), not to exceed $1,000.00. If the price of the land exceeds the $20,000.00, the veteran must pay the Board, in cash, a down payment equal to that portion of the sales price in excess of $20,000.00. The veteran may either purchase land owned by the Board, or the veteran may designate certain

Texas Veterans Land Fund

land which the Board may purchase in his behalf and then resell to him under the installment land contract.

Veterans' Housing Assistance Program

Another program that the Texas Veterans Land Board has made available is the Veterans' Housing Assistance Program (VHAP). You will note that the TREC promulgated contract forms have special provisions under the "Financing Conditions" section to provide for the Veterans' Housing Assistance Program. The program is made available to eligible veterans who wish to purchase a new or existing home and must be the primary residence of the veteran for at least three (3) years. The VHAP loan is used in conjunction with any other type of financing, and enables the veteran to borrow up to $20,000.00 as a first or second lien mortgage. There is a maximum loan of $20,000.00 on the loan, so if there is going to be a single mortgage of less than $20,000.00 the Veterans Land Board will be the only noteholder on the loan. If more than $20,000.00 is borrowed, the Veterans Land Board and the first lien lender share the first lien position, and the first lien lender services and originates the loan.

If the VHAP loan is used in conjunction with another conventional first lien, there is required five percent (5%) down payment of the purchase price. If it is used in conjunction with a VA loan there is no down payment if the veteran has full VA eligibility. As with other veteran loans, the veteran can transfer the loan to another veteran or non veteran so long as the original veteran has lived in the house for a minimum of three (3) years.

Additional information on both of these Veterans Land Board approved loans can be obtained by calling the Texas Veterans Land Board at their toll free number: 1-800-252-VETS.

Texas Housing Agency

In an effort to stimulate the construction and sale of low and middle income housing, the Texas Housing Agency was established. This agency sells bonds to establish a fund to make loans for housing development for families of low income or families of moderate income. The loan from the Housing Development must be submitted and recommended by a mortgage lender and the amortization period of the loan can not exceed forty (40) years. The interest rate is set at the sole discretion of the Board of Directors of the Agency. If the project is a multifamily housing development and contains at least twenty (20) units, at least five percent (5%) of the units must be occupied by an elderly individual or by a family of lower and moderate income, or homes that an elderly individual is head of the household. Detailed information can be obtained by writing the Texas Housing Agency, P. O. Box 13941, Austin, Texas 78711.

Texas also provides a mechanism whereby which a local governmental unit can authorize the creation of a Housing Finance Corporation within that governmental unit. This corporation is a nonprofit corporation which can sell bonds and utilize other methods of incurring income to provide financing to local lending institutions for low- and middle-income housing, similar to a state sponsored program administered by the Texas Housing Agency. There are also similar criteria for providing housing for the elderly. These corporations can only be enabled by the local governing body such as a city council. The determination must be made from town to town as to whether or not a housing financing corporation is available as a source for these types of funds.

Housing Finance Corporation

Mortgage brokers, in contrast to mortgage bankers, specialize in bringing together borrowers and lenders, just as real estate brokers bring together buyers and sellers. The mortgage broker does not lend money, and usually does not service loans. The mortgage broker's fee is expressed in points and is usually paid by the borrower. Mortgage brokers are locally oriented and often are small firms of from 1 to 10 persons.

MORTGAGE BROKERS

In some cities, **municipal bonds** provide a source of mortgage money for home buyers. The special advantage to borrowers is that municipal bonds pay interest that is tax-free from federal income taxes. Knowing this, bond investors will accept a lower rate of interest than they would if the interest were taxable—as it normally is on mortgage loans. This saving is passed on to the home buyer. Those who qualify will typi-

MUNICIPAL BONDS

cally pay about 2% less than if they had borrowed through conventional channels.

The objective of such programs is to make home ownership more affordable for low- and middle-income households. Also, a city may stipulate that loans be used in neighborhoods the city wants to revitalize. The loans are made by local lenders who are paid a fee for originating and servicing these loans. Although popular with the real estate industry, the U.S. Treasury has been less than enthusiastic about the concept because it bears the cost in lost tax revenues. As a result, federal legislation has been passed to limit the future use of this source of money.

OTHER LENDERS   **Pension funds** and **trust funds** traditionally have channeled their money to high-grade government and corporate bonds and stocks. However, the trend now is to place more money into real estate loans. Already active buyers in the secondary market, the pension and trust funds will likely become still larger sources of real estate financing in the future. In some localities, pension fund members can tap their own pension funds for home mortgages at very reasonable rates. This is an often overlooked source of primary market financing.

Finance companies that specialize in making business and consumer loans also provide limited financing for real estate. As a rule, finance companies seek second mortgages at interest rates 2% to 5% higher than the rates prevailing on first mortgages. First mortgages are also taken as collateral; however, the lenders already discussed usually charge lower interest rates for these loans and thus are more competitive.

Credit unions normally specialize in consumer loans. However, real estate loans are becoming more and more important as many of the country's 16,000 credit unions have branched out into first and second mortgage loans. Credit unions are an often overlooked but excellent source of home loan money.

Individuals are sometimes a source of cash loans for real estate, with the bulk of these loans made between relatives or friends. Generally, loan maturities are shorter than those obtainable from the institutional lenders already described.

In some cities, persons can be found who specialize in making or buying second and third mortgage loans of up to 10-year maturities. Individuals are beginning to invest substantial amounts of money in secondary mortgage market securities. Ironically, these investments are often made with money that would have otherwise been deposited in a savings and loan.

Individuals are heavily involved in seller financing. This method allows the seller to take some monthly payments from the buyer rather than the whole purchase price in cash. Because of its importance, seller financing is discussed under its own heading later in this chapter.

SECONDARY MARKET

The **secondary market** (also called the **secondary mortgage market**) provides a way for a lender to sell a loan. It also permits investment in real estate loans without the need for loan origination and servicing facilities. Although not directly encountered by real estate buyers, sellers and agents, the secondary market plays an important role in getting money from those who want to lend to those who want to borrow. In other words, think of the secondary market as **a pipeline for loan money.** Now visualize that pipeline running via the Wall Street financial district in New York City, since Wall Street is now a major participant in residential mortgage lending. Figure 12:1 illustrates this pipeline and diagrams key differences between the traditional mortgage delivery system and the secondary market system.

MORTGAGE LOAN DELIVERY SYSTEMS

Figure 12:1

Traditional System

Secondary Market System

Traditional Delivery
System

Notice in Figure 12:1 that in the traditional system the lender is a local institution gathering deposits from the community and then lending that money as real estate loans in the same community. Traditionally, each lender (S&L, mutual savings bank, commercial bank, credit union) was an independent unit that developed its own appraisal technique, loan application form, loan approval criteria, note and mortgage forms, servicing method and foreclosure policy. Nonetheless, three major problems needed solving. The first problem was the institution that had an imbalance of depositors and borrowers. Rapidly growing areas of the United States often needed more loan money than their savers were capable of depositing. Stable regions had more depositors than loan opportunities. Thus it was common to see correspondent relationships between lenders where, for example, a lender in Los Angeles would sell some of its mortgage loans to a savings bank in Brooklyn. This provided loans for borrowers and interest for savers. The system worked well but required individual correspondent relationships.

The second problem occurred when depositors wanted to withdraw money from their accounts and invest it elsewhere. To meet withdrawals, lenders needed a marketplace in which to convert theirs loans to cash. Third and last, the experiences of the 1970s and early 1980s taught S&Ls and mutual savings banks (also called **thrifts**) the hard lessons of borrowing short and lending long. Savers are now encouraged to leave their money on deposit longer, and lenders are looking for ways to better manage the maturities on the loans they make.

Secondary Market
Delivery Systems

As shown in Figure 12:1, with the secondary market system the borrower obtains a loan from a mortgage originator. This includes mortgage companies as well as banks and thrifts that originate loans they intend to sell. The mortgage originator packages the loan with other loans and then either sells the package as a whole or keeps the package and sells securities which are backed by the loans in the package. If the originator is not large enough to package its own mortgages, it will sell the loans to someone who can. Next, investment bankers (including some of the largest stockbrokers in the

United States) locate investors with money to invest. These investors are pension funds, life insurance companies, trust funds, private individuals, and thrifts. Interestingly, the thrifts, especially the S&Ls, are the biggest sellers and the biggest buyers.

A major stumbling block to a highly organized and efficient secondary market has been the uniqueness of both lend-
ers and loans. Traditionally, each lender developed its own special loan forms and procedures. Moreover, each loan is a unique combination of real estate and borrower. No two are exactly alike. How do you package such diversity into an attractive package for investors? A large part of the answer has come through standardized loan application forms, stan-
dardized appraisal forms, standardized credit report forms, standardized closing statements, standardized loan approval criteria and standardized promissory notes, mortgages and trust deeds. Loan terms have been standardized into catego-
ries, for example, fixed-rate 30-year loans, fixed-rate 15-year loans and various adjustable rate combinations. Additionally, nearly all loans must be insured. This can take the form of FHA or private mortgage insurance, or a VA guarantee, on each loan in the package. Additionally, there will be some form of assurance of timely repayment of the mortgage package as a whole. The net result is a mortgage security that is attractive to investors who in the past have not been interested in investing in mortgages.

Standardized Loan
Procedures

Let us now look at some of the key secondary market participants including the three giants of the industry: the FNMA, GNMA and FHLMC.

The **Federal National Mortgage Association (FNMA)** was organized by the federal government in 1938 to buy FHA mortgage loans from lenders. This made it possible for lenders to grant more loans to consumers. Ten years later it began purchasing VA loans. FNMA (fondly known in the real estate business and to itself as **"Fannie Mae"**) was successful in its mission.

FNMA

In 1968 Congress divided the FNMA into two organizations: the Government National Mortgage Association (to be

discussed in the next section) and the FNMA as we know it today. As part of that division, the FNMA changed from a government agency to a private profit-making corporation, chartered by Congress but owned by its shareholders and managed independently of the government. There are some 60 million shares of Fannie Mae stock in existence, and it is one of the most actively traded issues on the New York Stock Exchange. Fannie Mae buys FHA and VA loans and, since 1972, conventional whole loans from lenders across the United States. Money to buy these loans comes from the sale of FNMA stock plus the sale of FNMA bonds and notes. FNMA bond and note holders look to Fannie Mae for timely payment of principal and interest on these bonds and notes, and Fannie Mae looks to its mortgagors for principal and interest payments on the loans it owns. Thus, Fannie Mae stands in the middle and, although it is very careful to match interest rates and maturities between the loans it buys and the bonds and notes it sells, it still takes the risk of the middleman. In this respect, it is like a giant thrift institution.

Commitments   Fannie Mae's method of operation is to sell commitments to lenders pledging to buy specified dollar amounts of mortgage loans within a fixed period of time and usually at a specified yield. Lenders are not obligated to sell loans to Fannie Mae if they can find better terms elsewhere. However, Fannie Mae must purchase all loans delivered to it under the terms of the commitments. Loans must be made using FNMA-approved forms and loan approval criteria. The largest loan Fannie Mae would buy in 1985 was $115,300. This limit is adjusted each year as housing prices change. Fannie Mae will also buy loans on duplexes, triplexes and fourplexes— all at larger loan limits. Although the FNMA loan limit may seem inadequate for some houses and neighborhoods, the intention of Congress is that Fannie Mae cater to the mid-range of housing prices and leave the upper end of the market to others.

In addition to purchasing first mortgages, Fannie Mae also purchases second mortgages from lenders. FNMA forms and criteria must be followed and the loan-to-value ratio of the combined first and second mortgages cannot exceed 80%

if owner-occupied and 70% if not owner-occupied. This is a very helpful program for a person who has watched the value of his or her home increase and wants to borrow against that increase without first having to repay the existing mortgage loan.

Another innovation of Fannie Mae to help real estate is the **home seller program.** This is a secondary market for sellers who carryback mortgages. To qualify, the note and mortgage must be prepared by a FNMA-approved lender using standard FNMA loan qualification procedures. The note and mortgage may be kept by the home seller as an investment or sold to a FNMA-approved lender for possible resale to the FNMA.

Home Seller Program

In other developments, Fannie Mae has standardized the terms of adjustable rate mortgages it will purchase. This is a major step forward in reducing the proliferation of variety in these loans. Fannie Mae is also test marketing mortgage-backed securities in $1,000 increments to appeal to individuals, particularly for Individual Retirement Accounts. Additionally, Fannie Mae has started a collateralized mortgage obligation program and begun a mortgage pass-through program, both of which will be defined momentarily.

The **Government National Mortgage Association** (**GNMA,** popularly known to the industry and to itself as "**Ginnie Mae**") was created in 1968 when the FNMA was partitioned into two separate corporations. Ginnie Mae is a federal agency entirely within the Department of Housing and Urban Development (HUD). Although Ginnie Mae has some low-income housing functions, it is best known for its mortgage-backed securities (MBS) program. The purpose of the MBS program is to attract new sources of credit to FHA, VA and FmHA mortgages. Ginnie Mae does this by guaranteeing timely repayment of privately issued securities backed by pools of these mortgages.

To create a **mortgage-backed security,** the security issuer (such as a bank or S&L) obtains an MBS commitment from Ginnie Mae. The issuer either originates or acquires mortgage loans and creates a pool of mortgages of similar interest rate

Mortgage-Backed Security

and maturity. The minimum pool size is $1 million, and the loans are deposited with an independent custodian. Certificates representing undivided ownerships in the pool and carrying Ginnie Mae's guarantee of timely repayment are sold to investors. Minimum purchase is $25,000 and security dealers handle the sales. Each month the investor receives a check from the issuer for a share of the principal and interest scheduled to be made that month and a pro rata share of any prepayments of principal. These are classified as **pass-through securities** as the investors receive a "pass-through" of principal and interest payments due on the pool of mortgages.

The interest rate paid to the investor is ½% less than the interest rate on the loans in the pool. Because this represents a very attractive return and because the individual loans are government insured or guaranteed and because the pool as a whole is guaranteed by Ginnie Mae, these pass-throughs have become very popular investments not only for pension funds and other institutional investors but also for individuals. For an individual who does not have the $25,000 minimum, there are mutual funds that buy Ginnie Mae's and reoffer them in units as small as $1,000.

FHLMC

The **Federal Home Loan Mortgage Corporation (FHLMC,** also known to the industry and to itself as **"Freddie Mac"** or the "Mortgage Corporation") was created by Congress in 1970. Its goal, like that of the FNMA and GNMA, is to increase the availability of financing for residential mortgages. Where it differs is that Freddie Mac deals primarily in conventional mortgages, and it was initially established to serve as a secondary market for S&L members of the Federal Home Loan Bank System. Other differences are that unlike Ginnie Mae, which guarantees securities issued by others, Freddie Mac issues its own securities against its own mortgage pools. These securities are its participation certificates and collateralized mortgage obligations.

Participation Certificates and Collateralized Mortgage Obligators

Participation Certificates (PCs) allow a mortgage originator to deliver to Freddie Mac either whole mortgages or part interest in a pool of whole mortgages. In return, Freddie Mac gives the mortgage originator a PC representing an undivided interest in a pool of investment-quality conventional mortgages created from mortgages and mortgage interests purchased by Freddie Mac. Freddie Mac guarantees that the interest and principal on these PC's will be repaid in full and on time, even if the underlying mortgages are in default. (Freddie Mac reduces its losses by setting strict loan qualification criteria and requiring mortgage insurance on high loan-to-value loans.) The PCs can be kept as investments, sold for cash or used as collateral for loans. PCs are popular investments for S&Ls, pension funds and other institutional investors looking for high-yield investments. Individuals who can meet the $25,000 minimum also find PCs attractive. Freddie Mac also has a collateralized mortgage obligation program and the 1986 Tax Reform Act allows for the creation of a Real Estate Mortgage Investment Corporation. These are designed to deal with the unpredictability of mortgage maturities caused by early repayment. This is accomplished by dividing the cash flows from a mortgage pool into separate securities with separate maturities which are then sold to investors.

The financial success of the three giants of the secondary mortgage market (FNMA, GNMA and FHLMC) has brought private mortgage packagers into the marketplace. These are organizations such as MGIC Investment Corporation (a subsidiary of Mortgage Guaranty Investment Corporation); Residential Funding Corporation (a subsidiary of Norwest Mortgage Corp.); financial subsidiaries of such household-names as General Electric, Lockheed Aircraft, and Sears, Roebuck and Company; and mortgage packaging subsidiaries of state Realtor associations. These organizations both compete with the big three and specialize in markets not served by them. For example, Residential Funding will package mortgage loans as large as $500,000, well above the limits imposed by FNMA and FHLMC (same as FNMA) and limits on FHA and VA loans. All of these organizations will buy from loan originators who are not large enough to create their own pools. At least one specializes in helping to originate seller carryback loans that can be sold on the secondary market.

PRIVATE CONDUITS

Before leaving the topic of the secondary market, it is important to note that without electronic data transmission

COMPUTERIZATION

and computers, the programs just described would be severely handicapped. There are currently thousands of mortgage pools each containing from $1 million to $500 million (and more) in mortgage loans. Each loan in a pool has its own monthly payment schedule, and each payment must be broken down into its principal and interest components and any property tax and insurance impounds. Computers do this work as well as issue receipts and late notices. The pool, in turn, will be owned by several dozen to a hundred or more investors each with a different fractional interest in the pool. Once a month incoming mortgage payments are tallied, a small fee deducted for the operation of the pool and the balance allotted among the investors, all by computer. A computer is also used to print and mail checks to investors and provide them with an accounting of the pool's asset level.

Electronic Transfers   With advanced computer programs now available, secondary market operators are dispensing with the monthly mailing of checks to large investors. Instead, funds are electronically transmitted directly to the investor's bank account and the investor receives a notice that this has been done. If an investor is in more than one pool, the computer combines all payments due into one statement and one automatic deposit. Keeping track of the numbers is no small matter when a single large investor can be in as many as 1,000 different pools, and Freddie Mac, for example, is issuing 12 to 40 new pools a day. (By comparison, Fannie Mae does about as much business—$20 billion a year—as Freddie Mac. Ginnie Mae does about $50 billion a year.)

MORTGAGE
NETWORKS   Old timers to real estate will remember when a weekly sheet listing mortgage lenders in town with their current loan rates was passed around each real estate office. As interest rates began to fluctuate wildly in the late 1970s, this sheet was updated and circulated more often. In some real estate offices one person was given the job of calling lenders daily for quotes on loan availability and interest rates. Since then, rate changes have become a bit less frequent and, more importantly, the weekly loan sheet is being replaced by a computer

terminal. A salesperson simply types in words that request loan information, and the computer screen shows lenders' names plus their current loan offerings and interest rates. A salesperson can shop by computer for the best loan for a buyer and the buyer can watch. The salesperson (or buyer) then makes telephone contact with the lender and arranges for a loan interview.

Some of the more sophisticated mortgage networks go further. The salesperson can touch additional keys, and the computer will prequalify the buyer, match the buyer with a loan and tell the lender to mail loan application papers to that real estate office. If the real estate office has a printer, a loan application and loan agreement can be typed out on the spot.

There are currently a dozen computerized mortgage networks in the United States and more are being formed. Some networks are local and some are national. Some offer information only, and others allow the real estate office to interact with the lender. Some networks will issue a loan commitment by computer in the real estate office. With loan formats becoming more standardized because of the secondary mortgage market, shopping for a mortgage loan by computer is beginning to resemble shopping for generic brands at discount stores. Note that a lender will not be listed on a computer network unless he chooses to be and pays a fee. Nonmember lenders would still have to be contacted by telephone. The networks also charge real estate offices to list on the network.

Thus far we have been concerned with the money pipelines between lenders and borrowers. Ultimately though, money must have a source. These sources are savings generated by individuals and businesses as a result of their spending less than they earn **(real savings),** and government-created money, called **fiat money** or "printing press money." This second source does not represent unconsumed labor and materials; instead it competes for available goods and services alongside the savings of individuals and businesses.

In the arena of money and capital, real estate borrowers must compete with the needs of government, business and consumers. Governments, particularly the federal govern-

AVAILABILITY AND PRICE OF MORTGAGE MONEY

ment, compete the hardest when they borrow to finance a deficit. Not to borrow would mean bankruptcy and the inability to pay government employees and provide government programs and services. Strong competition also comes from business and consumer credit sectors. In the face of strong competition for loan funds, home buyers must either pay higher interest or be outbid.

One "solution" to this problem is for the federal government to create more money, thus making competition for funds easier and interest rates lower. Unfortunately, the net result is often "too much money chasing too few goods," and prices are pulled upward by the demand caused by the newly created money. This is followed by rising interest rates as savers demand higher returns to compensate for losses in purchasing power. Many economists feel that the higher price levels and interest rates of the 1970s were due to applying too much of this "solution" to the economy since 1965.

The alternative solution, from the standpoint of residential loans, is to increase real savings or decrease competing demands for available money. A number of plans and ideas have been put forth by civic, business and political leaders. They include proposals to simplify income taxes and balance the federal budget, incentives to increase productive output and incentives to save money in retirement accounts.

Usury

Usury is defined as the charging of an interest rate that is in excess of that allowed by law. In Texas, a statute that became effective May 8, 1981, has dramatically changed the usury ceiling in Texas. This law provides for different methods of calculating interest rates to determine what that ceiling will be.

The first calculation to determine the usury ceiling is termed the **indicated rate ceiling.** The indicated rate ceiling is the auction average rate quoted on a bank discount basis for 26-week treasury bills issued by the United States government for the week preceding the week in which the rate is contracted for, multiplied by two, and rounded to the nearest one-quarter of one percent.

As an alternative, the usury ceiling can be determined as an **annualized** or **quarterly ceiling.** If the computations of indicated rate ceiling, annualized ceiling or quarterly ceiling is less than 18% per year, the ceiling for interest on that loan will be 18% per year. If the computations are more than 24% a year the ceiling under that provision is 24% per year. This creates two ceilings, one at 18% and one at 24% depending on the calculations as defined under the new statute. In no event will the interest rate ceiling go below 18% a year.

If however, a loan is made on any contract under which credit in an amount in excess of $250,000 is or is to be extended, or any extension or renewal of any such contract, and which credit is extended for business, commercial, investment or other similar purpose but excluding any contract that is not for any of those purposes and is primarily for personal, family, household or agricultural use, the 24% limitations do not apply and the limitations on the ceiling determined by those computations are 28% per year.

For certain variable rate mortgage contracts which are not made for personal, family or household use, a monthly ceiling is available. The computation for the monthly ceiling is computed from auctions occurring during the preceding calendar month computed by the state consumer credit commissioner on the first business day of a calendar month on which the rate applies.

There are further requirements and criteria relating to variable rate mortgages, open-end mortgages and closed-end mortgages. Before any transaction is entered into, competent legal counsel should be consulted for the application of the new Texas law.

On March 31, 1980 and October 8, 1980 federal laws were passed which declared that the constitutional laws of any state expressly limiting the rate or amount of interest shall not apply to any loan which is:

1. secured by a first lien on residential property, by a first lien on stock in residential cooperative housing corporations, or by a first lien on a residential manufactured home;
2. made after March 31, 1980; and
3. is described in Section 527(b) of the National Housing Act, or an individual who finances the sale or exchange of residential real property which such individual owns

and which such individual has occupied as his principal residence.

In interpreting the statute, the Federal Home Loan Bank Board has taken the position that residential real property means real estate improved or to be improved by structures or structure designed for dwelling, as opposed to primarily commercial use.

What constitutes interest has been a heavily litigated area over the past several years in Texas because of the varying costs of obtaining loans. What is generally being discovered is that unless the loan instruments on their face indicate an interest rate in excess of that allowed by law, the loan will not be considered a usurious transaction. However, determination of what constitutes usury is a technical legal question.

Interest is statutorily defined in Texas as "compensation allowed by law for the use or forbearance or detention of money." This is very strictly construed in Texas to mean that only that amount charged for the forbearance of money is actually interest. Therefore, "points" (1 percent of the loan amount) for loan brokerage, initiation fees, loan origination fees, or loan commitment fees are not considered as interest in this state, except under certain circumstances where those fees go directly to the lender as part of the applicant's cost for the loan. If the points are construed to be interest, they can be "spread" over the 30-year term of the loan in determining the final rate of interest that the loan applicant pays. So a 30-year loan quoted at 10 percent interest and 2 "points" is not 12 percent, but about 10¼ percent per annum, since the 2 points are distributed over the 30-year period.

On the other hand, corporations are allowed by statute to pay interest at a rate not to exceed 1½ percent per month on the unpaid principal balance of the loan. It is not uncommon to find applicants forming corporations or incorporating themselves in order to take advantage of a loan which may be in excess of 12 percent but below the 1½ percent per month rate ceiling for corporations.

Price to the Borrower

Ultimately, the rate of interest the borrower must pay to obtain a loan is dependent on the cost of money to the lender, reserves for default, loan servicing costs, and available investment alternatives. For example, go to a savings institution and see what they are paying depositors on various accounts. To this add 2% for the cost of maintaining cash in the tills, office space, personnel, advertising, free gifts for depositors, deposit insurance, loan servicing, loan reserves for defaults and a ¼% profit margin. This will give you an idea of how much borrowers must be charged.

Life insurance companies, pension funds and trust funds do not have to "pay" for their money like thrift institutions. Nonetheless, they do want to earn the highest possible yields, with safety, on the money in their custody. Thus, if a real estate buyer wants to borrow in order to buy a home, the buyer must compete successfully with the other investment opportunities available on the open market. To determine the rate for yourself, look at the yields on newly issued corporate bonds as shown in the financial section of your daily newspaper. Add ½ of 1% to this for the extra work in packaging and servicing mortgage loans and you will have the interest rate home borrowers must pay to attract lenders.

From an investment risk standpoint, when a lender makes   *DUE-ON-SALE*
a loan with a fixed interest rate, the lender recognizes that, during the life of the loan, interest rates may rise or fall. When they rise, the lender remains locked into a lower rate. Most loans contain a **due-on-sale clause** (also called an **alienation clause** or a **call clause**). In the past, these were inserted by lenders so that if the borrower sold the property to someone considered uncreditworthy by the lender, the lender could call the loan balance due. Today lenders use these clauses to increase the rate of interest on the loan when the property changes hands. They enforce the clause by threatening to accelerate the balance of the loan unless the new owner will accept a higher rate of return.

Two important legal events have established lenders'   *Garn-St Germain*
rights to enforce due-on-sale clauses. One occurred in June 1982, when the U.S. Supreme Court decided the *Fidelity Federal Savings and Loan* vs. *de la Cuesta* case. The Court found in favor of Fidelity Federal ruling that federally chartered savings and loan associations have the right to enforce due-on-sale

clauses. In October of the same year, Congress passed the Garn-St Germain Depository Institutions Act (the Act). The Act makes all due-on-sale clauses in mortgage loans made by deposit institutions enforceable. In 39 states, this has been less than a major issue because those states have always upheld the enforceability of due-on-sale clauses. Where the Act made a big difference was in the other 11 states: Arkansas, Arizona, California, Colorado, Georgia, Iowa, Michigan, Minnesota, New Mexico, Utah and Vermont. These states had taken legislative or court action to stop due-on-sale clauses from being enforced. The Act reversed this through a "window period" provision that lasted through October 15, 1985. Unless a state legislature acted to preserve its nonenforceability stand before that date, due-on-sale clauses in existing loans are now fully enforceable. Due-on-sale clauses are also enforceable in any mortgage loan made after October 15, 1982, by any deposit institution anywhere in the United States. The Act does not apply to sellers who carryback a loan or to mortgage companies; they are still controlled by state law regarding due-on-sale enforceability.

The Issue   Why is all this an important issue? The answer is that when interest rates are high, a seller can sell more quickly and for a higher price if the seller is able to pass along to the buyer an existing low-interest rate loan. A lender, however, takes a financial loss whenever the lender receives less interest on a loan than it is paying to borrow money from savers. With enough loans like this a lender can go bankrupt. And if enough lenders go bankrupt, loans will be harder to find. So there is no simple solution. Meanwhile, lenders are writing new loan contracts that specifically allow for interest rate increases upon alienation. Therefore, it is important to understand what constitutes an alienation that will allow a lender to accelerate a loan.

The Act uses the words "sale or transfer" to define alienation and gives the Federal Home Loan Bank Board the power to interpret this very broadly. The obvious example is the sale of a property wherein the seller delivers a deed to the buyer and the buyer records it. But, due-on-sale enforcement can also result from the creation of an installment contract, the creation of a lease with option to buy, the creation of a lease of more than 3 years, the creation or refinancing of a junior lien (owner-occupied single-family homes excluded), the foreclosure of a junior lien, and a transfer into a trust (owner-occupied single-family homes excluded). Before undertaking any of these transactions, the wise real estate owner or investor will obtain a written statement from the lender agreeing not to accelerate the loan. The wise real estate agent will point out the Act to clients and customers before suggesting a deal that would trigger due-on-sale.

If loan rates drop it becomes worthwhile for a borrower to shop for a new loan and repay the existing one in full. To compensate, loan contracts sometimes call for a **prepayment penalty** in return for giving the borrower the right to repay the loan early. A typical prepayment penalty amounts to the equivalent of 6 months interest on the amount that is being paid early. However, this can vary from loan to loan and from state to state. Some loan contracts permit up to 20% of the unpaid balance to be paid in any one year without penalty. Other contracts make the penalty stiffest when the loan is young. In certain states, laws do not permit prepayment penalties on loans more than 5 years old. By federal law, prepayment penalties are not allowed on FHA and VA loans. Although there is some conflict in the Texas usury statutes, it is often contended that Texas does not permit prepayment penalties on loans that carry interest rates above 10% per year.

PREPAYMENT PENALTIES

As we have already seen, a major problem for savings institutions is that they are locked into long-term loans while being dependent on short-term savings deposits. As a result, savings institutions now prefer to make mortgage loans that allow the interest rate to rise and fall during the life of the loan. To make this arrangement more attractive to borrowers, these loans are offered at a lower rate of interest than a fixed-rate loan of similar maturity.

The first step toward mortgage loans with adjustable interest rates came in the late 1970s. The loan was called a **variable rate mortgage** and the interest rate could be adjusted by the

VARIABLE AND ADJUSTABLE RATE MORTGAGES

lender up or down during the 30-year life of the loan to reflect the rise and fall in interest rates paid to savers by the lender. The Federal Home Loan Bank Board (FHLBB) limited adjustments to no more than ½ of 1% each 6 months and a maximum of 2½% over the life of the loan. Any changes in the interest rate on the loan were reflected each 6 months in the monthly payments on the loan. Then in 1980, the FHLBB approved the use of a **renegotiable rate mortgage** loan. This was a 30-year loan with a requirement that every 1, 3, or 5 years the interest rate be adjusted to reflect current market conditions. Monthly payments were then adjusted up or down accordingly.

Current Format for ARMs

In 1981, the FHLBB authorized savings institutions to make the type of adjustable mortgage loan you are most likely to encounter in today's loan marketplace. This loan format is called an **adjustable rate mortgage (ARM)** or **adjustable mortgage loan (AML).** In authorizing ARMs the FHLBB's main requirement is that the interest rate on these loans be tied to some publicly available index that is mutually acceptable to the lender and the borrower. Basically, the concept is the same as the variable rate mortgage: as interest rates rise and fall in the open market, then the interest rate the lender is entitled to receive from the borrower rises and falls. The purpose is to more closely match what the savings institution receives from borrowers to what it must pay savers to attract funds.

Figure 12:2
ADJUSTABLE RATE MORTGAGES

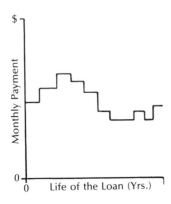

The benefit of an ARM to a borrower is that ARMs carry an initial interest rate that is lower than the rate on a fixed-rate mortgage of similar maturity. This often makes the difference between being able to qualify for a desired home and not qualifying for it. Other advantages to the borrower are that if market interest rates fall, the borrower's monthly payments will fall. (This is done without the cost of prepayment penalties and new loan origination costs as with a fixed-rate loan.) Most ARMs allow assumption by a new buyer at the terms in the ARM, and most allow total prepayment without penalty, particularly if there has been an upward adjustment in the interest rate.

The disadvantage of an ARM to the borrower is that if interest rates rise, the borrower is going to pay more. In periods of rising interest rates, property values and wages presumably will rise. But the possibility of progressively larger monthly payments for the family home often remains unattractive. As a result, various compromises have been worked out between lenders and borrowers so that rates can rise on loans, but not by too much. In view of the fact that about one-half of all mortgage loans being originated by thrifts, banks and mortgage companies are now adjustable, let us take a closer look at what a borrower gets with this loan format.

The interest rate on an ARM is tied to an **index rate.**   *Interest Rate*
When the index rate moves up or down, so do the borrower's payments when adjustment time arrives. Lenders and borrowers alike want a rate that genuinely reflects current market conditions for interest rates and which can be easily verified. By far, the most popular index is the interest rate on 1-year U.S. Treasury securities. Next most popular is the cost of funds to thrift institutions as measured by the FHLBB. A few loans use 6-month Treasury bills as an index rate.

To the index rate is added the margin. The **margin** is   *Margin*
calculated for the lender's cost of doing business, risk of loss on the loan and profit. Currently this runs from 2% to 3%, depending on the characteristics of the loan. This is a useful comparison device because if two lenders are offering the same loan terms and the same index, but one loan has a margin of 2% and the other 3%, then the one with the 2% margin will have lower loan payments. As a rule, the margin stays constant during the life of the loan. At each adjustment point in the loan's life, the lender takes the index rate and adds the margin. The total becomes the interest the borrower will pay until the next adjustment occurs.

The amount of time that elapses between adjustments   *Adjustment Period*
is called the adjustment period. By far, the most common adjustment period is 1 year. Less commonly used are 6-month,

3-year, and 5-year adjustment periods. When market rates are rising, the longer adjustment periods benefit the borrower. When market rates are falling, the shorter periods benefit the borrower because index decreases will show up sooner in their monthly payments.

Interest Rate Cap   Many lenders offer an **interest rate cap** or ceiling on how much the interest rate can increase for any one adjustment period during the life of the loan. If the cap is very low, say ½% per year, the lender does not have much more flexibility than if holding a fixed-rate loan. Thus, there would be little reduction of initial rate on the loan compared to a fixed-rate loan. If there is no cap at all, the borrower may feel quite uneasy. Compromises have prevailed, and the two most popular caps are 1% or 2% per year. In other words, the index rate may rise by 3%, but the cap limits the borrower's rate increase to 1% or 2%. Any unused difference may be added the next year, assuming the index rate has not fallen in the meantime.

Most borrowers also like to have a **lifetime cap** on interest. The purpose is to relieve the borrower's concern of interest rates rising without limit. A popular arrangement is a 5% life-of-loan interest rate cap. Thus, if an ARM is written at 10% interest, the maximum it could go to during its life is 15% interest.

Payment Cap   What if a loan's index rate rises so fast that the annual rate cap is reached each year and the lifetime cap is reached soon in the life of the loan? A borrower might be able to handle a modest increase in payments each year, but not big jumps in quick succession. To counteract this possibility, a **payment cap** sets a limit on how much the borrower's monthly payment can increase in any one year. A popular figure now in use is 7½%. In other words, no matter how high a payment is called for by the index rate, the borrower's monthly payment can only rise, at the most, 7½% per year. For example, given an initial rate of 10% on a 30-year ARM for $100,000, the monthly payment of interest and principal is $878 (see Table 11:1). If the index rate calls for a 2% upward adjustment at the end of 1 year, the payment on the loan would be $1,029. This is an increase of $151 or 17.2%. A 7½% payment cap would limit the increase to 107.5% × $878 = $943.85.

Negative Amortization

Although the 7½% payment cap in the above example protects the borrower's monthly payment from rising too fast, it does not make the difference between what's called for ($1,029) and what's paid ($943.85). The difference ($85.15) is added to the balance owed on the loan and earns interest just like the original amount borrowed. This is called **negative amortization:** instead of the loan balance dropping each month as loan payments are made, the balance owed rises. This can bring concern to the lender who can visualize the day the loan balance exceeds the value of the property. A popular arrangement is to set a limit of 125% of the original loan balance. At that point, either the lender accrues no more negative amortization or the loan is reamortized depending on the wording of the loan contract. Reamortized in this situation means the monthly payments will be adjusted upward by enough to stop the negative amortization.

Choosing Loan Rates Wisely

When a lender makes an ARM loan, the lender must explain to the borrower, in writing, the **worst-case scenario.** In other words, the lender must explain what will happen to the borrower's payments if the index rises the maximum amount each period up to the lifetime interest cap. If there is a payment cap, that and any possibility of negative amortization must also be explained. If the borrower is uneasy with these possibilities, then a fixed-rate loan should be considered. Most lenders offer fixed-rate loans as well as adjustable rate loans. Additionally, FHA and VA loans are fixed-rate loans.

"**Teaser rate**" adjustables have been offered from time to time by a few lenders and are best avoided. This is an ARM with an enticingly attractive initial rate below the market. For example, the teaser rate may be offered at 2% below market. A borrower who cannot qualify at the market rate might be able to do so at the teaser rate. However, in a year the loan contract calls for a 2% jump followed by additional annual increases. This overwhelms the borrower who, unable to pay, allows foreclosure to take place.

GRADUATED PAYMENT [MORTGAGES]

The objective of a **graduated payment mortgage** is to help borrowers qualify for loans by basing repayment schedules on salary expectations. With this type of mortgage, the interest rate and maturity are fixed but the monthly payment gradually rises. For example, a 10%, $60,000, 30-year loan normally requires monthly payments of $527 for complete amortization. Under the graduated payment mortgage, payments could start out as low as $437 per month the first year, then gradually increase to $590 in the eleventh year and then remain at that level until the thirtieth year. Since the interest alone on this $60,000 loan is $500 per month, the amount owed on the loan actually increases during its early years. Only when the monthly payment exceeds the monthly interest does the balance owed on the loan decrease.

Figure 12:3
GRADUATED PAYMENT MORTGAGE

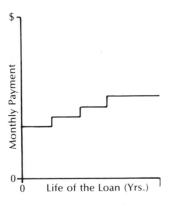

The FHA insures graduated payment mortgages under Section 245 and offers five repayment plans. This program is designed to appeal to first-time home buyers in the $15,000 to $25,000 income range because it enables them to tailor their installment payments to their expanding incomes, and thus buy a home sooner than under regular mortgage financing. An **adjustable graduated payment mortgage** combines variable interest with graduated payment features.

A variation of the graduated payment mortgage is the **growing equity mortgage.** This is a 30-year fixed-rate mortgage with monthly payments that are increased 3% to 7% each year. This loan is designed to parallel the borrower's income and fully repay itself in 12 to 15 years.

SHARED APPRECIATION MORTGAGES

The basic concept of a **shared appreciation mortgage (SAM)** is that the borrower gives the lender a portion of the property's appreciation in return for a lower rate of interest. To illustrate, a lender who would otherwise charge 12% interest might agree to take 8% interest plus one-third of the appreciation of the property. The lender is accepting what amounts to a speculative investment in the property in return for a reduced interest rate. The borrower is able to buy and occupy a home that he or she might not otherwise be able to afford, but gives up part of any future price appreciation.

Despite the apparent advantages of the SAM, there are some major pitfalls. For example, at what point in the future is the gain recognized and the lender paid off? If the home is sold, the profits can be split in accordance with the agreement. However, what if the lender feels the home is being sold at too low a price? What if the home is not sold for cash? What if the borrower does not want to sell? One answer to the last situation is that the lender may set a time limit of 10 years on the loan. If the home has not been sold by that time, the home is appraised and the borrower pays the lender the lender's share of the appreciation. At a 10% appreciation rate, a $93,750 house would be worth $243,164 ten years later. If the lender was entitled to one-third of the $149,414 appreciation, the borrower would owe the lender $49,805 in appreciation plus the remaining $70,000 balance on the loan. Unless the borrower can pay cash, this would have to be refinanced at then current rates of interest. On the other hand, if the property experiences no appreciation in value, the borrower will have enjoyed a below-market-rate loan for 10 years and be responsible only for refinancing the remaining loan balance at that time. These types of loans are questionable in Texas, as they could violate the Texas Homestead laws by forcing a sale of the homestead.

Figure 12:4
SHARED APPRECIATION MORTGAGES

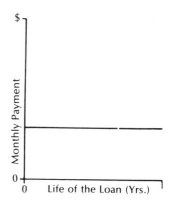

EQUITY SHARING

Giving the party that provides the financing a "piece of the action in the deal" is not a new innovation. Insurance companies financing shopping centers and office buildings have long used the idea of requiring part of the rental income and/or part of the profits plus interest on the loan itself. In other words, the lender wants to share in some of the benefits normally reserved for the equity holder in return for providing financing. The equity holder would agree to this either to get a lower rate of interest, such as in the SAM above, or to get financing when financing was scarce, or where the equity holder was not big enough to handle the deal alone. For example, on a $5 million project, the lender might agree to make a loan of $4 million at a very attractive rate if it can buy a half interest in the equity for $500,000.

Equity sharing is also found in residential financing. One variation is for an enterprising real estate person to find attractive income properties and sell a 50% equity interest to someone who wants to invest in real estate, but who has more money than time. The investor makes half of the down payment and signs for the loan. For this, the investor gets half of the income and profits and all of the tax deductions. The entrepreneur gets the other half in return for the remaining down payment and the effort of finding and managing the property. This type of financing, too, may encounter some difficulty with Texas homestead laws if one party occupies the house as their homestead.

"Rich Uncle" Financing

A second variation of equity sharing is often called "rich uncle" financing. The investor may be a parent helping a son or daughter buy a home or a son or daughter buying a parent's present home while giving the parent(s) the right to occupy it. A third variation is for an investor to provide most of the down payment for a home buyer, collect rent from the home buyer, pay the mortgage payments and property taxes and claim depreciation. Each party has a right to a portion of any appreciation and the right to buy out the other. The FHLMC now recognizes the importance of equity sharing and will buy mortgage loans on shared-equity properties. The FHLMC requires that the owner-occupant contribute at least 5% of the equity, that the owner-occupant and the owner-investor sign the mortgage and note, that both be individuals and that there be no agreement requiring sale or buy-out within 7 years of the loan date. Equity sharing can provide attractive tax benefits; however, you must seek competent tax advice before involving yourself or someone else.

PACKAGE MORTGAGES

Normally, we think of real estate mortgage loans as being secured solely by real estate. However, it is possible to include items classed as personal property in a real estate mortgage, thus creating a **package mortgage.** In residential loans, such items as the refrigerator, clothes washer and dryer can be pledged along with the house and land in a single mortgage. The purpose is to raise the value of the collateral in order to raise the amount a lender is willing to loan. For the borrower, it offers the opportunity of financing major appliances at the same rate of interest as the real estate itself. This rate is usually lower than if the borrower finances the appliances separately. Once an item of personal property is included in a package mortgage, selling it is a violation of the mortgage without the prior consent of the lender.

A mortgage secured by two or more properties is called a **blanket mortgage.** Suppose you want to buy a house plus the vacant lot next door, financing the purchase with a single mortgage that covers both properties. The cost of preparing one mortgage instead of two is a savings. Also, by combining the house and lot, the lot can be financed on better terms than if it were financed separately, as lenders more readily loan on a house and land than on land alone. Note, however, if the vacant lot is later sold separately from the house before the mortgage loan is fully repaid, it will be necessary to have it released from the blanket mortgage. This is usually accomplished by including a partial release clause in the original mortgage agreement that specifies how much of the loan must be repaid before the lot can be released.

BLANKET MORTGAGES

With a regular mortgage, the lender makes a lump sum payment to the borrower, who in turn repays it through monthly payments to the lender. With a **reverse mortgage,** also known as a reverse annuity mortgage or RAM, the lender makes a monthly payment to the homeowner who later repays in a lump sum. The reverse mortgage can be particularly valuable for an elderly homeowner who does not want to sell, but whose retirement income is not quite enough for comfortable living. The homeowner receives a monthly check, has full use of the property, and is not required to repay until he sells or dies. If he sells the home, money from the sale is taken to repay the loan. If he dies first, the property is sold through the estate and the loan repaid. There is some concern that the borrower may outlive his loan term. This may also encounter problems with Texas homestead laws.

REVERSE MORTGAGES (RAMs)

Under a **construction loan,** also called an interim loan, money is advanced as construction takes place. For example, a vacant lot owner arranges to borrow $60,000 to build a house. The lender does not advance all $60,000 at once because the value of the collateral is insufficient to warrant that amount

CONSTRUCTION OR INTERIM LOANS

until the house is finished. Instead, the lender will parcel out the loan as the building is being constructed, always holding a portion until the property is ready for occupancy, or in some cases actually occupied. Some lenders specialize only in construction loans and do not want to wait 20 or 30 years to be repaid. If so, it will be necessary to obtain a permanent long-term mortgage from another source for the purpose of repaying the construction loan. This is known as a permanent commitment or a **take-out loan,** since it takes the construction lender out of the financial picture when construction is completed and allows him to recycle his money into new construction projects.

BLENDED-RATE LOANS   Many real estate lenders still hold long-term loans that were made at interest rates below the current market. One way of raising the return on these loans is to offer borrowers who have them a **blended-rate loan.** Suppose you owe $50,000 on your home loan and the interest rate on it is 7%. Suppose further that the current rate on home loans is 12%. Your lender might offer to refinance your home for $70,000 at 9%, presuming the property will appraise high enough and you have the income to qualify. The $70,000 refinance offer would put $20,000 in your pocket (less loan fees), but would increase the interest you pay from 7% to 9% on the original $50,000. This puts the cost of the $20,000 at 14% per year. The arithmetic is as follows: you will now be paying 9% × $70,000 = $6,300 in interest. Before you paid 7% × $50,000 = $3,500 in interest. The difference, $2,800, is what you pay to borrow the additional $20,000. This equates to $2,800 ÷ $20,000 = 14% interest. This is the figure you should use in comparing other sources of financing (such as a second mortgage) or deciding whether you even want to borrow.

A blended-rate loan can be very attractive in a situation where you want to sell your home and you do not want to help finance the buyer. Suppose your home is worth $87,500 and you have the above-described $50,000, 7% loan. A buyer would normally expect to make a down payment of $17,500 and pay 12% interest on a new $70,000 loan. But with a blended loan your lender could offer the buyer the needed

$70,000 financing at 9%, a far more attractive rate and one that requires less income in order to qualify. Blended loans are available on FHA, VA and conventional loans held by the FNMA. Other lenders also offer them on fixed-rate assumable loans they hold.

Buy-downs are used to reduce the rate of interest a buyer must pay on a new mortgage loan. For example, suppose a builder has a tract of homes for sale and the current interest rate on home loans is 12%. At that interest rate, there are few buyers. What the builder can do is to arrange with a lender to pay the lender discount points so that the lender can offer a loan at a lower interest to the buyer. This can be done for the life of the loan at the cost of about 8 discount points for every point of interest rate reduction. Or, it can be done for a shorter period, such as the first 3 years of the loan's life. For example, the builder could offer 9% interest for the first 3 years of the loan. Not only is 9% more attractive than 12%, but more buyers can qualify for loans at 9% than at 12%. Although the buy-down is costly to the builder, it will help sell homes that might otherwise go unsold. Moreover, a buy-down will usually boost sales more than a price reduction of like amount. The builder offering the buy-down will usually take a price reduction equal to the discount points if the buyer will forego the buy-down. The disadvantage of a short-term buy-down is that market rates may not drop to allow refinancing and/or the buyer's income may not rise enough.

BUY-DOWNS

An **equity mortgage** is a loan arrangement wherein the lender agrees to extend a line of credit based on the amount of equity in a person's home. The maximum amount of the loan is generally 70% to 80% of the appraised value of the home minus any first mortgage or other liens against the property. The borrower need not take all the credit available, but rather can draw against the mortgage as needed. Some lenders specify a minimum amount per withdrawal. The borrower pays interest only on the amount actually borrowed, not the maximum available. The borrower then has several

EQUITY MORTGAGES

Figure 12:5
BUY-DOWN MORTGAGES

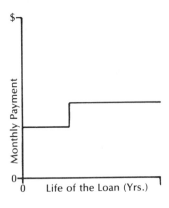

Life of the Loan (Yrs.)

years to repay the amount borrowed. The interest rate is adjustable and tends to be 1 to 3 percentage points above the "prime rate" paid by large corporations.

The equity mortgage will typically be a second mortgage that is used to tap the increase in equity resulting from rising home prices and first loan paydown. It's all done without having to refinance the first loan and uses the home as an asset against which the homeowner can borrow and repay as needed. Equity mortgages are very popular as a source of home improvement loans, money for college expenses, money to start a business, money for a major vacation and money to buy more real estate. The 1986 Tax Reform Act has made equity mortgages even more attractive by repealing the tax deductibility of interest paid on personal loans. Real estate interest is still deductible up to the limits described in Chapter 13.

Equity mortgages are unenforceable as liens in Texas, of course, because of the Texas homestead laws. As you will recall from Chapter 2, the only liens enforceable against the homestead in Texas are loans for purchase money, taxes, and home improvements. Simply stated, one *cannot* finance the equity in his homestead in Texas unless he can find a lender who is willing to suffer the potential consequences of an unenforceable lien.

SELLER FINANCING   When a seller is willing to accept part of the property's purchase price in the form of the buyer's promissory note accompanied by a mortgage or deed of trust, it is called **seller financing.** This allows the buyer to substitute a promissory note for cash, and the seller is said to be "taking back paper." Seller financing is popular for land sales (where lenders rarely loan), on property where an existing mortgage is being assumed by the buyer, and on property where the seller prefers to receive his money spread out over a period of time, with interest, instead of lump-sum cash. For example, a retired couple sells a rental home they own. The home is worth $120,000 and they owe $20,000. If they need only $60,000 in cash, they might be more than happy to take $60,000 down, let the buyer assume the existing mortgage and accept the remaining $40,000 in monthly payments at current interest rates. Alternatively, the buyer and seller can agree to structure the $40,000 as an adjustable, graduated, partially amortized or interest-only loan.

If the seller receives the sales price spread out over two or more years, income taxes are calculated using the installment reporting method discussed in Chapter 13. Being able to spread out the taxes on a gain may be an incentive to use seller financing. The seller should be aware, however, that he may not be able to convert his "paper" to cash without a long wait or without having to sell it at a substantial discount to an investor. Additionally, the seller is responsible for servicing the loan and is subject to losses due to default and foreclosure.

Note that some real estate agents and lenders refer to a loan that is carried back by a seller as a **purchase money** loan. Others define a purchase money loan as any loan, carry-back or institutional, that is used to finance the purchase of real property.

An alternative method of financing a real estate sale such as the one just reviewed is to use a **wraparound mortgage** or **wraparound deed of trust.** A "wraparound" encompasses existing mortgages and is subordinate (junior) to them. The existing mortgages stay on the property and the new mortgage wraps around them.

WRAPAROUND MORTGAGES

To illustrate, presume the existing $20,000 loan in the previous example carries an interest rate of 7% and that there are 10 years remaining on the loan. Presume further that current interest rates are 12%. With a wraparound it is possible for the buyer to pay less than 12% and at the same time for the seller to receive more than 12% on the money owed him. This is done by taking the buyer's $60,000 down payment and then creating a new junior mortgage that includes not only the $20,000 owed on the existing first mortgage but also the $40,000 the buyer owes the seller. In other words, the wraparound mortgage will be for $60,000, and the seller continues to remain liable for payment of the first mortgage. If the interest rate on the wraparound is set at 10%, the buyer saves by not having to pay 12% as he would on an entirely new loan. The advantage to the seller is that he is earning 10% not only on his $40,000 equity, but also on the $20,000 loan for which he is paying 7% interest. This gives the seller an actual yield of 11½% on his $40,000. (The calculation is as follows. The seller receives 10% on $60,000, which amounts to $6,000. He pays 7% on $20,000, which is $1,400. The difference, $4,600 is divided by $40,000 to get the seller's actual yield of 11½%.)

Wraparounds are not limited to seller financing. If the seller in the above example did not want to finance the sale, a third-party lender could provide the needed $40,000 and take a wraparound mortgage. The wraparound concept will not work when the mortgage debt to be "wrapped" contains an enforceable due-on-sale clause.

SUBORDINATION   Another financing technique is **subordination.** For example, a person owns a $200,000 vacant lot suitable for building, and a builder wants to build an $800,000 building on the lot. The builder has only $100,000 cash and the largest construction loan available is $800,000. If the builder can convince the lot owner to take $100,000 in cash and $100,000 later, he would have the $1 million total. However, the lender making the $800,000 loan will want to be the first mortgagee to protect its position in the event of foreclosure. The lot owner must be willing to take a subordinate position, in this case a second mortgage. If the project is successful, the lot owner will receive $100,000, plus interest, either in cash after the building is built and sold or as monthly payments. If the project goes into foreclosure, the lot owner can be paid only if the $800,000 first mortgage claim is satisfied in full from the sale proceeds. As you can surmise here, the lot owner must be very careful that the money loaned by the lender actually goes into construction and that whatever is built is worth at least $800,000 in addition to the land.

CONTRACTS FOR DEED   A **contract for deed,** also called an **installment contract**
OR INSTALLMENT   or **land contract,** enables the seller to finance a buyer by
CONTRACTS   permitting him to make a down payment followed by monthly payments. However, title remains in the name of the seller. In addition to its wise use in financing land sales, it has

also been a very effective financing tool in several states as a means of selling homes. For example, a homeowner owes $25,000 on his home and wants to sell it for $85,000. A buyer is found but does not have the $60,000 down payment necessary to assume the existing loan. The buyer does have $8,000, but for one reason or another cannot or chooses not to borrow from an institutional lender. If the seller is agreeable, the buyer can pay the seller $8,000 and enter into an installment contract with the seller for the remaining $77,000. The contract will call for monthly payments by the buyer to the seller that are large enough to allow the seller to meet the payments on the $25,000 loan plus repay the $52,000 owed to the seller, with interest. Unless property taxes and insurance are billed to the buyer, the seller will also collect for these and pay them. When the final payment is made to the seller (or the property refinanced through an institutional lender), title is conveyed to the buyer. Meanwhile the seller continues to hold title and is responsible for paying the mortgage. In addition to wrapping around a mortgage, an installment contract can also be used to wrap around another installment contract, provided it does not contain an enforceable due-on-sale clause. (Please see Chapter 8 for more about the contractual side of installment contracts.)

OPTION

When viewed as a financing tool, an **option** provides a method by which the need to immediately finance the full price of a property can be postponed. For example, a developer is offered 100 acres of land for a house subdivision but is not sure that the market will absorb that many houses. The solution is to buy 25 acres outright and take three 25-acre options at preset prices on the remainder. If the houses on the first 25 acres sell promptly, the builder can exercise the options to buy the remaining land. If sales are not good, the builder can let the remaining options expire and avoid being stuck with unwanted acreage.

A popular variation on the option idea is the **lease with option to buy** combination. Under it an owner leases to a tenant who, in addition to paying rent and using the property, also obtains the right to purchase it at a preset price for a fixed period of time. Homes are often sold this way, particularly when the resale market is sluggish. (Please see Chapter 8 for more about a lease with option to buy.)

Options can provide speculative opportunities to persons with limited amounts of capital. If prices do not rise, the optionee loses only the cost of the option; if prices do rise, the optionee exercises the option and realizes a profit.

CREATIVE FINANCING

The decade of the 1980s started with a shortage of money for real estate loans and an abundance of financing ideas. Many of these involved seller-assisted financing. At one point in 1982 it was estimated that 80% of home mortgage financing was by way of assumptions and seller financing.

The wraparound mortgage and installment contract are considered forms of creative financing. Most were designed to pass along the benefits of a low-interest loan in a high-interest market. With the Garn Act and the *de la Cuesta* case fewer loans are suitable for wrapping. If interest rates fall, wrapping will be less attractive and new financing more attractive. Nonetheless, there is plenty of room for creative ideas to solve financing problems. For example, a $400,000 apartment building with a $200,000 first mortgage against it is for sale. The seller wants $120,000 in cash and will carry paper for the rest as long as the loan-to-value ratio does not exceed 80%. A buyer has $40,000 in cash plus a house worth $80,000 with a $20,000 loan against it. The solution is to refinance the apartment building with the lender for 70%. This is a standard L/V ratio for apartment buildings and creates $80,000 in cash. The buyer gives the seller $40,000 in cash, a $40,000 second mortgage against the apartment building and a $40,000 second mortgage against the house. This will not work if the house is the buyer's homestead, though.

In another example of creative financing, consider the builder with many unsold homes but plenty of buyers who would like to buy if they could finance buyers for their present homes. The builder offers to help finance the sale of a buyer's property in order to make his own sale. Two parties get the homes they want and the builder is relieved of unsold inventory.

One seller-financing arrangement that deserves special attention because of its traps for the unwary is the **overencumbered property.** Institutional lenders are closely regulated regarding the amount of money they can loan against the appraised value of the property. Individuals are not regulated. The following example will illustrate the potential problem. Suppose a seller owns a house that is realistically worth $100,000 and the mortgage balance is $10,000. A buyer offers to purchase the property with the condition that he be allowed to obtain an $80,000 loan on the property from a lender. The $80,000 is used to pay off the existing $10,000 loan and to pay the broker's commission, loan fees and closing costs. The remaining $62,000 is split $30,000 to the seller and $32,000 to the buyer. The buyer also gives the seller a note, secured by a second mortgage against the property, for $80,000. The seller may feel good about getting $30,000 in cash and an $80,000 mortgage, for this is more than the property is worth, or so it seems.

But the $80,000 second mortgage stands junior to the $80,000 first mortgage. That's $160,000 of debt against a $100,000 property. The buyer might be trying to resell the property for $160,000 or more, but the chances of this are slim. More likely the buyer will wind up walking away from the property. This leaves the seller the choice of taking over the payments on the first mortgage or losing the property completely to the holder of the first.

Although such a scheme sounds crazy when viewed from a distance, the reason it can be performed is that the seller wants more for the property than it's worth. Someone then offers a deal showing that price, and the seller looks the other way from the possible consequences. Real estate agents who participate in such transactions are likely to find their licenses suspended. State licensing authorities take the position that a real estate agent is a professional who should know enough not to take part in a deal that leaves the seller holding a junior lien on an overencumbered property. This, too, seems logical when viewed from a distance. But when sales are slow and commissions thin, it is sometimes easy to put commission income ahead of fiduciary responsibility.

OVERLY CREATIVE FINANCING?

If in doubt about the propriety of a transaction, the Golden Rule of doing unto others as you would have them do unto you still applies. (Or as some restate it: "What goes around, comes around.")

INVESTING IN
MORTGAGES

Individuals can invest in mortgages in two ways. One is to invest in mortgage loan pools through certificates guaranteed by Ginnie Mae and Freddie Mac and available from stockbrokers. These yield about ½ of 1% below what FHA and VA borrowers are paying. In 1985, for example, this was approximately 11%, and the certificates are readily convertible to cash at current market prices on the open market if the investor does not want to hold them through maturity.

Individuals can also buy junior mortgages at yields above Ginnie Mae and Freddie Mac certificates. These junior mortgages are seconds, thirds and fourths offered by mortgage brokers. They yield more because they are riskier as to repayment and much more difficult to convert to cash before maturity. "There is," as the wise old adage says, "no such thing as a free lunch." Thus, it is important to recognize that when an investment of any kind promises above-market returns, there is some kind of added risk attached. With junior mortgages, it is important to realize that when a borrower offers to pay a premium above the best loan rates available from banks and thrift institutions, it is because the borrower and/ or the property does not qualify for the best rates.

Before buying a mortgage as an investment, one should have the title to the property searched. This is the only way to know for certain what priority the mortgage will have in the event of foreclosure. There have been cases where investors have purchased what they were told to be first and second mortgages only to find in foreclosure that they were actually holding third and fourth mortgages where the amount of debt exceeded the value of the property.

And how does one find the value of a property? By having it appraised by a professional appraiser who is independent of the party making or selling the mortgage investment. This value is compared to the existing and proposed debt against the property. The investor should also run a credit check on the borrower. The investor's final protection is, however, in making certain that the market value of the property is well in excess of the loans against it and that the property is well-constructed, well-located and functional.

Even though tenants do not acquire fee ownership, **rentals** and **leases** are a means of financing real estate. Whether the tenant is a bachelor receiving the use of a $30,000 apartment for which he pays $350 rent per month or a large corporation leasing a warehouse for 20 years, leasing is an ideal method of financing when the tenant does not want to buy, cannot raise the funds to buy or prefers to invest available funds elsewhere. Similarly, **farming leases** provide for the use of land without the need to purchase it. Some farm leases call for fixed rental payment. Other leases require the farmer to pay the landowner a share of the value of the crop that is actually produced—say 25%—and the landowner shares with the farmer the risks of weather, crop output and prices.

RENTAL

Under a **sale and leaseback** arrangement, an owner-occupant sells the property and then remains as a tenant. Thus, the buyer acquires an investment and the seller obtains capital for other purposes while retaining the use of the property. A variation is for the tenant to construct a building, sell it to a prearranged buyer, and immediately lease it back.

Although **leased land** arrangements are common throughout the United States for both commercial and industrial users and for farmers, anything other than fee ownership of residential land is unthinkable in many areas. Yet in some parts of the United States (for example, Baltimore, Maryland; Orange County, California; throughout Hawaii; and in parts of Florida) homes built on leased land are commonplace. Typically, these leases are at least 55 years in length and, barring an agreement to the contrary, the improvements to the land become the property of the fee owner at the end of the lease. Rents may be fixed in advance for the life of the lease, renegotiated at preset points during the life of the lease, or a combination of both.

LAND LEASES

To hedge against inflation, when fixed rents are used in a long-term lease, it is common practice to use **step-up rentals.** For example, under a 55-year house-lot lease, the rent may be set at $400 per year for the first 15 years, $600 per year for the next 10 years, $800 for the next 10 years, and so forth. An alternative is to renegotiate the rent at various points during the life of a lease so that the effects of land value changes are more closely equalized between the lessor and the lessee. For example, a 60-year lease may contain renegotiation points at the fifteenth, thirtieth, and forty-fifth years. At those points the property would be reappraised and the lease rent adjusted to reflect any changes in the value of the property. Property taxes and any increases in property taxes are paid by the lessee.

OVERVIEW OF FINANCING OPTIONS

If people always paid cash for real estate, the last four chapters would not have been necessary. But 95% of the time they don't; so means have been devised to finance their purchases. This has been true since the beginning of recorded history and will continue into the future. The financing methods that evolve will depend on the problems to be solved. For example, long-term fixed-rate amortized loans were the solution to foreclosures in the 1930s, and they worked well as long as interest rates did not fluctuate greatly. Graduated payment loans were devised when housing prices rose faster than buyer's incomes. Adjustable rate loans were developed so that lenders could more closely align the interest they receive from borrowers with the interest they pay their savers. Extensive use of loan assumptions, wraparounds and seller financing became necessary in the early 1980s because borrowers could not qualify for 16% and 18% loans and sellers were unwilling to drop prices.

With regard to the future, if mortgage money is expensive or in short supply, seller financing will play a large role. With the experience of rapidly fluctuating interest rates fresh in people's minds, loans with adjustable rates will continue to be widely offered. Fixed-rate loans will either have short maturities or carry a premium to compensate the lender for being locked into a fixed rate for a long period. When interest rates turn down again, borrowers with adjustable loans will benefit from lower monthly payments. If rates stay down long enough, fixed-rate loans will become more popular again.

Match terms **a–z** *with statements* **1–26.**

1. **a.** Adjustment period
24 **b.** Adjustable rate mortgage
2 **c.** Blanket mortgage
8 **d.** Blended-rate loan
10 **e.** Buy-down
16 **f.** Carryback financing
21 **g.** Contract for deed
15 **h.** Due-on-sale clause
9 **i.** Equity mortgage
17 **j.** Equity sharing
22 **k.** Fannie Mae
25 **l.** Graduated payment
    mortgage
12 **m.** Index rate

13 **n.** Interest rate cap
20 **o.** Mortgage company
7 **p.** Negative amortization
18 **q.** Option
5 **r.** Overencumbered property
3 **s.** Package mortgage
14 **t.** Payment cap
11 **u.** Reverse mortgage
6 **v.** Sale and leaseback
19 **w.** Secondary mortgage
    market
4 **x.** Subordination
23 **y.** Usury
26 **z.** Wraparound mortgage

VOCABULARY
REVIEW

1. The amount of time that elapses between interest rate changes on a loan.
2. A mortgage secured by two or more properties.
3. A mortgage secured by real and personal property.
4. To voluntarily give up a higher mortgage priority for a lower one.
5. A situation where the loans against a property exceed the value of the property.
6. A financing arrangement whereby an owner-occupant sells the property and then remains as a tenant.
7. Results when monthly interest exceeds monthly payment and the difference is added to the principal.
8. A refinanced loan wherein the lender combines the interest rate of the existing loan with a current rate.
9. A mortgage wherein the lender extends a line of credit based on the amount of equity in a person's home.
10. A payment by the seller to the lender in order to reduce the interest rate for the buyer.
11. A loan wherein the lender makes monthly payments to the property owner who later repays in a lump sum.
12. The interest rate, such as on U.S. Treasury securities, to which an adjustable loan is tied.
13. The ceiling to which the interest rate on a loan can rise.
14. A limit on how much a borrower's payment can increase in any one year.
15. Requires immediate repayment of the loan if ownership transfers; also called an alienation clause.
16. A note is accepted by a seller instead of cash.
17. An arrangement whereby a party providing financing gets a portion of the ownership.

18. A right, for a given period of time, to buy, sell or lease property at preset price and terms.
19. A market where mortgage loans can be sold to investors.
20. A firm that makes mortgage loans and then sells them to investors.
21. A method of selling and financing property whereby the buyer obtains possession but the seller retains the title.
22. A lending industry name for the Federal National Mortgage Association.
23. Charging a rate of interest higher than that permitted by law.
24. A mortgage loan on which the rate of interest can rise and fall with changes in prevailing interest rates.
25. A mortgage repayment plan that allows the borrower to make smaller monthly payments at first and larger ones later.
26. A debt instrument that encompasses existing mortgages and is subordinate to them.

QUESTIONS AND PROBLEMS

1. What is the most significant difference between a mortgage broker and a mortgage banker?
2. In the secondary mortgage market, who provides the loan money?
3. What is meant by the term "loan servicing"?
4. What is an adjustable rate mortgage?
5. What was the significance to real estate lending of the *de la Cuesta* case and the Garn Act?
6. By what financing methods do FNMA and GNMA provide money for real estate loans?
7. If a dollar is a dollar no matter where it comes from, what difference does it make if the source of a real estate loan was real savings or fiat money?
8. Regarding adjustable rate mortgage loans, what are the advantages and disadvantages to the borrower and lender?
9. Explain why rentals and leases are considered forms of real estate financing.
10. What is the single most important precaution an investor can make before buying a junior mortgage?

Taxes and Assessments

KEY TERMS

Adjusted sales price: the sales price of a property less commissions, fix-up, and closing costs
Ad valorem taxes: taxes charged according to the value of a property
Assessed value: a value placed on a property for the purpose of taxation
Assessment appeal board: local governmental body which hears and rules on property owner complaints of overassessment
Basis: the price paid for property; used in calculating income taxes

Documentary tax: a fee or tax on deeds and other documents payable at the time of recordation
Gain: the profit on the sale of an appreciated asset
Installment: a sale wherein the seller receives part (or all) of the purchase price in later taxable years
Mill rate: property tax rate that is expressed in tenths of a cent per dollar of assessed valuation
Tax lien: a charge or hold by the government against property to insure the payment of taxes

PROPERTY TAXES

The largest single source of income in America for local government programs and services is the property tax. Schools (from kindergarten through two-year colleges), fire and police departments, local welfare programs, public libraries, street maintenance, parks, and public hospital facilities are mainly supported by property taxes. Some state governments also obtain a portion of their revenues from this source.

Property taxes are **ad valorem** taxes. This means that they are levied according to the value of one's property; the more valuable the property, the higher the tax, and vice versa. The underlying theory of ad valorem taxation is that those owning the more valuable properties are wealthier and hence able to pay more taxes.

Determining how much tax a property owner will be charged involves three basic steps: (1) local government budget determination and appropriation, (2) appraisal of all taxable property within the taxation district, and (3) allocation

315

among individual property owners of the revenue that needs to be collected.

Appropriation

Each taxing body with the authority to tax prepares its budget for the coming year. Taxing bodies include the State of Texas, counties, cities, towns and villages, school districts, utility districts, water districts, and, in some counties, levee districts, sanitation districts, and other improvement districts. Each budget along with a list of sources from which the money will be derived is enacted into law. This is the **appropriation process.** Then estimated sales taxes, state and federal revenue sharing, business licenses, and city income taxes are subtracted from the budget. The balance must come from property taxes.

Assessment

Next, the valuation of the taxable property within each taxing body's district must be determined. To assure uniformity in appraisals, the Texas Property Tax Code provides for an **appraisal district** in each county. All taxing districts are required to use the appraisal district's value in determining the taxes to be paid. The county appraisal district appraises each taxable parcel of land and the improvements thereon. In Texas, the appraised value is the estimated fair market cash value of the property. This is the cash price one would expect a buyer and a seller to agree upon in a normal open market transaction.

The appraised value is converted into an assessed value upon which taxes are based. In Texas, the **assessed value** is set equal to the fair market value; in some other states, it is a percentage of the appraised value. Mathematically, the percentage selected makes no difference as long as each property is treated equally. Consider two houses with appraised values of $60,000 and $120,000, respectively. Whether the assessed values are set equal to appraised values or at a percentage of appraised values, the second house will still bear twice the property tax burden of the first.

Tax Rate Calculation

Certain types of property are exempt from taxation. The assessed values of the remaining taxable properties are then added together in order to calculate the tax rate. To explain this process, suppose that a building lies within the taxation districts of the Westside School District, the city of Rostin, and the county of Pearl River. The school district's budget for the coming year requires $800,000 from property taxes, and the assessed value of taxable property within the district is $20,000,000. By dividing $800,000 by $20,000,000, we see that the school district must collect a tax of 4 cents for every dollar of assessed valuation. This levy can be expressed three ways: (1) as a mill rate, (2) as dollars per hundred, or (3) as dollars per thousand. All three rating methods are found in the United States. The State of Texas uses dollars per hundred.

As a **mill rate,** this tax rate is expressed as mills per dollar of assessed valuation. Since 1 mill equals one-tenth of a cent, a 4-cent tax rate is the same as 40 mills. Expressed as **dollars per hundred,** the same rate would be $4 per hundred of assessed valuation. As **dollars per thousand,** it would be $40 per thousand.

The city of Rostin also calculates its tax rate by dividing its property tax requirements by the assessed value of the property within its boundaries. Suppose that its needs are $300,000 and the city limits enclose property totaling $10,000,000 in assessed valuation. (In this example, the city covers a smaller geographical area than the school district.) Thus the city must collect 3 cents for each dollar of assessed valuation in order to balance its budget.

The county government's budget requires $2,000,000 from property taxes and the county contains $200,000,000 in assessed valuation. This makes the county tax rate 1 cent per dollar of assessed valuation. Table 13:1 shows the school district, city, and county tax rates expressed as mills, dollars per hundred, and dollars per thousand.

EXPRESSING PROPERTY TAX RATES   Table 13:1

	Mill rate	Dollars per hundred	Dollars per thousands
School district	40 mills	$4.00	$40.00
City	30	3.00	30.00
County	10	1.00	10.00
Total	80 mills	$8.00	$80.00

The final step is to apply the tax rate to each property. So applying the mill rate to a home with an assessed value of $20,000, is simply a matter of multiplying the 80 mills (the equivalent of 8 cents) by the assessed valuation to arrive at property taxes of $1,600 per year. On a dollars per hundred basis, divide the $20,000 assessed valuation by $100 and multiply by $8. The result is $1,600. To insure collection, a lien for this amount is placed by the taxing authority against the property. It is removed when the tax is paid. Property tax liens are superior to other types of liens. Also, a mortgage foreclosure does not clear property tax liens; they still must be paid.

To avoid duplicate tax bill mailings, it is a common practice for all taxing bodies in a given county to have the county collect for them at the same time that the county collects on its own behalf.

The property tax year in Texas for state and county taxes is the calendar year. County and state taxes are billed once a year, are payable on October 1, and become delinquent on February 1 of the following year. Other taxing jurisdictions vary. A small discount is allowed for early payment of state and county taxes. Penalties are charged for late payment in all taxing jurisdictions.

UNPAID PROPERTY TAXES

All tax liens in Texas are, by law, superior to any other liens in existence on real estate. When an owner fails to pay his property taxes, the property is sold at a public tax auction; this extinguishes all other liens. However, unlike most liens in Texas, if foreclosure is due to unpaid taxes, the tax statutes provide a two-year period for the taxpayer to pay his taxes and have his property returned to him.

Texas statute provides that the period of redemption in all suits brought under the authority of the tax foreclosure statute shall be within two years from the date of the filing for record of the purchaser's deed, on the following basis:

(1) Within the first year of the redemption period, upon the payment of the amount of the bid for the property by the purchaser at such sale, including a One Dollar ($1) tax deed recording fee and all taxes, penalties, interest and costs thereafter paid thereon, plus twenty-five per cent (25%) of the aggregate total.

(2) Within the last year of the redemption period, upon the payment of the amount bid for the property at such sale, including a One Dollar ($1) tax deed recording fee and all taxes, penalties, interest and costs thereafter paid thereon, plus fifty per cent (50%) of the aggregate total; and no further or additional amount than herein specified shall be required to be paid to effect any such redemption.

Subject to the owner's right to redeem, any lienholder or party interested may redeem the property under the same provisions. The reason that a lienholder (such as a mortgage lender) is allowed to redeem a property is that if he does not do so, his creditor rights in the property are cut off because of the superiority of the tax lien.

There are other provisions for redemption if the land is sold under a decree and judgment of a court. The purchaser at such a foreclosure sale shall not be entitled to possession of the property sold for taxes until the expiration of two years after the date of recording the tax deed.

The right of government to divorce a property owner from his land for nonpayment of property taxes is well established by law. However, if the sale procedure is not properly followed, the purchaser may later find the property's title successfully challenged in court. Thus, it behooves the purchaser to obtain a title search and title insurance and, if necessary, to conduct a quiet title suit or file a suit to foreclose the rights of anyone previously having a right to the property.

ASSESSMENT APPEAL

By law, assessment procedures must be uniformly applied to all properties within a taxing jurisdiction. To this end, the values of all lands and buildings, as determined by the tax assessors, are made available for public inspection. These are the **assessment rolls.** They permit a property owner to compare the assessed valuation on his property with assessed valuations on similar properties. If an owner feels overassessed, he can file an appeal before the **Appraisal Review Board.** Texas also permits appeal to a court of law, if the property owner remains dissatisfied with the assessment. Note that the appeal process deals only with the method of assessment and taxation, not with the tax rate or the amount of tax.

PROPERTY TAX
EXEMPTIONS

More than half the land in many cities and counties is exempt from real property taxation. This is because governments and their agencies do not tax themselves or each other. Thus, government-owned offices of all types, public roads and parks, schools, military bases, and government-owned utilities are exempt from property taxes. Also exempted are properties owned by religious and charitable organizations (so long as they are used for religious or charitable purposes), hospitals, and cemeteries. In rural areas of Texas, large tracts of land are owned by federal and state governments, and these too are exempt from taxation. Texas also exempts from taxation: poorhouses, public libraries, art galleries, property of Boy Scouts, prison farms, veterans' organizations, fraternal organizations, public charities, certain nonprofit organizations, and volunteer fire departments. There are certain additional property tax exemptions for veterans of the armed forces.

Property tax exemptions are also used to attract industries and to appease voters. In the first instance, a local government agency may buy industrial land and buildings, and lease them to industries at a price lower than would be possible if they were privately owned and hence taxed. Alternatively, outright property tax reductions may be granted for a certain length of time to newly established or relocating firms. The rationale is that the cost to the public is outweighed by the economic boost that the new industry brings to the community. In the second instance, a number of states, including Texas, grant assessment reductions to resident homeowners for homestead property. This increases the tax burden for owners of rented houses and owners of households that rent and for commercial properties.

PROPERTY TAX
VARIATIONS

Property taxes on similarly priced homes within a city or county can vary widely when prices change faster than the assessor's office can reappraise. As a result, a home worth $90,000 in one neighborhood may receive a tax bill of $1,800 per year, while a $90,000 home in another neighborhood will be billed $2,400. When the appraisal district conducts a reappraisal, taxes in the first neighborhood will suddenly rise 33%, undoubtedly provoking complaints from property owners who were unaware that they were previously under-assessed. In times of slow-changing real estate prices, reappraisals were made only once every 10 years. Today, appraisal districts are developing computerized assessment systems that can adjust assessments to the market annually.

As an aid to keeping current on property value changes, some states are enacting laws that require a real estate buyer to advise the assessor's office of the price and terms of his purchase within 90 days after taking title. This information, coupled with building permit records and on-site visits by assessor's office employees, provides the data necessary to regularly update assessments. Such laws have not yet been enacted in Texas.

The amount of property taxes a property owner may expect to pay varies quite widely across the United States. On a home worth $90,000, for example, property taxes range from less than $900 per year to more than $3,600 per year. Why do differences exist and why are they so great? The answers fall into four basic categories: level of services offered, other sources of revenue, type of property, and government efficiency. Generally, cities with low property taxes offer fewer services to their residents. This may be by choice, such as smaller welfare payments, lower school expenditures per student, no subsidized public transportation, fewer parks and libraries, or because the city does not include the cost of some services in the property tax. For example, sewer fees may be added to the water bill and trash may be hauled by private firms. Lower rates can also be due to location. Wage rates are lower in some regions of the country, and a city not subject to ice and snow will have lower street maintenance expenses. Finally, a city may have other sources of revenue, such as oil royalties from wells on city property.

Supplemental Funding

Property tax levels are also influenced by the ability of local tax districts to obtain federal revenue sharing funds and money from state revenues (especially for schools), and to share in collections from sales taxes, license fees, liquor and tobacco taxes, and fines.

The amount and type of taxable property in a community greatly affects local tax rates. Taxable property must bear the burden avoided by tax-exempt property whereas privately owned vacant land, stores, factories, and high-priced homes generally produce more taxes than they consume in local government services and help to keep rates lower. Finally, one must look at the efficiency of the city under review. Has it managed its affairs in prior years so that the current budget is not burdened with large interest payments on debts caused by deficits in previous years? Is the city or county itself laid out in a compact and efficient manner, or does its sheer size make administration expensive? How many employees are required to perform a given service?

TAX LIMITATION MEASURES

Texas restricts increases in property taxes by local taxing units. The statute basically provides that the governing body may not adopt a tax rate that exceeds the rate for the previous year by more than 3 percent until the governing body has: (1) given public notice of its intention to adopt a higher rate; and (2) held a public hearing on the proposed increase. The hearing must be on a weekday that is not a public holiday and must begin after 5:00 P.M. and before 9:00 P.M. There are also provisions for notice to the property owners if the property value has been increased over the preceding tax year. The governing body of the taxing unit may decrease the official tax rate for the current year at any time.

SPECIAL ASSESSMENTS

Often the need arises to make local municipal improvements that will benefit property owners within a limited area, such as the paving of a street, the installation of street lights, curbs, storm drains, and sanitary sewer lines, or the construction of irrigation and drainage ditches. Such improvements can be provided through special assessments on property.

The theory underlying special assessments is that the improvements must benefit the land against which the cost will be charged, and the value of the benefits must exceed the cost. The area receiving the benefit of an improvement is the **improvement district** or **assessment district,** and the property within that district bears the cost of the improvement. This is different from a **public improvement.** A public improvement, such as reconstruction of the city's sewage plant, benefits the public at large and is financed through the general (ad valorem) property tax. A local improvement, such as extending a sewer line into a street of homes presently using septic tanks or cesspools, does not benefit the public at large and should properly be charged only to those who directly benefit. Similarly, when streets are widened, owners of homes lining a 20-foot-wide street in a strictly residential neighborhood would be expected to bear the cost of widening it to 30 or 40 feet and to donate the needed land from their frontyards. But a street widening from two lanes to four to accommodate traffic not generated by the homes on the street is a different situation, as the widening benefits the public at large. In this case the street widening is funded from public monies and the homeowners are compensated for any land taken from them.

An improvement district can be formed by the action of a group of concerned citizens who want and are willing to pay for an improvement. Property owners desiring the improvement take their proposal to the state legislature, city council, or other similar public body in charge of levying assessments. A public notice showing the proposed improvements, the extent of the improvement district, and the anticipated costs is prepared by the board. This notice is mailed to landowners in the proposed improvement district, posted conspicuously in the district, and published in a local newspaper. The notice also contains the date and place of public hearings on the matter at which property owners within the proposed district are invited to voice their comments and objections.

Forming an Improvement District

Special assessments pose a particular problem in Texas because of the constitutional nature of the homestead laws. There are only three reasons for which a homestead can be foreclosed on and sold for amounts due against that homestead:

Texas Homestead

1. Purchase money mortgage;
2. Ad valorem taxes due upon the homestead; and
3. Mechanics' and materialmen's liens, provided they are properly subscribed to and perfected pursuant to the constitutional provisions.

Therefore, assessments for water districts, homeowners' association dues, street improvements, or any other assessment district may not necessarily operate as a lien on a homestead to force a sale of the home to satisfy the amounts due. In an effort to make these liens more enforceable, lenders often put requirements for maintenance fees, homeowners' association dues, and special district assessments in the homeowner's mortgage. Defaulting in the payment of such special assessments might then be considered to be a default in the payment of the purchase money mortgage. To date, however, this theory has only been successfully enforced in condominiums.

Confirmation   If the hearings result in a decision to proceed, then under the authority granted by Texas law regarding special improvements, a local government ordinance is passed that describes the project and its costs and the improvement district boundaries. An assessment roll is also prepared that shows the cost to each parcel in the district. Hearings are held regarding the assessment roll. When everything is in order, the roll is **confirmed** (approved). Then the contract to construct the improvements is awarded and work is started.

The proposal to create an improvement district can also come from a city council, board of trustees, or board of supervisors. Whenever this happens, notices are distributed and hearings held to hear objections from affected parties. Objections are ruled upon by a court of law and if found to have merit, the assessment plans must be revised or dropped. Once approved, assessment rolls are prepared, more hearings held, the roll confirmed, and the contract awarded.

Bond Issues   Upon completion of the improvement, each landowner receives a bill for his portion of the cost. If the cost to a landowner is less than $100, the landowner either pays the amount in full to the contractor directly or to a designated public official who, in turn, pays the contractor. If the assessment is larger, the landowner can immediately pay it in full or let it **go to bond.** If he lets it go to bond, local government officials prepare a bond issue that totals all the unpaid assessments in the improvement district. These bonds are either given to the contractor as payment for his work or sold to the public through a securities dealer and the proceeds are used to pay the contractor. The collateral for the bonds is the land in the district upon which assessments have not been paid.

The bonds spread the cost of the improvements over a period of 5 to 10 years and are payable in equal annual (or semiannual) installments plus accumulated interest. Thus, a $2,000 sewer and street-widening assessment on a 10-year bond would be charged to a property owner at the rate of $200 per year (or $100 each 6 months) plus interest. As the bond is gradually retired, the amount of interest added to the regular principal payment declines.

Like property taxes, special assessments are a lien against the property. Consequently, if a property owner fails to pay his assessment, the assessed property can be sold in the same manner as when property taxes are delinquent.

Apportionment

Special assessments are apportioned according to benefits received, rather than by the value of the land and buildings being assessed. In fact, the presence of buildings in an improvement district is not usually considered in preparing the assessment roll; the theory is that the land receives all the benefit of the improvement. Several illustrations can best explain how assessments are apportioned. In a residential neighborhood, the assessment for installation of storm drains, curbs, and gutters is made on a **front-foot basis.** A property owner is charged for each foot of his lot that abuts the street being improved.

In the case of a sanitary sewer line assessment, the charge per lot can either be based on front footage or on a simple count of the lots in the district. In the latter case, if there are 100 lots on the new sewer line, each would pay 1% of the cost. In the case of a park or playground, lots nearest the new facility are deemed to benefit more and thus are assessed more than lots located farther away. This form of allocation is very subjective, and usually results in spirited objections at public hearings from those who do not feel they will use the facility in proportion to the assessment that their lots will bear.

INCOME TAXES ON THE SALE OF A RESIDENCE

We now turn to the income taxes that are due if a home is sold for more than it cost. Income taxes are levied by the federal government, by 44 states (the exceptions are Florida, Nevada, South Dakota, Texas, Washington, and Wyoming), and by 48 cities, including New York City, Baltimore, Pittsburgh, Philadelphia, Cincinnati, Cleveland, and Detroit. The discussion here centers on the federal income tax and includes key provisions of the Internal Revenue Code of 1986, as it applies to owner-occupied residences. Aspects of this Act that apply to real estate investments are located in Chapter 23.

Calculating a Home's Basis   The first step in determining the amount of taxable gain upon the sale of an owner-occupied residence is to calculate the home's **basis.** This is the price originally paid for the home plus any fees paid for closing services and legal counsel, and any fee or commission paid to help find the property. If the home was built rather than purchased, the basis is the cost of the land plus the cost of construction, such as the cost of materials and construction labor, architect's fees, building permit fees, planning and zoning commission approval costs, utility connection charges, and legal fees. The value of labor contributed by the homeowner and free labor from friends and relatives cannot be added. If the home was received as compensation, a gift, an inheritance, or in a trade, or if a portion of the home was depreciated for business purposes, special rules apply that will not be covered here and the seller should consult the Internal Revenue Service (IRS).

Assessments for local improvements and any improvements made by the seller during his occupancy are added to the original cost of the home. An improvement is a permanent betterment that materially adds to the value of a home, prolongs its life, or changes its use. For example, finishing an unfinished basement or upper floor, building a swimming pool, adding a bedroom or bathroom, installing new plumbing or wiring, installing a new roof, erecting a new fence, and paving a new driveway are classed as improvements and are added to the home's basis. Maintenance and repairs are not added as they merely maintain the property in ordinary operating condition. Fixing gutters, mending leaks in plumbing, replacing broken windowpanes, and painting the inside or outside of the home are considered maintenance and repair items. However, repairs, when done as part of an extensive remodeling or restoration job, may be added to the basis.

Calculating the Amount Realized

The next step in determining taxable gain is to calculate the **amount realized** from the sale. This is the selling price of the home less selling expenses. Selling expenses include brokerage commissions, advertising, legal fees, title services, escrow or closing fees, and mortgage points paid by the seller. If the sale includes furnishings, the value of those furnishings is deducted from the selling price and reported separately as personal property. If the seller takes back a note and mortgage which is immediately sold at a discount, the discounted value of the note is used, not its face amount.

Calculating Gain on the Sale

The **gain on the sale** is the difference between the amount realized and the basis. Table 13:2 illustrates this with an example. Unless the seller qualifies for tax postponement or tax exclusion as discussed next, this is the amount he reports as gain on his annual income tax forms.

Income Tax Postponement

The income tax law of the United States provides that if a seller purchases another home, the gain on the sale of the first home shall be postponed. To qualify for this postponement, the seller must meet two conditions. One deals with time and the other deals with purchase price. With regard to time, another home must be purchased and occupied within the time period beginning 24 months before the closing date of the old home and ending 24 months after the closing date

CALCULATION OF GAIN			**Table 13:2**
May 1, 1982	*Buy home for $90,000, closing costs are $500*	Basis is	$ 90,000
July 1, 1983	*Add landscaping and fencing for $3,500*	Basis is	$ 94,000
Dec. 1, 1985	*Add extra bedroom and bathroom for $15,000*	Basis is	$109,000
June 1, 1986	*Sell home for $125,000; sales commissions and closing costs are $8,000*	Amount realized is	$117,000
	Calculation of gain:	Amount realized	$117,000
		Less basis	$109,000
		Equals gain	$ 8,000

of the old home. A seller who decides to build his/her next home has 24 months to finish and occupy the home.

The second requirement for postponement is that in order to postpone all the gain, the next home must cost more than the adjusted sales price of the previous home. **Adjusted sales price** is the selling price of the old home less selling expenses and fix-up expenses. Fix-up expenses are expenditures for fix-up and repair work performed on the home to make it more salable. For fix-up and repair work to be deductible the work must be performed during the 90-day period ending on the day the contract to sell is signed, and it must be paid for before another 30 days elapses after that date. Table 13:3 illustrates the method for calculating adjusted sales price.

If the new home costs less than the adjusted sales price of the old, there will be a taxable gain. For example, if the old home had a basis of $150,000 and an adjusted sales price of $225,000, and the new home cost $215,000 then there would be a taxable gain of $10,000 and a postponed gain of $65,000. The basis of the new home is $215,000 minus the postponed gain of $65,000; i.e., $150,000.

Postponement of gain is continued from one home to the next as long as the cost of each subsequent home exceeds the adjusted sales price of the previous home, and as long as 24 months elapse between sales. (A shorter turnover period is usually allowed for work-related moves.) The basis of the first home is simply carried forward and included in the basis of the second home, which in turn is carried forward to the third home, and so on. Note that it is not the amount of cash one puts into a home, or the size of the mortgage that counts, but the sales price. Thus it is possible to move from a home with a small mortgage to a slightly more expensive home with a large mortgage, and finish the transaction with cash in the pocket and postponed taxes. Additionally, the

Table 13:3

ADJUSTED SALES PRICE

Selling price of old home	$250,000
Less selling expenses	−18,000
Less fix-up costs	−7,000
Equals adjusted sales price	$225,000

law does not restrict the type of home one may own and occupy. Thus the seller of a single-family residence can buy another house, or a condominium, or a cooperative (or vice versa) and still qualify for postponement. Table 13:4 illustrates a progression of tax-deferred residence replacements.

LIFETIME EXCLUSION

The postponement of taxes on gains as one moves from one home to the next works well as long as consistently more expensive homes are purchased. However, there may come a time in the homeowner's life when a smaller and presumably less expensive home is needed. To soften the tax burden that such a move usually causes, Congress has enacted legislation that allows a once-in-a-lifetime election to avoid tax on up to $125,000 of gain on the sale of one's residence. To qualify for this, one must be 55 years of age or older on the date of sale and have owned and occupied the residence for at least 3 of the 5 years preceding the sale. Any profit over $125,000 is taxable, but may be postponed if another residence is purchased in accordance with the rules previously described. For example, a person owning a $225,000 home with a basis of $50,000 could sell and move to a $100,000 home with no taxable gain. A person owning a $175,000 home with a $50,000 basis could sell and rent an apartment and have no taxable gain. By combining postponement with this $125,000 exclusion it is quite possible to eliminate the taxable gain from a lifetime of homeownership.

TAXABLE GAIN

Prior to January 1, 1987, any gain of a capital asset (which includes the sale of a home) was given preferential long-term

TAX-DEFERRED RESIDENCE REPLACEMENT	**Table 13:4**
1. *Cost and improvements for first home*	$ 50,000
2. *Adjusted sales price of first home*	80,000
3. *Gain on sale of first home*	30,000
4. *Cost of second home*	105,000
5. *Basis in second home (line 4 minus line 3)*	75,000
6. *Adjusted sales price of second home*	130,000
7. *Gain on sale of second house (line 6 minus line 5)*	55,000
8. *Cost of third home*	160,000
9. *Basis in third home (line 8 minus line 7)*	$105,000

capital gain treatment, provided the property had been owned more than 6 months. This treatment excluded 60% of the gain from one's income, thus lowering the income taxes due on the gain. As of January 1, 1987, the 60% exclusion was repealed and one's gain is now 100% taxable at ordinary income tax rates. Although ordinary rates are reduced in 1987 and 1988, the net effect is still a higher tax on gains.

INSTALLMENT METHOD

When a gain cannot be postponed by purchasing a more expensive home, or excluded using the lifetime exclusion, the seller can spread out the payment of taxes on the gain by selling on the **installment method.** This means the seller accepts a note or an installment contract for part (or all) of the purchase price, and receives one or more payments in later taxable years. When this occurs, the seller reports that proportion of the gain that is received in each year as it is received. We will not go through the calculations (which are different for homes versus investment property) as these are available on IRS forms should you be involved in an installment sale. The point to know for now is that a seller can postpone some of the taxes due on a gain by agreeing with the buyer to accept some of the purchase price in subsequent taxable years.

PROPERTY TAX AND INTEREST DEDUCTIONS

The Internal Revenue Code of 1986 retains the deductibility of state and local real estate taxes. A homeowner can deduct real property taxes and personal property taxes from other income when calculating income taxes. This applies to single-family residences, condominiums and cooperatives. The deduction does not extend to special assessment taxes for improvement districts.

The Internal Revenue Code of 1986 also retains the deductibility of interest, but subject to two limitations that will be discussed momentarily. The basic rule is that interest paid to finance the purchase of a home is deductible against a homeowner's other income. Also deductible are interest paid on improvement district bonds, loan prepayment penalties, and the deduction of points on new loans that are clearly distinguishable as interest and not service fees for making the loan. Loan points paid by a seller to help a buyer obtain an FHA or VA loan are not deductible as interest (it is not the seller's debt), but can be deducted from the home's selling price in computing a gain or loss on the sale. FHA mortgage insurance premiums are not deductible, nor are those paid to private mortgage insurers.

From an individual taxpayer's standpoint, the ability to deduct property taxes and mortgage interest on a personal residence becomes more valuable in successively higher tax brackets. At the 28% bracket, every dollar spent for something tax-deductible costs the taxpayer only 72¢ in after-tax money. Or seen from another viewpoint, the taxpayer obtains the full enjoyment of the money he spends on interest and property taxes without having to first pay income taxes on it. Although progressively less dramatic, the same argument applies to persons in the 15% tax brackets. As viewed from a national standpoint, the deductibility of interest and property taxes encourages widespread ownership of the country's land and buildings.

BELOW-MARKET INTEREST

In 1984 and 1985, Congress enacted legislation requiring sellers to charge market rates of interest or be taxed as if they had. This legislation requires minimum rates tied to prevailing rates on federal securities, i.e., U.S. Treasury notes and bonds. Effective July 1, 1985, if the amount of seller financing in a transaction is $2.8 million or less, the seller must charge no less than 9% interest or a rate equal to the applicable federal rate (AFR). If the amount of seller financing in a transaction is greater than $2.8 million, the seller must charge a rate equal to or greater than the AFR. This rule applied to home sellers as well as investors. Investing in real estate and its tax implications are discussed in Chapter 23.

Because tax rules for real estate are continually changing, only the major rules are reported and discussed here and in Chapter 23. As a real estate owner or agent you need a source of more frequent and more detailed information such as the annual income tax guide published by the Internal Revenue Service (free) or the privately published guides available in most bookstores. Additionally, you may wish to subscribe to a tax newsletter for up-to-the-minute tax information.

AGENT'S LIABILITY FOR TAX ADVICE

The real estate industry's desire for professional recognition coupled with the results of several key court cases strongly suggests that a real estate agent ought to be reasonably knowledgeable about taxes. This does not mean the agent must have knowledge of tax laws at the level of an accountant or tax attorney. Neither does it mean an agent can plead ignorance of tax laws. Rather it means a real estate agent is now liable for tax advice (or lack of it) if the advice is material to the transaction—and giving such advice is common in the brokerage business. What this means is that an agent should have enough general knowledge of real estate tax laws so as to be able to answer basic questions accurately and to warn clients and recommend tax counsel if the questions posed by the transaction are beyond the agent's knowledge. Note that the obligation to inform exists even when a client fails to ask about tax consequences. This is to avoid situations where after the deed has been recorded the client says, "Gee, I didn't know I'd have to pay all these taxes, my agent should have warned me," and then sues the agent. Lastly, if the agent tries to fill the role of accountant or tax attorney for the client, then the agent will be held liable to the standards of an accountant or tax attorney.

To summarize, a real estate agent must be aware of tax laws that affect the properties the agent is handling. A real estate agent has a responsibility to alert clients to potential tax consequences, liabilities, and advantages whether they ask for it or not. Lastly, an agent is responsible for the quality and accuracy of tax information given out by the agent.

VOCABULARY REVIEW

Match terms **a–j** *with statements* **1–10.**

a. *Mill rate*	**f.** *Special assessments*
b. *Ad valorem*	**g.** *Front-foot basis*
c. *Appropriation process*	**h.** *Adjusted sales price*
d. *Assessment roll*	**i.** *Conveyance tax*
e. *Assessed valuation*	**j.** *Installment method*

1. A tax rate expressed in tenths of a cent per dollar of assessed valuation.

2. According to value.

3. The enactment of a taxing body's budget and sources of money into law.
4. A book that contains the assessed valuation of each property in the county or taxing district.
5. A value placed on a property for the purpose of taxation.
6. Assessments levied to provide publicly built improvements that will primarily benefit property owners within a limited geographical area.
7. A charge or levy based directly on the measured distance that a parcel of land abuts a street.
8. Sales price of a property less fix-up costs and sales commissions, closing and other selling costs.
9. A tax charged by some states and localities upon recordation of a deed.
10. Sale of an appreciated property structured to spread out the payment of income taxes on the gain.

QUESTIONS AND PROBLEMS

1. Explain the process for calculating the property tax rate for a taxation district.
2. The Southside School District contains property totalling $120,000,000 in assessed valuation. If the district's budget is $960,000, what will the mill rate be?
3. Continuing with Problem 2 above, if a home situated in the Southside School District carries an assessed valuation of $40,000, how much will the homeowner be required to pay to support the district this year?
4. The Lakeview Mosquito Abatement District levies an annual tax of $0.05 per $100 of assessed valuation to pay for a mosquito-control program. How much does that amount to for a property in the district with an assessed valuation of $10,000?
5. In your county, if a property owner wishes to appeal an assessment, what procedure must he follow?
6. If the property taxes on your home were to rise 90% in 1 year, where would you go to protest the increase: to the board of equalization, to the city council, or to the county government? Explain.
7. How does the amount of tax-exempt real estate in a community affect nonexempt property owners?
8. What methods and techniques are used by your local assessor's office to keep up to date with changing real estate prices?
9. The Smiths bought a house in 1963 for $21,000, including closing costs. Five years later they made improvements costing $2,000 and 5 years after that more improvements that cost $5,000. Today they sell the house; the sales price is $68,000 and commissions and closing costs total $5,000. For income tax purposes, what is their gain?

10. Continuing with Problem 9, a month after selling, the Smiths purchase a two-bedroom condominium for $58,000, including closing costs. What is their taxable gain now? (Assume that the Smiths are less than 55 years of age.)

ADDITIONAL
READINGS

"Broker Liability for Tax Advice" by **Michael Hesse.** (*First Tuesday*, April 84, p. 20). This article points out that a client can collect from a broker if taxes were avoidable in a transaction and the broker failed to alert the client or gave the client wrong information.

"Property Taxation—a Complicated Process" by **Richard Darling.** (*Real Estate Today*, Nov/Dec 84, p. 19). Article describes how property owners can challenge their property valuations.

Tax Information for Homeowners. (Internal Revenue Service, Publication 530, 1987, 8 pages). Discusses income tax aspects of settlement costs, itemized deductions, rental and business use, repairs, improvements, buying, selling, record keeping, casualty losses, etc., for owners of houses, condominiums and cooperatives. Published annually and available free from the IRS.

Tax Information on Selling Your Home. (Internal Revenue Service, Publication 523, 1987, 12 pages). Provides instructions on how to report taxable income from the sale of one's residence. Published annually and available free from the IRS.

Texas Real Estate Law, 4th ed. by **Charles J. Jacobus.** (Reston, 1985, 560 pages). Provides up-to-date explanations of law pertinent to the daily operation of a real estate brokerage office in Texas. See Chapter 19 on Real Estate Taxation.

*   *   *

The following periodicals may also be of interest to you: *Journal of Taxation, Kiplinger Tax Letter, Monthly Digest of Tax Articles, National Tax Journal, Property Tax Journal, Property Tax Newsletter, Real Estate Tax Digest, Real Estate Tax Ideas, Tax Adviser, Tax Shelter Letter, Tax Shelter Opportunities in Real Estate, Tax Sheltered Investments Law Report and Taxes and the Tax Magazine.*

Title Closing and Escrow

Closing meeting: a meeting at which the buyer pays for the property, receives a deed to it, and all other matters pertaining to the sale are concluded

Closing statement: an accounting of funds to the buyer and the seller at the completion of a real estate transaction

Escrow closing: the deposit of documents and funds with a neutral third party along with instructions as to how to conduct the closing

Escrow agent: the person placed in charge of an escrow

Prorating: the division of ongoing expenses and income items between the buyer and the seller

RESPA, Real Estate Settlement Procedures Act: a federal law that deals with procedures to be followed in certain types of real estate closings

Title closing: the process of consummating a real estate transaction

Walk-through: a final inspection of the property by the buyer just before the closing or settlement

Numerous details must be handled between the time a buyer and seller sign a sales contract and the day title is conveyed to the buyer. Title must be searched (Chapter 6), a decision made as to how to take title (Chapter 4), a deed prepared (Chapter 5), loan arrangements made (Chapters 9 through 12), property tax records checked (Chapter 13) and so forth. In this chapter we will look at the final steps in the process, in particular the buyer's walk-through, the closing meeting or escrow, prorations and the settlement statement.

To protect both the buyer and the seller, it is good practice for a buyer to make a **walk-through.** This is a final inspection of the property just prior to the settlement date. It is quite possible the buyer has not been on the parcel or inside the structure since the initial offer and acceptance. Now, several weeks later, the buyer wants to make certain that the premises has been vacated, that no damage has occurred, that the seller has left behind personal property agreed upon and

BUYER'S WALK-THROUGH

that the seller has not removed and taken any real property. If the sales contract requires all mechanical items to be in normal working order, then the seller will want to test the heating and air-conditioning systems, dishwasher, disposal, stove, garage door opener, etc., and the refrigerator, washer and dryer if included. The buyer will also want to test all the plumbing to be certain the hot water heater works, faucets and showers run, toilets flush and sinks drain. A final inspection of the structure is made, including walls, roof, gutters, driveway, decks, patios, etc., as well as the land and landscaping.

Note that a walk-through is not the time for the buyer to make the initial inspection of the property. That is done before the contract is signed and if there are questions in the buyer's mind regarding the structural soundness of the property, a thorough inspection (possibly with the aid of a professional real estate inspector) should be conducted within ten days of signing the purchase contract. The walk-through is for the purpose of giving the buyer the opportunity to make certain that agreements regarding the condition of the premises have been kept. If during the walk-through the buyer notes the walls were damaged when the seller moved out, or the furnace does not function, the buyer (or the buyer's agent) notes these items and asks that funds be withheld at the closing to pay for repairs.

TITLE CLOSING

Title closing refers to the completion of a real estate transaction. This is when the buyer pays for the property and the seller delivers the deed. The day on which this occurs is called the **closing date.** Depending on where one resides in the United States, the title closing process is referred to as a **closing, settlement,** or **escrow.** All accomplish the same basic goal, but the method of reaching that goal can follow one of two paths.

In some parts of the United States, particularly in the East, and to a certain extent in the Mountain states, the Midwest, and the South, the title closing process is concluded at a meeting at which each party to the transaction, or his/her representative, is present. Elsewhere, title closing is conducted by an escrow agent, who is a neutral third party mutually selected by the buyer and seller to carry out the closing. With an escrow, there is no necessity for a closing meeting; in fact, most of the closing process is conducted by mail. In Texas the escrow closing is quickly becoming the fastest, safest, and most convenient method of carrying out the title closing process. The escrow agent is usually a title company. Let us look at the operation of each method.

When a meeting is used to close a real estate transaction, the seller (or his representative) meets in person with the buyer and delivers the deed. At the same time, the buyer pays the seller for the property. To ascertain that everything promised in the sales contract has been properly carried out, it is customary for the buyer and seller to each have an attorney present. The real estate agents who brought the buyer and seller together are also present, along with a representative of the firm that conducted the title search. If a new loan is being made or an existing one is being paid off at the closing, a representative of the lender will be present.

CLOSING OR SETTLEMENT MEETING

The location of the meeting and the selection of the person responsible for conducting the closing will depend on local custom and the nature of the closing. It is the custom in some states for the real estate agent to conduct the closing at his office. In other localities, the attorney for the seller conducts it in his office. An alternative is to have the title company responsible for the title search and title policy conduct the closing at its office.

To assure a smooth closing, each person attending is responsible for bringing certain documents. The seller and his attorney are responsible for preparing and bringing the deed, together with the most recent property tax bill (and receipt if it has been paid). If required by the sales contract, they also bring the insurance policy for the property, the termite and wood-rot inspection report, documents showing the removal of unacceptable liens and encumbrances, a title insurance policy, a bill of sale for personal property, a survey map, and a statement showing the remaining balance on any loan that the buyer will assume. The loan payment booklet, keys to the property, garage door opener, and the like

Seller's Responsibilities at Closing

are also brought to the meeting. If the property produces income, existing leases, rent schedules, current expenditures, and letters advising the tenants of the new owner must also be furnished.

Buyer's Responsibilities at Closing

The buyer's responsibilities include having adequate settlement funds ready, having an attorney present to protect his interests, and, if borrowing, obtaining the loan commitment and advising the lender of the meeting's time and place. The real estate agent is present because it is the custom in some localities that the agent be in charge of the closing and prepare the proration calculations, although this is not generally done in Texas. The agent also receives a commission check at the time and, as a matter of good business, will make certain that all goes well.

If a new loan is involved, the lender provides the required funds along with a note and mortgage for the borrower to sign. If an existing loan is to be paid off as part of the transaction, the lender is present to receive a check and release the mortgage held on the property. If a lender elects not to attend, the check and/or loan papers are given to the person in charge of the closing, along with instructions for their distribution and signing. A title insurance representative is also present to provide the latest status of title and the title insurance policy. If title insurance is not used, the seller is responsible for bringing an abstract or asking the abstractor to be present.

Agent's Duties

The seller and the seller's attorney may be unaware of all the things expected of them at the closing meeting. Therefore, it is the duty of the agent who listed the property to make certain that they are prepared for the meeting. Similarly, it is the duty of the agent who found the buyer to make certain that the buyer and the buyer's attorney are prepared for the closing meeting. If the agent both lists and sells the property, the agent assists both the buyer and seller. If more than one agent is involved in the transaction, each should keep the other(s) fully informed so the transaction will go as well as possible. At all times the buyer and seller are to be kept informed as to the status of the closing. An agent should provide them with a preview of all actions that will take place, explain the amounts of money involved and the purpose served by each payment or receipt, and in general prepare the parties for informed participation at the closing meeting.

When everyone concerned has arrived at the meeting place, the closing begins. Those present record each other's names as witnesses to the meeting. The various documents called for by the sales contract are exchanged for inspection. The buyer and his attorney inspect the deed the seller is offering, the title search and/or title policy, the mortgage papers, survey, leases, removals of encumbrances, and proration calculations. The lender also inspects the deed, survey, title search, and title policy. This continues until each party has a chance to inspect each document of interest.

The Transaction

As the title search will usually have been prepared a day or more before the meeting, the buyer and lender both want protection against any changes in title condition since then. A common solution is for the seller to sign a **seller's affidavit.** In this affidavit, the seller states that he is the true owner of the property, that there are no liens or proceedings currently against him, and that he has done nothing to damage the quality of title since the title search. If a defect caused by the seller later appears, he may be sued for damages. Furthermore, he may be liable for criminal charges if it can be shown that he was attempting to obtain money under false pretenses by signing the affidavit. Another solution is to require the person in charge of the closing to hold the money being paid to the seller until a final title search is made and the new deed recorded.

A settlement statement (discussed in detail later) is given to the buyer and seller to summarize the financial aspects of their transaction. It is prepared by the person in charge of the closing either just before or at the meeting. It provides a clear picture of where the buyer's and seller's monies are going at the closing by identifying each party to whom money is being paid.

If everyone involved in the closing has done his or her homework and comes prepared to the meeting, the closing usually goes smoothly. When everything is in order, the seller hands a completed deed to the buyer. The buyer then gives the seller a check that combines the down payment and net result of the prorations. The lender has the buyer sign the mortgage and note, and hands checks to the seller and the existing lender if one is involved. The seller writes a check to his real estate broker, attorney, and the abstractor. The buyer writes a check to his attorney for his services. This continues until every document is signed and everyone is paid. The deed, new mortgage, and release of the old mortgage are then recorded, and the transaction is complete.

Closing Into Escrow   Occasionally an unavoidable circumstance can cause delays in a closing. Perhaps an important document, known to be in the mail, has not arrived. Yet it will be difficult to reschedule the meeting. In such a situation, the parties concerned may agree to **close into escrow.** In such a closing, all parties sign their documents and entrust them to the escrow agent for safekeeping. No money is disbursed and the deed is not delivered until the missing paperwork has arrived. When it does, the escrow agent completes the transaction and delivers the money and documents by mail or messenger. The use of escrow to close a real estate transaction involves a neutral third party, called an **escrow agent,** escrow holder, or escrowee, who acts as a trusted stakeholder for all the parties to the transaction. Instead of delivering his deed directly to the buyer at a closing meeting, the seller gives the deed to the escrow agent with instructions that it be delivered only after the buyer has completed all his promises in the sales contract. Similarly, the buyer hands the escrow agent the money for the purchase price plus instructions that it be given to the seller only after fulfillment of the seller's promises. Let us look closer at this arrangement.

A typical real estate escrow closing starts when a sales contract is signed by the buyer and seller. They select a neutral escrow agent to handle the closing. This may be the escrow department of a bank or savings and loan or other lending agency, an attorney, or a title insurance company. Sometimes real estate brokers offer escrow services. However, if the broker is earning a sales commission in the transaction, the broker cannot be classed as neutral and disinterested. Because escrow agents are entrusted with valuable documents and large sums of money, most states have licensing and bonding requirements that escrow agents must meet.

The escrow agent's task begins with the deposit of the buyer's earnest money in a special bank trust account. In most commercial closings and almost all residential closings in Texas, the escrow agent's duties are very seldom written out as formal escrow instructions. An exception to this is the lender who furnishes a **Mortgagee's Information Letter** (MIL) to direct the escrow agent as to how to disburse the funds for the loan proceeds.

Escrow Agent's Duties

When the title search is completed, the escrow agent forwards it to the buyer or his attorney for approval. The property insurance and tax papers the seller would otherwise bring to the closing meeting are sent to the escrow agent for proration. Leases, service contracts, and notices to tenants are also sent to the escrow agent for proration and delivery to the buyer. The deed conveying title to the buyer is prepared, signed by the seller, and given to the escrow agent. Once delivered into escrow, even if the seller dies, marries, or is declared legally incompetent before the close of escrow, the deed will still pass title to the buyer.

As the closing date draws near, if all the instructions are otherwise complete, the escrow agent requests any additional money the buyer and lender must deposit in order to close. The day before closing the escrow agent orders a last minute check on the title. If no changes have occurred since the first (preliminary) title search, the deed, mortgage, mortgage release, and other documents to be recorded as part of the transaction are recorded first thing the following morning. As soon as the recording is confirmed, the escrow agent hands or mails a check to every party to whom funds are due from the escrow (usually the seller, real estate broker, and previous lender), along with any papers or documents which must be delivered through escrow (such as the fire insurance policy, copy of the property tax bill, and tenant leases). Several days later the buyer and lender will receive

The Closing

a title insurance policy in the mail from the title company. The public recorder's office also mails the documents it recorded to each party. The deed is sent to the buyer, the mortgage release to the seller, and the new mortgage to the lender.

In the escrow closing method, the closing, delivery of title, and recordation usually all take place at the same moment. Technically, the seller does not physically hand a deed to the buyer on the closing day. However, once all the conditions of the escrow are met, the escrow agent becomes an agent of the seller as to the money in the transaction, and an agent of the buyer as to the deed. Thus, a buyer, through an agent, receives the deed, and the law regarding delivery is fulfilled.

It is not necessary for the buyer and seller to meet face-to-face during the escrow period or at the closing. This can eliminate personality conflicts that might be detrimental to an otherwise sound transaction. The escrow agent, having previously accumulated all the documents, approvals, deeds, and monies prior to the closing date, does the closing alone.

In a brokered transaction, the real estate agent may be the only person who actually meets the escrow agent. All communication can be handled through the broker, by mail, or by telephone. If a real estate agent is not involved, the buyer and/or seller can open the escrow, either in person or by mail. The use of an escrow agent does not eliminate the need for an attorney. Although there might be no closing meeting for the attorneys to attend, they play a vital role in advising the buyer and seller on each document sent by the escrow agent for approval and signature.

DELAYS AND FAILURE TO CLOSE

When a real estate purchase contract is written, a closing date is also negotiated and placed in the contract. The choice of closing date will depend on when the buyer wants possession, when the seller wants to move out, and how long it will take to obtain a loan, title search and termite report and otherwise fulfill the contract requirements. In a typical residential sale this is 30 to 60 days, with 45 days being a popular choice when new financing is involved. The Texas Real Estate Commission promulgated earnest money form simply states that the closing will be "on or before" a specified date.

Delays along the way are sometimes encountered and may cause a delay in the closing. This is usually not a problem as long as the buyer still intends to buy, the seller still intends to sell and the delay is for a reasonable cause and a justifiable length of time. Note that the TREC form provides for extensions beyond the specified closing date to cure title objections or to complete loan requirements. These are common delays which are often beyond the control of either buyer or seller. This allows for some reasonable flexibility when these problems occur without requiring extensive or stress-filled renegotiation.

The delay might be quite lengthy, however. For example, there may be a previously undisclosed title defect that will take months to clear or perhaps there are unusual problems in financing or there has been major damage to the premises. In such cases, relieving all parties from further obligation to each other may be the wisest choice for all involved. This is one of the remedies provided for in Paragraph 16 of the TREC promulgated form. If so, it is essential that the buyer and seller sign mutual release papers. These are necessary to rescind the purchase contract and cancel the escrow if one has been opened. The buyer's deposit is also returned. Without release papers, the buyer still has a vaguely defined liability to buy and the seller can still be required to convey the property, so the escrow agent will refuse to disburse to either party. A mutual release gives the buyer the freedom to choose another property and the seller the chance to fix the problem and remarket the property later.

A stickier problem occurs when one party wants out of the contract and attempts to use any delay in closing as grounds for contract termination. The buyer may have found a preferable property for less money and better terms. The seller may have received a higher offer since signing the purchase contract. Although the party wishing to cancel may threaten with a lawsuit, courts might not enforce cancellation of valuable contract rights due to reasonable delays that are not the fault of the other party. Conversely, courts might not go along with a reluctant buyer or seller who manufactures delays so as to delay the closing and then claim default and cancellation of the contract. If the reluctance continues and negotiations to end it fail, the performing party may choose to complete its requirements and then ask the courts to force the reluctant party to the closing table.

Loan Escrows

Escrows can be used for purposes other than real estate or sales transactions. For example, a homeowner who is refinancing his property could enter into an escrow with the lender. The conditions of the escrow would be that the homeowner deliver a properly executed note and mortgage to the escrow agent and that the lender deposit the loan money. Upon closing, the escrow agent delivers the documents to the lender and the money to the homeowner. Or, in reverse, an escrow could be used to pay off the balance of a loan. The conditions would be the borrower's deposit of the balance due and the lender's deposit of the mortgage release and note. Even the weekly office sports pool is an escrow—with the person holding the pool money acting as escrow agent for the participants.

Reporting Requirements

All sales of real estate must now be reported to the Internal Revenue Service on their Form 1099. The responsibility for filing Form 1099 goes in the following order: the person responsible for the closing, the mortgage lender, the seller's broker, the buyer's broker, and any person designated by the U.S. Treasury. It is important to be clear at the closing who is to file the Form 1099. This rule went into effect on January 1, 1987.

PRORATING AT THE CLOSING

Ongoing expenses and income items must be prorated between the seller and buyer when property ownership changes hands. Items subject to proration include property insurance premiums, property taxes, accrued interest on assumed loans, and rents and operating expenses if the property produces income. If heating is done by oil and the oil tank is partially filled when title transfers, that oil can be prorated, as can utility bills when service is not shut off between owners. The TREC promulgated forms state that all prorations are made "through the closing date," indicating that for the day of closing, seller is responsible for payments, and is entitled to income prorations also. The prorating process has long been a source of considerable mystery to real estate newcomers. Several sample prorations common to most closings are set out below to help clarify the process.

Hazard insurance policies for such things as fire, wind, storm, and flood damage are paid for in advance. At the beginning of each year of the policy's life, the premium for that year's coverage must be paid. When real estate is sold, the buyer may ask the seller to transfer the remaining coverage to him. The seller usually agrees if the buyer reimburses him for the value of the remaining coverage on a prorated basis.

Hazard Insurance

The first step in prorating hazard insurance is to find out how often the premium is paid, how much it is, and what period of time it covers. Suppose that the seller has a 1-year policy that cost $180 and started on January 1 of the current year. If the property is sold and the closing date is June 30, the policy is half used up. Therefore, if the buyer wants the policy transferred to him, he must pay the seller $90 for the remaining 6 months of coverage.

Because closing dates do not always occur on neat, evenly divided portions of the year, nor do most items that need prorating, it is usually necessary to break the year into months and the months into days to make proration calculations. Suppose, in the previous hazard insurance example, that prorations are to be made on June 29 instead of June 30. This would give the buyer 6 months and 1 day of coverage. How much does he owe the seller? The first step is to calculate the monthly and daily rates for the policy: $180 divided by 12 is $15 per month. Dividing the monthly rate of $15 by 30 days gives a daily rate of 50¢. The second step is to add 6 months at $15 and 1 day at 50¢. Thus, the buyer owes the seller $90.50 for the unused portion of the policy.

When a buyer agrees to assume an existing loan from the seller, an interest proration is necessary. For example, a sales contract calls for the buyer to assume a 9% mortgage loan with a principal balance of $31,111 at the time of closing. Loan payments are due the 10th of each month, and the sales contract calls for a July 3 closing date, with interest on

Loan Interest

the loan to be prorated through the closing date. How much is to be prorated and to whom?

First, we must recognize that interest is normally paid in arrears. On a loan that is payable monthly, the borrower pays interest for the use of the loan at the end of each month he has had the loan. Thus, the July 10 monthly loan payment includes the interest due for the use of $31,111 from June 10 through July 9. However, the seller owned the property through July 3, and from June 10 through July 3 is 24 days. At the closing the seller must give the buyer enough money to pay for 24 days interest on the $31,111. If the annual interest rate is 9%, one month's interest is $31,111 times 9% divided by 12, which is $233.33. Divide this by 30 days to get a daily interest rate of $7.7777. Multiply the daily rate by 24 to obtain the interest for 24 days, $186.66.

30-Day Month   In Texas, it is the custom when prorating interest, property taxes, water bills, and insurance to use a 30-day month because it simplifies proration calculations. Naturally, using a 30-day month produces some inaccuracy when dealing with months that do not have 30 days. If this inaccuracy is significant to the buyer and seller, they can agree to prorate either by using the exact number of days in the closing month or by dividing the yearly rate by 365 to find a daily rate.

Rents   It is the custom in Texas to prorate rents on the basis of the actual number of days in the month, however. Using the July 3 closing date again, if the property is currently rented for $450 per month, paid in advance on the first of each month, what would the proration be? If the seller has already collected the rent for the month of July, he is obligated to hand over to the buyer that portion of the rent earned between July 4 and July 31, inclusive, a period of 28 days. To determine how many dollars this is, divide $450 by the number of days in July. This gives $14.516 as the rent per day. Then multiply the daily rate by 28 days to get $406.45, the portion of the July rent that the seller must hand over to the buyer. If the renter has not paid the July rent by the July 3 closing date, no proration is made. If the buyer later collects the July rent, he must return 3 days rent to the seller.

Prorated property taxes are common to nearly all real estate transactions. The amount of proration depends on when the property taxes are due, what portion has already been paid, and what period of time they cover. Property taxes are levied on an annual basis, but depending on the locality they may be due at the beginning, middle, or end of the tax year. In Texas, property owners are permitted to pay half their property taxes during the first 6 months of the tax year and the other half during the second 6 months. Although this is seldom done, prorations are usually made on an annual basis. The state and county tax year is concurrent with the calendar year. Property bills are sent out in early October and are due October 1, but are not delinquent until February 1 of the following year. If a transaction calls for property taxes to be prorated to September 4, how is the calculation made?

Property Taxes

Our problem is complicated by the fact that the new property tax bill will not have been issued by the September 4 closing date. The solution is to use the previous year's tax bill as the best estimate available. Suppose that it was $1,080 for the year. The proration would be from January 1 through September 5, a period of 8 months and 4 days. One month's taxes would be one-twelfth of $1,080, or $90. Dividing $90 by 30 gives a daily rate of $3. If you take 8 months at $90 each and 5 days at $3 each, the total is $735. The seller pays the buyer $735 because he owned the property through September 5; yet the buyer will later receive a property tax bill for the period starting January 1. If there is a possibility that the October property tax bill will change substantially from the previous year, the buyer and seller can agree to make another adjustment between themselves when the new bill is available.

In the event there is a miscalculation of the taxes, most title companies and escrow agents require the buyer and seller to settle their differences between themselves.

Let us work one more property tax proration example. Presume that the annual property taxes are $1,350, the tax year runs from January 1 through the following December 31, and the closing and proration date is December 28, and the day of closing belongs to the seller. First, determine how much of the annual property tax bill has been paid by the seller. If the seller has paid the taxes for January 1 through December 31, the buyer must reimburse the seller for the taxes from December 29 through December 31, a period of 3 days. The amount is calculated by taking one-twelfth of $1,350 to find the monthly tax rate of $112.50, and dividing by 30 to get the daily rate of $3.75. Then by multiplying the daily rate by 3 days we get $11.25, the amount that the buyer must give the seller.

Homeowners' Association   If the property being sold is a condominium unit or in a cooperative or a planned unit development, there will be a monthly homeowners' association payment to be prorated. Suppose the monthly fee is $120 and is paid in advance on the first of the month. If the closing takes place two-thirds of the way through the month, the buyer owes the seller $40 for the unused portion of the month.

Proration Date   Prorations need not be calculated as of the closing date. In the sales contract, the buyer and seller can mutually agree to a different proration date if they wish. If nothing is said, local law and custom will prevail. As stated previously, this means the seller pays for the day of closing in Texas.

Special assessments for such things as street improvements, water mains, and sewer lines are not usually prorated. As a rule, the selling price of the property reflects the added value of the improvements, and the seller pays any assessments in full before closing. This is not an ironclad rule, however; the buyer and seller in their sales contract can agree to do whatever they want about the assessment.

Proration Summary   Table 14:1 summarizes the most commonly found proration situations found in real estate closings. The table also shows who is to be charged and who is to be credited and whether the proration is to be worked forward from the closing date or backward. As a rule, items that are paid in advance by the seller are prorated forward from the closing date; for example, prepaid fire insurance. Items that are paid in arrears, such as interest on an existing loan, are prorated backward from the closing date.

SUMMARY OF COMMON PRORATIONS			Table 14:1
Accumulated interest on existing loan assumed by buyer	Charge seller	Credit buyer	*Prorate backward*
Insurance premium paid in advance	Charge buyer	Credit seller	*Prorate forward*
Property taxes paid in advance	Charge buyer	Credit seller	*Prorate forward*
Property taxes in arrears	Charge seller	Credit buyer	*Prorate backward*
Condominium or homeowner's fees paid in advance	Charge buyer	Credit seller	*Prorate forward*
Rent paid in advance	Charge seller	Credit buyer	*Prorate forward*
Interest on a new loan	Charge buyer	Credit lender	*Prorate forward*
Interest on a loan to be paid off at the closing	Charge seller	Credit lender	*Prorate backward*

SAMPLE CLOSING

To illustrate the arithmetic involved, let us work through a residential closing situation. Note that this example is not particular to any region of the United States, but is rather a composite that shows you how the most commonly encountered residential closing items are handled.

Homer Leavitt has listed his home for sale with List-Rite Realty for $125,000, and the sales commission is to be 6% of the selling price. A salesperson from Quick-Sale Realty learns about the property through the multiple listing service and produces a buyer willing to pay $123,000 with $33,000 down. The offer is conditioned on the seller paying off the existing $48,000, 12% interest mortgage loan and the buyer obtaining a new loan for $90,000. Property taxes, hazard insurance, and heating oil in the home's oil tank are to be prorated as of the closing date. The buyer also asks the seller to pay for a termite inspection and repairs if necessary, a title search, an owner's title insurance policy, and one-half of the closing fee. The seller accepts this offer on August 15, and they agree to close on September 15.

The property-tax year for this home runs from January 1 through December 31. Mr. Leavitt has paid the taxes for last year, but not for the current year as yet. Newly issued tax bills show that $1,680 will be due on October 1 for the current year. The hazard insurance policy (fire, windstorm, etc.) that the buyer wishes to assume was purchased by the seller for $240 and covers the period June 15 through the following June 14. The Charter Title Insurance Company will charge the seller $400 for a combined title search, title examination, and owner's title policy package.

The buyer obtains a loan commitment from the Park Tower National Bank for $90,000. To make this loan, the bank will charge a $900 loan origination fee, $100 for an appraisal, and $25 for a credit report on the buyer. The bank also requires a lender's title policy in the amount of $90,000 (added cost $40), 12 months of property tax reserves, and 4 months of hazard insurance reserves. The loan is to be repaid in equal monthly installments beginning November 1. The termite inspection by Dead-Bug Pest Company costs $39, and recording fees are $5 for deeds and mortgage releases and $10 for mortgages. The title company charges the buyer and the seller $110 each to conduct the closing and an attorney charges $60 to prepare a deed for the seller, although this may be prepared by one of the party's attorneys and included in their fees for representation. The seller is leaving $130 worth of fuel oil for the buyer.

The buyer and seller have each hired an attorney to advise them on legal matters in connection with the sales contract and closing. They are to be paid $250 and $300 respectively, out of the settlement. List-Rite Realty and Quick-Sale Realty have advised the closing agent they are splitting the $7,380 sales commission equally.

Finally, the $3,000 earnest money deposit that the buyer made with the offer is to be credited toward the down payment. Using this information, which is summarized in Table 14:2 for your convenience, let us see exactly how a settlement statement is prepared.

RESIDENTIAL Figure 14:1 is the most widely used residential settlement
SETTLEMENT form in the United States and it is filled out to reflect the
STATEMENT transaction outlined in Table 14:2. Let us work through this

TRANSACTION SUMMARY   Table 14:2

	Amount	Comments
Sale Price	$123,000	
Down Payment	$ 33,000	
Deposit (Earnest Money)	$ 3,000	Credit to buyer's down payment.
Existing Loan	$ 48,000	Seller to pay off through settlement. Interest rate is 12%.
New Loan	$ 90,000	Monthly payments begin Nov. 1. Interest rate is 9.6%.
Loan Orig. Fee	$ 900 ⎫	
Appraisal Fee	$ 100 ⎬	Paid by buyer in connection with obtaining $90,000 loan.
Credit Report	$ 25 ⎭	
Owner's Title Policy	$ 400	Seller pays Charter Title Co.
Lender's Title Policy	$ 40	Buyer pays Charter Title Co.
County Property Taxes	$ 1,680/yr	Not yet paid.
Hazard Insurance	$ 240/yr	Existing policy with 9 months to run. Transfer to buyer.
Heating Oil	$ 130	Remaining heating oil in tank.
Pest Inspection	$ 39	Seller pays Dead-Bug Pest Co.
Property Tax Reserves	$ 840	6 months at $140 for lender.
Hazard Insurance Reserves	$ 80	4 months at $20 for lender.
Buyer's Attorney	$ 250	
Seller's Attorney	$ 300	
Closing Fee	$ 220	Charter Title Company; buyer & seller each pay $110.
Deed Preparation	$ 60	Seller pays attorney.
Record Deed	$ 5	Buyer pays.
Record Mortgage Release	$ 5	Seller pays.
Record Mortgage	$ 10	Buyer pays.
Brokerage Commission	$ 7,380	Seller pays; to be split equally between List-Rite Realty and Quick-Sale Realty.

Settlement and Proration date is September 15.
All prorations are to be based on a 30-day banker's month.

Figure 14:1

SETTLEMENT STATEMENT

Form Approved
OMB NO. 63 R1501

A.	U.S. DEPARTMENT OF HOUSING AND URBAN DEVELOPMENT	B. TYPE OF LOAN:
		1. ☐ FHA 2. ☐ FMHA 3. ☐ CONV. UNINS 4. ☐ VA 5. ☐ CONV. INS
		6. FILE NUMBER 7. LOAN NUMBER
		8. MORTG. INS. CASE NO.

SETTLEMENT STATEMENT

C. **NOTE:** This form is furnished to give you a statement of actual settlement costs. Amounts paid to and by the settlement agent are shown. Items marked (p.o.c.) were paid outside the closing, they are shown here for informational purposes and are not included in the totals.

D. NAME OF BORROWER	E. NAME OF SELLER	F. NAME OF LENDER
Neidi d'Moni 2724 East 22nd Street City, State 00000	Homer Leavitt 1654 West 12th Street City, State 00000	Park Tower National Bank 1111 West 1st Street City, State 00000

G. PROPERTY LOCATION	H. SETTLEMENT AGENT	I. SETTLEMENT DATE:
1654 West 12th Street City, State 00000	Park Tower National Bank	Sept. 15, 19xx
	PLACE OF SETTLEMENT Park Tower National Bank	

J. SUMMARY OF BORROWER'S TRANSACTION		K. SUMMARY OF SELLER'S TRANSACTION	
100 GROSS AMOUNT DUE FROM BORROWER:		400 GROSS AMOUNT DUE TO SELLER:	
101 Contract sales price	123,000.00	401 Contract sales price	123,000.00
102 Personal property		402 Personal property	
103 Settlement charges to borrower (line 1400)	3,880.00	403	
104		404	
105		405	
Adjustments for items paid by seller in advance:		Adjustments for items paid by seller in advance:	
106 City/town taxes to		406 City/town taxes to	
107 County taxes to		407 County taxes to	
108 Assessments to		408 Assessments to	
109 Hazard Insurance 9/15 to 6/15	180.00	409 Hazard Insurance 9/15 to 6/15	180.00
110 Heating Oil to	130.00	410 Heating Oil to	130.00
111 to		411 to	
112 to		412 to	
120 GROSS AMOUNT DUE FROM BORROWER:	127,190.00	420 GROSS AMOUNT DUE TO SELLER:	123,310.00
200 AMOUNTS PAID BY OR IN BEHALF OF BORROWER:		500 REDUCTIONS IN AMOUNT DUE TO SELLER:	
201 Deposit or earnest money	3,000.00	501 Excess deposit (see instructions)	8,648.50
202 Principal amount of new loan(s)	90,000.00	502 Settlement charges to seller (line 1400)	
203 Existing loan(s) taken subject to		503 Existing loan(s) taken subject to	48,000.00
204		504 Payoff of first mortgage loan	
205		505 Payoff of second mortgage loan	
206		506 Accrued interest 9/1 to 9/15	200.00
207		507	
208		508	
209		509	
Adjustments for items unpaid by seller:		Adjustments for items unpaid by seller:	
210 City/town taxes to		510 City/town taxes to	
211 County taxes 1/1 to 9/15	1,190.00	511 County Taxes 1/1 to 9/15	1,190.00
212 Assessments to		512 Assessments to	
213 to		513 to	
214 to		514 to	
215 to		515 to	
216 to		516 to	
217 to		517 to	
218 to		518 to	
219 to		519 to	
220 TOTAL PAID BY/FOR BORROWER:	94,190.00	520 TOTAL REDUCTION AMOUNT DUE SELLER:	58,038.50
300 CASH AT SETTLEMENT FROM/TO BORROWER		600 CASH AT SETTLEMENT TO/FROM SELLER:	
301 Gross amount due from borrower (line 120)	127,190.00	601 Gross amount due to seller (line 420)	123,310.00
302 Less amounts paid by/for borrower (line 20)	94,190.00	602 Less total reductions in amount due seller (line 520)	58,038.50
303 CASH ☒ (FROM) ☐ (TO) BORROWER	33,000.00	603 CASH ☒ (TO) ☐ (FROM) SELLER	65,271.50

HUD-1 Rv. 5-76
(10M 7-82)

L. SETTLEMENT CHARGES

			PAID FROM BORROWER'S FUNDS AT SETTLEMENT	PAID FROM SELLER'S FUNDS AT SETTLEMENT
700 TOTAL SALES/BROKER'S COMMISSION Based on price $ 123,000.00 @ 6 %= 7,380.00				
Division of commission (line 700) as follows				
701 $ 3,690.00	to	List-Rite Realty		3,690.00
702 $ 3,690.00	to	Quick-Sale Realty		3,690.00
703 Commission paid at settlement				
704				
800 ITEMS PAYABLE IN CONNECTION WITH LOAN				
801 Loan Origination fee			900.00	
802 Loan Discount	%			
803 Appraisal Fee	to		100.00	
804 Credit Report	to		25.00	
805 Lender's inspection fee				
806 Mortgage insurance application fee	to			
807 Assumption Fee				
808				
809				
810				
811				
900 ITEMS REQUIRED BY LENDER TO BE PAID IN ADVANCE				
901 Interest from Sept 15 to Sept 30 @ $ 28.00 /day			420.00	
902 Mortgage insurance premium for mo to				
903 Hazard insurance premium for yrs to				
904				
905				
1000 RESERVES DEPOSITED WITH LENDER				
1001 Hazard insurance	4 mo @ $ 20.00 per mo		80.00	
1002 Mortgage insurance	mo @ $ per mo			
1003 City property taxes	mo @ $ per mo			
1004 County property taxes	12 mo @ $ 140.00 per mo		1,680.00	
1005 Annual assessments (Maint)	mo @ $ per mo			
1006	mo @ $ per mo			
1007	mo @ $ per mo			
1008	mo @ $ per mo			
1100 TITLE CHARGES:				
1101 Settlement or closing fee	to	Charter Title Company	110.00	110.00
1102 Abstract or title search	to			
1103 Title examination	to			
1104 Title insurance binder	to			
1105 Document preparation	to	Attorney	60.00	
1106 Notary fees	to			
1107 Attorney's fees to	to			
(includes above items No				
1108 Title insurance	to	Charter Title Company	40.00	814.50
(includes above items No				
1109 Lender's coverage	$ 90,000.00			
1110 Owner's coverage	$123,000.00			
1111 Buyer's Attorney			450.00	
1112 Seller's Attorney				300.00
1113				
1200 GOVERNMENT RECORDING AND TRANSFER CHARGES				
1201 Recording fees Deed $ 5.00 Mortgage $ 10.00 Releases $ 5.00			15.00	5.00
1202 City/county tax/stamps Deed $ Mortgage $				
1203 State tax/stamps Deed $ Mortgage $				
1204				
1205				
1300 ADDITIONAL SETTLEMENT CHARGES				
1301 Survey	to			
1302 Pest inspection	to	Dead-Bug Pest Company		39.00
1303				
1304				
1305				
1400 TOTAL SETTLEMENT CHARGES (entered on lines 103, Section J and 502, Section K)			3,880.00	8,648.50

SELLER'S AND/OR PURCHASER'S STATEMENT

Seller's and Purchaser's signature hereon acknowledges his/their approval of tax prorations, and signifies their understanding that prorations were based on figures for preceding year, or estimates for current year, and in event of any change for current year, all necessary adjustments must be made between Seller and Purchaser direct, likewise any DEFICIT in delinquent taxes will be reimbursed to Title Company by the Seller.

We approve the foregoing settlement statement, in its entirety, authorize payments in accordance therewith and acknowledge receipt of a copy thereof

Signature_____   _____

_____   _____

_____   _____
Seller   Purchaser

_____
Escrow Officer

sample transaction in order to see where each item is placed on the settlement statement. (You will notice that the buyer is referred to as the borrower throughout Figure 14:1. This is not important for the moment and will be explained at the end of the chapter.)

Lines 101 (Section J) and 401 (Section K) of the settlement statement show identically the price the buyer is paying and the seller is receiving for the property. On line 103 is the $3,512 total of the buyer's settlement charges from the reverse side of this form. (The reverse side will be discussed in a moment.) On lines 109 and 409 we find the hazard insurance proration. The existing policy cost the seller $240 and has 9 months to run. For these 9 months the buyer is being charged $180 on line 109 and the seller is credited the same amount on line 409. The heating oil remaining in the heating system tank is charged to the buyer on line 110 and credited to the seller on line 410. The gross amount of $126,822 that is due from the buyer is tallied on line 120.

On line 201 the buyer is credited with the $3,000 earnest money paid at the time the purchase contract was written. On the next line, the buyer is credited with the principal amount of the new $90,000 loan. On line 211 there is a property tax proration credit for the buyer; on line 511 the same proration is shown as a charge to the seller. This is because $1,680 in property taxes are due on October 1 for the period January 1 through December 31. Not yet paid for the year, the buyer must pay these taxes on October 1. However, the seller owned the property from January 1 to September 15, a period of $8\frac{1}{2}$ months. At the rate of $140 per month, this means the seller must give the buyer $1,190 as part of the closing costs.

On line 220 we see the $94,190 total of the buyer's credits. Line 301 shows the gross amount that is due from the buyer for this transaction. The difference, on line 303, is the amount of cash that is needed from the buyer (borrower) to close the transaction.

Seller's Side   On the seller's side of the settlement statement (Section K) at line 420 we have the gross amount due to the seller from the sales price and proration credits. On line 502 is the $8,189 total of the seller's settlement costs from the reverse side of the form (line 1400). Continuing, on line 504 the seller is charged for the existing mortgage loan that is being paid off as part of the closing. Accrued interest of $240 on that loan for the first half of September is charged to the seller on line 506. On line 520 the $57,619 total is what must come out of the seller's funds at the closing. This is subtracted from the gross amount due to the seller on line 601. The difference, on line 603, is the $65,691 cash the seller will receive at the closing.

Continuing on the next page of Figure 14:1 (reverse side of the actual form), the real estate commission is detailed on lines 700, 701, and 702. Note that if a closing agent makes the commission split shown here, that closing agent must have written instructions to do so from the real estate broker who is being paid by the seller. Otherwise, all the commission goes to the seller's broker and the seller's broker pays the cooperating broker according to whatever agreement they have.

Settlement Charges

Lines 801, 803, and 804 show the charges incurred by the buyer in connection with obtaining the new $90,000 loan. Line 901 carries the interest on the $90,000 loan as it is calculated from the date of closing to September end. This charge brings the loan up to the first day of the next month and simplifies future bookkeeping for the monthly loan payments. At 12% the interest on $90,000 is $24.00 a day and the buyer is charged $360 for 15 days.

As a condition for the loan, the lender requires impound accounts for hazard insurance and property taxes. In order to have enough on hand to make the property tax payment on October 1, the lender requires an immediate reserve of $1,680 (line 1004). Beginning November 1, one-twelfth of the estimated taxes for next year will be added to the buyer's monthly payment so as to have money in the impound account from which to pay taxes next year. The same concept applies to the hazard insurance. It comes due in 8 months, therefore the lender requires 4 months worth of reserves in advance (line 1001).

Lines 1101, 1105, and 1106 show the settlement (closing fee), and the document preparation fee, associated with this closing. Title insurance charges of $400 to the seller for the owner's policy and $40 to the buyer for the lender's policy are itemized on line 1108. Lines 1109 and 1110 show the coverage for each. The amounts paid from settlement funds to the attorneys of the buyer and seller are listed on lines 1111 and 1112 ($90,000 and $123,000 respectively). Note that the buyer and seller can choose to pay their attorneys outside of the closing. **Outside of the closing** or **outside of escrow** means a party to the closing has paid someone directly and not through the closing agent.

Government recording fees and conveyance taxes necessary to complete this transaction are itemized on lines 1201 and 1203 and charged to the buyer and seller as shown. On line 1302 the settlement agent pays the pest inspection company $39 on behalf of the seller. This is another item that is sometimes paid outside of the closing; i.e., the seller can write a check directly to the termite company once the inspection has been made. On line 1400, the totals for both the buyer (borrower) and seller are entered. The same totals ($3,512 & $8,189) are transferred to page 1 or obverse of the settlement statement on lines 103 and 502 respectively.

Note that Figure 14:1 shows both the buyer's side of the transaction and the seller's side. In actual practice, the seller will receive this settlement statement with lines 101 through 303 (Section J) blacked out, and the buyer will receive this statement with lines 401 through 603 (Section K) blacked out.

REAL ESTATE SETTLEMENT PROCEDURES ACT

In response to consumer complaints regarding real estate closing costs and procedures, Congress passed the Real Estate Settlement Procedures Act (RESPA) effective June 20, 1975 throughout the United States. The purpose of RESPA, which is administered by the U.S. Department of Housing and Urban Development (HUD), is to regulate and standardize real estate settlement practices when "federally related" first mortgage loans are made on one- to four-family residences, condominiums, and cooperatives. Federally related is defined to include FHA or VA or other government-backed or assisted loans, loans from lenders with federally insured deposits, loans that are to be purchased by FNMA, GNMA, FHLMC or other federally controlled secondary mortgage market institutions, and loans made by lenders who make or invest more than $1 million per year in residential loans. As the bulk of all home loans now made fall into one of these categories, the impact of this law is far-reaching.

RESPA prohibits kickbacks and fees for services not per- *Restrictions* formed during the closing process. For example, in some regions of the United States prior to this act, it was common practice for attorneys and closing agents to channel title business to certain title companies in return for a fee. This increased settlement costs without adding services. Now there must be a justifiable service rendered for each closing fee charge. The act also prohibits the seller from requiring that the buyer purchase title insurance from a particular title company.

The Real Estate Settlement Procedures Act also contains restrictions on the amount of advance property tax and insurance payments that a lender can collect and place in an impound or reserve account. The amount is limited to the property owner's share of taxes and insurance accrued prior to settlement, plus one-sixth of the estimated amount that will come due for these items in the twelve-month period beginning at settlement. This requirement assures that the lender has an adequate but not excessive amount of money impounded when taxes and insurance payments fall due. If the amount in the reserve account is not sufficient to pay an item when it comes due, the lender must temporarily use its own funds to make up the difference. Then the lender bills the borrower or increases the monthly reserve payment. If there is a drop in the amount the lender must pay out, then the monthly reserve requirement can be reduced.

Considerable criticism and debate have raged over the topic of reserves. Traditionally, lenders have not been required to pay interest to borrowers on money held as reserves, effectively creating an interest-free loan to themselves. This, in turn, tempted many lenders to require overly adequate reserves. HUD's RESPA sets a reasonable limit on reserve requirements and some states now require that interest be paid on reserves. Although not always required to do so, some lenders now voluntarily pay interest on reserves.

Benefits   To the typical home buyer who is applying for a first mortgage loan the most obvious benefits of RESPA are that (1) he will receive from the lender a special HUD information booklet explaining RESPA, (2) he will receive a good faith estimate of closing costs from the lender, (3) the lender will use the HUD Uniform Settlement Statement, and (4) he the buyer as the borrower has the right to inspect the Uniform Settlement Statement one business day before the day of closing.

The primary reason lenders are required to promptly give loan applicants an estimate of closing costs is to allow the loan applicant an opportunity to compare prices for the various services his transaction will require. Additionally, these estimates help the borrower calculate how much his total closing costs will be. Figure 14:2 illustrates a good faith estimate form. Note that it is primarily concerned with settlement services.

RESPA does not require estimates of escrow impounds for property taxes and insurance, although the lender can voluntarily add these items to the form. Note also that RESPA allows lenders to make estimates in terms of ranges. For example, escrow fees may be stated as $150 to $175 to reflect the range of rates being charged by local escrow companies for that service.

HUD SETTLEMENT   The HUD Settlement Statement you saw in Figure 14:1 *STATEMENT* is required of all federally related real estate lenders. Because it is actually a lender requirement, it uses the word "borrower" instead of "buyer." However, if the loan is in connection with a sale, and most are, the buyer and the borrower are one and the same person. This is not true when an owner is refinancing a property, however.

The HUD Settlement Statement has become so widely accepted that it is now used even when it is not required. Closing agents who handle high volumes of closings use computers with special HUD Settlement Statement programs to fill out these forms. Typically, the closing agent types the numbers onto a video screen and a tractor-fed printer with continuous-feed HUD forms takes over the rest of the typing task.

GOOD FAITH ESTIMATES OF CLOSING COSTS   **Figure 14:2**

The charges listed below are our Good Faith Estimate of some of the settlement charges you will need to pay at settlement of the loan for which you have applied. These charges will be paid to the title or escrow company that conducts the settlement. This form does not cover all items you will be required to pay in cash at settlement, for example, deposit in escrow for real estate taxes and insurance. You may wish to inquire as to the amounts of such other items. You may be required to pay other additional amounts at settlement. This is not a commitment to make a loan.

	Services		Estimated Fees
801.	Loan Origination Fee ____ % + $ _____		$
802.	Loan Discount %		$
803.	Appraisal Fee		$
804.	Credit Report		$
806.	Mortgage Insurance Application Fee		$
807.	Assumption Fee		$
808.	Tax Service Fee		$
901.	Interest		$
902.	Mortgage Insurance Premium		$
1101.	Settlement or Closing Fee		$
1106.	Notary Fees		$
1109.	Title Insurance, Lender's Coverage	List only those items borrower will pay	$
1110.	Title Insurance, Owner's Coverage		$
1201.	Recording Fees		$
1202.	County Tax/Stamps		$
1203.	City Tax/Stamps		$
1302.	Pest Inspection		$
1303.	Building Inspection		$
			$
These numbers correspond to the HUD Settlement Statement		TOTAL	$

VOCABULARY REVIEW

*Match terms **a–g** with statements **1–7**.*

a. Closing statement   **e.** Prorate
b. Deed delivery   **f.** Seller's affidavit of title
c. Documentary transfer tax **g.** RESPA
d. Escrow closing

1. An accounting of funds to the borrower (buyer) and seller at the completion of a real estate transaction.
2. Deposit of documents and funds with a neutral third party plus instructions as to how to conduct the closing.
3. A source of state and local revenue derived from taxing conveyance documents.
4. A document provided by the seller at a settlement meeting stating that he has done nothing to encumber title since the title search was made for this sale.
5. The moment at which title passes from the seller to the borrower (buyer).
6. To divide the ongoing income and expenses of a property between the borrower (buyer) and seller.
7. A federal law that deals with procedures to be followed in certain types of real estate closings.

QUESTIONS AND PROBLEMS

1. What are the duties of an escrow agent?
2. As a means of closing a real estate transaction, how does an escrow differ from a settlement meeting?
3. Is an escrow agent the agent of the borrower (buyer) or the seller? Explain.
4. The borrower (buyer) agrees to accept the seller's fire insurance policy as part of the purchase agreement. The policy cost $180, covers the period January 16 through the following January 15, and the settlement date is March 12. How much does the borrower (buyer) owe the seller (closest whole dollar)?
5. A borrower (buyer) agrees to assume an existing 8% mortgage on which $45,000 is still owed; the last monthly payment was made on March 1 and the next payment is due April 1. Settlement date is March 12. Local custom is to use a 30-day month and charge the borrower (buyer) interest beginning with the settlement day. Calculate the interest proration. To whom is it credited? To whom is it charged?
6. In real estate closing, does the borrower (buyer) or seller normally pay for the following items: deed preparation, lender's title policy, loan appraisal fee, mortgage recording, and mortgage release?

California Escrow Procedure: A Blueprint for the Nation. (Prentice-Hall, 1981, 227 pages). Book provides a thorough look at the escrow system of closing and the firms that do it. Valuable reading in other states where escrow closings are becoming popular.

"Going to Escrow" and "Closing Escrow" by **Laura Ann Davis.** *(First Tuesday,* Feb 85, p. 6 and Mar 85, p. 23). This two article series explains how escrow works, what documents are required, responsibilities of the parties, modifying escrow instructions, handling delays and cancellations and completing the closing.

"Interim Occupancy" by **Laura Ann Davis.** *(First Tuesday,* Feb 85, p. 22). Article discusses how to arrange for occupancy by the buyer before title transfers. Includes sample interim occupancy agreement.

Realty Bluebook by **Robert DeHeer.** (Professional Publishing Co., 1986, 756 pages). Contains 397 pages of amortization tables, 130 pages of financing techniques, 66 pages of checklists, 102 pages of contract clauses and 61 pages of tax information. New editions issued annually.

Settlement Costs and You. (U.S. Department of Housing and Urban Development, 31 pages). Explains borrowers' rights under RESPA. Demonstrates sample closings using the HUD settlement forms. Available free from lenders.

Texas Real Estate Law, 4th ed. by **Charles J. Jacobus.** (Reston, 1985, 560 pages). Chapters 13 and 14 deal with title assurance and closings in Texas.

*   *   *

Note to readers: Most title insurance companies have booklets describing local settlement procedures and title insurance services that are free for the asking.

Real Estate Leases

KEY TERMS

Escalation clause: provision in a lease for upward and downward rent adjustments

Ground rent: rent paid to occupy a plot of land

Lessee: the tenant

Lessor: the landlord

Option clause: the right at some future time to purchase or lease a property at a predetermined price

Quiet enjoyment: the right of possession and use of property without undue disturbance by others

Reversionary interest: the right to retake possession of a leased property at some future time

Sublease: a lease that is given by a lessee

Sublessee: a lessee who rents from another lessee

Sublessor: a lessee who rents to another lessee

Earlier chapters of this book discussed leases as estates in land (Chapter 3) and as a means of financing (Chapter 12). This chapter looks at leases from the standpoint of the tenant, the property owner, and the property manager. (During your lifetime you may be in any one of these roles, and perhaps all three.) Our discussion begins with some important terminology. Then comes a sample lease form with explanation, information on locating, qualifying and keeping tenants and finally, some information on job opportunities available in professional property management. Emphasis is on residential property, although a number of key points regarding commercial property leases are also included.

THE LEASEHOLD ESTATE

A lease conveys to the **lessee** (tenant) the right to possess and use another's property for a period of time. During this time, the **lessor** (the landlord or fee owner) possesses a **reversion** that entitles him to retake possession at the end of the lease period. This is also called a **reversionary right** or **reversionary interest.**

The tenant's right to occupy land is called a leasehold estate. There are four categories of leasehold estates: estate

363

for years, periodic estate, estate at will, and tenancy at sufferance. An **estate for years** must have a specific starting time and a specific ending time. It can be for any length of time, and it does not automatically renew itself. A **periodic estate** has an original lease period of fixed length that continually renews itself for like periods of time until the tenant or landlord acts to terminate it. A month-to-month lease is an example. In an **estate at will** all the normal landlord-tenant rights and duties exist except that the estate can be terminated by either party at any time. A **tenancy at sufferance** occurs when a tenant stays beyond his legal tenancy without the consent of the landlord. The tenant is commonly called a **holdover tenant** and no advance notice is required for eviction. He differs from a trespasser in that his original entry onto the property was legal.

CREATING
A VALID LEASE

A lease is both a conveyance and a contract. As a conveyance it transfers or conveys rights of possession to the tenant in the form of a leasehold estate. As a contract it establishes legally enforceable provisions for the payment of rent and any other obligations the landlord and tenant have to each other.

For a valid lease to exist, it must meet the usual requirements of a contract as described in Chapter 7. That is to say, the parties involved must be legally competent, and there must be mutual agreement, lawful objective, and sufficient consideration. The main elements of a lease are (1) the names of the lessee and lessor, (2) a description of the premises, (3) an agreement to convey (let) the premises by the lessor and to accept possession by the lessee, (4) provisions for the payment of rent, (5) the starting date and duration of the lease, and (6) signatures of the parties to the lease.

Statute of Frauds

The Statute of Frauds in Texas provides that a lease of real estate for a term which cannot be performed within one year must be in writing. This implies that a lease of one year or less need not be in writing to be enforceable. A lease for one year or less or a month-to-month lease could be oral and still be valid, but as a matter of good business practice, all leases should be written and signed. This gives all parties involved a written reminder of their obligations under the lease and reduces chances for dispute. A real estate agent should remember, however, that there is no promulgated form for a lease (other than those shown in Appendix—for temporary occupancy). An agent should not use another lease form without legal assistance.

Figure 15:1 illustrates a lease document that contains provisions typically found in a residential lease. These provisions are presented in simplified language to help you more easily grasp the rights and responsibilities created by a lease.

THE LEASE DOCUMENT

The first paragraph is the conveyance portion of the lease. At ① and ② the lessor and lessee are identified. At ③, the lessor conveys to the lessee and the lessee accepts the property. A description of the property follows at ④, and the **term** of the conveyance at ⑤. The property must be described so that there is no question as to the extent of the premises the lessee is renting. If the lease illustrated here were a month-to-month lease instead, the term of the lease would be changed to read, "commencing April 15, 19xx and continuing on a month-to-month basis until terminated by either the lessee or the lessor." During his tenancy, the lessee is entitled to **quiet enjoyment** of the property. This means uninterrupted use of the property without interference from the owner, lessor or other third party.

Conveyance

A month-to-month rental is the most flexible arrangement. It allows the owner to recover possession of the property on one-month notice and the tenant to leave on one-month notice with no further obligation to the owner. In rental agreements for longer periods of time, each party gives up some flexibility to gain commitment from the other. Under a one-year lease, a tenant has the property committed to him for a year. This means that the tenant is committed to paying rent for a full year, even though he may want to move out before the year is over. Similarly, the owner has the tenant's commitment to pay rent for a year, but loses the flexibility of being able to regain possession of the property until the year is over.

The balance of the lease document is concerned with contract aspects of the lease. At number ⑥, the amount of rent that the lessee will pay for the use of the property is

Figure 15:1

LEASE

This lease agreement is entered into the ___10th___ day
of ___April___ , 19_xx_ between ___John and Sally___
___Landlord ①___ *(hereinafter called the Lessor) and* ___Gary and___
___Barbara Tenant ②___ *(hereinafter called the Lessee). The Lessor*
hereby leases to the Lessee ③ and the Lessee hereby leases from
the Lessor the premises known as ___Apartment 24,___
___1234 Maple St., City, State ④___ *for the term of* ___one ⑤___
year beginning 12:00 noon on ___April 15, 19xx___ *and ending*
12:00 noon on ___April 15, 19xx___ *unless sooner terminated*
as herein set forth.

The rent for the term of this lease is $ ___3,600.00 ⑥___
payable in equal monthly installments of $ ___300.00 ⑦___ *on the*
___15th___ *day of each month beginning on* ___April 15, 19xx___ .
Receipt of the first monthly installment and $ ___300.00 ⑧___ *as*
a security, damage and clean-up deposit is hereby acknowledged.
It is furthermore agreed that:

⑨ *The use of the premises shall be as a residential dwell-*
ing for the above named Lessee only.

⑩ *The Lessee may not assign this lease or sublet any*
portion of the premises without written permission from the Lessor.

⑪ *The Lessee agrees to abide by the house rules as*
posted. A current copy is attached to this lease.

⑫ *The Lessor shall furnish water, sewer and heat as*
part of the rent. Electricity and telephone shall be paid for by
the Lessee.

⑬ *The Lessor agrees to keep the premises structure main-*
tained and in habitable condition.

⑭ *The Lessee agrees to maintain the interior of said*
premises and at the termination of this lease to return said premises
to the Lessor in as good condition as it is now except for ordinary
wear and tear.

⑮ *The Lessee shall not make any alterations or improve-*
ments to the premises without the Lessor's prior written consent.
Any alterations or improvements become the property of the Lessor
at the end of this lease.

Figure 15:1 *continued*

⑯ *If the premises are not ready for occupancy on the date herein provided, the Lessee may cancel this agreement and the Lessor shall return in full all money paid by the Lessee.*

⑰ *If the Lessee defaults on this lease agreement, the Lessor may give the Lessee three days notice of intention to terminate the lease. At the end of those three days the lease shall terminate and the Lessee shall vacate and surrender the premises to the Lessor.*

⑱ *If the Lessee holds over after the expiration of this lease without the Lessor's consent, the tenancy shall be month-to-month at twice the monthly rate indicated herein.*

⑲ *If the premises are destroyed or rendered uninhabitable by fire or other cause, this lease shall terminate as of the date of the casualty.*

⑳ *The Lessor shall have access to the premises for the purpose of inspecting for damage, making repairs, and showing to prospective tenants or buyers.*

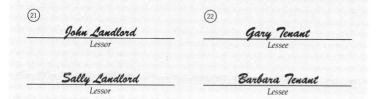

㉑

John Landlord
Lessor

Sally Landlord
Lessor

㉒

Gary Tenant
Lessee

Barbara Tenant
Lessee

set forth. In a lease for years it is the usual practice to state the total rent for the entire lease period. This is the total number of dollars the lessee is obligated to pay to the lessor. If the lessee wants to leave the premises before the lease period expires, he is still liable for the full amount of the contract. The method of payment of the obligation is shown at number ⑦. Unless the contract calls for rent to be paid in advance, under common law it is not due until the end of the rental period. At number ⑧, the lessor has taken a deposit in the form of the first monthly installment and acknowledges receipt of it. The lessor has also taken additional money as security against the possibility of uncollected rent or damage to the premises and for clean-up expenses. (The tenant is supposed to leave the premises clean.) The deposit is refunded, less legitimate charges, when the tenant leaves.

Items ⑨ through ⑳ summarize commonly found lease clauses. At ⑨ and ⑩, the lessor wants to maintain control over the use and occupancy of the premises. Without this he might find the premises used for an entirely different purpose by people he did not rent to. At ⑪, the tenant agrees to abide by the house rules. These normally cover such things as use of laundry and trash facilities, swimming pool rules, noise rules, etc. Number ⑫ states the responsibility of the lessee and lessor with regard to the payment of utilities.

The strict legal interpretation of a lease as a conveyance means the lessee is responsible for upkeep and repairs during his tenancy unless the lessor promises to do so in the lease contract. The paragraph at number ⑬ is that promise. Note however that with regard to residential properties, Texas courts and the Texas Legislature now take the position that the landlord is obligated to keep a residential property repaired and habitable even if this is not specifically stated in the contract. Commercial property still goes by the traditional lease interpretation.

Number ⑭ is the lessee's promise to maintain the interior of the dwelling. If the lessee damages the property, he is to repair it. Normal wear and tear are considered to be part of the rent. At paragraph ⑮, the lessor protects himself against unauthorized alterations and improvements and then goes on to point out that anything the tenant affixes to the building becomes realty. As realty it remains a part of the building when the tenant leaves.

Paragraphs ⑯ through ⑲ deal with the rights of both parties if the premises are not ready for occupancy, if the lessee defaults after moving in, if the lessee holds over, or if the premises are destroyed. The lessor also retains the right (paragraph ⑳) to enter the leased premises from time to time for business purposes.

Finally, at ㉑ and ㉒, the lessor and lessee sign. It is not necessary to have these signatures notarized. That is done only if the lease is to be recorded. The purpose of recording is to give constructive notice that the lessee has an estate in the property. Recording is usually done only when the lessee's rights are not apparent from inspection of the property for actual notice or where the lease is to run many years. From the property owner's standpoint, the lease is an encumbrance on the property. If the owner should subsequently sell the property or mortgage it, the lessee's tenancy remains undisturbed. The buyer or lender must accept the property subject to the lease.

If one of the lessors dies, the lease is still binding on the remaining lessor(s) and upon the estate of the deceased lessor. Similarly, if one of the lessees dies, the lease is still binding on the remaining lessee(s) and upon the estate of the deceased lessee. This is based on common law doctrine that applies to contracts in general. The lessee and lessor can, however, agree to do otherwise. The lessee could ask the lessor to **waive** (give up) the right to hold the lessee's estate to the lease in the event of the lessee's death. For example, an elderly tenant about to sign a lease might want to add wording to the lease whereby the tenant's death would allow his estate to terminate the lease early.

LANDLORD-TENANT LAWS

Traditionally, a lease was enforceable in court based solely on what it contained. This philosophy still prevails with regard to leases on commercial property. However, with regard to residential rental property, the trend today is for the legislature to establish special landlord-tenant laws. The intent is to strike a reasonable balance between the responsibilities of landlords to tenants and vice versa. Typically, these laws limit the amount of security deposit a landlord can require, tell the tenant how many days notice he has to give before vacating a periodic tenancy, and require the landlord to deliver possession on the date agreed. The landlord must maintain the premises in a fit condition for living and the tenant is to keep his unit clean and not damage it. The tenant is to obey the house rules and the landlord must give advance notice before entering an apartment except in legitimate emergencies. Additionally the laws set forth such things as the procedure for accounting for any deposit money not returned, the right of the tenant to make needed repairs and bill the landlord, the right of the landlord to file court actions for unpaid rent, and the proper procedure for evicting a tenant.

Since 1967, there have been a number of statutes passed to provide protection to the tenant in residential leasehold situations.

These laws, very generally summarized, specify:

1. **Notice must be provided before a tenancy may be terminated.** This is generally 30 days on a month-to-month tenancy. This does not apply to eviction proceedings, but rather to termination of tenancies.

2. **Interruption and exclusion by the landlord of the tenant's right to the premises.** This basically provides that the landlord may not exclude the tenant from his premises, but may only change the door locks to the tenant's premises. If the landlord does change the door locks to the tenant's premises, he must post a written notice on the tenant's door indicating that the tenant may pick up the new key to his premises at any time upon request, 24 hours a day.

3. **Landlord's lien for rent.** However, the exemptions provided under this statute are very extensive and ultimately allows very little of the furniture and household goods as those on which the landlord may obtain a lien as security for his rent.

4. **Security deposits.** There are very strict provisions now for the landlord's retaining security deposits. Basically, the landlord must return the security deposit within 30 days or give the tenant an explanation of why the security deposit was not returned and what the funds were used to repair. There are some strict provisions for the landlord's failure to comply with the statute.

5. **Habitable premises.** The landlord must provide habitable premises and may not evict a tenant for the purposes of retaliation for tenant's notice to repair the premises. The term habitable is determined by the facts in any given situation and varies from case to case.

6. **Installation of security devices.** The landlord has an obligation, upon request of tenant, to install security devices. The law defines security devices as window latches, deadbolt locks, pen locks, and night latches. The initial installation of these devices must be at the landlord's expense. Any installation of additional security devices will be at the tenant's expense.

7. **Disclosure of ownership and management of dwelling unit.** The landlord has the duty to disclose to the tenant the name and address of the owner of the dwelling unit in the manner specified in the statute. The same is true

of the name and address of any property management company which is currently managing the dwelling unit.

8. **Smoke detectors in dwelling units.** For dwelling units constructed after September 1, 1981, at least one smoke detector must be installed by the landlord outside of each separate bedroom in the immediate vicinity of the bedroom, with certain specified exceptions. For dwelling units constructed on or before September 1, 1981, at least one smoke detector must be installed by the landlord.

Note that these statutes apply to all landlord-tenant residential situations. Even when the TREC promulgated leases are used, these rights exist, regardless of the term of the tenancy.

METHODS FOR SETTING RENTS

There are several methods for setting rents. The first is the **fixed rental fee,** also called a **flat rent** or **gross lease.** The tenant agrees to pay a specified amount of money for the use of the premises. A tenant paying $300 per month on a month-to-month apartment lease or a dentist paying $5,000 per year for office space are both examples of fixed rents. A second method of setting rents is called the **step-up or graduated rental.** For example, a five-year office lease might call for monthly rents of 70¢ per square foot of floor space the first year, 73¢ the second year, 77¢ the third year, 81¢ the fourth year, and 85¢ the fifth.

Because of inflation, most lessors (particularly in office buildings) add an **escalation clause.** This allows the landlord to pass along to the tenant increases in such items as property taxes, utility charges or janitorial fees. Another variation is to have the tenant pay for all property taxes, insurance, repairs, utilities, etc., in addition to the base rent. This arrangement is called a **net lease** and it is commonly used when an entire building is being leased. Long-term ground leases.

Another system for setting rents is the **percentage basis** wherein the owner receives a percentage of the tenant's gross receipts as rent. For example, a farmer who leases land may give the landowner 20% of the value of the crop when it is sold. The monthly rent for a small hardware store might be $600 plus 6% of gross sales above $10,000. A supermarket may pay $7,500 plus 1½% of gross above $50,000 per month. By setting rents this way, the tenant shares some of his business risk with the property owner. Also, there is a built-in inflation hedge to the extent that inflation causes the tenant's receipts to increase.

OPTION CLAUSES

Option clauses give the tenant the right at some future time to lease the property at a predetermined price. This gives a tenant flexibility. For example, suppose that a prospective tenant is starting a new business and is not certain how successful it will be. Thus, in looking for space to rent, he will want a lease that allows an "out" if the new venture does not succeed, but will permit him to stay if the venture is successful. The solution is a lease with options. The landlord could offer a one-year lease, plus an option to stay for 2 more years at a higher rent plus a second option for an additional 5 years at a still higher rent. If the venture is not successful, the tenant is obligated for only one year. But if successful, he has the option of staying 2 more years, and if still successful, for 5 years after that.

Another option possibility offers the tenant a lease that also contains an option to buy the property for a fixed period of time at a preset price. This is called a **lease with option to buy** and is discussed in Chapter 8.

ASSIGNMENT &
SUBLETTING

Unless provided in the lease contract, in Texas the tenant may not assign his lease or sublet the premises without the landlord's prior written consent. An **assignment** is the total transfer of the tenant's rights to another person. These parties are referred to as the **assignor** and the **assignee,** respectively. The assignee acquires all the right, title and interest of the assignor, no more and no less. However, the assignor remains liable for the performance of the contract unless he is released by the landlord. To **sublet** means to transfer only a portion of the rights held under a lease. The sublease thereby created may be for a portion of the premises, or part of the lease term. The party acquiring those rights is called the **sublessee.** The original lessee is the **sublessor** with respect to the sublessee. The sublessee pays rent to the lessee who in turn remains liable to the landlord for rent on the entire premises.

GROUND LEASE

A **ground lease** is a lease of land alone. The lessor is the fee simple owner of the land, and conveys to the lessee an estate for years, typically lasting from 25 to 99 years. The lessee pays for and owns the improvements. Thus a ground lease separates the ownership of land from the ownership of buildings on that land. The lease rent, called the **ground rent,** is on a net lease basis. As a hedge against inflation, the rent is usually increased every 5 to 10 years. This is done either by a graduated lease or by requiring a reappraisal of the land and then by charging a new rent based on that valuation.

A lease need not be restricted to the use of the earth's surface. In Chapter 2 it was shown that land extends from the center of the earth skyward. Consequently it is possible for one person to own the mineral rights, another the surface rights, and a third the air rights. This can also be done with leases. A landowner can lease to an oil company the right to explore and extract minerals, oil and gas below his land and, at the same time, lease the surface rights to a farmer. In Chicago and New York City, railroads have leased surface and air rights above their downtown tracks for the purpose of constructing office buildings.

The amount specified in the lease is the rent that the tenant must pay the landlord for the use of the premises and is called the **contract rent.** The rent which the same property can command in the competitive open market is called the **economic rent**. When a lease contract is negotiated the contract rent and economic rent are nearly always the same. However as time passes, the market value of the right to use the premises may increase while the contract rent stays the same. When this occurs the lease itself becomes valuable. That value is determined by the difference between the contract rent and the economic rent, and how long the lease has to run. An example would be a 5 year lease with 3 years left at a contract rent of $300 per month where the current rental value of the premises is now $400 per month. If the lease is assignable, the fact that it offers a $100 per month savings for 3 years makes it valuable. Similarly, an oil lease obtained for $50 per acre before oil was discovered might be worth millions after its discovery. Conversely, when contract rent exceeds economic rent, the lease takes on a negative value.

CONTRACT RENT, ECONOMIC RENT

*LEASE
TERMINATION*

Most leases terminate because of the expiration of the term of the lease. The tenant has received the use of the premises and the landlord has received rent in return. However, a lease can be terminated if the landlord and the tenant mutually agree. The tenant surrenders the premises and the landlord releases him from the contract. Under certain conditions, destruction of the premises is cause for lease termination. Abandonment of the premises by the tenant can be grounds for lease termination provided the tenant's intention to do so is clear.

If either the tenant or the landlord fails to live up to the lease contract, termination can occur. Where the tenant is at fault, the landlord can evict him and recover possession of the premises. If the premises are unfit for occupancy, the tenant can claim **constructive eviction** as his reason for leaving. The government, under its right of eminent domain can also terminate a lease, but must provide just compensation. An example of this would be construction of a new highway that requires the demolition of a building rented to tenants. The property owner and the tenants would both be entitled to compensation.

A mortgage foreclosure can also bring about lease termination. It all depends on priority. If the mortgage was recorded before the lease was signed, then foreclosure of the mortgage also forecloses the lease. If the lease was recorded first, then the lease still stands. Because a lease can cloud a lender's title, wording is sometimes inserted in leases that makes them subordinate to any future financing of the property. This is highly technical, but nonetheless a very significant matter for long-term shopping center, office building and industrial leases.

Eviction Process

Under Texas law, the Forcible Entry and Detainer statutes provide for eviction proceedings. "Forcible Entry and Detainer" is a legal term referring to a tenant who takes possession of the premises without the consent of the landlord and then refuses to give up possession after demand is made by the landlord. According to the statutes the landlord must give the tenant a minimum of three days' written notice to vacate the premises before filing an action for Forcible Entry and Detainer. A person cannot be guilty of Forcible Entry and Detainer until he has been adjudged so by the Justice of the Peace Court in the precinct where the real estate is situated. The lawsuit must be heard within ten days after the filing. As in all other legal proceedings, there are additional procedural laws pertaining to the Forcible Entry and Detainer statutes, which could provide for quite a lengthy tenancy while eviction proceedings are in process.

There are two federal laws that deal with discrimination in housing. They are (1) the Civil Rights Act of 1866 which prohibits discrimination on the basis of race only, and (2) the Fair Housing Act of 1968 which prohibits discrimination based on race, color, religion, sex, or national origin.

FAIR HOUSING

So far as real estate licensees are concerned, these laws specify that they are not to accept sale or rental listings where they are asked to discriminate, nor are they permitted to make, print, or publish any statement or advertisement with respect to a sale or rental of a dwelling which suggests discrimination because of race, color, religion, or national origin.

So far as owners are concerned, the 1968 Act made exemptions for owners of three or fewer houses or two to four apartment units (one of which must be owner-occupied) provided the sale or lease was arranged without the aid of a real estate agent and without discriminatory advertising. The 1866 Act, however, effectively voids these exemptions with respect to racial discrimination. Seeking legal remedy under the 1866 Act requires a personal lawsuit and support from government agencies is not provided. Moreover, the property owner faces no statutory penalty for damages and no fine under the 1866 Act. The 1968 Act does provide for government legal action and support and for financial penalties against a property owner. At the end of Chapter 17 you will find a longer and more detailed discussion of federal fair housing laws including steering, blockbusting and testers. Note also that many states, counties and cities have fair housing laws that go beyond the federal laws. For example, in some jurisdictions it is illegal to discriminate on the basis of age, marital status, presence of children, physical handicaps, sexual preference, and welfare status.

RENT CONTROL   For the most part, until 1970, the concept of residential **rent control** was reserved for wartime use in the United States. During World War I, six states and several major cities and, in World War II, the federal government imposed limits on how much rent an owner could charge for the use of his real property. The purpose was twofold: (1) to discourage the construction of new housing so that the resources could be channeled to war needs, and (2) to set ceilings so that American householders would not drive up prices by bidding against each other for available rental housing. With limits on rents, but no price controls on the cost of construction materials and labor, the construction of new housing was slowed without the need for a direct government order to stop building.

Within a few years after World War I, and again after World War II, rent controls disappeared in nearly all parts of the country. The notable exception was New York City, where they have survived since the end of World War II and are still in use. However, beginning in the 1970s a number of other cities have enacted rent control laws. This time the major attraction is inflation protection.

Although it is true that since 1956 residential rents in the United States have not risen as rapidly as the general level of consumer prices, any relief from rent increases would nonetheless be welcomed by the 36% of American households that rent. Most tenants recognize that newly constructed properties must command higher rents to meet higher construction, land, and interest costs. However, in existing buildings they resent rent increases that have nothing to do with the original cost of the building or the cost of operating it. The argument of rent control supporters is that only increases in such things as property taxes, utilities, and maintenance should be passed on to tenants. The tenant's assumption in this argument is that rent alone is enough to attract dollars into housing investments. In reality, rents would have to be even higher if the investor could not also look forward to price appreciation of his property.

Rent Control Experience   Experience to date strongly suggests that rent control creates more problems than it solves. In New York City and

Washington, D.C., for example, it is generally agreed that controlled rents have caused existing dwelling units to be taken out of circulation. Despite relatively low vacancy rates thousands of dwelling units are abandoned each year by their owners at a cost of millions of dollars in lost property taxes. With controls on rents but no controls on expenses, property owners are often better off abandoning their properties than operating them.

Another problem with controlled rents is that a vacating tenant may demand a substantial cash payment from a tenant who wants to move in. Although this is illegal, the vacating tenant may sometimes attempt to circumvent the law by requiring the incoming tenant to purchase his furniture for several times its actual worth. Sometimes this payment is called a "key fee" as if to suggest the new tenant is purchasing the key. This pushes the actual cost of the controlled apartment much closer to the value of the unit on the open market, and the advantage of low, controlled rents is lost to the incoming tenant.

A side effect of rent control has been the conversion by many owners of existing rental apartments to condominiums since there are no controls on sales prices of such dwelling units. Some cities responded by restricting conversions. Owners then began to demolish and build new condominiums; however, laws have been enacted to restrict demolition permits.

Other side effects of rent control in the United States are that lenders prefer not to lend on rent-controlled buildings. This is because lenders do not like to loan unless the investor is assured of reasonable returns. Developers find it hard to attract tenants to new rental units from rent-controlled buildings where they are enjoying below-market rents. Owner-occupied properties and non-controlled properties are charged higher property taxes to make up for the falling values of controlled properties. Also there is a significant cost to the public to operate the government offices that administer the controls.

One of the ironies of rent control is that although controlled rents are very attractive to the tenant, he soon finds that the number of people like himself who want to buy at controlled prices exceeds the number who want to sell. Consequently a shortage develops. A better solution is to pursue public policies that encourage the construction of housing rather than discourage it.

VOCABULARY REVIEW

Match terms **a–l** *with statements* **1–12.**

4 **a.** *Assignment*

8 **b.** *Ground rent*

5 **c.** *Holdover tenant*

2 **d.** *Lessee*

1 **e.** *Lessor*

6 **f.** *Month-to-month rental*

11 **g.** *Option clause*

10 **h.** *Participation clause* (Escalation Clause)

12 **i.** *Percentage lease*

7 **j.** *Reversionary interest*

9 **k.** *Step-up rent*

3 **l.** *Sublet*

1. The landlord.
2. The tenant.
3. Partial transfer of rights held under a lease.
4. Complete transfer of rights held under a lease.
5. One who holds a tenancy at sufferance.
6. Example of a periodic estate.
7. The right of the landowner to retake possession at the end of the lease.
8. Rent charged for the use of land.
9. A lease that calls for specified rent increases at various points in time during the life of the lease.
10. A lease clause that allows the landlord to add to the tenant's rent any increases in property taxes, maintenance, and utilities during the life of the lease.
11. A lease clause that gives a tenant the opportunity of renewing his lease at a predetermined rental, but does not obligate him to do so.
12. A lease which relates the amount of rent to the income the lessee obtains by using the leased property.

QUESTIONS AND PROBLEMS

1. From the standpoint of the tenant, what are the advantages and disadvantages of a lease versus a month-to-month rental?
2. What remedies does a property manager in Texas have when a tenant does not pay his rent and/or refuses to move out?
3. In Texas, how many days does a landlord have to return a tenant's security deposit?
4. What is the difference between contract rent and economic rent?
5. On what basis could a tenant claim constructive eviction? What would the tenant's purpose be in doing this?

6. Is an option to renew a lease to the advantage of the lessor or the lessee?

7. What effects do the Civil Rights Act of 1866 and the Fair Housing Act of 1968 have on real estate licensees who handle rentals?

8. Is rent control currently in effect in your community? If so, what effects have these controls had on the sales of investment properties and on the construction of new rental buildings in your community?

9. In Texas, how many days notice must be given before terminating a month-to-month tenancy?

ADDITIONAL READINGS

Computer Applications in Property Management Accounting, rev. ed. (Institute of Real Estate Management, 1983, 64 pages). Explains computer uses in property management.

Handbook for Building Maintenance Management by **Mel Shear.** (Reston, 1983, 612 pages). Contains guidelines to effective as well as preventative maintenance. Includes security, safety, fire prevention, housekeeping, grounds keeping, plumbing, heating and energy management.

Income and Expense Analysis. (Institute of Real Estate Management, Chicago, 1986). Issued annually for apartment buildings and office buildings, these reports show typical rental income and operating expenses across the United States. Very useful for comparing buildings.

Managing Your Rental House for Increased Income by **Doreen Bierbrier.** (McGraw-Hill, 1985, 287 pages). A hands-on, practical guide to renting houses to unrelated single persons on a room-by-room basis. Includes choosing the right house, selecting tenants, rental agreements, record keeping and neighbor relations.

''The Rental Resurgence'' by **Leanne Lachman.** (*Real Estate Today,* Sep 84, p. 23). Article points out that today's housing costs, increased demand and restoration efforts are making rentals a renewed source of investment opportunity.

Texas Real Estate Law, 4th ed. by **Charles J. Jacobus.** (Reston, 1985, 560 pages). Provides up-to-date explanations of law pertinent to the daily operation of a real estate brokerage office in Texas. Chapter 14 deals with landlord and tenant relationships.

*　　*　　*

The following periodicals may also be of interest to you: *Apartment Journal, Apartment Management Newsletter, Apartment News, National Rental Housing Council Newsletter, Real Estate Perspectives, Journal of Property Management, Landlord-Tenant Law Bulletin, Managing Housing Letter* and *Skyscraper Management.*

Real Estate Appraisal

Appraise: to estimate the value of something

Capitalize: to convert future income to current value

Comparables: properties similar to the subject property that have sold recently

Cost approach: land value plus current construction costs minus depreciation

Depreciation: loss in value due to deterioration and obsolescence

Gross rent multiplier (GRM): a number that is multiplied by a property's gross rents to produce an estimate of the property's worth; an economic factor used to estimate a property's market value

Highest and best use: that use of a parcel of land which will produce the greatest current value

Income approach: a method of valuing a property based on the monetary returns it can be expected to produce

Market approach: a method of valuing property based on recent sales of similar properties

Market value: the cash price that a willing buyer and a willing seller would freely agree upon, given reasonable exposure of the property to the marketplace, full information as to the potential uses of the property and no undue compulsion to act

Operating expenses: expenditures necessary to operate a property and maintain the production of income

Scheduled gross, or **Projected gross:** the estimated rent a fully occupied property can be expected to produce on an annual basis

KEY TERMS

To **appraise** real estate means to estimate its value. There are three approaches to making this estimate. The first is to locate similar properties that have sold recently and use them as bench marks in estimating the value of the property you are appraising. This is the **market approach,** also called the market-data approach or market comparison approach. The second approach is to add together the cost of the individual components that make up the property being appraised. This is the **cost approach;** it starts with the cost of a similar parcel of vacant land and adds the cost of the lumber, concrete, plumbing, wiring, labor, etc., necessary to build a similar building. Depreciation is then subtracted. The third approach is to consider only the amount of net income that the property can reasonably be expected to produce for its owner plus any anticipated price increase or decrease. This is the **income approach.** For the person who owns or plans to own real estate, knowing how much a property is worth is a crucial part of the buying or selling decision. For the real estate agent, being able to estimate the value of a property is an essential part of taking a listing and conducting negotiations.

MARKET VALUE

In this chapter you will see demonstrations of the market, cost, and income approaches and how they are used in determining market value. **Market value,** also called **fair market value,** is the highest price in terms of money that a property will bring if (1) payment is made in cash or its equivalent, (2) the property is exposed on the open market for a reasonable length of time, (3) the buyer and seller are fully informed as to market conditions and the uses to which the property may be put, (4) neither is under abnormal pressure to conclude a transaction, and (5) the seller is capable of conveying marketable title. Market value is at the heart of nearly all real estate transactions.

MARKET COMPARISON APPROACH

Let us begin by demonstrating the application of the **market comparison approach** to a single-family residence. The residence to be appraised is called the **subject property** and is described as follows:

The subject property is a one-story, wood-frame house of 1,520 square feet containing three bedrooms, two bathrooms, a living room, dining room, kitchen, and utility room. There is a two-car garage with concrete driveway to the street, a 300-square-foot concrete patio in the backyard and an average amount of landscaping. The house is located on a 10,200-square-foot, level lot that measures 85 by 120 feet. The house is 12 years old, in good repair and located in a well-maintained neighborhood of houses of similar construction and age.

Comparables

After becoming familiar with the physical features and amenities of the subject property, the next step in the market approach is to locate houses with similar physical features and amenities that have sold recently under market value conditions. These are known as **comparables** or "comps." The more similar they are to the subject property, the fewer and smaller the adjustments that must be made in the comparison process and hence the less room for error. As a rule it is best to use comparable sales no more than 6 months old. During periods of relatively stable prices, this can be extended to 1 year. However, during periods of rapidly changing prices even a sale 6 months old may be out of date.

To apply the market comparison approach, the following information must be collected for each comparable sale: date of sale, sales price, financing terms, location of the property and a description of its physical characteristics and amenities. Recorded deeds at public records offices can provide dates and locations of recent sales. Although a deed seldom states the purchase price, nearly all states levy a deed transfer fee or conveyance tax, the amount of which is shown on the recorded deed. This tax can sometimes provide a clue as to the purchase price.

Sales Records

Records of past sales can often be obtained from title and abstract companies. Property tax assessors keep records on changes in ownership as well as property values. Where these records are kept up to date and are available to the public, they can provide information on what has sold recently and for how much. Assessors also keep detailed records of improvements made to land. This can be quite helpful in making adjustments between the subject property and the comparables. For real estate salespeople, locally operated multiple listing services provide asking prices and descriptions of properties currently offered for sale by member brokers along with descriptions, sales prices and dates for properties that have been sold. In some cities, commercially operated financial services publish information on local real estate transactions and sell it on a subscription basis.

To produce the most accurate appraisal possible, each sale used as a comparable should be inspected and the price and terms verified. An agent who specializes in a given neighborhood will have already visited the comparables when they

Verification

were still for sale. The agent can verify price and terms with the selling broker or from multiple listing service sales records.

Number of Comparables   Three to five comparables usually provide enough basis for reliable comparison. To use more than five, the additional accuracy must be weighed against the extra effort involved. When the supply of comparable sales is more than adequate, one should choose the sales that require the fewest adjustments.

It is also important that the comparables selected represent current market conditions. Sales between relatives or close friends may result in an advantageous price to the buyer or seller, and sales prices that for some other reason appear to be out of line with the general market should not be used. Listings and offers to buy should not be used in place of actual sales. They do not represent a meeting of minds between a buyer and a seller. Listing prices do indicate the upper limit of prices, whereas offers to buy indicate lower limits. Thus, if a property is listed for sale at $80,000 and there have been offers as high as $76,000, it is reasonable to presume the market price lies somewhere between $76,000 and $80,000.

Adjustment Process   Let's now work through the example shown in Table 16:1 to demonstrate the application of the market comparison approach to a house. Begin at lines 1 and 2 by entering the address and sale price of each comparable property. For convenience, refer to these as comparables A, B and C. On lines 3 through 10, make time adjustments to the sale price of each comparable to make it equivalent to the subject property today. **Adjustments** are made for price changes since each comparable was sold, as well as for differences in physical features, amenities and financial terms. The result indicates the market value of the subject property.

Time Adjustments   Returning to line 3 in Table 16:1, let's assume that house prices in the neighborhood where the subject property and comparables are located have risen 5% during the 6 months that have elapsed since comparable A was sold. If it were for sale today, comparable A would bring 5% or $4,590 more.

Table 16:1   VALUING A HOUSE BY THE MARKET COMPARISON APPROACH

Line	Item	Comparable Sale A		Comparable Sale B		Comparable Sale C	
1	**Address**	1702 Brookside Ave.		1912 Brookside Ave.		1501 18th Street	
2	**Sales price**		$91,800		$88,000		$89,000
3	**Time adjustment**	*sold 6 mos. ago, add 5%*	+4,590	*sold 3 mos. ago, add 2½%*	+2,200	*just sold*	0
4	**House size**	*160 sq ft larger at $40 per sq ft*	−6,400	*20 sq ft smaller at $40 per sq ft*	+ 800	*same size*	0
5	**Garage/carport**	*carport*	+4,000	*3-car garage*	−2,000	*2-car garage*	0
6	**Other**	*larger patio*	− 300	*no patio*	+ 600	*built-in bookcases*	− 500
7	**Age, upkeep, & overall quality of house**	*superior*	−2,000	*inferior*	+ 400	*equal*	0
8	**Landscaping**	*inferior*	+1,000	*equal*	0	*superior*	− 700
9	**Lot size, features, & location**	*superior*	−3,890	*inferior*	+ 900	*equal*	0
10	**Terms & conditions of sale**	*equal*	0	*special financing*	−1,500	*equal*	0
11	**Total adjustments**		−3,000		+1,400		−1,200
12	**ADJUSTED MARKET PRICE**		$88,800		$89,400		$87,800

13	**Correlation process:**						
	Comparable A	$88,800 × 20%	= $17,760				
	Comparable B	$89,400 × 30%	= $26,820				
	Comparable C	$87,800 × 50%	= $43,900				
14	**INDICATED VALUE**		$88,480				
	Round to		$88,500				

Therefore, you must add $4,590 to bring it up to the present. Comparable B was sold 3 months ago, and to bring it up to the present we need to add 2½% or $2,200 to its sales price. Comparable C was just sold and needs no time correction, as its price reflects today's market.

When using the market comparison approach, all adjustments are made to the comparable properties, not to the subject property. This is because we cannot adjust the value of something for which we do not yet know the value.

House Size   Because house A is 160 square feet larger than the subject house, it is logical to expect that the subject property would sell for less money. Hence a deduction is made from the sales price of comparable A on line 4. The amount of this deduction is based on the difference in floor area and the current cost of similar construction, minus an allowance for depreciation. If we value the extra 160 square feet at $40 per square foot, we must subtract $6,400. For comparable B, the house is 20 square feet smaller than the subject house. At $40 per square foot, we add $800 to comparable B, as it is reasonable to expect that the subject property would sell for that much more because it is that much larger. Comparable C is the same-sized house as the subject property, so no adjustment is needed.

Garage and Patio Adjustments   Next, the parking facilities (line 5) are adjusted. Let's first look at the current cost of garage and carport construction and the condition of these structures. Assume that the value of a carport is $2,000; a one-car garage, $4,000; a two-car garage, $6,000; and a three-car garage, $8,000. Adjustments would be made as follows. The subject property has a two-car garage worth $6,000 and comparable A has a carport worth $2,000. Therefore, based on the difference in garage facilities, we can reasonably expect the subject property to command $4,000 more than comparable A. By adding $4,000 to comparable A, we effectively equalize this difference. Comparable B has a garage worth $2,000 more than the subject property's garage. Therefore, $2,000 must be subtracted from comparable B to equalize it with the subject property. For comparable C, no adjustment is required, as comparable C and the subject property have similar garage facilities.

At line 6, the subject property has a 300-square-foot patio in the backyard worth $600. Comparable A has a patio worth $900; therefore, $300 is deducted from comparable A's selling price. Comparable B has no patio. As it would have sold for $600 more if it had one, a +$600 adjustment is required. The patio at comparable C is the same as the subject property's. However, comparable C has $500 worth of custom built-in living room bookcases that the subject property does not have. Therefore, $500 is subtracted from comparable C's sales price. Any other differences between the comparables and the subject property such as swimming pools, fireplaces, carpeting, drapes, roofing materials and kitchen appliances would be adjusted in a similar manner.

On line 7, recognize differences in building age, wear and tear, construction quality and design usefulness. Where the difference between the subject property and a comparable can be measured in terms of material and labor, the adjustment is the cost of that material and labor. For example, the $400 adjustment for comparable B reflects the cost of needed roof repair at the time B was sold. The adjustment of $2,000 for comparable A reflects the fact it has better-quality plumbing and electrical fixtures than the subject property. Differences that cannot be quantified in terms of labor and materials are usually dealt with as lump-sum judgments. Thus, one might allow $1,000 for each year of age difference between the subject and a comparable, or make a lump-sum adjustment of $2,000 for an inconvenient kitchen design.

Building Age, Condition and Quality

Keep in mind that adjustments are made on the basis of what each comparable property was like on the day it was sold. Thus, if an extra bedroom was added or the house was painted after its sale date, these items are not included in the adjustment process.

Line 8 shows the landscaping at comparable A to be inferior to the subject property. A positive correction is necessary here to equalize it with the subject. The landscaping at comparable B is similar and requires no correction; that at comparable C is better and thus requires a negative adjustment. The dollar amount of each adjustment is based on the market value of lawn, bushes, trees and the like.

Landscaping

Line 9 deals with any differences in lot size, slope, view and neighborhood. In this example, all comparables are in the same neighborhood as the subject property, thus eliminating the need to judge, in dollar terms, the relative merit of

Lot Features and Location

one neighborhood over another. However, comparable A has a slightly larger lot and a better view than the subject property. Based on recent lot sales in the area, the difference is judged to be $890 for the larger lot and $3,000 for the better view. Comparable B has a slightly smaller lot judged to be worth $900 less, and comparable C is similar in all respects.

Terms and Conditions Line 10 in Table 16:1 accounts for differences in financing.
of Sale As a rule, the more accommodating the terms of the sale to the buyer, the higher the sales price, and vice versa. We are looking for the highest cash price the subject property may reasonably be expected to bring, given adequate exposure to the marketplace and a knowledgeable buyer and seller not under undue pressure. If the comparables were sold under these conditions, no corrections would be needed in this category. However, if it can be determined that a comparable was sold under different conditions, an adjustment is necessary. For example, if the going rate of interest on home mortgages is 12% per year and the seller offers to finance the buyer at 9% interest, it is reasonable to expect that the seller can charge a higher selling price. Similarly, the seller can get a higher price if he has a low-interest loan that can be assumed by the buyer. Favorable financing terms offered by the seller of comparable B enabled him to obtain an extra $1,500 in selling price. Therefore, we must subtract $1,500 from comparable B. Another situation that requires an adjustment on line 10 is if a comparable was sold on a rush basis. If a seller is in a hurry to sell, a lower selling price usually must be accepted than if the property can be given more time in the marketplace.

Adjusted Market Price Adjustments for each comparable are totaled and either added or subtracted from its sale price. The result is the **adjusted market price** shown at line 12. This is the dollar value of each comparable sale after it has gone through an adjustment process to make it the same as the subject property. If it were possible to precisely evaluate every adjustment, and if the buyers of comparables A, B and C had paid exactly what their properties were worth at the time they purchased them, the three prices shown on line 12 would be the same.

However, buyers are not that precise, particularly in purchasing a home where amenity value influences price and varies considerably from one person to the next.

While comparing the properties, it will usually become apparent that some comparables are more like the subject property than others. The **correlation** step gives the appraiser the opportunity to assign more weight to the more similar comparables and less to the others. At line 13, comparable C is given a weight of 50% since it is more like the subject and required fewer adjustments. Moreover, this sameness is in areas where adjustments tend to be the hardest to estimate accurately: time, age, quality, location, view and financial conditions. Of the remaining two comparables, comparable B is weighted slightly higher than comparable A because it is a more recent sale and overall required fewer adjustments.

Correlation Process

In the correlation process, the adjusted market price of each comparable is multiplied by its weighting factor and totaled at line 14. The result is the **indicated value** of the subject property. It is customary to round off to the nearest $50 or $100 for properties under $10,000; to the nearest $250 or $500 for properties between $10,000 and $100,000; to the nearest $1,000 or $2,500 for properties between $100,000 and $250,000; and to the nearest $2,500 or $5,000 above that.

The process for estimating the market value of a condominium, townhouse or cooperative living unit by the market approach is similar to the process for houses except that fewer steps are involved. For example, in a condominium complex with a large number of two-bedroom units of identical floor plan, data on a sufficient number of comparable sales may be available within the building. This would eliminate adjustments for differences in unit floor plan, neighborhood, lot size and features, age and upkeep of the building, and landscaping. The only corrections needed would be those that make one unit different from another. This would include the location of the individual unit within the building (end units and units with better views sell for more), the upkeep and interior decoration of the unit, a time adjustment and an adjustment for terms and conditions of the sale.

CONDOMINIUM, TOWNHOUSE AND COOPERATIVE APPRAISALS

When there are not enough comparable sales of the same floor plan within the same building and it is necessary to use different-sized units, an adjustment must be made for floor area. If the number of comparables is still inadequate and units in different condominium buildings must be used, adjustments will be necessary for neighborhood, lot features, management, upkeep, age and overall condition of the building.

MARKET APPROACH TO VACANT LAND VALUATION

Subdivided lots zoned for commercial, industrial or apartment buildings are usually appraised and sold on a square foot basis. Thus, if apartment land is currently selling for $3.00 per square foot, a 100,000-square-foot parcel of comparable zoning and usefulness would be appraised at $300,000. Another method is to value on a front-foot basis. For example, if a lot has 70 feet of street frontage and if similar lots are selling for $300 per front foot, that lot would be appraised at $21,000. Storefront land is often sold this way. House lots can be valued either by the square foot, front foot, or lot method. The lot method is useful when one is comparing lots of similar size and zoning in the same neighborhood. For example, recent sales of 100-foot by 100-foot house lots in the $18,000 to $20,000 range would establish the value of similar lots in the same neighborhood.

Rural land and large parcels that have not been subdivided are usually valued and sold by the acre. For example, how would you value 21 acres of vacant land when the only comparables available are 16-acre and 25-acre sales? The method is to establish a per acre value from comparables and apply it to the subject land. Thus, if 16- and 25-acre parcels sold for $32,000 and $50,000, respectively, and are similar in all other respects to the 21-acre subject property, it would be reasonable to conclude that land is selling for $2,000 per acre. Therefore, the subject property is worth $42,000.

4–3–2–1 Rule

The 4–3–2–1 rule is a depth adjustment that appraisers sometimes use when valuing vacant lots. It states that the land at the back of the lot is worth less than the land at the front. To illustrate, consider a single-family residential lot that has 75 feet of frontage on a street and is 200 feet deep.

Across the street and in an equally desirable location are two lots for sale that are each 75 feet on the street and 100 feet deep. Would you pay as much for the single 75′ × 200′ lot as you would for two 75′ × 100′ lots? Let us omit the arithmetic and just remember the principle: the land at the back of a lot is worth less than the land at the front.

A variation of the market comparison approach and one that is very popular with agents who list and sell residential property is the **competitive market analysis (CMA).** This method is based on the principle that value can be estimated not only by looking at similar homes that have sold recently but also by taking into account homes presently on the market plus homes that were listed for sale but did not sell. The CMA is a listing tool that a sales agent prepares in order to show a seller what the home will likely sell for and the CMA helps the agent decide whether or not to accept the listing.

Figure 16:1 shows a competitive market analysis form published by the National Association of Realtors. The procedure in preparing a CMA is to select homes that are comparable to the subject property. The greater the similarity, the more accurate the appraisal will be and the more likely the client will accept the agent's estimate of value and counsel. It is usually best to use only properties in the same neighborhood; this is easier for the seller to relate to and removes the need to compensate for neighborhood differences. The comparables should also be similar in size, age and quality. Although a CMA does not require that individual adjustments be shown as in Table 16:1, it does depend on the agent's understanding of the process illustrated in that table. That is why Table 16:1 and its explanation are important. A residential agent may not be called upon to make a presentation as is done in Table 16:1; nonetheless, all those steps are considered and consolidated in the agent's mind before entering a probable final sales price on the CMA.

In section ① of the CMA shown in Figure 16:1, similar homes presently offered for sale are listed. This information is usually taken directly from the agent's multiple listing service (MLS) book, and ideally the agent will already have

COMPETITIVE MARKET ANALYSIS

Homes for Sale

Figure 16:1

COMPETITIVE MARKET ANALYSIS

Property Address _____ Date _____

For Sale Now:	Bed-rms.	Baths	Den	Sq. Ft.	1st Loan	List Price	Days on Market	Terms		

Sold Past 12 Mos.	Bed-rms.	Baths	Den	Sq. Ft.	1st Loan	List Price	Days on Market	Date Sold	Sale Price	Terms

Expired Past 12 Mos.	Bed-rms.	Baths	Den	Sq. Ft.	1st Loan	List Price	Days on Market	Terms		

F.H.A — V.A. Appraisals

Address	Appraisal	Address	Appraisal

Buyer Appeal

Marketing Position

(Grade each item 0 to 20% on the basis of desirability or urgency)

Buyer Appeal		Marketing Position	
1 Fine Location _____ %		1 Why Are They Selling _____ %	
2 Exciting Extras _____ %		2 How Soon Must They Sell _____ %	
3 Extra Special Financing _____ %		3 Will They Help Finance .... Yes____ No____ %	
4 Exceptional Appeal _____ %		4 Will They List at Competitive Market Value ... Yes____ No____ %	
5 Under Market Price _____ Yes___ No___ %		5 Will They Pay for Appraisal .... Yes____ No____ %	

Rating Total _____ %   Rating Total _____ %

Assets _____

Drawbacks _____

Area Market Conditions _____

Recommended Terms _____

Selling Costs

Brokerage	$	Top Competitive Market Value	$ _____
Loan Payoff	$		
Prepayment Privilege	$		
FHA — VA Points	$		
Title and Escrow Fees: IRS Stamps. Recons. Recording	$		
Termite Clearance	$	Probable Final Sales Price	$ _____
Misc. Payoffs: 2nd T.D., Pool, Patio, Water Softener, Fence, Improvement Bond.	$		
	$	Total Selling Costs	$ _____
	$		
Total	$	Net Proceeds	$ _____ Plus or Minus $ _____

toured these properties and have first-hand knowledge of their condition. These are the homes the seller's property will compete against in the marketplace.

In section ② the agent lists similar properties that have sold in the past several months. Ideally, the agent will have toured the properties when they were for sale. Sale prices are usually available through MLS sales records. Section ③ is for listing homes that were offered for sale, but did not sell. In other words, buyers were unwilling to take these homes at the prices offered.

In section ④ recent FHA and VA appraisals of comparable homes can be included if it is felt that they will be useful in determining the price at which to list. Two words of caution are in order here. First, using someone else's opinion of value is risky. It is better to form your own opinion based on actual facts. Second, FHA and VA appraisals often tend to lag behind the market. This means in a rising market they will be too low; in a declining market they will be too high.

Buyer Appeal

In section ⑤ buyer appeal, and in section ⑥ marketing position, the agent evaluates the subject property from the standpoint of whether or not it will sell if placed on the market. It is important to make the right decision to take or not to take a listing. Once taken, the agent knows that valuable time and money must be committed to get it sold. Factors which make a property more appealing to a buyer include good location, extra features, small down payment, low interest, meticulous maintenance and a below market price. Similarly, a property is more saleable if the sellers are motivated to sell, want to sell soon, will help with financing and will list at or below market. A busy agent will want to avoid spending time on overpriced listings, listings for which no financing is available and listings where the sellers have no motivation to sell. With the rating systems in sections ⑤ and ⑥, the closer the total is to zero, the less desirable the listing; the closer to 100%, the more desirable the listing.

Section ⑦ provides space to list the property's high and low points, current market conditions and recommended terms of sale. Section ⑧ shows the seller how much to expect in selling costs. Section ⑨ shows the seller what to expect in the way of a sales price and the amount of cash that can be expected from the sale.

The emphasis in CMA is on a visual inspection of the data on the form in order to arrive at market value directly. No pencil and paper adjustments are made. Instead, adjustments are made in a generalized fashion in the minds of the agent and the seller. In addition to its application to single-family houses, CMA can also be used on condominiums, cooperative apartments, townhouses and vacant lots—provided sufficient comparables are available.

GROSS RENT
MULTIPLIERS

A popular market comparison method that is used when a property produces income is the **gross rent multiplier,** or **GRM.** The GRM is an economic comparison factor that relates the gross rent a property can produce to its purchase price. For apartment buildings and commercial and industrial properties, the GRM is computed by dividing the sales price of the property by its gross annual rent. For example, if an apartment building grosses $100,000 per year in rents and has just sold for $700,000, it is said to have a GRM of 7. The use of a GRM to value single-family houses is questionable since they are usually sold as owner-occupied residences rather than as income properties. Note that if you do work a GRM for a house, it is customary to use the monthly (not yearly) rent.

Where comparable properties have been sold at fairly consistent gross rent multiples, the GRM technique presumes the subject property can be valued by multiplying its gross rent by that multiplier. To illustrate, suppose that apartment buildings were recently sold in your community as shown in Table 16:2. These sales indicate that the market is currently paying seven times the gross. Therefore, to find the value of a similar apartment building grossing $24,000 per year, multiply by 7.00 to get an indicated value of $168,000.

The GRM method is popular because it is simple to apply. Having once established what multiplier the market is paying, one need only know the gross rents of a building to set a value. However, this simplicity is also the weakness of the GRM method because the GRM takes into account only the gross rent a property produces. Gross rent does not allow

CALCULATING GROSS RENT MULTIPLIERS   Table 16:2

Building	Sales Price		Gross Annual Rents		Gross Rent Multiplier
No. 1	$245,000	÷	$ 34,900	=	7.02
No. 2	$160,000	÷	$ 22,988	=	6.96
No. 3	$204,000	÷	$ 29,352	=	6.95
No. 4	$196,000	÷	$ 27,762	=	7.06
As a Group:	$850,000	÷	$115,002	=	7.00

for variations in vacancies, uncollectible rents, property taxes, maintenance, management, insurance, utilities or reserves for replacements.

Weakness of GRM

To illustrate the problem, suppose that two apartment buildings each gross $100,000 per year. However, the first has expenses amounting to $40,000 per year and the second, expenses of $50,000 per year. Using the same GRM, the buildings would be valued the same, yet the first produces $10,000 more in net income for its owner. The GRM also overlooks the expected economic life span of a property. For example, a building with an expected remaining life span of 30 years would be valued exactly the same as one expected to last 20 years, if both currently produce the same rents. One method of partially offsetting these errors is to use different GRMs under different circumstances. Thus, a property with low operating expenses and a long expected economic life span might call for a GRM of 7 or more, whereas a property with high operating expenses or a shorter expected life span would be valued using a GRM of 6 or 5 or even less.

COST APPROACH

There are times when the market approach is an inappropriate valuation tool. For example, the market approach is of limited usefulness in valuing a fire station, school building, courthouse or highway bridge. These properties are rarely placed on the market and comparables are rarely found. Even with properties that are well-suited to the market approach, there may be times when it is valuable to apply another valuation approach. For example, a real estate agent may find that comparables indicate a certain style and size of house is selling in a particular neighborhood for $150,000. Yet the astute agent discovers through the cost approach that the same house can be built from scratch, including land, for $125,000. The agent builds and sells ten of these and concludes that, yes, there really is money to be made in real estate. Let us take a closer look at the cost approach.

Table 16:3 demonstrates the **cost approach.** Step 1 is to estimate the value of the land upon which the building is located. The land is valued as though vacant using the market comparison approach described earlier. In Step 2, the cost of constructing a similar building at today's costs is estimated. These costs include the current prices of building materials, construction wages, architect fees, contractor's services, building permits, utility hookups and the like, plus the cost of financing during the construction stage and the cost of construction equipment used at the project site. Step 3 is the calculation of the amount of money that represents the subject building's wear and tear, lack of usefulness and obsolescence when compared to the new building of Step 2. In Step 4, with depreciation subtracted from today's construction cost, the current value of the subject building is given on a used basis. Step 5 is to add this amount to the land value. Let us work through these steps.

Estimating New Construction Costs   In order to choose a method of estimating construction costs, one must decide whether cost will be approached on a reproduction or on a replacement basis. **Reproduction cost** is the cost at today's prices of constructing an *exact replica* of the subject improvements using the same or very similar materials. **Replacement cost** is the cost, at today's prices and using today's methods of construction, for an improvement

Table 16:3

COST APPROACH TO VALUE

Step 1:	Estimate land as if vacant		$30,000
Step 2:	Estimate new construction cost of similar building	$120,000	
Step 3:	Less estimated depreciation	−12,000	
Step 4:	Indicated value of building		108,000
Step 5:	Appraised property value by the cost approach		$138,000

having the same or *equivalent usefulness* as the subject property. Replacement cost is the more practical choice of the two as it eliminates nonessential or obsolete features and takes full advantage of current construction materials and techniques. It is the approach that will be described here.

The most widely used approach for estimating construction costs is the **square-foot method.** It provides reasonably accurate estimates that are fast and simple to prepare.

Square-Foot Method

The square-foot method is based on finding a newly constructed building that is similar to the subject building in size, type of occupancy, design, materials and construction quality. The cost of this building is converted to cost per square foot by dividing its current construction cost by the number of square feet in the building.

Cost information is also available from construction cost handbooks. Using a **cost handbook** starts with selecting a handbook appropriate to the type of building being appraised. From photographs of houses included in the handbook along with brief descriptions of the building's features, the appraiser finds a house that most nearly fits the description of the subject house. Next to pictures of the house is the current cost per square foot to construct it. If the subject house has a better quality roof, floor covering, heating system, greater or fewer built-in appliances, plumbing fixtures, or has a garage, basement, porch or swimming pool, the handbook provides costs for each of these. Figure 16:2 illustrates the calculations involved in the square-foot method.

Cost Handbooks

Having estimated the current cost of constructing the subject improvements, the next step in the cost approach is to estimate the loss in value due to depreciation since they were built. In making this estimate, we look for three kinds of **depreciation:** physical deterioration, functional obsolescence and economic obsolescence.

Estimating Depreciation

Physical deterioration results from wear and tear through use, such as wall-to-wall carpet that has been worn thin or a dishwasher, garbage disposal or water heater that must be replaced. Physical deterioration also results from the action

Figure 16:2   SQUARE-FOOT METHOD OF COST ESTIMATING

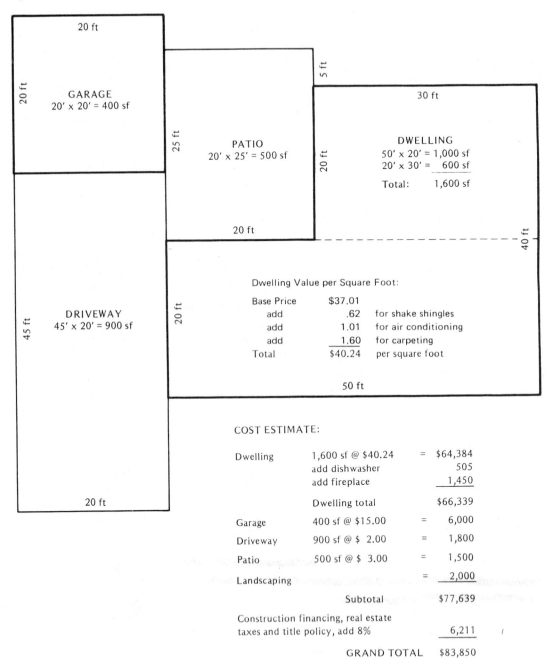

20 ft

20 ft

GARAGE
20' x 20' = 400 sf

5 ft

30 ft

25 ft

PATIO
20' x 25' = 500 sf

20 ft

DWELLING
50' x 20' = 1,000 sf
20' x 30' =   600 sf

Total: 1,600 sf

20 ft

40 ft

Dwelling Value per Square Foot:

Base Price	$37.01	
add	.62	for shake shingles
add	1.01	for air conditioning
add	1.60	for carpeting
Total	$40.24	per square foot

DRIVEWAY
45' x 20' = 900 sf

45 ft

20 ft

50 ft

20 ft

COST ESTIMATE:

Dwelling	1,600 sf @ $40.24	=	$64,384
	add dishwasher		505
	add fireplace		1,450
	Dwelling total		$66,339
Garage	400 sf @ $15.00	=	6,000
Driveway	900 sf @ $ 2.00	=	1,800
Patio	500 sf @ $ 3.00	=	1,500
Landscaping		=	2,000
	Subtotal		$77,639

Construction financing, real estate
taxes and title policy, add 8%   6,211

GRAND TOTAL $83,850

of nature in the form of sun, rain, heat, cold and wind, and from damage due to plants and animal life such as tree roots breaking sidewalks and termites eating wood. Physical deterioration can also result from neglect (an overflowing bathtub) and from vandalism.

Functional obsolescence results from outmoded equipment (old-fashioned plumbing fixtures in the bathrooms and kitchen), faulty or outdated design (a single bathroom in a three- or four-bedroom house or an illogical room layout), inadequate structural facilities (inadequate wiring to handle today's household appliance loads), and overadequate structural facilities (high ceilings in a home). Functional and physical obsolescence can be separated into curable and incurable components. **Curable** is something that can be fixed at reasonable cost such as worn carpeting, a leaky roof or outdated faucets in bathrooms. **Incurable** is something that cannot be reasonably fixed and must simply be lived with, for example, an illogical room layout.

Economic obsolescence is the loss of value due to external forces or events. For example, a once-popular neighborhood becomes undesirable because of air or noise pollution or because surrounding property owners fail to maintain their properties. Or, a city that is dependent on a military base finds the base closed and with it a big drop in demand for real estate. Or, the motel district in town loses customers because a new interstate highway is built several miles away. Far more often, however, properties experience economic appreciation and not economic obsolescence. The appreciation can come from new industries moving into town, city growth in a new direction, a shortage of land in beach or waterfront areas, etc. Thus it is quite possible for the economic appreciation of a property to more than offset the depreciation it experiences. The result is a building that is physically and functionally depreciating and at the same time appreciating in value. Consequently, while the chronological age of a building is important to value, what is more important is the remaining economic life of the building and whether it is functionally adequate for use in the future. This is what real estate investors look for.

Final Steps in the   After calculating the current construction cost of the sub-
Cost Approach   ject improvements and estimating the amount of depreciation,
the next step is to subtract the amount of depreciation from
the current construction cost to get the depreciated value of
the improvements. This is added to the value of the land
upon which the subject improvements rest. The total is the
value of the property by the cost approach.

INCOME APPROACH   The market approach is very useful in connection with
the sale or purchase of a home. The cost approach is very
useful for someone planning to build. But what about someone planning to invest? For investors the income approach
is the most popular method of valuing a property. The **income
approach** considers the monetary returns a property can be
expected to produce and converts that into a value the property should sell for if placed on the market today. This is
called capitalizing the income stream. To **capitalize** means
to convert future income to current value. To illustrate, suppose that an available apartment building is expected to return, after expenses, $18,000 per year. How much would
you, as an investor, pay for the building? The answer depends
on the return you require on each dollar you invest. Suppose
you will accept a return of 9% per year. In that case you
will pay $200,000 for this building. The calculation is as fol-
lows:

("*Present Worth Factor*")

$$\frac{\text{Income}}{\text{Rate}} = \text{Value} \qquad \frac{\$18,000}{.09} = \$200,000$$

This is the basic principle of capitalization. The appraisal
work comes in estimating the net income a property will
produce and looking at recent sales of similar properties to
see what capitalization rates are currently acceptable to investors. Let us look at the techniques one would use in estimating
a property's income. Pay close attention because each $1 error
in projected annual income or expenses can make a difference
of from $8 to $15 in the market value of the property.

Income and Expense   The best starting point is to look at the actual record of
Forecasting   income and expenses for the subject property over the past

3 to 5 years. Although the future will not be an exact repetition of the past, the past record of a property is usually the best guide to future performance. These historical data are blended with the current operating experience of similar buildings in order to estimate what the future will bring. The result is a projected operating statement, such as the one shown in Table 16:4, which begins with the estimated rents that the property can be expected to produce on an annual basis. This is the **projected gross,** or **scheduled gross,** and represents expected rentals from the subject property on a fully occupied basis. From this, vacancy and collection losses are subtracted. These are based partly on the building's past experience and partly on the operating experience of similar buildings.

The next step is to itemize anticipated operating expenses for the subject property. These are expenses necessary to

Operating Expenses

PROJECTED ANNUAL OPERATING STATEMENT   Table 16:4
(Also called a Pro Forma Statement)

Scheduled gross annual income	$84,000	
Vacancy allowance and collection losses	4,200	
Effective Gross Income		$79,800
Operating Expenses		
Property taxes	9,600	
Hazard and liability insurance	1,240	
Property management	5,040	
Janitorial services	1,500	
Gardener	1,200	
Utilities	3,940	
Trash pickup	600	
Repairs and maintenance	5,000	
Other	1,330	
Reserves for replacement		
Furniture & furnishings	1,200	
Stoves & refrigerators	600	
Furnace &/or air-conditioning	700	
Plumbing & electric	800	
Roof	750	
Exterior painting	900	
Total Operating Expenses		$34,400
Net Operating Income		$45,400

Operating Expense Ratio: $34,400 ÷ $79,800 = 43.1%

maintain the production of income. For an apartment building without recreational facilities or an elevator, the list in Table 16:4 is typical. Again, we must consider both the property's past operating expenses and what we expect those expenses to be in the future. For example, even though a property is currently being managed by its owner and no management fee is being paid, a typical management fee, say 6% of the gross rents, is included.

Not included as operating expenses are outlays for capital improvements, such as the construction of a new swimming pool, the expansion of parking facilities and assessments for street improvements. Improvements are not classified as expenses because they increase the usefulness of the property, which increases the rent the property will generate and therefore the property's value.

Reserves   **Reserves for replacement** are established for items that do not require an expenditure of cash each year. To illustrate, lobby furniture (and furniture in apartments rented as "furnished") wears out a little each year, eventually requiring replacement. Suppose that these items cost $7,200 and are expected to last 6 years, at which time they must be replaced. An annual $1,200 reserve for replacement not only reflects wear and tear of the furniture during the year, but also reminds us that to avoid having to meet the entire furniture and furnishings replacement cost out of one year's income, money should be set aside each year. In a similar manner, reserves are established for other items that must be replaced or repaired more than once during the life of the building, but not yearly.

Net Operating Income   The operating expense total is then subtracted from the effective gross income. The balance that remains is the **net operating income.** From the net operating income the property owner receives both a return *on* and a return *of* investment. The return *on* investment is the interest received for investing money in the property. The return *of* investment is compensation for the fact that the building is wearing out.

Operating Expense Ratio   At this point, the **operating expense ratio** can be calculated. It is obtained by dividing the total operating expenses by the effective gross income. The resulting ratio provides a handy yardstick against which similar properties can be compared. If the operating expense ratio is out of step compared to similar properties, it signals the need for further investigation. A range of 25% to 45% is typical for apartment buildings. The Institute of Real Estate Management of the National Association of Realtors publishes books and articles that give typical operating ratios for various types of income properties across the United States. Local inquiry to appraisers and brokers who specialize in income properties will also provide typical ratios for buildings in a community.

The final step in the income approach is to capitalize the net operating income. In other words, what price should an investor offer to pay for a property that produces a given net income per year? The solution is: income + rate = value. If the annual net operating income is $45,400 and if the investor intends to pay all cash, expects to receive a 10% return on his investment, and anticipates no change in the value of the property while he owns it, the solution is to divide $45,400 by 10%. However, most investors today borrow much of the purchase price and usually expect an increase in property value. Under these conditions, how much should the investor pay?

Capitalizing Income

The best known method for solving this type of investment question involves using the Ellwood Tables, published in 1959 by L. W. Ellwood, MAI. However, for the person who does not use these tables regularly, the arithmetic involved can prove confusing. As a result mortgage-equity tables are now available from bookstores. These allow the user to look up a single number, called an **overall rate,** and divide it into the net operating income to find a value for the property.

For example, suppose an investor who is interested in buying the above property can obtain an 11%, fully amortized 25-year mortgage loan for 75% of the purchase price. He wants an 18% return on his equity in the property, plans to hold it 10 years, and expects it will increase 50% in value (after selling costs) during that time. How much should he offer to pay the seller? In Table 16:5, we look for an interest rate of 11% and for appreciation of 50%. This gives an overall rate of .10756 and the solution is:

$$\frac{\text{Income}}{\text{Overall rate}} = \text{Value} \quad \frac{\$45,400}{.10756} = \$422,090$$

Further exploration of the numbers in Table 16:5 shows that as loan money becomes more costly, the overall rate rises, and as interest rates fall, so does the overall rate. If the investor can anticipate appreciation in value, the overall rate drops; if he can't, the overall rate climbs. You can experiment by dividing some of the other overall rates in this table into $45,400 to see how the value of this property changes under different circumstances.

DEPRECIATION

The pro forma in Table 16:4 provides reserves for replacement of such items as the roof, furnace, air-conditioning, plumbing, electrical and exterior paint and so forth. Nonetheless, as the building ages the style of the building will become dated, the neighborhood will change and the structure will experience physical deterioration. Allowance for this is usually accounted for in the selection of the capitalization rate. The less functional, economic and physical obsolescence that

Table 16:5

OVERALL RATES—10-YEAR HOLDING PERIOD
25-Year Loan for 75% of the Purchase Price, 18% Investor Return

Appreciation, Depreciation	Loan Interest Rate			
	9%	10%	11%	12%
+100%	.07251	.07935	.08631	.09338
+ 50%	.09376	.10060	**.10756**	.11463
+ 25%	.10439	.11123	.11819	.12526
+ 15%	.10864	.11548	.12244	.12951
+ 10%	.11077	.11761	.12457	.13164
+ 5%	.11289	.11973	.12669	.13376
0	.11502	.12186	.12882	.13589
+ 5%	.11715	.12399	.13095	.13802
+ 10%	.11927	.12611	.13307	.14014
+ 15%	.12140	.12824	.13520	.14227
+ 25%	.12565	.13249	.13945	.14652
+ 50%	.13628	.14312	.15008	.15715
+100%	.15753	.16437	.17133	.17840

Source: *Financial Capitalization Rate Tables,* Financial Publishing Company, Boston, Mass. By permission.

is expected to take place, the lower the acceptable "cap" rate and vice versa.

In contrast to actual depreciation, there is the **fictional depreciation** that the U.S. Treasury allows income property owners to deduct as an expense when calculating income taxes. In late 1985, for example, the Treasury allowed the purchaser of an apartment building to completely depreciate the structure over a period of 19 years regardless of the age or condition of the structure. More often than not, 19 years was an understatement of the remaining life of the structure; but it was chosen by Congress as an incentive to invest in real estate, and not as an accurate gauge of a property's life. Thus it was quite common to see depreciation claimed on buildings that were in reality appreciating because of rising income from rents and/or falling capitalization rates.

Fictional Depreciation

For certain types of real property, some approaches are more suitable than others. This is especially true for single-family residences. Here you must rely almost entirely on the market and cost approaches as very few houses are sold on their ability to generate cash rent. Unless you can develop a measure of the "psychic income" in home ownership, relying heavily on rental value will lead to a property value below the market and cost approaches. Applying all three approaches to special-purpose buildings may also prove to be impractical. For example, in valuing a college or university campus or a state capitol building, the income and market approaches have only limited applicability.

CHOICE OF APPROACHES

When appraising a property that is bought for investment purposes such as an apartment building, shopping center, office building or warehouse, the income approach is the primary method of valuation. As a cross-check on the income approach, an apartment building should be compared to other apartment buildings on a price per apartment unit basis or price per square foot basis. Similarly, an office, store or warehouse can be compared to other recent office, store or warehouse sales on a price per square foot basis. Additionally, the cost approach can be used to determine if it would be cheaper to buy land and build rather than buy an existing building.

APPRAISER'S BEST ESTIMATE

It is important to realize that the appraised value is the appraiser's best *estimate* of the subject property's worth. Thus, no matter how painstakingly it is done, property valuation requires the appraiser to make many subjective judgments. Because of this, it is not unusual for three highly qualified appraisers to look at the same property and produce three different appraised values. It is also important to recognize that an appraisal is made as of a specific date. It is not a certificate of value, good forever until used. If a property was valued at $115,000 on January 5th of this year, the more time that has elapsed since that date, the less accurate that value is as an indication of the property's current worth.

An appraisal does not take into consideration the financial condition of the owner, the owner's health, sentimental attachment or any other personal matter. An appraisal does not guarantee the property will sell for the appraised market value. (The buyer and the seller determine the actual selling price.) Nor does buying at the appraised market value guarantee a future profit for the purchaser. (The real estate market can change.) An appraisal is not a guarantee that the roof will not leak, that there are no termites, or that everything in the building works. An appraisal is not an offer to buy, although a buyer can order one made so as to know how much to offer. An appraisal is not a loan commitment, although a lender can order one made so as to apply a loan-to-value ratio when making a loan.

THE APPRAISAL REPORT

There are four methods by which valuation findings and conclusions are reported: oral, letter, form and narrative.

Oral Report

An **oral report** is an appraisal delivered to a client orally without supporting written evidence. It is often given over the telephone or at a meeting. The advantage is that time is saved by not having to write a description of all the comparables and the adjustments made. The disadvantage of an oral report is the lack of written evidence as to what was said. Consequently, it is good practice not to make oral reports without written follow-up as there is too much chance of being misquoted—intentionally or unintentionally.

An **appraisal letter** is a report in the form of a business letter. In it the appraiser identifies the property and the rights being appraised, states his value conclusion and provides highlights of the facts used in drawing that conclusion. An appraisal letter is usually one or two pages long.

Appraisal Letter

A **form appraisal** report is an appraisal made on a pre-printed form. The objective is to reduce the amount of time the appraiser must spend on reporting findings and conclusions and to standardize the information the lender is seeking. For example, the FHA and VA have developed a form that must accompany all FHA and VA loan applications. Freddie Mac and Fannie Mae also have a jointly developed appraisal form to be used for loans sold to them. Standardized appraisal forms have been a major factor in making it possible to have a large secondary mortgage market. Standardized forms also allow greater use of computers in making and preparing appraisals for home loan applications. There are computer programs on the market that allow a person to enter appraisal data on a computer terminal and have the resulting appraisal typed out on appraisal forms that are tractor-fed through a printer.

Form Appraisal

A **narrative appraisal** is a complete report by the appraiser and typically runs 10 to 100 pages and sometimes longer. In it the appraiser reports on everything pertinent to the property and the market for the property and gives his value conclusion. This thoroughness allows the reader to follow in detail the appraiser's reasoning. After identifying the property and the rights being appraised, a narrative report will include detailed information on the objective of the appraisal assignment; the definition of value as used in the report; regional, city and neighborhood influences on value; economic trends; the physical characteristics of the land and its improvements; the condition of title; the zoning; a survey or map; photographs of the property; and a statement as to the property's highest and best use. Each comparable sale

Narrative Appraisal

is reported with its sale details and all facts used are identified as to their sources. The appraiser concludes by showing how the information was analyzed in order to value the property.

Format Choice Choosing an appraisal format depends on the information needed and how much money can be spent to obtain it. A person desiring to list a home for sale will probably choose a competitive market analysis. A lender asked to make a home loan will want a form appraisal that will satisfy the secondary mortgage market. A prospective buyer who wants to know the value of a four-unit apartment building (fourplex) would probably select an appraisal letter. An out-of-state investor considering a 200-unit apartment building would probably want a narrative report. A government agency purchasing under eminent domain will usually require a narrative report.

PROFESSIONAL LIABILITY If you offer to appraise property for others, make certain you have the training and experience necessary to do the job correctly. Do not imply expertise if you do not possess it. Always conclude an appraisal with a written report of the facts you used and your analysis. These are strongly worded statements; however, a real estate practitioner can quickly get into trouble with clients and licensing authorities by giving offhand estimates of value upon which someone relies and thereby suffers a loss. Practitioners who expect to prepare competitive market analysis forms should develop expertise in order to do this accurately.

CHARACTERISTICS OF VALUE Up to this point we have been concerned primarily with value based on evidence found in the marketplace and how to report it. Before concluding this chapter, let us briefly touch on what creates value, the principles of real property valuation and appraisal for purposes other than market value.

For a good or service to have value in the marketplace it must possess four characteristics: demand, utility, scarcity and transferability. **Demand** is a need or desire coupled with the purchasing power to fill it, whereas **utility** is the ability of a good or service to fill that need. **Scarcity** means there must be a short supply relative to demand. Air, for example, has utility and is in demand, but it is not scarce. Finally, goods or service must be **transferable** to have value to anyone other than the person possessing it.

The **principle of anticipation** reflects the fact that what a person will pay for a property depends on the expected benefits from the property in the future. Thus, the buyer of a home anticipates receiving shelter plus the investment and psychic benefits of home ownership. The investor buys property in anticipation of future income.

The **principle of substitution** states that the maximum value of a property in the marketplace tends to be set by the cost of purchasing an equally desirable substitute property provided no costly delay is encountered in making the substitution. In other words, substitution sets an upper limit on price. Thus, if there are two similar houses for sale, or two similar apartments for rent, the lower priced one will generally be purchased or rented first. In the same manner, the cost of buying land and constructing a new building sets a limit on the value of existing buildings.

PRINCIPLES OF VALUE

The **highest and best use** of a property is that use which will give the property its greatest current value. This means you must be alert to the possibility that the present use of a parcel of land may not be the use that makes the land the most valuable. Consider a 30-year-old house located at a busy intersection in a shopping area. To place a value on that property based on its continued use as a residence would be misleading if the property would be worth more with the house removed and shopping or commercial facilities built on the land instead.

Principle of Highest and Best Use

The principle of competition recognizes that where substantial profits are being made, competition will be encouraged. For example, if apartment rents increase to the point where owners of existing apartment buildings are making substantial profits, builders and investors will be encouraged to build more apartment buildings.

Applied to real estate, the **principle of supply and demand** refers to the ability of people to pay for land coupled

Supply and Demand

with the relative scarcity of land. This means that attention must be given to such matters on the demand side as population growth, personal income and preferences of people. On the supply side, you must look at the available supply of land and its relative scarcity. When the supply of land is limited and demand is great, the result is rising land prices. Conversely, where land is abundant and there are relatively few buyers, supply and demand will be in balance, with prices differing by only a few cents per square foot.

The **principle of change** reminds us that real property uses are always in a state of change. Although it may be imperceptible on a day-to-day basis, change can easily be seen when longer periods of time are considered. Because the present value of a property is related to its future uses, the more potential changes that can be identified, the more accurate the estimate of its present worth.

Diminishing Marginal Returns

The principle of **diminishing marginal returns,** also called the **principle of contribution,** refers to the relationship between added cost and the value it returns. It tells us that we should invest dollars whenever they will return to us more than $1 of value and should stop when each dollar invested returns less than $1 in value.

The **principle of conformity** holds that maximum value is realized when a reasonable degree of homogeneity is present in a neighborhood. This is the basis for zoning laws across the country; certain tracts in a community are zoned for single-family houses, others for apartment buildings, stores and industry. Within a tract there should also be a reasonable amount of homogeneity. For example, a $200,000 house would be out of place in a neighborhood of $90,000 houses.

MULTIPLE MEANINGS OF THE WORD "VALUE"

When we hear the word "value," we tend to think of market value. However, at any given moment in time, a single property can have other values too. This is because value or worth is very much affected by the purpose for which the valuation was performed. For example, **assessed value** is the value given a property by the county tax assessor for purposes of property taxation. **Estate tax value** is the value that federal and state taxation authorities establish for a deceased person's property; it is used to calculate the amount of estate taxes that must be paid. **Insurance value** is concerned with the cost of replacing damaged property. It differs from market value in two major respects: (1) the value of the land is not included, as it is presumed only the structures are destructible, and (2) the amount of coverage is based on the replacement cost of the structures. **Loan value** is the value set on a property for the purpose of making a loan.

When two or more adjoining parcels are combined into one large parcel it is called **assemblage.** The increased value of the large parcel over and above the sum of the smaller parcels is called **plottage value.** For example, local zoning laws may permit a six-unit apartment building on a single 10,000-square-foot lot. However, if two of these lots can be combined, zoning laws permit 15 units. This makes the lots more valuable if sold together.

Plottage Value

Rental value is the value of a property expressed in terms of the right to its use for a specific period of time. The fee simple interest in a house may have a market value of $80,000, whereas the market value of one month's occupancy might be $600. **Replacement value** is value as measured by the current cost of building a structure of equivalent utility. **Salvage value** is what a structure is worth if it has to be removed and taken elsewhere, either in whole or dismantled for parts. Because salvage operations require much labor the salvage value of most buildings is usually very low.

This list of values is not exhaustive, but it points out that the word "value" has many meanings. When reading an appraisal report, always read the first paragraph to see why the appraisal was prepared. Before preparing an appraisal, make certain you know its purpose and then state it at the beginning of your report.

Whenever supply and demand are unbalanced because of excess supply, a **buyer's market** exists. This means a buyer can negotiate prices and terms more to his liking and a seller, who wants to sell, must accept them. When the imbalance

BUYER'S AND SELLER'S MARKETS

occurs because demand exceeds supply, it is a **seller's market** and sellers are able to negotiate prices and terms more to their liking as buyers compete for the available merchandise.

A **broad market** means that many buyers and sellers are in the market at the same time. This makes it relatively easy to establish the price of a property and for a seller to find a buyer quickly, and vice versa. A **thin market** is said to exist when there are only a few buyers and a few sellers in the market at the same time. It is oftentimes difficult to appraise a property in a thin market because there are so few sales to use as comparables.

PROFESSIONAL
APPRAISAL SOCIETIES

During the 1930s, two professional appraisal societies were organized: The **American Institute of Real Estate Appraisers** (AIREA) and the **Society of Real Estate Appraisers.** Although a person offering services as a real estate appraiser need not be associated with either of these groups, there are advantages in membership. Now well-known, both organizations have developed designation systems to recognize appraisal education, experience and competence. Within the AIREA, the highest-level designation is the MAI (Member of the Appraisal Institute). To qualify, an MAI needs a 4-year college degree or equivalent education, various AIREA courses, examinations, an income property demonstration appraisal and at least 5 years of appraisal experience, including 3 years in non-single-family real estate. There are about 5,000 MAIs in the United States. The AIREA has also developed the RM (Residential Member) designation. Members at this level need a high school education, appraisal course work, a passing appraisal examination score, a residential demonstration appraisal and 3 years of experience in residential real estate.

The highest designations offered by the Society of Real Estate Appraisers are the SREA (Senior Real Estate Analyst) and SRPA (Senior Real Property Appraiser). For members specializing in residential appraisal, the professional designation is SRA (Senior Residential Appraiser). The SRA designation requires completion of basic courses in real estate appraisal, economics and statistics, an examination on appraising and a residential appraisal demonstration report.

To this the SRPA designation adds requirements for advanced course work in real estate appraisal plus an income property demonstration appraisal. For the SREA designation, further advanced course work and written and oral examinations on real estate market analysis are necessary. For all designations, the applicant must have field experience and submit actual appraisals for review by the Society.

In addition to the Institute and the Society there are several other professional appraisal organizations in the United States. They are the National Association of Independent Fee Appraisers, the Farm Managers and Rural Appraisers, the National Society of Real Estate Appraisers and the American Society of Appraisers. All work to promote and maintain high standards of appraisal services and all offer a variety of appraisal education and designation programs.

Appraisal License

Several states require that any person who appraises real estate for a fee must hold a license to do so. Depending on the state, this may be a regular real estate sales or broker license or a special appraiser's license. If you plan to make appraisals for a fee (apart from appraisal in connection with listing or selling a property as a licensed real estate salesperson or broker) make inquiry to your state's real estate licensing department as to appraisal licensing requirements.

VOCABULARY REVIEW

*Match terms **a–z** with statements **1–26.***

a. Adjustments
b. Appraise
c. Buyer's market
d. Capitalize
e. Comparables
f. Competitive market analysis
g. Cost approach
h. Curable depreciation
i. Depreciation
j. Functional obsolescence
k. Gross rent multiplier
l. Highest and best use
m. Income approach

n. Incurable depreciation
o. Market approach
p. Market value
q. Net operating income
r. Operating expenses
s. Physical deterioration
t. Principle of substitution
u. Replacement cost
v. Reproduction cost
w. Scheduled gross
x. Square-foot method
y. Subject property
z. Thin market

1. Properties similar to the subject property that have sold recently.
2. Cost, at today's prices and using today's methods of construction, to build an improvement having the same usefulness as the subject property.
3. Cost at today's prices of constructing an exact replica of the subject improvements using the same or similar methods.
4. A method of valuing property based on the prices of recent sales of similar properties.
5. Land value plus current construction costs less depreciation.
6. The property that is being appraised.
7. Corrections made to comparable properties to account for differences between them and the subject property.
8. A property valuation and listing technique that looks at properties currently for sale, recent sales and properties that did not sell, and which does not make specific dollar adjustments for differences.
9. Depreciation resulting from wear and tear of the improvements.
10. Depreciation resulting from improvements that are inadequate, overly adequate or improperly designed for today's needs.
11. The estimated rent a fully occupied property can be expected to produce on an annual basis.
12. To convert future income to current value.
13. Gross income less operating expenses, vacancies and collection losses.
14. Expenditures necessary to maintain the production of income.
15. Acts as an upper limit on prices; the lower priced of two similar properties will usually sell first.
16. To estimate the value of something.
17. A method of valuing property based on the monetary return it is expected to produce.

18. A number that is multiplied by a property's gross rents to produce an estimate of its worth.

19. A method for estimating construction costs that is based on the cost per square foot to build a structure.

20. Depreciation that can be fixed at reasonable cost.

21. Depreciation that cannot be fixed at reasonable cost.

22. A market with more sellers than buyers.

23. A market where there are few buyers and few sellers.

24. That use of a parcel of land that will produce the greatest current value for the parcel.

25. Loss in value due to deterioration and obsolescence.

26. The cash price that a willing buyer and a willing seller would agree upon, given reasonable exposure of the property to the market-place, full information as to the potential uses of the property and no undue compulsion to act.

QUESTIONS AND PROBLEMS

1. When making a market comparison appraisal, how many comparable properties should be used?

2. How useful are asking prices and offers to buy when making a market comparison appraisal?

3. In the market approach, are the adjustments made to the subject property or to the comparables? Why?

4. Why is it important when valuing vacant land that comparable properties have similar zoning, neighborhoods, size and usefulness?

5. Explain the use of gross rent multipliers in valuing real properties. What are the strengths and the weaknesses of this method?

6. What are the five steps used in valuing an improved property by the cost approach?

7. Briefly explain the concept of the income approach to valuing real property.

8. Explain how the competitive market analysis method differs from the standard market approach method. Which method is better? And for what?

9. What precaution does the principle of diminishing marginal returns suggest to a real estate owner?

10. With regard to appraising a single-family house, what type of appraisal format would most likely be requested by a lender? A prospective buyer? An executor of an estate? A highway department?

ADDITIONAL READINGS

Appraising Real Property by **Byrl Boyce** and **William Kinnard, Jr.** (The Society of Real Estate Appraisers, 1984, 514 pages). Provides a first exposure to the principles and techniques of real property valuation with special emphasis on residential properties. Follows the Society's Appraisal 101 course.

Base 1000: The Vaughn Method of Appraising Houses by **Charles Vaughn.** (Reston, 1984, 224 pages). Book covers essential factors in appraising houses including site, neighborhood, size, construction, quality, financing, and market conditions. Teaches how to make allowances for positive or negative influences on value and how to arrive at separate values for land and improvements.

Basic Real Estate Appraisal by **Richard Betts** and **Silas Ely.** (Wiley, 1982, 367 pages). A readable and attractively laid-out book that explains appraisal theory and its application in the field. Numerous photographs and illustrations.

Fundamentals of Real Estate Appraisal, 3rd ed. by **William Ventolo, Jr.,** and **Martha Williams.** (Real Estate Education Co., 1983, 338 pages). Book relates appraisal theory to practical application. Generous use of examples to illustrate market, cost and income approaches.

"Pricing Practicalities" by **David Beson.** (*Real Estate Today,* Sep 84, p. 42). Article explains the realities of a competitive market to prospective home sellers.

Residential Cost Handbook. (**Marshall** and **Swift,** 1986, 200 pages). Provides cost of construction information for residential structures. Binder-style book is updated every three months and contains adjustments for various cities in the United States.

The Appraisal of Real Estate, 8th ed. (American Institute of Real Estate Appraisers, Chicago, 1983, 750 pages). Covers the fundamental concepts of real estate value and its estimation by the market, cost and income approaches.

The Appraisal of Rural Property. (American Institute of Real Estate Appraisal, Chicago, 1983, 434 pages). Contains principles, data collection and value estimation for farms, ranches, vineyards, orchards, dairyland, timberland and agricultural land in transition. One of many specialized appraisal books, monographs and articles published by the AIREA.

*   *   *

The following periodicals may also be of interest to you: *Appraisal Journal, Appraisal Review, Appraisal Review Journal, Appraisal Digest, Appraisal Institute Digest, Appraisal Institute Magazine, Boeckh Building Cost Index Numbers, Real Estate Appraiser and Analyst* and *Real Estate Appraiser.*

The Owner-Broker Relationship

Agent: the person empowered to act by and on behalf of the principal

Commingling: the mixing of clients' or customer's funds with an agent's personal funds

Dual agency: representation of two or more parties in a transaction by the same agent

Exclusive right to sell: a listing that gives the broker the right to collect a commission no matter who sells the property during the listing period

Listing: a contract wherein a broker is employed to perform real estate brokerage services

Middleman: a person who brings two or more parties together but does not conduct negotiations

Principal: a person who authorizes another to act for him; also refers to a property owner

Puffing: nonfactual or extravagant statements a reasonable person would recognize as such

Ready, willing and able buyer: a buyer who is ready to buy now without further coaxing, and who has the financial capability to do so

Third parties: persons who are not parties to a contract but who may be affected by it

THE PRINCIPAL, THE AGENT, AND THIRD PARTIES

When a property owner gives a real estate broker a listing authorizing the broker to find a buyer or a tenant and promising compensation if he does, an **agency relationship** is created. For an agency to exist, there must be a principal and an agent. The **principal** is the person who empowers another to act as his representative; the **agent** is the person who is empowered to act. When someone speaks about the "laws of agency," he refers to those laws that govern the rights and duties of the principal, agent, and the persons (called **third parties)** with whom they deal.

Agencies are divided into three categories: universal, general, and specific. A **universal agency** is very broad in scope, as the principal gives his agent the legal power to transact matters of all types for him. A **general agency** gives the agent the power to bind his principal in a particular trade or business. For example, the relationship between a real estate broker (principal) and his salesperson (agent) is considered a general agency. With a **special agency** the principal empowers his agent to perform only specific acts and no others. The special agent may not bind the principal by his acts. Applications of special agency include real estate listings, the topic we shall discuss next.

LISTING AGREEMENT

A **real estate listing** is an *employment contract* between a property owner and a real estate broker. By it the property owner appoints the broker as the owner's agent for the specific purpose of finding a buyer or tenant for his property who is willing to meet the conditions set forth in the listing. It does not authorize the broker to actually sell or convey title to the property, or to sign contracts.

Note that although persons licensed as real estate salesmen perform listing and sales functions, they are actually functioning as extensions of the broker. A seller may conduct all the aspects of a listing and sale through a salesman licensee, but it is the broker behind the salesman with whom the seller has the listing contract and who is legally liable for its proper execution. If you plan to be a salesman for a broker, be aware of what is legally and ethically required of a broker since you are that broker's eyes, ears, hands and mouth. If your interest is in listing your property through a broker, know that it is the broker with whom you have the listing contract even though your day-to-day contact is with the broker's salesmen. **Sales associates** are the licensed salespersons or brokers who work for a broker.

Although some states still do not require that listing agreements be in writing to be valid, Texas requires that they be written and signed to be enforceable in a court of law.

When a property owner signs a listing, all the essential elements of a valid contract must be present. The owner and broker must be legally capable of contracting, there must be mutual assent, and the agreement must be for a lawful purpose. An exception is mutual consideration: in Texas the contract is considered to be unilateral and the owner promises to pay a commission if a buyer is found, but the broker usually does not promise to find one. It is assumed that when a broker takes a listing, he intends to work on it. The Texas

Real Estate Licensing Act further provides that the listing agreement must have a definite termination date, or the agent's license may be suspended or revoked.

Figure 17:1 illustrates a simplified exclusive right-to-sell listing agreement. Actual listing contracts tend to be longer and more complex and vary in detail from one contract to the next. The Figure 17:1 document is an educational introduction to listings that give in plain English the contract provisions commonly found in an exclusive right-to-sell listing. Beginning at ①, there is a description of the property plus the price and terms at which the broker is instructed to find a buyer. At ②, the broker promises to make reasonable efforts to find a buyer. The period of time that the listing is to be in effect is shown at ③.

At ④, the owner agrees not to list the property with any other brokers, permit other brokers to have a sign on the property, or advertise it during the listing period. Also, the owner agrees not to revoke the broker's exclusive right to find a buyer as set forth by this contract.

The broker recognizes that the owner may later accept a price and terms that are different from those in the listing. The wording at ⑤ states that the broker will earn a commission no matter what price and terms the owner ultimately accepts.

At ⑥, the amount of compensation the owner agrees to pay the broker is established. The usual arrangement is to express the amount as a percentage of the sale or exchange price, although a stated dollar amount could be used if the owner and broker agreed. In any event, the amount of the fee is negotiable between the owner and the broker. If the owner feels the fee is too high, he can list with someone who charges less or sell the property himself. The broker recognizes that if the fee is too low it will not be worthwhile spending time and effort finding a buyer. The typical commission fee in the United States at present is 5% to 7% of the selling price for houses, condominiums, and small apartment buildings, and 6% to 10% on farms, ranches, and vacant land. On multimillion dollar improved properties, commissions usually drop to the 2% to 4% range. Brokerage commissions are not set by a state regulatory agency or by local

Brokerage Commissions

Figure 17:1

EXCLUSIVE RIGHT TO SELL LISTING CONTRACT

(1) *Property Description:* A single-family house at 2424 E. Main Street, City, State. Legally described as Lot 17, Tract 191, County, State.

Price: $105,000

Terms: Cash

(2) *In consideration of the services of* ABC Realty Company *(herein called the "Broker"), to be rendered to* Roger and Mary Leeving *(herein called the "Owner"), and the promise of said Broker to make reasonable efforts to obtain a purchaser, therefore, the Owner hereby grants to the Broker*

(3) *for the period of time from noon on* April 1, 19xx, *to noon on* July 1, 19xx *(herein called the "listing period")*

(4) *the exclusive and irrevocable right to advertise and find a purchaser for the above described property at the price and terms shown*

(5) *or for such sum and terms or exchange as the owner later agrees to accept.*

(6) *The Owner hereby agrees to pay Broker a cash fee of* 6% *of the selling or exchange price:*

(7) *(A) in case of any sale or exchange of the above property within the listing period either by the Broker, the Owner or any person, or*

(8) *(B) upon the Broker finding a purchaser who is ready, willing, and able to complete the purchase as proposed by the owner, or*

(9) *(C) in the event of a sale or exchange within 60 days of the expiration of the listing period to any party shown the above property during the listing period by the Broker or his representative and where the name was disclosed to the Owner.*

(10) *The Owner agrees to give the Broker access to the buildings on the property for the purposes of showing them at reasonable hours and allows the Broker to post a "For Sale" sign on the premises.*

⑪ *The Owner agrees to allow the Broker to place this listing information in any multiple listing organization of which he is a member and to engage the cooperation of other brokers to bring about a sale.*

⑫ *The Owner agrees to refer to the Broker all inquiries regarding this property during the listing period.*

⑬ *Accepted:*   ABC Realty Company

By: *Kurt Kwiklister*   Owner: *Roger Leeving*

                                   Owner: *Mary Leeving*

Date: April 1, 19xx

Figure 17:1 *continued*

real estate boards. In fact, any effort by brokers to set commission rates among themselves is a violation of federal antitrust laws. The penalty can be as much as triple damages and criminal liability.

The conditions under which a commission must be paid by the owner to the broker appear next. At ⑦, a commission is deemed to be earned if the owner agrees to a sale or exchange of the property, no matter who finds the buyer. In other words, even if the owner finds his own buyer, or a friend of the owner finds a buyer, the broker is entitled to a full commission fee. If the owner disregards his promise at ④ and lists with another broker who then sells the property, the owner is liable for two full commissions.

Protecting the Broker

The wording at ⑧ is included to protect the broker against the possibility that the owner may refuse to sell after the broker has expended time and effort to find a buyer at the price and terms of the listing contract. The listing itself is not an offer to sell property. It is strictly a contract whereby the owner employs the broker to find a buyer. Thus, even though a buyer offers to pay the exact price and terms shown in the listing, the buyer does not have a binding sales contract until the offer is accepted in writing by the owner. However, if the owner refuses to sell at the listed price and terms, the broker is still entitled to a commission. If the owner does not pay the broker voluntarily, the broker can file a lawsuit against the owner to collect.

Protecting the Owner   At ⑨, the broker is protected against the possibility that the listing period will expire while still working with a prospective purchaser. In fairness to the owner, however, two limitations are placed on the broker. First, a sales contract must be concluded within a reasonable time after the listing expires, and second, the name of the purchaser must have been given to the owner before the listing period expires.

Continuing at ⑩, the owner agrees to let the broker enter the property at reasonable hours to show it and put a "For Sale" sign on the property. At ⑪ the property owner gives the broker specific permission to enter the property into a multiple listing service and to engage the cooperation of other brokers to bring about a sale.

At ⑫, the owner agrees to refer all inquiries regarding the availability of the property to the broker. The purpose is to discourage the owner from thinking that he might be able to save a commission by selling it himself during the listing period, and to increase the broker's chances of generating a sale of the property. Finally, at ⑬, the owner and the broker (or the broker's sales associates if authorized to do so) sign and date the agreement.

EXCLUSIVE RIGHT-TO-SELL LISTING   The listing illustrated in Figure 17:1 is called an **exclusive right to sell,** or an **exclusive authority to sell,** listing. Its distinguishing characteristic is that no matter who sells the property during the listing period, the listing broker is entitled to a commission. This is the most widely used type of listing in the United States. Once signed by the owner and accepted by the broker, the primary advantage to the broker is that the money and effort the broker expends on advertising and showing the property will be to the broker's benefit. The advantage to the owner is that the broker will usually put more effort into selling a property on which the broker holds an exclusive right to sell than on one for which the broker has only an exclusive agency or an open listing.

EXCLUSIVE AGENCY LISTING   The **exclusive agency listing** is similar to the listing shown in Figure 17:1, except that the owner may sell the property himself during the listing period and not owe a commission to the broker. The broker, however, is the only broker who can act as an agent during the listing period; hence the term exclusive agency. For an owner, this may seem like the better of two worlds: the owner has a broker looking for a buyer, but if the owner finds a buyer first, he can save a commission fee. The broker is less enthusiastic, because the broker's efforts can too easily be undermined by the owner. Consequently, the broker may not expend as much effort on advertising and showing the property as with an exclusive right to sell.

Open listings carry no exclusive rights. An owner can give an open listing to any number of brokers at the same time, and the owner can still find a buyer and avoid a commission. This gives the owner the greatest freedom of any listing form, but there is little incentive for the broker to expend time and money showing the property as the broker has little control over who will be compensated if the property is sold. The broker's only protection is that, if the broker does find a buyer at the listing price and terms, the broker is entitled to a commission. This reluctance to develop a sales effort usually means few, if any, offers will be received and may result in no sale or a sale below market price. Yet, if a broker does find a buyer, the commission earned may be the same as with an exclusive right to sell.

OPEN LISTING

A **net listing** is created when an owner states the price he wants for his property and then agrees to pay the broker anything he can get above that price as his commission. It can be written in the form of an exclusive right to sell, an exclusive agency, or an open listing. If a homeowner asks for a "net $60,000" and the broker sells the home for $75,000, the commission would be $15,000. By using the net listing method, many owners feel that they are forcing the broker to look to the buyer for the commission by marking up the price of the property. In reality though, a buyer will rarely pay $75,000 for a home that, compared to similar properties for sale, is worth only $60,000 or $65,000. Consequently, we must conclude that the home is actually worth $75,000 and the $15,000 (in effect a 20% commission) came from the seller. If other brokers in the area are charging 4% to 7% of the

NET LISTING

sales price, a 20% commission invites both public criticism and a lawsuit questioning the broker's loyalty to his seller for accepting such a low listing price.

Because of widespread misunderstanding regarding net listings and because they provide such fertile ground for questionable commission practices, some states prohibit them outright (Texas does not), and most brokers strenuously avoid them even though requested by property owners. There is no law that says a broker must accept a listing; a broker is free to accept only those listings for which the broker can perform a valuable service and earn an honest profit.

MULTIPLE LISTING SERVICE (MLS)

Multiple listing service (MLS) organizations enable a broker with a listing to make a blanket offering of subagency to other brokers, thus broadening the market exposure for a given property. Member brokers are authorized to show each others' properties to their prospects. If a sale results, the commission is divided between the broker who found the buyer and the broker who obtained the listing, less a small deduction for the cost of operating the multiple listing service.

Market Exposure

A property listed with a broker who is a multiple listing service member receives the advantage of greater sales exposure, which, in turn, means a better price and a quicker sale. For the buyer, it means learning about what is for sale at many offices without having to visit each individually. For the salesman and broker, it means that, if his own office does not have a suitable property for a prospect, the opportunity to make a sale is not lost, because the prospect can be shown the listings of other brokers.

To give a property the widest possible market exposure and to maintain fairness among its members, most multiple listing organizations obligate each member broker to provide information to the organization on each of his listings within three to seven days after the listing is taken. To facilitate the exchange of information, multiple listing organizations have developed customized listing forms. These forms are a combination of an exclusive right-to-sell listing agreement (with authority to place the listing into multiple) plus a data sheet on the property. The data sheet, which describes all the physical and financial characteristics of the property, and a photograph of the property are published weekly in a multiple listing book which is distributed to MLS members. Then, if Broker B has a prospect interested in a property listed by Broker A, Broker B telephones Broker A and arranges to show the property. If Broker B's prospect makes an offer on the property, Broker B contacts Broker A and together they call on the seller with the offer.

MLS organizations have been taken to court for being open only to members of local real estate boards. This has now changed, and any licensed broker can join. The role that multiple listing services play directly or indirectly in commission splitting is also being tested in the courts. Another idea that has been tested in the courts is that an MLS be open to anyone who wants to list a property, whether broker or owner. Although proponents say that an owner should be able to list and advertise in an MLS just as in a newspaper. The accepted view is that owners lack real estate "sophistication" and would place much inaccurate information in the MLS, and that the use of the MLS by non-members is a violation of federal copyright laws. Allowing the use of information without regard to standards would do considerable harm to MLS members who must rely on such information as being correct when describing and showing properties.

Court Issues

In addition to publishing MLS books, a number of multiple listing services store their listing information in computers. Thus a salesperson with a briefcase-sized MLS terminal can use a telephone to dial the MLS computer and request up-to-the minute information for any property in the computer listing. This is a popular system with salespeople who are constantly in the field showing property or in their cars (where they can link up by cellular telephone). It is also quicker than waiting for updated printed MLS information.

Computerized MLS

Electronic advances now make it possible to give a prospective buyer a visual tour by videodisc through a neighborhood without leaving the broker's office. A single videodisc

Videodisc

can store over 100,000 still photographs of individual properties for sale, as well as the neighborhoods, schools, shopping centers, recreation facilities, etc. These discs are imaged commercially and then duplicated and sold to real estate offices. So large is the storage capacity of such a disc that often every property in a community can be photographed and placed on the disc. Thus, a salesperson in a real estate office can select any image on the disc and play it onto a television screen. In other words, with MLS book in hand, the salesperson can show a prospect a color picture of each property for sale along with pictures of the street and neighborhood, plus nearby schools and shopping facilities. Realty offices with computerized access to MLS files can also interface the videodisc with the MLS computer listing so the prospective buyer can see how the property fits into a community.

LISTING PERIOD

It is to the broker's advantage to make the listing period as long as possible, since it provides more time to find a buyer. Sometimes, even an overpriced property will become saleable if the listing period is long enough and prices rise fast enough. From a legal standpoint, an owner and a broker can agree to a listing period of several years if they wish. However, most owners are reluctant to be committed for that long and prefer a better balance between their flexibility and the amount of time needed for a broker to conduct a sales campaign. In residential sales, 3 to 4 months is a popular compromise; farm, ranch, commercial, and industrial listings are usually made for 6 months to 1 year.

AGENT'S AUTHORITY

A written listing agreement is an example of an expressed contract. It outlines on paper the extent of the agent's *express authority* to act on behalf of the principal and the principal's obligations to the agent. A written agreement is the preferred method of creating an agency because it provides a document to evidence the existence of the agency relationship.

Agency authority may also arise from custom in the industry, common usage, and the conduct of the parties involved. For example, the right of an agent to post a "For Sale" sign on the listed property may not be expressly stated in the listing. However, if it is the custom in the industry to do

so, and presuming there are no deed covenants or city ordinances to the contrary, the agent has **implied authority** to
post the sign. A similar situation exists with regard to showing
a listed property to prospects. A home seller can expect to
have his home shown to clients on weekends and evenings
whereas a commercial property owner would expect showings
only during business hours.

Ostensible authority is conferred when a principal gives
a third party reason to believe that another person is his
agent even though that person is unaware of the appointment.
If the third party accepts this as true, the principal may well
be bound by the acts of his agent. For example, you give
your house key to a plumber with instructions that when
he has finished unstopping the waste lines he is to lock the
house and give the key to your next door neighbor. Even
though you do not call and expressly appoint your neighbor
as your agent to receive your key, once the plumber gives
the key to your neighbor, your neighbor becomes your agent
with regard to that key. Since you told the plumber to leave
the key there, he has every reason to believe that you appointed your neighbor as your agent to receive the key. This
can also be referred to as an **agency by estoppel.** It can also
result when a principal fails to maintain due diligence over
his agent and the agent exercises powers not granted to him.
If this causes a third party to believe the agent has these
powers, an agency by estoppel has been created.

An **agency by ratification** is one established after the fact.
For example, if an agent secures a contract on behalf of a
principal and the principal subsequently ratifies or agrees
to it, a court may hold that an agency was created at the
time the initial negotiations started. An **agency coupled with
an interest** is said to exist when the agent holds an interest
in the property he is representing. It is an irrevocable agency.

When a real estate broker accepts a listing, a **fiduciary
relationship** is created. This requires that the agent exhibit
trust and honesty and exercise good business judgment when
working on behalf of his principal. Specifically, the broker
must faithfully perform the agency agreement, be loyal to
his principal, exercise competence, and account for all funds

*BROKER'S
OBLIGATIONS TO
HIS PRINCIPAL*

handled by him in performing the agency. The broker also has certain obligations toward the third parties he deals with. Let us look at these requirements more closely.

Broker responsibility in the State of Texas has mainly been guided by the Canons of Professional Ethics and Conduct for Brokers and Salesmen as established by the Texas Real Estate Commission, and as recently codified by regulations adopted by the Texas Real Estate Commission. There had been many attempts to legally define the duty of a broker to his principal and his capacity as a fiduciary. Recent changes in the Texas Real Estate Licensing Act have codified some specific points in each of these areas.

Faithful Performance   Faithful performance (also referred to as **obedience**) means that the agent is to obey all legal instructions given to him by his principal and apply his best efforts and diligence to carry out the objectives of the agency. For a real estate broker this means performance as promised in the listing contract. A broker who promises to make a "reasonable effort" or apply "diligence" in finding a buyer, and who then does nothing to promote the listing, gives the owner legal grounds for terminating the listing. Faithful performance also means not departing from the principal's instructions. If the agent does so (except in extreme emergencies not foreseen by the principal), it is at his own risk. If the principal thereby suffers a loss, the agent is responsible for that loss. For example, a broker accepts a personal note from a buyer as an earnest money deposit, but fails to tell the seller that the deposit is not in cash. If the seller accepts the offer and the note is later found to be worthless, the broker is liable for the amount of the note.

Another aspect of performance is that the agent must personally perform the tasks delegated to him. This protects the principal who has selected an agent on the basis of trust and confidence from later finding that the agent has delegated that responsibility to another person. However, a major question arises on this point in real estate brokerage, as a large part of the success in finding a buyer for a property results from the cooperative efforts of other brokers and their salesmen. To eliminate the possibility of the owner refusing to pay a commission if a cooperating broker finds a buyer, listing agreements often include a statement that the listing broker is authorized to secure the cooperation of other brokers and pay them part of the commission from the sale.

Probably no other area of agency is as fertile ground for lawsuits as the requirement that, once an agency is created, the agent must be loyal to his principal. The law is clear in all states that in a listing agreement the broker (and the broker's sales staff) occupy a position of trust, confidence, and responsibility. As such, the agent is legally bound to keep the property owner fully informed as to all matters that might affect the sale of the listed property and to promote and protect the owner's interests.

Loyalty to Principal

Unfortunately, greed and expediency sometimes get in the way. As a result, numerous laws have been enacted for the purpose of protecting the principal and threatening the agent with court action for misplaced loyalty. For example, an out-of-town landowner not fully up-to-date on the value of his land might visit a local broker and ask him to list it for $30,000. The broker being much more knowledgeable of local land prices would be aware of a recent city council decision to extend roads and utilities to the area of this property. As a result, he would know that the land is now worth $50,000. If that broker remained silent on the matter, the property would be listed for sale at $30,000. At this price, the broker could find a buyer before the end of the day and have a commission on the sale. However, the opportunity for a quick $20,000 might be too tempting to let pass. He could either buy the property himself or, to hide his identity, in his wife's name or that of a friend and shortly thereafter resell it for $50,000. Whether he sold the property to a buyer for $30,000 or bought it himself and sold it for $50,000, the broker would not be exhibiting loyalty to the principal. Laws and penalties for breach of loyalty are stiff. Such a broker can be sued for recovery of the price difference and the commission paid, his real estate license can be suspended or revoked, and he may be required to pay additional fines and money damages.

If a licensee intends to purchase a property listed for sale by his agency or through a cooperating broker, he is under both a moral and a legal obligation to make certain that the price paid is the fair market value and that the seller knows who the buyer is.

Protecting the Owner's Interest

Loyalty to the principal also means that, whether seeking a buyer or negotiating a sale, the broker must continue to protect the owner's financial interests. Suppose that an owner lists his home at $82,000 but confides in the broker, "If I cannot get $82,000, anything over $79,000 will be fine." The broker shows the home to a prospect who says, "Eighty-two thousand is too much. What will the owner really take?" or "Will he take seventy-nine thousand?" Loyalty to the principal requires the broker to say that the owner will take $82,000, for that is the price in the listing agreement. If the buyer balks, the broker can suggest that the buyer submit an offer for the seller's consideration. All offers must be submitted to the owner, no matter what the offering price and terms. This prevents the agent from rejecting an offer that the owner might have accepted if he had known about it. If the seller really intends for the broker to quote $79,000 as an acceptable price, the listing price should be changed; then the broker can say, "The property was previously listed for $82,000, but is now priced at $79,000."

A broker's loyalty to his principal includes keeping the principal informed of changes in market conditions during the listing period. If, after a listing is taken, an adjacent land-owner is successful in rezoning his land to a higher use and the listed property becomes more valuable, the broker's responsibility is to inform the seller. Similarly, if a buyer is looking at a property priced at $30,000 and tells the broker, "I'll offer $27,000 and come up if need be," it is the duty of the broker to report this to the owner. The owner can then decide if he wants to accept the $27,000 offer or try for more. If the broker does not keep the owner fully informed, he is not properly fulfilling his duties as the owner's agent.

Although the law is clear in requiring the broker to report to the owner all facts that may have a bearing on the property's ultimate sale, it is less clear about the broker-buyer relationship. This ambiguity sometimes places the broker in a difficult position if a prospective buyer is not fully aware of this and thinks instead that the broker is *his* agent in the transaction. It is true that the broker owes the buyer honesty, integrity and fair business dealings, but the broker must also make it clear to the buyer that he is the agent of the owner, and therefore loyal to the owner. Otherwise the broker becomes a dual agent, in which case the law requires that he make this known to everyone concerned.

In Texas the Real Estate Licensing Act specifically prohibits certain misplaced loyalties, such as:

1. *". . . conduct which constitutes dishonest dealings, bad faith, or untrustworthiness [Section 15(6)(V)]."*

2. *". . . the offering of real property for sale or lease without the knowledge and consent of the owner, or on terms other than those authorized by the owner or his agent [Section 15(6)(O)]."*

3. *". . . accepting, receiving, or charging an undisclosed commission rebate or making a direct profit on expenditures made for the principal [Section 15(6)(H)]."*

4. *". . . failing to make clear to all parties to a transaction which party the agent is acting for, or receiving compensation from more than one party, except with the full knowledge and consent of all parties [Section 15(6)(D)]."*

Dual Agency

If a broker represents a seller, it is his duty to obtain the highest price and the best terms possible for the seller. If a broker represents a buyer, the broker's duty is to obtain the lowest price and terms for the buyer. When the same broker represents two or more principals in the same transaction, it is a **dual agency,** and a conflict of interest results. If the broker represents both principals in the same transaction, to whom does he owe his loyalty? Does he work equally hard for each principal? This is an unanswerable question; therefore, the law requires that each principal be informed that he cannot expect the broker's full allegiance and thus each is responsible for looking after his own interest personally. If a broker represents more than one principal and does not obtain their consent, he cannot claim a commission and the defrauded principal(s) may be able to rescind the transaction itself. Moreover, his real estate license may be suspended or revoked. This is true even though the broker does his best to be equally fair to each principal.

Dual agency automatically results when one broker represents two or more parties in a real estate exchange. Consequently, the broker must take care to inform his principals of his dual agency in writing before negotiations begin.

A dual agency also develops when a buyer agrees to pay a broker a fee for finding a property and the broker finds one, lists it, and earns a fee from the seller as well as the buyer. Again, both the buyer and seller must be informed of the dual agency in advance of negotiations. If either principal does not approve of the dual agency, he can refuse to participate.

The Texas Real Estate Licensing Act provides that a license may be revoked if the broker or salesman fails to make clear to all parties to a transaction which party he is acting for, or if he receives compensation from more than one party, except with the full knowledge and consent of all parties [Section 15(6)(D)]. If he acts in the dual capacity of broker and undisclosed principal in a transaction [Section 15(6)(J)] (for instance, if the broker is also the purchaser, and takes advantage of a client by making a purchase below market value), he would violate this provision of the Act.

Middleman

A **middleman** is a person who brings together two or more parties who conduct negotiations between themselves without the help of the middleman. If it is clearly understood by all parties involved that the middleman's only purpose was to bring them together, no one expects the middleman's loyalty. If, however, the middleman assists or influences the negotiations, he becomes an agent of one of the parties, and is subject to the laws of agency.

Reasonable Care

The duty of **reasonable care** implies competence and expertise on the part of the broker. It is the broker's responsibility to disclose all knowledge and material facts concerning a property to his principal. Also, the broker must not become a party to any fraud or misrepresentation likely to affect the sound judgment of the principal.

Although the broker has a duty to disclose all material facts of a transaction to his principal, he may not give legal interpretations. Giving legal interpretations of documents involved in a transaction can be construed as practicing law without a license, an act specifically prohibited by real estate licensing acts. Moreover, the broker can be held financially responsible for any wrong legal information he gives to a client.

The duty of reasonable care also requires an agent to take proper care of property entrusted to him by his principal. For example, if a broker is entrusted with a key to an owner's building to show it to prospects, it is the broker's responsibility to see that it is used for only that purpose and that the building is locked upon leaving. Similarly, if a broker receives a check as an earnest money deposit, he must properly deposit it in a bank and not carry it around for several weeks.

The earnest money that accompanies an offer on a property does not belong to the broker, even though he possesses a check made out to him. For the purpose of holding money for clients and customers, laws in Texas require a broker to maintain a special **trust** or **escrow account.** All monies received by a broker as agent for his principal are to be promptly deposited in this account or the account of an attorney or title company handling the transaction. Texas Real Estate Commission Regulations require that this account be a demand deposit (checking account) at a bank or a trust account at a trust company. There is a new trend under way to allow brokers to deposit trust funds in savings accounts where the money can earn interest. The broker's trust account must be separate from his personal bank account, and the broker is required by law to accurately account for all funds received into and paid out of the trust account. State-conducted surprise audits are made on broker's trust accounts to ensure compliance with the law. One trust account is adequate for all the monies received on behalf of all principals. Failure to comply with trust fund requirements can result in the loss of one's real estate license.

There are several provisions in the new Texas Real Estate Licensing Act which specifically address the broker's obligations to account for funds received. Section 15(6)(E) of the Act states that the broker could have his license revoked or suspended for:

Accounting for Funds Received

". . . failing within a reasonable time to properly account for or remit money coming into his possession that belongs to others, or commingling money belonging to others with his own funds."

Section 15(6)(Y) of the Act provides the same penalties for:

". . . failing within a reasonable time to deposit money received as escrow agent in a real estate transaction, either in trust with a title company authorized to do business in this state, or in a custodial, trust, or escrow account maintained for that purpose."

Section 15(6)(Z) of the act further specifies the same penalties for:

". . . disbursing money deposited in the custodial, trust, or escrow account . . . before the transaction has been consummated or finally otherwise terminated."

Commingling

If a broker places money belonging to a client or customer in his own personal account, it is called **commingling** and is grounds for suspension or revocation of the broker's real estate license. The reason for such severe action is that in the past some brokers have used money belonging to others for short-term loans to themselves and then have been unable to replace the money. Also, clients' and customers' money placed in a personal bank account can be attached by a court of law to pay personal claims against the broker.

If a broker receives a check as an earnest money deposit, along with instructions from the buyer that it remain uncashed, the broker may comply with the buyer's request as long as the seller is informed of this fact when the offer is presented. Similarly, the broker can accept a promissory note, if he informs the seller. The objective is to disclose to the seller all material facts that might influence his decision to accept or reject the offer. The fact that the deposit accompanying the offer is not cash is a material fact. If the broker withholds this information, he violates the laws of agency.

BROKER'S OBLIGATIONS TO THIRD PARTIES

A broker's fiduciary obligations are to the principal who has employed him. State law nonetheless makes certain demands on the broker in relation to the third parties the broker deals with on behalf of the principal. Foremost among these are honesty, integrity and fair business dealing. This includes the proper care of deposit money and offers, and the responsibility for written or verbal statements made by the broker or his sales staff or any impression made by withholding information. Misrepresenting a property by omitting vital information is as wrong as giving false information. Disclosure of such misconduct usually results in a broker losing his right to a commission. He may also lose his real estate license, and can be sued by any party to the transaction who suffered a financial loss because of the misrepresentation.

In guarding against misrepresentation, a licensee must be careful not to make statements not known to be true. For example, a prospect looks at a house listed for sale and asks if it is connected to the city sewer system. The agent does not know the answer, but sensing it is important to making a sale, says, "Yes." This is fraud. If the prospect relies on this statement, purchases the house, and finds out that there is no sewer connection, the agent may be at the center of litigation regarding sale cancellation, commission loss, damage lawsuit, and state license discipline. The answer should be, "I don't know, but I will find out for you."

Suppose instead, that the property owner has told the broker that the house is connected to the city sewer system, and the broker, having no reason to doubt the statement, accepts it in good faith and gives that information to prospective buyers. If this statement is not true, the owner is at fault, owes the broker a commission, and is subject to legal action from the buyer for sale cancellation and money damages. When a broker must rely on information supplied by the owner, it is best to have it in writing. However, relying on the owner for information does not completely relieve the broker of responsibility to third parties. If an owner says his house is connected to the city sewer system and the broker knows that is impossible because there is no sewer line on that street, it is the broker's responsibility to correct the erroneous statement.

Disclosure

In addition to fair and honest business dealings, Texas law requires real estate licensees to disclose latent defects in the property, to disclose any interest in the real estate held by the licensee, to disclose any additional commissions received from someone other than the principal, and to advise the purchaser, in writing, to obtain title insurance or have an abstract examined. Although the licensee owes a duty of confidence and loyalty to his principal, he cannot be a part of any fraud on the principal's behalf. If his principal should request that he make any misrepresentations, the licensee should terminate his employment and refuse to engage in any such acts.

Section 15(6)(A) of the Texas Real Estate Licensing Act states that a licensee may have his license revoked or suspended for failing to disclose to a potential purchaser any latent structural defect that would be a significant factor to a reasonable and prudent purchaser in making a decision to purchase. This may seem to conflict with the licensee's fiduciary obligation to his principal not to disclose information entrusted to him. However, the licensee must remember that if the principal requires him to do anything which is in violation of the Licensing Act, it would be illegal. Therefore, it is assumed that the prudent licensee, when in doubt, would prefer to disclose a potential defect rather than risk the chance of performing an illegal act.

Section 15(6)(D) of the Licensing Act subjects the licensee to penalties for failing to make clear whom he represents. It is not uncommon for a purchaser who has asked a licensee to help him in locating a house to think that the licensee is working for him. The purchaser should be informed that the licensee is working for the seller and the listing agent. Thus, the purchaser remains a third party and the agent should treat him as such. (Note, a buyer can employ a broker, just as a seller can. The arrangement should be in writing.)

Section 15(6)(U) subjects a licensee to penalties for failing to advise the purchaser in writing before the closing of a transaction that he should (1) have the property abstract examined by an attorney of his own choosing, or (2) be furnished with or obtain a policy of title insurance.

The foregoing obligations to third parties are a part of a constantly growing list in this age of consumerism. When coupled with the provisions of the Deceptive Trade Practices—Consumer Protection Act and Texas statutes relating to real estate fraud, they illustrate the increasing concern for Texas real estate brokers and salesmen regarding their obligations to those they serve.

Since a broker is a special agent of his principal rather than a general agent, he has no power to bind his principal. Therefore, if there is an aggrieved third party who feels damaged because of a material misrepresentation, the third party cannot sue the principal and recover. He can, however, sue the broker.

A recent case that typifies current legal thinking held that facts not known by the buyer must be disclosed to him by the seller, or the broker representing him, if they materially affect the desirability of the property. Even the use of an "as is" clause in the purchase contract does not excuse a broker from disclosing material facts regarding a property. The court went on to say that a buyer of real estate has every right to rescind a contract when the agent by his silence has allowed the transaction to proceed without informing the buyer of all facts relevant to the property.

In another case, the buyers of a home built on filled land sued the seller because the lot settled and damaged the house. Their complaint against the seller was that they had not been told of the filled land. The seller in turn sued the broker because the broker had made no mention of that fact to the buyers. In court, the buyers were able to rescind their deal with the seller. In turn the seller successfully sued the broker and recovered the real estate commission, attorney fees and earnings lost while defending the buyer's suit. The court said the broker violated his duty to his principal by not informing the purchasers that the house was on filled land.

In another case, Mrs. Widow was interested in buying an income property. She visited a broker who showed her a number of income and expense statements from listed properties. He recommended one in particular that he claimed would yield a monthly income to her of $700 to $900. This estimate was based on unverified statements made by the current owner. She bought the property only to learn that, in fact, the property's income was insufficient to meet fixed expenses. Subsequently she lost the property through foreclosure. In years past, she would have been simply called foolish for not personally investigating and verifying the income and expenses of the property herself and would have had to bear the loss herself. Today, however, courts look upon real estate licensees as professionals who possess superior knowledge or special information regarding real property and to which their clients are legally entitled. (This is especially significant in that "professional" status is what the real estate industry has been working hard to achieve in recent years.) Mrs. Widow sued the broker for withholding information that should have been disclosed, and she won. As a result, the broker is responsible for reimbursing her loss.

Puffing

Puffing (or **puffery**) has traditionally been recognized as a reference to nonfactual or extravagant statements that a reasonable person would recognize as such. Thus, a buyer may have no legal complaint against a broker who told him that a certain hillside lot had the most beautiful view in the world, or that a listed property had the finest landscaping in the county. However, if a broker in showing a rural property says it has "fantastic" well water, there had better be plenty of good water when the buyer moves in. The line between puffery and misrepresentation is almost nonexistent in Texas. If a consumer believes the broker and relies on the representation, the broker has liability. Puffing should simply be avoided.

OWNER-BROKER OVERVIEW

Because the owner-broker relationship is so important, let us stop for an overview of it. When a seller and a broker enter into a listing agreement, a contract is created that appoints the broker as the special agent of the seller for the purpose of finding a purchaser who is ready, willing, and able to buy at the price and terms set forth in the listing. The listing creates a fiduciary relationship between the broker and the owner. The term **fiduciary** describes the faithful relationship owed by an agent to his principal. Specifically these are the duties of faithful performance, loyalty, competence, accounting, and disclosure. When an agent breaches these fiduciary responsibilities the principal can bring a civil suit to recover losses, and the agent's license to operate may be revoked or suspended by the state.

The principal or owner also has certain obligations to the agent. Although these do not receive much statutory attention in most states, they are important when the principal fails to live up to those obligations. The principal's primary obligation from the agent's standpoint is **compensation.** However, the agent is also eligible for **reimbursement** for expenses not related to the sale itself. For example, if an agent had to pay a plumber to fix a broken pipe for the owner, the agent could expect reimbursement from the owner over and above the sales commission.

The other two obligations of the principal are indemnification and performance. An agent is entitled to **indemnification** when he suffers a loss through no fault of his own; for example, because a misrepresentation by the principal to the agent was passed on in good faith to the buyer. The duty of **performance** means the principal is expected to do whatever he reasonably can to accomplish the purpose of the agency, such as referring inquiries by prospective buyers to the broker.

Principal's Obligations

Although the broker has no contracts with third parties, the broker is nonetheless responsible for the honesty, integrity and fairness of all his business dealings with them. In fact, courts today are bending over backwards to protect buyers from misleading or missing information, undisclosed fees, and hidden broker identity.

Third Parties

The sales associates working with a broker are general agents of the broker. This agency is created by way of an employment contract between the broker and each sales associate. The salesman owes the broker the duties of performance, accounting, loyalty, and reasonable care. The broker's obligations to the sales associate as a subagent are compensation, reimbursement, indemnification and performance. In addition, the employment contract will state the extent to which the sales associate can bind the broker. For example, is the sales associate's signature by itself sufficient to bind the broker to a listing or must the broker also sign it? With regard to third parties, the sales associate also owes them honesty, integrity, and fair business dealings.

BROKER'S SUBAGENTS

COOPERATING   In approximately 70% of all sales made through multiple
BROKER   listing services, the broker who locates the buyer is not the
broker who listed the property. This results in a dilemma:
Is the broker who located the buyer (the **cooperating broker**)
an agent of the buyer or the seller? There are three schools
of thought on this. The traditional one is illustrated in Figure
17:2.

The traditional view is that everyone is an agent (or subagent) of the seller. This view is also reflected in the Texas
Real Estate Commission promulgated forms, which state that
any cooperating broker represents the seller. A second school
of thought is that since the cooperating broker has no contract
with the seller (only an agreement to share with the listing
broker) and none with the buyer, he is the agent of neither.
The third school of thought is that the cooperating broker
represents the buyer by virtue of the fact that the cooperating
broker is trying to locate a suitable property for the buyer.
In fact, a recent Federal Trade Commission study found 71%
of buyers surveyed believe this to be the case. Buyers may
come to believe this because it is the cooperating broker who
spends time with them, takes them to see properties, and
who usually writes and presents the offer and, if needed,
comes back with a counteroffer. Moreover, the cooperating
broker hopes to make a good impression so a sale will be
made and so the buyer will return to that same broker for
future real estate dealings.

Figure 17:2   **TRADITIONAL VIEW OF AGENCY**

The vertical links in this illustration must be
clearly disclosed to buyers and sellers.

The problem arises when the buyer takes the cooperating broker into confidence not knowing that the cooperating broker's loyalty is to the seller. To avoid becoming a dual agent, the wise course is for the cooperating broker to be very clear with the buyer and the seller as to his loyalty as the cooperating broker. If it is with the seller, then the buyer must be informed of this early in the showing process, not at the time the offer is written. If it is with the buyer, then the seller must be made aware that, although there will be a commission split, the seller is not to expect the cooperating broker's loyalty. The payment of fees is a matter of contract, not agency, and there is nothing illegal about the seller paying the fee of a broker who is an agent of the buyer. What the law does say is that undisclosed dual agencies are illegal; yet this is what often happens in cooperative sales. The simple solution is early disclosure in writing to the seller and buyer as to where the cooperating broker's loyalty lies. This will go a long way in deciding what to do if the seller states he will take $115,000 on a $120,000 listing and the buyer is ready to offer $117,500 but wants to start the bidding at $112,500.

Disclosure

Another solution to the representation dilemma is for the buyer to hire a broker whose task is to find properties for sale and present them to the buyer for consideration. In this case, it is clear that the **buyer's broker** is loyal to the buyer and working to get the best deal possible for the buyer. Another benefit of buyer representation is that buyers are not limited to "listed properties." A buyer's broker can investigate properties offered for sale by owners and can approach owners who have not yet put their properties on the market.

BUYER'S BROKER

The biggest drawback of a buyer's brokerage is that most people are accustomed to a system wherein the seller pays the full cost of marketing a property. One solution is for this buyer's broker to present an offer based on the net amount the seller will receive. Consider, for example, a $100,000 property listed at 6% commission and sold the traditional way using a cooperating broker and a 50/50 split. The buyer pays the seller $100,000 and the seller pays the listing broker $6,000 who, in turn, pays $3,000 of that to the cooperating broker. Using a buyer's broker, the buyer pays his broker $3,000 and the seller $97,000. The seller's broker gets $3,000 and splits with no one. The net result is that either way, the seller receives $94,000 and the brokers each get $3,000. The difference is that in the second case, the buyer has a broker whose loyalty and effort are clearly for the buyer.

BROKER COMPENSATION

To be legally eligible for compensation, the broker must be able to clearly show that he was employed. Usually, this requirement is fulfilled by using a preprinted listing form approved for use by the local multiple listing service. The broker fills in the blank spaces with the information that applies to the property he is listing. If listings come in the letter form from property owners, the broker must make certain that all the essential requirements of a valid listing are present and clearly stated. If they are not, the broker may expend time and money finding a buyer only to be denied a commission because he was not properly employed. To guard against this, the broker should transfer the owner's request to the preprinted listing form he uses and then have the owner sign it.

In Texas, the Real Estate Licensing Act sets specific requirements that the broker must comply with to maintain an action for a commission. Section 20(a) specifies that a broker may not file a lawsuit for the collection of compensation for his performance without alleging and proving that he is a duly licensed real estate broker or salesman. Section 20(b) states that an action may not be brought in a court of this state for recovery of a commission unless the promise for such commission is in writing and signed by the party to be charged, or by a person lawfully authorized to sign the commission agreement. Section 20(c) requires that the licensee shall advise the purchaser, in writing, that the purchaser should have the abstract examined by an attorney of purchaser selection, or that purchaser should be furnished with or obtain a policy of title insurance.

"Ready, Willing, and Able"

There is considerable authority in Texas for the view that— once a real estate broker has met the foregoing statutory requirements and produces a **ready, willing, and able buyer** —the broker, at that time, has earned his commission and is owed that commission even if the listing agreement says that the commission is contingent upon the closing of the transaction. The theory is that a listing is usually a unilateral contract ("I'll pay you *if* you perform the agency objective"). Once the broker has produced a ready, willing, and able buyer, the broker has performed as required in the contract; if the seller chooses not to close the transaction, the seller still owes the broker the commission. There is further authority that in the event a broker must sue for his commission, he may also recover his attorney's fees in pursuing this cause of action against his principal.

The difference between the two arrangements becomes important when a buyer is found at the price and terms acceptable to the owner, but no sale results. The "ready, willing, and able" contract provides more protection for the broker since his commission does not depend on the deal reaching settlement. The "no sale, no commission" approach is to the owner's advantage, for he is not required to pay a commission unless there is a completed sale. However, with the passage of time, court decisions have tended to blur the clear-cut distinction between the two. For example, if the owner has a "no sale, no commission" agreement, it would appear that, if the broker brought a ready, willing, and able buyer at the listing price and terms and the owner refused to sell, the owner would owe no commission, for there was no sale. However, a court of law would find in favor of the broker for the full amount of the commission if the refusal to sell was arbitrary and without reasonable cause or in bad faith. Under a "ready, willing, and able" listing, traditionally, if a broker produced a buyer, it was up to the owner to decide if the buyer was, in fact, financially able to buy. If the owner accepted the buyer's offer and subsequently the buyer did not have the money to complete the deal, the owner still owed the broker a commission. The legal thinking today is that the broker should be responsible, because he is in a much better position to analyze the buyer's financial ability than the owner.

PROCURING CAUSE

A broker who possesses an open listing or an exclusive agency listing is entitled to a commission if he can prove that the resulting sale was primarily due to his efforts. That is, he has to have been the **procuring cause,** the one whose efforts originated procurement of the sale. Suppose that a broker shows an open-listed property to a prospect and, during the listing period or an extension, that prospect goes directly to the owner and concludes a deal. Even though the owner negotiates his own transaction and prepares his own sales contract, the broker is entitled to a full commission for finding the buyer. This would also be true if the owner and the buyer used a subterfuge or strawman to purchase the property to avoid paying a commission. Texas law protects the broker who has in good faith produced a buyer at the request of an owner.

When an open listing is given to two or more brokers, the first one who produces a buyer is entitled to the commission. For example, Broker 1 shows a property to Prospect P but no sale is made. Later P goes to Broker 2 and makes an offer, which is accepted by the owner. Although two brokers have attempted to sell the property, only one has succeeded, and that one is entitled to the commission. The fact that Broker 1 receives nothing, even though he may have expended considerable effort, is an important reason why brokers dislike open listings.

TERMINATING THE LISTING CONTRACT

The usual situation in a listing contract is that the broker finds a buyer acceptable to the owner. Thus, in most listing contracts the agency terminates because the objective of the contract has been completed. In the bulk of the listings for which a buyer is not found, the agency is terminated because the listing period expires (remember that if no termination date is specified in the listing agreement, the Texas Real Estate License Act provides that the agent's license can be suspended or revoked).

Even when a listing calls for mutual consideration and has a specific termination date, it is still possible to revoke the agency aspect of the listing before the termination date. However, liability for breach of contract still remains, and money damages may result. Thus, an owner who has listed his property may tell the broker not to bring any more offers, but the owner still remains liable to the broker for payment for the effort expended by the broker up to that time. Depending on how far advanced the broker is at that point, the amount could be as much as a full commission.

A listing can be terminated by mutual agreement of both the owner and broker without money damages. Because listings are the stock in trade of the brokerage business, brokers do not like to lose listings, but sometimes this is the only logical alternative since the time and effort in setting and collecting damages can be very expensive. Suppose, however, that a broker has an exclusive right-to-sell listing and suspects that the owner wants to cancel because he has found a buyer and wants to avoid paying a commission. The broker can stop showing the property, but the owner is still obligated to pay a commission if the property is sold before the listing period expires. Whatever the broker and seller decide, it is best to put the agreement into writing and sign it.

Mutual Agreement

With regard to open listings, once the property is sold by anyone, broker or owner, all listing agreements pertaining to the property are automatically terminated; the objective has been completed, there is no further need for the agency to exist. Similarly, with an exclusive agency listing, if the owner sells the property himself, the agency with the exclusive broker is terminated.

Agency can also be terminated by improper performance or abandonment by the agent. Thus, if a broker acts counter to his principal's best financial interests, the agency is terminated, no commission is payable, and the broker may be subject to a lawsuit for any damages suffered by the principal. If a broker takes a listing and then does nothing to promote it, the owner can assume that the broker abandoned it and has grounds for revocation. The owner should keep written documentation in the event the matter ever goes to court.

Abandonment, etc.

An agency is automatically terminated by the death of either the principal or the agent, or if either is judged legally incompetent by virtue of insanity, and might also be terminated if the owner becomes bankrupt.

The full-service real estate broker who takes a listing and places it in multiple listing, advertises the property at his

BARGAIN BROKERS

expense, holds open house, qualifies prospects, shows property, obtains offers, negotiates, opens escrow and follows through until closing is the mainstay of the real estate selling industry. The vast majority of all open-market sales are handled that way. The remainder are sold by owners, some handling everything themselves and some using flat-fee brokers who oversee the transaction but do not do the actual showing and selling.

Flat-Fee Brokers   For a fee that typically ranges from $400 to $1,500, a **flat-fee broker** will list a property, suggest a market price, write advertising, assist with negotiations, draw up a sales contract and turn the signed papers over to an escrow company for closing. The homeowner is responsible for paying for advertising, answering inquiries, setting appointments with prospects, showing the property and applying whatever salesmanship is necessary to induce the prospect to make an offer. Under the flat-fee arrangement, also called self-help brokerage, the homeowner is effectively buying real estate services on an à la carte basis. Some brokerage firms have been very successful in this—offering sellers a choice of à la carte or full service.

Discount Broker   A **discount broker** is a full-service broker who charges less than the prevailing commission rates in his community. In a seller's market a real estate agent's major problem is finding salable property to list, not finding buyers. The discount broker attracts sellers by offering to do the job for less money; for example, 3% or 4% instead of 5% to 7%. Charging less means a discount broker must sell more properties to be successful. Consequently, most discount brokers may be careful to take listings only on property that will sell quickly, and to reject those that won't.

PROPERTY   In addition to other laws controlling the owner-broker
DISCLOSURE   relationship, the U.S. Congress has enacted legislation aimed
STATEMENTS   at protecting purchasers of property in new subdivisions from misrepresentation, fraud and deceit. This law is administered through federal regulations promulgated by the Department of Housing and Urban Development (HUD). The HUD re-

quirements, administered by the Office of Interstate Land Sales Registration (OILSR), apply primarily to subdivision lots. The purpose of this law, effective in 1969 and amended in 1979, is to require that developers give prospective purchasers extensive disclosures regarding the lots in the form of a **property report.**

The requirement that a property report be prepared according to HUD specifications was the response of Congress to the concern that, all too often, buyers were receiving inaccurate or inadequate information. A color brochure handed to prospects might picture an artificial lake and boat marina within the subdivision, yet the developer has not obtained the necessary permits to build either and may never do so. Or, a developer implies that the lots being offered for sale are ready for building when in fact there is no sewer system and the soil cannot handle septic tanks. Or prospects are not told that many roads in the subdivision will not be built for several years, and, when they are, lot owners will face a hefty paving assessment followed by annual maintenance fees because the county has no intention of maintaining them as public roads.

Property Report

In addition to addressing the above issues, the property report also discloses payment terms, what happens if there is a default, any soil problems, distance to school and stores, any additional costs to expect, availability of utilities, restrictive covenants, oil and mineral rights, etc. The property report must be given to each purchaser before a contract to purchase is signed. Failure to do so gives the purchaser the right to cancel any contract or agreement.

Not an Approval

The property report is *not* a government approval of the subdivision. It is strictly a disclosure of pertinent facts that the prospective purchaser is strongly encouraged to read before buying. A number of states also have enacted their own disclosure laws. Typically these apply to developers of housing subdivisions, condominiums, cooperatives and vacant lots. In these reports the developer is required to make a number of pertinent disclosures about the lot, structure, owners' association, neighborhood, financing terms, etc., and this must be given to the prospective purchaser before a purchase contract can be signed. Once signed, HUD and most states allow the buyer a "cooling-off" period of from 3 to 7 days during which the buyer can cancel the contract and receive all his money back. Like the HUD property report, a state-required property report does not mean the state has approved or disapproved the subdivision. The property report is strictly a disclosure statement designed to help the prospective purchaser make an informed decision about buying.

Government's Position   In enforcing disclosure requirements, neither HUD nor OILSR takes a position as to whether a particular subdivision is a good investment or a bad one, and a statement to this effect is printed on the first page of every property report given to a prospective buyer. The statement also urges the prospective buyer to read the property report before signing anything. The primary purpose of the property report is to ensure that the developer and his sales agents disclose to third parties pertinent facts regarding the property before a sale is made.

A number of states have also enacted their own disclosure laws. Typically these apply to developers of house subdivisions, condominiums, cooperatives, and vacant lots, whereas the federal laws are primarily concerned with vacant land sales. Also, state disclosure laws deal with developments sold entirely within a state and in some cases with developments in other states sold to their residents, whereas HUD and OILSR deal only with lots in one state sold to residents of another state.

CONSTITUTIONAL IMPACT ON OWNERSHIP OF REAL PROPERTY   The most fundamental rights in real property are contained in the U.S. Constitution. These rights are so firmly established and so broadly affect real estate that they deserve discussion at the outset. The Declaration of Independence declared that "all men are created equal" and set the stage for an attitude of the government which we enjoy in the United States. It was with this forethought that our founders wrote the United States Constitution which instilled in all citizens certain inalienable rights of which they can never be deprived. As far as real property ownership is concerned, the most significant of these are the Fifth, Fourteenth and the Thirteenth Amendments to the Constitution.

The Fifth Amendment clearly states that no person shall ". . . be deprived of life, liberty, or property without due process of law, . . ." It was from this fundamental statement that we have developed the inherent right that nobody can have their property taken from them without court proceedings. This concept has been expanded over the last 25 years or so to include the prohibition of certain types of discrimination.

To date, the types of discrimination which have been deemed "suspect" by the United States Supreme Court have included discrimination on the basis of race, color, religion, national origin and alienage. This is logical in that a citizen of the United States cannot alter his race, color, national origin or alienage, and is entitled to practice the religion of his choice. Therefore very strict constitutional prohibitions have been established by the courts to assure these people of their rights to be the same as the rights of any other citizen in the United States. It should be emphasized that there is no constitutional prohibition for discrimination on the basis of sex, age, or marital status.

One of the most significant areas of litigation has been based on racial discrimination. This has been applied to state and individual actions through enforcement of interpretation of the Thirteenth and Fourteenth Amendments to the Constitution.

The Fourteenth Amendment prohibits any state from depriving a person of life, liberty or property without due process of law and prohibits any State from denying any person within its jurisdiction the equal protection of the laws. The significant case in interpreting the Fourteenth Amendment as it applies to the States was *Shelley* v. *Kraemer*. In this Supreme Court case, some white property owners were attempting to enforce a deed restriction which required that all property owners must be Caucasian. The state courts granted the relief sought. The Supreme Court, however, reversed the case stating that the action of state courts in imposing penalties are depriving parties of other substantive rights without providing adequate notice. The opportunity to defend has long been regarded as a denial of due process of law as guaranteed by the Fourteenth Amendment. The court stated that equality and the enjoyment of property rights was regarded by the framers of the Fourteenth Amendment as an essential precondition to realization of other basic civil rights and liberties which the Fourteenth Amendment was intended to guaranty, and therefore concluded that the "equal protection" clause of the Fourteenth Amendment should prohibit the judicial enforcement by state courts of restrictive covenants based on race or color.

The Thirteenth Amendment to the United States Constitution prohibits slavery and involuntary servitude. This amendment formed the basis for the most significant landmark case on discrimination, *Jones* v. *Alfred H. Mayer Company.* That case basically held that any form of discrimination, *even by individuals,* creates a "badge of slavery" which in turn results in the violation of the Thirteenth Amendment. The Supreme Court stated that in enforcing the Civil Rights Act of 1866, Congress is empowered under the Thirteenth Amendment to secure to all citizens the right to buy whatever a white man can buy and the right to live wherever a white man can live. The court further stated, "If Congress cannot say that being a free man means at least this much, then the Thirteenth Amendment had a promise the Nation cannot keep." This case effectively prohibits discrimination of all types and is applicable to real estate transactions.

FAIR HOUSING LAWS

In addition to the constitutional problem, there are two major federal laws that prohibit discrimination in housing. The first is the Civil Rights Act of 1866. It states that, "All citizens of the United States shall have the same right in every State and Territory, as is enjoyed by the white citizens thereof to inherit, purchase, lease, sell, hold, and convey real and personal property." In 1968, the Supreme Court affirmed that the 1866 Act prohibits "all racial discrimination, private as well as public, in the sale of real property." The second is the **Fair Housing Law,** officially known as Title VIII of the Civil Rights Act of 1968, as amended. This law makes it illegal to discriminate based on race, color, religion, sex, or national origin in connection with the sale or rental of housing and any vacant land offered for residential construction or use.

Specifically, what do these two laws prohibit and what do they allow? The 1968 Fair Housing Law provides protection against the following acts if they are based on race, color, religion, sex, or national origin:

(1) Refusing to sell or rent to, deal or negotiate with any person;

(2) Discriminating in the terms or conditions for buying or renting housing;

(3) Discriminating by advertising that housing is available only to persons of a certain race, color, religion, sex, or national origin;

(4) Denying that housing is available for inspection, sale or rent when it really is available;

(5) Denying or making different terms or conditions for home loans by commercial lenders;

(6) Denying to anyone the use of or participation in any real estate services, such as brokers' organizations, multiple listing services or other facilities related to the selling or renting of housing;

(7) Steering and blockbusting.

Steering is the practice of directing home seekers to particular neighborhoods based on race, color, religion, sex or national origin. Steering includes efforts to exclude minority members from one area of a city as well as to direct them to minority or changing areas. Examples include showing only certain neighborhoods, slanting property descriptions, and down-grading neighborhoods. Steering is often subtle, sometimes no more than a word, phrase, or facial expression. Nonetheless, steering accounts for the bulk of the complaints filed against real estate licensees under the Fair Housing Act.

Steering

Blockbusting is the illegal practice of inducing panic selling in a neighborhood for financial gain. Blockbusting typically starts when one person induces another to sell his property cheaply by stating that an impending change in the racial or religious composition of the neighborhood will cause prop-

Blockbusting

erty values to fall, school quality to decline, and crime to increase. The first home thus acquired is sold (at a mark-up) to a minority member. This event is used to reinforce fears that the neighborhood is indeed changing. The process quickly snowballs as residents panic and sell at progressively lower prices. The homes are then resold at higher prices to incoming residents.

Note that blockbusting is not limited to fears over people moving into a neighborhood. In a Virginia case, a real estate firm attempted to gain listings in a certain neighborhood by playing upon residents' fears regarding an upcoming express-way project.

Housing Covered by the 1968 Fair Housing Law

The 1968 Fair Housing Law applies to the following types of housing:

- Single-family houses owned by private individuals when (1) a real estate broker or other person in the business of selling or renting dwellings is used and/or (2) discriminatory advertising is used;
- Single-family houses not owned by private individuals;
- Single-family houses owned by a private individual who owns more than three such houses or who, in any two-year period, sells more than one in which the individual was not the most recent resident;
- Multifamily dwellings of five or more units;
- Multifamily dwellings containing four or fewer units, if the owner does not reside in one of the units.

Acts Not Prohibited by the 1968 Fair Housing Law

Not covered by the 1968 Fair Housing Law are the sale or rental of single-family houses owned by a private individual who owns three or fewer such single-family houses if (1) a broker is not used, (2) discriminatory advertising is not used, and (3) no more than one house in which the owner was not the most recent resident is sold during any two-year period. Not covered by the 1968 Act are rentals of rooms or units in owner-occupied multidwellings for two to four families, if discriminatory advertising is not used. Also the 1968 Act does not cover the sale, rental or occupancy of dwellings which a religious organization owns or operates for other than a commercial purpose to persons of the same religion, if membership in that religion is not restricted on account of race, color, or national origin. And the 1968 Act does not cover the rental or occupancy of lodgings which a private club owns or operates for its members for other than a commercial purpose.

Note, however, the above listed acts not prohibited by the 1968 Fair Housing Law are prohibited by the 1866 Civil Rights Act when discrimination based on race occurs in connection with such acts.

There are three ways that adherence to the 1968 Act can be enforced by someone who feels discriminated against. The first is to file a written complaint with the Department of Housing and Urban Development in Washington, D.C. The second is to file court action directly in a U.S. District Court or state or local court. The third is to file a complaint with the U.S. Attorney General. If a complaint is filed with HUD, HUD may investigate to see if the law has been broken, may attempt to resolve the problem by conference, conciliation or persuasion, may refer the matter to a state or local fair housing authority, or may recommend that the complaint be filed in court. A person seeking enforcement of the 1866 Act must file a suit in a Federal Court.

Fair Housing Enforcement

No matter which route is taken, the burden of proving illegal discrimination is the responsibility of the person filing the complaint. If successful, the following remedies are available: (1) an injunction to stop the sale or rental of the property to someone else and make it available to the complainant, (2) money for actual damages caused by the discrimination, (3) punitive damages, and (4) court costs. There are also criminal penalties for those who coerce, intimidate, threaten or interfere with a person's buying, renting or selling of housing.

A real estate agent's duties are to uphold the 1968 Fair Housing Act and the 1866 Civil Rights Act. If a property owner asks an agent to discriminate, the agent must refuse to accept the listing. An agent is in violation of fair housing laws by giving a minority buyer or seller less than favorable treatment or by ignoring him or by referring him to an agent

Agent's Duties

of the same minority. Violation also occurs when an agent fails to use best efforts, does not submit an offer, delays submitting an offer or induces a seller to reject an offer because of race, color, religion, sex or national origin.

Testers

From time-to-time a licensee may be approached by fair housing testers. These are individuals or organizations that respond to advertising and visit real estate offices to test for compliance with fair housing laws. The tester does not announce himself or herself as such and then ask if the office follows fair housing practices. Rather, the tester plays the role of a person looking for housing to buy or rent and observes if fair housing laws are being followed. If not followed, the tester lodges a complaint with the appropriate fair housing agency.

State Laws

What has been said so far has to do with federal housing laws. In addition, many states, counties and cities have enacted their own fair housing laws. You will need to contact local fair housing authorities as these laws often go beyond the federal laws. For example, within some states it is illegal to discriminate on the basis of age, marital status, presence of children, physical handicap, sexual preference, and welfare status. Within other states an owner-occupant may discriminate only in his own single-family or two-family home, not in the four-family dwelling allowed in the 1968 Act.

Texas has no statutes dealing specifically with fair housing practices, except for recent changes in the Real Estate Licensing Act to prohibit discrimination by licensees. Cities, however, such as Houston and Dallas, have enacted fair housing ordinances. All licensees should be familiar with their local ordinances pertaining to this area of the law.

VOCABULARY REVIEW

Match Terms **a–n** *with statements* **1–14.**

a. *Agent*
b. *Commingling*
c. *Dual agency*
d. *Exclusive agency*
e. *Exclusive right to sell*
f. *Middleman*
g. *Multiple listing service*
h. *Net listing*
i. *Open listing*
j. *Principal*

k. *Procuring cause*   **m.** *Special agency*
l. *Puffing*   **n.** *Third parties*

1. A person who authorizes another to act for him.
2. Listing giving a broker a nonexclusive right to find a purchaser.
3. Persons who are not parties to a contract but who may be affected by it.
4. An agency created for the performance of specific acts only.
5. A person who brings two or more parties together but does not assist in conducting negotiations.
6. Listing giving the broker the right to collect a commission no matter who sells the property during the listing period.
7. A listing wherein the owner reserves the right to sell the property himself, but agrees to list with no other broker during the listing period.
8. Person empowered to act by and on behalf of the principal.
9. A listing for which the commission is the difference between the sales price and a minimum price set by the seller.
10. An organization of real estate brokers that exists for the purpose of exchanging listing information.
11. One broker representing two or more parties in a transaction.
12. Mixing of clients' funds with an agent's personal funds.
13. Broker who is the primary cause of a real estate transaction.
14. Nonfactual or extravagant statements that a reasonable person would recognize as such.

QUESTIONS AND PROBLEMS

1. When we speak of an agency relationship, to what are we referring?
2. How does a universal agency differ from a general agency?
3. What does broker cooperation refer to? How is it achieved?
4. Why do brokers strongly prefer to take exclusive right-to-sell listings rather than exclusive agency or open listings?
5. What advantages and disadvantages does the open listing offer a property owner?
6. The laws of agency require that the agent be faithful and loyal to the principal. What does this mean to a real estate broker who has just taken a listing?
7. What does the phrase "ready, willing, and able buyer" mean in a real estate contract?
8. If a person holds a real estate license in Texas, is he or she required to disclose that fact when acting as a principal?
9. How are listings terminated?
10. What is the purpose of HUD property disclosure statements?
11. Briefly define the terms steering and blockbusting.
12. What impact did the *Jones* v. *Mayer* case have on fair housing laws?

ADDITIONAL
READINGS

"Avoid Civil Rights Litigation" by **Armin Guggenheim.** (*Real Estate Today,* Sept 84, p. 38). Article points out how recent court decisions in civil rights cases are beginning to clarify many of the problems faced by real estate agents.

"Buying Lots from Developers" from the **U.S. Department of Housing and Urban Development.** (Government Printing Office, 1975, 26 pages). This is must reading for anyone planning to buy a vacant lot. Contains what to watch out for, what questions to ask, and HUD property report requirements.

Classified Secrets: Writing Real Estate Ads that Work by **William Pivar.** (Real Estate Education Co., 1984, 373 pages). Book emphasizes the need to write ads that attract. Includes where to advertise, motivating action, selling special properties, analyzing results, etc.

The Condominium Home: A Special Marketing Challenge by **Janet Scaro.** (Realtors National Marketing Institute, 1981, 253 pages). Looks at condominium listing, marketing, selling, and opportunities for agents.

How to List and Sell Real Estate by **Danielle Kennedy** and **Warren Jamison.** (Reston, 1983, 524 pages). A very popular guide that contains prospecting hints, ideas for letters, role plays, actual situations, time planning, promotions and closing techniques.

Strategies for Success in Real Estate by **Sam Young.** (Reston, 1983, 237 pages). Topics include public relations, creating referral business, listing presentations, telephone techniques, listing property, showing property and closing the sale.

Texas Real Estate Law, 4th ed. by **Charles J. Jacobus.** (Reston, 1985, 560 pages). Provides up-to-date explanations of law pertinent to the daily operation of a real estate brokerage office in Texas. Chapters 5 and 6 deal with agency and real estate brokerage.

"When the Seller Wants Out" by **Shari Lyn Anderson.** (*First Tuesday,* Apr 85, p. 6). Covers the practical and legal aspects of what a broker can do when a seller wants to cancel the listing. Includes sample cancellation form.

Licensing Laws and Professional Affiliation

Broker: a person or legal entity licensed to act independently in conducting a real estate brokerage business

Independent contractor: one who contracts to do work according to his own methods and is responsible to his employer only as to the results of that work

License revocation: to recall and make void a license

License suspension: to temporarily make a license ineffective

Licensee: one who holds a license from a government or other agency and which permits a person to pursue some occupation according to certain standards, such as real estate sales

Realtor: a registered trademark owned by the National Association of Realtors for use by its members

Reciprocity: an arrangement whereby one state honors licenses issued by another state and vice versa

Recovery fund: a state-operated fund that can be tapped to pay for uncollectible judgments against real estate licensees

Sales associate: a salesman or broker employed by a broker

Salesman: a person employed by a broker to list, negotiate, sell or lease real property for others

RATIONALE FOR REAL ESTATE LICENSING

Does the public have a vested interest in seeing that real estate salespersons and brokers have the qualifications of honesty, truthfulness, good reputation and real estate knowledge before they are allowed to negotiate real estate transactions on behalf of others? It was this concern that brought about real estate licensing laws as we know them today.

The first attempt in the United States to license persons acting as agents in real estate transactions was in the year 1917 in California. Opponents claimed that the new law was an unreasonable interference with the right of every citizen to engage in a useful and legitimate occupation and were successful in having the law declared unconstitutional by the courts on a technicality. Two years later, in 1919, the California legislature passed a second real estate licensing act; this time it was upheld by the Supreme Court. That

same year, Michigan, Oregon, and Tennessee also passed
real estate licensing acts. Today all 50 states and the District
of Columbia require that persons who offer their services as
real estate agents be licensed.

The Real Estate License Act (the "Act") of Texas (Art.
6573a, V.A.T.S.) was first passed in 1939. A revised Act became effective May 19, 1975 and new amendments have been
added in every legislative session since 1975. These have
materially changed and upgraded the requirements for obtaining and maintaining a license. In addition, the Act clearly
defines the functions and duties of a Broker, and establishes
explicit provisions for license revocation and suspension. It
is anticipated that the interpretation of the Act will be administered literally, thus requiring a higher standard of care from
the Broker.

Although licensing laws do prevent complete freedom
of entry into the profession, the public has a vested interest
in seeing that salesmen and brokers have the qualifications
of honesty, truthfulness, and good reputation. This was the
intent of the first license laws. Some years later the additional
requirements of license examinations and real estate education
were added in the belief that a person who wants to be a
real estate agent should meet special knowledge qualifications.

Experience to date clearly indicates that the Texas Real
Estate License Act has helped to upgrade technical competency and has increased public confidence in brokers and
salesmen. Moreover, the Act is an important and powerful
tool in reducing fraudulent real estate practices because a
state can suspend or revoke a person's license to operate.
A complete copy of the Act is shown in Appendix B-1. It is
suggested that it be read several times, in detail. It is a primary
basis for test questions at every level, and there is no excuse
for not knowing it.

BROKER DEFINED   There are currently two levels of license under the Act.
A *Real Estate Broker*, as statutorily defined in Texas, means
a person (*person* is defined as an "individual, partnership,
or corporation") who, for another person and for a fee, commission, or other valuable consideration, or with the intention

or in the expectation or on the promise of receiving or collecting a fee, commission, or other valuable consideration from another person:

1. *sells, exchanges, purchases, rents, or leases real estate;*

2. *offers to sell, exchange, purchase, rent, or lease real estate;*

3. *negotiates, or attempts to negotiate, the listing, sale, exchange, purchase, rental, or leasing of real estate;*

4. *lists, or offers or attempts or agrees to list, real estate for sale, rental, lease, exchange, or trade;*

5. *appraises, or offers or attempts or agrees to appraise, real estate;*

6. *auctions, or offers or attempts or agrees to auction, real estate;*

7. *buys or sells, or offers to buy or sell, or otherwise deals in options on real estate;*

8. *aids, attempts, or offers to aid, in locating or obtaining for purchase, rent, or lease any real estate;*

9. *procures, or assists in the procuring of, prospects for the purpose of effecting the sale, exchange, lease, or rental of real estate; or*

10. *procures, or assists in the procuring of, properties for the purpose of effecting the sale, exchange, lease, or rental of real estate.*

In addition to the foregoing, clarification of certain licensing provisions have been set out in recent amendments to the Rules pertaining to the provisions of The Texas Real Estate Licensing Act. These amendments state that an office sales manager who deals only with licensees and office personnel does not have to be licensed, nor does an officer of a corporation acting in behalf of the Board of Directors of the corporation, provided he receives no special compensation therefor.

The statutory definition of *Broker* in Texas also includes a person employed by, or on behalf of, the owner or owners of lots or other parcels of real estate, at a salary, fee, commission, or any other valuable consideration, employed to sell real estate in lots or parcels, or any other disposition thereof. Broker also includes a person who charges an advance fee, or contracts for collection of a fee in connection with a contract, whereby he undertakes primarily to promote the sale of real estate either through its listing in a publication issued primarily for such purpose, or for referral of information concerning the real estate to brokers, or both.

SALESMAN DEFINED   The definition of *Real Estate Salesman* means a person associated with a Texas-licensed real estate broker for the purposes of performing acts or transactions comprehended by the term of *Real Estate Broker* as defined in the Act. It is specifically provided that a salesman shall not accept compensation for real estate transactions from any person other than the broker under whom he is licensed at the time that he is paid, or under whom he was licensed when he has earned his right to compensation. Thus, a salesman who takes a listing on a property does so in the name of his broker. In the event of a legal dispute caused by a salesman, the dispute would be between the principal and the broker. Thus, some brokers take considerable care to oversee the documents that their salesmen prepare and sign. Other brokers do not, relying instead on the knowledge and sensibility of their salesmen, and accepting a certain amount of risk in the process.

The above definitions are intended to be all inclusive, so that almost any act affecting real property is construed to be one which constitutes brokerage. The objective is to maintain higher standards in the real estate industry through licensing. The only people not required to be licensed are specifically exempted from the Act, and are persons operating in unique capacities, such as:

Exemptions from Licensing

1. *an attorney-at-law licensed in this state or in any other state;*

2. *an attorney in fact under a duly-executed power of attorney authorizing the consummation of a real estate transaction (however not to circumvent the licensing requirements of the Act);*

3. *a public official in the conduct of his official duties;*

4. *a person acting officially as a receiver, trustee, administrator, executor, or guardian;*

5. *a person acting under a court order or under the authority of a will or a written trust instrument;*

6. *a salesperson employed by an owner in the sale of structures and land on which said structures are situated, provided such structures are erected by the owner in the due course of his business (such as a builder);*

7. *an on-site manager of an apartment complex;*

8. *transactions involving the sale, lease, or transfer of any mineral or mining interest in real property;*

9. *an owner or his employees in renting or leasing his own real estate whether improved or unimproved;*

10. *transaction involving the sale, lease, or transfer of cemetery lots.*

The term **sales associate** is not a license category. It merely refers to anyone with a real estate license who is employed by and "associated" with a broker. Most often this associate will be a real estate salesman. However, a person who holds a broker license can work for another broker. Such a person is a regular member of the employing broker's sales force just like someone with a salesman license. The salesmen and brokers who work for a broker are known collectively as the broker's sales associates or sales force or sales staff. You will also hear the term real estate agent used in a general sense. Correctly speaking, the broker is a special agent of the property owner and the sales associate is a general agent of the broker. In nontechnical language, real estate agent today means anyone, broker or salesman, who negotiates real estate transactions for others.

Sales Associate

To be eligible in Texas for a real estate salesman's license, an individual must have been a resident of Texas for at least 60 days, and be at least 18 years of age. An applicant for a brokerage license shall additionally have not less than two years active experience as a licensed real estate practitioner. He must further satisfy the Commission, through its application procedures, as to his honesty, trustworthiness, integrity, and competency. Competency is determined by passing the licensing examination.

License Eligibility

The Act, made effective September 1, 1979, further requires that any applicant for broker licensure shall furnish the Commission satisfactory evidence: (1) that he has satisfied the educational requirements required by the Act; (2) that he has satisfied the requirements for broker licensure effective on or after January 1, 1985; (3) that he was a licensed real estate broker in another state and that he has had not less than two years active experience in that other state as a licensed real estate broker or salesman during the 36-month period immediately preceeding the filing of his application and that he satisfied the educational requirements for broker licensure provided for by the Act; or (4) he has within one year previous to the filing of his application been licensed in the state as a broker.

Examination   Examination of the license applicant's knowledge of real estate law and practices, mathematics, valuation, finance, and the like, is now an accepted prerequisite for license granting in all states. The Texas salesman exam is two hours in length. The broker exam is three hours. Salesman exams cover the basic aspects of state license law, contracts and agency, real property interests, subdivision map reading, fair housing laws, real estate mathematics, and the ability to follow written instructions. Broker exams cover the same topics in more depth and test the applicant's ability to prepare listings, offer and accept contracts, leasing contracts, and closing statements. The applicant's knowledge of real estate finance and appraisal is also tested.

Education Requirements—   In recent years, the education requirements have also
Brokers   become an increasingly important part of license qualifications. Nearly all states (including Texas) require that applicants take real estate education courses at community colleges, universities, private real estate schools, or through adult education programs at high schools.

As of January 1, 1985, an applicant for a Texas real estate brokerage license must furnish evidence of successful completion of 60 semester hours (900 classroom hours) of real estate core courses or related courses accepted by the Real Estate Commission.

An applicant for real estate salesman license must furnish evidence of successful completion of 12 semester hours (180 classroom hours) of post secondary education. Six hours of these 12 hours must be in real estate core courses as defined by the Act. At least two of the six hours must be completed in a course described as Principles of Real Estate as defined by the Act. Additional educational requirements for the subsequent certifications are as follows:

Education Requirements for Salesmen

Annual Certification	Semester Hours That Must Be Completed	Hours of Required Real Estate Core Courses	Classroom Hours Equivalent*
2nd	14	8	210
3rd	16	10	240
4th	18	12	260

* The Texas Real Estate Commission currently considers each semester hour to be equivalent to 15 classroom hours, and each quarter hour to be equivalent to 10 classroom hours.

In addition to the other educational requirements, all applicants for licensure must complete at least three classroom hours of course work on federal, state and local laws governing housing discrimination, housing credit discrimination, and community reinvestment, or at least three semester hours of course work on constitutional law.

Table 18:1 shows the education and experience requirements in effect in the United States at the time this book was printed. The table is included to give you an overview of the emphasis currently being placed on education and experience by the various states. For up-to-the-minute information on education and experience requirements in Texas, you should contact the Texas Real Estate Commission, Education Division, in Austin.

Licensing authorities in a number of states now feel that in addition to meeting the original education requirement to obtain a license, a real estate licensee should continue to take courses in order to renew his license. States that require continuing education for license renewal are identified in Table 18:1. Texas is considering the matter and will undoubtedly require continuing education before long.

Table 18:1   REAL ESTATE EDUCATION AND EXPERIENCE REQUIREMENTS

STATE	SALESPERSON LICENSE		BROKER LICENSE		
	Education Requirement	Continuing Education	Education Requirement	Experience Requirement	Continuing Education
Alabama	45 hours	No	45 hours	2 years	No
Alaska	None	No	None	2 years	No
Arizona	45 hours	Yes	180 hours	3 years	Yes
Arkansas	30 hours	No	90 hours or 2 yrs + 30 hrs.		No
California	45 + 90 hours	Yes	360 hours	2 years	Yes
Colorado	48 hours	No	96 hours	2 yrs	No
Connecticut	30 hours	Yes	90 hours	2 years	Yes
Delaware	126 hours	Yes	201 hours	5 years	Yes
Dist. of Col.	45 hours	Yes	135 hours	2 years	Yes
Florida	63 hours	Yes	135 hours	1 year	Yes
Georgia	24 + 80 hours	Yes	164 hours	3 years	Yes
Hawaii	40 hours	No	46 hours	2 years	No
Idaho	45 hours	No	135 hours	2 years	No
Illinois	30 hours	No	90 hours	1 year	No
Indiana	40 hours	No	64 hours	1 year	No
Iowa	30 hours	Yes	90 hours	2 years	Yes
Kansas	30 hours	Yes	24 hours	2 years	Yes
Kentucky	96 hours	No	336 hours	2 years	No
Louisiana	90 hours	Yes	150 hours	2 years	Yes
Maine	None	Yes	90 hours or 1 year		Yes
Maryland	45 hours	Yes	135 hours	3 years	Yes
Massachusetts	24 hours	No	30 hours	1 year	No
Michigan	40 hours	Yes	90 hours	3 years	Yes
Minnesota	90 hours	Yes	90 hours	2 years	Yes
Mississippi	60 + 30 hours	No	135 hours	1 year	No

Explanation: Hours are clock-hours in the classroom; experience requirement is experience as a licensed real estate salesperson; continuing education refers to education required for license renewal. Some states credit completed salesperson education toward the broker education requirement. Xns = transactions.

LICENSING
PROCEDURE

When a license applicant has completed or is close to completing the education and experience requirements, he begins his formal application for licensure by filling out a license application form furnished by the Texas Real Estate Commission. When the application is completed, it is returned to the Commission along with a fee to cover application processing and the examination charge. After the Commission receives the application, an examination authorization letter is issued that gives the applicant one year in which to take and pass the exam.

REAL ESTATE EDUCATION AND EXPERIENCE REQUIREMENTS   **Table 18:1** *continued*

STATE	SALESPERSON LICENSE		BROKER LICENSE		
	Education Requirement	Continuing Education	Education Requirement	Experience Requirement	Continuing Education
Missouri	60 hours	Yes	140 hours	None	Yes
Montana	None	No	None	2 years	No
Nebraska	60 hours	Yes	120 hours	2 years	Yes
Nevada	90 hours	Yes	960 hours	2 years	Yes
New Hampshire	None	Yes	None	1 year	Yes
New Jersey	75 hours	No	165 hours	2 years	No
New Mexico	60 hours	No	90 hours	2 years	No
New York	45 hours	Yes	90 hours	2 years	Yes
North Carolina	30 hours	No	120 hours *or* 2 years		No
North Dakota	30 hours	Yes	90 hours	2 years	Yes
Ohio	60 + 60 hours	Yes	240 hours	2 yrs + 20 Xns	Yes
Oklahoma	45 hours	Yes	90 hours	1 year	Yes
Oregon	90 hours	Yes	150 hours	3 years	Yes
Pennsylvania	60 hours	No	240 hours	3 years	No
Rhode Island	None	No	90 hours	1 year	No
South Carolina	30 + 30 hours	No	90 hours	3 years	No
South Dakota	30 hours	Yes	90 hours	2 years	Yes
Tennessee	30 hours	Yes	90 hours	2 years	Yes
Texas	180 hours	Yes	900 hours	2 years	No
Utah	90 hours	No	120 hours	3 years	No
Vermont	None	No	None	1 year	No
Virginia	45 hours	No	180 hours	3 years	No
Washington	30 + 30 hours	Yes	90 hours	2 years	No
West Virginia	90 hours	No	180 hours	2 years	No
Wisconsin	30 hours	Yes	60 hours	None	Yes
Wyoming	30 hours	Yes	60 hours	2 years	Yes

Source: National Association of Real Estate License Law Officials, 50 South Main Street, Suite 600, Salt Lake City, Utah 84144. Check with your state for any subsequent changes.

Next, the Commission schedules a written examination for the applicant. Exams are held in various parts of the state so the applicant need not travel to the state capital. The applicant is not allowed to bring any books or notes into the testing room. However, an applicant is allowed to use a noiseless, non-programmable, battery-operated calculator. Exams are machine scored and applicants should bring pencils and an eraser. The exam is offered at least once a month and is written and administered by the Texas Real Estate Commission.

Examination

No later than the 30th day after the day on which the person completes an examination administered by the Commission, the Commission sends to the person his or her results. If so requested by the applicant, the Commission shall send to the person the analysis of that person's performance on the examination no later than the 30th day after the date the request is received by the Commission.

If the applicant fails the written examination, the usual procedure is to allow him to repeat it until he passes. The original application fee does not have to be paid each time; however, a fee is charged to retake the exam and the applicant may then take any scheduled exam in the state.

Renewal   Once licensed, as long as a person remains active in real estate he may renew his license by paying the required annual certification fee. If the licensee has met all of the educational requirements, his license renewal is put on a biennial renewal (every two years). No additional exam is required. If a license is not renewed before it expires, Texas allows a grace period of one year before requiring reexamination. Once the grace period is passed, all license rights lapse and the individual must meet current application requirements and take another written exam.

Inactive Status   When the association of a salesman with his sponsoring broker is terminated, the broker must immediately return the salesman's license to the Commission. The salesman is then placed on "inactive" status by the Commission. That salesman's license may be activated if, within the calendar year, a request, accompanied by the required fee, is filed with the Commission by a licensed broker advising that he assumes sponsorship of the salesman. A salesman may also elect to remain inactive indefinitely so long as he continues to pay his annual fee to the Commission.

NONRESIDENT LICENSING   The general rule regarding license requirements is that a person must be licensed in the state within which he negotiates. Thus, if a broker or one of his salesmen sells an out-of-state property, but conducts the negotiations entirely within the borders of his own state, he does not need to be licensed to sell in the state where the land is actually located. State laws also permit the broker of one state to split a commission with the broker of another state provided each conducts negotiations only within the state where he is licensed. Therefore, if Broker B, licensed in State B, takes a listing at his office on a parcel of land located in State B, and Broker C in State C sells it to one of his clients, conducting the sale negotiations within State C, then Brokers B and C can split the commission. If, however, Broker C comes to State B to negotiate a contract, then a license in State B is necessary. The standard practice has been to apply for a **nonresident license** and meet substantially the same exam and experience requirements as demanded of resident brokers.

The Texas Real Estate Licensing Act allows a licensed real estate broker in another state to apply for broker licensure if he has been a licensed real estate broker in another state with not less than 2 years' active experience during the 36-month period immediately preceeding the filing of his application, and if he has satisfied the educational requirements for broker licensure in the State of Texas.

License Reciprocity

In recent years, there has been considerable effort to design real estate licensing systems that permit a broker and his sales staff to conduct negotiations in other states without having to obtain nonresident licenses. The result is **license reciprocity** and it applies when one state honors another's license. In permitting reciprocity, state officials are primarily concerned with the nonresident's knowledge of real estate law and practice as it applies to the state in which he wishes to operate.

A few states accept real estate licenses issued by other states. This is called **full reciprocity** and means that a licensee can operate in another state without having to take that state's examination and meet its education and experience requirements. More commonly, most states have **partial reciprocity** which gives credit to the licensees of another state for experience, education and examination. The 1979 amendment to the Real Estate License Act discarded the term "reciprocity" and technically, Texas does not reciprocate with any state. Instead, the Texas Real Estate License Act provides that a resident broker in another state may apply for a nonresident Texas broker license by meeting the nonresident broker requirements.

Notice of Consent   When a broker operates outside of his home state, he may be required to file a **notice of consent** in each state in which he intends to operate, usually with the secretary of state. This permits the secretary of state to receive legal summonses on behalf of the nonresident broker and provides a state resident an avenue by which he can sue a broker who is a resident of another state. Texas has this requirement.

LICENSING THE
BUSINESS FIRM   When a real estate broker wishes to establish a brokerage business of his own, the simplest method is a sole proprietorship under his own name, such as, John B. Jones, Real Estate Broker. Some states, including Texas, permit a broker to operate out of his residence. However, operating a business in a residential neighborhood can be bothersome to neighbors, and many states require brokers to maintain a place of business in a location that is zoned for businesses.

Assumed Name   When a person operates under a name other than his own, he must register that name by filing an **assumed name certificate** with his county clerk and the state real estate licensing authority. Thus, if John B. Jones wishes to call his brokerage business Great Texas Realty, his business certificate would show "John B. Jones, doing business as Great Texas Realty." (Sometimes "doing business as" is shortened to dba or d/b/a.)

A sole proprietorship, whether operated under the broker's name or an assumed name, offers a broker advantages in the form of absolute control, flexibility, ease of organization, personal independence, ownership of all the profits and losses, and the freedom to expand by sponsoring all the salespeople and staff he can manage and afford. Against this the sole proprietor must recognize that he is the sole source of capital for the business and the only owner available to manage it.

Recognizing the need to accumulate capital and management expertise within a single brokerage operation, Texas also permits corporations and partnerships to be licensed. Since a corporation is an artificial being (not an individual), it cannot take a real estate examination. Therefore, Texas laws require that an officer of the corporation be a Texas-licensed real estate broker and qualified to act as the designated person for a corporation holding Texas broker licensure. A corporation incorporated in a state other than Texas may be accepted as a Texas resident for purposes of licensure if it is qualified to do business in Texas; its corporate officers, its principal place of business and all of its assets are located in Texas; and all of its officers and directors are Texas residents. Texas law does not require that a partnership be licensed, provided that each individual partner or non-partner employee who acts as a real estate agent in the partnership's name is licensed as a real estate broker or salesman. The partnership must also file an assumed name certificate showing the names of the partners and the name of the partnership.

Branch Offices

If a broker expands by establishing branch offices that are geographically separate from the main or home office, each branch must have a branch office license.

LICENSING REAL ESTATE INSPECTORS

A common problem for real estate purchasers, and an area of continuing liability for real estate agents, has been that of defective property. Purchasers frequently feel that the expertise of real estate agents should shield them from the duty to investigate too closely, since the agent sees and inspects property all the time. The agent also has a duty to disclose material defects in the property under the License Act. The difficulty in relying on the agent is that the agent often doesn't have the expertise, and, in many cases, the defect is too technical or complicated to be discovered by the agent.

In an effort to alleviate this situation, Texas has passed a recent amendment to the Real Estate License Act that provides for the licensing of **real estate inspectors.** The statute now provides that a person may not act as a real estate inspector for a buyer or seller unless the person possesses a real estate inspector license issued by the Texas Real Estate Commission. The statute further provides for minimum standards of education and a recovery fund, similar to that required of real estate salesmen or brokers. The new law is also designed to eliminate certain potential for conflicts of interest, specifically prohibiting the inspector from:

(1) *accepting an assignment if the employment is contingent on the reporting of a specific, predetermined condition, or on reporting findings other than those known to the inspector to be facts at the time of accepting the assignment; or*

(2) *acting in a manner or engaging in a practice that is dishonest or fraudulent or that involves deceit or misrepresentation; or*

(3) *performing the inspection in a negligent or incompetent manner; or*

(4) *acting in the dual capacity of inspector and undisclosed principal; or*

(5) *acting in the dual capacity of real estate inspector and real estate broker or salesman; or*

(6) *performing any repairs in connection with the real estate inspection.*

There are additional prohibitions, and specific references to prohibiting the inspector's violations of the Deceptive Trade Practices Act. The statute also provides for recovery of attorney's fees, at the discretion of the court, if they are incurred in obtaining a recovery from a licensed inspector for a violation of the Act.

Since the statute has been in effect, it has opened a whole new industry in the real estate profession. In addition, it has given the home purchaser a licensed, competent person for protection against defects in the property. The real estate licensee, too, has a person he can recommend for the inspections of a more technical nature, which may help to eliminate another potential liability.

TEXAS REAL ESTATE COMMISSION

The administration of the provisions of the Texas Real Estate Licensing Act is vested in the Texas Real Estate Commission. The Commission consists of nine members appointed by the Governor with the consent of two-thirds of the Senate present. The commissioners hold office for staggered terms of six years, with the terms of three members expiring every two years.

Six members of the Commission must have been engaged in the real estate brokerage business as licensed real estate brokers as their major occupation for at least five years next preceeding their appointments to the Commission. The other three members must be representatives of the general public who are not licensed under the Texas Real Estate Licensing Act and who do not have, other than as consumers, a financial interest in the practice of real estate broker or real estate salesman, and who are not acting for anyone holding such an interest.

Commission Membership

Existing commissioners can be removed from the Commission if as broker member he or she ceases to be a licensed real estate broker or if as a public member he or she acquires a real estate license or financial interest in the practice of real estate, or if that commissioner becomes an employee or paid consultant of any real estate trade association or an officer in a state wide real estate trade association. All appointments to the Commission must be made without regard to the race, creed, sex, religion or national origin of the appointee.

The Commission has a regular meeting in October of each year, although it may meet more often. It has the power to make and enforce all rules and regulations in performance of its duties, and institute actions to enjoin any violation of any provision of the Texas Real Estate License Act.

Any rule promulgated by the Commission may be blocked or rescinded by a majority vote of the standing committee of the Texas House or Texas Senate having jurisdiction over the affairs of the Texas Real Estate Commission.

The duties of the Commissioners do not normally include the daily operation of the Real Estate Commission. Their compensation as Commissioners is only token compensation for time actually spent on their duties, and they are not employees of the Commission. Therefore, to administer the day-to-day activities of the Commission, the Commission selects an Administrator, who has the complete authority to exercise the powers, rights, and duties of the Commission. The Adminis-

Commissioners' Duties

trator and his staff are salaried employees of the Commission and all business of the Commission, service of process, notices, and applications are considered filed with the Administrator or Assistant Administrator.

LICENSE SUSPENSION AND REVOCATION

The most important control a state has over its real estate salesmen and brokers is that it can **suspend** (temporarily make ineffective) or **revoke** (recall and make void) a real estate license. Without one, it is unlawful for a person to engage in real estate activities for the purpose of earning a commission or fee. Unless an agent has a valid license, a court of law will not uphold his claim for a commission from a client.

The Texas Real Estate Licensing Act gives certain reasons for which a license can be revoked or suspended:

1. *(A)   The licensee has entered a plea of guilty or nolo contendere, or been found guilty or been convicted of, a felony, in which fraud is an essential element, and the time for appeal has elapsed or the judgment or conviction has been affirmed on appeal, irrespective of an order granting probation following such conviction, suspending the imposition of sentence; or*

   (B)   A final money judgment has been rendered against the licensee resulting from contractual obligations of the licensee incurred in the pursuit of his business, and such judgment remains unsatisfied for a period of more than six months after becoming final; or

2. *The licensee has procured, or attempted to procure, a real estate license for himself or a salesman, by fraud, misrepresentation or deceit, or by making a material misstatement of fact in an application for a real estate license; or*

3. *The licensee, when selling, trading, or renting real property in his own name, engaged in misrepresentation or dishonest or fraudulent action; or*

4. *The licensee, while performing an act constituting a broker or salesman, as defined by this Act, has been guilty of:*

   (A)   Making a material misrepresentation, or failing to disclose to a potential purchaser any latent structural defect or any other defect known to the broker or salesman. Latent structural defects

and other defects do not refer to trivial or insignificant defects, but refer to those defects which would be significant factors to a reasonable and prudent purchaser in making a decision to purchase; or

(B)   Making a false promise of a character likely to influence, persuade, or induce any person to enter into a contract or agreement when the licensee could not or did not intend to keep such promise; or

(C)   Pursuing a continued and flagrant course of misrepresentation or making false promises through agents, salesmen, advertising, or otherwise; or

(D)   Failing to make clear, to all parties to a transaction, which party he is acting for, or receiving compensation from more than one party except with the full knowledge and consent of all parties; or

(E)   Failing within a reasonable time properly to account for or remit money coming into his possession which belongs to others or commingling money belonging to others with his own funds; or

(F)   Paying a commission or fees to, or dividing a commission or fee with, anyone not licensed as a real estate broker or salesman in this state or in any other state, or not an attorney at law licensed in this state or any other state, for compensation for services as a real estate agent; or

(G)   Failing to specify in a listing contract a definite termination date which is not subject to prior notice; or

(H)   Accepting, receiving, or charging an undisclosed commission, rebate, or direct profit on expenditures made for a principal; or

(I)   Soliciting, selling, or offering for sale real property under a scheme or program that constitutes a lottery or deceptive practice; or

(J)   Acting in the dual capacity of broker and undisclosed principal in a transaction; or

(K)   Guaranteeing, authorizing, or permitting a person to guarantee that future profits will result from a resale of real property; or

(L)   Placing a sign on real property offering it for sale, lease, or rent without the written consent of the owner or his authorized agent; or

(M)   Inducing or attempting to induce a party to a contract of sale or lease to break the contract for the purpose of substituting in lieu thereof a new contract; or

(N)   Negotiating or attempting to negotiate the sale, exchange, lease, or rental of real property with an owner or lessor, knowing that the owner or lessor had a written outstanding contract, granting exclusive agency in connection with the property to another real estate broker; or

(O)   Offering real property for sale or for lease without the knowledge and consent of the owner or his authorized agent, or on terms other than those authorized by the owner or his authorized agent; or

(P)   Publishing, or causing to be published, an advertisement including, but not limited to, advertising by newspaper, radio, television, or display which is misleading, or which is likely to deceive the public, or which in any manner tends to create a misleading impression, or which fails to identify the person causing the advertisement to be published as a licensed real estate broker or agent; or

(Q)   Having knowingly withheld from or inserted in a statement of account or invoice, a statement that made it inaccurate in a material particular; or

(R)   Publishing or circulating an unjustified or unwarranted threat of legal proceedings, or other action; or

(S)   Establishing an association, by employment or otherwise, with an unlicensed person who is expected or required to act as a real estate licensee, or aiding or abetting or conspiring with a person to circumvent the requirements of this Act; or

(T)   Failing or refusing on demand to furnish copies of a document pertaining to a transaction dealing with real estate to a person whose signature is affixed to the document; or

(U)   Failing to advise a purchaser in writing before the closing of a transaction that the purchaser should either have the abstract

*covering the real estate which is the subject of the contract exam-
ined by an attorney of the purchaser's own selection, or be furnished with or obtain a policy of title insurance; or*

*(V)   Conduct which constitutes dishonest dealings, bad faith,
or untrustworthiness; or*

*(W)   Acting negligently or incompetently in performing an act
for which a person is required to hold a real estate license; or*

(X)   Disregarding or violating a provision of this Act; or

*(Y)   Failing within a reasonable time to deposit money received
as escrow agent in a real estate transaction, either in trust with
a title company authorized to do business in this state, or in a
custodial, trust, or escrow account maintained for that purpose
in a banking institution authorized to do business in this state;
or*

*(Z)   Disbursing money deposited in a custodial, trust, or escrow
account, as provided in Subsection (y) before the transaction
concerned has been consummated or finally otherwise terminated;
or*

*(AA)   Failing or refusing on demand to produce a document,
book, or record in his possession concerning a real estate transaction conducted by him for inspection by the Real Estate Commission or its authorized personnel or representative; or*

*(BB)   Failing within a reasonable time to provide information
requested by the Commission as a result of a formal or informal
complaint to the Commission which would indicate a violation
of this Act; or*

*(CC)   Failing without just cause to surrender to the rightful
owner, on demand, a document or instrument coming into his
possession.*

*(DD)   Discriminating against an owner, potential purchaser,
lessor, or potential lessee on the basis of race, color, religion,
sex, national origin, or ancestry. Prohibited discrimination shall
include but not be limited to directing prospective home buyers
or lessees interested in equivalent properties to different areas
according to the race, color, religion, sex, national origin, or
ancestry of the potential owner or lessee.*

BONDS AND RECOVERY FUNDS

The fact that a salesman or broker can lose his or her license for a wrongdoing strongly encourages licensees to operate within the law. However, the threat and loss of a license do nothing to provide financial compensation for any losses suffered by a wronged party. This must be recovered from the licensee or his employer, either through a mutually agreed upon monetary settlement or a court judgment resulting from a civil lawsuit brought by the wronged party. But even with a court-ordered settlement in his favor, all too often court judgments turn out to be uncollectible because the defendant has no money.

Two solutions to the uncollectible judgment problem are in common use. Some states require that a person post a **bond** with the state before a salesman's or broker's license is issued to him. In the event of an otherwise uncollectible court judgment against a licensee, the bond money is used to provide payment. Bond requirements vary from $1,000 to $10,000, with $5,000 to $10,000 being the most popular range. Licensees either can obtain these bonds from bonding companies for an annual fee, or they can post the required amount of cash or securities with the state.*

The second method of protecting the public is through a state sponsored **recovery fund.** A portion of the money that each licensee pays for his real estate license is set aside in a fund which is made available for the payment of otherwise uncollectible judgments. The number of states that use such recovery funds is growing rapidly.**

Recovery Fund

The Texas Real Estate Commission has established a recovery fund, with specified limits, to pay damages in the event a judgment is obtained against the licensee and there

---

* Bonds are used in Alabama, Alaska, Massachusetts, Montana, Tennessee, and West Virginia.

** Recovery funds are used in Alabama, Alaska, Arizona, Arkansas, California, Colorado, Connecticut, Delaware, District of Columbia, Florida, Georgia, Hawaii, Idaho, Illinois, Kansas, Kentucky, Louisiana, Maryland, Minnesota, Nevada, New Jersey, New Mexico, North Carolina, North Dakota, Ohio, Oklahoma, Pennsylvania, Rhode Island, South Dakota, Tennessee, Texas, Utah, Virginia, and Wyoming.

are no other funds recoverable from the licensee. The recovery fund is funded solely from fees paid by licensees. It is important to note that in order to proceed against the recovery fund the complainant must have received a final judgment in a court of competent jurisdiction. The amounts to be recovered are limited to $20,000 per transaction or $50,000 against any one licensed real estate broker or salesman. The complainant must also prove that there were no attachable assets belonging to the broker or salesman.

The Texas Real Estate License Act provides that if a person files a complaint with the Commission relating to a real estate broker or salesman, the Commission shall furnish to that complainant an explanation of the remedies that are available to that person under the Real Estate Licensing Act. The Commission must also provide information about appropriate state or local agencies or officials with which the person may file a complaint. The Commission shall furnish the same explanation information to the person against whom the complaint is filed. The Commission is required to keep an information file about each complaint filed with the Commission and it shall inform the complainant and person against whom the complaint is filed as to the status of the complaint at least as often as every three months. If the Commission revokes a person's license issued under the Act, the Commission may not issue another license to that person for one year after the revocation.

The requirement for bonds and the establishment of recovery funds are not perfect solutions to the problem of uncollectible judgments because the wronged party must expend considerable effort to recover his loss, and it is quite possible that the maximum amount available per transaction or licensee will not fully compensate for the losses suffered. However, either system is better than none at all, which is still the case in some states.

Be aware that there may be times when a real estate licensee also needs a securities license. This is so whenever the property being sold is an investment contract in real estate rather than real estate itself. A prime example is a real estate partnership. Timeshare units and rental pools where condo-

SECURITIES LICENSE

minium owners put their units into a pool for a percentage of the pool's income may also fall into this category. Securities licenses are issued by the National Association of Securities Dealers based on successful completion of their examination. Legal counsel is advised if there is the possibility you may be selling securities. Counsel will also advise on state and federal laws requiring the registration of real estate securities before they are sold.

AFFILIATING WITH
A BROKER

If you plan to enter real estate sales, selecting a broker to work for is one of the most important decisions you must make. The best way to approach it is to stop and carefully consider what you have to offer the real estate business and what you expect in return. And look at it in that order! It is easy to become captivated by the big commission income you visualize coming your way. But if that is your only perspective, you will meet with disappointment. People are willing to pay you money because they expect to receive some product or service in return. That is their viewpoint and it would probably be yours if you were in their position. Your clients are not concerned with your income goal, it is only incidental to their goals. If you help them attain their goals, you will reach yours.

Before applying for a real estate license ask yourself if the working hours and conditions of a real estate agent are suitable to you. Specifically, are you prepared to work on a commission-only basis? Evenings and weekends? On your own? With people you've never met before? If you can comfortably answer "Yes" to these questions, then start looking for a broker to sponsor you. (Salesman license educational requirements can be completed without broker sponsorship, but a salesperson must have a sponsoring broker in order to make application for a salesman license.)

Training

Your next step is to look for those features and qualities in a broker that will complement, enhance, and encourage your personal development in real estate. If you are new to the industry, training and education will most likely be at the top of your list. Therefore, in looking for a broker you will want to find one who will in one fashion or another teach you the trade. (What you have learned to date from books, classes and license examination preparation will be helpful, but you will need additional specific training.) Real estate franchise operations and large brokerage offices usually offer extensive training. In smaller offices, the broker in charge is usually responsible for seeing that newcomers receive training. An office that offers no training to a newcomer should be avoided.

Another question high on your list will be compensation. Very few offices provide a newcomer with a guaranteed minimum wage or even a draw against future commissions. Most brokers feel that one must produce to be paid and the hungrier the salesperson, the quicker he will produce. A broker who pays salespersons regardless of sales produced simply must siphon the money from those who are producing. The old saying, "There's no such thing as a free lunch" applies to sales commissions.

Compensation

Compensation for salespersons is usually a percentage of the commissions they earn for the broker. How much each receives is open to negotiation between the broker and each salesperson working for him. A broker who offers his sales staff office space, extensive secretarial help, a large advertising budget, a mailing program, and generous long-distance telephone privileges might take 40% to 50% of each incoming commission dollar for office overhead. A broker who provides fewer services might take 25% or 30%.

Salespersons with proven sales records can sometimes reduce the portion that must go to the broker of each earned commission dollar. This is because the broker may feel that with an outstanding sales performer, a high volume of sales will offset a smaller percentage for overhead. Conversely, a new and untried salesperson, or one with a mediocre past sales record, may have to give up a larger portion of each dollar for the broker's overhead.

When one brokerage agency lists a property and another locates the buyer, the commission is split according to any agreement the two brokers wish to make. After splitting, each broker pays a portion of the money he receives to the salesperson involved in accordance with his commission agreements.

While investigating commission arrangements, one should also inquire about incentive and bonus plans, automobile expense reimbursement, health insurance, life insurance, and retirement plans.

An alternative commission arrangement is the **100% commission** wherein the salesperson does not share his commission with the broker. Instead the salesperson is charged a fee for office space, advertising, telephone, multiple listing and any other expenses the broker incurs on behalf of the salesperson. Generally speaking, 100% arrangements are more popular with proven performers than with newcomers.

Broker Support

Broker support will have an impact on any salesperson's success. Specifically: Will you have your own desk to work from? Are office facilities efficient and modern? Does the broker provide secretarial services? What is the broker's advertising policy and who pays for ads? Does the broker have sources of financing for clients? Does the broker allow his salespersons to invest in real estate? Does the broker have a good reputation in the community? Who pays for signs, business cards, franchise fees, and realty board dues?

Finding a Broker

Many salespersons associate with a particular broker as a result of a friendship or word-of-mouth information. However, there are other ways to find a suitable position. An excellent way to start your search is to decide what geographical area you want to work in. If you choose the same community or neighborhood in which you live, you will already possess a valuable sense and feel for that area.

Having selected a geographical area to specialize in, look in the Sunday newspaper real estate advertisements section and the telephone book Yellow Pages for names of brokers. Hold interviews with several brokers and as you do, remember that you are interviewing them just as intensively as they are interviewing you. At your visits with brokers be particularly alert for your feelings. Intuition can be as valuable a guide to a sound working relationship as can a list of questions and answers regarding the job.

As you narrow your choices, revisit the offices of brokers who particularly impressed you. Talk with some of the salespersons who have worked or are working there. They can be very candid and valuable sources of information. Be wary of individuals who are extreme in their opinions: rely instead on the consensus of opinion. Locate clients who have used the firm's services and ask them their opinions of the firm. You might also talk to local appraisers, lenders, and escrow agents for candid opinions. If you do all this advance work, the benefits to you will be greater enjoyment of your work, more money in your pocket, and less likelihood of wanting to quit or move to another office.

Having selected a broker with whom to associate, your next step is to make an employment contract. An **employment contract** formalizes the working arrangement between the broker and his salespersons. An oral contract may be satisfactory, but a written one is preferred because it sets forth the relationship with a higher degree of precision. This greatly reduces the potential for future controversy and litigation.

Employment Contract

The employment contract will cover such matters as compensation (how much and under what circumstances), training (how often and if required), hours of work (including assigned office hours and open houses), company identification (distinctive articles of clothing and name tags), fees and dues (license and realty board), expenses (automobile, advertising, telephone), fringe benefits (health and life insurance, pension and profit-sharing plans), withholding (income taxes and social security), territory (assigned area of the community), termination of employment (quitting and firing), federal tax obligations, and general office policies and procedures (office manual).

Is the real estate sales associate an employee of the broker or an independent contractor? The answer is both. On one hand, the sales associate acts like an **employee** because the associate works for the broker, usually at the broker's place

INDEPENDENT CONTRACTOR STATUS

of business. There the associate prepares listings and sales documents on forms specified by the broker and upon closing receives payment from the broker. On the other hand, the sales associate acts like an **independent contractor** because the associate is paid only if the associate brings about a sale that produces a commission. An important distinction between the two is whether or not the broker must withhold income taxes and social security from the associate's commission checks. If the sales associate is considered by the Internal Revenue Service (IRS) to be an employee for tax purposes, the broker must withhold. If classed as an independent contractor for tax purposes, the sales associate is responsible for his own income taxes and social security. The IRS prefers employee status because it is easier to collect taxes from an employer than an employee and because the combined social security contribution of employer and employee is greater than that paid by a self-employed person earning the same amount.

As a result of federal legislation that took effect January 1, 1983, the IRS will treat real estate sales associates as independent contractors if they meet all of the following three requirements. First, the associate must be a licensed real estate agent. Second, substantially all of the associate's payment for services as a real estate agent must be directly related to sales and not to hours worked. Third, a written agreement must exist between the associate and the broker stating that the associate will be treated as an independent contractor for tax purposes.

These are highlights of the issue. If you plan to work for a broker, you may find it valuable to have this matter as well as your entire employment contract reviewed by an attorney before you sign it.

FRANCHISED OFFICES

Prior to the early 1970s, a real estate brokerage was typically a small business. In fact, most brokerages were one office firms. A brokerage was considered large if it had four or five branch offices, handling perhaps 200 properties a year. Then real estate franchise organizations entered the real estate business in a big way. By offering **franchises,** large organizations such as Century-21, Red Carpet, and Gallery of Homes offered national identification, large-scale advertising, sales staff training programs, management advice, customer referrals, financing help for buyers and guaranteed sales plans to small brokerage offices. In return, the brokerage firm (the **franchiser**) paid a fee to the national organization of from 3% to 8% of its gross commission income. The new marketing system flourished, (the idea became popular) and by the mid-1980s approximately half of the real estate licensees affiliated with the National Association of Realtors were working as franchised offices. Meanwhile, the number of franchisers grew since more than 60 such large organizations including Realty World, ERA, International Real Estate Network, Better Homes and Gardens Realty, and Mayflower Realty, offered attractive franchises to the small firms.

Statistics show that franchising appeals mostly to middle-sized firms with 10 to 50 sales associates. Larger firms are able to provide the advantages of a franchise for themselves, while the smallest firms tend to occupy special market niches and often consist of one or two licensees who do not bring in additional sales associates. For a newly licensed salesperson wishing to affiliate with a firm, a franchised firm can offer immediate public recognition, extensive training opportunities, established office routines, regular sales meetings and access to a nationwide referral system. Franchise affiliation is not magic however. Success still depends on the individual who makes sales calls, values property, gets listings, advertises, shows property, qualifies, negotiates, and closes transactions.

National Real Estate Firms

During the late 1970s a large real estate firm in California— Coldwell Banker—began an expansion program by purchasing multi-branch real estate firms in other states. Today, the Coldwell Banker chain, owned in turn by Sears, Roebuck, has several hundred offices across the United States. Merrill Lynch, the Wall Street stock brokerage firm, has also entered the real estate brokerage business. It, too, has bought existing real estate brokerage firms to accomplish this. Other Wall Street firms are looking into the real estate brokerage business as are several large retailers like Sears. Between the national firms and the local firms in size are several well-established regional firms such as Henry S. Miller and Co. in Dallas, and the Horne Co. in Houston.

For a newcomer, affiliation with a national or regional real estate firm offers benefits like those of a franchised firm (recognition, training, routines, etc.). The main difference is who owns the firm. A franchised firm will be locally owned and locally managed; that is, it is an independent firm. Regional and national firms are locally managed but not locally owned. The sales associates will only occasionally, if ever, meet the owner(s).

PROFESSIONAL REAL ESTATE ASSOCIATIONS

Even before laws required real estate agents to have licenses, there were professional real estate organizations. Called real estate boards, they joined together agents within a city or county on a voluntary basis. The push to organize came from real estate people who saw the need for some sort of controlling organization that could supervise the activities of individual agents and elevate real estate sellers to professional status in the public's mind. Next came the gradual grouping of local boards into state associations, and finally, in 1908, the National Association of Real Estate Boards (NAREB) was formed. In 1914, NAREB developed a model license law that became the basis for real estate license laws in many states.

National Association of Realtors (NAR)

Today the local boards are still the fundamental units of the National Association of Realtors (NAR; the name was changed from NAREB on January 1, 1974). Local board membership is open to anyone holding a real estate license. Called boards of Realtors, real estate boards, and realty boards, they promote fair dealing among their members and with the public, and protect members from dishonest and irresponsible licensees. They also promote legislation that protects property rights, offer short seminars to keep members up to date with current laws and practices, and, in general, do whatever is necessary to build the dignity, stability, and professionalization of the industry. Local boards often operate the local multiple listing service, although in some communities it is a privately owned and operated business.

State associations are composed of the members of local boards plus salesmen and brokers who live in areas where no local board exists. The purposes of the state associations are to unite members statewide, to encourage legislation that benefits and protects the real estate industry and safeguards the public in their real estate transactions, and to promote economic growth and development in the state. Also, state associations hold conventions to educate members and foster contacts among them.

The Texas Association of Realtors (TAR), with over 50,000 members, is the Texas organization of Realtors authorized to use the Realtor emblem. They maintain an active program of continuing education throughout the NAR Institute and its Real Estate Institute. They publish and distribute information on state legislation (material legislation), licensing laws, and professional standards.

Texas Association of Realtors (TAR)

A great deal of information is available through the TAR library of tapes and books. Standardized legal forms are available through the Texas Association of Realtors. The mailing address is

> Texas Association of Realtors
> P.O. Box 14488
> Austin, Texas 78761

The NAR is made up of local boards and state associations in the United States. The term **"Realtor"** is a registered trade name that belongs to NAR. Realtor is not synonymous with real estate agent. It is reserved for the exclusive use of members of the National Association of Realtors, who as part of their membership pledge themselves to abide by the Association's Code of Ethics. The term Realtor cannot be used by nonmembers and in some states the unauthorized use of the term is a violation of the real estate law. Prior to 1974, the use of the term Realtor was primarily reserved for principal brokers. Then in November of that year, by a national membership vote, the decision was made to create an additional membership class, the **Realtor-Associate,** for salespersons working for member Realtors.

Realtor and NAR

The Code of Ethics has been revised several times since it was developed in 1913, and it now contains 23 Articles

Code of Ethics

that pertain to the Realtor's relation to his clients, to other real estate agents, and to the public as a whole. The full Code is reproduced in Figure 18:1.

Although a complete review of each article is beyond the scope of this chapter, it can be seen in the Code that some articles parallel existing laws. For example, Article 10 speaks against racial discrimination and Article 12 speaks for full disclosure. However, the bulk of the Code addresses itself to the obligations of a Realtor that are beyond the written law. For example, in Article 2, the Realtor agrees to keep himself informed regarding laws and regulations, proposed legislation, and current market conditions so that he may be in a position to advise his clients properly. In Article 5, the Realtor agrees to willingly share with other Realtors the lessons of his own experience. In other words, to be recognized as a Realtor, one must not only comply with the letter of the law, but also observe the ethical standards by which the industry operates.

In some states, ethical standards such as those in the NAR Code of Ethics have been legislated into law. Called **canons,** their intent is to promote ethical practices by all brokers and salesmen, not just by those who join the National Association of Realtors. The Texas Real Estate Commission promulgates its own Course of Professional Ethics, set out in Appendix D.

In addition to its emphasis on real estate brokerage, the National Association of Realtors also contains a number of specialized professional groups within itself. These include the American Institute of Real Estate Appraisers, the Farm and Land Institute, the Institute of Real Estate Management, the Realtors National Marketing Institute, the Society of Industrial Realtors, the Real Estate Securities and Syndication Institute, the American Society of Real Estate Counselors, the American Chapter of the International Real Estate Federation, and the Women's Council of Realtors. In each case, membership is open to Realtors interested in these specialties.

Realtist and NAREB   The National Association of Real Estate Brokers (NAREB) is a national trade association representing minority real estate professionals actively engaged in the industry. Founded in

CODE OF ETHICS

Figure 18:1

Preamble . . .

Under all is the land. Upon its wise utilization and widely allocated ownership depend the survival and growth of free institutions and of our civilization. The REALTOR® should recognize that the interests of the nation and its citizens require the highest and best use of the land and the widest distribution of land ownership. They require the creation of adequate housing, the building of functioning cities, the development of productive industries and farms, and the preservation of a healthful environment.

Such interests impose obligations beyond those of ordinary commerce. They impose grave social responsibility and a patriotic duty to which the REALTOR® should dedicate himself, and for which he should be diligent in preparing himself. The REALTOR®, therefore, is zealous to maintain and improve the standards of his calling and shares with his fellow-REALTORS® a common responsibility for its integrity and honor. The term REALTOR® has come to connote competency, fairness, and high integrity resulting from adherence to a lofty ideal of moral conduct in business relations. No inducement of profit and no instruction from clients ever can justify departure from this ideal.

In the interpretation of his obligation, a REALTOR® can take no safer guide than that which has been handed down through the centuries, embodied in the Golden Rule, "Whatsoever ye would that men should do to you, do ye even so to them."

Accepting this standard as his own, every REALTOR® pledges himself to observe its spirit in all of his activities and to conduct his business in accordance with the tenets set forth below.

ARTICLE 1

The REALTOR® should keep himself informed on matters affecting real estate in his community, the state, and nation so that he may be able to contribute responsibly to public thinking on such matters.

ARTICLE 2

In justice to those who place their interests in his care, the REALTOR® should endeavor always to be informed regarding laws, proposed legislation, governmental regulations, public policies, and current market conditions in order to be in a position to advise his clients properly.

ARTICLE 3

It is the duty of the REALTOR® to protect the public against fraud, misrepresentation, and unethical practices in real estate transactions. He should endeavor to eliminate in his community any practices which could be damaging to the public or bring discredit to the real estate profession. The REALTOR® should assist the governmental agency charged with regulating the practices of brokers and salesmen in his state.

ARTICLE 4

The REALTOR® should seek no unfair advantage over other REALTORS® and should conduct his business so as to avoid controversies with other REALTORS®.

ARTICLE 5

In the best interests of society, of his associates, and his own business, the REALTOR® should willingly share with other REALTORS® the lessons of his experience and study for the benefit of the public, and should be loyal to the Board of REALTORS® of his community and active in its work.

ARTICLE 6

To prevent dissension and misunderstanding and to assure better service to the owner, the REALTOR® should urge the exclusive listing of property unless contrary to the best interest of the owner.

ARTICLE 7

In accepting employment as an agent, the REALTOR® pledges himself to protect and promote the interests of the client. This obligation of absolute fidelity to the client's interests is primary, but it does not relieve the REALTOR® of the obligation to treat fairly all parties to the transaction.

Figure 18:1 *continued*

ARTICLE 8

The REALTOR® shall not accept compensation from more than one party, even if permitted by law, without the full knowledge of all parties to the transaction.

ARTICLE 9

The REALTOR® shall avoid exaggeration, misrepresentation, or concealment of pertinent facts. He has an affirmative obligation to discover adverse factors that a reasonably competent and diligent investigation would disclose.

ARTICLE 10

The REALTOR® shall not deny equal professional services to any person for reasons of race, creed, sex, or country of national origin. The REALTOR® shall not be a party to any plan or agreement to discriminate against a person or persons on the basis of race, creed, sex, or country of national origin.

ARTICLE 11

A REALTOR® is expected to provide a level of competent service in keeping with the Standards of Practice in those fields in which the REALTOR® customarily engages.

The REALTOR® shall not undertake to provide specialized professional services concerning a type of property or service that is outside his field of competence unless he engages the assistance of one who is competent on such types of property or service, or unless the facts are fully disclosed to the client. Any person engaged to provide such assistance shall be so identified to the client and his contribution to the assignment should be set forth.

The REALTOR® shall refer to the Standards of Practice of the National Association as to the degree of competence that a client has a right to expect the REALTOR® to possess, taking into consideration the complexity of the problem, the availability of expert assistance, and the opportunities for experience available to the REALTOR®.

ARTICLE 12

The REALTOR® shall not undertake to provide professional services concerning a property or its value where he has a present or contemplated interest unless such interest is specifically disclosed to all affected parties.

ARTICLE 13

The REALTOR® shall not acquire an interest in or buy for himself, any member of his immediate family, his firm or any member thereof, or any entity in which he has a substantial ownership interest, property listed with him, without making the true position known to the listing owner. In selling property owned by himself, or in which he has any interest, the REALTOR® shall reveal the facts of his ownership or interest to the purchaser.

ARTICLE 14

In the event of a controversy between REALTORS® associated with different firms, arising out of their relationship as REALTORS®, the REALTORS® shall submit the dispute to arbitration in accordance with the regulations of their board or boards rather than litigate the matter.

ARTICLE 15

If a REALTOR® is charged with unethical practice or is asked to present evidence in any disciplinary proceeding or investigation, he shall place all pertinent facts before the proper tribunal of the member board or affiliated institute, society, or council of which he is a member.

ARTICLE 16

When acting as agent, the REALTOR® shall not accept any commission, rebate, or profit on expenditures made for his principal-owner, without the principal's knowledge and consent.

Figure 18:1 *continued*

ARTICLE 17

The REALTOR® shall not engage in activities that constitute the unauthorized practice of law and shall recommend that legal counsel be obtained when the interest of any party to the transaction requires it.

ARTICLE 18

The REALTOR® shall keep in a special account in an appropriate financial institution, separated from his own funds, monies coming into his possession in trust for other persons, such as escrows, trust funds, clients' monies, and other like items.

ARTICLE 19

The REALTOR® shall be careful at all times to present a true picture in his advertising and representations to the public. He shall neither advertise without disclosing his name nor permit any person associated with him to use individual names or telephone numbers, unless such person's connection with the REALTOR® is obvious in the advertisement.

ARTICLE 20

The REALTOR®, for the protection of all parties, shall see that financial obligations and commitments regarding real estate transactions are in writing, expressing the exact agreement of the parties. A copy of each agreement shall be furnished to each party upon his signing such agreement.

ARTICLE 21

The REALTOR® shall not engage in any practice or take any action inconsistent with the agency of another REALTOR®.

ARTICLE 22

In the sale of property which is exclusively listed with a REALTOR®, the REALTOR® shall utilize the services of other brokers upon mutually agreed upon terms when it is in the best interests of the client.

Negotiations concerning property which is listed exclusively shall be carried on with the listing broker, not with the owner, except with the consent of the listing broker.

ARTICLE 23

The REALTOR® shall not publicly disparage the business practice of a competitor nor volunteer an opinion of a competitor's transaction. If his opinion is sought and if the REALTOR® deems it appropriate to respond, such opinion shall be rendered with strict professional integrity and courtesy.

The Code of Ethics was adopted in 1913. Amended at the Annual Convention in 1924, 1928, 1950, 1951, 1952, 1955, 1956, 1961, 1962, 1974 and 1982.

1947, its 5,000 members use the trade name **Realtist.** The organization extends through 14 regions across the country with more than 60 active local boards. NAREB education and certification programs include the Real Estate Management Brokers Institute, National Society of Real Estate Appraisers, Real Estate Brokerage Institute, and United Developers Council. The organization's purposes are to promote high standards of service and conduct and to protect the public against unethical, improper or fraudulent real estate practices.

GRI Designation

To help encourage and recognize professionalism in the real estate industry, state Boards of Realtors sponsor education courses leading to the GRI designation. Course offerings typically include real estate law, finance, appraisal, investments, office management, and salesmanship. Upon completion of the prescribed curriculum, the designation, Graduate Realtor's Institute, is awarded.

VOCABULARY REVIEW

Match terms **a–m** *with statements* **1–13.**

a. *Assumed name certificate*	**h.** *Realty board*
b. *Broker*	**i.** *Reciprocity*
c. *Certification fee*	**j.** *Recovery fund*
d. *dba*	**k.** *Respondent*
e. *Real estate commissioner*	**l.** *Revoke*
f. *Real estate salesman*	**m.** *Suspend*
g. *Realtor*	

1. Annual license renewal fee.
2. A person who is licensed to handle real estate transactions for a fee, but who must do so only as the employee of a real estate broker.
3. A copyrighted and registered term owned by the National Association of Realtors for exclusive use by its members.
4. Indicates that an assumed name is being used.
5. An arrangement whereby states honor each other's licenses.
6. A business operated under any name other than the owner's name.
7. An independent agent who negotiates transactions for a fee.
8. A person appointed by the governor to implement and carry out those laws enacted by the state legislature that pertain to real estate.
9. To temporarily make ineffective.
10. To recall and make void.

11. A real estate licensee against whom a complaint has been filed with the real estate commission.
12. A local trade organization for real estate licensees and other persons allied with the real estate industry.
13. A state-operated fund that can be tapped to pay for uncollectible judgments against real estate licensees.

QUESTIONS AND PROBLEMS

1. What was the purpose of early real estate license laws?
2. When is a person required to hold a real estate license?
3. What factors does a broker consider when deciding what percentage of commissions should be paid to the salespersons in his office?
4. A person applying for a Texas salesman's license in 1985 would need how many hours of education?
5. What trends are apparent in Texas with regard to real estate education requirements?
6. In Texas, what requirements must be met to qualify for the GRI designation?
7. What is the name of the person currently serving as real estate administrator for Texas? What are his (her) duties and responsibilities?
8. How is the real estate commission selected in Texas? What are its duties and responsibilities?
9. Under what circumstances are real estate licenses suspended or revoked in Texas?

ADDITIONAL READINGS

Business Opportunities Brokerage by **Edward Bernd.** (Prentice-Hall, 1983, 169 pages). A practical, readable book on what to do when a client asks you to sell a muffler shop, wine and cheese store, country-western lounge, or yarn and knitting shop, and you don't want to turn down the listing because you don't know how.

Design-a-Day. (Page Unlimited, 1–800–368–5045, 1986). This is a three-ring calendar notebook designed for real estate agents. Has daily pages for appointments, expenses, mileage, notes and important reminders. Also has sections for commission records, telephone numbers, loan tables, appraisal checklist and common abbreviations. Published annually.

Digest of Real Estate License Laws. (National Association of Real Estate License Law Officials, 1986, 165 pages). Contains summaries of real estate license laws for each of the United States and the Canadian Provinces. Published annually.

"Price Competition for Residential Brokerage" by **John Crockett.** (*Real Estate Review,* Winter 84, p. 98). Article states that when the commission rate is fixed, the competition among brokerage firms leads to excessive hiring of sales agents who then stay busy by spending significant amounts of time at tasks that add little to the services they produce.

Protecting Your Sales Commission: Professional Liability in Real Estate by **Ronald Friedman** and **Benjamin Henszy.** (Real Estate Education Co., 1982, 280 pages). Book alerts real estate licensees to their professional liability in misrepresentation, conflict of interest, standard of care and fiduciary duties. Also covers broker's right to compensation and what a broker should do if sued.

"The Code of Ethics." (*Real Estate Today,* Feb 85, pp. 46–59). This feature section contains the following articles: "Ethics: The Starting Point of Success," "Wait! Let's Arbitrate," "Complaints: Handle With Care," "The Value of Your Reputation" and "How to Create a Client/Customer Relations Department."

"Unlawful, Unethical or Unbusinesslike?" by **Fred Crane** and **Simon Sykes.** (*First Tuesday,* Nov 83 through June 84). This is an eight-part series on the dividing line between unlawful, unethical, and unbusinesslike behavior, and lawful, ethical, and businesslike behavior for real estate brokers and salespersons.

*   *   *

The following periodicals may also be of interest to you: *Affirmative Action Register, Civil Rights Update, Real Estate Business, Real Estate Perspectives, Real Estate Selling, Real Estate Success Secrets, Real Estate Today* and *Realtor News.*

Condominiums, Cooperatives, PUDs, and Timeshares

Bylaws: rules that govern how an owners' property association will be run

CC&Rs: covenants, conditions and restrictions by which a property owner agrees to abide

Common elements: those parts of a condominium in which each unit owner holds an undivided interest

Condominium: individual ownership of separate portions of a building plus joint ownership of the common elements

Condominium declaration: a document that converts a given parcel of land into a condominium subdivision

Cooperative: land and building owned or leased by a corporation which in turn leases space to its shareholders

Limited common elements: common elements, the use of which is limited to certain owners; for example walls and ceilings between individual units

Planned unit development (PUD): individually owned houses with community ownership of common areas

Proprietary lease: a lease issued by a cooperative corporation to its shareholders

Time-sharing: part ownership of a property coupled with a right to exclusive use of it for a specified number of days per year

HISTORY

The idea of combining community living with community ownership is not new. Two thousand years ago, the Roman Senate passed condominium laws that permitted Roman citizens to own individual dwelling units in multi-unit buildings. This form of ownership resulted because land was scarce and expensive in Rome. After the fall of the Roman Empire, condominium ownership was used in the walled cities of the Middle Ages. However, this was primarily a defensive measure as residing outside the walls was dangerous due to roving bands of raiders. With the stabilization of governments after the Middle Ages, the condominium concept became dormant until the early twentieth century, when the idea was revived in Western Europe in response to land scarcity in cities. From there the concept spread to several Latin American countries and, in 1951, to Puerto Rico.

UNITED STATES
HOUSING LAW

Puerto Rican laws and experience became the basis for the passage by the U.S. Congress in 1961 of Section 234 of the National Housing Act. This section provides a legal model for condominium ownership and makes available FHA mortgage loan insurance on condominium units. Currently, one in four new residences being built in the United States is a condominium. Additionally, many existing apartment buildings are being converted to condominium ownership.

Condominium ownership is not the only legal framework available that combines community living with community ownership, although it is currently the best known. Prior to the enactment of condominium legislation, cooperative ownership of multifamily residential buildings was popular in the United States, particularly in the states of Florida, New York, and Hawaii. A more recent variation is the individually owned house combined with community ownership of common areas in what is called a planned unit development or PUD.

Of the forces responsible for creating the need for condominiums, cooperatives, and PUDs, the most important are land scarcity in desirable areas, continuing escalation in construction costs, disenchantment with the work of maintaining the grounds around a house, and the desire to own rather than rent.

Land-use Efficiency

When constructing single-family houses on separate lots, a builder can usually average four to five houses per acre of land. In a growing number of cities, the sheer physical space necessary to continue building detached houses either does not exist or, if it does, it is a long distance from employment centers or is so expensive as to eliminate all but a small portion of the population from building there. As in ancient Roman times, the solution is to build more dwellings on the same parcel of land. Instead of four or five dwellings, build 25 or 100 on an acre of land. That way not only is the land more efficiently used, but the cost is divided among more owners. From the standpoint of construction costs, the builder does not have the miles of streets, sewers, or utility lines that would be necessary to reach every house in a subdivision. Furthermore, the facts that there are shared walls, that one dwelling unit's ceiling is often another's floor, and that one roof can cover many vertically stacked units can produce savings in construction materials and labor.

For some householders, the lure of "carefree living," wherein such chores as lawn mowing, watering, weeding, snow shoveling, and building maintenance are provided, is the major attraction. For others, it is the security often associated with clustered dwellings or the extensive recreational and social facilities that are not economically possible on a single-dwelling-unit basis. It is commonplace to find swimming pools, recreation halls, tennis and volleyball courts, gymnasiums, and even social directors at some condominium, cooperative, and PUD projects.

Amenities

A large rental apartment project can also produce the same advantages of land and construction economy and amenities. Nevertheless, we cannot overlook the preference of most American households to own rather than rent their dwellings. This preference is typically based on a desire for a savings program, observation of inflation in real estate prices, and advantageous income tax laws that allow owners, but not renters, to deduct property taxes and mortgage interest.

Figure 19:1 illustrates the estate in land created by a condominium, cooperative, and planned unit development and compares each with the estate held by the owner of a house. Notice in Figure 19:1 that the ownership of house A extends from lot line B across to lot line C. Except where limited by zoning or other legal restrictions, the owner of house A has full control over and full right to use the land between his lot lines from the center of the earth to the limits of the sky. Within the law, he can choose how to use his land, what to build on it or add to it, what color to paint his house and garage, how many people and animals will live there, what type of landscaping to have, from whom to purchase property insurance, and so on. The owner of house D has the same control over the land between lot lines C and E.

DIVIDING THE LAND OF AN ESTATE

The owner of A cannot dictate to his neighbor what color to paint his house, what kind of shrubs and trees to grow,

Figure 19:1

COMPARISON OF ESTATES

(Presume fee simple ownership in each case)

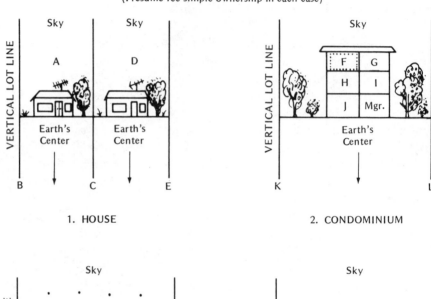

1. HOUSE

2. CONDOMINIUM

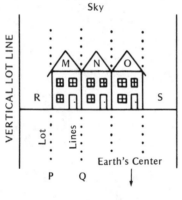

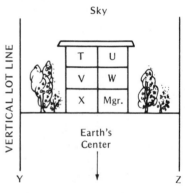

3. TOWNHOUSE

4. COOPERATIVE

or from whom to buy hazard insurance if he buys it at all. (Occasionally, one will find deed restrictions in housing subdivisions that give the owners a limited amount of control over each other's land uses in the subdivision.)

Condominium   In a **condominium,** each dwelling unit owner owns as his fee estate the cubicle of air space that his unit occupies. This is the space lying between the interior surfaces of the unit sides and between the floor and the ceiling. The remainder of the building and the land are called the **common elements** or common areas. Each unit owner holds an undivided interest in the common elements.

In Figure 19:1, the owner of dwelling unit F owns as his separate property the air space enclosed by the dotted lines. Except for the individual unit owners' air spaces, F, G, H, I, and J each owns an undivided interest in everything between lot lines K and L. This includes the land and the shell of the building, plus such things as the manager's apartment, lobby, hallways, stairways, elevators, and recreation facilities. In Texas, the Condominium Act also recognizes **limited common elements.** These are common elements reserved for the use of a certain number of apartments to the exclusion of other apartments, such as special corridors, stairways, elevators, and services common to apartments of a particular floor.

In a **planned unit development** (PUD) each owner owns as his individual property the land that his dwelling unit occupies. For example, the owner of house M in Figure 19:1 owns the land between lot lines P and Q from the center of the earth skyward. A homeowners' association consisting of M, N, and O owns the land at R and S and any improvements thereon, such as recreation facilities or parking lots. The most distinguishing feature of a PUD is the ownership of land by the unit owner. In both condominiums and cooperatives, there is no land attributable to the unit owner.

Planned Unit Development (PUD) Estate

In a **cooperative** there is no individually owned property at all. Rather, the owners hold shares of stock in a cooperative corporation, which, in turn, owns the land and building and issues proprietary leases to the owners to use specific apartments. A **proprietary lease** differs from the usual landlord-tenant lease in that the "tenant" is also an owner of the building. In the cooperative in Figure 19:1, all the land and building lying between lot lines Y and Z are owned by a corporation that is owned by shareholders T, U, V, W, and X. Ownership of the corporation's shares carries the right to occupy apartment units in the building.

Cooperative Estate

Having now briefly illustrated the estates created by the condominium, and PUD forms of real estate ownership, let us take a closer look at their organization, financing, and management.

THE CONDOMINIUM DECLARATION

In Texas, a condominium is created when a person, usually a real estate developer, files a **condominium declaration** with the county clerk that converts a parcel of land held under a single deed into a number of individual condominium estates, plus an estate that includes the common elements. Included in the declaration is a description of the location of each individual unit with respect to the land, identification of the common elements to be shared, and the percentage interest each unit owner will have in the common elements. If the condominium is to be on leasehold land, the declaration converts the single leasehold interest into individual leases or subleases. In Texas a condominium must have at least four units. The right of a person to file a condominium declaration is outlined in the Texas Condominium Act. The declaration can only be amended at a meeting of the unit owners, and at least 67% of the ownership must approve the change.

Owners' Association

In addition to filing the condominium declaration, also known as the **master deed,** the developer must provide a legal framework by which the unit owners can govern themselves. Often, a nonprofit condominium **council of co-owners** or **owners' association** is incorporated, and each unit purchaser automatically becomes a member. The association can also be organized as a trust or unincorporated association. However, in the event of a lawsuit against the association, these may not offer the members the legal protection normally provided by a corporation. The main purpose of the owners' association is to control, regulate, and maintain the common elements.

Finally, the developer must file in the declaration a list of regulations by which anyone purchasing a unit in the condominium must abide. These are known as **covenants, conditions, and restrictions** in the declaration and tell a unit owner such things as what color the exterior of his living room drapes must be and whether or not he can have children or pets living in his apartment. Typically, these also govern such things as when the swimming pool and other recreation facilities will be open for use and when quiet hours will be observed in the building.

Bylaws may also be recorded with the declaration. They provide the rules by which the association's board of directors or executive committee is elected from among the association members and set the standards by which the board must rule. They also set forth how association dues (maintenance fees) will be established and collected, how contracts will be let for maintenance, management, and repair work, and how personnel will be hired.

Bylaws

Each purchaser of a condominium unit receives a deed to his or her unit from the developer. The deed describes the size and location of the unit, both in terms of the unit number in the building and its surveyed airspace. Usually this is done by referring to the parcel map which was filed with the declaration. The deed will also recite the percentage interest in the common elements that the grantee is receiving. The deed is recorded upon closing just as one would record a deed to a house.

Unit Deed

When the owner sells, he has a new deed prepared that describes the unit and the common element interest, and delivers it to the purchaser at closing. If the condominium is on leased land, the developer will deliver a lease (or sublease) to the unit buyer. When he later sells, he assigns that lease to the buyer.

Once the units in the building have been sold and the association turned over to the unit owners, the council of co-owners can change the bylaws. Voting rights are specified in the declaration or the bylaws.

Voting Rules

Votes are weighted in accordance with the bylaws, and three variations are presently in use. The most straightforward method is to give each unit owner one vote. In other associations, the weight of one's vote depends on the percentage of the building he owns. Thus, in a condominium composed of 1,000- and 1,500-square-foot apartments, the owners of the 1,500-square-foot units would have one and one-half times the vote of those with 1,000-square-foot units. In the third variation, the weighting is by the sales price of the unit. The argument for weighted voting is that the bylaws often require the owners of the larger and more expensive units to bear a proportionately larger share of the cost of maintaining the building.

CONDOMINIUM MANAGEMENT

For condominium owners to enjoy maintenance-free living, the association must employ the services of a building manager. If the project contains only a few units, the association may elect to employ one of its members on a part-time basis to take care of the landscaping, hallways, trash, and the like and to keep records of his expenses. For major maintenance items such as painting, roof repairs, and pool refurbishing, independent contractors are hired.

In larger projects, the association can either hire a full-time manager or a professional management firm. A management firm supplies a management package that combines an on-site resident manager plus off-site services, such as accounting for the building's expenses and handling the payroll. The management firm will also contract for gardening, trash hauling, and janitorial services. Each month the firm bills the association for the package of services rendered.

Whether hired directly by the association or by the management firm, the resident manager is usually responsible for enforcing the house rules, handling complaints or problems regarding maintenance, and supervising such matters as the handling of the mail and the use of the swimming pool and recreation areas. The extent of his duties and responsibilities is set by the owners' association. The association should also retain the right to fire the resident manager and the management firm if their services are not satisfactory.

MAINTENANCE FEES

The costs of maintaining the common elements in a condominium are allocated among the unit owners in accordance with percentages set forth in the enabling declaration. These **maintenance fees** or **association dues** are collected monthly. Failure to pay creates a lien against the delinquent owner's unit. The amount collected is based on the association's budget. This in turn is based on the association's estimate of the cost of month-to-month maintenance, insurance, legal counsel, and accounting services, plus reserves for expenses that do not occur monthly.

The importance of setting aside reserves each month is illustrated by the following example. Suppose it is estimated that the exterior of a 100-unit building will have to be painted every 5 years, and that the cost, allowing for inflation, will be $18,000. The association has two choices: the members can either wait until the paint job is needed and then divide the $18,000 cost among the 100 owners, or they can pay a small amount each month into a reserve fund so that in 5 years there will be $18,000 available. The first choice means a special assessment averaging $180 per owner at the time the job needs to be done. The second choice requires an average of $3 per month from each owner for 60 months. If the reserves are kept in an interest-bearing savings account, as they should be, less than $3 per month would need to be collected.

Since condominium law recognizes each condominium dwelling unit as a separate legal ownership, property taxes are assessed on each unit separately. Property taxes are based on the assessed value of the unit, which is based on its market value. As a rule, it is not necessary for the taxing authority to assess and tax the common elements separately. The reason is that the market value of each unit reflects not only the value of the unit itself, but also the value of the fractional ownership in the common elements that accompanies the unit.

PROPERTY TAXES AND INSURANCE

The association is responsible for purchasing hazard and liability insurance covering the common elements. Each dwelling unit owner is responsible for purchasing hazard and liability insurance for the interior of his dwelling. Owners should be cautioned to be sure the association has insurance in force, and in sufficient amounts. If damages exceed the policy coverage in Texas, the unit owners are proportionally liable for the damage.

Thus, if a visitor slips on a banana peel in the lobby or a hallway of the building, the association is responsible. If the accident occurs in an individual's unit, the unit owner is responsible. In a high-rise condominium, if the roof breaks during a heavy rainstorm and floods several apartments below, the association is responsible. If an apartment owner's dishwasher overflows and soaks the apartments below him, he is responsible.

If the condominium unit is being rented, the owner will want to have landlord insurance, and the tenant, for his own protection, will want a tenant's hazard and liability policy.

CONDOMINIUM FINANCING

Because each condominium unit can be separately owned, each can be separately financed. Thus, a condominium purchaser can choose whether or not to borrow against his unit. If he borrows, he can choose a large or small down payment and a long or short amortization period. Once in his unit, if he wants to repay early or refinance, that is his option too. When he sells, the buyer can elect to assume the loan, pay it off, or obtain new financing. In other words, while association bylaws, restrictions, and house rules may regulate how an owner may use his unit, in no way does the association control how a unit may be financed.

Since each unit is a separate ownership, if a lender needs to foreclose against a delinquent borrower in the building, the remaining unit owners are not involved. They are neither responsible for the delinquent borrower's mortgage debt, nor are they parties to the foreclosure.

Loan Terms

Loan terms offered condominium buyers are quite similar to those offered on houses. Typically, lenders will make conventional, uninsured loans for up to 80% of value. With private mortgage insurance, this can be raised to 90% or 95%. On FHA-approved buildings, the FHA will insure up to 97% of the first $25,000 of appraised value, and 95% above that to a maximum loan guarantee of $90,000. Amortization periods typically run 25 to 30 years. Financing can also be in the form of an installment contract or a purchase money mortgage.

When a condominium is being sold by a developer to private buyers for the first time, the usual procedure is for the developer to find a lender who will advance the money the developer needs to build and offer to finance the unit purchasers. As purchasers sign their mortgage papers, the lender is credited on his loan. Although a buyer can still pay cash or obtain his own lender, having a loan package ready for the buyer is a valuable marketing tool.

Deposit Practices

If a project is not already completed and ready for occupancy when it is offered for sale, it is common practice for the developer to require a substantial deposit. The best practice is to place this in an escrow account payable to the developer upon completion. However, some developers use deposits to help pay the expenses of construction while the building is being built. Unfortunately, if such deposits are spent by a developer who goes bankrupt before the project is completed, the buyer receives neither a finished unit nor the return of his deposit. If the deposits are held in escrow, the buyers do not receive a unit but they do get their deposits back.

LEGISLATION AGAINST ABUSES

The legal documents involved in purchasing a house are few in comparison to those involved in purchasing a condominium. Because the master deed, bylaws, and restrictions often total 100 or more pages of legal language, unit purchasers who are not concerned with "details" often do not read them. As a result, in numerous cases developers have buried in these documents the fact that they are retaining substantial rights and title in their projects, even after all the units have been sold.

Two specific areas of abuse have been recreation and management. Some developers retain title to recreation areas and then charge unit owners escalating monthly-use fees that are far more than actual costs. The developer then keeps the difference. If a unit owner protests by refusing to pay, the developer can place a lien against the unit and ultimately have it sold at foreclosure. In the second area of abuse, the fine print appoints the developer as manager of the project for 25 years. When the unit owners find their management fees out of proportion to the level of services received, the developer points out the clause appointing him manager and reminds them that he cannot be fired.

In some instances, developers have used declaration fine print to bury the fact that they are retaining the fee title to the land and that the unit owners are lessees. Thus, not only are unit owners required to pay a lease fee to the developer each month, but they will never own the land beneath them. There is nothing fundamentally wrong with having a condominium on leased land; it is the intentional burying of this fact with the hope that it will not be detected before the sales contracts are signed that creates trouble.

CONDOMINIUM
CONVERSIONS

During the late 1970s the idea of condominium ownership became very popular in the United States. Builders constructed new condominiums at a rapid pace, but not enough to fill demand. Soon enterprising developers found that existing apartment buildings could be converted to condominiums and sold to the waiting public. Compared to new construction, a condominium conversion is often simpler, faster and more profitable for the developer. The procedure involves finding an attractively built existing building that is well-located and has good floor plans. The developer does a facelift on the outside, adds more landscaping, paints the interior, and replaces carpets and appliances. The developer also files the necessary legal paperwork to convert the building and land into condominium units and common elements.

There are, however, some significant problems which have surfaced. One of these is the plight of the tenants who are forced to move out when a building is converted. Initially, they found other rentals available. But as more and more buildings were converted there were progressively more evicted tenants looking for progressively fewer remaining rentals. This caused rents to rise and worked a particular hardship on the elderly and handicapped. Tenants prevailed upon their political representatives, and numerous "protection" laws were passed at state and local levels. Rent control laws were enacted. Developers were required to give tenants more time to move; e.g., 120 days and up to a year in some cases. Some jurisdictions passed laws requiring developers to help tenants find new quarters. Others require developers to set aside 20% of their units at below market prices for the elderly and the handicapped. Some cities require that one-third to one-half of the tenants in a building approve of the conversion before it can proceed. And in a few cities, there have been outright moratoriums on conversions. Interestingly though, it was the real estate market itself that put the brakes on conversions. Rising real estate prices coupled with rising interest rates slowed conversions to a trickle by 1982.

Another potential problem area with condominium conversions, and one that a prospective buyer should be aware of, is that converted buildings are used buildings that were not intended as condominiums when built. As used buildings, there may be considerable deferred maintenance and the building may have thermal insulation suitable to a time when energy costs were lower. If the building was originally built for rental purposes, sound-deadening insulation in the walls, floors and ceilings may be inadequate. Fire protection between units may also be less than satisfactory. In contrast, newly built condominiums must meet current building code requirements regarding thermal and sound insulation, fire-wall construction, and so forth.

Lastly, it is worth noting that not all condominium conversions are carried out by developers. Enterprising tenants have successfully converted their own buildings and saved considerable sums of money. It is not uncommon for the value of a building to double when it is converted to a condominium. Tenants who are willing to hire the legal, architectural, and construction help they need can create valuable condominium homes for themselves in the same building where they were previously renters.

Before we turn our attention from condominiums, let it be reemphasized that a condominium is first and foremost a legal concept. It tells how title to real property is owned. It does not, by itself, tell us what a condominium looks like. Physically, a condominium can take the shape of a two-story garden apartment building, a 20-story tower, row houses, or four or more clustered houses. You will hear them called low-rise and high-rise condominiums, town-homes, garden-rises, walled garden apartments, villas, and cluster housing.

Condominiums are not restricted to residential uses. In recent years, a number of developers across the nation have

PHYSICAL APPEARANCE OF CONDOMINIUMS

built office buildings and sold individual suites to doctors, dentists, and lawyers. The same idea has been applied to shopping centers and industrial space. A condominium does not have to be a new building. Many existing apartment houses have been converted from rental status to condominium ownership with only a few physical changes to the building.

ADVANTAGES OF CONDOMINIUM LIVING

Compared to detached dwellings condominium living offers a number of advantages and some disadvantages. Let's take a look.

On the advantage side, instead of four or five detached dwellings on an acre of land a condominium builder can place 25 or even 100 living units. This spreads the cost of the site among more dwellings and the builder does not have the miles of streets, sewers or utility lines that would be necessary to reach every house in a spread-out subdivision. Furthermore, the use of shared walls and foundations and the fact that one dwelling unit's ceiling is another's floor and that one roof can cover many vertically stacked units can produce savings in construction materials and labor. In central city districts where a single square foot of vacant land can cost $100 or more, only a high-rise condominium can make housing units possible. In the near suburbs where land is somewhat cheaper, a condominium often permits the choice of buying rather than renting.

Other advantages for some are the lure of "carefree living," wherein such chores as lawn mowing, watering, weeding, snow removal and building maintenance are provided. For other people, it is the security often associated with clustered dwellings and nearby neighbors. For many, other advantages include extensive recreational and social facilities that are not economically feasible on a single-dwelling basis. It is commonplace to find swimming pools, recreation halls, tennis and volleyball courts, gymnasiums and even social directors at condominiums.

Lastly, we cannot overlook the psychological and financial advantages of ownership. Many large rental apartment projects produce the same economies of scale and amenities just described. Nonetheless, most Americans prefer to own rather than rent their dwellings. In part, this is the pride of owning something. In part, it comes from a desire for a savings program, the potential for capital appreciation, and income tax laws that favor owners over renters.

A major disadvantage of condominium living is the permanent close proximity of one's neighbors and the extra level of government. In other words, buying into a condominium means buying into a group of people whose lifestyles may differ from yours and whose opinions as to how to run the association will differ from yours. By way of contrast, if you buy a single-family detached house on a lot you will have sole control over the use of it (subject to zoning and legal restrictions). You can choose to remodel or add on. You can choose what color to paint your house and garage, how many people and animals will live there, what type of landscaping to have, from whom to purchase property insurance, whether to rent it out or live in it and so on. Your next door neighbor will have the same rights over his land. You cannot dictate to him what color to paint his house, what kind of shrubs to grow or from whom to buy hazard insurance if he buys it at all.

In a condominium the owners have a considerable degree of control over each other in matters that "overlap" and affect the common good of the association. Moreover, certain decisions must be made as a group, such as what kinds of common element hazard and liability insurance to carry, how much to carry and from whom to purchase it. If there is an outdoor swimming pool, a decision must be made as to what months it should be heated and how warm it should be kept. The group as a whole must decide on how the landscaping is to be maintained, who will do it and how much should be spent. If there is to be security service, again there must be a group decision as to how much, when and who should be hired. If a large truck runs into a unit on the other end of the building, it's an association problem because each owner has an undivided interest in the whole building.

All matters affecting the condominium must be brought to the attention of the board of directors, often by way of a committee. All committee and board positions are filled by

DISADVANTAGES OF CONDOMINIUM LIVING

volunteers from the association. Thus, owning a condominium is not entirely carefree. There will be times when the board of directors will do things differently than an individual owner would like. Another possibility is that there may be a lack of interested and talented people to serve as directors and on committees. Consequently, things that need to be done may go undone, possibly posing a hazard to the association. Sometimes, individual unit owners may be unaware of the management and maintenance requirements for a multi-million dollar building, and they may have hired a management firm that knows (or does) even less.

THINGS TO CHECK BEFORE BUYING

If you are considering the purchase of a condominium unit consider the advantages and disadvantages with care before buying. Also, look closely at the association's finances. The association may not have adequate reserves for painting the building, putting on a new roof, and other upcoming maintenance work. If so, both current owners and prospective buyers will be in for a rude surprise in the form of a special assessment. Check the budget to see if it covers everything adequately and ask about any pending lawsuits against the association that might drain its finances.

If you offer to buy a condominium unit you should make the offer contingent on your reading and approving the articles of incorporation, the CC&Rs, and the bylaws, even though they make boring reading. These are the rules you agree to live by and it's better to read them before committing to buy than after. You may find prohibitions against your pet cat or dog or against renting your unit while you are temporarily transferred overseas. (At the closing the seller must give you a current set of these documents along with the deed and keys to the unit. When you sell, you must give a current set to your buyer.)

Before buying pay special attention to construction quality. Will ongoing maintenance be expensive? Is there deferred maintenance? Ask if the clubhouse and recreation facilities are owned by the association or by the developer who will continue to charge you for their use year after year? Is soundproofing between units adequate or will you hear your neighbor's piano, snoring, and arguments? What is the owner-tenant mix? The most successful condominiums are predominantly owner-occupied rather than renter-occupied. This is because owners usually take more interest and care in their properties. This in turn boosts resale values. The list of things to look for and ask about when buying into a condominium is longer than the space here allows. But bookstores have good books that will help you. However, before moving on, consider the following two recommendations which apply to any purchase of a condominium, cooperative, planned unit development or timeshare. First, keep a balance between your heart and your head. It is easy to be enchanted to the point that you make no further investigation, perhaps because what you would know in advance might sour the deal. Then, after the closing you discover the problems you should have asked about earlier. Second, ask those who have already bought if they would buy again.

Prior to the availability of condominium enabling legislation in the United States, owner-occupied community housing took the form of the cooperative housing corporation. Although the condominium is dominant today, there are still substantial numbers of cooperative apartments in New York City, Miami, Chicago, San Francisco, and Honolulu. They are rarely found in Texas.

COOPERATIVE APARTMENTS

A **cooperative apartment** is organized by forming a non-profit corporation. This is usually done by a developer who is either planning to convert an existing rental building to cooperative ownership or to build a new structure. Sometimes, the tenants in a rental building will organize a cooperative corporation to buy their building from the owner. To raise the funds necessary to pay for the building, the corporation borrows as much as it can by mortgaging the building. The balance is raised by selling shares of stock in the corporation.

The shareholder, or **cooperator,** receives a proprietary lease from the corporation to occupy a certain apartment in the building. The more desirable apartments require the purchase of more shares than the less desirable ones.

The Cooperator

In return for this lease, the cooperator does not pay rent; instead, he agrees to pay to the corporation his share of the cost of maintaining the building and his share of the monthly mortgage payments and annual property taxes. This sharing of expenses is a unique and crucial feature of this form of ownership. If one or more cooperators fail to pay their pro rata share, the remaining cooperators must make up the difference. Suppose that the monthly loan payment on a 10-unit cooperative building is $4,000 and it is shared equally by its 10 cooperators, each contributing $400 per month. If one shareholder fails to contribute his $400, only $3,600 is available for the required payment. If the lender is paid $3,600 rather than $4,000, the loan is delinquent and subject to foreclosure. The lender does not take the position that, since 9 of the 10 cooperators made their payments, nine-tenths of the building is free from foreclosure threat. Therefore, it is the responsibility of the remaining nine to continue making the $4,000 monthly payments or lose the building. They can seek voluntary reimbursement by the tardy cooperator, or, if that does not work, terminate him as a shareholder.

In most cooperative leases written today, shareholder termination is the worst that can happen to a nonpaying cooperator, because under American corporation law a shareholder is not liable for the debts of the corporation. Thus, even if the cooperative corporation owes more than it owns and is in foreclosure or bankruptcy, the shareholders cannot be dunned for deficiency payments. The lender can look only to the value of the corporation's property for recovery of its loan. In view of this, lenders are especially cautious when making loans to cooperatives, and this has made it difficult for cooperatives to raise money. To counteract this situation, the FHA, under Section 213 of the National Housing Act, will insure lenders against losses on loans made to nonprofit housing cooperatives.

Refinancing Methods   Since the entire building serves as collateral for the loan, it is impossible to obtain new financing on an individual apartment unit in a cooperative building. So, if there is to be new mortgage financing, it must be on the entire building. When the original mortgage loan is substantially reduced and/or apartment prices have risen, as evidenced by a rise in the value of shares, this can be a severe handicap if a cooperator wants to sell. To illustrate, suppose that a family buys into a cooperative for $15,000. Several years later the family wants to sell, and is offered $80,000 for its shares. Unlike the purchaser of a house or a condominium who can obtain most of the money he needs by mortgaging the dwelling he is buying, the cooperative purchaser cannot mortgage his unit. Consequently, if the buyer does not have $80,000 in cash, he would be forced to mortgage other assets or seek an unsecured personal loan at an interest rate higher than for regular home mortgage loans.

In an effort to help cooperators obtain financing, New York and California have passed legislation allowing state-regulated lenders to make loans using cooperative stock as collateral. An alternative for institutional lenders is seller financing. If the seller is willing to help the buyer with financing, the shares can be sold on an installment contract.

Board of Directors

How a cooperative will be run is set forth in its articles of incorporation, bylaws, covenants and restrictions, and house rules. The governing body is a board of directors elected by a vote of the cooperators, and voting can either be based on shares held or on a one-vote-per-apartment basis. The board hires the services needed to maintain and operate the building and decides on how cooperative facilities will be used by shareholders. The annual budget and other matters of importance are submitted to all shareholders for a vote. Between shareholder meetings, normally scheduled annually, unhappy cooperators can approach board members and ask that a desired change be made. Or, at election time, they can vote for more sympathetic contenders for board membership or can run for board positions themselves.

Owners' Association

In two very significant areas, the authority of a cooperative owners' association and its board differs from that found in a condominium. First, as the interior of a cooperator's apartment is not his separate property, the association can control how he uses it. This right is based on the principle that the entire building is owned jointly by all cooperators for their mutual benefit. Thus, if a cooperator damages his apartment or is a constant nuisance, his lease can be terminated. As a rule, this requires at least a two-thirds vote of the shareholders and return of the cooperator's investment.

Second, in a cooperative, the owners' association has the right to accept or reject new shareholders and sublessees. (The latter occurs when a shareholder rents his apartment to another.) If there is much turnover in the building, the association will delegate this right to the board. Thus, whenever a shareholder wishes to sell or rent, the transaction is subject to approval by the board. Except in cases of unlawful discrimination, this feature has been upheld by the courts. The legal basis is that cooperators share not only mutual ownership in their building, but also a joint financial responsibility. However, the board cannot be capricious or inconsistent.

From a social standpoint, the right to approve purchasers and renters helps to foster and maintain the economic and social status of residents, which some persons find attractive. It is also a very useful feature when a person wants ownership in an adult-only building or one that excludes pets.

Income Tax Treatment

Although owners of houses and condominium units have always enjoyed deductions for mortgage interest and property taxes on their federal income tax returns, such was not always the case with cooperatives. Originally, cooperators were excluded because it was the corporation, not the shareholder, that was liable for interest and taxes. Now, however, if 80% of a cooperative's income is derived from tenant-owner payments, the individual cooperators may deduct their proportionate share of property taxes and loan interest. If the land or building is leased to the corporation and the fee owner pays the taxes, he is entitled to the deduction, not the cooperators.

Other Cooperative Forms

Most cooperatives are organized as corporations. It is a practical way to take title, select and control management, administer the day-to-day affairs of the cooperative, and at the same time insulate the individual members from direct liability for the obligations of the corporation. It is also possible to form a cooperative as a general or limited partnership, or as a trust arrangement with the cooperators as trust beneficiaries, or as a tenancy in common. None of these has been widely used, primarily because partnerships and trusts do not provide the legal protection of a corporation, and because the tenancy in common idea has now been replaced by the condominium concept.

Low-cost cooperatives can be found in a number of United States cities. Sponsored by the FHA or by the city itself, these cooperatives are subsidized by public tax revenues and provide low- and moderate-income families with an opportunity for home ownership. Leases in these buildings are usually written for only 1 to 3 years and are not automatically renewable by the cooperator. This feature reflects the possibility that public funds may be cut back in the future. Also, when a cooperator sells, he is not permitted to retain any profits made upon resale. Rather, he is restricted to recovering only the money he has actually invested (that is, his down payment, mortgage amortization, and improvements).

As illustrated in Figure 19:1, each owner in a planned unit development (PUD) owns as separate property the land beneath his or her dwelling. In addition, each unit owner is a shareholder in a nonprofit, incorporated owners' association that holds title to the common areas surrounding the dwelling units. The common areas can be as minimal as a few green spaces or might include parks, pools, golf courses, clubhouses, and jogging trails.

PLANNED UNIT DEVELOPMENT

Since each owner in a planned unit development owns his land and dwelling as separate property, presumably he may use and maintain it as he wishes. However, there may be mutual restrictions upon all separately owned lots and dwellings. The right to establish and enforce these restrictions is usually vested in the owners' association. The association can dictate what color an owner can paint his window shutters, how he can landscape the front of his lot, and how many children and pets can reside in his dwelling. Additionally, the association maintains the common areas and governs how these areas shall be used by the residents and their guests.

From a structural standpoint, the dwellings in a residential PUD typically look more like houses than apartment buildings and generally contain more living area than apartment units. Because vertical stacking is limited to one owner, densities are usually limited to eight or ten units per acre. Even though this is twice the density of a typical detached house subdivision, by careful planning, a developer can give each owner the feeling of more spaciousness. One way is by taking advantage of uneven terrain. If a parcel contains some flat land, some hilly land, some land covered with trees, and a running stream, the dwellings can be clustered on the land best suited for building and thus preserve the stream, woods, and steep slopes in their natural state. With a standard subdivision layout the developer would have to remove the groves of trees, fill in the stream, and terrace the slopes, and would still be able to provide homes for only half the number of families.

Such thoughtful planning is not limited to single-family PUDs. Some of the most attractive planned residential developments in the United States combine natural surroundings with detached houses, row houses, clustered houses, apartment buildings, condominiums, and stores for shopping. So skillfully has this been done that residents are far more aware of the project's green vistas and lakes than they are of neighboring buildings. Reston in Virginia and Columbia in Maryland are city-sized examples of the planned unit development concept. A PUD can also consist of just one or two dozen homes on six acres in surburbia.

Comparison   When comparing a PUD to a condominium, note that a condominium is a creature of state statute, whereas a PUD is a creature of local zoning. Typically a PUD is an overlay zoning (that is, a zoning that overlays an existing residential zoning). This allows a developer to increase the dwelling density of one part of his development so long as he leaves another part as open space. Also note that in a condominium the owners own an undivided interest in all the common elements in the project. The owners' association owns nothing but is responsible for seeing that the project is managed properly. In a PUD, the owners' association has title to the common areas. In both the condominium and the planned unit development, membership in the owners' association is automatic upon purchase of a unit in the project.

Resort timesharing is a method of dividing up and selling private occupancy of a living unit at a vacation facility for specified lengths of time each year. The idea started in Europe in the 1960s when groups of people jointly purchased ski resort lodgings and summer vacation villas so each individual owner could enjoy a week or two of exclusive occupancy. U.S. resort developers quickly recognized the market potential of the idea, and in 1969 the first resort timeshare opened in the United States. Since then hotels, motels, condominiums, townhouses, lodges, villas, recreational vehicle parks, campgrounds, houseboats, and even a cruise ship have been time-shared.

RESORT TIMESHARING

Nearly all timeshares fall into one of two legal formats. The first is the **right-to-use** format. This gives the buyer a contractual right to occupy a living unit at a resort property for one week a year for a specific term of 20 to 40 years. The cost for the entire period is paid in advance. At the end of the contract term all of the buyer's possessory rights terminate unless the contract contains a renewal clause or a right to buy. The developer creates these contracts by either buying or leasing a resort property and then selling 50 one-week-a-year right-to-use contracts on each living unit. (The other two weeks of the year are reserved for maintenance). Approximately 30% of the timeshare market is right-to-use.

Right-to-Use

The second format is **fee simple** ownership. Here each timeshare purchaser obtains a fee ownership in the unit purchased. Thus, each purchaser owns the whole property for one week a year in perpetuity. The sale is handled like any sale of real estate. There is a formal closing, a title policy, execution of a mortgage and note, and delivery of a recordable deed that conveys the timeshare interest. A developer offers fee timeshares by either building or buying a resort property and then selling 50 one-week-a-year fee simple slices in each unit, with the remaining two weeks for maintenance. Approximately 70% of the timeshare market is fee simple.

Fee Simple

The initial cost to the buyer-owner of a timeshare week at a U.S. resort is typically $6,000 to $10,000—depending on the quality and location of the resort, the time of year

Timesharing Costs

(low season or high season) and form of ownership (right-to-use is usually less expensive). Additionally, there will be an annual maintenance fee of $140 to $280 per timeshare week. Buyers can purchase two or more timeshare weeks if they want a longer vacation. Some buyers purchase one week in the summer and one week in the winter.

Benefits of Timesharing   The appeal of timesharing to developers is that a resort or condominium complex that can be bought and furnished for $100,000 per unit can, typically, be resold in 50 timeshare slices of $6,000 each; that is, $300,000 a unit. The primary appeal of timesharing to consumers is they have a resort to go to every year at a prepaid price. This is particularly appealing during inflationary times, although the annual maintenance fee can change upwards. There may be certain tax benefits if the timeshare is financed and for property taxes on fee simple timeshares. There may also be appreciation of the timeshare unit if it is in a particularly popular and well-run resort.

Then again, some or all of these benefits may not materialize. First, the lump sum paid for a timeshare week is usually much lower than hotel bills added up year after year. However, the timeshare buyer must pay in full in advance (or finance at interest), whereas the vacationer at a hotel pays only for what is used each year. Also, for timesharing there is a maintenance fee of approximately $20 to $40 per day that goes for clerk and maid service, linen laundry and replacement, structural maintenance and repairs, swimming pool service, hazard and liability insurance, reservations, collections and accounting services, general management, etc.

Second, going to the same resort for the same week every year for the next 30 or 40 years may become wearisome for some people. Yet that is what a timeshare buyer is agreeing to do. And, if the week is unused because of schedule problems the maintenance fee must still be paid. To offset this, two large resort exchange services and several smaller ones and some of the larger timeshare developers help their buyers exchange weeks among their various projects. There is a cost, however, to exchanging. There may be as many as three fees to pay: an initiation fee, an annual membership fee, and a fee when an exchange is made. These can amount to $100 or more for each exchange. Moreover, someone else with an unwanted timeshare week that you do want must also be in the exchange bank and at the right time of the year. Satisfaction is usually achieved in exchanging by being flexible in accepting an exchange. Note too, if you own an off-season week at Lake Conroe, do not count on exchanging it for a peak-season vacation in Hawaii. Exchange banks usually require members to accept periods of equal or lesser popularity.

Third, through 1985 the tax laws allowed deductions for interest expense on financed timeshares and for property taxes on fee timeshares. At the time this book was scheduled to print, however, there were federal tax reform proposals that may eliminate those deductions. Timeshares have occasionally been touted as tax shelter vehicles; however that has already aroused the ire of the Internal Revenue Service.

Fourth, although there have been several reported instances of timeshare appreciation, it is generally agreed in the timeshare industry and by consumer groups that the primary reason to purchase a resort timeshare is to obtain a vacation, not price appreciation. In fact, a timeshare industry rule-of-thumb is that one-third of the retail price of a timeshare unit goes to marketing costs. This acts as a damper on timeshare resale prices and even suggests that a prospective buyer might be able to purchase a timeshare on the resale market for less than from a developer.

Contrasted with the comfort of knowing that as a timeshare owner one has a commitment to long-term resort use, there is the sobering thought of one's commitment to long-term maintenance, repair, refurbishing and management. This is similar to ownership in a condominium, except with ownership split among as many as 50 owners for each unit, does any owner have a large enough stake to want to take an active part in overseeing the management? Often, one result is that management falls to the developer who, having once sold off the project, may no longer have much incentive to oversee things as carefully as during the sales period. At this point the developer can and often does turn the job

Commitment—
Pros and Cons

over to a management firm, but who oversees them to make certain the timeshare owners get good service at a fair price?

TEXAS TIMESHARE ACT

In 1985, the Texas legislature adopted the Texas Timeshare Act. All transaction interests under the Timeshare Act are defined as an interest in land within the meaning of the Texas Real Estate License Act. Therefore all Brokers and Salesmen who market timeshares must be licensed, unless they are otherwise exempt from licensure under the Real Estate License Act. The Timeshare Act further requires that all timeshare properties must be registered with the Texas Real Estate Commission before they can be offered for sale, although a developer can accept a reservation request from a prospective purchaser if the reservation deposit is placed in an escrow account which is fully refundable at any time at the request of the purchaser. A timeshare registration requires extensive disclosures to the Commission. The Commission has the power to investigate all aspects of the development and to suspend the registration (stopping sales) for any violation of the Timeshare Act.

The Timeshare Act also requires three sets of disclosures to the prospective purchaser. The first set of disclosures must be made prior to the use of any promotion and advertising. The second set of disclosures must be made to the prospective purchaser prior to the signing of any agreement or contract. The third set of disclosures must be made to prospective purchasers prior to the signing of any agreement or contract to participate in any exchange program.

Prior to the signing of any agreement or contract to acquire a timeshare interest in which a prospective purchaser is also offered participation in any exchange program, the developer shall also deliver to the prospective purchaser the exchange disclosure statement of any exchange company whose service is advertised or offered by the developer or other person in connection with the disposition. If participation in an exchange program is offered for the first time after a disposition has occurred, any person offering such participation shall also deliver an exchange disclosure statement to the purchaser prior to the execution by the purchaser of any instrument relating to participation in the exchange program.

In all cases, the person offering such participation shall obtain from the purchaser a written acknowledgment of receipt of the exchange disclosure statement. The exchange disclosure statement shall include the following information:

(1) the name and address of the exchange company;

(2) if the exchange company is not the developer, a statement describing the legal relationship, if any, between the exchange company and the developer;

(3) a statement indicating the conditions under which the exchange program might terminate or become unavailable;

(4) whether membership or participation or both in the exchange program is voluntary or mandatory;

(5) a complete description of the required procedure for executing an exchange of timeshare periods;

(6) the fee required for membership or participation or both in the program and whether such fee is subject to change;

(7) a statement to the effect that participation in the exchange program is conditioned upon compliance with the terms of a contract between the exchange company and the purchaser;

(8) a statement in conspicuous and bold-faced print to the effect that all exchanges are arranged on a space-available basis and that neither the developer nor the exchange company guarantees that a particular timeshare period can be exchanged; and

(9) a description of seasonal demand and unit occupancy restrictions employed in the exchange program.

All disclosure statements require that the developer obtain written acknowledgment of their receipt from the purchaser.

The Timeshare Act also gives the purchaser who has not visited the timeshare unit a right to cancel the contract to purchase the Timeshare interest before the fourth day after the date the contract is executed. The right to cancel must be stated in the contract in bold face, conspicuous print that is larger than the print in the remaining text of the contract. This statement disclaiming the prospective purchaser's right to cancel must be placed immediately prior to the space reserved for the purchaser's signature.

The Timeshare Act has specific provisions applicable to exchange programs, handling of escrow accounts, penalties for violation, and insurance requirements. The Act is new, and, in many areas, is rather vague. The expansion of time-share interest in Texas, however, is going to make this new statute the subject of many controversies.

VOCABULARY REVIEW

Match terms **a–t** *with statements* **1–20.**

a. *Annual meeting*	**k.** *House rules*
b. *Board of directors*	**l.** *Maintenance fees*
c. *Bylaws*	**m.** *Management company*
d. *CC&Rs*	**n.** *Owners' association*
e. *Common elements*	**o.** *Proprietary lease*
f. *Condominium*	**p.** *PUD*
g. *Condominium act*	**q.** *Reserves*
h. *Condominium subdivision*	**r.** *Right-to-use*
i. *Cooperative*	**s.** *Separate property*
j. *Cooperator*	**t.** *Timesharing*

1. Individual ownership of the air space and the building unit it occupies in a multi-unit building, plus undivided ownership of the common elements.
2. Ownership by a corporation which in turn leases space to its shareholders.
3. Roof, stairs, elevator, lobby, etc., in a condominium.
4. An organization composed of unit owners in which membership is automatic upon purchase of a unit.
5. Type of lease issued by a cooperative corporation to its shareholders.
6. A document that converts a parcel of land into a stratified subdivision; also called a master deed.
7. Rules that govern how the owners' association will be run.
8. A shareholder in a cooperative apartment.
9. Charges levied against unit owners to cover the costs of maintaining the common areas. Also called association dues.
10. Form of community ownership where the houses and lots are privately owned but title to common areas is held by an owners' association.
11. State legislation which creates the legal framework for condominium subdivisions.
12. That portion of a condominium that is the exclusive property of an individual unit owner.
13. Covenants, conditions, and restrictions by which an owner must abide.
14. Rules for the use of the swimming pool and recreation facilities would be found here.
15. A governing body elected by association members.

16. A once-a-year business meeting of the entire association member-ship.
17. Whoever advises the board of directors and takes care of day-to-day tasks.
18. The exclusive use of a property for a specified number of days each year.
19. A contractual right to occupy a living unit at a timeshare resort.
20. Money set aside from the budget for expenses that do not occur every month.

QUESTIONS AND PROBLEMS

1. Why are condominiums a popular alternative to single-family houses?
2. Who owns the land in a fee simple condominium project? In a cooperative?
3. What is the key difference between a proprietary lease in a cooperative and a landlord-tenant lease?
4. What is the purpose of the master deed in a condominium project?
5. To whom does the wall between two condominium units belong?
6. What are CC&Rs and what is their purpose?
7. What are maintenance fees? What happens if they are not paid?
8. If the owners' association carries hazard and liability insurance, why is it also advisable for each unit owner to purchase a hazard and liability policy?
9. Briefly explain the concept of right-to-use and fee simple timesharing.
10. Briefly explain how title to land in a PUD is held.

ADDITIONAL READINGS

Condominium Development Guide, rev. ed. by **Keith Romney** and **Brad Romney.** (Warren, Gorham and Lamont, 1983, 896 pages). Lengthy, legal, readable, practical, and detailed. This is the type of information one needs before developing a condominium. Contains procedures, analysis and forms. Annual updates issued.

Condominium Contract Stresses Full Disclosure (*Chipman*) Explanation of a standardized condominium sales contract (1984).

"The Condominium: A Home For All Seasons." (*Real Estate Today,* Feb 85, pp. 10–28). This feature section contains these articles: "Condoeconomics," "Condominium Housing: A Bright Future Ahead," and "Farming Condo Resales."

The Condominium and Cooperative Apartment Buyer's Guide by **David Kennedy.** (Wiley & Sons, 1983, 314 pages). This is a consumer's guide that includes what to look for, what questions to ask, rights and responsibilities of owners, tax considerations, using a broker, conversions and tips on buying and selling.

A Guide for Condo Buyers (*Harris*). Condominium ownership is accompanied by a special set of rights and obligations (1981).

Real Estate Broker's Guide to Resort Time Sharing by **Richard Lynge** and **Keith Trowbridge.** (Real Estate Education Co., 1984, 262 pages). Book explains the field to anyone considering joining a timeshare sales program. Explains broker developer relationship, resort quality, sales methods, commissions and management procedures.

"Same Time, Same Place, Next Year." (*Consumer Reports,* Aug 84, p. 464). Explains timesharing and swapping timeshares plus economics and pitfalls of timesharing. This magazine frequently has consumer-oriented articles on real estate.

Texas Real Estate Law, 4th ed. by **Charles J. Jacobus.** (Reston, 1985, 560 pages). Provides up-to-date explanations of law pertinent to the daily operation of a real estate brokerage office in Texas. See Chapter 17 on Condominiums and Co-operatives.

The Owner's and Manager's Guide to Condominium Management, rev. ed. (Institute of Real Estate Management, 1984, 323 pages). Readable and helpful for condominium purchasers and the board of directors. Discusses the government, management and human relations that are part of condominium living. Coverage includes association meetings, building maintenance, legal liability, budgeting and taxes.

*　　*　　*

The following periodicals may also be of interest to you: *Community Management Report, Condominium Comment, Resort Management, Resort Timesharing Today* and *Timesharing Law Reporter Briefs.*

Property Insurance

All-risks policy: all perils, except those excluded in writing, are covered

Broad-form: an insurance term that describes a homeowner's policy that covers a large number of named perils

Endorsement: a policy modification; also called a rider or an attachment

Homeowner policy: a combined property and liability policy designed for residential use

Insurance premium: the amount of money one must pay for insurance coverage

Perils: hazards or risks

Public liability: the financial responsibility one has toward others

PERILS OR RISKS TO PROPERTY

As an owner of real estate, the owner must take the risk that his property may be damaged due to fire or other catastrophe. Additionally there is the possibility that someone may injure himself while on the property and hold the owner responsible. Insurance to cover losses from either of these sources is available.

The basic property damage policy is the New York fire form developed by the New York State Legislature and now used throughout the United States. Its 165 lines of court-tested language cover (1) loss by fire, (2) loss by lightning, and (3) losses sustained while removing property from an endangered premises. Coverage can be on real property improvements, personal property, or both. Let us briefly discuss these **perils** (also called hazards or risks).

PROPERTY DAMAGE BY CATASTROPHES

To be covered for loss by fire, there must be flames. Smoke or heat damage or damage by explosion, no matter how severe, does not qualify unless preceded by flames. Also, the fire must be hostile as opposed to friendly. A hostile fire is a fire burning where it is not intended. A friendly fire is a fire burning in a place designed for it, such as a furnace, fireplace, gas stove, or water heater. However, if a friendly fire gets out of control, it is then classed as hostile and resulting losses are covered. Insurers are required to pay whether the fire was purely accidental or the result of negligence by the insured or some other person. For example, suppose that you have a fire in the fireplace of your home and do not bother to close the fireplace screen. If, while you have left the room, the fire throws out a live ember onto a rug and starts a fire, you are covered even though you were negligent in not closing the screen. However, if the insured intentionally starts a hostile fire, the insurer is excused from paying for the damage.

Damage caused by lightning is covered whether or not an actual fire develops. However, man-made electrical discharges are not covered. For example, melted wires caused by an electrical short circuit are not covered unless the cause was lightning or a fire on the premises.

To encourage the removal of personal property from an endangered building, the New York form also covers certain types of loss or damage resulting from removal and storage elsewhere. Coverage is good for 5 days at a new location, after which a new policy must be obtained.

Endorsements   Although fire is the single most important cause of property damage in the United States, property is also exposed to many other perils, including hail, tornado, earthquake, riot, windstorm, smoke damage, explosion, glass breakage, waterpipe leaks, vandalism, freezing, and building collapse. Coverage for each peril can be purchased with a separate policy or it can be added to the fire form as an **endorsement.** An endorsement, also called a **rider** or **attachment,** is an agreement by the insurer to extend coverage to losses by perils not included in the basic policy. Using endorsements, a policyholder can create a single policy that covers only the perils he is exposed to and not pay for coverage he does not need. The amount of money the policyholder pays for coverage is called the **insurance premium.**

PUBLIC LIABILITY   **Public liability** is the financial responsibility one has toward others as a result of one's actions or failure to take action. For example, if you are trimming the limbs from a tall tree in your backyard and a limb falls on your neighbor's roof and damages it, you are liable to your neighbor for damages. Or, if you have a swimming pool in your backyard and a neighbor child drowns in it, the child's parents may be able to successfully sue you for money damages.

Generally, you are liable when there exists a legal duty to exercise reasonable care and you fail to do so, thereby causing injury to an innocent party. Even though you did not intend for the limb to fall on your neighbor's roof or the child to drown in your pool, you are not excused from liability. You can be held accountable, in money, for the amount of damage caused.

HOMEOWNER PACKAGE POLICIES

For major commercial and industrial property owners and users, carefully identifying each risk exposure and then insuring for it is a logical and economic approach to purchasing insurance. But for the majority of homeowners, owners of small apartment and business properties, and their tenants, purchasing insurance piecemeal is a confusing process. As a result, package policies have been developed for owners and tenants of specific kinds of properties.

Of these, the best known and most widely used is the **homeowner's package policy,** which contains the coverages deemed by insurance experts to be most useful to persons who own or rent the home in which they live. Not only does this approach avoid overlaps and lessen the opportunity for gaps in coverage, but the cost is less than purchasing separate, individual policies with the same total coverage. Moreover, homeowner policies go beyond covering only damage and public liability directly connected with the insured property. They also include coverage for theft of the insured's real and personal property and public liability arising from the personal activities of the insured. Let us take a closer look.

Policy Formats

There are standardized homeowner policy forms promulgated for use in Texas by the State Board of Insurance. The basic conditions of the policy are contained in the Texas Standard Homeowner's Policy form. The forms defining specific coverage are added to the basic conditions. (They will be reviewed later in this text.) Each of these added forms contains two sections. **Section I** deals with property insurance and includes a standard fire policy with a wide variety of endorsements, plus a theft policy. Buildings and their contents and, to a certain extent, personal property when it is taken off the insured premises are covered. **Section II** deals with liability on the premises, plus personal liability.

Form HO-A

Form HO-A covers damage and loss to buildings and contents caused by such perils as fire, lightning, hail, windstorm, explosion, riot, smoke, vandalism, theft, sonic boom, falling objects, weight of ice, snow, or sleet, building cracking or collapse, accidental plumbing leakage or overflow, freezing of pipes, artificial electrical discharge, and hot-water-system malfunction.

Major HO-A exclusions are loss or damage caused by an enemy attack, insurrection, rebellion, revolution, civil war, or usurped power. As a group, these exceptions are sometimes referred to as a **war clause exemption.** Also excluded are the perils of earthquake, flood, landslide, mudflow, tidal waves, or underground seepage. If a property owner expects to be exposed to these perils, he must buy additional insurance. With regard to theft, major exceptions to coverage are motorized vehicles, business property, and animals. These require separate policies or endorsements.

Section II of the policy includes liability insurance, medical payments coverage for injuries to others, and insurance for physical damage to the property of others. This section covers such incidents as a homeowner's tree falling onto a neighbor's house, the family dog biting a visitor, a guest slipping on a freshly waxed kitchen floor, and the insured or the insured's child kicking a football through someone's window. Not covered is damage to, or damage caused by the homeowner's automobile.

HO-B

Homeowner **Form HO-B** is a homeowner policy that provides all risk coverage for the dwelling and named-peril coverage on the contents.

HO-C

Form HO-C covers more perils to the building structure than HO-A and is sometimes referred to as an **all-risks** policy for both dwelling and contents. However, property damage by flood, earthquake, war, termites, rodents, wear and tear, marring and scratching, rust, mold, and contamination (nuclear, for example) are still excluded. The difference between an all-risks policy and a **named-peril** policy, such as HO-A or HO-B, is that in a named-peril policy each peril must be named in the policy in order to be covered. In an all-risks policy, all perils except those excluded are covered. The term **broad-form** is used to describe policies that cover a large number of named perils.

Forms **HO-B-Tenant,** and **HO-C-Tenant,** often referred to as a **tenant's policy,** provides the same coverages as HO-B and HO-C except that there is no coverage on building structures. It is designed for the personal property of renters.

Tenant's Policies

Form **HO-C-Con-1** is designed for condominium and cooperative owners where the owners' association carries property damage and public liability insurance on the common elements. This form covers the same perils as the tenant's form, but increases the additional living expense limit and puts addition and alteration coverage on a replacement cost basis with a maximum recovery of $1,000. Endorsements can be added to increase these coverages, cover appurtenant structures on the premises that are solely owned by the insured, and pay for special assessments levied against the policyholder for uninsured property or liability losses of the association.

Condominium and Cooperative Policies

Section II in all home insurance forms is a liability policy for you and all family members who live with you. This coverage is designed to protect you from a financially crippling claim or lawsuit. The falling limb and freshly waxed floor examples mentioned earlier in this chapter are events that would be covered by this coverage. If a liability claim arises, the insurance company will pay the legal costs of defending you as well as any damages up to the limits of the policy. Note that this section also provides you and your family with liability protection away from your premises. Thus, if you accidentally hit someone with a golf ball on a golf course

Liability Coverage

or your child accidentally kicks a football through a neighbor's window, this part of the policy covers you. If you have a pet who takes a bite out of a visitor to your home or out of a neighbor's leg while you are walking that pet, you are covered.

Medical Payments

The cost of treating minor injuries for which you may be liable is paid by **medical payments coverage** found in home insurance policies. The main difference between this and liability coverage is that medical payments coverage provides payment regardless of who is at fault. However, it covers only relatively minor injuries, say $500 or $1,000. Major injuries would come under the liability coverage. The liability and medical payments coverage in a home insurance policy do not apply to your motor vehicles nor to your business pursuits. Those require separate policies. Additionally, your home insurance policy does not cover injuries to you or your family. Those must be insured separately.

Endorsements

Any home policy can be endorsed for additional coverage. For example, **inflation guard** endorsements are available that automatically increase property damage coverage by $1\frac{1}{2}\%$, 2% or $2\frac{1}{2}\%$ per quarter, as selected by the insured. Another popular endorsement is **worker's compensation** insurance. This is designed to pay for injuries suffered by persons employed by the insured to do work on the premises, such as babysitters and cleaning help. If the property is to be rented out, tenant coverage can be added. Alternatively, a policy specifically designed for rental property can be purchased.

NEW FOR OLD

A special problem in recovering for damages to a building is that, although the building may not be new, any repairs are new made. For example, if a 20-year-old house burns to the ground, it is absurd to think we can put back a used house, even though a used house is exactly what the insured lost. Thus, the question is whether insurance should pay for the full cost of fixing the damage, in effect replace "new for old," or simply pay the actual cash value of the loss. **Actual cash value** is the new price minus accumulated depreciation and is, in effect, "old for old." Under "old for old," if the owner rebuilds, he pays the difference between actual cash value and the cost of the repairs. As this can be quite costly to the insured, the alternative is to purchase a policy that replaces "new for old."

For the owner of an apartment building, store, or other property operated on a business basis, obtaining "new for old" coverage is a matter of substituting the term "replacement cost" for "actual cash value" wherever it appears in the policy. Also, the policyholder must agree to carry coverage amounting to at least 80% of current replacement cost and to use the insurance proceeds to repair or replace the damaged property within a reasonable time. Most Texas underwriters require a "new for old" policy.

Under a homeowner's policy, if the amount of insurance carried is 80% or more of the cost to replace the house today, the full cost of repair will be paid by the insurer, up to the face amount of the policy. If the face amount is less than 80% of replacement costs, the insured is entitled to the higher of (1) the actual cash value of the loss or (2) the amount calculated as follows:

$$\frac{\text{Insurance carried}}{\left(\begin{array}{c}80\% \text{ of today's cost} \\ \text{to replace whole structure}\end{array}\right)} \times \left(\begin{array}{c}\text{Today's cost to replace} \\ \text{the damaged portion}\end{array}\right) = \text{Recovery}$$

LENDER REQUIREMENTS

Real estate lenders such as savings and loans, banks, mortgage companies, etc., require that a borrower carry fire and extended coverage on the mortgaged structures. The reason, of course, is to protect the value of the security for the loan. The lender will be named on the policy along with the property owner, and any checks from the insurance company for damages will be made out to the borrower and the lender jointly. Note that the lender does not require liability and medical payments coverage since as the lender he is not concerned with that aspect of the borrower's exposure. Nonetheless, most borrowers will choose a homeowner policy that has Section I coverage satisfactory to the lender rather than fire and extended coverage only.

The borrower must have a policy that meets the lender's requirements before the loan is made and must keep the policy in force at all times while the loan is outstanding. Some lenders collect one-twelfth of the annual premium each month and forward the money to the insurer annually. Other lenders allow the homeowner to maintain the policy so long as he mails proof of the policy to the lender each year. The lender on a condominium unit will require proof that the condominium association carries insurance on the common elements.

Guaranteed Replacement Cost

Because of the nearly constant increase in the cost of construction over the past several decades, lenders require either a replacement cost policy that guarantees adequate money to rebuild the entire structure at today's costs or coverage for the full amount of the loan. (The land is not insured as it is assumed it will survive any damage to the structures upon it.) The borrower, for peace of mind, will choose replacement cost coverage. This is especially true where the loan is less than the cost of replacement.

It is difficult to overemphasize the need for a policy review every one to three years. (The insurance agent will do this on request as part of the policy service.) Many a sad tale has been told by a homeowner who bought 20 years ago, has dutifully paid the insurance premium every year, has not revised the coverage to reflect current construction costs, and then has a major loss. Caution is also advised when a seller carries back financing or an individual buys mortgages as investments. If you fall into this category, make certain that any structures on the property serving as collateral are adequately insured so that if the structures are destroyed, there will be enough insurance money to fully pay you off. Also make certain you are named on the policy as a lender and that the borrower renews the policy each year.

FLOOD INSURANCE

In 1968 Congress created the National Flood Insurance Program. This program is a joint effort by the nation's insurance industry and the Federal Insurance Administration to offer property owners coverage for losses to real and personal property resulting from the inundation of normally dry areas from (1) the overflow of inland or tidal waters, (2) the unusual and rapid accumulation or runoff of surface waters, (3) mudslides resulting from accumulations of water on or under the ground, and (4) erosion losses caused by abnormal water runoff.

Pursuant to the Flood Control Act of 1973, federally regulated lenders are not permitted to finance property in federally-designated flood-prone areas without flood insurance. Flood insurance for all types of structures and their contents is available through private insurance agents.

A property damage or public liability policy can be canceled by the insured at any time. Since the policy is billed in advance, the insured is entitled to a refund for any unused coverage. This is computed at short rates, which are somewhat higher than a simple pro rata charge. For example, the holder of a 1-year policy who cancels one-third of the way through the year is charged 44% of the 1-year price, not $33\frac{1}{3}$%.

POLICY CANCELLATION

The insurer also has the right to cancel a policy. However, unlike the policyholder, who can cancel on immediate notice, the Texas form requires the insurer to give the policyholder 10-day notice. Also, the cost of the policy, and hence the refund of unused premium, must be calculated on a pro rata basis. For example, the insured would be charged one-half the annual premium for 6 months of coverage.

If a property is rented, the landlord should make certain that adequate property damage and liability coverage is purchased. If a loan is involved, the lender will require property damage coverage for the amount of the loan. But the lender is not concerned with liability over and above the loan amount nor if someone is injured on your property and holds you liable. Landlord coverage can be obtained by endorsement to an existing homeowner policy or by purchasing a landlord package policy that combines property damage, liability, medical expenses and loss of rents. The latter pays you what you would normally collect in rent when damage is severe enough that the tenant has to move out while repairs are made.

LANDLORD POLICIES

An insurance company cannot cancel a policy if it has been in effect for ninety days. Certain acts of the policyholder,

Policy Suspension

however, may cancel his coverage without the necessity of a written notice from the insurer. Cancellation can occur if the insured allows the hazard exposure to the insurer to increase beyond the risks normally associated with the type of property being insured, for example, converting a dwelling to a restaurant. Cancellation may also occur if the insured fails to make the premium payments, or if there is a determination by the State Board of Insurance that the policy violates the insurance code.

Willful concealment or misrepresentation by the insured of any material fact or circumstance concerning the policy, the property, or the insured, either before or after a loss, makes the policy void. Thus, if a person operates a business in the basement of his house and conceals this from the insurer for fear of being charged more for insurance, the money he pays for insurance could be wasted.

Oftentimes in a real estate transaction the buyer will ask to assume the seller's existing insurance policy for the property. This way the buyer avoids having to pay a full year's premium in advance and the seller benefits by avoiding a short-rate cancellation charge. To avoid a break in coverage, the insurer must accept the buyer as the new policyholder before the closing takes place. This is done with an endorsement issued by the insurer naming the buyer as the insured party. The reason for this requirement is that an insurance policy does not protect the property, but the insured's financial interest in the property. This is called an **insurable interest.**

Suppose the property is destroyed by fire immediately after the closing. Once title has passed, the seller no longer has an insurable interest in the property. If the insurance company has not endorsed the policy over to the buyer, the company is under no obligation to pay for the damage. If there is doubt that the endorsement to the buyer can be obtained in time for the closing, the buyer should purchase a new policy in his/her own name.

Note that anyone holding a mortgage on an improved property has an insurable interest and should require the borrower to carry a policy that names both the borrower and lender as insured parties. This is a standard requirement of institutional lenders.

A long-standing concern of home buyers has been the possibility of finding structural or mechanical defects in a home after buying it. In new homes, the builder can usually be held responsible for repairs, and in many states he is required to give a 1-year warranty of his product. Additional protection is available from builders associated with the Home Owners Warranty Corporation (HOW). Under this program, the builder warrants against defects caused by faulty workmanship or materials for the first year and against defects in wiring, piping, ductwork and major structural defects in the second year. If the builder cannot or will not honor this warranty, the HOW program underwriter will do so. Then for 8 more years, the underwriter directly insures the home buyer against major structural defects.

In a growing number of cities, the purchaser of a used house can obtain a warranty for 12 to 18 months to cover most things that can go wrong. Available through real estate brokers, this coverage is sold through two plans. Under one plan, the insurer makes an inspection of the home and issues a policy covering all defects not identified by the inspection. Under the second plan, there is no inspection. However, a participating broker must agree to insure all homes he sells.

Ongoing insurance is also available to homeowners. For an annual fee of approximately $250, the insurer will repair or replace defective systems in previously-owned homes, including electrical, plumbing, heating, air conditioning, built-in appliances, and structural components.

HOME BUYER'S INSURANCE

VOCABULARY REVIEW

Match terms **a–k** *with statements* **1–11.**

a. *Actual cash value*   **g.** *Perils*
b. *Friendly fire*   **h.** *Premium*
c. *Homeowner's policy*   **i.** *Replacement cost*
d. *Hostile fire*   **j.** *Tenant's policy*
e. *Inflation guard*   **k.** *War clause*
f. *Liability*

1. A fire that is burning in a place intended for it.
2. A fire that is burning in a place not intended for it.
3. A policy endorsement that automatically increases the amount of insurance coverage periodically during the life of the policy.
4. Also called hazards or risks.
5. Words inserted in an insurance policy to limit the extent of coverage for damages caused by warfare, insurrection, etc.
6. A combined property and liability policy designed for persons who do not own the dwelling in which they live.
7. Current cost of replacing damaged property less depreciation; in effect, "old for old."
8. Cost of replacing damaged property at current prices; in effect, "new for old."
9. A combined property and liability policy designed for residential owner-occupants.
10. The financial responsibility one has toward others.
11. The amount of money paid for insurance coverage.

QUESTIONS AND PROBLEMS

1. Do fire policies cover losses caused by negligence? Losses intentionally caused by the insured?
2. What role does an endorsement or rider play in an insurance policy?
3. What is the purpose of public liability insurance?
4. In a homeowner's policy, what type of loss does Section I deal with? Section II?
5. How do all-risk insurance policies differ from broad-form policies?
6. What does the phrase "new for old" refer to when talking about insurance policies that cover property damage?
7. Why will an insurer suspend coverage if a property is left vacant too long?

ADDITIONAL READINGS

"Choosing Tenant or Condo Coverage" by **Richard Lynch.** (*Money*, July 84, p. 127). Covers finding and buying the right policy to protect you and your possessions as a tenant or condominium owner. Discusses policy costs, coverage, perils, exclusions and personal liability.

"Guarding the Lender's Interest" by **Richard Clarke.** (*Mortgage Banking,* Feb 84, p. 37). Mortgage lenders require hazard insurance on property used as collateral. This article explains the how and why of policies that meet this requirement.

"Homeowners Insurance." (*Consumer Reports,* Aug 85, p. 473). This excellent 10-page article explains homeowner policies, what they cover and how much they cost. Includes ratings of 23 insurance companies as to accessibility, courtesy, claim handling, speed of payment and customer satisfaction.

Insurance Principles and Practices, 2nd ed. by **F. G. Crane.** (Wiley, 1984, 550 pages). A very readable survey of risk and insurance from a consumer's viewpoint. Includes insurance for the homeowner.

"People and Property: Destruction Clauses Revisited" by **Emmanuel Halper.** (*Real Estate Review,* Winter 84, p. 78 and Spring 84, p. 58). This is a delightfully humorous two-part article that deals with the serious business of insurance and property destruction as it pertains to shopping center leases.

*   *   *

The following general interest periodicals may be of interest to you: *Architectural Digest, Better Homes and Gardens, Home and Garden, Homeowner* and *Sunset.*

Building codes: local and state laws that set minimum construction standards

Certificate of occupancy: a government issued document that states a structure meets local zoning and building code requirements and is ready for use

Downzoning: rezoning of land from a higher density use to a lower density use

Environmental impact statement: a report that contains information regarding the effect of a proposed project on the environment of an area

Land-use control: any legal restriction that controls how a parcel of land may be used

Nonconforming use: an improvement that is inconsistent with current land use zoning regulations

Restrictive covenants: clauses placed in deeds to control how future landowners may or may not use the property; also used in leases

Variance: a permit granted to an individual property owner to vary slightly from strict compliance with the local zoning requirements

Zoning: public regulations that control the specific use of land in a given district

KEY TERMS

Land-use control is a broad term that describes any legal restriction that controls how a parcel of land may be used. Land-use controls can be divided by origin into two broad categories: public controls and private controls. Examples of public controls are zoning, building codes, subdivision regulations and master plans. Private controls come in the form of deed restrictions.

No other aspect of land-use control affects the American public to a greater degree than **zoning.** Since the first zoning law went into effect in 1916 in New York City, nearly every town and city in the United States, plus a large number of counties, has adopted zoning ordinances. (The original purpose for adopting zoning in New York City was to keep the expanding garment industry out of the fashionable Fifth

ZONING

Avenue business and residential areas.) Zoning laws divide land into zones (districts) and within each zone regulate the purpose for which buildings may be constructed, the height and bulk of the buildings, the area of the lot that they may occupy, and the number of persons that they can accommodate. Through zoning, a community can protect existing land users from encroachment by undesirable uses, ensure that future land uses in the community will be compatible with each other, and control development so that each parcel of land will be adequately serviced by streets, sanitary and storm sewers, schools, parks, and utilities.

The authority to control land use is derived from the basic police power each state has in order to protect the public health, safety, morals, and general welfare of its citizens. Through an enabling act passed by the Texas legislature, the authority to control land use is also given to individual towns, cities, and counties. These local government units then pass zoning ordinances that establish the boundaries of the various land-use zones and determine the type of development that will be permitted in each of them according to a comprehensive plan. By going to his local government offices, a landowner can see on a map how his land is zoned. Once he knows the zoning for his land, he can consult the zoning ordinance to see how he will be allowed to use it.

In Texas it has often been said that the planning and zoning commission does not zone, but only plans. It is the local governing body or city council which does the actual zoning because of the procedures that the zoning statutes and enabling acts have established.

Zoning Symbols   For convenience, zones are usually identified by code abbreviations such as R (residential), C (commercial), I or M (industrial-manufacturing), and A (agriculture). Within each general category there are subcategories, such as R-1 (single-family residence), R-2 (two-family residence), R-3 (low-density, garden-type apartments), R-4 (high-density, high-rise apartments), PUD (multi-use, planned use development) and RPD (residential planned development). Similarly, there are usually three or four manufacturing zones ranging from light, smoke-free industry (I-1 or M-1) to heavy industry

(I-4 or M-4). However, there is no mandatory uniformity in zoning classifications in the United States. One city may use R-4 to designate high-rise apartments, while another uses R-4 to designate single-family homes on 4,000-square-foot lots and the letter A to designate apartments.

Besides specifying how the landowner may use his land, the zoning ordinance includes additional rules. For example, land zoned for low-density apartments may require 1,500 square feet of land per living unit, a minimum of 600 square feet of living space per unit for one bedroom, 800 square feet for two bedrooms, and 1,000 square feet for three bedrooms. The zoning ordinance may also contain a set-back requirement which states that a building must be placed at least 25 feet back from the street, 10 feet from the sides of the lot, and 15 feet from the rear lot line. The ordinance may also limit the building's height to 2½ stories and require that the lot be a minimum of 10,000 square feet in size. As can be seen, zoning encourages uniformity even as it serves the common good.

Land-Use Restrictions

Zoning laws are enforced by virtue of the fact that in order to build upon his land a person must obtain a building permit from his city or county government. Before a permit is issued, the proposed structure must conform with government-imposed structural standards and comply with the zoning on the land. If a landowner builds without a permit, he can be forced to tear down his building.

Enforcement of Zoning Laws

When an existing structure does not conform with a new zoning law, it is "grandfathered-in" as a **nonconforming use.** Thus, the owner can continue to use the structure even though it does not conform to the new zoning. However, the owner is not permitted to enlarge or remodel the structure or to extend its life. When the structure is ultimately demolished, any new use of the land must be then in accordance with the zoning law. If you are driving through a residential neighborhood and see an old store or service station that looks very much out of place, it is probably a nonconforming use that was allowed to stay because it was built before the current zoning on the property went into effect.

Zoning Changes   Once an area has been zoned for a specific land use, changes are made by **amending the zoning ordinance** or by obtaining a variance. The amendment approach is taken when a change in zoning is necessary. An amendment can be initiated by a property owner in the area to be rezoned or by local government. Either way, if there is a proposed change in the zoning ordinance, the zoning commission, after giving proper public notice, holds a public hearing to provide a forum for public input and response. After the public hearing, the zoning commission makes a recommendation to the city council. The city council then, after posting proper public notices, holds its own public hearing. After the city council's public hearing, the city council does the actual enactment of the zoning ordinance or zoning change legislation, which ultimately becomes of record in the municipal ordinances. The city council has the right to overrule the planning and zoning commission by a majority vote, unless the city charter provides otherwise.

By comparison, **variances** allow an individual landowner to deviate somewhat from zoning code requirements and do not involve a zoning change. For example, a variance might be granted to the owner of an odd-shaped lot to reduce the set-back requirements slightly so that he can fit a building on it. Variances usually are granted where strict compliance with the zoning ordinance or code would cause undue hardship. However, the variance must not change the basic character of the neighborhood, and it must be consistent with the general objectives of zoning as they apply to that neighborhood.

Conditional Use Permit   A **conditional use permit** allows a land use that does not conform with existing zoning provided the use is within the limitations imposed by the permit. A conditional use permit is usually quite restrictive, and if the conditions of the permit are violated the permit is no longer valid. For example, a neighborhood grocery store operating under a conditional use permit can only be a neighborhood grocery. The structure cannot be used as an auto parts store.

Spot Zoning   **Spot zoning** refers to the rezoning of a small area of land in an existing neighborhood. For example, a neighborhood convenience center (grocery, laundry, barbershop) might be allowed in a residential neighborhood provided it serves a useful purpose for neighborhood residents and is not a nuisance.

Downzoning means that land previously zoned for higher-density uses (or more active uses) is rezoned for lower-density uses (or less active uses). Examples are downzoning from high-rise commercial to low-rise commercial, apartment zoning to single-family, and single-family to agriculture. Although a landowner's property value may fall as a result of downzoning, there is no compensation to the landowner as there is no taking of land as with eminent domain.

Downzoning

A **buffer zone** is a strip of land that separates one land use from another. Thus, between a large shopping center and a neighborhood of single-family homes, there may be a row of garden apartments. Alternatively, between an industrial park and a residential subdivision, a developer may leave a strip of land in grass and trees rather than build homes immediately adjacent to the industrial buildings. Note that "buffer zone" is a generic term and not necessarily a zoning law category.

Buffer Zone

A zoning law can be changed or struck down if it can be proved in court that it is unclear, discriminatory, unreasonable, not for the protection of the public health, safety, and general welfare, or not applied to all property in a similar manner.

It must be recognized that zoning alone does not create land value. For example, zoning a hundred square miles of lonely desert or mountain land for stores and offices would not appreciably change its value. Value is created by the concerted effort of a number of people who want to use a particular parcel of land for a specific purpose. To the extent that zoning channels that demand to certain parcels of land and away from others, zoning does have an important impact on property value.

Because zoning can greatly influence the value of a property, it is absolutely essential that you be aware of the zoning

PRECAUTIONS

for that parcel when you purchase any real estate. You will want to know what the zoning will allow and what it will not; whether the parcel is under a restrictive or temporary permit; and what the zoning and planning departments might allow on the property in the future. Where there is any uncertainty or where a zone change or variance will be necessary in order to use the property the way you want to, a conservative approach is to make the offer to buy contingent on obtaining planning and zoning approval before going to settlement.

If you are a real estate agent you must stay abreast of zoning and planning and building matters regarding the properties you list and sell. A particularly sensitive issue that occurs regularly is a property listed for sale which does not meet zoning and/or building code requirements. For example, suppose the current (or previous) owner of a house has converted the garage to a den or bedroom without obtaining building permits and without providing space for parking elsewhere on the parcel. Legally this makes the property unmarketable. If you, as agent, sell this property without telling the buyer about the lack of permits, you've given the buyer grounds to sue you for misrepresentation and the seller for rescission. When faced with a situation like this you should ask the seller to obtain the necessary permits. If the seller refuses, and the buyer still wants to buy, make the problem very clear to the buyer and have the buyer sign a statement indicating acceptance of title under these conditions. You can also refuse to accept the listing if it looks as though it will create more trouble than it's worth.

Professional Obligations Toward Property Zoning

The point here is that the public has a right to expect real estate agents to be professionals in their field. Thus the agent is expected to be fully aware of the permitted uses for a property and whether or not current uses comply. This is necessary to properly value the property for listing and to provide accurate information to prospective buyers. Note too that even if the seller in the above example was unaware of his zoning and building violations, it is the agent's responsibility to recognize the problem and inform the seller. An agent cannot take the position that if the seller didn't mention it, then the agent needn't worry about it *and* if the buyer later complains, it's the seller's problem, not the agent's. Recent court decisions clearly indicate that the agent has a responsibility to inform the seller of a problem so that the seller cannot later complain to the agent, "You should have told me about that when I listed the property with you and certainly before I accepted the buyer's offer."

Before a building lot can be sold, a subdivider must comply with local government regulations concerning street construction, curbs, sidewalks, street lighting, fire hydrants, storm and sanitary sewers, grading and compacting of soil, water and utility lines, minimum lot size, and so on. In addition, the subdivider may be required to either set aside land for schools and parks or provide money so that land may be purchased nearby for that purpose. Until he has complied with all state and local regulations, the subdivider cannot receive his subdivision approval. Without approval he cannot record his plat map, which in turn means he cannot sell his lots to the public. If he tries to sell his lots without approval, he can be stopped by a government court order and in some states fined. Moreover, permits to build will be refused to lot owners, and anyone who bought from the subdivider is entitled to a refund.

SUBDIVISION REGULATIONS

Recognizing the need to protect public health and safety against slipshod construction practices, state and local governments have enacted building codes. These establish minimum acceptable material and construction standards for such things as structural load and stress, windows and ventilation, size and location of rooms, fire protection, exits, electrical installation, plumbing, heating, lighting, and so forth.

Before a building permit is granted, the design of a proposed structure must meet the building-code requirements. During construction, local building department inspectors visit the construction site to make certain that the codes are being observed. Finally, when the building is completed, a **certificate of occupancy** is issued to the building owner to show that the structure meets the code. Without this certificate, the building cannot be legally occupied.

BUILDING CODES

DEED RESTRICTIONS   Although property owners tend to think of land-use controls as being strictly a product of government, it is possible to achieve land-use control through private means. In fact, Houston, Texas, with a population of more than 2 million persons, operates without zoning and relies almost entirely upon private land-use controls and building permits to achieve a similar effect.

Private land-use controls take the form of deed and lease restrictions. In the United States, it has long been recognized that the ownership of land includes the right to sell or lease it on whatever legally acceptable conditions the owner establishes, including the right to dictate to the buyer or lessee how he shall or shall not use it. For example, a developer can sell the lots in his subdivision subject to a restriction written into each deed that the land cannot be used for anything but a single-family residence containing at least 1,200 square feet of living area. The legal theory is that, if the buyer or lessee agrees to the restrictions, he is bound by them. If they are not obeyed, any lot owner in the subdivision can obtain a court order to enforce compliance. The only limit to the number of restrictions that an owner may place on his land is economic. If there are too many restrictions, the landowner may find that no one wants his land.

Deed restrictions, also known as **restrictive covenants,** can be used to dictate such matters as the purpose of the structure to be built, architectural requirements, set-backs, size of the structure, and aesthetics. In neighborhoods with view lots, they are often used to limit the height to which trees may be permitted to grow. Deed restrictions cannot be used to discriminate on the basis of sex, race, color, or creed; if they do they are unenforceable by the courts.

In Texas, and particularly Houston, **deed restrictions** have been one of the mainstays of land use control.

Since deed restrictions are enforced pursuant to contract law, only those who benefit from that contract (i.e., previous owners who may have reserved restrictions or subsequent purchasers in the property affected by the deed restrictions), have the right to enforce these deed restrictions. They must be enforced judicially, since judicial interpretation is generally required for proper construction of the deed restrictions and normally involve lawsuits and expensive litigation. To help facilitate the enforcement of deed restrictions, the Texas legislature passed a statute which enabled incorporated cities, towns, or villages who do not have zoning ordinances to enforce deed restrictions on behalf of the people affected by those deed restrictions.

The City of Houston, pursuant to this enabling act, has made some attempt at enforcing deed restrictions pursuant to its municipal authority. It is an attempt to enforce deed restrictions through the municipal power without the necessity of the homeowners or other beneficiaries of the deed restrictions having to go to court to enforce same, using their own personal funds.

There has been another statute enacted applying only to cities of 900,000 or more (namely Houston) which prohibits the obtaining of commercial building permits in deed restricted areas if they are in violation of the restrictive covenant. There are some serious legal questions as to whether or not these ordinances and statutes are enforceable or constitutional, but it is important that the effort has been made and that the City of Houston is in the process of trying to enforce deed restrictions in a number of situations in Houston under the authority of these laws.

Restrictive covenants normally carry a time limit so that they can be subject to periodic review. However, there has been a judicial interpretation that deed restrictions can run forever, providing that the limitation on the use is not unreasonable. Once the deed restrictions have been filed and are of record, they may not be subsequently modified without the consent of all the property owners, unless the power to amend the restrictions has been reserved or some other procedure for amending the property restrictions is contained in those restrictions.

Deed restrictions can be more functional than zoning restrictions because there is no control over what provisions can be contained in deed restrictions. Virtually anything, providing that it is not unconstitutional or illegal, can be in deed restrictions, and can provide a very tight land-use control. Zoning ordinances, on the other hand, generally have to promote the public health, safety, and welfare and cannot deal with more detailed aspects of land-use control, such as types of shingles and wood fences, or other aspects of architectural style that could be comfortably enforced through the deed restriction mechanism of land-use control.

ENVIRONMENTAL
IMPACT STATEMENTS

The purpose of an **environmental impact statement** (EIS), also called an **environmental impact report** (EIR), is to gather into one document enough information about the effect of a proposed project on the total environment so that a neutral decision maker can judge the environmental benefits and costs of the project. For example, a city zoning commission that has been asked to approve a zone change can request an EIS that will show the expected impact of the change on such things as population density, automobile traffic, noise, air quality, water and sewage facilities, drainage, energy consumption, school enrollments, employment, public health and safety, recreation facilities, wildlife, and vegetation. The idea is that with this information at hand better decisions can be made about land uses. When problems can be anticipated in advance, it is easier to make modifications or explore alternatives.

The EIS requirement has the greatest effect on private development at the city and county level. Usually the EIS accompanies the development application that is submitted to the planning or zoning commission. Where applicable, copies are also sent to affected school districts, water and sanitation districts, and highway and flood control departments. The EIS is then made available for public inspection as part of the hearing process on the development application. This gives concerned civic groups and the public at large an opportunity to voice their opinions regarding the anticipated benefits and costs of the proposed development. If the proposed development is partially or wholly funded by state or federal funds, state or federal hearings are also held.

Content of an EIS

Typically an EIS will contain a description of present conditions at the proposed development site, plus information on the following five points: (1) the probable impact of the proposed project on the physical, economic, and social environment of the area, (2) any unavoidable adverse environmental effects, (3) any alternatives to the proposed project, (4) the short-term versus long-term effects of the proposed project on the environment, and (5) a listing of any irreversible commitment of resources if the project is implemented. For a government-initiated project, the EIS is prepared by a government agency, sometimes with the help of private consultants. In the case of a private development, it may be prepared by the developer, a local government agency for a fee, or by a private firm specializing in the preparation of impact statements.

Match terms **a–h** *with statements* **1–8.**

VOCABULARY REVIEW

a. *Building codes*
b. *Certificate of occupancy*
c. *EIS or EIR*
d. *Land-use control*

e. *Nonconforming use*
f. *Restrictive covenants*
g. *Variance*
h. *Zoning*

1. A broad term used to describe any legal restriction (such as zoning) that controls how a parcel of land may be used.
2. Public regulations that control the specific use to which land in a given district may be put.
3. An improvement that is inconsistent with current zoning regulations.
4. Local and state laws that set minimum construction standards.
5. Clauses placed in deeds to control how future landowners may or may not use the property.
6. A document issued by a building department stating that a structure meets local zoning and building code requirements and is ready for use.
7. A report that contains information regarding the effect of a proposed project on the environment.
8. A permit granted to an individual property owner to vary slightly from strict compliance with zoning requirements.

QUESTIONS AND PROBLEMS

1. For land-use control to be successful, why is it necessary to consider the rights of individual property owners as well as the public as a whole?
2. Explain how a city obtains its power to control land use through zoning.
3. What is the purpose of a variance? How does it differ from a zoning ordinance amendment?
4. In your community, what are the letter/number designations for the

following: high-rise apartments, low-rise apartments, single-family houses, stores, duplexes, industrial sites?

5. How does Houston control land-use without zoning regulations?

ADDITIONAL READINGS

"America's Innovative Communities" by **Gregg Logan** and **Bonni Hahlbeck.** (*Real Estate Today*, Sep 84, p. 31). Article discusses the benefits of master planned communities and the importance of having a variety of housing styles and prices in the same community.

Buying Lots From Developers. (U.S. Department of Housing and Urban Development, 26 pages). This is must reading for anyone planning to buy a vacant lot. Includes what to be wary of, what questions to ask and HUD property report requirements.

The Citizens Guide to Zoning, rev. ed. by **Herbert H. Smith.** (Planners Press, 1983, 242 pages). Book stresses the value of citizen involvement in good zoning. Explains zoning and its philosophy and the nuts and bolts of zoning ordinances and administration, variances, hearings, PUDs and TDRs.

"Debunking the Mythology of Zoning" by **Jack Harris** and **William Moore.** (*Real Estate Review*, Winter 84, p. 94). Although zoning is accepted as a requisite for a modern city, there may be better methods. Moreover, present zoning laws often add substantially to housing costs.

Dictionary of Zoning Terms in Texas (*Ordway & Smith*, 1982, 82 pages). Reference work defining terms commonly used in Texas zoning ordinances.

A Guide to the Zoning Process in Texas (*Ordway & Smith*, 1982, 83 pages). Technical report based on a survey of ordinance of 36 Texas cities.

"Living With Deed Restrictions" by **Judon Fambrough** and **Cindy Dickson.** (*Guarantor*, Nov/Dec 84, p. 6). Article shows how deed restrictions have become a popular tool of developers to protect land values thereby making the property more attractive to buyers.

Respectful Rehabilitation. (Preservation Press, 1982, 185 pages). Contains methods and techniques for rehabilitating, preserving and maintaining historic buildings. Generously illustrated with examples.

Texas Real Estate Law, 4th ed. by **Charles J. Jacobus.** (Reston, 1985, 560 pages). Provides up-to-date explanations of law pertinent to the daily operation of a real estate brokerage office in Texas. See Chapter 18 on state, local, and private land-use control in Texas.

Zero Lot Line Housing by **David Jensen.** (Urban Land Institute, 1981, 150 pages). Using a zero lot line is the alternative when people prefer single family houses and land is too expensive for large lots. Book discusses site selection, development, building design, landscaping and legal considerations.

*   *   *

The following periodicals may also be of interest to you: *Automation in Housing, Community Development Journal, Journal of the American Planners Association, Land Use Abstracts, Land Use Controls, Land Use Digest, Land Use Law and Zoning Digest* and the *Zoning and Planning Law Report.*

Real Estate and the Economy

KEY TERMS

Base industry: an industry that produces goods or services for export from the region

Cost-push inflation: higher prices driven up by increased costs of labor and supplies

Demand-pull inflation: higher prices driven up by buyers bidding against each other

Economic base: the ability of a region to export goods and services to other regions and receive money in return

Federal Reserve Board: the governing board of the nation's central bank

Monetize the debt: the creation of money by the Federal Reserve to purchase Treasury securities

Real: inflation adjusted

Real-cost inflation: higher prices due to greater effort needed to produce the same product today versus several years ago

Service industry: an industry that produces goods and services to sell to local residents

Earlier chapters of this book described real estate from the standpoints of what it is, how you convey it, how you finance it, how it is taxed, how you rent it, how you value it, how you insure it and how you brokerage it. In this chapter we will look at the very important role of regional and national economics in giving value to real estate. In particular, this chapter will discuss the need for an economic base to support real estate values, short-run changes in housing demand when a new industry moves into town or an old one closes, long-run effects on housing demand caused by population and income changes, and the impact of federal tax, fiscal and monetary policies. The chapter will conclude with a look at inflation, a review of the 1975–1985 period for real estate, the importance of watching the Federal Reserve and the outlook for the future.

ECONOMIC BASE

In order to survive, a city (or town or region) must export goods and services so that its residents may purchase goods and services not produced locally. To illustrate, Hollywood produces films for theaters and television stations across the country. Income from these films permits residents in Hollywood to purchase things not produced in Hollywood such as cars and trucks made in Detroit. The money Detroit receives is used to buy farm products. A farming region produces farm products in order to generate income with which to buy farm machinery, gasoline, fertilizer, clothing and vacations. In turn, the economy of a resort area is kept alive with the money spent there by vacationers and on and on.

The ability of a city or region to produce a commodity or service that can bring in money from outside its area is called its **economic base.** Industries that produce goods and services for export are called **base, export** or **primary industries.** Thus, film making is a base industry for Hollywood, automobile manufacturing is a base industry for Detroit, and agriculture is a base industry in the Midwest. Producers of goods and services that are not exported are called **service, filler** or **secondary industries.** This category includes local school systems, supermarkets, medical centers, drugstores, and real estate offices.

Effect on Property Values   Because land is immovable, the existence of base industries is *absolutely essential* to maintaining local real estate values. Unless a region or city exports, it will die economically, and the value of local real estate will fall. An extreme example of this can be found in the abandoned mining towns of yesteryear. Before the discovery of mineral riches, land was often worth but a few dollars an acre for grazing purposes. With the discovery of minerals and subsequent mine development, land that was suitable for townsites zoomed in value. A new and far richer economic base industry than grazing brought wealth and people into the area, and grazing land was suddenly in demand for homesites, stores and offices. Years later, when the mines played out and mineral wealth could no longer be exported from the area, outside money ceased to flow into the town. Miners were laid off and moved to other towns where jobs could be found. Without the miners' money, service industries folded and their employees left. The demand for real estate dropped and real estate prices fell, often to their old value as grasslands.

The extent to which regions and cities are vulnerable to changes in economic base depends on how many different kinds of base industries are present and the ability of those industries to consistently export their products. Thus, a city that relies on a single base industry is much more vulnerable than a city with a diversified group of base industries. For example, a city or town that has grown up around a military base will suffer if that base is cut back in size or closed down. Real estate prices in Texas have been directly influenced by the rise and fall of oil prices. The economy of Detroit has been hurt by the change in consumer buying preferences to foreign-made cars. The steel-making region that spans Indiana, Ohio, Pennsylvania, and West Virginia has been adversely impacted by steel mill shutdowns due to lower prices for steel from abroad. Towns that rely heavily on the lumber industry have seen their economies, and real estate prices, hurt by the drop in demand for lumber following the end of the last housing boom. The economies of farm communities and the prices of farm land are tied to the rise and fall of farm product prices.

Vulnerability

Sometimes these events galvanize concerned citizens, property owners, and business people into action. Seattle and Tacoma have been busy attracting industries other than aircraft manufacturing so as to smooth out the ups and downs of the aircraft business. Oregon repealed its unitary tax on business firms and is actively courting electronics companies. Some steel mills have been bought by employees determined to keep them open and competitive with foreign operations.

Just how important is a base industry job to a local economy? As a rule, for each additional person employed in a base industry, another two persons will be employed in local service industries. Thus, if an electronics firm moves into a community and creates 100 new base industry jobs, opportunities will be created for another 200 persons in jobs such as retail store clerks, restaurant services, gas station operators, gardeners, bankers, doctors, dentists, lawyers, police, fire fighting, school teaching, and local government—to name only a few.

Employment Multiplier

If you understand what is happening in local base industries, you can calculate the need for land and housing. For example, the 100 base industry jobs created by the electronics firm result in 200 service jobs, for a total of 300 new job opportunities in the community. If every three jobs require two households (more than one person working in some families) and each household averages 2.9 persons, then 300 jobs will provide income for 200 households containing a total of 580 persons. The ultimate effect of the 300 new jobs on local employment and housing demand will depend on what portion of the jobs can be filled from within the community and the extent of vacant housing. If the community is already operating at full employment and has no vacant housing to speak of, the addition of 100 base jobs will result in a demand for land, building materials and labor necessary to provide 200 new housing units. From the standpoint of local government, 580 more people must be supplied with schools, parks, streets, libraries, water, sewage treatment, police and fire protection.

SHORT-RUN DEMAND
FOR HOUSING

Because it takes time to develop raw land into sites for homes, offices and stores, the supply of developed real estate cannot immediately respond to sudden changes in demand. As a result, price changes for already developed real property can be rapid and dramatic over short periods of time.

Increase in Demand

To illustrate, suppose that in a given community there are presently 5,000 single-family houses and their average value is $82,000. A new industry moves into the community and increases the demand for houses by 100. Local builders, recognizing the new demand, set to work adding 100 houses to the available housing stock. However, it will take time to acquire land, file subdivision maps, acquire building permits, grade the land and construct the houses. The entire process typically takes 10 to 36 months. Meanwhile the available supply of houses remains fixed. The result will be an increase in house prices as the newly arriving employees bid against each other for a place to live in the existing housing stock. The result is diagrammed in Figure 22:1. Demand Curve 1 represents the demand for houses at various prices before

SHORT-RUN SUPPLY—DEMAND PICTURE   **Figure 22:1**

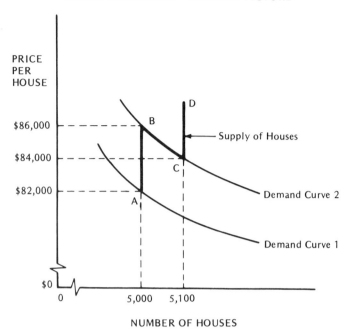

NUMBER OF HOUSES

the new employees arrive. Supply and demand are in balance at $82,000 per house, as shown at A.

Next, the new industry moves in. The new employees added to the housing market produce Demand Curve 2. Prices rise owing to competition for the existing houses. This increase literally rations the existing stock of 5,000 houses among 5,100 households. Prices rise until enough current owners decide to sell and enough new buyers are priced out of the market. Once again, supply and demand are in balance with 5,000 houses occupied by 5,000 families. This is point B at $86,000.

At last, the 100 new houses that were started in response to the new demand are completed and are on the market. At what price must these be offered in order to sell them all? It would appear that $86,000 is the answer, as that is what houses are now selling for. However, the supply-demand relationship in Figure 22:1 shows that only 5,000 houses are in demand at $86,000, not 5,100 houses. To find out at what price the additional 100 houses will be absorbed by

Increase in Supply

the market, we must travel along Demand Curve 2 to 5,100 houses. At point C, the market will absorb 5,100 houses if they are priced at $84,000 each. Thus, a temporary glut of homes causes prices to be reduced slightly. This price softening applies to the builders of the 100 new houses and to the owners of the other 5,000 homes if they wish to sell during this temporary oversupply situation.

Aware of the oversupply of houses on the market, builders will react by halting building activity until those units are sold and demand starts pushing prices upward again to D at which time the process repeats itself. Over a period of years, the supply pattern for houses takes on a stair-step appearance as temporary shortages and temporary excesses alternate.

Decrease in Demand   Just as a short-run increase in demand can cause a quick run-up in prices, a short-run decrease in demand has the opposite effect because supply cannot be decreased as fast as demand falls. This situation is diagrammed in Figure 22:2

Figure 22:2   **SHORT-RUN DROP IN DEMAND**

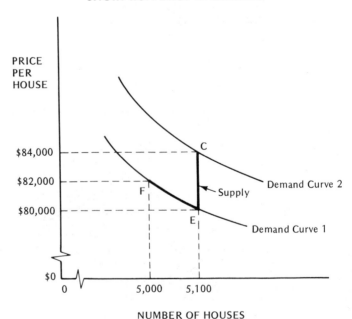

with supply and demand in balance at 5,100 houses at $84,000 each. Suppose there is an overnight cutback of jobs and, as a result, 100 homeowners decide to sell and move out of the community. This would cause demand to shift downward from Demand Curve 2 to Demand Curve 1. To sell 100 houses, it is necessary for prices to fall from $84,000 at point C to $80,000 at point E. Without an increase in the economic base of the community, only a reduction in the supply of existing houses through demolition, disasters and conversions to other uses will push prices back up along Demand Curve 1. If supply falls to 5,000 houses, prices will go to $82,000 at point F.

The presence of inflation will cushion the drop in dollar values when demand shifts to Demand Curve 1 in Figure 22:2. Similarly, the drop in prices from B to C in Figure 22:1 will be milder in the presence of moderate inflation. In the presence of high inflation, prices may not drop, but actually rise. However, if you strip away the masking effect of inflation, Figures 22:1 and 22:2 accurately portray what actually happens when demand suddenly changes and supply cannot react fast enough. Although we have been talking in terms of houses, the same concept applies to vacant lots, apartment buildings, townhouses, condominiums, office buildings, factories, hotels and motels, store space and so forth.

Effect of Inflation

Future demand for housing in the United States can be seen by looking at the population in terms of age distribution, and the ability of people to obtain income at various age levels. As shown in Figure 22:3, during the first 10 years of life a person earns no income and is dependent on others, usually parents, for sustenance. During junior high school, high school and college (if any) a person has part-time jobs but usually is still dependent on others for financial support.

Upon leaving school and entering the labor market on a full-time basis, a person's income rises quickly, reflecting increased productive capacity in society. As skills increase, income continues to rise rapidly. In another decade the rise stops increasing as rapidly, although it still advances. Then, somewhere between the ages of 40 and 60, depending on a

LONG-RUN DEMAND FOR HOUSING

Figure 22:3

LIFETIME INCOME CURVE

Based on Median Dollar Income of all Persons
in the United States

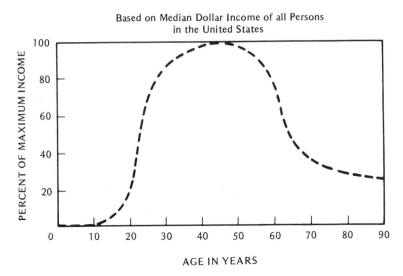

AGE IN YEARS

person's skills and the usefulness of those skills in society, health and/or the desire to slow down, the peak earning year occurs. For those with 4 years of college or the equivalent, this occurs around age 55. For the nation as a whole, it occurs in the mid-forties. The peak earning year is followed at first by mild decreases in income and then by more rapid decreases as retirement approaches.

Buying Pattern   With this earning pattern in mind, you can see the progression of housing demand. When a person is young and setting up a household for the first time, income is low and so are accumulated assets. Thus, housing that requires no equity investment at a minimum cost is needed; that is, an inexpensive rental with no frills. During the next decade income increases and the household can increase the quality of its rental unit. At the same time savings accumulate, which, coupled with the ability to make loan payments, enable the household to meet the down payment and loan requirements for a modest housing purchase. As the household grows and income increases, the family can move to larger, more expensive quarters. Typically this occurs between the ages of 35 and 45. Another upward move in house size and price usually occurs between 45 and 55 when the family reaches its maximum income.

As the children move out and income peaks and then begins to recede, the household begins to consider a smaller and less expensive dwelling unit. The need for less expensive housing becomes even more compelling upon retirement and a further reduction in income. Retirement income typically is not sufficient to support the large house bought during the peak earning years. However, the homeowner has an equity that can now be consolidated in a smaller residence that is fully or nearly fully paid for.

With the above pattern in mind, let us now turn our attention to Figure 22:4 where the population of the United States is graphed according to its age distribution. The lines labeled 1970 and 1980 are based on the U.S. census; the 1990 and 2000 lines are government-prepared population projections. The 1990 and 2000 lines are based on the fact that persons on the 1980 line will be 10 and 20 years older, respectively, minus losses due to deaths and additions due to immigration.

Age Distribution

Figure 22:4

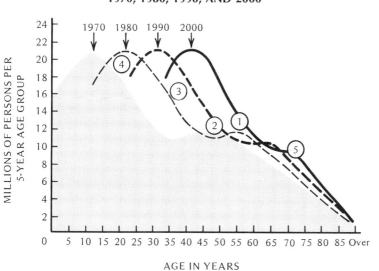

**AGE DISTRIBUTION OF THE U.S.
POPULATION FOR THE YEARS
1970, 1980, 1990, AND 2000**

There are two peaks in the 1980 age distribution line. The smaller of the two, identified as ①, represents persons aged 50 to 60 years in 1980. These persons were born during the decade of the 1920s, a period of economic prosperity in most parts of the United States. Moving to the left, the dip at ② represents children born during the economic depression that spanned the 1930s. By 1980, they were 40 to 50 years old. Moving again to the left, a substantial upward rise is encountered at ③. This is the famed World War II and postwar "baby boom." It started in 1940 and lasted until 1960. In 1960, the number of births per year began to decline and continued to decline in each subsequent year through 1978. This is shown at ④.

Housing Demand

Of particular interest is the huge wave of demand from the 1940–1960 baby boom that is working its way across Figure 22:4. How does this translate into housing demand? Beginning in the early 1960s, the United States experienced a growing demand for inexpensive rentals by persons under 25 years of age. By 1985, that demand peaked as all children born from 1940 to 1960 became 25 years or older. Between 1965 and 1975, the number of persons in the United States aged 25 through 34 increased by 9 million and resulted in the formation of 5 million households. Each household required a housing unit suitable to its income characteristics. Between 1975 and 1985, this age group grew by another 9 million persons and created an additional 5 million households, each of which required a place to live.

More Homeowners

In addition to producing new households, the 1940–1960 children are climbing the income ladder and have more money to spend on housing. And, as they get older they want to own, not rent. Government statistics show that 60% of all households aged 35 through 44 are homeowners, and among those 45 through 54 years old, 75% are owners. (Percentages are even higher if there are children present.) The purchase of more expensive homes will continue until the year 2015 at which time persons born in 1960 will reach the age of 55. Because personal income patterns decline after that age, a retrenchment into more modest housing will then be observed.

Although the dominant factor in housing demand in the   *Over 65*
next several decades will be the maturing members of the
1940–1960 baby boom, we must not overlook the present
steady growth in households over the age of 65 years. Households aged 65 and above are growing in numbers and, as
may be seen at ⑤, will continue to do so until 1995. At that
time there will be a 10-year pause in growth due to persons
born during the 1930 decade reaching the age of 65. Following
that, the over-65 group will again grow in numbers as those
born between 1940 and 1960 reach this age level. As less
than one-fifth of the population over 65 remains in the labor
force, the housing demand created by these age groups will
primarily be the result of their investments, pensions, social
security income, public welfare and assets accumulated earlier
in life such as the family home.

When the children born after 1960 reach the age at which   *Another Wave*
they want to have a residence of their own (usually 18 to
25 years of age), they will find large amounts of housing
available as the persons born between 1940 and 1960 climb
the lifetime income curve and upgrade their housing. Unless
some of the housing being abandoned by the 1940–1960 group
can be used to accommodate households over the age of
65, this situation will probably cause a slowdown in new
housing construction. The United States has already experienced a virtual halt in new elementary school construction
because of the drop in births after 1960. And this came after
a 15-year-long frantic effort to build schoolrooms.

In 1978, the drop in births that began in 1960 began to
reverse itself. Now the baby-boom children are having children of their own. This will make a third wave in the age
distribution of the U.S. population and, with it, a new wave
of housing demand when those children form households.

Thus far we have talked about the economic base needed   *GOVERNMENTAL*
to support local land values and the effect on housing demand   *IMPACT*

by population age groups and income levels. Now let us look at the influence on real estate caused by the federal government's tax rules, laws, deficits and monetary policies.

TAX LAWS   Real estate has long been favored with special income tax treatment. For years, tax laws have allowed homeowners to deduct property taxes and mortgage loan interest when calculating state and federal taxes. To illustrate, for a person in a 28% tax bracket, a 10% interest rate costs, after taxes, only 6%. Similarly, property taxes of $1,500 per year cost, after taxes, only $1080.

Owners of improved investment property can deduct the costs of operating and maintaining their investment property plus depreciation on the improvements up to the amount of total income earned on the property. For most investment properties since 1940, depreciation expense has been more of an accounting entry than a market reality. This has been a result of rising real estate prices coupled with tax rules that allowed improvements to be depreciated over accounting lives shorter than their useful lives. Since depreciation is deductible at tax time and not repaid until years later when the property is sold, tax policies regarding depreciation have made real estate an attractive investment.

Due to the new Internal Revenue Code of 1986, Congress has taken away in whole or in part the special tax treatment given to real estate owners. This has made real estate a much less attractive investment than in prior years. For example, before the Economic Recovery Tax Act of 1981, improved property bought for business or investment could be depreciated for tax purposes over a life of 20 to 40 years depending on the age and condition of the property. In 1981, the depreciation period was reduced to 15 years for both used and new buildings. In 1984, this was raised to 18 years and in 1985 to 19 years, with talk of it going higher. Since a faster depreciation period makes real estate more attractive and a longer period makes it less attractive, you can see how Congress can influence real estate values. The President and Congress have now limited the amount of mortgage interest individuals can deduct on real estate partnerships. This detracts from the attractiveness of these real estate investments and, in turn, has an impact on values. Other real estate tax areas changed are accelerated depreciation, and preferred tax treatment for capital gains. The key point to remember here is that tax treatment of the expenses and profits from real estate greatly influence what a person can and will pay for a property. Generous tax treatment creates an upward influence on values and vice versa.

Few home buyers can afford to pay all cash for a place to live; most must borrow. As a result, the housing industry is very sensitive to the price and availability of loan money. Not only does this affect contractors and construction workers, but also appliance and furniture manufacturers, lumber mills, cement factories, real estate appraisers and real estate agents. Anyone connected with the manufacture, sale or resale of housing is directly affected by the price and availability of mortgage loan money to home buyers.

FISCAL POLICY

If federal, state or local governments cannot balance their budgets, they too must borrow. When they do, they compete with home buyers and businesses for available savings in the capital markets. Of these, government gets its needs filled first at whatever the interest cost. This is because if a government did not borrow it would not have enough to pay its bills and would be bankrupt. This leaves home buyers and businesses to compete for what is left over. For the most part, state and local governments have learned to live within their budgets. But the federal government has not. Defense spending and social spending in excess of income has produced federal deficits in nearly every year since 1940. Not terribly worrisome at first, by the 1970s financing the federal deficit was taking progressively larger and larger chunks of money out of the capital markets. By the middle of the 1980 decade, annual federal deficits were $200 billion and absorbing that much of the country's, indeed the world's, capital. What was left was available to businesses and home buyers but at high interest rates. In view of this, it is generally agreed among economists that if the federal government learns to live within its means, interest rates will come down for everyone.

Through the Federal Reserve Banks the Federal Reserve Board has the ability to create and destroy money. This is

MONETARY POLICY

done by any of the following mechanisms: (1) open-market purchases and sales of Treasury securities, (2) changes in the discount rate charged to banks, and (3) changes in the reserve requirements of banks. We will omit a detailed explanation of each of these and go directly to the point: the Federal Reserve can create money. This is useful because in an economy that grows 3% a year, a 3% increase in the money supply is necessary to keep prices from falling. At the same time, however, there is the temptation to print more money than needed for economic growth because this new money can be used to buy back Treasury securities that were created to fund the federal deficit. The short-term result of such purchases is that interest rates drop, and the government, business and housing are all beneficiaries. Unfortunately, the longer-run effect (beyond two years) is more inflation as there is now more money in circulation without a corresponding increase in goods and services to buy.

When inflation is apparent, savers become wise and respond by buying equity assets, such as real estate, to hedge against further inflation and by raising the rate of interest they will accept so as to compensate for inflation. Thus, any benefits of creating extra money by the Federal Reserve are lost.

FEDERAL PROGRAMS

A number of federal programs and laws have been enacted to help people buy homes. Two of the oldest and most far-reaching have been the Federal Housing Administration and the Veterans Administration. FHA loan insurance programs have helped persons with modest incomes to qualify for low down payment loans and therefore buy homes they might not otherwise be able to buy. Similarly, the VA has guaranteed loans so that qualifying veterans could buy with little or no money down. Again, many who might have otherwise not been able to qualify found they could buy a home using the VA's guarantee. To stay abreast of rising home prices, both the FHA and VA have regularly raised their loan limits. Additionally, the FHA offers graduated payment loan programs to squeeze the last ounce of borrowing power out of a loan applicant's income.

A far-reaching law passed in 1974 was the federal Equal   *Equal Credit*
Credit Opportunity Act (ECOA). This law requires that all
the income of a woman must be counted in full regardless
of marital status or children. Prior to the ECOA, it was common for lenders to refuse to count a married woman's income
if she was pregnant and discount it by 50% if she was not
pregnant, but in the prime child-bearing years. Coupled with
prevailing lower wages for women, the size of loan a couple
could get was mainly limited by the husband's income. Additionally, widows, divorcees, and singles were considered
high-risk borrowers and either did not get credit or did in
small amounts only.

The Equal Credit Opportunity Act created borrowing
power that did not exist before. Husband-wife families could
qualify for larger loans. Mothers and daughters living together, brothers owning together, single persons, divorced
and widowed persons all suddenly found themselves with
new and greater borrowing power; and with it, the ability
to bid up prices. At the same time, women began to earn
more money because of laws requiring equal pay for equal
work and laws prohibiting sex discrimination in hiring. Furthermore, more women were going into the labor force and
many were choosing higher-paying career-oriented jobs.

A very important influence on real estate activity and   *SECONDARY*
prices in the United States has been the secondary mortgage   *MORTGAGE MARKET*
market. Prior to the 1970 decade, home loan money came
mostly from savings and loans, mutual savings banks, commercial banks and life insurance companies. This was a relatively limited source of money that tended to keep a lid on
real estate prices. With the advent of the Federal National
Mortgage Association, the Government National Mortgage
Association, the Federal Home Loan Mortgage Corporation
and other secondary mortgage market operators, previously
untapped sources of loan money were now available to real
estate borrowers. Individuals and pension funds that had
avoided making mortgage loans because of the work involved
could now invest with ease and a guarantee of safety. Additionally, a secondary market provides a place to sell a mortgage that a lender does not want to hold until maturity.

Much of the money raised in the secondary market has been used (and will continue to be used) to fund the 1940–1960 baby boom children as they buy housing. However, a lot of that money also helped fuel real estate speculation and inflation in the late 1970s. (By the way, the secondary market now is producing some drag on prices. Because of substantial foreclosure losses in the early 1980s, loan qualification standards were tightened in 1985.)

TYPES OF INFLATION

In nearly all years since World War II, prices of consumer commodities and real estate have risen. Although inflation is currently not as pressing an issue as it was in the 1970s, there are four concepts with which you should be familiar: cost-push inflation, demand-pull inflation, monetary inflation and real-cost inflation.

Cost-push Inflation

The increasing cost of inputs necessary to manufacture a product or offer a service results in what is called **cost-push inflation.** To illustrate, an automobile manufacturer increases the price of cars because labor and materials cost more. Similarly, a builder of new homes will include any increases in the prices of lumber, bricks, concrete, metal, construction labor, construction loans and government permits.

Demand-pull Inflation

When buyers bid against each other to buy something that has been offered for sale, **demand-pull inflation** results. For example, three buyers for a choice lot may bid $75,000, $76,000 and $77,000, respectively. Demand-pull inflation is basically the result of too much money chasing too few goods. This type of inflation usually has little to do with the actual cost of producing the particular goods or services being sought. Instead, it reflects what buyers feel they would have to pay elsewhere for the same thing.

Monetary Inflation

Monetary inflation results from the creation of excessive amounts of money by government. The classic example of this was in Germany during the first 5 years after World War I. In an effort to provide money to solve all the war-torn country's problems at once, the German government created and spent money on a grand scale. However, there was no parallel increase in goods and services to be purchased with that money. The result was demand-pull inflation as millions of people with pockets, and later wheelbarrows, stuffed with newly printed currency fought to buy everything from bread and vegetables to real estate. Within the space of a few short years, prices rose on the order of one million percent before the printing presses were finally shut down.

To a lesser degree monetary inflation is used today by many countries. Allowing the money supply to grow faster than the available supply of goods and services causes a temporary economic stimulus by placing more money in peoples' hands. But the ultimate result is a reduction in the purchasing power of that money.

Real-cost inflation is inflation caused by the increased effort necessary to produce the same quantity of a good or service. For example, much easy-to-develop land has already been built upon and that forces developers to use land requiring more effort to bulldoze into usable lots. Another example is water service to new lots. Local water districts that once could supply the town's population from a few wells or a nearby lake or river must now travel many miles to find water. The additional cost of the water system and pumping charges must be added to the user's water bill.

Real-cost Inflation

The period from 1975 to 1985 has been one of the most dramatic in American economic history. Real estate prices doubled and tripled between 1975 and 1980. Inflation zoomed upward, interest rates reached record highs and real estate was the favored investment. Then in the early 1980s, inflation fell dramatically, real estate prices stalled, and interest rates retreated but remained historically high. What the country witnessed was a combination of what's been discussed thus far in this chapter at work in the marketplace. Let's take a closer look at what happened then and what may happen in the future.

1975–1985 PERIOD

In 1975 members of the leading edge of the 1940–1960 baby boom were in the market as adults ready for their first

1975 to 1980

housing purchases. Simultaneously, the Equal Credit Opportunity Act made it easier to qualify for loans, and the secondary mortgage market opened previously untapped sources of loan money. Added to this was the lack of new housing for sale due to a drop in housing starts in connection with a credit crunch and recession in 1974–1975.

As federal spending and money growth policies designed to end the recession took hold, interest rates fell, people regained jobs and the mood of the country turned bullish. People began buying homes again and against a backdrop of limited supply quickly pulled prices upward. Rising prices usually dampen demand. But several other factors were involved that made buying real estate, and in particular buying homes, very attractive.

Low Real Interest   The first factor was the low **real** (i.e., inflation adjusted) cost of interest. Although interest rates for homes ranged from 8% to 10% between 1975 and 1978, inflation and home prices were rising faster. Thus, it made sense to borrow and buy real estate; in fact, the more the better. Since it was possible to buy with as little as 10% down, buyers were realizing enormous returns on their investments. Persons who received $60,000 for houses bought earlier for $40,000 were now making down payments on $80,000 houses. These sellers were taking their money into $110,000 houses while those sellers were buying $150,000 houses and so on.

Tax Benefits   As already noted, tax laws allow the deduction of interest. During the 1970s, wage increases of 10% per year and more were common. This pushed wage earners into higher tax brackets and made interest deductions even more valuable. Meanwhile, increases from appreciation were not taxable until the property sold and then received preferential long-term capital gains treatment. Thus, despite higher interest and higher home prices, as long as prices continued to rise substantially real estate seemed to be an assured ticket to quick wealth.

Reversal   The boom came to a turning point in late 1979. Politically, high inflation (reaching at one point a rate of 18% per year) became a national issue and something to be halted and reversed. Federal Reserve policy changed from one of generous monetary growth to one of restrained monetary growth. Those who loaned money to real estate buyers were either investing in real estate themselves or charging high enough interest rates to counteract inflation. In the process, mortgage loan rates reached 18% per year and the bank prime rate went even higher. Thus, the inflation that had spawned the late 1970s real estate boom was also its downfall. Residential developers who had responded with new construction to meet the market demand now found themselves with homes to sell in the face of 16% to 18% interest rates and few buyers. Many experienced stunning losses, foreclosure and bankruptcy as interest charges on unsold homes bled them financially.

Giveth and Taketh

What was such an irresistible investment from 1975 to 1979 was no longer as attractive by the early 1980s. Inflation rates dropped below interest rates, home prices stopped rising 20% to 30% per year, and higher home prices coupled with higher interest rates now priced many home buyers out of the market. What inflation had given, it was now taking away. Even the creative financing that kept sales going at successively higher prices was disappearing. Fewer and fewer loans became assumable, a process that the 1982 *de la Cuesta* case and the 1982 Garn Act accelerated. Lenders, stuck badly and sometimes forced out of business, now wanted to loan on adjustable rate terms.

Looking Ahead

Expectations about inflation (or the lack of it) and interest rates lag the actual changes. At the mid-point of the 1980 decade, much of the home buying public was still unsure what to make of things. House prices, on average, essentially remained stable for the first half of the decade while interest rates were slow to drop. Many investors were left with high-priced properties that could not be sold except at below-market interest rates. More generous depreciation schedules offered by the 1981 tax act did help real estate's attractiveness. But, investors and speculators remained unimpressed with housing and turned to office buildings with depreciation as the carrot. However, even this carrot produced a problem as millions of square feet of office space built between 1981 and 1985 stood vacant at mid-decade while interest payments continued to come due.

Owner-Occupants

No longer a speculator's market, the housing market is again an owner-occupant market. Owner-occupants receive the benefits of occupancy and the psychic value of owning their home. As such, they are less demanding of appreciation potential compared to investors who, sensing an unrewarding investment, will avoid it or sell out of it and go elsewhere with their capital. Thus, it appears that for the foreseeable future, success in new construction will go to those who appeal best to the owner-occupant's needs, tastes and pocketbook. With falling interest rates, more owner-occupants will be able to qualify for loans and buy homes. This will especially help the resale market and those owners who need to refinance existing loans. Investors, unless they can get a combination of appreciation, tax benefits and rental income that exceeds other investment opportunities will look elsewhere.

Expensive Housing

During the 1975–79 period, escalating wage increases, interest rates below inflation, and attractive tax benefits encouraged home buyers to buy homes larger and more expensive than they otherwise could afford. By the early 1980s, wages were not rising as rapidly, and appreciation was no longer offsetting interest rates. Although persons already owning could usually move to another home of equal value, new entrants to the housing market were much less fortunate. The result has been a demand for smaller houses on smaller lots that has not been seen since the days of the FHA-VA tract houses of the late 1940s and early 1950s. Some of the most dramatic sales success stories of the mid-1980s are coming from developers who are offering single-family detached homes of less than 1,000 square feet. (This is the equivalent of a good-sized 2-bedroom, 2-bath apartment.) Interestingly, developers are finding that although condominiums can provide this size of unit very easily, the American dream is still for a single-family home with its own private backyard; even if the home and yard are both postage-stamp size. Compared with a national median for new houses of 1,600 square feet in the late 1970s, a 1,000 square-foot home costs enough less that even with 10% to 12% interest rates it is affordable for many new home buyers. Given a choice between buying a small house or continuing to rent an apartment unit, the small house is the first-time buyer's choice. To make small houses look bigger than they are, builders and their architects make better use of every square foot. Popular building techniques utilize raised ceilings, sunken floors, blended-space, built-in furniture, more light, more windows and personal touches such as lofts and curved walls.

WATCHING THE FED

If you plan to develop or invest in real estate, it is very helpful to watch Federal Reserve statistics so as to better anticipate changes in interest rates. Although the marketplace is the ultimate decider of interest rates, the actions of the **Federal Reserve Board** can and do provide a powerful push on rates. For example, even though mortgage rates were already rising by 1978 as lenders tried to stay ahead of inflation, Federal Reserve action in 1979 and 1980 to slow money supply growth helped interest rates go higher. By 1985 the Board was carefully increasing the money supply in order to reduce interest rates and thus keep the U.S. economy from falling into another recession.

To understand the Federal Reserve Board, you need to know that the Board has four objectives for the American economy: (1) high employment, (2) stable prices, (3) steady growth in the nation's productive capacity, and (4) a stable foreign exchange value for the dollar. During a recession, employment and economic growth are of primary importance, and the Board adds extra money to the banking system as it did to pull out of the 1974–1975 recession. In the late 1970s, stable prices and a stable dollar were the prime concerns. This required a slowdown in the growth of the money supply, which the Board did. By the end of 1984, inflation was down to 4% and the dollar was very strong. In 1985, the Board was gingerly touching the money accelerator to buoy a banking industry beleaguered by high interest rates, ward off recession, and take the edge off what many considered to be an overly strong dollar.

Monetary Base   Week-to-week changes in the results of Federal Reserve monetary policy can be found each Friday in the *Wall Street Journal* under "Federal Reserve Data." Of these, the most important is the **monetary base** figure. This shows the legal reserves of banks at the Federal Reserve plus cash in the hands of the public. If this grows faster than the real (i.e., inflation adjusted) rate of growth of the country's gross national product (GNP), one can assume that the nation's money supply will soon be expanding at a greater rate than real gross national product. This will cause, for the time being, interest rates to fall and economic growth to be stimulated. Two years down the road it will turn to inflation.

THE OUTLOOK   As this text is being written, there are two likely economic scenarios pending and the federal deficit plays a leading role in both. The first scenario is that Congress will not balance its budget. This means the Federal Reserve Board must decide whether or not to expand the money supply in order to buy back the deficit, i.e., **monetize the debt.** Failure to expand the money supply will allow interest rates to rise dramatically and cause a recession worse than the 1981–1982 recession, which itself was the worst since the 1930s. Yet creating money in excess of increases in goods and services will cause inflation and high interest costs just as it did in the 1975–1979 period.

   The second scenario is that Congress will bring about a meaningful reduction in the size of the federal deficit. This would reduce the need of the U.S. Treasury to compete with businesses and home buyers for available loan funds. With less competition interest rates will fall. This will attract more loan funds as lenders become confident that rates won't soon be rising. Lower rates will reduce the federal deficit still further as interest paid on existing government debt gradually drops. The cost of this attractive scenario is overall fiscal belt tightening: recipients of social spending programs would have to receive less as would the military. Alternatively, Congress could raise taxes to pay for its spending or it could apply a combination of the two.

A Parallel   There is a very close parallel between the federal government's money problems and the money problems of a free-spending married couple who discovered credit cards. At first, the couple found that a credit card could help them buy a few things that their monthly paychecks would not have covered. But instead of repaying the credit card balance, more items were purchased until the limit on the card was reached. Flushed with the pleasures of living beyond their monthly paychecks, another credit card was obtained. Purchases were made with it until it, too, reached its maximum. Now the first two credit card companies were demanding monthly payments, so a third credit card, this one with cash borrowing privileges, was obtained. This card was used to make payments on the previous two cards and buy still more on credit. Soon all three credit card companies wanted monthly repayments so the couple took out a loan at the bank, mortgaging the appreciation in their house to do so. The buying continued and soon another loan was taken out with a finance company to make payments on the existing loans and buy more things. Then one day, there were simply no more places to borrow, yet the payments on all those loans kept coming due. The couple was advised by a credit counselor that they had two choices: declare bankruptcy or adopt an austerity budget and start repaying the loans. If you were in their shoes, which would you choose? If you were in the U.S. Congress, which would you choose for the country? Or, would you look for one more lender to keep the deficits going a little while longer?

There is no lack of household formation potential in the United States. Additionally there is a large stock of existing housing in the country plus the capacity to build two million new housing units every year. The main question will continue to be who gets what; i.e., how housing will be distributed. Because real estate is so sensitive to the price and availability of loanable funds, the answer will depend heavily on competition from the government.

VOCABULARY REVIEW

Match terms **a–j** *with statements* **1–10.**

a. Base industry

b. Cost-push inflation

c. Demand-pull inflation

d. Economic base

e. Federal Reserve Board

f. Monetary inflation

g. Monetize the debt

h. Real

i. Real-cost inflation

j. Service industry

1. An industry that produces goods or services for export from the region.

2. An industry that produces goods or services to sell to local residents.

3. The ability of a region to export goods and services to other regions.

4. Higher prices due to buyers bidding against each other.

5. Higher prices due to greater effort needed to produce the same product today.

6. Higher prices due to increased costs of labor and supplies.

7. Results from increasing the money supply faster than increases in goods and services to buy.

8. Governing board of the nation's central bank.

9. Inflation adjusted.

10. The creation of money by the Federal Reserve to purchase Treasury securities.

QUESTIONS AND PROBLEMS

1. List and rank in order of importance the base industries that support your community. How stable are they? Are any new ones coming? Are any existing ones leaving?

2. What would be the effect of a new industry creating 500 new jobs in your community? Is there sufficient vacant housing available? What would be the effect of a loss of 500 jobs?

3. Does the population age distribution of your community differ from the United States as a whole? How would this affect demand for housing in your area?

4. What is the after-tax cost of a 15% mortgage loan to a person in a 28% income tax bracket? A 10% loan? A 5% loan?

5. What was the intent of government in passing the Equal Credit Opportunity Act?

6. Identify three specific examples of cost-push inflation that you have personally observed or read about during the past 12 months.

7. Why are large federal deficits considered bad for home buyers?

8. What are the economic goals of the Federal Reserve Board?

9. What is the advantage and the disadvantage of monetizing the federal debt?

10. If money supply grows slower than real gross national product, would the result be rising prices or falling prices?

"Computers to the Rescue." (*Real Estate Today*, May 85, pp. 12–27). This section features the following articles: "Fight Fear of Automation," "Basics of Property Management Software," "Negotiate Before You Automate" and "Practical Protection for Your Software."

Historical Chart Book. (Federal Reserve Board). Published annually, this book contains easy-to-read graphs and charts of money, finance, prices, real estate, production and labor statistics. Most go back 50 years or more to give the reader an excellent historical perspective.

"In Search of Dreams". (*Real Estate Today*, Sep 84, p. 8). Looks forward at how Americans will satisfy their housing needs in the 1980s. In the same issue are articles on trends in population shifts, manufactured housing and older homes.

Statistical Abstract of the United States. (Bureau of the Census, 1987, 1,010 pages). Contains statistics on nearly every facet of life in the United States. Includes such real estate-related statistics as housing prices, value of construction, construction wages, new housing starts, occupied housing units, occupant characteristics, homes sold and mortgage loans. Published annually.

Savings and Loan Fact Book. (United States League of Savings Associations, 1987). An excellent reference source for statistics on savings, home ownership, residential construction and financing. Published annually.

*   *   *

The following periodicals may also be of interest to you: *American Real Estate and Urban Economics Association Journal, Business Conditions Digest, Growth and Change, Housing Market Report, Housing Starts (Census), Journal of Housing, Journal of Urban Economics, New One-Family Houses Sold and For Sale (Census), Survey of Current Business, Trends in Housing, Urban Growth and Urban Land.*

ADDITIONAL
READINGS

Investing in Real Estate

KEY TERMS

Cash flow: the number of dollars remaining each year after an investor collects rents and pays operating expenses and mortgage payments

Cash-on-cash: the cash flow produced by a property divided by the amount of cash necessary to purchase it

Downside risk: the possibility that an investor will lose his money in an investment

Equity build-up: the increase of one's equity in a property due to mortgage balance reduction and price appreciation

Investment strategy: a plan that balances returns available with risks that must be taken in order to enhance the investor's overall welfare

Leverage: the impact that borrowed funds have on investment return

Negative cash flow: a condition wherein the cash paid out exceeds the cash received

Prospectus: a disclosure statement that describes an investment opportunity

Straight-line depreciation: depreciation in equal amounts each year over the life of the asset

Tax shelter: the income tax savings that an investment can produce for its owner

The monetary returns that are possible from real estate ownership make it a very attractive investment. However, at the same time the real estate investor takes two risks: he may never obtain a return on his investment and he may never recover his investment. There are no simple answers as to what is a "sure-fire" real estate investment. Rather, success depends on intelligently made decisions. With that in mind, we shall consider investment benefits, tax consequences, property selection, investment timing, investment strategy, and limited partnerships.

BENEFITS OF REAL ESTATE INVESTING

The monetary benefits of investing in real estate come from cash flow, tax shelter, mortgage reduction, and appreciation.

Appreciation is the increase in property value that the owner hopes will occur while owning it. Enough appreciation can offset underestimated expenses, overestimated rents and a rising adjustable loan. Without appreciation, a property must produce enough rental income to pay the operating expenses and loan interest, cover wear and obsolescence, and give the investor a decent return.

Mortgage reduction occurs when an investor uses a portion of a property's rental income to reduce the balance owing on the mortgage. At first, the reduction may be quite small because most of the loan payments might be applied more to payments of interest rather than the reduction of principal. But, eventually the balance owing begins to fall at a more rapid rate. Some investors invest with the idea that if they hold a rental property for the entire life of the loan, the tenants will have paid for the property. This presumes the investor is patient, and that the other elements of cash flow and income tax consequences are conducive to holding the property. Let's look at cash flow, tax shelter, depreciation, taxation of gains, and other real estate tax topics.

CASH FLOW

Cash flow refers to the number of dollars remaining each year after you collect rents and pay operating expenses and mortgage payments. For example, suppose you own an apartment building that generates $30,500 per year in rents. The operating expenses (including reserves) are $10,000 per year and mortgage payments are $20,000 per year. Given these facts, your cash flow picture is shown in Figure 23:1.

The purpose of calculating cash flow is to show the cash-in-the-pocket effect of owning a particular property. In Figure 23:1, $500 per year is going into your pocket. When money is flowing to you it is called a **positive cash flow.** If you must dip into your pocketbook to keep the property going, you have a **negative cash flow,** also called an "alligator." For example, if in Figure 23:1, the mortgage payments were $21,000 per year, there would be a negative cash flow. A

Figure 23:1

Rent receipts for the year	**$30,500**
Less operating expenses	10,000
Less mortgage loan payments	20,000
Equals cash flow	**$ 500**

negative cash flow does not automatically mean a property is a poor investment. There may be mortgage reduction, tax benefits and appreciation that more than offset this.

Two terms that are related to cash flow are net spendable and cash-on-cash. **Net spendable** is the same thing as cash flow and refers to the amount of spendable income a property produces for its owner. **Cash-on-cash** is the cash flow (or net spendable) that a property produces in a given year divided by the amount of cash required to buy the property. For example, if a property has a cash flow of $5,000 per year and can be purchased with a $50,000 down payment (including closing costs), the cash-on-cash figure for that property is 10%. For many real estate investors, this is the heart of the investment decision, namely, "How much do I have to put down and how much will I have in my pocket at the end of each year?"

TAX SHELTER

Broadly defined, **tax shelter** describes any tax-deductible expense generated by an investment property. Examples most often utilized for real estate investment are interest, maintenance, insurance, property taxes and depreciation. More narrowly defined, tax shelter refers only to **depreciation** (a noncash expense, discussed later in this chapter) that a taxpayer can report as a taxable deduction against other income.

The United States Congress has a decades-long history of tinkering with depreciation rules for income tax calculation. During the 1960s and 1970s, Congress wanted to encourage investment in real estate, especially residential real estate, and made income tax rules that allowed very generous treatment of depreciation expenses. Laws passed made it possible to deduct depreciation on property that was, in fact, appreciating in value. Moreover, tax laws made it possible to take a larger portion of depreciation early in the life of a building, and less later. This produced paper losses for tax purposes that could offset income from one's job, or from other investments. The tax benefits became so attractive that they were often a compelling force in choosing a property. In other words, not only did an investor look forward to the rents a property could produce, but also the tax savings it would produce, as well as mortgage reduction and anticipated appreciation. This, plus favorable tax status upon trade or sale, made real estate the hottest investment around.

The height of quick write-off came with a 1981 federal tax law that permitted a building to be entirely depreciated in 15 years, no matter how old or new it was. This depreciation method was called the Accelerated Cost Recovery System (ACRS). Then the tide started to change direction. There was concern in Congress that real estate had become an immense tax loophole that needed tightening. In 1984, the depreciation period was lengthened to 18 years. In 1985, it went to 19 years and rules were added regarding below-market interest rates on seller carryback financing (see Chapter 13). Then in the Fall of 1986, a new Internal Revenue Code was passed by Congress that took away nearly all the extra tax benefits previously given to real estate. Now, Congress said, real estate investments would have to stand more on their economic merits, not on favorable tax treatment. Let's look at some of the important changes regarding taxation of real estate investments as brought by the Internal Revenue Code of 1986.

1987–1988 TAX RULES   One of the important changes in how real estate investors will calculate and pay their income taxes for 1987, 1988 and beyond, has to do with depreciation. Under the new tax rules that took effect on January 1, 1987, the minimum depreciation period for real estate changed from 19 years to 27½ years for residential, and from 19 years to 31½ years for commercial. (Property already owned and being depreciated before that date continues to use whatever rules were in effect when its depreciation was started, i.e., they were **"grandfathered-in."**) Also, as of January 1, 1987, accelerated depreciation is repealed and only straight-line can be used. (Again, existing investments continue to use whatever depreciation method they started with.)

Loss Limitations   Another aspect of the new tax rules is that there are now stricter limits on how much loss can be deducted from a person's other income. This is true whether the property was purchased before or after January 1, 1987. This is now a major consideration in whether to buy or sell or hold real estate as an investment, and in choosing what types of real estate to own. Using our investment example, suppose that the $20,000 mortgage payment consists of $19,500 in interest (which is an expense for tax purposes) and $500 in loan reduction (which is not an expense for tax purposes). Suppose also that tax law allows $8,000 in depreciation on the property for the year. The result is a taxable loss as shown in Figure 23:2.

Under the old (pre-1987) tax rules, all of the operating expenses, the interest, and the depreciation was deductible against other income, with relatively little restriction. Under the new rules, i.e., those beginning January 1, 1987, there are substantial restrictions, and a distinction is made between "passive investors" and "active investors." If you are a **passive investor,** you can deduct your loss only against income from other passive investments. A passive investor is one who does not materially participate on a "regular, substantial and continuous basis," for example, a limited partner. For passive investments made before 1987, this rule is phased in over four years, from 1987 through 1990.

If you are an **active investor** (for example, you manage the rentals you own), it is possible to use as much as $25,000 of your losses to offset your other income (such as your job income). However, this only applies to taxpayers with up to $100,000 of adjusted gross income (as defined on one's annual IRS Form 1040). Above that, the loss deduction gradually is reduced and is eliminated at $150,000 of adjusted gross income. This aspect of the tax law change will have little effect on the middle-income person who owns a rental house or two, or a small apartment building, and has a hand in managing them. But, for persons with larger income who

Figure 23:2

Rent receipts for the year	$30,500
Less operating expenses	10,000
Less interest on loan	19,500
Less depreciation	8,000
Equals taxable income	**($ 7,000)***

* In accounting language, parentheses indicate a negative or minus amount.

are affected by the new Internal Revenue Code, one can expect to see some restructuring of investments and more investor participation. For example, non-active investors with passive losses will look for properties with passive income, such as parking lots. Those who do not actively manage their real estate holdings may take a more active role so as to qualify as an active investor. Loss-producing partnerships may be attractive acquisitions only for income-producing investors.

DEPRECIATION
CALCULATION

As noted several paragraphs earlier, under tax rules effective January 1, 1987, depreciation is to be straight-line. **Straight-line depreciation** is calculated by taking the total amount of anticipated depreciation and dividing by the number of years. For example, a building valued at $275,000 for depreciation purposes and depreciated over 27½ years using straight-line will have $10,000 in depreciation each year. (Note that only improvements are depreciable, land is not. Therefore, when buying investment real estate, it is necessary to subtract the value of the land from the purchase price before calculating depreciation.)

In contrast to straight-line depreciation, **accelerated depreciation** is any method of depreciation that allows depreciation at a rate faster than straight-line during the first several years of ownership. Although this is not allowed for real property placed in service starting January 1, 1987, it is retained for certain types of personal property used in business (such as a real estate agent's automobile) and for real property started under accelerated depreciation before 1987. Figure 23:3 illustrates straight-line (so-called because it is a straight line on a graph as shown), and accelerated depreciation. Neither method allows a taxpayer to depreciate more than the cost of the asset.

Passive losses (including depreciation) that are unusable in any given year can be carried forward from year-to-year and used later. Any losses carried forward into the year of sale can be deducted in full at that time. Depreciation recapture, a tax rule used in some past years to counter-balance the benefits of accelerated depreciation, phases out during 1987 and is repealed in 1988.

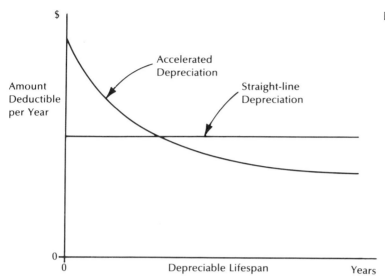

Figure 23:3

Straight-line depreciation allocates depreciation equally to each year of ownership. Accelerated depreciation allows more depreciation to be claimed sooner and less later.

CAPITAL GAIN

A major tax law change that went into effect starting January 1, 1987, is the repeal of the long-term capital gain exclusion. For real and personal property sold before that date, and provided it was owned more than six months, 60% of the gain was excluded from income. The new rule is that all gains are included and taxed as ordinary income, regardless of how long the property has been owned. At the same time, ordinary income tax rates are reduced, but the net effect is a higher tax on gains.

ADDITIONAL TAX LAW CHANGES

The most highly-advertised aspect of tax reform is that income tax rates will drop. Before 1987, rates for individuals ranged from 11% to 50%, and for corporations from 15% to 46%. For 1988, individual rates are 15% and 28%, and corporate rates are 15% to 34%. Additionally, taxpayers with joint taxable income above $71,900, and single taxpayers with taxable income above $43,150 pay a 5% surtax on top of the

28% rate. During 1987 there is a transition that mixes old and new rates to give a top rate of 38.5%. (This is called tax simplification!)

At-Risk Rules   Over the past several years, Congress has enacted **at-risk rules** for investors. The issue was that an investor could invest $1, and borrow $4 that did not require personal repayment, and take tax write-offs on the full $5. Congress passed rules that limited write-off to the amount actually invested plus **recourse financing,** i.e., the investor is personally obligated to repay. Under the old rules, this applied to nearly every investment, except real estate. Under the new rules, it applies to real estate. But, real estate sales nearly always require financing, and it is often **nonrecourse financing,** i.e., there is no personal obligation, only the value of the property secures the debt. Therefore, Congress considers the amount at risk in real estate to be the sum of third-party financing (note that this does not include seller financing), recourse indebtedness, and cash.

Installment Sales   In the past, a seller of real estate who had a substantial gain might choose to sell on the **installment method** to spread out receipt of the gain, and, therefore the taxes on it. The new rules limit the benefits of using installment sales. Now, for rental property a minimum installment payment will be imputed to the seller for tax purposes, regardless of the amount actually received. This will be equal to the product of the seller's total debt-to-assets ratio times the face amount of the obligation. The wise seller will seek competent tax advice before agreeing to carry back a mortgage.

Construction-Period   In past years, Congress has set various policies as to
Expenses   whether or not interest paid during construction could be taken as an immediate expense or had to be added to the cost of the building and amortized. Beginning January 1, 1987, the rule changed from amortization over 10 years to amortization over the depreciable life of the asset, even though the interest is an actual, paid expense during the construction period. This tax change is a major disincentive for new construction.

In past years, it was possible to receive a credit against income taxes of as much as 10% of the purchase price of personal property used for business purposes. Real estate did not qualify, but sometimes personal property, such as individual air-conditioning units placed in windows, and stand-alone stoves and refrigerators, did qualify. The new Internal Revenue Code eliminates investment tax credits for all types of property.

Investment Tax Credit

In an effort to encourage individuals to rebuild older structures rather than tear them down or let them decay, Congress has had a policy of giving rehabilitation tax credits. Under the 1986 law, tax credits of 15%, 20% and 25% were available on the rehabilitation of certain old and/or historic structures. The new law continues rehabilitation tax credits and now historic structures are allowed a credit of 20%. (This effectively means the federal government will pick up 20% of the cost of rehabilitating an historic structure.) Non-historic structures constructed prior to 1935 receive a 10% tax credit. (The investor needs to have other income against which to claim the credit, and the passive loss rules apply.)

Rehabilitation Tax Credits

Whereas the new tax law mostly tightens the rules on real estate, there is one area that has loosened: low-income housing. A number of inducements such as tax-exempt bond financing, accelerated depreciation, and five-year amortization have been used in the past. The rules now allow a tax credit to owners of buildings that provide low-income rental housing. On new and newly rehabilitated housing, the credit is a maximum of 9% per year for 10 years. (Effectively, the government pays for most of the building.) On existing housing the credit is a maximum of 4% for 10 years.

Low-Income Housing Credit

Tax law changes have been made in the past decade with increasing frequency and impact. In fact, one of the biggest risks in real estate in the mid-1980s has been, and continues to be, tax law changes. The values of land and buildings can, and do, go up and down with changes in tax rules. (This is in addition to the marketplace risks that an investor must take.) Therefore, it is of great importance that you stay

WATCH LIST

abreast of tax law changes, impending tax law changes, and even swings in the mood of Congress toward real estate. As noted earlier in this chapter, the 1960s and 1970s saw exceptionally favorable treatment of real estate by the tax laws. In the 1980s, real estate will have to stand on its own as an economic investment. Keep this in mind as you continue to read this chapter. Also keep in mind that because approximately two-out-of-three households in the United States own their homes, home ownership is likely to continue its favored tax status. Thus, as reported in Chapter 13, the new tax rules have pretty much left intact the personal deduction for home loan interest and property taxes, the 2-year rollover privilege and the $125,000 gain exclusion for persons over 55.

EQUITY BUILD-UP

An owner's **equity** in a property is defined as the market value of the property less all liens or other charges against the property. Thus, if you own a property worth $125,000 and owe $75,000, your equity is $50,000. If you own that property with your brother or sister, each with a one-half interest, your equity is $25,000 and his/her equity is $25,000.

Equity build-up is the change in your equity over a period of time. Suppose you purchase a small apartment building for $200,000, placing $60,000 down and borrowing the balance. Your beginning equity is your down payment of $60,000. If after 5 years you have paid the loan down to $120,000 and you can sell the property for $220,000, your equity is now $100,000. Since you started with $60,000, your equity build-up is $40,000. Figure 23:4 recaps this calculation.

Figure 23:4

CALCULATING EQUITY BUILD-UP

Equity at Time of Purchase		Equity 5 Years Later		Equity Build-up	
Purchase price	$200,000	Market value	$220,000	Current equity	$100,000
Mortgage loan	−140,000	Less loan balance	−120,000	Less beginning equity	−60,000
Down payment (equity)	$ 60,000	Equals current equity	$100,000	Equals equity build-up	$ 40,000

Leverage is the impact that borrowed funds have on investment return. The purpose of borrowing is to earn more on the borrowed funds than the funds cost. For example, suppose you are an investor and you have $250,000 to invest in an apartment building. If you use all your money to buy a $250,000 building there is zero leverage. If you use your $250,000 to buy a $500,000 building, there is 50% leverage. If you use your $250,000 to buy a $2,500,000 building there is 90% leverage.

LEVERAGE

Whether or not to try leverage depends on whether the property can reasonably be expected to produce cash flow, tax benefits, mortgage reduction and appreciation in excess of the cost of the borrowed funds. The decision also depends on your willingness to take risk. For example, the $250,000 building would have to fall to zero value before you lost all your money. Moreover, the building could experience a vacancy rate on the order of 60% and there would still be enough cash to meet out-of-pocket operating expenses. In other words, with zero leverage there is very little likelihood of a total financial wipe-out.

In contrast, if you buy the $2,500,000 building a 10% drop in the property's value to $2,250,000 wipes out your entire equity. Moreover, even the slightest drop-off in occupancy from 95% down to 85% will cause great strain on your ability to meet mortgage loan payments and out-of-pocket operating expenses.

But, suppose apartment building values increase by 10%. If you had bought the $250,000 building with borrowed funds, it will now be worth $275,000, an increase of $25,000 on your investment of $250,000. Similarly, if you had bought the $2,500,000 building it will now be worth $2,750,000, an increase of $250,000 on your investment of $250,000. As you can see, leverage can work both against you and for you. If the benefits from borrowing exceed the costs of borrowing, it is called **positive leverage.** If the borrowed funds cost more than they are producing, it is called **negative leverage.**

The real estate market offers a wide selection of properties for investments, including vacant land, houses, condominiums, small, medium, and large apartment buildings, office

PROPERTY SELECTION

buildings, stores, industrial property, and so forth. Selecting a suitable type of property is a matter of matching an investor's capital with his attitudes toward risk taking and the amount of time he is willing to spend on management. Let's begin by looking at the ownership of vacant land.

Vacant Land   The major risk of owning vacant land as an investment is that one will have to wait too long for an increase in value. Vacant land produces no income, yet it consumes the investor's dollars in the form of interest, property taxes, insurance, and eventually selling costs. The rule of thumb is that the market value of vacant land must double every 5 years for the investor to break even. If this increase does not occur, the owner will have spent more on interest, insurance, property taxes, brokerage fees, and closing costs than is made on the price increase.

The key to successful land speculating is in outguessing the general public. If the public feels that development of a vacant parcel to a higher use is 10 years in the future, the market price will reflect the discounted cost at current interest rates and property taxes for that waiting period. If the land speculator buys at these prices, and the higher use occurs in 5 years, there is a good chance the purchase will be profitable. However, the speculator will lose money if the public expects the higher use to occur in 5 years and it actually takes 10 years.

Finally, land speculators expose themselves to an extra risk that owners of improved property can usually avoid. When it comes time to sell, unless buildings will immediately be placed upon the land by the purchaser, very few lenders will loan the purchaser money to buy the land. This may force the seller to accept the purchase price in the form of a down payment plus periodic payments for the balance. If the interest rate on the balance is below prevailing mortgage rates, as often happens in land sales, the seller is effectively subsidizing the buyer. Furthermore, if the payments are made over several years, the seller takes the risk that the money he receives will buy less because of inflation.

Houses and   Houses and condominiums are the smallest properties
Condominiums   available in income-producing real estate and as such are

within the financial reach of more prospective investors than apartment buildings, stores, or offices. Moreover, they can usually be purchased with lower down payments and interest rates, because lenders feel that loans on houses and condominiums are less prone to default than on larger buildings. With a small property, the investor can fall back upon salary and other income to meet loan payments in the event rents fall short. With larger buildings, the lender knows he must rely more on the rental success of the property and less on the owner's other sources of income.

Houses and condominiums are usually overpriced in relation to the monthly rent they can generate. This is because their prices are influenced both by the value of the shelter they provide and the amenity value of home ownership. Thus, an investor must pay what prospective owner-occupants are willing to pay, yet when the property is rented, a tenant will pay only for the shelter value. However, when the investor sells, the sale price will be higher than would be justified by rents alone. What this means is that the investor can usually expect a negative cash flow during ownership. Consequently, there must be a substantial increase in property value to offset the monthly negative cash flow, and give the investor a good return on investment.

Because considerable appreciation must occur to make house and condominium investments profitable, many investors who start with these move to more income-oriented properties as their capital grows. Particularly popular with investors who have modest amounts of investment capital are duplexes (two units), triplexes (three units), and fourplexes (four units).

Small Apartment Buildings

If it were necessary to hire professional management, such small buildings would be uneconomical to own. However, for most owners of two- to four-unit apartment buildings, management is on a do-it-yourself basis. Moreover, it is possible for the owner to live on the premises. This eliminates a cash outlay for management and allows the owner to reduce repair and maintenance expenses by handling them himself. Also, with the owner living on the property, tenants are encouraged to take better care of the premises and discouraged from moving out without paying their rent. Finally, the ownership of a residential rental property provides the owner with a wealth of experience and education in property management.

Medium-size Buildings   Apartment buildings containing 5 to 24 units also present good investment opportunities for those with sufficient down payment. However, in addition to analyzing the building, rents, and neighborhood, thought must be given to the matter of property management before a purchase is made. An apartment building of this size is not large enough for a full-time manager; therefore, the owner must either do the job or hire a part-time manager to live on the property. An owner who does the job should be willing to live on the property and devote a substantial amount of time to management, maintenance, and upkeep activities. If a part-time manager is hired, the task is to find one who is knowledgeable and capable of maintaining property, showing vacant units, interviewing tenants, collecting rents on time, and handling landlord-tenant relations in accordance with local landlord-tenant laws. As the size of an apartment building increases, so does its efficiency. As a rule of thumb, when a building reaches 25 units, it will generate enough rent so that a full-time professional manager can be hired to live on the premises. With a live-in manager, the property owner need not reside on the property nor be involved in day-to-day management chores. This is very advantageous if the owner has another occupation where time is better spent.

Larger Apartment   As the number of apartment units increases, the cost of
Buildings   management per unit drops. Beyond 60 units, assistant managers can be hired. This makes it possible to have a representative of the owner on the premises more hours of the day to look after the investment and keep the tenants happy. Size also means it is possible to add recreational facilities and other amenities that are not possible on a small scale. The cost of having a swimming pool in a 10-unit building might add so much to apartment rents that they would be priced out of the market. The same pool in a 50- or 100-unit building would make relatively little difference in rent. As buildings reach 200 or more units in size, it becomes economical to

add such things as a children's pool, gymnasium, game room, lounge, and a social director.

Since larger apartment buildings cost less to manage per unit and compete very effectively in the market for tenants, they tend to produce larger cash flows per invested dollar. However, errors in location selection, building design, and management policy are magnified as the building grows in size. Also, many lenders, particularly small- and medium-sized banks and savings associations, are simply not large enough to lend on big projects. Finally, the number of investors who can single-handedly invest a down payment of $500,000 or more is limited. This has caused the widespread growth of the limited partnership as a means of making the economies of large-scale ownership available to investors with as little as $2,000 to invest.

Office buildings offer the prospective investor not only a higher rent per square foot of floor space than any of the investments discussed thus far, but also larger cash flows per dollar of property worth. This is because office buildings are costlier to build and operate than residential structures, and because they expose the owner to more risk.

Office Buildings

The higher construction and operating costs of an office building reflect the amenities and services office users demand. To be competitive today, an office building must offer air-conditioning to all tenants on a room-by-room basis, thus adding to construction and operating costs. Office users also expect and pay for daily office housecleaning services, such as emptying waste baskets, cleaning ashtrays, dusting, and vacuuming. Apartment dwellers neither expect these services nor pay for them.

Tenant turnover is more expensive in an office building than an apartment building because a change in office tenants usually requires more extensive remodeling. To offset this, building owners include the cost of remodeling in the tenant's rent. Another consideration is that it is not unusual for office space to remain vacant for long periods of time. Also, if a building is rented to a single tenant, a single vacancy means there is no income at all. To reduce tenant turnover, incentives such as lower rent may be offered if a tenant agrees to sign a longer lease, such as 5 years instead of 1 or 2 years. Care, however, must be taken on longer leases so that the owner does not become locked into a fixed monthly rent while operating costs escalate.

The risk in properly locating an office building is greater than with a residential property since office users are very particular about where they locate. If a residential building is not well located, the owner can usually drop rents a little and still fill the building. To do the same with an office building may require a much larger drop; then, even with the building full, it may not generate enough rent to pay the operating expenses and mortgage payments. Finally, the tax shelter benefits available from offices may not be as attractive as comparably priced apartments. This is because compared to office buildings, residential properties tend to have a higher percentage of their value in depreciable improvements and less in nondepreciable land.

INVESTMENT TIMING

The potential risks and rewards available from owning improved real estate depend to a great extent on the point in the life of a property at which an investment is made. Should one invest while a project is still an idea? Or is it better to wait until it is finished and fully rented? That depends on the risks one can afford and the potential rewards.

Land Purchase

The riskiest point to invest in a project is when it is still an idea in someone's head. At this point, money is needed to purchase land. But beyond the cost of the land, there are many unknowns, including the geological suitability of the land to support buildings, the ability to obtain the needed zoning, the cost of construction, the availability of a loan, the rents the market will pay, how quickly the property will find tenants, the expenses of operating the property, and finally the return the investor will obtain. Even though the investor may have a feasibility study that predicts success for the project, such a report is still only an educated guess. Therefore, the anticipated returns to an investor entering a project at this point must be high to offset the risks he takes. As the project clears such hurdles as zoning approval, obtaining construction cost bids, and finding a lender, it becomes less risky. Therefore, a person who invests after these hurdles are cleared would expect somewhat less potential reward. Nonetheless, the investor is buying into the project at a relatively low price; if it is successful, he will enjoy a developer's profit upon which no income tax must be paid until the property is finally sold. Against this, he takes the risk that the project may stall along the way or that, once completed, it will lose money.

Another major milestone is reached when the project is completed and opens its doors for business. At this point, the finished cost of the building is known, and during the first 12 months of operations the property owners learn what rents the market will pay, what level of occupancy will be achieved and what actual operating expenses will be. As estimates are replaced with actual operating experience, the risk to the investor decreases. As a result, the investor entering at this stage receives a smaller dollar return on his investment, but is more certain of his return than if he had invested earlier.

Project Completion

A building is new only once, and after its first year it begins to face competition from newer buildings. However, if an inflationary economy forces up the construction cost of newer buildings, existing buildings will be able to charge less rent. Furthermore, newer buildings may be forced to use less desirable sites. During the first 10 years, occupancy rates are stable, operating expenses are well established, tax benefits are good, and the building is relatively free of major repairs or replacements.

First Decade

As a building passes its tenth birthday, the costs and risks it presents to a prospective investor change. Before buying, he must ask whether the neighborhood is still expected to remain desirable to tenants and whether the building's location will increase in value enough to offset wear and tear and obsolescence. A careful inspection must be made of the structure to determine whether poor construction quality will soon result in costly repairs. Also, the investor must be prepared for normal replacements and expenses such as

Second Decade

new appliances, water heaters, and a fresh coat of paint. As a result, an investor buying a 10-year-old building will seek a larger return than when the building was younger.

Third & Fourth Decades   Larger returns are particularly important as a building reaches its twentieth year and major expense items such as a new roof, replacement of plumbing fixtures, repair of parking areas, and remodeling become necessary. As a building approaches and passes its thirtieth year, investors must consider carefully the remaining economic life of the property and whether rents permit a return on investment as well as a return of investment. Also, maintenance costs climb as a building becomes older, and decisions will be necessary regarding whether or not major restoration and remodeling should be undertaken. If it is, the cost must be recovered during the balance of the building's life. The alternative is to add little or no money to the building, a decision the surrounding neighborhood may already be forcing upon the property owner. Older properties may offer attractive tax benefits and have been a strong magnet to real estate investors who hope to find properties that can be fixed up for a profit. However, care must be taken not to overpay for this privilege.

Building Recycling   More buildings are torn down than fall down, and this phase in a building's life also represents an investment opportunity. However, like the first stage in the development cycle, raw land, the risks are high. In effect, when the decision is made to purchase a structure with the intention of demolishing it, the investor is counting on the value of the land being worth more in another use. That use may be a government-sponsored renewal program, or the investor may be accumulating adjoining properties with the ultimate intention of creating plottage value by demolishing the structures and joining the lots. Because the risks of capital loss in this phase are high, the potential returns should be too.

"GLITAMAD"   The acronym GLITAMAD, developed by Maury Seldin and Richard Swesnick, is a helpful way to remember the various phases in the life cycle of improved real estate investments. (See Figure 23:5.)

"GLITAMAD"	Figure 23:5

G = Ground (the raw land stage)

L = Loan (long-term loan
      commitment)   Increasing risk,
                                     Increasing returns

I = Interim (short-term loan and
      construction)

T = Tenancy (building filled
      with tenants)   Least risk,
                                     Least returns
A = Absorption (second through
      tenth year)

M = Maturity (eleventh through
      thirtieth year)   Increasing risk,
                                     Increasing returns
A = Aging (more than 30 years)

D = Demise (demolition, reuse
      of the land)

As the risk that an investor will suffer a loss increases, the expected returns must increase.

Source: Maury Seldin and Richard H. Swesnik, *Real Estate Investment Strategy,* copyright © 1970, John Wiley & Sons, Inc., New York. Used by permission.

The objective in developing a personal investment strategy is to balance the returns available with the risks that must be taken so that the overall welfare of the investor is enhanced. To accomplish this, it is very helpful to look at lifetime income and consumption patterns.

DEVELOPING A PERSONAL INVESTMENT STRATEGY

In Figure 23:6 the broken line represents the income that a person can typically expect to receive at various ages during his or her life. It includes income from wages, pensions, and investments, and is the same income curve that was discussed in Chapter 22. The solid line represents a person's lifetime consumption pattern. Taken together, the two lines show that, during the first 20 to 25 years, consumption exceeds income. Then the situation reverses itself and income outpaces consumption. If one is planning an investment program, these are the years to carry it out.

Figure 23:6 shows that an investment opportunity offering a high risk of loss is better suited for a person under the age of 45. Then, even if the investment does turn sour, the

Risk Taking

Figure 23:6   **LIFETIME INCOME AND CONSUMPTION PATTERNS**

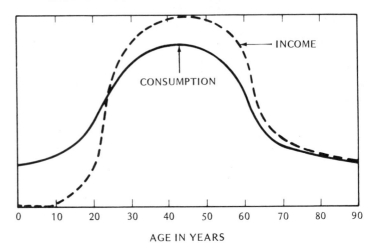

investor still has a substantial amount of working life remaining to recover financially. An investor between 45 and 55 years of age should be somewhat more cautious in terms of risk taking, since there is less time to make a financial recovery if the need arises. Above the age of 55, high-risk investments are even less appropriate for the same reason. Therefore, as a person reaches 55, 60, and 65, there should be a program of moving toward relatively risk-free investments, even though the returns will be smaller. Upon retirement, the investor can live off the investments he or she made when younger.

Debt Repayment   Mortgage debt commitments that require a portion of the investor's personal income should also be considered in light of one's position on the lifetime income and consumption curves. This is done to ascertain whether there will be sufficient income in the future to meet the loan payments. Not to consider the future may force a premature sale, perhaps in the midst of a very sluggish market at a distressed price. For the investor who has passed his income peak, financing with less debt and more equity means a higher probability that the properties will generate enough income to meet monthly loan payments. Also, with fewer dollars going to debt repayment, more can be kept by the investor for living expenses. By comparison, a relatively young investor may be handicapped by the lack of starting capital; however, he has the advantages of time and increasing income on his side.

The same points made here in connection with investments can also be applied to one's home. If a homeowner can purchase a home with a mortgage and then pay down the mortgage during those years in life when income substantially exceeds consumption, the home can be carried debt free into retirement to provide a place to live without mortgage payments. The home then becomes an investment in every sense of the word.

VALUING AN INVESTMENT

Chapter 16, "Real Estate Appraisal," discussed value from the standpoint of an appraiser or listing agent who uses current marketplace facts to estimate the value of a property. An investor's valuation problem is somewhat different. An investor knows the seller's asking price, can find information relating to the current income and expenses of a property and can project future income based on these. Additionally, an investor will have information on how the property can be financed and will have some figure in mind as to how much appreciation to expect. From these, the investor calculates the anticipated return on investment. If this return is more appealing than alternative investments, the property is purchased. If not, no sale results. Figure 23:7 illustrates the different viewpoints of the appraiser and the investor.

LIMITED PARTNERSHIPS

As discussed earlier in this chapter, large investment properties have a number of economic advantages over small ones. Yet the vast majority of investors in the United States do not have the capital to buy a large project single-handedly. Moreover, many persons who would like to own real estate

Figure 23:7

Appraiser's Viewpoint	Investor's Viewpoint
$Value = \dfrac{Net\ Income}{Return}$	$Return = \dfrac{Net\ Income}{Price}$

The appraiser solves for value. The investor solves for return.

do not do so because they wish to avoid the work and responsibilities of property management. As a result, the United States has witnessed the widespread use of limited partnerships for real estate investment. This popular form of investment offers investors the following advantages:

1. Management of the property and financial affairs of the partnership by the general partner.
2. Financial liability limited to the amount invested.
3. The opportunity for a small investor to own a part of large projects and to diversify.

The organizers of a limited partnership are responsible for selecting properties, putting them into a financial package, and making it available to investors. As a rule, the organizers are the general partners and the investors are the limited partners. For their efforts in organizing the partnership, the general partners receive a cash fee from the limited partners and/or a promotional interest in the partnership.

Property Purchase Methods

Property is purchased by one of two methods. The organizers can either buy properties first and then seek limited partners, or they can find limited partners first and then buy properties. The first approach is a **specific property offering.** The second is a **blind pool.** The advantage of the specific property offering is that the prospective limited partner knows in advance precisely what properties will be owned. However, this approach requires the organizers either to find a seller who is willing to wait for a partnership to be formed or to buy the property in their own names using their own capital. If they use their own capital, the organizers risk the chance of financial loss if limited partners cannot be found.

The advantage of the blind pool is that the organizers do not buy until money has been raised from the limited partners. This requires less capital from the organizers, and avoids the problem of holding property but not being able to find sufficient investors. Also, the organizers can negotiate better prices from sellers when they have cash in hand. However, if the organizers are poor judges of property, the investors may wind up owning property that they would not have otherwise purchased.

Once property is purchased, the general partners are responsible for managing the property themselves or selecting a management firm to do the job. In addition, the general partners must maintain the accounting books and at least once a year remit to each investor his portion of the cash flow, an accounting of the partnership's performance for the year, and profit or loss data for income tax purposes. With regard to selling partnership property, the partnership agreement usually gives the limited partners the right to vote on when to sell, to whom to sell, and for how much. In practice, the general partners decide when to put the matter up to a vote, and the limited partners usually follow their advice.

Property Management

The word "limited" in limited partnership refers to the limited financial liability of the limited partner. In a properly drawn agreement, limited partners cannot lose more than they have invested. By comparison, the general partners are legally liable for all the debts of the partnership, up to the full extent of their entire personal worth. Being a limited partner does not eliminate the possibility of being asked at a later date for more investment money if the properties in the partnership are not financially successful. When this happens, each limited partner must decide between adding more money in hopes the partnership will soon make a financial turnaround, or refusing to do so and being eliminated from the partnership. By way of comparison, an individual investor who buys real estate in his own name takes the risks of both the limited and general partner.

Financial Liability

Investing with others can provide diversification. For example, a limited partnership of 200 members each contributing $5,000 would raise $1,000,000. This could be used as a down payment on one property worth $4,000,000 or on four different properties priced at $1,000,000 each. If the $4,000,000 property is purchased, the entire success or failure of the partnership rides on that one property. With four $1,000,000 properties, the failure of one can be balanced by the success of the others. Even greater diversification can be achieved by purchasing properties in different rental price ranges, in different parts of the same city, and in different cities in the country. Regard-

Investment Diversification

ing income tax benefits, a very important advantage of the limited partnership is that it allows the investor to be taxed as though he is the sole owner of the property, because the partnership itself is not subject to taxation. All income and loss items, including any tax shelter generated by the property, are proportioned to each investor directly.

Service Fees   The prospective investor should carefully look at the price the organizers are charging for their services. Is it adequate, but not excessive? To expect good performance from capable people, they must be compensated adequately, but to overpay reduces the returns from the investment that properly belong to those who provide the capital. When is the compensation to be paid? If management fees are paid in advance, there is less incentive for the organizers to provide quality management for the limited partners after the partnership is formed. The preferred arrangement is to pay for management services as they are received, and for the limited partners to reserve the right to vote for new management. Similarly, it is preferable to base a substantial portion of the fee for organizing the partnership on the success of the investment. By giving the organizers a percentage of the partnership's profits instead of a fixed fee, the organizers have a direct stake in the success of the partnership.

Pitfalls   Although the limited partnership form of real estate ownership offers investors many advantages, experience has shown that there are numerous pitfalls that can separate investors from their money. Most importantly, a limited partner should recognize that the success or failure of a limited partnership is dependent on the organizers. Do they have a good record in selecting, organizing, and managing real estate investments in the past? Are they respected in the community for prompt and honest dealings? Will local banks and building suppliers offer them credit? What is their rating with credit bureaus? Are they permanent residents of the community in which they operate? Do the county court records show pending lawsuits or other legal complaints against them?

With reference to the properties in the partnership, are the income projections reasonable and have adequate allowances been made for vacancies, maintenance, and management? Overoptimism, sloppy income and expense projections, and outright shading of the truth will ultimately be costly to the investor. Unless there is absolute confidence in the promoters, one should personally visit the properties in the partnership and verify the rent schedules, vacancy levels, operating expenses, and physical condition of the improvements. Consideration should also be given to the partnership's **downside risk** (that is, the risk of losing one's money).

The careful investor will consult with a lawyer to make certain that the partnership agreement does limit liability to the amount invested, and that the tax benefits will be as advertised. He will also want to know what to expect if the partnership suffers financial setbacks. Are the partnership's properties to be sold at a loss or at a foreclosure sale, or do the general partners stand ready to provide the needed money? Will the limited partners be asked to contribute? The prospective investor should also investigate to see if the properties are overpriced. Far too many partnerships organized to date have placed so much emphasis on tax shelter benefits that the entire matter of whether the investment was economically feasible has been overlooked. Even to a 28% bracket taxpayer, a dollar wasted before taxes is still 28¢ wasted after taxes.

Finally, to receive maximum benefits from his investment, the investor must be prepared to stay with the partnership until the properties are refinanced or sold. The resale market for limited partnership interests is almost nonexistent, and when a buyer is found, the price is usually below the proportional worth of the investor's interest in the partnership. Moreover, the partnership agreement may place restrictions on limited partners who want to sell their interests.

One major problem with limited partnerships has been that they are illiquid. Once an investor invests, the commitment is to stay in until the partnership dissolves, and this can be 5, 10, or even 15+ years later. Until then, the limited partner can convert to cash only by selling to someone else or sometimes back to the partnership. This is usually done

Master Limited Partnerships

at a substantial discount to the value of the property in the partnership, assuming a sale can even be arranged. Into this need has come the **master limited partnership** (MLP). MLPs are limited partnerships that can be traded on a stock exchange nearly as easily as corporate stock. Thus, an investor can buy into a partnership after it has been formed, and sell out of it before it is dissolved. Meanwhile, the investor receives the available tax advantages of a limited partnership. However, if the underlying partnership is not well run, has poorly-operating properties, or is uneconomic, simply making the partnership easily traded is no magic. MLPs do offer liquidity, but you must still carefully analyze the partnership's ability to perform before investing in it.

DISCLOSURE LAWS   Because investors are vulnerable to unsound investments and exploitation at the hands of limited partnership organizers, state and federal disclosure laws have been passed to protect them if the investment qualifies as a "security." Administered by the Securities & Exchange Commission at the federal level and by Texas Securities Board at the state level, these laws require organizers and sales staff to disclose all pertinent facts surrounding the partnership offering. Prospective investors must be told how much money the organizers wish to raise, what portion will go for promotional expenses and organizers' fees, what properties have been (or will be) purchased, from whom they were bought, and for how much. Also, prospective investors must be provided with a copy of the partnership agreement and given property income and expense records for past years. They must be told how long the partnership expects to hold its properties until selling, the partnership's policy on cash flow distribution, the right of limited partners to a voice in management, the names of those responsible for managing the partnership properties, and how profits (or losses) will be split when the properties are sold.

The Prospectus   The amount of disclosure detail required by state and federal laws varies with the number of properties and the partners' relationship. For a handful of friends forming a partnership among themselves, there would be little in the way of formal disclosure requirements. However, as the number of investors increases and the partnership is offered to investors across state lines, disclosure requirements increase dramatically. It is not unusual for a disclosure statement, called a **prospectus,** to be 50 to 100 pages long.

The philosophy of disclosure laws is to make information available to prospective investors and let them make their own decisions. Thus, an investor is free to invest in an unsound investment so long as the facts are explained to him in advance. An alternative point of view is that many investors do not read nor understand disclosure statements; therefore, it is the duty of government to pass on the economic soundness of an investment before it can be offered to the public. The result has been the passage of **blue-sky laws** in several states. The first of these was passed by the Kansas legislature in 1911 to protect purchasers from buying into dubious investment schemes that sold them nothing more than a piece of the blue sky. Texas has retained these laws and applies them to limited partnerships and other securities offered within its borders.

Blue-Sky Laws

As the opening paragraph of this chapter suggested, you can become rich by investing in real estate. It should be pointed out, however, that success won't drop in your lap; it takes effort and courage. Good properties and good opportunities are always available, but you will look at many opportunities to find one good investment. You will also need to know which ones you don't want, and why. That part that takes effort. All investors need to know what a good opportunity looks like, and this book is a step in that direction. After you finish this text, start reading articles and books on real estate investing from libraries and bookstores and take courses in real estate investing. But most important, now is the time to get out and start looking at properties if you have not already done so. Begin to get a sense in the field for what you are learning from your books and classes. Always ask questions as you go along, and demand straight, reasonable answers. After you've viewed several dozen properties and talked to appraisers, lenders, brokers, property managers,

EFFORT AND COURAGE

etc., you will begin to get a feel for the market—what's for sale, what a property can earn, how much mortgage money costs, etc. As you do this you will see everything you've learned in this book come to life.

As you continue you will recognize what a good investment property looks like. At this point your next big step is to muster the courage to acquire it. All the real estate investment education you've received will not translate into money in your pocket until you make an offer; until you put your money, reputation, and good judgment on the line. There is no "get rich quick" formula, and don't expect there to be one. If you have a good, informed investment strategy and the courage to take the risks, the rewards are certainly attainable.

VOCABULARY REVIEW

Match terms **a–n** *with statements* **1–14.**

a. *Accelerated depreciation*	**h.** *Equity build-up*
b. *Active investor*	**i.** *GLITAMAD*
c. *At-risk*	**j.** *Leverage*
d. *Blind pool*	**k.** *Negative cash flow*
e. *Cash flow*	**l.** *Prospectus*
f. *Cash-on-cash*	**m.** *Straight-line*
g. *Downside risk*	**n.** *Tax shelter*

1. Number of dollars remaining each year after collecting rents and paying operating expenses and mortgage payments.
2. Requires the investor to dip into his own pocket.
3. Income tax savings that an investment can produce for its owner.
4. Results from mortgage balance reduction and price appreciation.
5. An acronym that refers to the various phases in the life cycle of an improved property.
6. A method of calculating depreciation that takes equal amounts of depreciation each year.
7. Any method of depreciation that achieves a faster rate of depreciation than the straight-line method.
8. A limited partnership wherein properties are purchased after the limited partners have invested their money.
9. The possibility that an investor will lose his money in an investment.
10. A disclosure statement that describes an investment opportunity.
11. The cash-flow of a property divided by the amount of cash necessary to purchase it.
12. As defined by tax law, the amount an investor risks is an investment.

13. The impact that borrowed funds have on investment return.
14. An investor who takes an active role in property management, as defined by income tax law.

QUESTIONS AND PROBLEMS

1. What is a tax-sheltered real estate investment?
2. What monetary benefits do investors expect to receive by investing in real estate?
3. What is the major risk that a speculator in vacant land takes?
4. What advantages and disadvantages do duplexes and triplexes offer to a prospective investor?
5. Is an investor better off investing in a project before it is built or after it is completed and occupied? Explain.
6. As a building grows older, why should an investor demand a higher return per dollar invested?
7. How does a person's age affect investment goals and the amount of investment risk that may be taken?
8. An investor is looking at a property that produces a net operating income of $22,000 per year. He expects the property to appreciate 50% in ten years and plans to finance it with a 25-year, 11% interest, 75% loan-to-value loan. If the property is priced to produce an 18% return on the investor's equity, how much is the seller asking? (Use Table 16:5 in Chapter 16.)
9. Another investor looks at the property described in Problem 8, but feels it will appreciate only 25% in value. How much would he offer to pay the seller?

ADDITIONAL READINGS

A Compilation of Texas Real Estate Owned by Publicly Held Limited Partnerships as of June 30, 1983. (**Friedman,** 1984, 69 pages). Technical report identifying and cataloging Texas real estate ownership by publicly held partnerships as of June 30, 1983.

"Don't Get Burned by Securities Laws" by **Anne Hamblin Schiave.** (*Real Estate Today,* May 84). Discusses how to comply with securities laws when selling real estate syndications.

Fundamentals of Real Estate Investing by **Jerry Ferguson.** (Scott-Foresman, 1984, 352 pages). Looks at the selection, acquisition, management and disposition of real estate. Focus is on small properties that can be acquired by individuals.

Preservation and Tax Benefits. (**Crumbley & Shelton,** 1984). A technical report examining the rehabilitation of historical structure as a tax shelter.

Real Estate Investment by **John Wiedemer.** (Reston, 1985, 300 pages). Includes financing, depreciation, taxation, property analysis, syndication, charts, tables, glossary, etc.

Successful Leasing and Selling of Retail Property by **Grubb & Ellis Co.**

(Real Estate Education Co., 1984, 235 pages). Includes developing property, qualifying clients, marketing, signs, showing, site presentation, financing, etc. Same author and publisher also offer *Successful Industrial Real Estate Brokerage* (1984, 312 pages) and *Successful Leasing and Selling of Office Property* (1983, 243 pages).

"Ten Questions to Ask About a Limited Partnership" by **Greg Anrig, Jr.** (*Money*, May 85, p. 165). This article provides guidelines to help the investor make a sound decision. (*Money Magazine* regularly has articles on real estate for persons with modest amounts to invest.)

*   *   *

The following periodicals may also be of interest to you: *Commercial Investment Journal, Database, Historic Preservation, Investing in Real Estate, National Real Estate Investor, Old House Journal, Preservation News, Property Investment Review, Real Estate Insider Newsletter, Real Estate Investing Letter, Real Estate Investment Digest, Real Estate Investing Ideas, Real Estate Securities Journal, Real Estate Syndication Digest* and *RESSI Review.*

Construction Illustrations and Terminology

COMBINED SLAB AND FOUNDATION (thickened edge slab)   **Figure A:1**

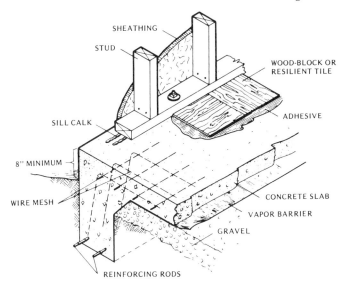

BASEMENT DETAILS   **Figure A:2**

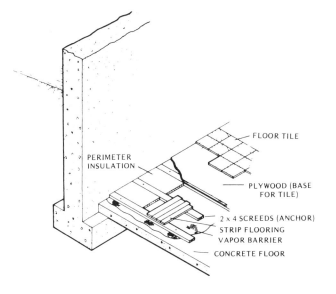

Figure A:3

FLOOR FRAMING
1. nailing bridging to joists;   2. nailing board subfloor to joists;
3. nailing header to joists;   4. toenailing header to sill

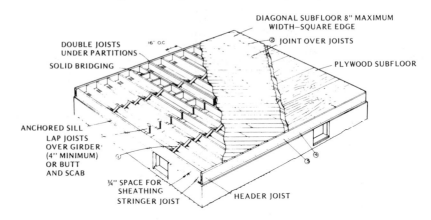

Figure A:4

WALL FRAMING USED WITH PLATFORM CONSTRUCTION

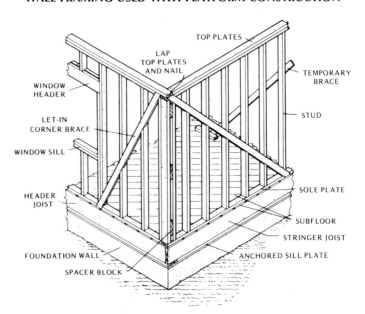

HEADERS FOR WINDOWS AND DOOR OPENINGS

Figure A:5

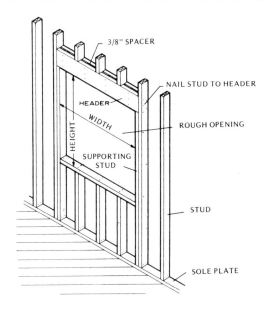

3/8" SPACER

NAIL STUD TO HEADER

HEADER

WIDTH

HEIGHT

ROUGH OPENING

SUPPORTING STUD

STUD

SOLE PLATE

VERTICAL APPLICATION OF PLYWOOD OR STRUCTURAL INSULATING BOARD SHEATHING

Figure A:6

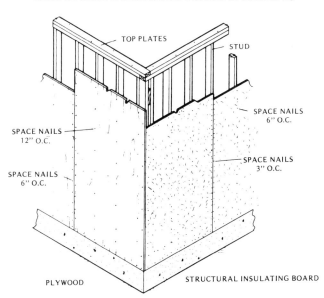

TOP PLATES

STUD

SPACE NAILS 6" O.C.

SPACE NAILS 12" O.C.

SPACE NAILS 3" O.C.

SPACE NAILS 6" O.C.

PLYWOOD

STRUCTURAL INSULATING BOARD

Figure A:7

EXTERIOR SIDING

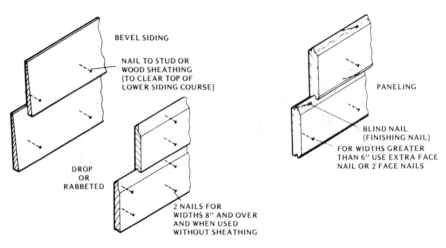

BEVEL SIDING

NAIL TO STUD OR
WOOD SHEATHING
(TO CLEAR TOP OF
LOWER SIDING COURSE)

PANELING

DROP
OR
RABBETED

BLIND NAIL
(FINISHING NAIL)
FOR WIDTHS GREATER
THAN 6" USE EXTRA FACE
NAIL OR 2 FACE NAILS

2 NAILS FOR
WIDTHS 8" AND OVER
AND WHEN USED
WITHOUT SHEATHING

Figure A:8

VERTICAL BOARD SIDING

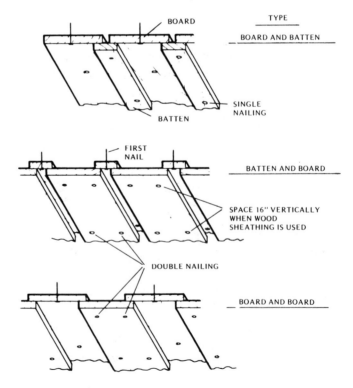

BOARD

TYPE

BOARD AND BATTEN

SINGLE
NAILING

BATTEN

FIRST
NAIL

BATTEN AND BOARD

SPACE 16" VERTICALLY
WHEN WOOD
SHEATHING IS USED

DOUBLE NAILING

BOARD AND BOARD

APPLICATION OF GYPSUM BOARD FINISH

A: vertical application;   B: horizontal application

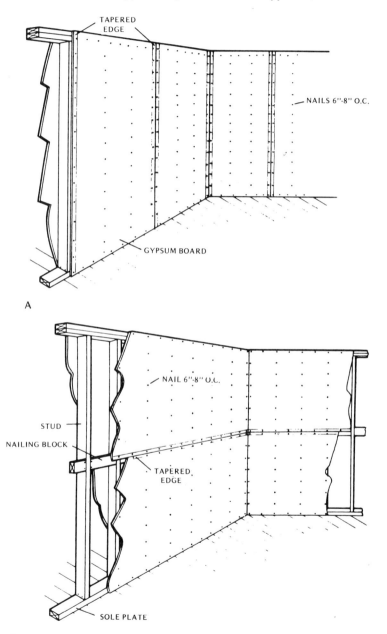

A

B

Figure A:10   **APPLICATION OF INSULATION**

A: wall section with blanket type;   B: wall section with "press-fit" insulation;   C: ceiling with full insulation

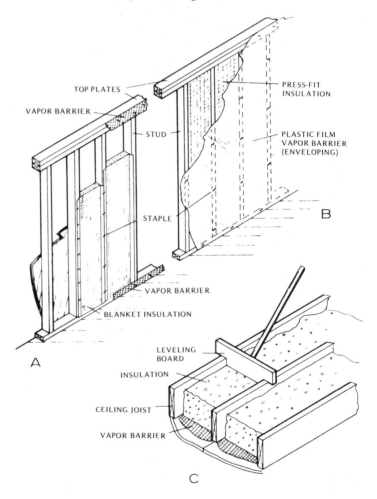

PLACEMENT OF INSULATION

A: in walls, floor, and ceiling;   B: in 1-1/2 story house;
C: at attic door;   D: in flat roof

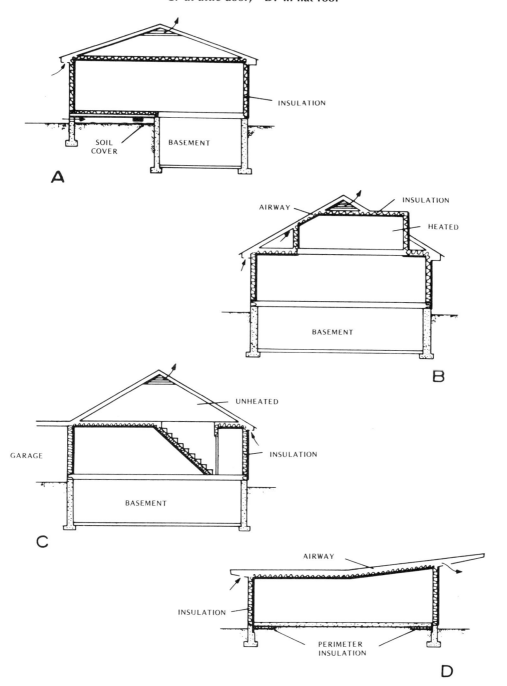

Figure A:12   **MASONRY FIREPLACE**

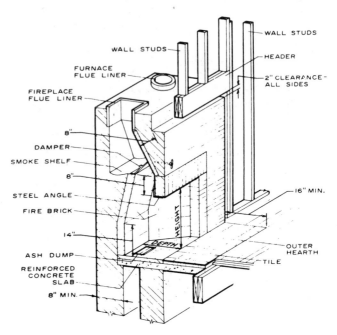

Figure A:13   **STAIRWAY DETAILS**

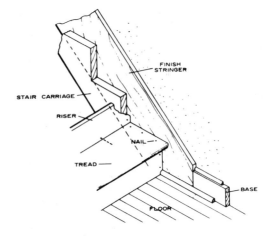

DOOR DETAILS

Figure A:14

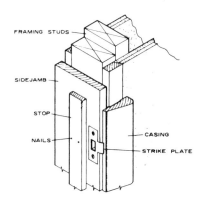

SOUND INSULATION

Figure A:15

WALL DETAIL	DESCRIPTION	STC RATING
	1/2" GYPSUM WALLBOARD	32
	5/8" GYPSUM WALLBOARD	37
	5/8" GYPSUM WALLBOARD (DOUBLE LAYER EACH SIDE)	45
	1/2" GYPSUM WALLBOARD 1 1/2" FIBROUS INSULATION	49
	RESILIENT CLIPS TO 3/8" GYPSUM BACKER BOARD 1/2" FIBERBOARD (LAMINATED) (EACH SIDE)	52

Figure A:16   **CEILING AND ROOF FRAMING**

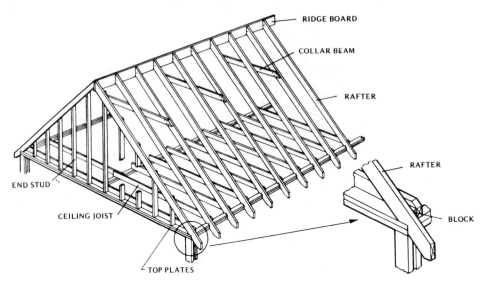

Figure A:17   **INSTALLATION OF BOARD ROOF SHEATHING, SHOWING BOTH**
CLOSED AND SPACED TYPES

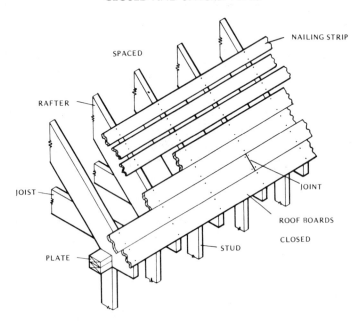

BUILT-UP ROOF

Figure A:18

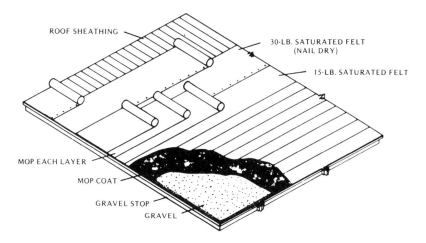

ROOF SHEATHING

30-LB. SATURATED FELT
(NAIL DRY)

15-LB. SATURATED FELT

MOP EACH LAYER

MOP COAT

GRAVEL STOP

GRAVEL

APPLICATION OF ASPHALT SHINGLES

Figure A:19

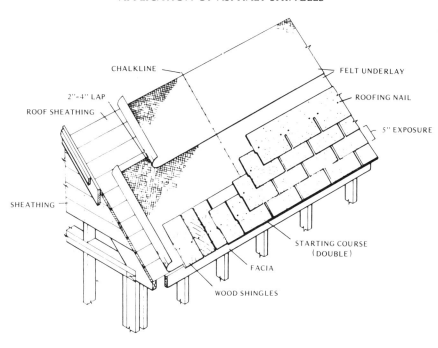

CHALKLINE

FELT UNDERLAY

2"-4" LAP

ROOFING NAIL

ROOF SHEATHING

5" EXPOSURE

SHEATHING

STARTING COURSE
(DOUBLE)

FACIA

WOOD SHINGLES

Figure A:20   **ROOFS USING SINGLE ROOF CONSTRUCTION**
                         A: flat roof;   B: low-pitched roof

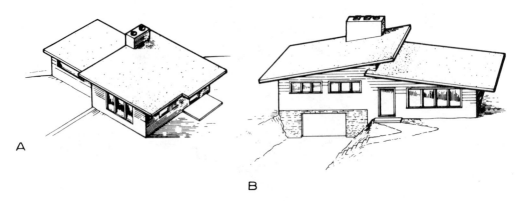

A

B

TYPES OF PITCHED ROOFS
A: gable;   B: gable with dormers;   C: hip

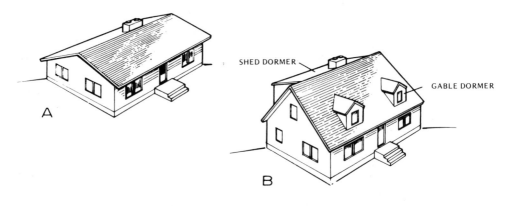

A

SHED DORMER

GABLE DORMER

B

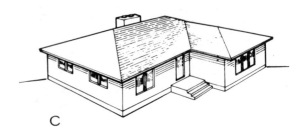

C

Title 113A—Real Estate Dealers

Art. 6573a. THE REAL ESTATE LICENSE ACT

Short title; license required; responsibility for acts and conduct; compensation and commissions

Section 1.

(a) This Act shall be known and may be cited as "The Real Estate License Act."

(b) It is unlawful for a person to act in the capacity of, engage in the business of, or advertise or hold himself out as engaging in or conducting the business of a real estate broker or a real estate salesman within this state without first obtaining a real estate license from the Texas Real Estate Commission. It is unlawful for a person licensed as a real estate salesman to act or attempt to act as a real estate agent unless he is, at such time, associated with a licensed Texas real estate broker and acting for the licensed real estate broker.

(c) Each real estate broker licensed pursuant to this Act is responsible to the commission, members of the public, and his clients for all acts and conduct performed under this Act by himself or by a real estate salesman associated with or acting for the broker.

(d) No real estate salesman shall accept compensation for real estate sales and transactions from any person other than the broker under whom he is at the time licensed or under whom he was licensed when he earned the right to compensation.

(e) No real estate salesman shall pay a commission to any person except through the broker under whom he is at the time licensed.

Definitions; prospective application of Act

Section 2.

As used in this Act:

(1) "Real estate" means a leasehold, as well as any other interest or estate in land, whether corporeal, incorporeal, freehold, or nonfree- **619**

hold, and whether the real estate is situated in this state or elsewhere.

(2) "Real estate broker" means a person who, for another person and for a fee, commission, or other valuable consideration, or with the intention or in the expectation or on the promise of receiving or collecting a fee, commission, or other valuable consideration from another person:

(A) sells, exchanges, purchases, rents, or leases real estate;

(B) offers to sell, exchange, purchase, rent, or lease real estate;

(C) negotiates or attempts to negotiate the listing, sale, exchange, purchase, rental, or leasing of real estate;

(D) lists or offers or attempts or agrees to list real estate for sale, rental, lease, exchange, or trade;

(E) appraises or offers or attempts or agrees to appraise real estate;

(F) auctions, or offers or attempts or agrees to auction, real estate;

(G) buys or sells or offers to buy or sell, or otherwise deals in options on real estate;

(H) aids, attempts, or offers to aid in locating or obtaining for purchase, rent, or lease any real estate;

(I) procures or assists in the procuring of prospects for the purpose of effecting the sale, exchange, lease, or rental of real estate; or

(J) procures or assists in the procuring of properties for the purpose of effecting the sale, exchange, lease, or rental of real estate.

(3) "Broker" also includes a person employed by or on behalf of the owner or owners of lots or other parcels of real estate, at a salary, fee, commission, or any other valuable consideration, to sell the real estate or any part thereof, in lots or parcels or other disposition thereof. It also includes a person who engages in the business of charging an advance fee or contracting for collection of a fee in connection with a contract whereby he undertakes primarily to promote the sale of real estate either through its listing in a publication issued primarily for such purpose, or for referral of information concerning the real estate to brokers, or both.

(4) "Real estate salesman" means a person associated with a Texas licensed real estate broker for the purposes of performing acts or transactions comprehended by the definition of "real estate broker" as defined in this Act.

(5) "Person" means an individual, a partnership, or a corporation, foreign or domestic.

(6) "Commission" means the Texas Real Estate Commission.

(7) If the sense requires it, words in the present tense include the future tense; in the masculine gender, include the feminine or neuter gender; in the singular number, include the plural number; in the plural number, include the singular number; the word "and" may be read "or"; and the word "or" may be read "and." This Act is substantive in character and is intended to be applied prospectively only.

Exemptions

Section 3.

The provisions of this Act shall not apply to any of the following persons and transactions, and each and all of the following persons and transactions are hereby exempted from the provisions of this Act, to wit:

(a) an attorney at law licensed in this state or in any other state;

(b) an attorney in fact under a duly executed power of attorney authorizing the consummation of a real estate transaction;

(c) a public official in the conduct of his official duties;

(d) a person acting officially as a receiver, trustee, administrator, executor, or guardian;

(e) a person acting under a court order or under the authority of a will or a written trust instrument;

(f) a salesperson employed by an owner in the sale of structures and land on which said structures are situated, provided such structures are erected by the owner in the due course of his business;

(g) an on-site manager of an apartment complex;

(h) transactions involving the sale, lease, or transfer of any mineral or mining interest in real property;

(i) an owner or his employees in renting or leasing his own real estate whether improved or unimproved;

(j) transactions involving the sale, lease, or transfer of cemetery lots.

Acts constituting broker or salesman

Section 4.

A person who, directly or indirectly for another, with the intention or on the promise of receiving any valuable consideration, offers, attempts, or agrees to perform, or performs, a single act defined in

Subdivisions 2 and 3, Section 2 of this Act, whether as a part of a transaction, or as an entire transaction, is deemed to be acting as a real estate broker or salesman within the meaning of this Act. The commission of a single such act by a person required to be licensed under this Act and not so licensed shall constitute a violation of this Act.

Real Estate Commission; disposition of fees; Research Center; application of Sunset Act

Section 5.

(a) *The administration of the provisions of this Act is vested in a commission, to be known as the "Texas Real Estate Commission," consisting of nine members to be appointed by the governor with the advice and consent of two-thirds of the senate present. The commissioners hold office for staggered terms of six years with the terms of three members expiring every two years. Each member holds office until his successor is appointed and has qualified. Within 15 days after his appointment, each member shall qualify by taking the constitutional oath of office and furnishing a bond payable to the Governor of Texas in the penal sum of $10,000, conditional on the faithful performance of his duties as prescribed by law. A vacancy for any cause shall be filled by the governor for the unexpired term. Notwithstanding any other provisions in this subsection, the six members of the commission in office on September 1, 1979, shall continue in office until the 5th day of October of the years in which their respective terms expire, or until their successors are appointed and have qualified. The terms of office of the appointees who fill the offices of incumbent members whose terms expire October 5, 1979, 1981, and 1983, expire on January 31, 1985, 1987, and 1989, respectively. Each succeeding term of office expires on January 31 of odd-numbered years. For the three public members initially appointed under this Act, the governor shall designate one member for a term expiring January 31, 1981, one member for a term expiring January 31, 1983, and one member for a term expiring January 31, 1985. At a regular meeting in February of each year, the commission shall elect from its own membership a chairman, vice-chairman, and secretary. Each member of the commission shall be present for at least one-half of the regularly scheduled meetings held each year by the commission. The failure of a member to meet this requirement* *automatically removes the member from the commission and creates a vacancy on the commission. A quorum of the commission consists of five members.*

(b) *All members, officers, employees, and agents of the commission are subject to the code of ethics and standards of conduct imposed by Chapter 421, Acts of the 63rd Legislature, Regular Session, 1973 (Article 6252–9b, Vernon's Texas Civil Statutes).*

(c) *Appointments to the commission shall be made without regard to the race, creed, sex, religion, or national origin of the appointees. Each member of the commission shall be a citizen of Texas and a qualified voter. Six members shall have been engaged in the real estate brokerage business as licensed real estate brokers as their major occupations for at least five years next preceding their appointments. Three members must be representatives of the general public who are not licensed under this Act and who do not have, other than as consumers, a financial interest in the practice of a real estate broker or real estate salesman. It is grounds for removal from the commission if:*

(1) a broker-member of the commission ceases to be a licensed real estate broker; or

(2) a person is required to register as a lobbyist under Chapter 305, Government Code, by virtue of his activities for compensation in or on behalf of a profession related to the operation of the commission.

(d) *Each member of the commission shall receive as compensation for each day actually spent on his official duties the sum of $75 and his actual and necessary expenses incurred in the performance of his official duties.*

(e) *The commission shall have the authority and power to make and enforce all rules and regulations necessary for the performance of its duties, to establish standards of conduct and ethics for its licensees in keeping with the purposes and intent of this Act or to insure compliance with the provisions of this Act. If the appropriate standing committees of both houses of the legislature acting under Subsection (g), Section 5, Administrative Procedure and Texas Register Act, as added (Article 6252–13a, Vernon's Texas Civil Statutes), transmit to the commission statements opposing adoption of a rule under that section, the rule may not take effect, or if the rule has already taken effect, the rule is repealed effective on the date the commission receives the committees' statements. In addition to any* *other action, proceeding, or remedy authorized by law, the commission shall have the right to institute an action in its own name to enjoin any violation of any provision of this Act or any rule or regulation of the commission and in order for the commission to sustain such action it shall not be necessary to allege or prove, either that an adequate remedy at law does not exist, or that substantial or irreparable damage would result from the continued violation thereof. Either party to such action may appeal to the appellate court having jurisdiction of said cause. The commission shall not be required to give any appeal bond in any action or proceeding to enforce the provisions of this Act.*

(f) The commission is empowered to select and name an administrator, who shall also act as executive secretary, and to select and employ such other subordinate officers and employees as are necessary to administer this Act. The salaries of the administrator and the officers and employees shall be fixed by the commission not to exceed such amounts as are fixed by the applicable general appropriations bill. The commission may designate a subordinate officer as assistant administrator who shall be authorized to act for the administrator in his absence. A person who is required to register as a lobbyist under Chapter 422, Acts of the 63rd Legislature, Regular Session, 1973, as amended (Article 6252–9c, Vernon's Texas Civil Statutes), may not act as the general counsel to the commission or serve as a member of the commission.

(g) The commission shall adopt a seal of a design which it shall prescribe. Copies of all records and papers in the office of the commission, duly certified and authenticated by the seal of the commission, shall be received in evidence in all courts with like effect as the original.

(h) Except as provided in Subsections (i) and (j) of this section, all money derived from fees, assessments, or charges under this Act, shall be paid by the commission into the State Treasury for safekeeping, and shall be placed by the State Treasurer in a separate fund to be available for the use of the commission in the administration of this Act on requisition by the commission. A necessary amount of the money so paid into the State Treasury is hereby specifically appropriated to the commission for the purpose of paying the salaries and expenses necessary and proper for the administration of this Act, including equipment and maintenance of supplies for the offices

or quarters occupied by the commission, and necessary travel expenses for the commission or persons authorized to act for it when performing duties under this Act. At the end of the state fiscal year, any unused portion of the funds in the special account, except such funds as may be appropriated to administer this Act pending receipt of additional revenues available for that purpose, shall be paid into the General Revenue Fund. The comptroller shall, on requisition of the commission, draw warrants from time to time on the State Treasurer for the amount specified in the requisition, not exceeding, however, the amount in the fund at the time of making a requisition. However, all money expended in the administration of this Act shall be specified and determined by itemized appropriation in the general departmental appropriation bill for the Texas Real Estate Commission, and not otherwise.

(i) *In the event that fees collected under the Residential Service Company Act (Article 6573b, Vernon's Texas Civil Statutes), are insufficient to fund the legislative appropriation for that activity, funds from the real estate license fund are hereby authorized to be used for the administration of that Act. In no event, however, will the total expenditures for that activity exceed the legislative appropriation therefor.*

(j) *Fifteen dollars received by the commission from fees received from real estate brokers and $7.50 received by the commission from fees received from real estate salesmen for licensure status shall be transmitted annually to Texas A & M University for deposit in a separate banking account. The money in the separate account shall be expended for the support and maintenance of the Texas Real Estate Research Center and for carrying out the purposes, objectives, and duties of the center. However, all money expended from the separate account shall be as determined by legislative appropriation.*

Texas Real Estate Research Center @ Texas A&M
Salesmen - $7.50/yr.
Brokers - $15.00/yr

(k) *The Texas Real Estate Commission is subject to the Texas Sunset Act (Chapter 325, Government Code). Unless continued in existence as provided by that Act, the commission is abolished and this Act expires September 1, 1991.*

(l) *The commission is subject to the open meetings law, Chapter 271, Acts of the 60th Legislature, Regular Session, 1967, as amended (Article 6252–17, Vernon's Texas Civil Statutes), and the Administrative Procedure and Texas Register Act, as amended (Article 6252–13a, Vernon's Texas Civil Statutes).*

Licenses; qualification

Section 6.

(a) A person desiring to act as a real estate broker in this state shall file an application for a license with the commission on a form prescribed by the commission. A broker desiring to engage a person to participate in real estate brokerage activity shall join the person in filing an application for a salesman license on a form prescribed by the commission.

(b) To be eligible for a license, an individual must be a citizen of the United States or a lawfully admitted alien, be at least 18 years of age, and be a legal resident of Texas for at least 60 days immediately preceding the filing of an application, and must satisfy the commission as to his honesty, trustworthiness, integrity, and competency. However, the competency of the individual, for the purpose of qualifying for the granting of licensure privileges, shall be judged solely on the basis of the examination referred to in Section 7 of this Act.

(c) To be eligible for a license, a corporation must designate one of its officers to act for it. The designated person must be a citizen of the United States or a lawfully admitted alien, be at least 18 years of age, and be a resident of Texas for at least 60 days immediately preceding the filing of an application, and must be qualified to be licensed individually as a real estate broker. However, the competency of the person shall be judged solely on the basis of the examination referred to in Section 7 of this Act.

Moral character checks

Section 6A.

(a) If, at any time before a person applies for a license under this Act, the person requests the commission to determine whether his moral character complies with the commission's moral character requirements for licensing under this Act and the person pays a $10 fee for the moral character determination, the commission shall make its determination of the person's moral character.

(b) Not later than the 30th day after the day on which the commission makes its determination, the commission shall give the person notice of the determination.

(c) If the person later applies for a license under this Act, the commission may conduct a supplemental moral character check of the person. The supplemental check may cover only the time since the day on which the person requested the original moral character determination.

Examinations, educational requirements; evidence of qualification

Section 7.

(a) Competency as referred to in Section 6 of this Act shall be established by an examination prepared by or contracted for by the commission. The examination shall be given at such times and at such places within the state as the commission shall prescribe. The examination shall be of scope sufficient in the judgment of the commission to determine that a person is competent to act as a real estate broker or salesman in a manner to protect the interest of the public. The examination for a salesman license shall be less exacting and less stringent than the examination for a broker license. The commission shall furnish each applicant with study material and references on which his examination shall be based. When an applicant for real estate licensure fails a qualifying examination, he may apply for reexamination by filing a request therefor together with the proper fee. The examination requirement shall be satisfied within one year from the date the application for a license is filed. Courses of study required for licensure shall include but not be limited to the following which shall be considered core real estate courses for all purposes of this Act:

(1) Principles of Real Estate (or equivalent) shall include but not be limited to an overview of licensing as a real estate broker and salesman, ethics of practice, titles to and conveyancing of real estate, legal descriptions, law of agency, deeds, encumbrances and liens, distinctions between personal and real property, contracts, appraisal, finance and regulations, closing procedures, and real estate mathematics.

(2) Real Estate Appraisal (or equivalent) shall include but not be limited to the central purposes and functions of an appraisal, social and economic determinant of value, appraisal case studies, cost, market data and income approaches to value estimates, final correlations, and reporting.

(3) Real Estate Law (or equivalent) shall include but not be limited to legal concepts of real estate, land description, real property rights and estates in land, contracts, conveyances, encumbrances, foreclosures, recording procedures, and evidence of titles.

(4) Real Estate Finance (or equivalent) shall include but not be limited to monetary systems, primary and secondary money markets, sources of mortgage loans, federal government programs, loan applications, processes and procedures, closing costs, alternative financial instruments, equal credit opportunity acts, community reinvestment act, and state housing agency.

(5) Real Estate Marketing (or equivalent) shall include but not be limited to real estate professionalism and ethics, characteristics of successful salesmen, time management, psychology of marketing, listing procedures, advertising, negotiating and closing, finanacing, and the Deceptive Trade Practices-Consumer Protection Act, as amended, Section 17.01 et seq., Business & Commerce Code.[1]

(6) Real Estate Mathematics (or equivalent) shall include but not be limited to basic arithmetic skills and review of mathematical logic, percentages, interest, time-valued money, depreciation, amortization, proration, and estimation of closing statements.

(7) Real Estate Brokerage (or equivalent) shall include but not be limited to law of agency, planning and organization, operational policies and procedures, recruiting, selection and training of personnel, records and control, and real estate firm analysis and expansion criteria.

(8) Property Management (or equivalent) shall include but not be limited to role of property manager, landlord policies, operational guidelines, leases, lease negotiations, tenant relations, maintenance, reports, habitability laws, and the Fair Housing Act.

(9) Real Estate Investments (or equivalent) shall include but not be limited to real estate investment characteristics, techniques of investment analysis, time-valued money, discounted and nondiscounted investment criteria, leverage, tax shelters depreciation, and applications to property tax.

***(b)** The commission shall waive the examination of an applicant for broker licensure who has, within one year previous to the filing of his application, been licensed in this state as a broker, and shall waive the examination of an applicant for salesman licensure who*

---

[1] See V.T.C.A. Bus. & C. § 17.41 et seq.

has, within one year previous to the filing of his application, been licensed in this state as either a broker or salesman.

(c) *From and after the effective date of this Act, each applicant for broker licensure shall furnish the commission satisfactory evidence that he has had not less than two years active experience in this state as a licensed real estate salesman practitioner during the 36-month period immediately preceding the filing of the application; and, in addition, shall furnish the commission satisfactory evidence of having completed successfully 36 semester hours of core real estate courses or related courses accepted by the commission. On January 1, 1983, the number of required semester hours shall be increased to 48. On or after January 1, 1985, the required semester hours shall be increased to 60. These qualifications for broker licensure shall not be required of an applicant who, at the time of making the application, is duly licensed as a real estate broker by any other state in the United States if that state's requirements for licensure are comparable to those of Texas. As a prerequisite for applying for broker licensure, those persons licensed as salesmen subject to the annual education requirements provided by Subsection (d) of this section shall, as part of the semester hours required by this subsection, furnish the commission satisfactory evidence of having completed all the requirements of Subsection (d) of this section.*

(d) *From and after the effective date of this Act, as a prerequisite for applying for salesman licensure each applicant shall furnish the commission satisfactory evidence of having completed 12 semester hours of postsecondary education, six semester hours of which must be completed in core real estate courses, of which a minimum of two semester hours must be completed in Principles of Real Estate as described in Subdivision (1) of Subsection (a) of Section 7. The remaining six semester hours shall be completed in core real estate courses or related courses. As a condition for the first annual certification of salesman licensure privileges, the applicant shall furnish the commission satisfactory evidence of having completed a minimum of 14 semester hours, eight semester hours of which must be completed in core real estate courses. As a condition for the second annual certification of salesman licensure privileges, the applicant shall furnish the commission satisfactory evidence of having completed a minimum of 16 semester hours, 10 semester hours of which must be completed in core real estate courses. As a condition for the third annual certification of salesman licensure privileges, the appli-*

cant shall furnish the commission satisfactory evidence of having completed a minimum of 18 semester hours, 12 semester hours of which must be completed in core real estate courses.

(e) Repealed by Acts 1981, 67th Leg., p. 160, ch. 71, § 3, eff. April 23, 1981.

(f) Insofar as is necessary for the administration of this Act, the commission is authorized to inspect and accredit educational programs or courses of study in real estate and to establish standards of accreditation for such programs conducted in the State of Texas, other than accredited colleges and universities. Schools, other than accredited colleges and universities, which are authorized to offer real estate educational courses pursuant to provisions of this section shall be required to maintain a corporate surety bond in the sum of $10,000 payable to the commission, for the benefit of a party who may suffer damages resulting from failure of a commission approved school or course to fulfill obligations attendant to the approval.

(g) A person licensed as a salesman on May 19, 1975, is not subject to the educational requirements or prerequisites of this Act as a condition for holding salesman licensure privileges. A person licensed as a broker on May 19, 1975, is not subject to the educational requirements or prerequisites of this Act as a condition for holding broker licensure privileges.

(h) Notwithstanding any other provision of this Act, from and after the effective date of this Act each applicant for broker licensure shall furnish the commission with satisfactory evidence:

(1) that he has satisfied the requirements of Subsection (c) of this section; or

(2) that he is a licensed real estate broker in another state, that he has not had not less than two years' active experience in the other state as a licensed real estate salesman or broker during the 36-month period immediately preceding the filing of the application, and that he has satisfied the educational requirements for broker licensure as provided by Subsection (c) of this section; or

(3) that he has, within one year previous to the filing of his application, been licensed in this state as a broker.

(i) Notwithstanding any other provision of this Act, the commission shall waive the requirements of Subsection (d) of Section 7 of this Act for an applicant for salesman licensure who has, within one year previous to the filing of his application, been licensed in

this state as a broker or salesman. However, with respect to an applicant for salesman licensure who was licensed as a salesman within one year previous to the filing of the application but whose original licensure privileges were issued under the provisions that second and third annual certification of the licensure privileges would be conditioned upon furnishing satisfactory evidence of successful completion of additional education, the commission shall require the applicant to furnish satisfactory evidence of successful completion of any additional education that would have been required if the licensure privileges had been maintained without interruption during the previous year.

(j) Not later than the 30th day after the day on which a person completes an examination administered by the commission, the commission shall send to the person his or her examination results. If requested in writing by a person who fails the examination, the commission shall send to the person not later than the 30th day after the day on which the request is received by the commission an analysis of the person's performance on the examination.

(k) All applicants for licensure must complete at least three classroom hours of coursework on federal, state, and local laws governing housing discrimination, housing credit discrimination, and community reinvestment or at least three semester hours of coursework on constitutional law.

Real estate recovery fund

Section 8. Part 1.

(a) The commission shall establish a real estate recovery fund which shall be set apart and maintained by the commission as provided in this section. The fund shall be used in the manner provided in this section for reimbursing aggrieved persons who suffer actual damages by reason of certain acts committed by a duly licensed real estate broker or salesman, or by an unlicensed employee or agent of a broker or salesman, provided the broker or salesman was licensed by the State of Texas at the time the act was committed and provided recovery is ordered by a court of competent jurisdiction against the broker or salesman. The use of the fund as provided in Part 1 of this section is limited to an act that is either a violation of Section 15(3) or (4) of this Act.

$10 fee for Recovery Fund

(b) *On the effective date of this Act, the commission shall collect from each real estate broker and salesman licensed by this state a fee of $10 which shall be deposited in the real estate recovery fund. The commission shall suspend a license issued under the provisions of this Act for failure to pay this fee. After the effective date of this Act, when a person makes application for an original license pursuant to this Act he shall pay, in addition to his original license application fee, a fee of $10 which shall be deposited in the real estate recovery fund. If the commission does not issue the license, this fee shall be returned to the applicant.*

Part 2. If on December 31 of any year the balance remaining in the real estate recovery fund is less than $300,000, each real estate broker and each real estate salesman, on recertification of his license during the following calendar year, shall pay, in addition to his license recertification fee, a fee of $10, which shall be deposited in the real estate recovery fund, or a pro rata share of the amount necessary to bring the fund to $1 million, whichever is less.

2 yr. limit on action for judgment

Part 3. **(a)** *No action for a judgment which subsequently results in an order for collection from the real estate recovery fund shall be started later than two years from the accrual of the cause of action. When an aggrieved person commences action for a judgment which may result in collection from the real estate recovery fund, the real estate broker or real estate salesman shall notify the commission in writing to this effect at the time of the commencement of the action.*

Broker or salesman must notify commission when an aggrieved person commences action for a judgment which may result in collection from the recovery fund.

(b) *When an aggrieved person recovers a valid judgment in a court of competent jurisdiction against a real estate broker, or real estate salesman, on the grounds described in Part 1(a) of this section that occurred on or after May 19, 1975, the aggrieved person may, after final judgment has been entered, execution returned nulla bona, and a judgment lien perfected, file a verified claim in the court in which the judgment was entered and, on 20 days' written notice to the commission, and to the judgment debtor, may apply to the court for an order directing payment out of the real estate recovery fund of the amount unpaid on the judgment, subject to the limitations stated in Part 8 of this section.*

(c) *The court shall proceed on the application forthwith. On the hearing on the application, the aggrieved person is required to show that:*

(1) the judgment is based on facts allowing recovery under Part 1(a) of this section;

(2) he is not a spouse of the debtor, or the personal representative of the spouse; and he is not a real estate broker or salesman, as defined by this Act, who is seeking to recover a real estate commission in the transaction or transactions for which the application for payment is made;

(3) he has obtained a judgment as set out in Part 3(b) of this section, stating the amount of the judgment and the amount owing on the judgment at the date of the application;

(4) the judgment debtor lacks sufficient attachable assets to satisfy the judgment; and

(5) the amount that may be realized from the sale of real or personal property or other assets liable to be sold or applied in satisfaction of the judgment and the balance remaining due on the judgment after application of the amount that may be realized.

(**d**) The court shall make an order directed to the commission requiring payment from the real estate recovery fund of whatever sum it finds to be payable on the claim, pursuant to and in accordance with the limitations contained in this section, if the court is satisfied, on the hearing, of the truth of all matters required to be shown by the aggrieved person by Part 3(c) of this section and that the aggrieved person has satisfied all of the requirements of Parts 3(b) and (c) of this section.

(**e**) A license granted under the provisions of this Act shall be revoked by the commission on proof that the commission has made a payment from the real estate recovery fund of any amount toward satisfaction of a judgment against a licensed real estate broker or salesman. No broker or salesman is eligible to receive a new license until he has repaid in full, plus interest at the current legal rate, the amount paid from the real estate recovery fund on his account. A discharge in bankruptcy shall not relieve a person from the penalties and disabilities provided in this Act.

Part 4. The sums received by the real estate commission for deposit in the real estate recovery fund shall be held by the commission in trust for carrying out the purposes of the real estate recovery fund. These funds may be invested and reinvested in the same manner as funds of the Texas State Employees Retirement System, and the interest from these investments shall be deposited to the credit of the real estate recovery fund, provided, however, that no investments shall be made which will impair the necessary liquidity required to satisfy judgment payments awarded pursuant to this section.

Part 5. When the real estate commission receives notice of entry of a final judgment and a hearing is scheduled under Part 3(d) of this section, the commission may notify the Attorney General of Texas of its desire to enter an appearance, file a response, appear at the court hearing, defend the action, or take whatever other action it deems appropriate on behalf of, and in the name of, the defendant, and take recourse through any appropriate method of review on behalf of, and in the name of, the defendant. In taking such action the real estate commission and the attorney general shall act only to protect the fund from spurious or unjust claims or to insure compliance with the requirements for recovery under this section.

Part 6. When, on the order of the court, the commission has paid from the real estate recovery fund any sum to the judgment creditor, the commission shall be subrogated to all of the rights of the judgment creditor to the extent of the amount paid. The judgment creditor shall assign all his right, title, and interest in the judgment up to the amount paid by the commission which amount shall have priority for repayment in the event of any subsequent recovery on the judgment. Any amount and interest recovered by the commission on the judgment shall be deposited to the fund.

Part 7. The failure of an aggrieved person to comply with the provisions of this section relating to the real estate recovery fund shall constitute a waiver of any rights under this section.

Part 8. (a) Notwithstanding any other provision, payments from the real estate recovery fund are subject to the conditions and limitations in Subsections (b) through (d) of this part.

(b) Payments may be made only pursuant to an order of a court of competent jurisdiction, as provided in Part 3, and in the manner prescribed by this section.

(c) Payments for claims, including attorneys' fees, interest, and court costs, arising out of the same transaction shall be limited in the aggregate to $20,000 regardless of the number of claimants.

(d) Payments for claims based on judgments against any one licensed real estate broker or salesman may not exceed in the aggregate $50,000 until the fund has been reimbursed by the licensee for all amounts paid.

[handwritten margin note: limit: $20,000 per transaction $50,000 per broker or salesman]

Part 9. Nothing contained in this section shall limit the authority of the commission to take disciplinary action against a licensee for a violation of this Act or the rules and regulations of the commission; nor shall the repayment in full of all obligations to the real estate recovery fund by a licensee nullify or modify the effect of any other disciplinary proceeding brought pursuant to this Act.

Part 10. Any person receiving payment out of the real estate recovery fund pursuant to Section 8 of this Act shall be entitled to receive reasonable attorney fees as determined by the court, subject to the limitations stated in Part 8 of this section.

Issuance of license; certification fees; expiration dates

Section 9.

(a) When an applicant has satisfactorily met all requirements and conditions of this Act, a license shall be issued which may remain in force and effect so long as the holder of the license remains in compliance with the obligations of this Act, which include payment of the annual certification fee as provided in Section 11 of this Act. Each salesman license issued shall be delivered or mailed to the broker with whom the salesman is associated and shall be kept under his custody and control.

(b) An applicant is not permitted to engage in the real estate business either as a broker or salesman until a license evidencing his authority to engage in the real estate business has been received.

(c) The commission by rule may adopt a system under which licenses expire on various dates during the year. Dates for payment of the annual certification fee shall be adjusted accordingly. For the year in which the certification date is changed, annual certification fees payable shall be prorated on a monthly basis so each licensee shall pay only that portion of the license fee which is allocable to the number of months during which the license is valid. On certification of the license on the new certification date, the total annual certification fee is payable.

(d) Any other provision of this Act notwithstanding, the commission may issue licenses valid for a period not to exceed 24 months and may charge and collect certification fees for such period; provided, however, that such certification fees shall not, calculated on an annual basis, exceed the amounts established in Section 11 of this Act,

*and further provided that the educational conditions for annual certifi-
cation established in Subsection (d) of Section 7 of this Act shall
not be waived by the commission.*

Refusal to issue license; review

Section 10.

*If the commission declines or fails to license an applicant, it
shall immediately give written notice of the refusal to the applicant.
Before the applicant may appeal to a district court as provided in
Section 18 of this Act, he must file within 10 days after the receipt
of the notice an appeal from the ruling, requesting a time and place
for a hearing before the commission. The commission shall set a
time and place for the hearing within 30 days from the receipt of
the appeal, giving 10 days' notice of the hearing to the applicant.
The time of the hearing may be continued from time to time with
the consent of the applicant. Following the hearing, the commission
shall enter an order which is, in its opinion, appropriate in the
matter concerned.*

*If an applicant fails to request a hearing as provided in this
section, the commission's ruling shall become final and not subject
to review by the courts.*

Fees

Section 11.

The commission shall charge and collect the following fees:

*(1) a fee not to exceed $100 for the filing of an original application
for real estate broker licensure;*

*(2) a fee not to exceed $100 for annual certification of real
estate broker licensure status;*

*(3) a fee not to exceed $50 for the filing of an original application
for salesman licensure;*

*(4) a fee not to exceed $50 for annual certification of real estate
salesman licensure status;*

(5) a fee not to exceed $25 for taking a license examination;

*(6) a fee not to exceed $10 for filing a request for a license for
each additional office or place of business;*

*(7) a fee not to exceed $20 for filing a request for a license for
a change of place of business or change of sponsoring broker;*

(8) a fee not to exceed $10 for filing a request to replace a license lost or destroyed;

(9) a fee not to exceed $400 for filing an application for approval of a real estate course pursuant to the provisions of Subsection (f) of Section 7 of this Act;

(10) a fee not to exceed $200 per annum for and in each year of operation of a real estate course, established pursuant to the provisions of Subsection (f) of Section 7 of this Act; and

(11) a fee of $15 for transcript evaluation.

Maintenance and location of offices; display of license

Section 12.

(a) Each resident broker shall maintain a fixed office within this state. The address of the office shall be designated on the broker's license. Within 10 days after a move from a previously designated address, the broker shall submit an application for a new license, designating the new location of his office, together with the required fee, whereupon the commission shall issue a license, reflecting the new location, provided the new location complies with the terms of this section.

(b) If a broker maintains more than one place of business within this state, he shall apply for, pay the required fee for, and obtain an additional license to be known as a branch office license for each additional office he maintains.

(c) The license or licenses of the broker shall at all times be prominently displayed in the licensee's place or places of business.

(d) Each broker shall also prominently display in his place or in one of his places of business the license of each real estate salesman associated with him.

Inactive licenses

Section 13.

(a) When the association of a salesman with his sponsoring broker is terminated, the broker shall immediately return the salesman license to the commission. The salesman license then becomes inactive.

(b) The salesman license may be activated if, before the license expires, a request, accompanied by the required fee, is filed with

the commission by a licensed broker advising that he assumes sponsorship of the salesman.

Unlawful employment or compensation; nonresident license

Section 14.

(a) It is unlawful for a licensed broker to employ or compensate directly or indirectly a person for performing an act enumerated in the definition of real estate broker in Section 2 of this Act if the person is not a licensed broker or licensed salesman in this state or an attorney at law licensed in this state or in any other state. However, a licensed broker may pay a commission to a licensed broker of another state if the foreign broker does not conduct in this state any of the negotiations for which the fee, compensation, or commission is paid.

(b) A resident broker of another state who furnishes the evidence required in Subsection (h) of Section 7 of this Act may apply for a license as a broker in this state. A nonresident licensee need not maintain a place of business in this state. The commission may in its discretion refuse to issue a broker license to an applicant who is not a resident of this state for the same reasons that it may refuse to license a resident of this state.

(c) Each nonresident applicant shall file an irrevocable consent that legal actions may be commenced against him in the proper court of any county of this state in which a cause of action may arise, or in which the plaintiff may reside, by service of process or pleading authorized by the laws of this state, or by serving the administrator or assistant administrator of the commission. The consent shall stipulate that the service of process or pleading shall be valid and binding in all courts as if personal service had been made on the nonresident broker in this state. The consent shall be duly acknowledged, and if made by a corporation, shall be authenticated by its seal. A service of process or pleading served on the commission shall be by duplicate copies, one of which shall be filed in the office of the commission and the other forwarded by registered mail to the last known principal address which the commission has for the nonresident broker against whom the process or pleading is directed. No default in an action may be taken except on certification by the commission that a copy of the process or pleading was mailed to the defendant as provided in this section, and no default judgment

may be taken in an action or proceeding until 20 days after the day of mailing of the process or pleading to the defendant.

Notwithstanding any other provision of this subsection, a nonresident of this state who resides in a city whose boundaries are contiguous at any point to the boundaries of a city of this state, and who has been an actual bona fide resident of that city for at least 60 days immediately preceding the filing of his application, is eligible to be licensed as a real estate broker or salesman under this Act in the same manner as a resident of this state. If he is licensed in this manner, he shall at all times maintain a place of business either in the city in which he resides or in the city in this state which is contiguous to the city in which he resides, and he may not maintain a place of business at another location in this state unless he also complies with the requirements of Section 14(b) of this Act. The place of business must satisfy the requirements of Subsection (a) of Section 12 of this Act, but the place of business shall be deemed a definite place of business in this state within the meaning of Subsection (a) of Section 12.

Investigations; suspension or revocation of license; civil or criminal liability

Section 15.

The commission may, on its own motion, and shall, on the verified complaint in writing of any person, provided the complaint, or the complaint together with evidence, documentary or otherwise, presented in connection with the complaint, provides reasonable cause, investigate the actions and records of a real estate broker or real estate salesman. The commission may suspend or revoke a license issued under the provisions of this Act at any time when it has been determined that:

(1)(A) the licensee has entered a plea of guilty or nolo contendere to, or been found guilty of, or been convicted of, a felony, in which fraud is an essential element, and the time for appeal has elapsed or the judgment or conviction has been affirmed on appeal, irrespective of an order granting probation following such conviction, suspending the imposition of sentence; or

(B) a final money judgment has been rendered against the licensee resulting from contractual obligations of the licensee incurred in

the pursuit of his business, and such judgment remains unsatisfied for a period of more than six months after becoming final; or

(2) the licensee has procured, or attempted to procure, a real estate license, for himself or a salesman, by fraud, misrepresentation or deceit, or by making a material misstatement of fact in an application for a real estate license; or

(3) the licensee, when selling, buying, trading, or renting real property in his own name, engaged in misrepresentation or dishonest or fraudulent action; or

(4) the licensee has failed within a reasonable time to make good a check issued to the commission after the commission has mailed a request for payment by certified mail to the licensee's last known business address as reflected by the commission's records; or

(5) the licensee has disregarded or violated a provision of this Act; or

(6) the licensee, while performing an act constituting an act of a broker or salesman, as defined by this Act, has been guilty of:

(A) making a material misrepresentation, or failing to disclose to a potential purchaser any latent structural defect or any other defect known to the broker or salesman. Latent structural defects and other defects do not refer to trivial or insignificant defects but refer to those defects that would be a significant factor to a reasonable and prudent purchaser in making a decision to purchase; or

(B) making a false promise of a character likely to influence, persuade, or induce any person to enter into a contract or agreement when the licensee could not or did not intend to keep such promise; or

(C) pursuing a continued and flagrant course of misrepresentation or making of false promises through agents, salesmen, advertising, or otherwise; or

(D) failing to make clear, to all parties to a transaction, which party he is acting for, or receiving compensation from more than one party except with the full knowledge and consent of all parties; or

(E) failing within a reasonable time properly to account for or remit money coming into his possession which belongs to others, or commingling money belonging to others with his own funds; or

(F) paying a commission or fees to or dividing a commission or fees with anyone not licensed as a real estate broker or salesman in this state, in any other state, or not an attorney at law licensed

in this state or any other state, for compensation for services as a real estate agent; or

(G) failing to specify in a listing contract a definite termination date which is not subject to prior notice; or

(H) accepting, receiving, or charging an undisclosed commission, rebate, or direct profit on expenditures made for a principal; or

(I) soliciting, selling, or offering for sale real property under a scheme or program that constitutes a lottery or deceptive practice; or

(J) acting in the dual capacity of broker and undisclosed principal in a transaction; or

(K) guaranteeing, authorizing, or permitting a person to guarantee that future profits will result from a resale of real property; or

(L) placing a sign on real property offering it for sale, lease, or rent without the written consent of the owner or his authorized agent; or

(M) inducing or attempting to induce a party to a contract of sale or lease to break the contract for the purpose of substituting in lieu thereof a new contract; or

(N) negotiating or attempting to negotiate the sale, exchange, lease, or rental of real property with an owner or lessor, knowing that the owner or lessor had a written outstanding contract, granting exclusive agency in connection with the property to another real estate broker; or

(O) offering real property for sale or for lease without the knowledge and consent of the owner or his authorized agent, or on terms other than those authorized by the owner or his authorized agent; or

(P) publishing, or causing to be published, an advertisement including, but not limited to, advertising by newspaper, radio, television, or display which is misleading, or which is likely to deceive the public, or which in any manner tends to create a misleading impression, or which fails to identify the person causing the advertisement to be published as a licensed real estate broker or agent; or

(Q) having knowingly withheld from or inserted in a statement of account or invoice, a statement that made it inaccurate in a material particular; or

(R) publishing or circulating an unjustified or unwarranted threat of legal proceedings, or other action; or

(S) establishing an association, by employment or otherwise, *with an unlicensed person who is expected or required to act as a real estate licensee, or aiding or abetting or conspiring with a person to circumvent the requirements of this Act; or*

(T) failing or refusing on demand to furnish copies of a document pertaining to a transaction dealing with real estate to a person whose signature is affixed to the document; or

(U) failing to advise a purchaser in writing before the closing of a transaction that the purchaser should either have the abstract covering the real estate which is the subject of the contract examined by an attorney of the purchaser's own selection, or be furnished with or obtain a policy of title insurance; or

(V) conduct which constitutes dishonest dealings, bad faith, or untrustworthiness; or

(W) acting negligently or incompetently in performing an act for which a person is required to hold a real estate license; or

(X) disregarding or violating a provision of this Act; or

(Y) failing within a reasonable time to deposit money received as escrow agent in a real estate transaction, either in trust with a title company authorized to do business in this state, or in a custodial, trust, or escrow account maintained for that purpose in a banking institution authorized to do business in this state; or

(Z) disbursing money deposited in a custodial, trust, or escrow account, as provided in Subsection (Y) before the transaction concerned has been consummated or finally otherwise terminated; or

(AA) discriminating against an owner, potential purchaser, lessor, or potential lessee on the basis of race, color, religion, sex, national origin, or ancestry. Prohibited discrimination shall include but not be limited to directing prospective home buyers or lessees interested in equivalent properties to different areas according to the race, color, religion, sex, national origin, or ancestry of the potential owner or lessee; or

(7) the licensee has failed or refused on demand to produce a document, book, or record in his possession concerning a real estate transaction conducted by him for inspection by the Real Estate Commission or its authorized personnel or representative; or

(8) the licensee has failed within a reasonable time to provide information requested by the commission as a result of a formal or informal complaint to the commission which would indicate a violation of this Act; or

(9) the licensee has failed without just cause to surrender to

the rightful owner, on demand, a document or instrument coming into his possession.

The provisions of this section do not relieve a person from civil liability or from criminal prosecution under this Act or under the laws of this state.

Issuance of license after revocation prohibited for one year

Section 15A.

If the commission revokes a person's license issued under this Act, the commission may not issue another license to the person for one year after the revocation.

Legislative intent; investigations; probation of license revocation, cancellation, or suspension

Section 15B.

It is the intent of the legislature that the commission only is vested with the authority and responsibility for the administration, implementation, and enforcement of this Act. Duties, functions, and responsibilities of the commission's administrative assistants, agents, investigators, and all other employees shall be those assigned and determined by the commission. Notwithstanding any other provision of the Act, there shall be no undercover or covert investigations conducted by authority of this Act unless expressly authorized by the commission after due consideration of the circumstances and determination by the commission that such measures are necessary to carry out the purposes of this Act. No investigations of licensees or any other actions against licensees shall be initiated on the basis of anonymous complaints whether in writing or otherwise but shall be initiated only upon the commission's own motion or a verified written complaint. Upon the adoption of such motion by the commission or upon receipt of such complaint, the licensee shall be notified promptly and in writing unless the commission itself, after due consideration, determines otherwise. Provided, however, that the commission shall have the right and may, upon majority vote, rule that an order revoking, cancelling, or suspending a license be probated upon reasonable terms and conditions determined by the commission.

Unauthorized practice of law; Texas Real Estate
Broker-Lawyer Committee

Section 16.

(a) *A license granted under the provisions of this Act shall be suspended or revoked by the commission on proof that the licensee, not being licensed and authorized to practice law in this state, for a consideration, reward, pecuniary benefit, present or anticipated, direct or indirect, or in connection with or as a part of his employment, agency, or fiduciary relationship as a licensee, drew a deed, note, deed of trust, will, or other written instrument that may transfer or anywise affect the title to or an interest in land, except as provided in the subsections below, or advised or counseled a person as to the validity or legal sufficiency of an instrument or as to the validity of title to real estate.*

(b) *Notwithstanding the provisions of this Act or any other law, the completion of contract forms which bind the sale, exchange, option, lease, or rental of any interest in real property by a real estate broker or salesman incident to the performance of the acts of a broker as defined by this article does not constitute the unauthorized or illegal practice of law in this state, provided the forms have been promulgated for use by the Texas Real Estate Commission for the particular kind of transaction involved, or the forms have been prepared by an attorney at law licensed by this state and approved by said attorney for the particular kind of transaction involved, or the forms have been prepared by the property owner or prepared by an attorney and required by the property owner.*

(c) *A Texas Real Estate Broker-Lawyer Committee is hereby created which, in addition to other powers and duties delegated to it, shall draft and revise contract forms capable of standardization for use by real estate licensees and which will expedite real estate transactions and reduce controversies to a minimum while containing safeguards adequate to protect the interests of the principals to the transaction.*

(d) *The Texas Real Estate Broker-Lawyer Committee shall have 12 members including six members appointed by the Texas Real Estate Commission and six members of the State Bar of Texas appointed by the President of the State Bar of Texas. The members of the committee shall hold office for staggered terms of six years with the terms of two commission appointees and two State Bar*

appointees expiring every two years. Each member shall hold office until his successor is appointed. A vacancy for any cause shall be filled for the expired term by the agency making the original appointment. Appointments to the committee shall be made without regard to race, creed, sex, religion, or national origin.

(e) In the best interest of the public the commission may adopt rules and regulations requiring real estate brokers and salesmen to use contract forms which have been prepared by the Texas Real Estate Broker-Lawyer Committee and promulgated by the Texas Real Estate Commission; provided, however, that the Texas Real Estate Commission shall not prohibit a real estate broker or salesman from using a contract form or forms binding the sale, exchange, option, lease, or rental of any interest in real property which have been prepared by the property owner or prepared by an attorney and required by the property owner. For the purpose of this section, contract forms prepared by the Texas Real Estate Broker-Lawyer Committee appointed by the commission and the State Bar of Texas and promulgated by the commission prior to the effective date of this Act shall be deemed to have been prepared by the Texas Real Estate Broker-Lawyer Committee. The commission may suspend or revoke a license issued under the provisions of this article when it has determined that the licensee failed to use a contract form as required by the commission pursuant to this section.

Hearings

Section 17.

(a) Before a license is suspended or revoked, the licensee is entitled to a public hearing. The commission shall prescribe the time and place of the hearing. However, the hearing shall be held, if the licensee so desires, within the county where the licensee has his principal place of business, or if the licensee is a nonresident, the hearing may be called for and held in any county within this state. The notice calling the hearing shall recite the allegations against the licensee and the notice may be served personally or by mailing it by certified mail to the licensee's last known business address, as reflected by the commission's records, at least 10 days prior to the date set for the hearing. In the hearing, all witnesses shall be duly sworn and stenographic notes of the proceedings shall be taken and filed as a part of the records in the case. A party to the proceeding

desiring it shall be furnished with a copy of the stenographic notes on the payment to the commission of a fee of $1.50 per page plus applicable sales tax and postage. After a hearing, the commission shall enter an order based on its findings of fact adduced from the evidence presented.

(b) The commission may issue subpoenas for the attendance of witnesses and the production of records or documents. The process issued by the commission may extend to all parts of the state, and the process may be served by any person designated by the commission. The person serving the process shall receive compensation to be allowed by the commission, not to exceed the fee prescribed by law for similar services. A witness subpoenaed who appears in a proceeding before the commission shall receive the same fees and mileage allowances as allowed by law, and the fees and allowances shall be taxed as part of the cost of the proceedings.

(c) If, in a proceeding before the commission, a witness fails or refuses to attend on subpoena issued by the commission, or refuses to testify, or refuses to produce a record or document, the production of which is called for by the subpoena, the attendance of the witness and the giving of his testimony and the production of the documents and records shall be enforced by a court of competent jurisdiction of this state in the same manner as the attendance, testimony of witnesses, and production of records are enforced in civil cases in the courts of this state.

(d) If a hearing relating to the denial, suspension, or revocation of a license under this Act is conducted by the administrator or assistant administrator, the applicant for the license or the licensee who is adversely affected by the decision of the administrator or assistant administrator is entitled to request a rehearing by the commission itself on making a timely motion for the rehearing.

Judicial Review

Section 18.

(a) A person aggrieved by a ruling, order, or decision of the commission has the right to appeal to a district court in the county where the hearing was held within 30 days from the service of notice of the action of the commission.

(b) The appeal having been properly filed, the court may request of the commission, and the commission on receiving the request

shall within 30 days prepare and transmit to the court, a certified copy of its entire record in the matter in which the appeal has been taken. The appeal shall be tried in accordance with Texas Rules of Civil Procedure.

(c) In the event an appeal is taken by a licensee or applicant, the appeal does not act as a supersedeas unless the court so directs, and the court shall dispose of the appeal and enter its decision promptly.

(d) If an aggrieved person fails to perfect an appeal as provided in this section, the commission's ruling becomes final.

Contents of listing contract forms

Section 18A.

(a) Any listing contract form adopted by the commission relating to the contractual obligations between a seller of real estate and a real estate broker or salesman acting as an agent for the seller shall include a section that informs the parties to the contract that real estate commissions are negotiable.

(b) When appropriate to the form it shall include a section explaining the availability of Texas coastal natural hazards information important to coastal residents.

Information given to complainants and subjects of complaints

Section 18B.

(a) If a person files a complaint with the commission relating to a real estate broker or salesman, the commission shall furnish to the person an explanation of the remedies that are available to the person under this Act and information about appropriate state or local agencies or officials with which the person may file a complaint. The commission shall furnish the same explanation and information to the person against whom the complaint is filed.

(b) The commission shall keep an information file about each complaint filed with the commission.

(c) If a written complaint is filed with the commission relating to a real estate broker or salesman, the commission, at least as frequently as quarterly and until the complaint is finally resolved, *shall inform the complainant and the person against whom the complaint is filed of the status of the complaint.*

Real estate inspectors; licensing; violations; penalties; real estate inspection recovery fund

Section 18C.

(a) For purposes of this section, the following definitions shall apply:

(1) "Real Estate Inspector" means a person or persons who hold themselves out to the public as being trained and qualified to inspect improvements to real property, including structural items and/or equipment and systems, and who accept employment for the purpose of performing such an inspection for a buyer or seller of real property.

(2) "Real Estate Inspection" means a written or oral opinion as to the condition of improvements to real property, including structural items and/or equipment and systems.

(3) "Commission" means the Texas Real Estate Commission.

(4) "Core Real Estate Inspection Courses" means educational courses approved by the commission, including, but not limited to, electrical, mechanical, plumbing, roofing, and structural courses of study.

(b) The commission shall promulgate and prescribe the following rules and regulations:

(1) the application forms and requirements for original and renewal licenses;

(2) the method and content of examinations administered under this section; and

(3) the fees for original and renewal license application as provided by Subsection (f) of this section and a fee for each licensing examination as provided by Subsection (f) of this section.

(c) A person may not act or attempt to act as a real estate inspector in this state for a buyer or seller of real property unless the person possesses a real estate inspector license issued under this section. To be eligible for a license, an applicant must be an individual, a citizen of the United States or a lawfully admitted alien and a resident of this state for at least 60 days immediately preceding the filing of an application. The applicant must be at least 18 years old and must satisfy the commission as to the applicant's

honesty, trustworthiness, integrity, and competency. An applicant for an original real estate inspector license must submit satisfactory evidence to the commission of successful completion of not less than 90 classroom hours of core real estate inspection courses. The commission shall determine the competency of an applicant solely on the basis of the examination required by Subsection (g) of this section. An applicant must file an application for a license with the commission on a form prescribed by the commission.

(d) The commission shall issue a real estate inspector license to an applicant who possesses the required qualifications, passes the appropriate licensing examination, pays the examination fee and original license application fee required by this section, and pays the fee required by Subdivision (2) of Subsection (1) of this section.

(e) A license issued under this section expires one year after the date it is issued. To renew a license, the licensee must submit a renewal application to the commission before the expiration date of the license. The renewal application must be on a form prescribed by the commission, and must be accompanied by the renewal fee. The commission shall notify the licensee of the expiration date of the license and the amount of the renewal fee. The notice shall be mailed not later than the 30th day before the expiration date. A licensee shall notify the commission within 30 days after a change of place of business and pay the applicable fee provided by Subsection (f) of this section.

(f) The commission shall charge and collect reasonable and necessary fees to administer this section as follows:

(1) a fee not to exceed $150 for the filing of an original application for license as a real estate inspector;

(2) a fee not to exceed $200 for the annual license renewal of a real estate inspector;

(3) a fee not to exceed $50 for taking a license examination;

(4) a fee not to exceed $20 for a request for a change of place of business or to replace a lost or destroyed license.
All fees paid to the commission shall be by cashier's check or money order.

(g) The commission shall prescribe the licensing examination, which shall be prepared by or contracted for by the commission. A licensing examination shall evaluate competency in the subject matter of all required core real estate inspection courses. The licensing examination shall be offered not less often than once every two months

in Austin. If a license applicant fails the examination, the applicant may apply for re-examination by filing a request with the commission and paying the examination fee. Each license applicant must satisfy the examination requirement not later than six months after the date on which the license application is filed. A license applicant who fails to satisfy the examination requirement within six months after the date on which the license application is filed must submit a new license application with the commission and pay the examination fee to be eligible for examination.

(h) A violation of this section or a rule adopted under this section is a ground for denial, suspension, or revocation of a license under this section. Proceedings for the denial, suspension, or revocation of a license and appeals from those proceedings are governed by the Administrative Procedure and Texas Register Act (Article 6252–13a, Vernon's Texas Civil Statutes).

(i) A real estate inspector licensed under this section may not:

(1) accept an assignment for real estate inspection if the employment or fee is contingent on the reporting of a specific, predetermined condition of the improvements to real property or is contingent on the reporting of specific findings other than those known by the inspector to be facts at the time of accepting such assignment; or

(2) act in a manner or engage in a practice that is dishonest or fraudulent or that involves deceit or misrepresentation; or

(3) perform a real estate inspection in a negligent or incompetent manner; or

(4) act in the dual capacity of real estate inspector and undisclosed principal in a transaction; or

(5) act in the dual capacity of real estate inspector and real estate broker or salesman; or

(6) perform or agree to perform any repairs or maintenance in connection with a real estate inspection pursuant to the provisions of any earnest money contract, lease agreement, or exchange of real estate; or

(7) perform a real estate inspection pursuant to a written contract for inspection which does not contain the following statement in the contract for inspection in at least 10-point bold type above or adjacent to the signature of the purchaser of the real estate inspection, to wit:

"NOTICE: YOU THE BUYER HAVE OTHER RIGHTS AND REMEDIES UNDER THE TEXAS DECEPTIVE

TRADE PRACTICES-CONSUMER PROTECTION ACT WHICH ARE IN ADDITION TO ANY REMEDY WHICH MAY BE AVAILABLE UNDER THIS CONTRACT.

FOR MORE INFORMATION CONCERNING YOUR RIGHTS, CONTACT THE CONSUMER PROTECTION DIVISION OF THE ATTORNEY GENERAL'S OFFICE, YOUR LOCAL DISTRICT OR COUNTY ATTORNEY, OR THE ATTORNEY OF YOUR CHOICE."

(8) violate the rules adopted by the commission, or any provisions of this section.

(j) A person commits an offense if the person knowingly or intentionally engages in the business of real estate inspecting without a license under this section or performs an inspection during a period in which the inspector's license is revoked or suspended. An offense under this subsection is a Class B misdemeanor.

(k) This section does not apply to any electrician, plumber, carpenter, any person engaged in the business of structural pest control in compliance with the Texas Structural Pest Control Act (Article 135b–6, Vernon's Texas Civil Statutes), or any other person who repairs, maintains, or inspects improvements to real property and who does not hold himself or herself out to the public through personal solicitation or public advertising as being in the business of inspecting such improvements. It is further provided that the provisions of this section shall not be construed so as to prevent any person from performing any and all acts which said person is authorized to perform pursuant to a license issued by the State of Texas or any governmental subdivision thereof.

(l)(1) The commission shall establish a real estate inspection recovery fund which shall be set apart and maintained by the commission as provided in this subsection. The fund shall be used in the manner provided in this subsection for reimbursing aggrieved persons who suffer actual damages by reason of certain acts committed by a duly licensed real estate inspector, provided the real estate inspector was licensed by the State of Texas at the time the act was committed and provided recovery is ordered by a court of competent jurisdiction against the real estate inspector. The use of the fund as provided in Subdivision (1) of this subsection is limited to an act that is a violation of either Subsection (i)(3), (4), (5), (6), or (7), of this section.

(2) After the effective date of this section, when a person receives notice that he has successfully completed the licensing examination provided by Subsection (g) of this section, he shall pay, in addition to any other fees required by this section, a fee of $250, which shall be deposited in the real estate inspection recovery fund prior to the commission issuing such person a real estate inspector license.

(3) If on December 31 of any year the balance remaining in the real estate inspection recovery fund is less than $50,000, each real estate inspector, on renewal of his license during the following calendar year, shall pay, in addition to his license renewal fee, a fee of $100, which shall be deposited in the real estate inspection recovery fund, or a pro rata share of the amount necessary to bring the fund to $75,000, whichever is less.

(4)(A) No action for a judgment which subsequently results in an order for collection from the real estate inspection recovery fund shall be started later than two years from the accrual of the cause of action. When an aggrieved person commences action for a judgment which may result in collection from the real estate inspection recovery fund, the real estate inspector shall notify the commission in writing to this effect at the time of the commencement of the action.

(B) When an aggrieved person recovers a valid judgment in a court of competent jurisdiction against a real estate inspector, on the grounds described in Subdivision (1) of this subsection that occurred on or after January 1, 1986, the aggrieved person may, after final judgment has been entered, execution returned nulla bona, and a judgment lien perfected, file a verified claim in the court in which the judgment was entered and, on 20 days' written notice to the commission, and to the judgment debtor, may apply to the court where the judgment was rendered for an order directing payment out of the real estate inspection recovery fund of the amount unpaid on the judgment, subject to the limitations stated in Subdivision (9) of this subsection.

(C) The court shall proceed on the application forthwith. On the hearing on the application, the aggrieved person is required to show:

(i) that the judgment is based on facts allowing recovery under Subdivision (1) of this subsection;

(ii) that he is not a spouse of the debtor, or the personal representative of the spouse; and he is not a real estate inspector, as defined by this section;

(iii) that he has obtained a judgment as set out in Subdivision (4)(B) of this subsection, stating the amount of the judgment and the amount owing on the judgment at the date of the application;

(iv) that based on the best information available, the judgment debtor lacks sufficient attachable assets to satisfy the judgment; and

(v) the amount that may be realized from the sale of real or personal property or other assets liable to be sold or applied in satisfaction of the judgment and the balance remaining due on the judgment after application of the amount that may be realized.

(D) The court shall make an order directed to the commission requiring payment out of the real estate inspection recovery fund of whatever sum it finds to be payable on the claim, pursuant to and in accordance with the limitations contained in this subsection, if the court is satisfied, on the hearing, of the truth of all matters required to be shown by the aggrieved person by Subdivision (4)(C) of this subsection and that the aggrieved person has satisfied all of the requirements of Subdivisions (4)(B) and (C) of this subsection.

(E) A license granted under the provisions of this section shall be revoked by the commission on proof that the commission has made a payment from the real estate inspection recovery fund of any amount toward satisfaction of a judgment against a licensed real estate inspector. No real estate inspector is eligible to receive a new license until he has repaid in full, plus interest at the current legal rate, the amount paid from the real estate recovery fund on his account. A discharge in bankruptcy shall not relieve a person from the penalties and disabilities provided in this subsection.

(5) The sums received by the real estate commission for deposit in the real estate inspection recovery fund shall be held by the commission in trust for carrying out the purpose of the real estate inspection fund. These funds may be invested and reinvested in the same manner as funds of the Employees Retirement System of Texas, and the interest from these investments shall be deposited to the credit of the real estate inspection recovery fund, provided, however, that no investments shall be made which will impair the necessary liquidity required to satisfy judgment payments awarded pursuant to this subsection.

(6) When the commission receives notice of entry of a final judgment in a hearing as scheduled under Subdivision (4)(C) of this subsection, the commission may notify the attorney general of Texas of its desire to enter an appearance, file a response, appear at the court hearing, defend the action, or take whatever other action

it deems appropriate on behalf of, and in the name of, the defendant, and take recourse through any appropriate method of review on behalf of, and in the name of, the defendant. In taking such action the commission and the attorney general shall act only to protect the fund from spurious or unjust claims or to insure compliance with the requirements for recovery under this subsection.

(7) When, on the order of the court, the commission has paid from the real estate inspection recovery fund any sum to the judgment creditor, the commission shall be subrogated to all of the rights of the judgment creditor to the extent of the amount paid. The judgment creditor shall assign all his right, title, and interest in the judgment up to the amount paid by the commission which amount shall have priority for repayment in the event of any subsequent recovery on the judgment. Any amount in interest recovered by the commission on the judgment shall be deposited to the fund.

(8) The failure of an aggrieved person to comply with the provisions of this subsection relating to the real estate inspection recovery fund shall constitute a waiver of any rights under this subsection.

(9)(A) Notwithstanding any other provision, payments from the real estate inspection recovery fund are subject to the conditions and limitations in Paragraphs (B) through (D) of this subdivision.

(B) Payments may be made only pursuant to an order of a court of competent jurisdiction, as provided in Subdivision (4) of this subsection, and in the manner prescribed by this subsection.

(C) Payments for claims, including attorney's fees, interest, and court costs, arising out of the same transaction shall be limited in the aggregate to $7,500 regardless of the number of claimants.

(D) Payments for claims based on judgments against any one licensed real estate inspector may not exceed in the aggregate $15,000 until the fund has been reimbursed by the licensee for all amounts paid.

(10) Nothing contained in this subsection shall limit the authority of the commission to take disciplinary action against a licensee for a violation of this section or the rules and regulations of the commission, nor shall the repayment in full of all obligations to the real estate inspection recovery fund by a licensee nullify or modify the effect of any other disciplinary proceeding brought pursuant to this section.

(11) Any person receiving payment out of the real estate inspection recovery fund pursuant to Subdivision (9) of this subsection

shall be entitled to receive reasonable attorney's fees as determined by the court, subject to the limitations stated in Subdivision (9) of this subsection.

(m) A person is not required to be licensed under this section to engage in the business of real estate inspecting until January 1, 1986. During the interim period between the effective date of this section and January 1, 1986, registration of real estate inspectors is covered by the law in effect on August 31, 1985, and that law is continued in effect for that purpose until midnight on December 31, 1985, at which time it shall cease to be operative.

Penalties; injunctions

Section 19.

(a) A person acting as a real estate broker or real estate salesman without first obtaining a license is guilty of a misdemeanor and on conviction shall be punishable by a fine of not less than $100 nor more than $500, or by imprisonment in the county jail for a term not to exceed one year, or both; and if a corporation, shall be punishable by a fine of not less than $1,000 nor more than $2,000. A person, on conviction of a second or subsequent offense, shall be punishable by a fine of not less than $500 nor more than $1,000, or by imprisonment for a term not to exceed two years, or both; and if a corporation, shall be punishable by a fine of not less than $2,000 nor more than $5,000.

(b) In case a person received money, or the equivalent thereof, as a fee, commission, compensation, or profit by or in consequence of a violation of Subsection (a) of this section, he shall, in addition, be liable to a penalty of not less than the amount of the sum of money so received and not more than three times the sum so received, as may be determined by the court, which penalty may be recovered in a court of competent jurisdiction by an aggrieved person.

(c) When in the judgment of the commission a person has engaged, or is about to engage, in an act or practice which constitutes or will constitute a violation of a provision of this Act, the county attorney or district attorney in the county in which the violation has occurred or is about to occur, or in the county of the defendant's residence, or the attorney general may maintain an action in the name of the State of Texas in the district court of such county to abate and temporarily and permanently enjoin the acts and practices

and to enforce compliance with this Act. The plaintiff in an action under this subsection is not required to give a bond, and court costs may not be adjudged against the plaintiff.

Actions for compensation or commission; abstracts or title insurance

Section 20.

(a) A person may not bring or maintain an action for the collection of compensation for the performance in this state of an act set forth in Section 2 of this Act without alleging and proving that the person performing the brokerage services was a duly licensed real estate broker or salesman at the time the alleged services were commenced, or was a duly licensed attorney at law in this state or in any other state.

(b) An action may not be brought in a court in this state for the recovery of a commission for the sale or purchase of real estate unless the promise or agreement on which the action is brought, or some memorandum thereof, is in writing and signed by the party to be charged or signed by a person lawfully authorized by him to sign it.

(c) When an offer to purchase real estate in this state is signed, the real estate broker or salesman shall advise the purchaser or purchasers, in writing, that the purchaser or purchasers should have the abstract covering the real estate which is the subject of the contract examined by an attorney of the purchaser's own selection, or that the purchaser or purchasers should be furnished with or obtain a policy of title insurance. Failure to advise the purchaser as provided in this subsection precludes the payment of or recovery of any commission agreed to be paid on the sale.

Texas Standard Contract Forms

1 Residential Earnest Money Contract (Resale)—FHA Insured or VA Guaranteed Financing

2 New Home Residential Earnest Money Contract—Conventional or VA Guaranteed Loan

3 New Home Residential Earnest Money Contract—FHA Insured Loan

4 Unimproved Property Earnest Money Contract

5 Sale of Other Property by Buyer

6 Second or "Back-up" Contract Addendum

7 VA Release of Liability/Restoration of Entitlement (Assumption of Loan Contract)

8 New Home Insulation Addendum

9 Financing Conditions Addendum

10 Seller's Temporary Residential Lease

11 Buyer's Temporary Residential Lease

12 Farm and Ranch Earnest Money Contract

13 Residential Condominium Earnest Money Contract (Resale)—All Cash, Assumption, Third Party Conventional or Seller Financing

14 Residential Condominium Earnest Money Contract (Resale)—FHA Insured or VA Guaranteed Financing

02-08-85

RESIDENTIAL EARNEST MONEY CONTRACT (RESALE)
FHA INSURED OR VA GUARANTEED FINANCING

PROMULGATED BY TEXAS REAL ESTATE COMMISSION

NOTICE: Not For Use For Condominium Transactions

1. PARTIES: _____ (Seller) agrees to sell
and convey to _____ (Buyer) and Buyer
agrees to buy from Seller the property described below.

2. PROPERTY: Lot _____, Block _____, _____
Addition, City of _____, _____ County, Texas, known as
_____ (Address); or as described on attached exhibit, together
with the following items, if any: curtains and rods, draperies and rods, valances, blinds, window shades, screens, shutters, awnings, wall-to-wall carpeting, mirrors fixed in place, ceiling fans, attic fans, mail boxes, television antennas, permanently installed heating and air conditioning units and equipment, built-in security and fire detection equipment, lighting and plumbing fixtures, water softener, trash compactor, garage door openers with controls, shrubbery and all other property owned by Seller and attached to the above described real property. All property sold by this contract is called the "Property".

3. CONTRACT SALES PRICE:
   A. Cash payable at closing .... $_____
   B. Sum of all financing described below excluding any VA Funding Fee or FHA Mortgage Insurance Premium (MIP) .... $_____
   C. Sales Price payable to Seller on Loan funding after closing (Sum of A and B) .... $_____

4. FINANCING: (Check applicable boxes below)
   ☐ A. FHA INSURED FINANCING:
   This contract is subject to approval for Buyer of a Section _____ FHA Insured Loan (the Loan) of not less than $_____,
   amortizable monthly for not less than _____ years, with interest not to exceed _____ % per annum for the first _____ year(s) of the Loan.
   As required by HUD-FHA, if FHA valuation is unknown, "It is expressly agreed that, notwithstanding any other provisions of this contract, the Purchaser (Buyer) shall not be obligated to complete the purchase of the Property described herein or to incur any penalty by forfeiture of Earnest Money deposits or otherwise unless the Seller has delivered to the Purchaser (Buyer) a written statement issued by the Federal Housing Commissioner setting forth the appraised value of the Property (excluding closing costs and MIP) of not less than $_____, which statement the Seller hereby agrees to deliver to the Purchaser (Buyer) promptly after such appraised value statement is made available to the Seller. The Purchaser (Buyer) shall, however, have the privilege and option of proceeding with the consummation of this contract without regard to the amount of the appraised valuation made by the Federal Housing Commissioner. The appraised valuation is arrived at to determine the maximum mortgage the Department of Housing and Urban Development will insure. HUD does not warrant the value or the condition of the property. The purchaser should satisfy himself/herself that the price and the condition of the property are acceptable."
   If the FHA appraised value of the Property (excluding closing costs and MIP) is less than the Sales Price (3C above). Seller may reduce the Sales Price to an amount equal to the FHA appraised value (excluding closing costs and MIP) and the parties to the sale shall close the sale at such lower Sales Price with appropriate adjustments to 3A and 3B above.

   ☐ B. VA GUARANTEED FINANCING:
   This contract is subject to approval for Buyer of a _____
   (type loan) VA guaranteed loan (the Loan) of not less than $_____, amortizable monthly for not less than _____ years,
   ☐ 1. with interest at maximum rate allowable at time of loan funding if the Loan is a fixed rate loan or
   ☐ 2. with interest not to exceed _____ % per annum for the first _____ year(s) of the Loan if such loan is not fixed rate.
   VA NOTICE TO BUYER: "It is expressly agreed that, notwithstanding any other provisions of this contract, the Buyer shall not incur any penalty by forfeiture of earnest money or otherwise or be obligated to complete the purchase of the Property described herein, if the contract purchase price or cost exceeds the reasonable value of the Property established by the Veterans Administration. The Buyer shall, however, have the privilege and option of proceeding with the consummation of this contract without regard to the amount of the reasonable value established by the Veterans Administration."
   If Buyer elects to complete the purchase at an amount in excess of the reasonable value established by VA, Buyer shall pay such excess amount in cash from a source which Buyer agrees to disclose to the VA and which Buyer represents will not be from borrowed funds except as approved by VA. If VA reasonable value of the Property is less than the Sales Price (3C above), Seller may reduce the Sales Price to an amount equal to the VA reasonable value and the parties to the sale shall close at such lower Sales Price with appropriate adjustments to 3A and 3B above.

   ☐ C. TEXAS VETERANS' HOUSING ASSISTANCE PROGRAM LOAN:
   This contract is also subject to approval for Buyer of a Texas Veterans' Housing Assistance Program Loan (the Program Loan) in an amount of
   $_____ for a period of at least _____ years at the interest rate established by the Texas Veterans' Land Board at the time of closing.
   NOTE: Describe special terms of any non-fixed rate loan in Paragraph 11.

182

TREC NO. 21-0

FHA or VA Residential Earnest Money Contract — Page Two   02-08-85

Buyer shall apply for all loan(s) within _____days from the effective date of this contract and shall make every reasonable effort to obtain approval. Such financing shall have been approved when Buyer has satisfied all of lender's financial conditions, e.g., sale of other property, requirements of a co-signer or financial verification. If all loan approvals have not been secured by the Closing Date, this contract shall terminate and Earnest Money shall be refunded to Buyer.

5.   EARNEST MONEY: $_____ is herewith tendered by Buyer and is to be deposited as Earnest Money with _____

_____ at _____ (Address) as Escrow Agent, upon execution

of the contract by both parties. ☐ Additional Earnest Money of $_____ shall be deposited by Buyer with the Escrow Agent on or

before _____, 19_____.

6.   TITLE: Seller shall furnish to Buyer at Seller's expense either:

    ☐ A.   Owner's Policy of Title Insurance (the Title Policy) issued by _____in
         the amount of the Sales Price and dated at or after closing: OR

    ☐ B.   Abstracts of Title certified by an abstract company (1) from the sovereignty to the effective date of this contract (Complete Abstract) and (2) supplemented
         to the Closing Date (Supplemental Abstract).

    NOTICE TO SELLER AND BUYER: AS REQUIRED BY LAW, Broker advises Buyer that Buyer should have the Abstract covering the Property examined by an attorney of Buyer's selection, or Buyer should be furnished with or obtain a Title Policy. If a Title Policy is to be obtained, Buyer should obtain a Commitment for Title Insurance (the Commitment) which should be examined by an attorney of Buyer's choice at or prior to closing. If the Property is situated in a Utility District, Section 50.301 Texas Water Code requires the Buyer to sign and acknowledge the statutory notice from Seller relating to the tax rate and bonded indebtedness of the District.

7.   PROPERTY CONDITION: (Check A or B)

    ☐ A.   Buyer accepts the Property in its present condition, subject only to FHA or VA required repairs and _____

    ☐ B.   Buyer requires inspections and repairs required by the FHA or VA and the Property Condition Addendum attached hereto.

    On Seller's receipt of all loan approvals and inspection reports, Seller shall commence repairs and termite treatment required of Seller by the contract, any lender and the Property Condition Addendum, if any, and complete such repairs prior to closing. Seller's responsibility for the repairs, termite treatment and repairs to termite damage shall not exceed $_____. If Seller fails to complete such repairs, Buyer may do so and Seller shall be liable up to the amount specified and the same paid from the proceeds of the sale. If the repair costs will exceed the stated amount and Seller refuses to pay such excess, Buyer may (1) pay the additional cost or (2) accept the Property with the limited repairs unless such repairs are required by FHA/VA or (3) Buyer may terminate this contract and the Earnest Money shall be refunded to Buyer. Buyer shall make his election within three (3) days after Seller notifies Buyer of Seller's refusal to pay such excess. Failure of Buyer to make such election within the time provided shall be deemed to be Buyer's election to accept the Property with the limited repairs as permitted by FHA/VA, and the sale shall be closed as scheduled. (NOTE: If VA Buyer pays additional costs of repairs, Buyer may be paying in excess of the VA Certificate of Reasonable Value.)

    If the repair costs will exceed five (5) percent of the Sales Price of the Property and Seller agrees to pay the cost of such repairs, Buyer shall have the option of closing the sale with the completed repairs, or terminating the sale and the Earnest Money shall be refunded to Buyer. Buyer shall make this election within three (3) days after Seller notifies Buyer of Seller's willingness to pay the cost of such repairs that exceed five (5) percent of the Sales Price. Failure of Buyer to make such election within the time provided shall be deemed to be Buyer's election to close the sale with the completed repairs.

    Broker(s) and sales associates have no responsibility or liability for inspections or repairs made pursuant to this contract.

8.   BROKER'S FEE: _____, Listing Broker, and any Co-Broker represent Seller unless otherwise specified herein. Seller agrees to pay Listing Broker the fee specified by separate agreement between Listing Broker and Seller. Escrow Agent is authorized and directed to pay Listing Broker's fee from the sale proceeds at closing.

9.   CLOSING: The closing of the sale shall be on or before _____, 19_____, or within seven (7) days after objections to title have been cured, whichever date is later (the Closing Date); however, if financing approval has been obtained pursuant to Paragraph 4, the Closing Date shall be extended daily up to fifteen (15) days if necessary to complete loan requirements. If either party fails to close this sale by the Closing Date, the non-defaulting party shall be entitled to exercise the remedies contained in Paragraph 16 immediately and without notice.

10.   POSSESSION: The possession of the Property shall be delivered to Buyer on _____ in its present or required improved condition, ordinary wear and tear excepted. Any possession by Buyer prior to or Seller after closing that is not authorized by the Buyer's Temporary Residential Lease or Seller's Temporary Residential Lease forms promulgated by the Texas Real Estate Commission shall establish a landlord-tenant at sufferance relationship between the parties.

11.   SPECIAL PROVISIONS: (Insert factual statements and business details applicable to this sale.)

12.   SALES EXPENSES TO BE PAID AT OR PRIOR TO CLOSING:

    A.   Loan appraisal fee shall be paid by _____.

    B.   (1) FHA Sale: The total of the loan discount and any buydown fees shall not exceed $_____ of which Buyer shall pay the first
          $_____ and Seller shall pay the remainder.

         (2) VA Sale: The total of the loan discount and buydown fees shall not exceed $_____ which shall be paid by Seller.

182

C. Seller's Expenses: (1) FHA or VA required repairs and any other inspections, reports or repairs required of Seller herein and in the Property Conditic Addendum (2) releases of existing loans, including prepayment penalties and recordation; tax statements; preparation of deed; ½ of escrow fee (3) expenses VA prohibits Buyer to pay (e.g., preparation of loan documents, copies of restrictions, photos, excess cost of survey, remaining ½ of escrow fee) (4) any Texas Veterans' Housing Assistance Program Participation Fee (5) other expenses stipulated to be paid by Seller under other provisions of this contract.

D. Buyer's Expenses: Interest on the note(s) from date of disbursement to one (1) month prior to date of first monthly payment, expenses stipulated to be paid by Buyer under other provisions of this contract and any customary Texas Veterans' Housing Assistance Program Loan costs for Buyers.

   (1) FHA Buyer: (a) All prepaid items required by applicable HUD-FHA or other regulations (e.g., required premiums for flood and hazard insurance, reserve deposits for other insurance, ad valorem taxes and special governmental assessments) (b) expenses incident to any loan (e.g., ½ of escrow fee, preparation of loan documents, survey, recording fees, copies of restrictions and easements, amortization schedule, Mortgagee's Title Policy, loan origination fee, credit reports, photos) (c) loan related inspection fees.

   (2) VA Buyer: (a) All prepaid items (e.g., required premiums for flood and hazard insurance, reserve deposits for other insurance, ad valorem taxes and special governmental assessments) (b) expenses incident to any loan (e.g., credit reports, recording fees, Mortgagee's Title Policy, loan origination fee, that portion of survey cost VA Buyer may pay by VA Regulation) (c) loan related inspection fees.

E. The VA Loan Funding Fee or FHA Mortgage Insurance Premium (MIP) in the amount of $_____ is to be paid by _____.

   If paid by Buyer, it is to be [ ] paid in cash at closing [ ] added to the amount of the loan to the extent permitted by lender. If financed, the amount is to be added to the loan amount in Paragraph 3-B by lender but is not part of the Contract Sales Price.

F. If any sales expenses exceed the maximum amount herein stipulated to be paid by either party, either party may terminate this contract unless the other party agrees to pay such excess. In no event shall Buyer pay charges and fees expressly prohibited by FHA/VA Regulations.

13. PRORATIONS: Taxes, flood and hazard insurance (at Buyer's option), any rents and maintenance fees shall be prorated through the Closing Date. If Buyer elects to continue Seller's insurance policy, it shall be transferred at closing.

14. TITLE APPROVAL:

A. If abstract is furnished, Seller shall deliver Complete Abstract to Buyer within twenty (20) days from the effective date hereof. Buyer shall have twenty (20) days from date of receipt of Complete Abstract to deliver a copy of the examining attorney's title opinion to Seller, stating any objections to title, and only objections so stated shall be considered.

B. If Title Policy is furnished, the Title Policy shall guarantee Buyer's title to be good and indefeasible subject only to (1) restrictive covenants affecting the Property (2) any discrepancies, conflicts or shortages in area or boundary lines, or any encroachments, or any overlapping of improvements (3) taxes for the current and subsequent years and subsequent assessments for prior years due to a change in land usage or ownership (4) existing building and zoning ordinances (5) rights of parties in possession (6) liens created as security for the sale consideration (7) utility easements common to the platted subdivision of which this Property is a part and (8) reservations or other exceptions contained in the Deed or permitted by the terms of this contract. Exceptions permitted in the Deed and zoning ordinances shall not be valid objections to title. If the Title Policy will be subject to exceptions other than those recited above in sub-paragraphs (1) through (7) inclusive, Seller shall deliver to Buyer the Commitment and legible copies of any documents creating such exceptions that are not recited in sub-paragraphs (1) through (7) above at least five (5) days prior to closing. If Buyer has objection to any such previously undisclosed exceptions, Buyer shall have five (5) days after receipt of such Commitment and copies to make written objections to Seller. If no Title Commitment is provided to Buyer at or prior to closing, it will be conclusively presumed that Seller represented at closing that the Title Policy would not be subject to exceptions other than those recited above in sub-paragraphs (1) through (7).

C. In either instance if title objections are raised, Seller shall have fifteen (15) days from the date such objections are disclosed to cure the same, and the Closing Date shall be extended accordingly. If the objections are not satisfied by the extended closing date, this contract shall terminate and the Earnest Money shall be refunded to Buyer, unless Buyer elects to waive the unsatisfied objections and complete the purchase.

D. Seller shall furnish tax statements showing no delinquent taxes, a Supplemental Abstract when applicable, showing no additional title exceptions and a General Warranty Deed conveying title subject only to liens securing payment of debt created as part of the consideration, taxes for the current year, restrictive covenants and utility easements common to the platted subdivision of which the Property is a part, and reservations and conditions permitted by this contract or otherwise acceptable to Buyer. Each note shall be secured by vendor's and deed of trust liens. In case of dispute as to the form of the deed, forms prepared by the State Bar of Texas shall be used.

15. CASUALTY LOSS: If any part of Property is damaged or destroyed by fire or other casualty loss, Seller shall restore the same to its previous condition as soon as reasonably possible, but in any event by Closing Date. If Seller is unable to do so without fault, Buyer may terminate this contract and the Earnest Money shall be refunded to Buyer.

16. DEFAULT: If Buyer fails to comply herewith, Seller may either (a) enforce specific performance and seek such other relief as may be provided by law or (b) terminate this contract and receive the Earnest Money as liquidated damages. If Seller is unable without fault, within the time herein required, to (a) make any non-casualty repairs or (b) deliver the Commitment or (3) deliver the Complete Abstract, Buyer may either terminate this contract and receive the Earnest Money as the sole remedy or extend the time for performance up to fifteen (15) days and the Closing Date shall be extended pursuant to other provisions of this contract. If Seller fails to comply herewith for any other reason, Buyer may either (a) enforce specific performance hereof and seek such other relief as may be provided by law or (b) terminate this contract and receive the Earnest Money, thereby releasing Seller from this contract.

17. ATTORNEY'S FEES: Any signatory of this contract, Broker or Escrow Agent who is the prevailing party in any legal proceeding brought under or with relation to this contract or transaction shall be additionally entitled to recover court costs and reasonable attorney fees from the nonprevailing party.

18. ESCROW: The Earnest Money is deposited with Escrow Agent with the understanding that Escrow Agent (a) is not a party to this contract and does not assume or have any liability for performance or non-performance of any signatory (b) has the right to require from all signatories a written release of liability of the Escrow Agent which authorizes the disbursement of the Earnest Money (c) is not liable for interest or other charge on the funds held and (d) is not liable for any losses of escrow funds caused by the failure of any banking institution in which such funds have been deposited, unless such banking institution is acting as Escrow Agent. If any signatory unreasonably fails to deliver promptly the document described in (b) above, then such signatory shall be liable to the other signatories as provided in Paragraph 17. At closing, the Earnest Money shall be applied first to any cash down payment required, then to Buyer's closing costs and any excess refunded to Buyer. Any refund or payment of the Earnest Money under this contract shall be reduced by the amount of any actual expenses incurred on behalf of the party receiving the Earnest Money, and Escrow Agent will pay the same to the creditors entitled thereto.

182

FHA or VA Residential Earnest Money Contract concerning _____ Page Four   02-08-85
(Address of Property)

19. REPRESENTATIONS: Seller represents that as of the Closing Date there will be no unrecorded liens, assessments or Uniform Commercial Code Security Interests against any of the Property which will not be satisfied out of the Sales Price. If any representation in this contract is untrue on the Closing Date, this contract may be terminated by Buyer and the Earnest Money shall be refunded to Buyer. All representations contained in this contract shall survive closing.

20. AGREEMENT OF PARTIES: This contract contains the entire agreement of the parties and cannot be changed except by their written consent. Texas Real Estate Commission promulgated addenda which are part of this contract are: (list) _____

_____

_____

21. NOTICES: All notices shall be in writing and effective when delivered at the addresses shown below.

22. CONSULT YOUR ATTORNEY: The Broker cannot give you legal advice. This is intended to be a legally binding contract. READ IT CAREFULLY. Federal law may impose certain duties upon Brokers or Signatories to this contract when any of the signatories is a foreign party, or when any of the signatories receives certain amounts of U.S. currency in connection with a real estate closing. If you do not understand the effect of any part of this contract, consult your attorney BEFORE signing.

SELLER'S   BUYER'S
ATTORNEY: _____   ATTORNEY: _____

EXECUTED in multiple originals effective the _____ day of _____, 19_____. **(BROKER: FILL IN THE DATE OF FINAL ACCEPTANCE.)**

_____   _____
Buyer   Seller

_____   _____
Buyer   Seller

_____   _____
Buyer's Address   Phone No.   Seller's Address   Phone No.

AGREEMENT BETWEEN BROKERS

Listing Broker agrees to pay _____, Co-Broker,

a fee of _____ of the total sales price when the Broker's fee described in Paragraph 8 is received. Escrow Agent is authorized and directed to pay Co-Broker from Listing Broker's fee at closing.

_____   _____
Co-Broker   License No.   Listing Broker   License No.

By: _____   By: _____

_____   _____
Co-Broker's Address   Phone No.   Listing Broker's Address   Phone No.

EARNEST MONEY RECEIPT

Receipt of $_____ Earnest Money is acknowledged in the form of _____

_____

Escrow Agent: _____   By: _____

Date: _____, 19_____.

The form of this contract has been approved by the Texas Real Estate Commission. Such approval relates to this contract form only. No representation is made as to the legal validity or adequacy of any provision in any specific transaction. It is not suitable for complex transactions. Extensive riders or additions are not to be used. (02-85) TREC NO. 21-0. This form replaces TREC NO. 2-0 and NO. 3-0.

182

NEW HOME RESIDENTIAL EARNEST MONEY CONTRACT
CONVENTIONAL or VA GUARANTEED LOAN

1. PARTIES: _____ (Seller) agrees to sell and convey to
_____(Buyer) and Buyer agrees to buy from Seller the following property.

2. PROPERTY: Lot _____ , Block _____ , _____
Addition, City of _____ , _____ , County, Texas, known as
_____(Address); or as described on attached exhibit, together with the improvements, fixtures
and all other property located thereon or placed thereon pursuant to Paragraph 7 below. All property sold by this contract is called "Property".

3. CONTRACT SALES PRICE:
   A. Cash down payment payable at closing . . . . $_____
   B. All notes described below in the amount of . . . . $_____
   C. Sales Price payable to Seller on Loan funding after closing (sum of A and B) . . . . $_____

4. FINANCING CONDITIONS: This contract is subject to approval for Buyer of a _____ (type of loan) loan
(the Loan) to be evidenced by a promissory note (the Note) in the amount of $_____ , amortizable monthly for not
less than _____ years, with interest not to exceed _____% per annum for a Conventional loan or with interest at the maximum rate allowable at
time of Loan funding for a VA loan. Buyer shall apply for the Loan within _____ days from the effective date of this contract and shall make
every reasonable effort to obtain approval from _____ , as lender, or any lender that will make
the Loan at no greater loan expense (including but not limited to points, discounts or other charges however designated) to Seller than charged by
the designated lender. If the Loan cannot be approved within _____ days from the effective date of this contract, this contract shall terminate and
the Earnest Money shall be refunded to Buyer without delay.

5. EARNEST MONEY: $_____ is herewith tendered and is to be deposited as Earnest Money with _____
_____ , as Escrow Agent, upon execution of this contract by both parties. Additional Earnest Money shall be
deposited with the Escrow Agent on or before _____ , 19____ , in the amount of $_____ .

6. TITLE: Seller shall furnish to Buyer at _____'s expense either:
   ☐ A. Owner's Policy of Title Insurance (the Title Policy) issued by _____
        in the amount of the Sales Price and dated at or after closing; OR
   ☐ B. Abstracts of Title certified by a reputable abstractor or abstractors (a) from the sovereignty to the effective date of this contract (Complete
        Abstract) and (b) supplemented to the closing date (Supplemental Abstract).
   NOTICE TO BUYER: (i) AS REQUIRED BY LAW, Broker advises that YOU should have the Abstract covering the Property examined by an
   attorney of YOUR selection, or YOU should be furnished with or obtain a Title Policy; (ii) if the Property is situated in any Utility District, Section
   50.301 of the Texas Water Code requires the Buyer to sign and acknowledge a statutory notice.

7. PROPERTY CONDITIONS: Improvements are ☐ completed   ☐ incomplete.
   A. COMPLETED IMPROVEMENTS: Buyer will accept the Property at closing in its present condition subject only to lender requirements
       and_____
   B. INCOMPLETE IMPROVEMENTS: All improvements shall be completed with due diligence in accordance with the plans and specifications
       initialed by the parties hereto, incorporated herein and identified as _____
       _____ , together with the following changes or alternates: _____

       _____
       and any other change orders subsequent hereto (all called Plans and Specifications). All change orders shall be signed by the parties. Seller may
       substitute materials, equipment and appliances of equal quality for those specified in the Plans and Specifications. Change orders or items selected
       by Buyer which increase the construction costs or exceed the allowance specified in the Plans and Specifications shall be paid by Buyer as follows:

       _____ .
       Buyer shall make required selections within _____ days after receipt of written notice from Seller. The improvements shall be substantially
       completed in accordance with the Plans and Specifications and ready for occupancy not later than _____ , 19____ . If
       construction has not already commenced, it shall be commenced on or before _____ , 19____ , or within _____ days after
       Loan approval, whichever is later. The improvements shall be deemed to be substantially completed in accordance with the Plans and Specifications
       upon the final inspection and approval by all applicable governmental authorities and the lender. If delay of construction is caused by reason of
       Buyer's acts or omissions, provided Seller has exercised reasonable and continued diligence, or by reason of acts of God, fire or other casualty loss,
       strikes, boycotts or non-availability of materials for which no substitute of equal quality and price is available, the time of such delays shall be
       added to the time allowed for substantial completion of the construction, but in no event shall such time extensions exceed a total period
       of _____ days.
   C. WARRANTIES: In connection with all improvements, fixtures and all other property located on or made a part of the Property: ☐ Seller makes
       no express warranties, OR ☐ Seller makes such express warranties as are stated herein or attached. Seller agrees to deliver or assign and pass
       through to Buyer at closing all manufacturer warranties that are assignable. (NOTE: Any warranties stated herein or attached have not been
       approved by the authorities preparing or promulgating this form).
   D. INSULATION: Unless included in the Plans and Specifications insulation information required under Federal Trade Commission Regulations is
       included in an attached addendum.

(Insert factual statements and business details applicable to this sale.)   070

8. BROKER'S FEE:_____ Listing Broker (_____ %) and

_____ Co-Broker (_____ %), as Real Estate Broker (the Broker),

has negotiated this sale and Seller agrees to pay Broker in _____ County, Texas, on consummation of this sale or on Seller's default

(unless otherwise provided herein) a total cash fee of _____ of the total Sales Price, which Escrow Agent shall pay from the sale proceeds.

9. CLOSING: If improvements have been completed, the closing of the sale (the Closing Date) shall be on or before _____,
or within seven (7) days after all objections to title have been cured, whichever date is later; but if the Property is damaged or destroyed by casualty loss, the Closing Date shall be extended, if necessary, a maximum of seven (7) days. If improvements are incomplete, closing shall be within _____ days after the improvements have been substantially completed in accordance with the Plans and Specifications and are ready for occupancy; or within seven (7) days after all objections to title have been cured, whichever date is later. Closing shall not relieve Seller of Seller's obligations hereunder to fully complete all improvements.

10. POSSESSION: Possession of the Property shall be delivered to Buyer on _____.

11. SPECIAL PROVISIONS:

12. SALES EXPENSES TO BE PAID IN CASH AT OR PRIOR TO CLOSING:

A. Loan appraisal fee shall be paid by_____.

B. Seller's Expenses:

(1.) Seller's discount points in connection with the Loan not exceeding_____.

(2.) Preparation of Deed; ½ of any escrow fee; costs of releasing any existing loan; tax statements; other expenses stipulated to be paid by Seller under other provisions of this contract.

(3.) If VA financed, any non-approved Buyer's expenses shall be paid by Seller at closing.

C. Buyer's Expenses:

(1.) Fees for loans (e.g., mortgage insurance application fee and premiums; loan application, origination and commitment fees; Buyer's loan discount points) not exceeding $_____.

(2.) Allowable expenses incidental to making any loan (e.g., preparation of loan documents, survey, recording fees, copies of restrictions and easements, Mortgagee's Title Policy, credit reports, photos); ½ of any escrow fee; and if required by lender; premiums for flood and hazard insurance, reserve deposits for insurance premiums, ad valorem taxes, maintenance fees and special assessments; and interest from date of disbursement to one month prior to date of first monthly payments on any notes; expenses stipulated to be paid by Buyer under other paragraphs of this contract.

D. Any exceptions to A through C above are _____.

If any sales expenses exceed the maximum amount herein stipulated to be paid by either party, either party may terminate this contract unless the other party agrees to pay such excess. In no event shall Buyer pay charges and fees other than those expressly permitted by VA, if applicable.

13. PRORATIONS: Taxes and any rents, maintenance fees or special assessments shall be prorated to the Closing Date.

14. TITLE APPROVAL: If abstracts are furnished, Seller shall deliver Complete Abstract to Buyer within twenty (20) days from the effective date hereof. Buyer shall have twenty (20) days from date of receipt of Complete Abstract to delivery a copy of the title opinion to Seller, stating any objections to title. If Title Policy is to be furnished, Seller shall deliver to Buyer within seven (7) business days from the effective date of this contract a Commitment for Title Insurance (the Commitment) and legible copies of all recorded instruments affecting the Property and recited as exceptions in the Commitment. If Buyer has reasonable objection to any such exception, Buyer shall have five (5) business days after receipt of such instruments to make written objections to Seller and the title company. If Buyer or a third party lender makes such objections or if objections are disclosed in the title opinion, Supplemental Abstract, the Commitment, Survey or by the issuer of the Title Policy, Seller shall have thirty (30) days from the date such objections are disclosed to cure the same, and the Closing Date shall be extended accordingly. If the objections are not satisfied by the extended Closing Date, this contract shall terminate and the Earnest Money refunded to Buyer, unless Buyer elects to waive the unsatisfied objections and complete the purchase. The Title Policy shall guarantee Buyer's title to be good and indefeasible subject only to (i) restrictive covenants and easements affecting the Property (ii) any discrepancies, conflicts or shortages in area or boundary lines or any encroachments, or any overlapping of improvements (iii) all taxes for the current and subsequent years, and subsequent assessments for prior years due to a change in land usage or ownership (iv) any existing building and zoning ordinances (v) rights of parties in possession (vi) any liens created as security for the sale consideration and (vii) any reservations or exceptions permitted in the Deed. Seller shall furnish tax statements showing no delinquent taxes and a General Warranty Deed conveying title subject only to liens securing payment of debt created as part of the consideration, taxes for the current year and easements, restrictions, reservations and conditions permitted by the contract or otherwise acceptable to the Buyer. Each note herein provided shall be secured by Vendor's and Deed of Trust liens. In case of dispute as to the form of the Deed, the form prepared by the State Bar of Texas shall be used.

15. CASUALTY LOSS: If any part of the Property is damaged or destroyed by fire or other casualty loss after completion, Seller shall restore the same to its previous condition as soon as reasonably possible, but in any event, in the time provided in Paragraph 9; and if Seller is unable to do so without fault, this contract shall terminate and the Earnest Money shall be refunded with no broker's fee due.

16. DEFAULT: If Buyer fails to comply herewith, Seller may either (a) terminate this contract and receive the Earnest Money as liquidated damages, one-half of which (but not exceeding the Broker's fee) be paid by Seller to Broker in full payment for Broker's services, or (b) seek such other relief as may be provided by law in which event the Broker's fee shall be payable only if and when Seller collects damages for such default by suit, compromise, settlement or otherwise, and after first deducting the expense of collection, and then only in an amount equal to one-half of that portion collected, but not exceeding the amount of the Broker's fee. If Seller is unable, without fault, to deliver Abstracts or Title Policy or to have the improvements substantially completed within the time stated in Paragraph 7B, this contract shall terminate, the Earnest Money shall be refunded to Buyer, and the Broker shall not be entitled to any fee. If Seller fails to comply with the provisions of this contract for any other reason, Buyer may either (i) terminate this contract and receive the Earnest Money or (ii) seek such other relief as may be provided by law.

17. ATTORNEY'S FEES: Any signatory to this contract who is the prevailing party in any legal proceeding against any other signatory brought under or with relation to this contract or transaction shall be additionally entitled to recover court costs and reasonable attorney fees from the non-prevailing party.

18. ESCROW: If Escrow Agent is Broker or other third party, the Earnest Money is deposited with Escrow Agent with the understanding that Escrow Agent (i) does not assume or have any liability for performance or non-performance of any party (ii) has the right to require the receipt, release and authorization in writing of all parties before paying the Earnest Money to any party and (iii) is not liable for interest or other charge on the funds held. If any party unreasonably fails to agree in writing to an appropriate release of Earnest Money, then such party shall be liable to the other parties to the extent provided in paragraph 17. At closing, Earnest Money shall be applied to any cash down payment required, next to Buyer's closing costs and any excess refunded to Buyer. The Escrow Agent or Broker may incur actual expenses on behalf of Seller or Buyer; therefore, any refund or payment of the Earnest Money under this

(Insert factual statements and business details applicable to this sale.)   070

contract shall be reduced by the amount of any actual expenses incurred on behalf of the party receiving the Earnest Money, and the Escrow Agent will pay the same to the creditors entitled thereto. To the extent that the Seller's share of the Earnest Money is insufficient to pay such expenses, the same will be deducted from the Broker's share of the Earnest Money.

19. REPRESENTATIONS: Seller represents that there will be no unrecorded liens, assessments or Uniform Commercial Code Liens against any of the Property on Closing Date which will not be satisfied out of the Sales Price, unless securing payment of any deferred consideration. Seller represents that all ad valorem taxes which have been or may be assessed against the Property by virtue of any change in use of the Property prior to Closing Date have been or will be paid by Seller. If any representation above is untrue, this contract may be terminated by Buyer and Earnest Money shall be refunded without delay.

20. VA NOTICE TO BUYER (If applicable): "It is expressly agreed that, notwithstanding any other provision of this contract, the Buyer shall not incur penalty by forfeiture of earnest money or otherwise be obligated to complete the purchase of the Property described herein, if the contract purchase price or cost exceeds the reasonable value of the Property established by the Veterans Administration. The Buyer shall, however, have the privilege and option of proceeding with the consummation of this contract without regard to the amount of the reasonable value established by the Veterans Administration." Buyer agrees that should Buyer elect to complete the purchase at an amount in excess of the reasonable value established by VA, Buyer shall pay such excess amount in cash from a source which Buyer agrees to disclose to the VA and which Buyer represents will not be from borrowed funds except as approved by VA.

21. AGREEMENT OF PARTIES: This contract contains the entire agreement of the parties and cannot be changed except by their written consent. The representations, obligations and warranties contained in this contract shall survive closing.

22. CONSULT YOUR ATTORNEY: This is intended to be a legally binding contract. READ IT CAREFULLY. If you do not understand the effect of any part, consult your attorney BEFORE signing. The Broker cannot give you legal advice—only factual and business details concerning land and improvements. Attorneys to represent parties may be designated below, and, so employment may be accepted, Broker shall promptly deliver a copy of this contract to such attorneys.

Seller's Atty:_____   Buyer's Atty:_____

EXECUTED in multiple originals effective the _____ day of _____, 19____ **(BROKER FILL IN THE DATE LAST PARTY SIGNS).**

Listing Broker _____ License No.	Seller _____	
By_____		
	Seller _____	
Co-Broker _____ License No.		
By_____	Seller's Address _____ Tel.	
Receipt of $_____ Earnest Money is acknowledged in the		
	Buyer _____	
form of_____		
	Buyer _____	
Escrow Agent _____ Date		
By_____	Buyer's Address _____ Tel.	

070

NEW HOME RESIDENTIAL EARNEST MONEY CONTRACT
FHA INSURED LOAN

1. PARTIES: _____ (Seller) agrees to sell and convey to
_____ (Buyer) and Buyer agrees to buy from Seller the following property.

2. PROPERTY: Lot _____ , Block _____ , _____
   Addition, City of _____ , _____ , County, Texas, known as
   _____ (Address); or as described on attached exhibit, together with the improvements, fixtures
   and all other property located thereon or placed thereon pursuant to Paragraph 7 below. All property sold by this contract is called "Property".

3. CONTRACT SALES PRICE:
   A. Cash down payment payable at closing . . . . $_____
   B. The Note described below in the amount of . . . . $_____
   C. Sales Price payable to Seller on Loan funding after closing (sum of A and B) . . . . $_____

4. FINANCING CONDITIONS: This contract is subject to approval for Buyer of a Section _____ FHA Insured Loan
   (the Loan) of not less than the amount of the Note, amortizable monthly for not less than _____ years, with interest at maximum rate allowable at
   time of Loan funding. Buyer shall apply for the Loan within _____ days from the effective date of this contract and shall make every reasonable
   effort to obtain approval from _____ ,
   as lender, or any lender that will make the Loan at no greater loan expense (including but not limited to points, discounts or other charges however
   designated) to Seller than charged by the designated lender. If the Loan cannot be approved within _____ days from the effective date of this
   contract, this contract shall terminate and the Earnest Money shall be refunded to Buyer without delay.

5. EARNEST MONEY: $_____ is herewith tendered and is to be deposited as Earnest Money with _____
   _____ , as Escrow Agent, upon execution of the contract by both parties. Additional Earnest Money shall be
   deposited with the Escrow Agent on or before _____ , 19____, in the amount of $_____ .

6. TITLE: Seller shall furnish to Buyer at _____ 's expense either:
   ☐ A. Owner's Policy of Title Insurance (the Title Policy) issued by _____
        in the amount of the Sales Price and dated at or after closing; OR
   ☐ B. Abstracts of Title certified by a reputable abstractor or abstractors (a) from the sovereignty to the effective date of this contract (Complete
        Abstract) and (b) supplemented to the closing date (Supplemental Abstract).
   NOTICE TO BUYER: (i) AS REQUIRED BY LAW, Broker advises that YOU should have the Abstract covering the Property examined by an
   attorney of YOUR selection, or YOU should be furnished with or obtain a Title Policy; (ii) if the Property is situated in any Utility District, Section
   50.301 of the Texas Water Code requires the Buyer to sign and acknowledge a statutory notice.

7. PROPERTY CONDITIONS: Improvements are ☐ completed ☐ incomplete.
   A. COMPLETED IMPROVEMENTS: Buyer will accept the Property at closing in its present condition subject only to lender requirements
      and_____
   B. INCOMPLETE IMPROVEMENTS: All improvements shall be completed with due diligence in accordance with the plans and specifications
      initialed by the parties hereto, incorporated herein and identified as _____
      _____ , together with the following changes or alternates: _____
      _____
      and any other change orders subsequent hereto (all called Plans and Specifications). All change orders shall be signed by the parties. Seller may
      substitute materials, equipment and appliances of equal quality for those specified in the Plans and Specifications. Change orders or items selected
      by Buyer which increase the construction costs or exceed the allowance specified in the Plans and Specifications shall be paid by Buyer as follows:
      _____ .
      Buyer shall make required selections within _____ days after receipt of written notice from Seller. The improvements shall be substantially
      completed in accordance with the Plans and Specifications and ready for occupancy not later than _____ , 19____ . If
      construction has not already commenced, it shall be commenced on or before _____ , 19____ , or within _____ days after Loan approval,
      whichever is later. The improvements shall be deemed to be substantially completed in accordance with the Plans and Specifications upon the final
      inspection and approval by all applicable governmental authorities and the lender. If delay of construction is caused by reason of Buyer's acts or
      omissions, provided Seller has exercised reasonable and continued diligence, or by reason of acts of God, fire or other casualty loss, strikes,
      boycotts or non-availability of materials for which no substitute of equal quality and price is available, the time of such delays shall be added to the
      time allowed for substantial completion of the construction, but in no event shall such time extensions exceed a total period of _____ days.
   C. WARRANTIES: In connection with all improvements, fixtures and all other property located on or made a part of the Property: ☐ Seller makes
      no express warranties, OR ☐ Seller makes such express warranties as are stated herein or attached. Seller agrees to deliver or assign and pass
      through to Buyer at closing all manufacturer warranties that are assignable. (NOTE: Any warranties stated herein or attached have not been
      approved by the authorities preparing or promulgating this form).
   D. INSULATION: Unless included in the Plans and Specifications insulation information required under Federal Trade Commission Regulations is
      included in an attached addendum.

(Insert factual statements and business details applicable to this sale.)   085

8. BROKER'S FEE: _____ Listing Broker (_____ %) and
_____ Co-Broker (_____ %), as Real Estate Broker (the Broker),
has negotiated this sale and Seller agrees to pay Broker in _____ County, Texas, on consummation of this sale or on Seller's default
(unless otherwise provided herein) a total cash fee of _____ of the total Sales Price, which Escrow Agent shall pay from the sale proceeds.

9. CLOSING: If improvements have been completed the closing of the sale (the Closing Date) shall be on or before _____,
or within seven (7) days after all objections to title have been cured, whichever date is later; but if the Property is damaged or destroyed by casualty loss, the
Closing Date shall be extended, if necessary, a maximum of seven (7) days. If improvements are incomplete, closing shall be within _____ days after
the improvements have been substantially completed in accordance with the Plans and Specifications and are ready for occupancy; or within seven (7) days
after all objections to title have been cured, whichever date is later. Closing shall not relieve Seller of Seller's obligations hereunder to fully complete all
improvements.

10. POSSESSION: Possession of the Property shall be delivered to Buyer on _____.

11. SPECIAL PROVISIONS:

12. SALES EXPENSES TO BE PAID IN CASH AT OR PRIOR TO CLOSING:
    A. Loan appraisal fee (FHA application fee) shall be paid by _____.
    B. Seller's Expenses:
       (1.) Seller's discount points in connection with the Loan not exceeding _____.
       (2.) FHA inspections required of Seller.
       (3.) Expenses incident to Loan (e.g., preparation of Loan documents, survey, recording fees, copies of restrictions and easements, amortization
            schedule, Mortgagee's Title Policy, Loan origination fee, credit reports, photographs).
       (4.) Releases of existing loans, including prepayment penalties and recordation; tax statements; preparation of Deed; escrow fee; and other
            expenses stipulated to be paid by Seller under other provisions of this contract.
    C. Buyer's Expenses: All prepaid items required by applicable HUD-FHA or other regulations (e.g., required premiums for flood and hazard
       insurance; required reserve deposits for FHA and other insurance, ad valorem taxes, maintenance fees and special assessments); interest on the
       Note from the date of disbursement to one month prior to date of first monthly payment; expenses stipulated to be paid by Buyer under other
       provisions of this contract.
    D. Any exceptions to A through C above are _____.
       If any sales expenses exceed the maximum amount herein stipulated to be paid by either party, either party may terminate this contract unless the
       other party agrees to pay such excess. In no event shall Buyer pay charges and fees other than those expressly permitted by FHA.

13. PRORATIONS: Taxes and any rents, maintenance fees or special assessments shall be prorated to the Closing Date.

14. TITLE APPROVAL: If abstracts are furnished, Seller shall deliver Complete Abstract to Buyer within twenty (20) days from the effective date hereof.
    Buyer shall have twenty (20) days from date of receipt of Complete Abstract to deliver a copy of the title opinion to seller, stating any objections to title.
    If Title Policy is to be furnished, Seller shall deliver to Buyer within seven (7) business days from the effective date of this contract a Commitment for
    Title Insurance (the Commitment) and legible copies of all recorded instruments affecting the Property and recited as exceptions in the Commitment. If
    Buyer has reasonable objection to any such exception, Buyer shall have five (5) business days after receipt of such instruments to make written
    objections to Seller and the title company. If Buyer or a third party lender makes such objections or if objections are disclosed in the title opinion,
    Supplemental Abstract, the Commitment, Survey or by the issuer of the Title Policy, Seller shall have thirty (30) days from the date such objections are
    disclosed to cure the same, and the Closing Date shall be extended accordingly. If the objections are not satisfied by the extended Closing Date, this
    contract shall terminate and the Earnest Money refunded to Buyer, unless Buyer elects to waive the unsatisfied objections and complete the purchase.
    The Title Policy shall guarantee Buyer's title to be good and indefeasible subject only to (i) restrictive covenants and easements affecting the Property
    (ii) any discrepancies, conflicts or shortages in area or boundary lines or any encroachments, or any overlapping of improvements (iii) all taxes for the
    current and subsequent years, and subsequent assessments for prior years due to a change in land usage or ownership (iv) any existing building and
    zoning ordinances (v) rights of parties in possession (vi) any liens created as security for the sale consideration and (vii) any reservations or exceptions
    permitted in the Deed. Seller shall furnish tax statements showing no delinquent taxes and a General Warranty Deed conveying title subject only to liens
    securing payment of debt created as part of the consideration, taxes for the current year and easements, restrictions, reservations and conditions
    permitted by the contract or otherwise acceptable to the Buyer. Each note herein provided shall be secured by Vendor's and Deed of Trust liens. In case of
    dispute as to the form of the Deed, the form prepared by the State Bar of Texas shall be used.

15. CASUALTY LOSS: If any part of the Property is damaged or destroyed by fire or other casualty loss after completion, Seller shall restore the same to its
    previous condition as soon as reasonably possible, but in any event, in the time provided in Paragraph 9; and if Seller is unable to do so without fault, this
    contract shall terminate and the Earnest Money shall be refunded with no broker's fee due.

16. DEFAULT: If Buyer fails to comply herewith, Seller may either (a) terminate this contract and receive the Earnest Money as liquidated damages,
    one-half of which (but not exceeding the Broker's fee) shall be paid by Seller to Broker in full payment for Broker's services, or (b) seek such other relief
    as may be provided by law in which event the Broker's fee shall be payable only if and when Seller collects damages for such default by suit,
    compromise, settlement or otherwise, and after first deducting the expense of collection, and then only in an amount equal to one-half of that portion
    collected, but not exceeding the amount of the Broker's fee. If Seller is unable, without fault, to deliver Abstracts or Title Policy or to have the
    improvements substantially completed within the time stated in Paragraph 7 B, this contract shall terminate, the Earnest Money shall be refunded to
    Buyer, and the Broker shall not be entitled to any fee. If Seller fails to comply with the provisions of this contact for any other reason, Buyer may either (i)
    terminate this contract and receive the Earnest Money or (ii) seek such other relief as may be provided by law. .

17. ATTORNEY'S FEES: Any signatory to this contract who is the prevailing party in any legal proceeding against any other signatory brought under or
    with relation to this contract or transaction shall be additionally entitled to recover court costs and reasonable attorney fees from the non-prevailing
    party.

18. ESCROW: If Escrow Agent is Broker or other third party, the Earnest Money is deposited with Escrow Agent with the understanding that Escrow
    Agent (i) does not assume or have any liability for performance or non-performance of any party (ii) has the right to require the receipt, release and
    authorization in writing of all parties before paying the Earnest Money to any party and (iii) is not liable for interest or other charge on the funds held. If
    any party unreasonably fails to agree in writing to an appropriate release of Earnest Money, then such party shall be liable to the other parties to the
    extent provided in paragraph 17. At closing, Earnest Money shall be applied to any cash down payment required, next to Buyer's closing costs and any
    excess refunded to Buyer. The Escrow Agent or Broker may incur actual expenses on behalf of Seller or Buyer; therefore, any refund or payment of the
    Earnest Money under this contract shall be reduced by the amount of any actual expenses incurred on behalf of the party receiving the Earnest Money,

(Insert factual statements and business details applicable to this sale.)   085

and the Escrow Agent will pay the same to the creditors entitled thereto. To the extent that the Seller's share of the Earnest Money is insufficient to pay such expenses, the same will be deducted from the Broker's share of the Earnest Money.

19. REPRESENTATIONS: Seller represents that there will be no unrecorded liens, assessments or Uniform Commercial Code Liens against any of the Property on Closing Date which will not be satisfied out of the Sales Price, unless securing payment of any deferred consideration. Seller represents that all ad valorem taxes which have been or may be assessed against the Property by virtue of any change in use of the Property prior to Closing Date have been or will be paid by Seller. If any representation above is untrue, this contract may be terminated by Buyer and Earnest Money shall be refunded without delay.

20. FHA CLAUSE: As required by HUD-FHA regulation, if FHA valuation is unknown, "It is expressly agreed that, notwithstanding any other provisions of this contract, the Purchaser (Buyer) shall not be obligated to complete the purchase of the Property described herein or to incur any penalty by forfeiture of Earnest Money deposits or otherwise unless the Seller has delivered to the Purchaser (Buyer) a written statement issued by the Federal Housing Commissioner setting forth the appraised value of the Property (excluding closing costs) of not less than \$_____, which statement the Seller hereby agrees to deliver to the Purchaser (Buyer) promptly after such appraised value statement is made available to the Seller. The Purchaser (Buyer) shall, however, have the privilege and option of proceeding with the consummation of this contract without regard to the amount of the appraised valuation made by the Federal Housing Commissioner. The appraised valuation is arrived at to determine the maximum mortgage the Department of Housing and Urban Development will insure. HUD does not warrant the value or the condition of the property. The Purchaser should satisfy himself/herself that the price and the condition of the property are acceptable."

21. AGREEMENT OF PARTIES: This contract contains the entire agreement of the parties and cannot be changed except by their written consent. The representations, obligations and warranties contained in this contract shall survive closing.

22. CONSULT YOUR ATTORNEY: This is intended to be a legally binding contract. READ IT CAREFULLY. If you do not understand the effect of any part, consult your attorney BEFORE signing. The Broker cannot give you legal advice—only factual and business details concerning land and improvements. Attorneys to represent parties may be designated below, and, so employment may be accepted, Broker shall promptly deliver a copy of this contract to such attorneys.

Seller's Atty: _____   Buyer's Atty: _____

EXECUTED in multiple originals effective the _____ day of _____, 19____. **(BROKER FILL IN THE DATE LAST PARTY SIGNS).**

Listing Broker _____ License No.   Seller _____
By_____

   Seller _____

Co-Broker _____ License No.
By_____

   Seller's Address _____ Tel.

Receipt of \$_____ Earnest Money is acknowledged in the

form of_____

   Buyer _____

   Buyer _____

Escrow Agent _____ Date
By_____

   Buyer's Address _____ Tel.

085

02-08-85

UNIMPROVED PROPERTY EARNEST MONEY CONTRACT

This Contract Is Limited To Transactions Where Intended Use Is For One To Four Family Residences

PROMULGATED BY TEXAS REAL ESTATE COMMISSION

1. PARTIES: _____(Seller) agrees to sell and convey to _____(Buyer) and Buyer agrees to buy from Seller the property described below.

2. PROPERTY: Lot _____, Block _____, _____Addition, City of _____, _____, County, Texas, or as described on attached exhibit (the Property).

3. CONTRACT SALES PRICE:

    A. Cash payable at closing .... $_____
    B. Sum of all financing described in Paragraph 4 below .... $_____
    C. Sales Price (Sum of A and B) .... $_____

4. FINANCING: (Check applicable boxes below)

    ☐ A. ALL CASH: This is an all cash sale; no financing is involved.
    ☐ B. ASSUMPTION:

        (1) Buyer's assumption of the unpaid principal balance of a first lien promissory note payable to _____ in present monthly installments of $_____, including principal, interest and any reserve deposits, with Buyer's first installment payment being payable on the first installment payment date after closing, the assumed principal balance of which at closing will be $_____.
        (2) Buyer's assumption of the unpaid principal balance of a second lien promissory note payable to _____ in present monthly installments of $_____, including principal, interest and any reserve deposits, with Buyer's first installment payment being payable on the first installment payment date after closing, the assumed principal balance of which at closing will be $_____.

        Buyer's assumption of an existing note includes all obligations imposed by the deed of trust securing the note.
        If the total principal balance of all assumed loans varies in an amount greater than $350.00 at closing either party may terminate this contract and the Earnest Money shall be refunded to Buyer. If the noteholder on assumption (a) requires Buyer to pay an assumption fee in excess of $_____ in B(1) above or $_____ in B(2) above and Seller declines to pay such excess or (b) raises the existing interest rate above _____% in B(1) above or _____% in B(2) above, Buyer may terminate this contract and the Earnest Money shall be refunded to Buyer. The cash payable at closing shall be adjusted by the amount of any variance in the loan balance(s) shown above.
        NOTICE TO BUYER: Monthly payments, interest rates or other terms of some loans may be adjusted after closing. Before signing the contract, examine the notes and deeds of trust to determine the possibility of future adjustments.

    ☐ C. THIRD PARTY FINANCED:
        ☐ 1. A third party first lien note of $_____, due in full in _____year(s), payable in initial monthly payments of principal and interest not exceeding $_____ for the first _____year(s) of the loan.
        ☐ 2. A third party second lien note of $_____, due in full in _____year(s), payable in initial monthly payments of principal and interest not exceeding $_____ for the first _____year(s) of the loan.
        NOTICE TO PARTIES: Before signing this contract Buyer is advised to determine the financing options from lenders. Certain loans have variable rates of interest, some have monthly payments which may not be sufficient to pay the accruing interest, and some have interest rate ''buydowns'' which reduce the rate of interest for part or all of the loan term at the expense of one or more of the parties to the contract.

    ☐ D. SELLER FINANCED: A promissory note from Buyer to Seller in the amount of $_____, bearing _____% interest per annum, and payable:

        ☐ 1. In one payment due _____after the date of the note with interest payable _____.
        ☐ 2. In installments of $_____ [ ] including interest [ ] plus interest beginning _____ after the date of the note and continuing at _____intervals thereafter for _____year(s) when the entire balance of the note shall be due and payable.
        ☐ 3. Interest only in _____installments for the first _____year(s) and thereafter in installments of $_____ [ ] including interest [ ] plus interest beginning _____after the date of the note and continuing at _____ intervals thereafter for _____year(s) when the entire balance of the note is due and payable.
        ☐ 4. This contract is subject to Buyer furnishing Seller evidence of good credit within _____days from the effective date of this contract. If notice of disapproval of Buyer's credit is not given within five (5) days thereafter, Seller shall be deemed to have approved Buyer's credit. Buyer hereby authorizes Buyer's credit report to be furnished to Seller.

Unimproved Property Earnest Money Contract — Page Two   02-08-85

Any Seller financed note may be prepaid in whole or in part at any time, without penalty. The lien securing payment of such note will be inferior to any lien securing any loan assumed or given in connection with third party financing. If an Owner's Policy of Title Insurance is furnished, Buyer shall furnish Seller with a Mortgagee's Title Policy.

Buyer shall apply for all third party financing or noteholder's approval of Buyer for assumption and waiver of the right to accelerate the note within _____ days from the effective date of this contract and shall make every reasonable effort to obtain the same. Such financing or assumption shall have been approved when

Buyer has satisfied all of lender's financial conditions, e.g., sale of other property, requirement of co-signer or financial verifications. If such financing or noteholder's approval and waiver is not obtained within _____ days from the effective date hereof, this contract shall terminate and the Earnest Money shall be refunded to Buyer.

5. EARNEST MONEY: $_____ is herewith tendered by Buyer and is to be deposited as Earnest Money with

_____, at _____ (Address),

as Escrow Agent, upon execution of the contract by both parties. ☐ Additional Earnest Money of $_____ shall be deposited by Buyer with

the Escrow Agent on or before _____, 19_____.

6. TITLE: Seller shall furnish to Buyer at Seller's expense either:

    ☐ A.   Owner's Policy of Title Insurance (the Title Policy) issued by _____
           in the amount of the Sales Price and dated at or after closing: OR

    ☐ B.   Abstracts of Title certified by an abstract company (1) from the sovereignty to the effective date of this contract (Complete Abstract) and (2) supplemented
           to the Closing Date (Supplemental Abstract).
    NOTICE TO SELLER AND BUYER: AS REQUIRED BY LAW, Broker advises Buyer that Buyer should have an Abstract covering the Property examined by an attorney of Buyer's selection, or Buyer should be furnished with or obtain a Title Policy. If a Title Policy is to be obtained, Buyer should obtain a Commitment for Title Insurance (the Commitment) which should be examined by an attorney of Buyer's choice at or prior to closing. If the Property is situated in a Utility District, Section 50.301 Texas Water Code requires the Buyer to sign and acknowledge the statutory notice from Seller relating to the tax rate and bonded indebtedness of the District.

7. PROPERTY CONDITION: Buyer accepts the Property in its present condition, subject only to _____

    _____

8. BROKER'S FEE: _____, Listing Broker, and any Co-Broker represent Seller unless otherwise specified herein. Seller agrees to pay Listing Broker the fee specified by separate agreement between Listing Broker and Seller. If there is

    no separate agreement, Seller agrees to pay Listing Broker in _____ County, Texas, on consummation

    of this sale or on Seller's default a total cash fee of _____ of the Total Sales Price or upon Buyer's default, one half of the Earnest Money paid to Seller not to exceed the amount of cash fee. Escrow Agent is authorized and directed to pay Listing Broker said fee from the sale proceeds.

9. CLOSING: The closing of the sale shall be on or before _____, 19_____, or within seven (7) days after objections to title have been cured, whichever date is later (the Closing Date); however, if financing or assumption approval has been obtained pursuant to Paragraph 4, the Closing Date shall be extended daily up to fifteen (15) days if necessary to complete loan requirements. If either party fails to close this sale by the Closing Date, the non-defaulting party shall be entitled to exercise the remedies contained in Paragraph 15 immediately and without notice.

10. POSSESSION: The possession of the Property shall be delivered to Buyer at closing.

11. SPECIAL PROVISIONS: (Insert factual statements and business details applicable to this sale.)

12. SALES EXPENSES TO BE PAID IN CASH AT OR PRIOR TO CLOSING:

    A.   Loan appraisal fees shall be paid by _____.
    B.   The total of the loan discount and buydown fees shall not exceed $_____ of which Buyer shall pay the first $_____ and Seller shall
         pay the remainder.
    C.   Seller's Expenses: Prepayment penalties on any existing loans paid at closing, plus cost of releasing such loans and recording releases; tax statements; ½ of any escrow fee; preparation of deed; preparation and recording of any deed of trust to secure assumption; other expenses stipulated to be paid by Seller under other provisions of this contract.
    D.   Buyer's Expenses: Application, origination and commitment fees; private mortgage insurance premiums and any loan assumption fee; expenses incident to new loan(s) (e.g., preparation of any note, deed of trust and other loan documents, survey [unless stipulated to be paid by Seller in Paragraph 20], recording fees, copies of restrictions and easements, Mortgagee's Title Policies, credit reports, photos); ½ of any escrow fee; any required reserve deposits for ad valorem taxes and special governmental assessments; interest on all monthly installment payment notes from date of disbursements to one (1) month prior to dates of first monthly payments; expenses stipulated to be paid by Buyer under other provisions of this contract.
    E.   If any sales expenses exceed the maximum amount herein stipulated to be paid by either party, either party may terminate this contract unless the other party agrees to pay such excess.

13. PRORATIONS AND TAXES: Interest on any assumed loan, current taxes, any rents and maintenance fees shall be prorated through the Closing Date. If ad valorem taxes for the year in which the sale is closed are not available on the Closing Date, proration of taxes shall be made on the basis of taxes assessed in the previous year.

    If this sale or Buyer's use of the Property after closing results in the assessment of additional taxes for periods prior to closing, such additional taxes shall be the obligation of the Buyer and such obligation shall survive closing. If Seller's change in use of the Property prior to closing or denial of a special use valuation claimed by Seller results in the assessment of additional taxes for periods prior to closing, such additional taxes shall be the obligation of Seller, and such obligation shall survive closing.

177

Unimproved Property Earnest Money Contract concerning _____ Page Three   02-08-85

(Address of Property)

14. TITLE APPROVAL:

A. If abstract is furnished, Seller shall deliver Complete Abstract to Buyer within twenty (20) days from the effective date hereof. Buyer shall have twenty (20) days from date of receipt of Complete Abstract to deliver a copy of the examining attorney's title opinion to Seller, stating any objections to title, and only objections so stated shall be considered.

B. If Title Policy is furnished, the Title Policy shall guarantee Buyer's title to be good and indefeasible subject only to (1) restrictive covenants affecting the Property (2) any discrepancies, conflicts or shortages in area or boundary lines, or any encroachments, or any overlapping of improvements (3) taxes for the current and subsequent years and subsequent assessments for prior years due to a change in land usage or ownership (4) existing building and zoning ordinances (5) rights of parties in possession (6) liens created or assumed as security for the sale consideration (7) utility easements common to the platted subdivision of which this Property is a part and (8) reservations or other exceptions permitted by the terms of this contract. Exceptions permitted in the Deed and zoning ordinances shall not be valid objections to title. If the Title Policy will be subject to exceptions other than those recited above in sub-paragraphs (1) through (7) inclusive, Seller shall deliver to Buyer the Commitment and legible copies of any documents creating such exceptions that are not recited in sub-paragraphs (1) through (7) above at least five (5) days prior to closing. If Buyer has objection to any such previously undisclosed exceptions, Buyer shall have five (5) days after receipt of such Commitment and copies to make written objections to Seller. If no Title Commitment is provided to Buyer at or prior to closing, it will be conclusively presumed that Seller represented at closing that the Title Policy would not be subject to exceptions other than those recited above in sub-paragraphs (1) through (7).

C. In either instance if title objections are raised, Seller shall have fifteen (15) days from the date such objections are disclosed to cure the same, and the Closing Date shall be extended accordingly. If the objections are not satisfied by the extended closing date, this contract shall terminate and the Earnest Money shall be refunded to Buyer, unless Buyer elects to waive the unsatisfied objections and complete the purchase.

D. Seller shall furnish tax statements showing no delinquent taxes, a Supplemental Abstract when applicable, showing no additional title exceptions and a General Warranty Deed conveying title subject only to liens securing payment of debt created or assumed as part of the consideration, taxes for the current year, restrictive covenants and utility easements common to the platted subdivision of which the Property is a part and reservations and conditions permitted by this contract or otherwise acceptable to Buyer. Each note shall be secured by vendor's and deed of trust liens. A vendor's lien and deed of trust to secure assumption shall be required, which shall automatically be released on execution and delivery of a release by noteholder. If Seller is released from liability on any assumed note, the vendor's lien and deed of trust to secure assumption shall not be required. In case of dispute as to the form of the Deed, note(s), deed of trust or deed of trust to secure assumption, forms prepared by the State Bar of Texas shall be used.

15. DEFAULT: If Buyer fails to comply herewith, Seller may either (a) enforce specific performance and seek such other relief as may be provided by law or (b) terminate this contract and receive the Earnest Money as liquidated damages. If Seller is unable without fault, within the time herein required, to (a) deliver the Commitment or (b) deliver the Complete Abstract, Buyer may either terminate this contract and receive the Earnest Money as the sole remedy or extend the time for performance up to fifteen (15) days and the Closing Date shall be extended pursuant to other provisions of this contract. If Seller fails to comply herewith for any other reason, Buyer may either (a) enforce specific performance hereof and seek such other relief as may be provided by law or (b) terminate this contract and receive the Earnest Money, thereby releasing Seller from this contract.

16. ATTORNEY'S FEES: Any signatory to this contract, Broker or Escrow Agent who is the prevailing party in any legal proceeding brought under or with relation to this contract or transaction shall be additionally entitled to recover court costs and reasonable attorney fees from the non-prevailing party.

17. ESCROW: The Earnest Money is deposited with Escrow Agent with the understanding that Escrow Agent (a) is not a party to this contract and does not assume or have any liability for performance or non-performance of any signatory (b) has the right to require from all signatories a written release of liability of the Escrow Agent which authorizes the disbursement of the Earnest Money (c) is not liable for interest or other charge on the funds held and (d) is not liable for any losses of escrow funds caused by the failure of any banking institution in which such funds have been deposited, unless such banking institution is acting as Escrow Agent. If any signatory unreasonably fails to deliver promptly the documents described in (b) above, then such signatory shall be liable to the other signatories as provided in Paragraph 16. At closing, the Earnest Money shall be applied first to any cash down payment required, then to Buyer's closing costs and any excess refunded to Buyer. Any refund or payment of the Earnest Money under this contract shall be reduced by the amount of any actual expenses incurred on behalf of the party receiving the Earnest Money, and Escrow Agent will pay the same to the creditors entitled thereto.

18. REPRESENTATIONS: Seller represents that as of the Closing Date (a) there will be no unrecorded liens, assessments or Uniform Commercial Code Security Interests against any of the Property which will not be satisfied out of the Sales Price, unless securing payment of any loans assumed by Buyer and (b) that assumed loan(s) will be without default. If any representation above is untrue on the Closing Date this contract may be terminated by Buyer and the Earnest Money shall be refunded to Buyer. All representations contained in this contract shall survive closing.

19. USE AND UTILITIES: The intended use of the Property by Buyer is [   ] single family dwelling [   ] multiple family dwelling of _____units [   ] mobile home. Utilities required at the Property for such use are [   ] water [   ] sanitary sewer [   ] gas [   ] electricity [   ] telephone [   ] _____. If Buyer ascertains that applicable zoning ordinances, restrictions or governmental laws, rules or regulations prevent such intended use or that such required utilities are not available, or that the Property is located within the 100 year flood plain as designated by the appropriate governmental authority, and Buyer so notifies Seller within _____days from the effective date of this contract, then the same shall terminate and the Earnest Money shall be refunded to Buyer; failure on the part of Buyer to give the notice within the required time shall constitute Buyer's acceptance of the Property for Buyer's intended use.

20. SURVEY: [   ] required [   ] not required. If required, then within _____days from the effective date of this contract a current survey of the Property shall be furnished by and at the expense of [   ] Seller [   ] Buyer by a mutually acceptable Registered Public Surveyor licensed by the State of Texas. A plat of the survey together with any appropriate field notes shall be furnished to Seller and Buyer. The survey shall locate all improvements, encroachments and overlapping of improvements on the Property, together with all easements and roadways adjoining or crossing the Property.

21. AGREEMENT OF PARTIES: This contract contains the entire agreement of the parties and cannot be changed except by their written agreement. Texas Real Estate Commission promulgated addenda which are a part of this contract are (list): _____

177

Unimproved Property Earnest Money Contract — Page Four   02-08-85

22. NOTICES: All notices shall be in writing and effective when delivered at the addresses shown below.

23. CONSULT YOUR ATTORNEY: The Broker cannot give you legal advice. This is intended to be a legally binding contract. READ IT CAREFULLY. Federal law may impose certain duties upon Brokers or Signatories to this contract when any of the signatories is a foreign party, or when any of the signatories receives certain amounts of U.S. currency in connection with a real estate closing. If you do not understand the effect of any part of this contract, consult your attorney BEFORE signing.

SELLER'S
ATTORNEY: _____

BUYER'S
ATTORNEY: _____

EXECUTED in multiple originals effective the _____ day of _____, 19_____. **(BROKER: FILL IN THE DATE OF FINAL ACCEPTANCE.)**

_____   _____
Buyer   Seller

_____   _____
Buyer   Seller

_____   _____
Buyer's Address   Phone No.   Seller's Address   Phone No.

AGREEMENT BETWEEN BROKERS

Listing Broker agrees to pay _____, Co-Broker,
a fee of _____ of the total sales price when the Broker's fee described in Paragraph 8 is received. Escrow Agent is authorized and directed to pay Co-Broker from Listing Broker's fee at closing.

_____   _____
Co-Broker   License No.   Listing Broker   License No.

By: _____   By: _____

_____   _____
Co-Broker's Address   Phone No.   Listing Broker's Address   Phone No.

EARNEST MONEY RECEIPT

Receipt of $_____ Earnest Money is acknowledged in the form of _____

_____

Escrow Agent: _____   By: _____

Date: _____, 19_____.

177

PROMULGATED BY TEXAS REAL ESTATE COMMISSION

SALE OF OTHER PROPERTY BY BUYER

**ADDENDUM TO EARNEST MONEY CONTRACT BETWEEN THE UNDERSIGNED PARTIES
CONCERNING PROPERTY AT** _____
(Street Address and City)

1. Sale of property at _____
    and Buyer's receipt of the sale proceeds by 5:00 p.m. on _____, 19____ is a condition of the contract (the Condition). If the
    Condition is not satisfied or waived by Buyer by the above time and date, the contract shall terminate and the Earnest Money shall be
    returned to Buyer.

2. The Property may continue to be shown and offered for sale.

3. If the Seller accepts a bona-fide written offer to purchase the Property, Buyer shall be notified that Seller requires removal of the Condition.
    Unless Buyer, by 5:00 p.m. on the _____ day after Seller's notice to Buyer, (i) delivers notice to the Listing Broker's office waiving the
    Condition and (ii) deposits $ _____ with Escrow Agent as additional Earnest Money, the contract shall terminate and
    the Earnest Money shall be returned to Buyer.

4. If Buyer waives the Condition, but approval of any loan or loan assumption requires sale of the property described in Paragraph 1 above,
    the Buyer shall be in default if such requirement is not satisfied within the time specified in Paragraph 9 of the contract, and all Earnest
    Money shall be forfeited by Buyer and paid in accordance with the default provisions of the contract.

5. All notices shall be in writing and effective when delivered at the following addresses:

Listing Broker: _____

Buyer: _____

<table>
<tr><td>_____</td><td>_____</td></tr>
<tr><td align="center">Seller</td><td align="center">Buyer</td></tr>
<tr><td>_____</td><td>_____</td></tr>
<tr><td align="center">Seller</td><td align="center">Buyer</td></tr>
</table>

167

PROMULGATED BY TEXAS REAL ESTATE COMMISSION

SECOND OR "BACK-UP" CONTRACT ADDENDUM

ADDENDUM TO EARNEST MONEY CONTRACT BETWEEN THE UNDERSIGNED PARTIES CONCERNING PROPERTY AT _____

(Street Address and City)

Seller has entered into an Earnest Money contract (First Contract) dated _____, 19 _____, with _____ _____ (First Buyer) for the sale of the Property. If the First Contract is not terminated by 5:00 p.m. on _____, 19_____, this contract (Second Contract) shall terminate and the Earnest Money shall be returned to Buyer. If the First Contract is terminated within the time specified above, the effective date of the Second Contract shall be the date of termination of the First Contract.

_____   _____
Seller   Buyer

_____   _____
Seller   Buyer

The form of this contract has been approved by the Texas Real Estate Commission. Such approval relates to this contract form only. No representation is made as to the legal validity or adequacy of any provision in any specific transaction. It is not suitable for complex transactions. Extensive riders or additions are not to be used. (6-82) TREC No. 11-0

167

PROMULGATED BY TEXAS REAL ESTATE COMMISSION

VA RELEASE OF LIABILITY/RESTORATION OF ENTITLEMENT (ASSUMPTION OF LOAN CONTRACT)

ADDENDUM TO EARNEST MONEY CONTRACT BETWEEN THE UNDERSIGNED PARTIES CONCERNING PROPERTY AT _____

(Street Address and City)

Buyer shall accept from Seller a deed containing the VA-required assumption clause and shall furnish promptly such information and documents required by VA to release Seller from VA liability or to restore Seller's VA entitlement as indicated below.

(Check A or B)

☐ A. VA RELEASE OF SELLER'S PERSONAL LIABILITY TO THE GOVERNMENT ON LOAN TO BE ASSUMED

(Check only 1 or 2)

☐ 1. This contract is contingent upon the approval of a release of Seller's VA liability being received by Seller on or before the Closing Date. If such approval is not received by this date, the contract shall terminate and Earnest Money shall be refunded to Buyer without delay.

☐ 2. If approval of the release of Seller's VA liability has not been received by Seller on or before the Closing Date, Buyer shall continue to aid in the receipt of same after closing.

☐ B. RESTORATION OF SELLER'S VA ENTITLEMENT FOR A VA GUARANTEED LOAN*

Buyer is a veteran and will apply promptly to VA for substitution of Buyer's entitlement for that of the Seller on the loan being assumed; and

(Check only 1 or 2)

☐ 1. This contract is contingent upon the approval of the restoration of Seller's VA entitlement being received by Seller on or before the Closing Date. If such approval is not received by this date, the contract shall terminate and Earnest Money shall be refunded to Buyer without delay.

☐ 2. If approval of the restoration of Seller's VA entitlement has not been received by the Seller on or before the Closing Date, Buyer shall continue to aid in the receipt of same after closing.

The provisions of this addendum shall survive closing.

*NOTICE: VA will not restore Seller's entitlement unless Buyer is a Veteran, has sufficient unused VA entitlement, and is otherwise qualified. If restoration is important to Seller, Seller should require receipt thereof prior to closing.

_____   _____
            Seller   Buyer

_____   _____
            Seller   Buyer

The form of this contract has been approved by the Texas Real Estate Commission. Such approval relates to this contract form only. No representation is made as to the legal validity or adequacy of any provision in any specific transaction. It is not suitable for complex transactions. Extensive riders or additions are not to be used. (6-82) TREC No. 12-0

167

PROMULGATED BY TEXAS REAL ESTATE COMMISSION

NEW HOME INSULATION ADDENDUM

ADDENDUM TO EARNEST MONEY CONTRACT BETWEEN THE UNDERSIGNED PARTIES CONCERNING PROPERTY AT _____

(Street Address and City)

As required by Federal Trade Commission Regulations, the information relating to the insulation installed or to be installed in the home being purchased under the contract is as follows:

A. Exterior walls of improved living areas insulated with _____ insulation to a thickness of _____ inches which yields an R-Value of _____ .

B. Walls in other areas of the home insulated with _____ insulation to a thickness of _____ inches which yields an R-Value of _____ .

C. Ceilings in improved living areas, insulated with _____ insulation to a thickness of _____ inches which yields an R-Value of _____ .

D. Floors of improved living areas not applied to a slab foundation insulated with _____ insulation to a thickness of _____ inches which yields an R-Value of _____ .

E. _____ insulated with _____ insulation to a thickness of _____ inches which yields an R-Value of _____ .

All stated R-Values are based on information provided by the manufacturer of the insulation.

_____   _____
                Seller   Buyer

_____   _____
                Seller   Buyer

168

PROMULGATED BY THE TEXAS REAL ESTATE COMMISSION

FINANCING CONDITIONS ADDENDUM
(To be used only for Conventional Loans)

ADDENDUM TO EARNEST MONEY CONTRACT BETWEEN THE UNDERSIGNED PARTIES CONCERNING THE PROPERTY AT _____

(Street Address and City)

Paragraph 4 of the contract is replaced and superseded by this Addendum.

4. FINANCING CONDITIONS: This contract is subject to approval for Buyer by a third party of a conventional loan (the Loan) of not less than the amount of the Note, ☐ with ☐ without private mortgage insurance, as described below:

☐   A.   A flexible interest rate Loan for a minimum term of _____ years with monthly payments based upon a _____ year amortization, with the initial interest rate not to exceed _____ % per annum, with the following provisions:

☐   (i)   None of the following.

☐   (ii)   The initial interest rate may be adjusted at the end of _____ years; and may be adjusted thereafter every _____ years to the rate determined by the lender.

☐   (iii)   The maximum interest rate adjustment at any adjustment period shall not exceed _____ % per annum.

☐   (iv)   The maximum interest rate that may be paid by the Buyer at any time during the Loan term shall not exceed _____ % per annum.

☐   (v)   The maximum payment adjustment for principal and interest at any adjustment period is _____ % of the previous payment for principal and interest.

☐   (vi)   The monthly principal and interest payment shall not exceed $_____ during the loan term. If the monthly payments will not amortize the Loan over its remaining term, the Loan term may be extended by the lender. If the monthly interest accruing on the Loan exceeds the amount of the monthly payments, the excess will be added to the Loan principal.

☐   B.   Buydown Loan for a minimum _____ year term with annual interest of _____ % for the first loan year, _____ % for the second loan year, _____ % for the third loan year, _____ % for the fourth loan year, _____ % for the fifth loan year and _____ % thereafter. In addition to the Sales Expenses in Paragraph 12, a buydown fee not to exceed $_____ shall be paid by _____.

This contract is also subject to the approval by the lender of any third party Second Note. Buyer shall apply for all financing within _____ days from the effective date of this contract and shall make every effort to obtain approval. If financing cannot be approved within _____ days from the effective date of this contract, this contract shall terminate and the Earnest Money shall be refunded to Buyer without delay.

_____	_____
Seller	Buyer
_____	_____
Seller	Buyer

167

02-08-85

SELLER'S TEMPORARY RESIDENTIAL LEASE

PROMULGATED BY TEXAS REAL ESTATE COMMISSION

1. PARTIES: The parties to this Lease are _____

(Landlord) and _____ (Tenant).

2. LEASE: Landlord leases to Tenant the property (the Property) described in the Earnest Money Contract (the Contract) between Landlord as Buyer

and Tenant as Seller dated _____ , 19____ , and known as _____

_____ (address).

3. TERM: The term of this Lease commences on the date the sale covered by the Contract is closed and terminates on _____ ,

19____ , unless terminated earlier by reason of other provisions hereof.

4. RENTAL: Tenant shall pay as rental the sum of $_____ per day, payable (   ) monthly (   ) weekly in advance,
or (   ) upon termination of this Lease. The rental shall be paid to Landlord or Landlord's agent at the address which appears by Landlord's signature
below.

5. SECURITY DEPOSIT: Tenant will pay to Landlord at closing as a deposit the sum of $_____ to secure performance of this Lease
by Tenant. The deposit shall be used by Landlord to the extent necessary to satisfy Tenant's obligations under this Lease, and the unused portion of
the deposit shall be refunded to Tenant, together with an itemized list of all deductions from the deposit, within thirty (30) days after Tenant surrenders
possession of the Property.

6. UTILITIES: Tenant shall pay all utility charges except _____

_____ , which shall be paid by Landlord

7. USE OF PROPERTY: The Property shall be used and occupied by Tenant for single family dwelling purposes only. The Tenant shall not assign
this Lease or sublet any part of the Property.

8. PETS: No pets shall be kept on the Property except _____

_____ .

9. CONDITION OF PROPERTY: Tenant accepts the Property in its condition and state of repair at the commencement of the lease term, and
Landlord shall not be obligated to make any repairs or improvements. Upon termination Tenant shall surrender the Property to the Landlord in its

required condition under the Contract at the time of closing, except normal wear and tear and loss by fire or other casualty and _____

_____ .

10. ALTERATIONS: No holes may be made or nails driven into the woodwork, floors, walls, or ceilings of the improvements, nor may Tenant alter,
paint or decorate the Property or install improvements or fixtures thereon without prior written consent of Landlord. Any additional improvements or
fixtures placed on the Property shall become the property of Landlord.

11. INSPECTIONS: During the lease term Landlord may enter the Property at all reasonable times to inspect the improvements.

171   TREC No. 15-1

12. LAWS: Tenant shall obey all applicable laws, restrictions, ordinances, rules and regulations with respect to the Property.

13. REPAIRS AND MAINTENANCE: Tenant shall bear all expense of repairing and maintaining the Property, including but not limited to yard, trees and shrubs. Tenant shall replace or repair at the expense of Tenant any damage to the Property caused directly or indirectly by the acts or omissions of the Tenant or any other person therein or thereon by the consent, invitation or sufferance of Tenant. The repair or replacement of such damage shall be commenced and prosecuted to completion with reasonable dispatch. Tenant hereby knowingly, voluntarily, specifically and for a valuable consideration waives all duties imposed on the Landlord that can be waived pursuant to Section 92.006 of the Texas Property Code.

14. INDEMNITY: Tenant shall indemnify Landlord from the claims of all third parties for injury or damage to the person or property of such third party arising from the use or occupancy of the Property by Tenant. This indemnification shall include all costs and expenses incurred by Landlord, including attorney's fees.

15. INSURANCE: Landlord and Tenant shall each maintain such insurance on the improvements and Property as each party may deem appropriate during the term of this Lease. NOTE: Possession of the Property by the Tenant changes policy rights. CONSULT YOUR INSURANCE AGENT prior to closing the Contract.

16. DEFAULT: If Tenant fails to perform or observe any provision of this Lease and fails to remedy same within three (3) days after notice by Landlord, or if bankruptcy proceedings are commenced by or against Tenant, or an assignment for the benefit of creditors is made by Tenant, the same shall constitute a default under this Lease.

17. TERMINATION: This Lease shall terminate upon expiration of the term or upon Tenant's default under this Lease. Upon termination, and after notice for possession by Landlord, Tenant shall vacate the Property within five (5) days.

18. HOLDING OVER: A. Any possession by Tenant after termination shall not operate to renew or extend the term but shall be construed as a

tenancy at sufferance of the Landlord. Tenant shall pay rental at a rate of $_____ per day during the period of any possession after termination.

   B. As an advance on any such hold over rental the Escrow Agent under the Contract shall retain from the sale proceeds under the Contract the

sum of $_____. When Tenant delivers possession of the Property to Landlord, the Escrow Agent shall pay to the Landlord the amount of any accrued and unpaid hold over rental and the balance shall be paid to Tenant. This fund is deposited with Escrow Agent with the understanding that Escrow Agent (1) is not a party to this contract and does not assume or have any liability for performance or non-performance of any party or other signatory (2) has the right to require from all signatories a written release of liability of the Escrow Agent which authorizes the dispersement of the fund (3) is not liable for interest or other charge on the funds held and (4) is not liable for any losses of escrow funds caused by the failure of any banking institution in which such funds have been deposited, unless such banking institution is acting as Escrow Agent. If any signatory unreasonably fails to deliver promptly the documents described in (2) above, then such signatory shall be liable to the other signatories as provided in Paragraph 19.

19. ATTORNEY'S FEES: Any signatory to this Lease, Broker or Escrow Agent who is the prevailing party in any legal proceeding brought under or with relation to this Lease or transaction shall be additionally entitled to recover court costs and reasonable attorney's fees from the non-prevailing party.

20. NOTICES: All notices by Landlord shall be in writing and effective when delivered to the Property. All notices by Tenants submitted as required by law shall be in writing and effective when delivered to the designated address for payment of rent.

21. NOTICE TO LANDLORD: You are hereby advised that Section 92.051 of the Texas Property Code requires the installation of smoke detectors in all rental property.

22. CONSULT YOUR ATTORNEY: This is intended to be a legally binding contract. READ IT CAREFULLY. If you do not understand the exact effect of any part consult your attorney before signing.

23. SPECIAL PROVISIONS:

DATED this _____ day of _____, 19_____

LANDLORD _____

Designated name and address
for payment of rent:

LANDLORD _____

TENANT _____

Name _____

TENANT _____

Street _____

Receipt of advance hold over rental is acknowledged in the form of

City _____ State _____ Zip _____

_____

_____

Escrow Agent   Date

By _____

The form of this contract has been approved by the Texas Real Estate Commission. Such approval relates to this contract form only. No representation is made as to the legal validity or adequacy of any provision in any specific transaction. It is not suitable for complex transactions. Extensive riders or additions are not to be used. (02-85) TREC No. 15-1

171

02-08-85

(NOTICE: For use only when BUYER occupies property PRIOR to closing)

BUYER'S TEMPORARY RESIDENTIAL LEASE

PROMULGATED BY TEXAS REAL ESTATE COMMISSION

1. PARTIES: The parties to this Lease are _____

(Landlord) and _____ (Tenant).

2. LEASE: Landlord leases to Tenant the property (the Property) described in the Earnest Money Contract (the Contract) between Landlord as Seller

and Tenant as Buyer dated _____, 19____, and known as _____

_____ (address).

3. TERM: The term of this Lease commences on _____
and terminates on the Contract Closing Date, unless terminated earlier by reason of other provisions hereof.

4. CONSIDERATION: A. Tenant shall pay as rental the sum of $_____ per day, payable ( ) monthly ( ) weekly in advance, or ( ) upon termination of this Lease. No portion of the rental paid shall be applied to payment of any items covered by the Contract. The rental shall be paid to Landlord or Landlord's agent at the address which appears by Landlord's signature below.

B. Tenant shall pay to the Escrow Agent in the Contract the sum of $_____ as additional Earnest Money prior to taking possession of the Property. This fund is deposited with Escrow Agent with the understanding that Escrow Agent (1) is not a party to this contract and does not assume or have any liability for performance or non-performance of any party or other signatory (2) has the right to require from all signatories a written release of liability of the Escrow Agent which authorizes the disbursement of the fund (3) is not liable for interest or other charge on the funds held and (4) is not liable for any losses of escrow funds caused by the failure of any banking institution in which such funds have been deposited, unless such banking institution is acting as Escrow Agent. If any signatory unreasonably fails to deliver promptly the documents described in (2) above, then such signatory shall be liable to the other signatories as provided in Paragraph 19.

5. SECURITY DEPOSIT: Tenant has paid to Landlord or his agent, _____

_____, as a deposit the sum of $_____ to secure performance of this Lease by Tenant. If this Lease is terminated before closing of the sale of the Property, the deposit shall be used by the Landlord to the extent necessary to satisfy Tenant's obligations under this Lease, and the unused portion of the deposit will be refunded to Tenant, together with an itemized list of all deductions from the deposit, within thirty (30) days after Tenant surrenders possession of the Property. If this Lease is terminated by the closing of the sale of the Property, the deposit will be refunded to Tenant at the closing. NOTICE: The security deposit must be in addition to the Earnest Money deposit under the terms of the Contract.

6. UTILITIES: The Tenant shall be responsible for all utility company connections and payment of all deposits and charges to utility companies,

except _____

_____, which shall be paid by Landlord.

7. USE OF PROPERTY: The Property shall be used and occupied by Tenant for single family dwelling purposes only. The Tenant shall not assign this Lease or sublet any part of the Property.

8. PETS: No pets shall be kept on the Property except _____

_____.

170 TREC No. 16-1

9. CONDITION OF PROPERTY: Tenant accepts the Property in its present condition and state of repair, but Landlord shall be obligated to make all repairs and improvements required by the Contract. If this Lease is terminated other than by the closing of the sale under the Contract, Tenant shall surrender the Property to Landlord in its present condition, or as may have been improved by Landlord, normal wear and tear and loss by fire or other casualty only excepted.

10. ALTERATIONS: No holes may be made or nails driven into the woodwork, floors, walls, or ceilings of the improvements, nor may Tenant alter, paint or decorate the Property or install improvements or fixtures thereon without prior written consent of Landlord. Any additional improvements or fixtures placed on the Property shall become the property of Landlord if this Lease is terminated other than by closing of the sale under the Contract. Such improvements or fixtures shall remain upon and be surrendered with the Property.

11. INSPECTIONS: Landlord may enter the Property at all reasonable times to inspect, complete, replace or repair the improvements.

12. LAWS: Tenant shall obey all applicable laws, restrictions, ordinances, rules and regulations with respect to the Property.

13. REPAIRS AND MAINTENANCE: Tenant shall bear all expense of repairing and maintaining the Property, including but not limited to yard, trees and shrubs, unless otherwise stipulated in the Contract. Notwithstanding the provision of the Contract relating to Casualty Loss, Tenant shall replace or repair at the expense of Tenant any damage to the Property caused directly or indirectly by the acts or omissions of the Tenant or any other person therein or thereon by the consent, invitation or sufferance of the Tenant. The repair or replacement of such damage shall be commenced and prosecuted to completion with reasonable dispatch. Tenant hereby knowingly, voluntarily, specifically and for a valuable consideration waives all duties imposed on the Landlord that can be waived pursuant to Section 92.006 of the Texas Property Code.

14. INDEMNITY: Tenant shall indemnify Landlord from the claims of all third parties for injury or damage to the person or property of such third party arising from the use or occupancy of the Property by Tenant. This indemnification shall include all costs and expenses incurred by Landlord, including attorney's fees.

15. INSURANCE: Landlord and Tenant shall each maintain such insurance on the improvements and Property as each party may deem appropriate during the term of this Lease. NOTE: Possession of the Property by the Tenant changes policy rights. CONSULT YOUR INSURANCE AGENT prior to change of possession.

16. DEFAULT: If Tenant fails to perform or observe any provision of this Lease and fails to remedy same within three (3) days after notice by Landlord, or if bankruptcy proceedings are commenced by or against Tenant, or an assignment for the benefit of creditors is made by Tenant, the same shall constitute a default under this Lease.

17. TERMINATION. This Lease shall terminate upon (a) expiration of the term, (b) closing of the sale under the Contract, (c) termination of the Contract prior to closing, (d) Tenant's default under this Lease, (e) Tenant's failure to close the sale after all conditions of the Contract necessary for the closing of the sale have been satisfied and the Landlord has given five (5) days notice of a date and time of closing, whichever occurs first. Upon termination other than by closing of the sale, Tenant shall vacate the Property within five (5) days after notice for possession.

18. HOLDING OVER: Any possession by Tenant after termination shall not operate or renew or extend the term but shall be construed as a tenancy at sufferance of the Landlord. Tenant shall pay rental at a rate of two (2) times the rental stipulated in Paragraph 4 above during the period of any possession after termination.

19. ATTORNEY'S FEES: Any signatory of this Lease, Broker or Escrow Agent who is the prevailing party in any legal proceeding brought under or with relation to this Lease or transaction shall be additionally entitled to recover court costs and reasonable attorney's fees from the non-prevailing party.

20. NOTICES: All notices by Landlord shall be in writing and effective when delivered to the Property. All notices by Tenants submitted as required by law shall be in writing and effective when delivered to the designated address for payment of rent.

21. NOTICE TO LANDLORD: You are hereby advised that Section 92.051 of the Texas Property Code requires the installation of smoke detectors in all rental property.

22. CONSULT YOUR ATTORNEY: This is intended to be a legally binding contract. READ IT CAREFULLY. If you do not understand the exact effect of any part consult your attorney before signing.

23. SPECIAL PROVISIONS:

170   TREC No. 16-1

DATED this _____ day of _____ , 19_____ .

LANDLORD _____

Designated name and address
for payment of rent:

LANDLORD _____

TENANT _____

Name

TENANT _____

Street

Receipt of additional Earnest Money is acknowledged in the form of

_____

City   State   Zip

_____

Escrow Agent   Date

By _____

The form of this contract has been approved by the Texas Real Estate Commission. Such approval relates to this contract form only. No representation is made as to the legal validity or adequacy of any provision in any specific transaction. It is not suitable for complex transactions. Extensive riders or additions are not to be used. (02-85) TREC No. 16-1

170

FARM AND RANCH EARNEST MONEY CONTRACT

1. PARTIES: _____(Seller) agrees to sell

   and convey to _____(Buyer) and Buyer

   agrees to buy from Seller the following property situated in _____County, Texas.

2. PROPERTY: The land described as _____

   _____

   or as described on attached Exhibit, together with all improvements thereon and all rights, privileges and appurtenances pertaining thereto; including, but not limited to, water rights, claims and permits, easements, all rights and obligations of applicable government programs and cooperative memberships; subject, however, to the following exceptions, reservations, conditions and restrictions: (if recorded, insert recording data).

   A. Minerals, royalties, and timber interests
       (i) Presently outstanding in third parties

       (ii) To be additionally retained by Seller

   B. Mineral Leases

   C. Surface Leases

   D. Easements

   E. Restrictions

   F. Other

   together with the following crops and equipment _____

   _____

   _____

   All property sold by this contract is called "Property".

140

3. CONTRACT SALES PRICE:
    A. Cash payable at closing . . . . $_____
    B. Sum of all notes described in Paragraph 4 below . . . . $_____
    C. Sales Price payable to Seller (Sum of A and B) . . . . $_____
    ☐ D. The Sales Price herein shall be adjusted, based on the survey required by Paragraph 20C, and the number of acres over or under _____ acres shall be multiplied by $_____ per acre, and the product thereof shall be added to or subtracted from the Sales Price, as the case may be, and Subparagraph 3A shall be adjusted accordingly.

4. FINANCING: (Check applicable boxes below)
    ☐ A. ASSUMPTION: Buyer shall assume the unpaid balance of that promissory note payable to _____
        _____ dated _____, and those obligations imposed by the Deed of Trust recorded in Volume _____, Page _____of the Deed of Trust Records in the county where the Property is situated. Buyer shall pay the installment payment due after the date of closing. The assumed principal balance at closing will be $_____allowing for an agreed $500.00 variance. The cash payable at closing shall be adjusted for the amount of such variance. Buyer shall apply for assumption approval within _____days from the effective date of this contract and shall make every reasonable effort to obtain the same. If the variance exceeds $500.00 or the existing interest rate is increased above _____% or Buyer is required to pay an assumption fee in excess of $_____, or assumption approval cannot be obtained within _____ days from the effective date hereof, this contract may be terminated at Buyer's option and the Earnest Money shall be refunded to Buyer without delay.
    ☐ B. THIRD PARTY FINANCING: This contract is subject to approval of a loan for Buyer by a third party in the amount of $_____ payable at _____intervals for not less than _____years with the initial interest rate not to exceed _____% per annum, and with each principal and interest installment not to exceed $_____ ☐ including interest ☐ plus interest, for the first _____years of the loan. Buyer shall apply for the loan within _____days from the effective date of this contract and shall make every reasonable effort to obtain approval. If the loan has not been approved within _____days from the effective date of this contract, this contract shall terminate and the Earnest Money shall be refunded to Buyer without delay.
    ☐ C. SELLER FINANCING: Buyer shall execute a promissory note to Seller in the principal sum of $_____, bearing _____% interest per annum, and payable: (Check 1, 2 or 3 below)
        ☐ 1. In one payment due _____after the date of the note with interest payable _____.
        ☐ 2. In installments of $_____ ☐ including interest ☐ plus interest beginning _____ _____after the date of the note and continuing at _____ intervals thereafter for _____years when the entire balance of the note shall be due and payable.
        ☐ 3. Interest only in _____installments for the first _____years and thereafter in installments of $_____ ☐ including interest ☐ plus interest beginning _____after the date of the note and continuing at _____intervals thereafter for _____years when the entire balance of the note is due and payable.
    Any Seller financed note may be prepaid in whole or in part at any time without penalty. The lien securing payment of such note will be inferior to any lien securing any loan assumed or given in connection with third party financing.

5. EARNEST MONEY: $_____ is herewith tendered and is to be deposited as Earnest Money with _____, _____, as Escrow Agent, upon execution of the contract by both parties.

6. TITLE: Seller shall furnish to Buyer at Seller's expense either:
    ☐ A. Owner's Policy of Title Insurance (the Title Policy) issued by _____ in the amount of the Sales Price and dated at or after closing; OR
    ☐ B. Abstracts of Title certified by a reputable abstractor or abstractors (a) from the sovereignty to the effective date of this contract (Complete Abstract) and (b) supplemented to the closing date (Supplemental Abstract).
    NOTICE TO BUYER: (i) AS REQUIRED BY LAW, Broker advises that YOU should have the Abstract covering the Property examined by an attorney of YOUR selection, or YOU should be furnished with or obtain a Title Policy; (ii) if the Property is situated in any Utility District, Section 50.301 of the Texas Water Code requires the Buyer to sign and acknowledge a statutory notice.

7. PROPERTY CONDITION: (Check "A" or "B")
    ☐ A. Buyer accepts the Property in its present condition, subject only to lender required repairs and _____
        _____.
    ☐ B. Buyer requires inspections and repairs required by the Property Condition Addendum (the Addendum) and any lender.
    Upon Seller's receipt of all loan approvals and inspection reports, Seller shall commence and complete prior to closing all required repairs at Seller's expense.
    All inspections, reports and repairs required of Seller by this contract and the Addendum shall not exceed $_____. If Seller fails to complete such requirements, Buyer may do so and Seller shall be liable up to the amount specified and the same paid from the proceeds of the sale. If such expenditures exceed the stated amount and Seller refuses to pay such excess, Buyer may pay the additional cost or accept the Property with the limited repairs and this sale shall be closed as scheduled, or Buyer may terminate this contract and the Earnest Money shall be refunded to Buyer. Broker and sales associates have no responsibility or liability for repair or replacement of any of the Property.

8. BROKER'S FEE: _____Listing Broker (_____%) and _____Co-Broker (_____%), as Real Estate Broker (the Broker), has negotiated this sale and Seller agrees to pay Broker in _____County, Texas, on consummation of this sale or on Seller's default (unless otherwise provided herein) a total cash fee of _____of the total Sales Price, which Escrow Agent shall pay from the sale proceeds.

9. CLOSING: The closing of the sale (the Closing Date) shall be on or before _____, 19_____, or within seven days after objections to title have been cured, whichever date is later.

10. POSSESSION: The possession of the Property shall be delivered to Buyer at closing.

11. SPECIAL PROVISIONS:

(Insert factual statements and business details applicable to this sale.)

140

12. SALES EXPENSES TO BE PAID IN CASH AT OR PRIOR TO CLOSING:
    A. SELLER'S EXPENSES: All cost of releasing existing loans and recording the releases; tax statements; ½ of any escrow fee; preparation of Deed; other expenses stipulated to be paid by Seller under other provisions of this contract.
    B. BUYER'S EXPENSES: All expenses incident to any loan (e.g., loan procurement fees, preparation of Note, Deed of Trust and other loan documents, recording fees, Mortgagee's Title Policy, prepayable interest, credit reports); ½ of any escrow fee; copies of restrictions, easements, reservations or conditions affecting the Property; and expenses stipulated to be paid by Buyer under other provisions of this contract.
13. PRORATIONS: Insurance (at Buyer's option), interest on any assumed debt, assessments, current taxes, and any rents and maintenance fees shall be prorated to the date of closing. If ad valorem taxes for the year in which the sale is closed are not available on the Closing Date, proration of taxes shall be made on the basis of taxes assessed in the previous year. If Buyer is assuming payment of any existing loan on the Property, all reserve deposits for the payment of taxes, insurance premiums, or other charges shall be transferred to Buyer by Seller and Buyer shall pay to Seller the amount of such reserve deposits.
14. TITLE APPROVAL: If abstracts are furnished, Seller shall deliver Complete Abstract to Buyer within twenty (20) days from the effective date hereof. Buyer shall have twenty (20) days from date of receipt of Complete Abstract to deliver a copy of the title opinion to Seller, stating any objections to title. If Title Policy is to be furnished, Buyer may request in writing from the title company within three (3) business days from the date of this contract a Commitment for Title Insurance (the Commitment) and legible copies of all recorded instruments affecting the Property and recited as exceptions in the Commitment. If Buyer has reasonable objection to any such exception, Buyer shall have five (5) business days after receipt of such instruments to make written objections to Seller and the title company. If buyer or a third party lender makes such objections or if objections are disclosed in the title opinion, Supplemental Abstract, the Commitment, Survey or by the issuer of the Title Policy, Seller shall have thirty (30) days from the date such objections are disclosed to cure the same, and the Closing Date shall be extended accordingly. If the objections are not satisfied by the extended Closing Date, this contract shall terminate and the Earnest Money refunded to Buyer, unless Buyer elects to waive the unsatisfied objections and complete the purchase. The Title Policy shall guarantee Buyer's title to be good and indefeasible subject only to (i) restrictive covenants and easements affecting the Property (ii) any discrepancies, conflicts or shortages in area or boundary lines or any encroachments, or any overlapping of improvements (iii) all taxes for the current and subsequent years, and subsequent assessments for prior years due to a change in land usage or ownership (iv) any existing building and zoning ordinances (v) rights of parties in possession (vi) any liens created or assumed as security for the sale consideration and (vii) any reservations or exception permitted in the Deed. Seller shall furnish tax statements showing no delinquent taxes and a General Warranty Deed conveying title subject only to liens securing payment of debt created or assumed as part of the consideration, taxes for the current year and easements, restrictions, reservations and conditions permitted by the contract or otherwise acceptable to the Buyer. Each note herein provided shall be secured by Vendor's and Deed of Trust liens. A Vendor's lien and Deed of Trust to secure any assumption shall be required, which lien shall be automatically released on execution and delivery of a release by note holder. In case of dispute as to the form of the Deed, Note(s), or Deed of Trust, forms prepared by the State Bar of Texas shall be used.
15. DEFAULT: If Buyer fails to comply herewith, Seller may either enforce specific performance or terminate this contract and receive the Earnest Money as liquidated damages, one-half of which (but not exceeding the herein recited Broker's fee) shall be paid by Seller to Broker in full payment of Broker's services. If Seller is unable without fault to deliver Abstract or Title Policy required herein within the time herein specified, Buyer may either terminate this contract and receive the Earnest Money as the sole remedy, and no Broker's fee shall be earned, or extend the time up to 30 days. If Seller fails to comply herewith for any other reason, Buyer may (i) terminate this contract and receive the Earnest Money, thereby releasing Seller from this contract (ii) enforce specific performance hereof or (iii) seek such other relief as may be provided by law. If completion of sale is prevented by Buyer's default, and Seller elects to enforce specific performance, the Broker's fee is payable only if and when Seller collects damages for such default by suit, compromise, settlement or otherwise, and after first deducting the expenses of collection, and then only in an amount equal to one-half of that portion collected, but not exceeding the amount of Broker's fee.
16. ATTORNEY'S FEES: Any signatory to this contract who is the prevailing party in any legal proceeding against any other signatory brought under or with relation to this contract or transaction shall be additionally entitled to recover court costs and reasonable attorney's fees from the non-prevailing party.
17. ESCROW: If Escrow Agent is Broker or other third party, the Earnest Money is deposited with Escrow Agent with the understanding that Escrow Agent (i) does not assume or have any liability for performance or non-performance of any party (ii) has the right to require the receipt, release and authorization in writing of all parties before paying the Earnest Money to any party and (iii) is not liable for interest or other charge on the funds held. If any party unreasonably fails to agree in writing to an appropriate release of Earnest Money, then such party shall be liable to the other parties as provided in Paragraph 16. At closing, Earnest Money shall be applied to any cash down payment required, next to Buyer's closing costs and any excess refunded to Buyer. In preparation for closing, the Escrow Agent or Broker may incur actual expenses on behalf of Seller or Buyer; therefore, any refund or payment of the Earnest Money under this contract shall be reduced by the amount of any actual expenses incurred on behalf of the party receiving the Earnest Money, and the Escrow Agent will pay the same to the creditors entitled thereto. To the extent that the Seller's share of the Earnest Money is insufficient to pay such expenses, the same will be deducted from the Broker's share of the Earnest Money.
18. REPRESENTATIONS: Seller represents that on Closing Date (i) all assumed loan(s) will not be in default, and (ii) unless securing payment of any deferred consideration, there will be no unrecorded liens or Uniform Commercial Code liens against any of the Property which will not be satisfied out of the Sale Price. If any representation above is untrue, this contract may be terminated by Buyer and Earnest Money shall be refunded without delay. All representations in this contract shall survive closing.
19. USE OF PROPERTY: If Seller has claimed the benefit of laws permitting a special use valuation for the purposes of payment of ad valorem taxes on the Property, the Seller represents that he was legally entitled to claim such benefits. If, after the purchase is closed, Buyer changes the use of the Property and the same results in the assessment of additional taxes, such additional taxes will be the obligation of the Buyer.
20. PROPERTY SURVEY:
    ☐ A. No survey is required.
    ☐ B. Seller shall furnish to Buyer within ten (10) days from the effective date of this contract Seller's existing survey of the Property dated _____, 19_____.
    ☐ C. A survey of the Property, dated subsequent to the effective date of this contract, shall be furnished within _____days from the effective date of this contract showing the location of the Property with respect to the original survey lines and the boundaries and visible conditions along the same, perimeter fences, easements, rights of way, roadways, and computation of area which shall be furnished by and at the expense of ☐ Seller ☐ Buyer by a mutually acceptable Registered Public Surveyor licensed by the State of Texas. Buyer shall furnish to surveyor a copy of the title opinion or Commitment for Title Insurance prior to the making of this survey.
21. CASUALTY LOSS: If any part of the Property is damaged or destroyed by fire or other casualty, Seller shall restore the same to its previous condition as soon as reasonably possible, but in any event by Closing Date; and if Seller is unable to do so without fault, this contract shall terminate at Buyer's option and Earnest Money shall be refunded with no Broker's fee due.
22. AGREEMENT OF PARTIES: This contract contains the entire agreement of the parties and cannot be changed except by their written consent.
23. CONSULT YOUR ATTORNEY: This is intended to be a legally binding contract. READ IT CAREFULLY. If you do not understand the effect of any part, consult your attorney BEFORE signing. The Broker cannot give you legal advice — only factual and business details concerning land and improvements. Attorneys to represent parties may be designated below; and, so employment may be accepted, Broker shall promptly deliver a copy of this contract to such attorneys.

Seller's Atty: _____   Buyer's Atty: _____

EXECUTED in multiple originals effective the _____ day of _____, 19_____. **(BROKER FILL IN THE DATE LAST PARTY SIGNS.)**

Listing Broker _____ License No.

By _____

Co-Broker _____ License No.

By _____

Receipt of $_____ Earnest Money is acknowledged in the

form of _____

_____

Escrow Agent _____ Date

By _____

Seller _____

Seller _____

Seller's Address _____ Tel.

Buyer _____

Buyer _____

Buyer's Address _____ Tel.

2-16-84

NOTICE: Not For Use Where Seller Owns Fee Simple Title To Land Beneath Unit

RESIDENTIAL CONDOMINIUM EARNEST MONEY CONTRACT (RESALE)
ALL CASH, ASSUMPTION, THIRD PARTY CONVENTIONAL OR SELLER FINANCING

1. PARTIES: _____(Seller) agrees to sell

   and convey to _____(Buyer) and Buyer

   agrees to buy from Seller the property described below.

2. PROPERTY AND CONDOMINIUM DOCUMENTS:

   A.   Condominium Unit _____, in Building _____, of _____,

   a condominium project, located at _____(Address),

   City of _____, _____County, Texas, described in the Condominium Declaration and Plat
   and any amendments thereto of record in said County; together with such Unit's undivided interest in the Common Elements designated by the Declaration,
   including those areas reserved as Limited Common Elements appurtenant to the Unit and such other rights to use the Common Elements which have been
   specifically assigned to the Unit in any other manner.
   The property shall include the following items, if any: curtains and rods, draperies and rods, valances, blinds, window shades, screens, shutters, awnings,
   wall-to-wall carpeting, mirrors fixed in place, ceiling fans, mail boxes, television antenna, permanently installed heating and air conditioning units and
   equipment, built-in security and fire detection equipment, lighting and plumbing fixtures, water softener, stove, trash compactor, garage door openers and all
   other personal property owned by Seller and attached to the Unit, or located in the Unit and given as collateral for any indebtedness which will remain in
   effect after closing. All property, interests and rights sold herein are called the "Property".

   B.   The Declaration and Plat, Articles of Association or Incorporation, By-Laws, Restrictions, any Rules and Regulations and amendments thereto are called
   "Condominium Documents". (Check 1, 2 or 3):

       ☐ 1.   Prior to signing this contract Buyer has received and approved a copy of the Condominium Documents and agrees to be bound thereby.

       ☐ 2.   Buyer has received but not approved a copy of the Condominium Documents prior to signing this contract. Buyer shall have five (5) days after the
   effective date hereof to terminate this contract for any reason and the Earnest Money shall be refunded to Buyer.

       ☐ 3.   Buyer has not received the Condominium Documents. Seller shall have five (5) days after the effective date hereof to deliver the Condominium
   Documents to Buyer or Buyer may terminate this contract and the Earnest Money shall be refunded to Buyer. Buyer shall have five (5) days after
   receipt of such documents to terminate this contract for any reason and the Earnest Money shall be refunded to Buyer.
   If Buyer does not give notice of termination as provided above, Buyer shall be deemed to have approved the Condominium Documents.

   C.   The Certificate from the condominium owners association (the Association) described in Paragraph 20 herein is called the "Certificate". (Check 1, 2 or 3):

       ☐ 1.   Buyer has received and approved a copy of the Certificate prior to signing this contract.

       ☐ 2.   Buyer has received but not approved a copy of the Certificate prior to signing this contract. Buyer shall have five (5) days after the effective date hereof
   to terminate this contract for any reason and the Earnest Money shall be refunded to Buyer.

       ☐ 3.   Buyer has not received the Certificate. Seller shall have five (5) days after the effective date hereof to deliver the Certificate to Buyer or Buyer may

   terminate this contract and the Earnest Money shall be refunded to Buyer. Buyer shall have five (5) days after receipt of such Certificate to terminate

   this contract for any reason and the Earnest Money shall be refunded to Buyer.

   If Buyer does not give notice of termination as provided above, Buyer shall be deemed to have approved the Certificate.

3. CONTRACT SALES PRICE:

   A.   Cash payable at closing . . . .$_____

   B.   Sum of all financing described in Paragraph 4 below . . . .$_____

   C.   Sales Price payable to Seller (Sum of A and B) . . . .$_____

4. FINANCING CONDITIONS: (Check applicable box below)

       ☐ A.   ALL CASH: This is an all cash sale; no financing is involved.

       ☐ B.   ASSUMPTION:

   (1) Buyer's assumption of the unpaid principal balance of a first lien promissory note payable to _____

   _____in present monthly installments of $_____, including principal,
   interest and any reserve deposits, with Buyer's first installment payment being payable on the first installment payment date after closing, the
   assumed principal balance of which at closing will be $_____.

   (2) Buyer's assumption of the unpaid principal balance of a second lien promissory note payable to _____

   _____in present monthly installments of $_____, including principal,
   interest and any reserve deposits, with Buyer's first installment payment being payable on the first installment payment date after closing, the assumed

   principal balance of which at closing will be $_____.
   Buyer's assumption of an existing note includes all obligations imposed by the deed of trust securing the note. If the principal balance of all assumed
   loans varies in an amount greater than $350.00 at closing from the total of the amount stated above, or if noteholders on assumption (i) require Buyer to
   pay an assumption fee in excess of $_____ in B(1) above and $_____ in B(2) above and Seller declines to pay

063

such excess or (ii) raise the existing interest rate above _____% in B(1) or _____% in B(2) above, Buyer may terminate this contract and the Earnest Money shall be refunded to Buyer. The cash payable at closing shall be adjusted by the amount of the variance from the loan balance(s) shown above.

NOTICE TO BUYER: Monthly payments, interest rates or other terms of some loans may be adjusted after closing. Before signing the contract, examine the note and deed of trust to determine the possibility of future adjustments.

☐ C.   THIRD PARTY FINANCED: A conventional third party fixed rate loan to Buyer in the amount of $_____ , payable in _____intervals for not less than _____years with the interest rate not to exceed _____% per annum, ☐ with ☐ without private mortgage insurance.

☐ D.   SELLER FINANCED: A promissory note from Buyer to Seller in the amount of $_____, bearing _____% interest per annum, principal and interest payable (Check 1 or 2):

     ☐ 1.   In one payment due _____after the date of the note with interest payable _____ .

     ☐ 2.   In installments of $_____ ☐ including interest ☐ plus interest beginning _____after the date of the note and continuing at _____ intervals thereafter for _____years when the entire balance of the note shall be due and payable.

     ☐ 3.   This contract is subject to Buyer furnishing Seller evidence of good credit within _____days from the effective date of this contract. If notice of disapproval of Buyer's credit is not given within three (3) days thereafter, Seller shall be deemed to have approved Buyer's credit. Buyer hereby authorizes Buyer's credit report to be furnished to Seller.

Any Seller financed note may be prepaid in whole or in part at any time without penalty. The lien securing payment of such note will be inferior / to any lien securing any loan assumed or given in connection with third party financing. Buyer shall furnish Seller with a Mortgagee's Title Policy.

NOTICE: If the term, interest rate or payment of a note is subject to change or additional assumptions are required, use Paragraph 11.

Buyer shall apply for all third party financing or noteholder's approval of Buyer for assumption and waiver of the right to accelerate the note within _____days from the effective date of this contract and shall make every reasonable effort to obtain the same. Such financing or assumption shall have been approved when Buyer has satisfied all of lender's or noteholder's financial requirements, including sale of other property, requirement of co-signature or financial verifications. If such financing or assumption approval and waiver of acceleration is not obtained within _____days from the effective date hereof, this contract shall terminate and the Earnest Money shall be refunded to Buyer.

5.   EARNEST MONEY: $_____ is herewith tendered and is to be deposited as Earnest Money with _____at _____(location) as Escrow Agent, upon execution of the contract by both parties. Additional Earnest Money in the amount of $_____ shall be deposited with the Escrow Agent on or before _____, 19_____.

6.   TITLE: Seller at Seller's expense shall furnish to Buyer an Owner's Policy of Title Insurance (the Title Policy) issued by _____in the amount of the Sales Price and dated at or after closing.

NOTICE TO BUYER: AS REQUIRED BY LAW, Broker advises that YOU should have the Abstract covering the Property examined by an attorney of YOUR selection, or YOU should be furnished with or obtain a Title Policy. If the Property is situated in a Utility District, Section 50.301 Texas Water Code requires the Buyer to sign and acknowledge a statutory notice relating to the tax rate and bonded indebtedness of the District.

7.   PROPERTY CONDITION (Check A or B):

☐ A.   Buyer accepts the Property in its present condition, subject to lender required repairs and _____.

☐ B.   Buyer requires inspections and repairs required by the Property Condition Addendum (attached hereto) and any lender.
On Seller's receipt of all loan approvals and inspection reports, Seller shall commence repairs required of Seller by the contract and the Property Condition Addendum, if any, and complete such repairs prior to closing. Seller's responsibility for the repairs shall not exceed $_____. If Seller fails to commence or complete such repairs, Buyer may do so and Seller shall be liable up to the amount specified and the same paid from the proceeds of the sale. If the repair costs will exceed the stated amount and Seller refuses to pay such excess, Buyer may pay the additional cost or accept the Property with the limited repairs and this sale shall be closed as scheduled, or Buyer may terminate this contract and the Earnest Money shall be refunded to Buyer. If the repair costs will exceed five (5) percent of the Sales Price of the Property and Seller agrees to pay the cost of such repairs, Buyer shall have the option of closing the sale with the completed repairs, or terminating the sale and the Earnest Money shall be refunded to Buyer. Seller's obligation to make repairs required by this contract and Property Condition Addendum shall be limited to those items which Seller has the sole obligation to maintain and repair under the terms of the Declaration. After Buyer receives all reports of needed common element repairs that are not the responsibility of Seller, Buyer shall have five (5) days to give written notice to Seller that Buyer will terminate this contract unless Buyer receives written confirmation from the Association that such repairs will be made in a reasonable time. If Buyer does give such notice, Seller shall have five (5) days after receipt of such notice to cause to be delivered to Buyer written confirmation of the Association's commitment to repair. If Buyer does not give such notice to Seller, Buyer will be deemed to have accepted the Property without such repairs. If required by Buyer and written confirmation of repairs is not delivered to Buyer as required above, Buyer may terminate this contract and the Earnest Money shall be refunded to Buyer.
Broker(s) and sales associates have no responsibility or liability for inspections or repairs made pursuant to this contract.

8.   BROKER'S FEE: _____, Listing Broker, and any Co-Broker represent Seller. Seller agrees to pay Listing Broker the fee specified by separate agreement between Listing Broker and Seller. Escrow Agent is authorized and directed to pay Listing Broker's fee from the sale proceeds at closing.

9.   CLOSING: The closing of the sale shall be on or before _____, 19_____, or within seven (7) days after objections to title have been cured, whichever date is later (the Closing Date); however, if financing or assumption approval has been obtained pursuant to Paragraph 4, the Closing Date shall be extended daily up to fifteen (15) days if necessary to complete other loan requirements.

10.   POSSESSION: The possession of the Property shall be delivered to Buyer on _____ in its present or required improved condition, ordinary wear and tear excepted.

Third page — Residential Condominium Earnest Money Contract   2-16-84

11. SPECIAL PROVISIONS: (BROKER: List addenda and insert factual statements and business details applicable to this sale.)

12. SALES EXPENSES TO BE PAID IN CASH AT OR PRIOR TO CLOSING:

    A.   Loan appraisal fees shall be paid by _____.

    B.   Any Condominium Association transfer or processing fee shall be paid by _____.

    C.   The total loan discount points shall not exceed _____points (not including origination fee) of which Buyer shall pay _____points and Seller shall pay the remainder.

    D.   Seller's Expenses: Prepayment penalties on any existing loans paid at closing, plus cost of releasing such loans and recording releases; tax statements; 1/2 of any escrow fee; preparation of deed; preparation and recording of any deed of trust to secure assumption; other expenses stipulated to be paid by Seller under other provisions of this contract.

    E.   Buyer's Expenses: Application, origination and commitment fees; private mortgage insurance premiums and any loan assumption fee; expenses incident to loan(s) (e.g., preparation of any note, deed of trust and other loan documents, survey, recording fees, copies of restrictions and easements, Mortgagee's Title Policies, credit reports, photos); 1/2 of any escrow fee; any required premiums for flood and hazard insurance; any required reserve deposits for insurance premiums, ad valorem taxes and special governmental assessments; interest on all monthly installment payment notes from date of disbursements to one (1) month prior to dates of first monthly payments; expenses stipulated to be paid by Buyer under other provisions of this contract.

    F.   If any sales expenses exceed the maximum amount herein stipulated to be paid by either party, either party may terminate this contract unless the other party agrees to pay such excess.

13. PRORATIONS: Ad valorem taxes, rents, insurance premiums, interest and any current regular condominium assessments shall be prorated to Closing Date. Cash reserves from regular condominium assessments for deferred maintenance or capital improvements established by the Association shall not be credited to Seller except as otherwise provided by the Declaration. Any unpaid special assessments due the Association shall be the obligation of Seller except as otherwise provided by the Condominium Documents.

14. TITLE APPROVAL: The Title Policy shall guarantee Buyer's title to be good and indefeasible subject only to (i) restrictive covenants affecting the Property (ii) any discrepancies, conflicts or shortages in area or boundary lines, or any encroachments, or any overlapping of improvements (iii) taxes for the current and subsequent years, and subsequent assessments for prior years due to change in land usage or ownership (iv) existing building and zoning ordinances (v) rights of parties in possession (vi) liens created or assumed as security for the sale consideration (vii) terms and provisions of the Condominium Documents including the platted easements and assessments set out therein and (viii) other exceptions permitted by the terms of this contract. Exceptions permitted in the deed and zoning ordinances shall not be valid objections to title. If the Title Policy will be subject to exceptions other than those recited above in sub-paragraph (i) through (vii) inclusive, Seller shall deliver to Buyer a Commitment for Title Insurance (the Commitment) and legible copies of any documents creating such exceptions that are not recited in sub-paragraph (i) through (vii) above. If Buyer has objection to any such previously undisclosed exceptions, Buyer shall have five (5) days after receipt of such Commitment and copies to make written objections to Seller. If Buyer makes such objections, Seller shall have fifteen (15) days from the date such objections are disclosed to cure the same, and the Closing Date shall be extended accordingly. If the objections are not satisfied by the extended closing date, this contract shall terminate and the Earnest Money shall be refunded to Buyer, unless Buyer elects to waive the unsatisfied objections and complete the purchase. Seller shall furnish tax statements showing no delinquent taxes and a General Warranty Deed conveying title subject only to liens securing payment of debt created or assumed as part of the consideration, taxes for the current year and easements, restrictions, reservations and conditions permitted by this contract or otherwise acceptable to Buyer. Each note herein provided shall be secured by vendor's and deed of trust liens. A vendor's lien and deed of trust to secure any assumption shall be required, which shall be automatically released on execution and delivery of a release by noteholder. If Seller is released from liability on an assumed note the vendor's lien and deed of trust to secure assumption shall not be required. In case of dispute as to the form of the deed, note(s), deed of trust or deed of trust to secure assumption, forms prepared by the State Bar of Texas shall be used.

15. CASUALTY LOSS: If any part of the Unit is damaged or destroyed by fire or other casualty loss, Seller shall restore the same to its previous condition as soon as reasonably possible, but in any event by Closing Date. If Seller is unable to do so without fault, Buyer may terminate this contract and the Earnest Money shall be refunded to Buyer. If any part of the Common Elements or any Unit adjoining the Unit described in Paragraph 2A is damaged or destroyed by fire or other casualty loss, Buyer shall have five (5) days from receipt of notice of such casualty loss within which to notify Seller in writing that the contract will be terminated unless Buyer receives written confirmation from the Association that the damaged condition will be restored to its previous condition within a reasonable time at no cost to Buyer. Unless Buyer gives such notice within such time, Buyer will be deemed to have accepted the Property without confirmation of such restoration. Seller shall have five (5) days from the date of receipt of Buyer's notice within which to cause to be delivered to Buyer such confirmation. If required by Buyer and written confirmation is not delivered to Buyer as required above, Buyer may terminate this contract and the Earnest Money will be refunded to Buyer.

NOTICE TO BUYER: CONSULT YOUR INSURANCE AGENT PRIOR TO THE CLOSING DATE DUE TO THE UNIQUE REQUIREMENTS OF THIS TYPE OF PROPERTY.

Fourth page   Residential Condominium Earnest Money Contract   2-16-84

16. DEFAULT: If Buyer fails to comply herewith, Seller may either (i) enforce specific performance and seek such other relief as may be provided by law or (ii) terminate this contract and receive the Earnest Money as liquidated damages. If Seller is unable without fault to deliver the Title Policy Commitment required herein, Buyer may either terminate this contract and receive the Earnest Money as the sole remedy or extend the Closing Date up to fifteen (15) days. If Seller is unable without fault to deliver the Certificate described in Paragraph 20 within the time herein specified, Buyer may either terminate this contract and receive the Earnest Money as the sole remedy or extend the time for delivery up to fifteen (15) days. If Seller fails to comply herewith for any other reason, Buyer may either (i) enforce specific performance hereof and seek such other relief as may be provided by law or (ii) terminate this contract and receive the Earnest Money, thereby releasing Seller from this contract.

17. ATTORNEY'S FEES: Any signatory of this contract who is the prevailing party in any legal proceeding against any other signatory brought under or with relation to this contract or transaction shall be additionally entitled to recover costs and reasonable attorney fees from the nonprevailing party.

18. ESCROW: The Earnest Money is deposited with Escrow Agent with the understanding that Escrow Agent (i) is not a party to this contract and does not assume or have any liability for performance or non-performance of any party or other signatory (ii) has the right to require from all signatories a written release of liability of the Escrow Agent, which terminates this contract and authorizes the disbursement of the Earnest Money and (iii) is not liable for interest or other charge on the funds held. If any signatory unreasonably fails to deliver promptly the document described in (ii) above, then such signatory shall be liable to the other signatories as provided in Paragraph 17. At closing, the Earnest Money shall be applied first to any cash down payment required, then to Buyer's closing costs and any excess refunded to Buyer. Any refund or payment of the Earnest Money under this contract shall be reduced by the amount of any actual expenses incurred on behalf of the party receiving the Earnest Money, and Escrow Agent will pay the same to the creditors entitled thereto.

19. REPRESENTATIONS: Seller represents that as of the Closing Date (i) there will be no unrecorded liens, assessments or Uniform Commercial Code Liens against any of the Property which will not be satisfied out of the Sales Price, unless securing payment of any deferred consideration (ii) loan(s) will be without default (iii) any reserve deposits held by the lender will not be deficient (iv) the present amount of the regular condominium assessment is $_____ which will be current and (v) Seller has no knowledge of any misrepresentation or errors in the Condominium Certificate or any material changes in the information contained therein. If any representation in this contract or the Certificate is untrue on the Closing Date, this contract may be terminated by Buyer and the Earnest Money shall be refunded to Buyer. All representations contained in this contract shall survive closing.

20. CERTIFICATE BY THE ASSOCIATION: The Certificate shall state or have attached thereto:
   A. Any right of first refusal held by the Association on the Unit;
   B. The amount of the monthly common expense assessment and the amount and effective date of any increase in such assessment;
   C. Any unpaid common expense or special assessment due and unpaid by the Seller to the Association;
   D. Any other unpaid amounts payable by Seller to the Association;
   E. Future capital expenditures approved by the Association;
   F. The amount of reserves for capital expenditures and any portion of those reserves allocated by the Association for specified projects;
   G. The most recent regularly prepared balance sheet and income and expense statement;
   H. The current operating budget of the Association;
   I. Any judgments against the Association and the nature of pending suits to which the Association is a party;
   J. A description of any insurance coverage provided for the benefit of Unit owners;
   K. The remaining term of any leasehold estate on which the condominium project is situated;
   L. Any knowledge by the governing body of the Association (the Board) of alterations or improvements to the Unit or to any other portions of the project which violate any provision of the Declaration;
   M. Any knowledge by the Board of violations of the Health or Building Codes with respect to the Unit or any other portion of the project; and
   N. Any knowledge of a condition which, in the good faith opinion of the Board, is a material physical defect in the Unit or in the common elements of the project.
   The Certificate may be in a form approved by the Texas Real Estate Commission for use with this contract.

21. AGREEMENT OF PARTIES: This contract contains the entire agreement of the parties and cannot be changed except by their written consent.

22. NOTICES: All notices shall be in writing and effective when delivered at the addresses shown below.

Fifth page   Residential Condominium Earnest Money Contract   2-16-84

23.   CONSULT YOUR ATTORNEY: The Broker cannot give you legal advice. This is intended to be a legally binding contract. READ IT CAREFULLY. If you do not understand the effect of any part, consult your attorney BEFORE signing.

Seller's Atty: _____   Buyer's Atty: _____

EXECUTED in multiple originals effective the _____ day of _____, 19_____. **(BROKER: <u>FILL IN THE DATE OF FINAL ACCEPTANCE.</u>)**

_____   _____
Buyer   Seller

_____   _____
Buyer   Seller

_____   Phone No.   _____   Phone No.
Buyer's Address   Seller's Address

Listing Broker agrees to pay _____, Co-Broker, a fee of _____ of the total sales price when the Broker's fee described in Paragraph 8 is received. Escrow Agent is authorized and directed to pay Co-Broker from Listing Broker's fee at closing.

_____   License No.   _____   License No.
Co-Broker   Listing Broker

By: _____   By: _____

_____   Phone No.   _____   Phone No.
Co-Broker's Address   Listing Broker's Address

Receipt of $_____ Earnest Money is acknowledged in the form of _____

_____

Escrow Agent: _____   By: _____

Date: _____, 19_____.

| This form has been approved by the Texas Real Estate Commission For Voluntary Use. |

02-08-85

RESIDENTIAL CONDOMINIUM EARNEST MONEY CONTRACT (RESALE)
FHA INSURED OR VA GUARANTEED FINANCING

NOTICE: Not For Use Where Seller Owns Fee Simple Title To Land Beneath Unit

1. PARTIES: _____(Seller) agrees to
    sell and convey to _____(Buyer) and Buyer
    agrees to buy from Seller the property described below.

2. PROPERTY AND CONDOMINIUM DOCUMENTS:

    A. Condominium Unit _____, in Building _____, of _____,
        a condominium project, located at _____(Address),
        City of _____, _____County, Texas, described in the Condominium Declaration and Plat
        and any amendments thereto of record in said County; together with such Unit's undivided interest in the Common Elements designated by the Declaration,
        including those areas reserved as Limited Common Elements appurtenant to the Unit and such other rights to use the Common Elements which have been
        specifically assigned to the Unit in any other manner.
        The property shall include the following items, if any: curtains and rods, draperies and rods, valances, blinds, window shades, screens, shutters, awnings,
        wall-to-wall carpeting, mirrors fixed in place, ceiling fans, mail boxes, television antenna, permanently installed heating and air conditioning units and
        equipment, built-in security and fire detection equipment, lighting and plumbing fixtures, water softener, stove, trash compactor, garage door openers with
        controls and all other personal property owned by Seller and attached to the Unit, or located in the Unit and given as collateral for any indebtedness which
        will remain in effect after closing. All property, interests and rights sold herein are called the "Property".

    B. The Declaration and Plat, Articles of Association or Incorporation, By-Laws, Restrictions, any Rules and Regulations and amendments thereto are called
        "Condominium Documents": (Check 1, 2 or 3)

        ☐ 1. Prior to signing this contract Buyer has received and approved a copy of the Condominium Documents and agrees to be bound thereby.

        ☐ 2. Buyer has received but not approved a copy of the Condominium Documents prior to signing this contract. Buyer shall have five (5) days after the
              effective date hereof to terminate this contract for any reason and the Earnest Money shall be refunded to Buyer.

        ☐ 3. Buyer has not received the Condominium Documents. Seller shall have five (5) days after the effective date hereof to deliver the Condominium
              Documents to Buyer or Buyer may terminate this contract and the Earnest Money shall be refunded to Buyer. Buyer shall have five (5) days after
              receipt of such documents to terminate this contract for any reason and the Earnest Money shall be refunded to Buyer.
        If Buyer does not give notice of termination as provided above, Buyer shall be deemed to have approved the Condominium Documents.

    C. The Certificate from the condominium owners association (the Association) described in Paragraph 20 herein is called the "Certificate": (Check 1, 2 or 3)

        ☐ 1. Buyer has received and approved a copy of the Certificate prior to signing this contract.

        ☐ 2. Buyer has received but not approved a copy of the Certificate prior to signing this contract. Buyer shall have five (5) days after the effective date hereof
              to terminate this contract for any reason and the Earnest Money shall be refunded to Buyer.

        ☐ 3. Buyer has not received the Certificate. Seller shall have five (5) days after the effective date hereof to deliver the Certificate to Buyer or Buyer may
              terminate this contract and the Earnest Money shall be refunded to Buyer. Buyer shall have five (5) days after receipt of such Certificate to terminate
              this contract for any reason and the Earnest Money shall be refunded to Buyer.
        If Buyer does not give notice of termination as provided above, Buyer shall be deemed to have approved the Certificate.

3. CONTRACT SALES PRICE:

    A. Cash payable at closing . . . . $_____
    B. Sum of all financing described below excluding any VA Funding Fee or FHA Mortgage Insurance Premium (MIP) . . . . $_____
    C. Sales Price payable to Seller (Sum of A and B) . . . . $_____

4. FINANCING: (Check applicable boxes below)

    ☐ A. FHA INSURED FINANCING:
          This contract is subject to approval for Buyer of a Section _____ FHA Insured Loan (the Loan) of not less than
          $_____, amortizable monthly for not less than _____ years, with interest not to exceed _____% per annum for
          the first _____ year(s) of the loan.
          As required by HUD-FHA, if FHA valuation is unknown, "It is expressly agreed that, notwithstanding any other provisions of this contract, the Purchaser
          (Buyer) shall not be obligated to complete the purchase of the Property described herein or to incur any penalty by forfeiture of Earnest Money deposits
          or otherwise unless the Seller has delivered to the Purchaser (Buyer) a written statement issued by the Federal Housing Commissioner setting forth the
          appraised value of the Property (excluding closing costs and MIP) of not less than $_____, which statement the Seller hereby
          agrees to deliver to the Purchaser (Buyer) promptly after such appraised value statement is made available to the Seller. The Purchaser (Buyer) shall,
          however, have the privilege and option of proceeding with the consummation of this contract without regard to the amount of the appraised valuation made
          by the Federal Housing Commissioner. The appraised valuation is arrived at to determine the maximum mortgage the Department of Housing and Urban
          Development will insure. HUD does not warrant the value or the condition of the property. The purchaser should satisfy himself/herself that the price and
          the condition of the property are acceptable."

    NOTE: Describe special terms of any non-fixed rate loan in Paragraph 11.

FHA or VA Financed Residential Condominium Earnest Money Contract — Page Two   02-08-85

If the FHA appraised value of the Property (excluding closing costs and MIP) is less than the Sales Price (3C above). Seller may reduce the Sales Price to an amount equal to the FHA appraised value (excluding closing costs and MIP) and the parties to the sale shall close the sale at such lower Sales Price with appropriate adjustments to 3A and 3B above.

☐ B.   VA GUARANTEED FINANCING:

This contract is subject to approval for Buyer of a _____ (type loan) VA guaranteed loan (the Loan) of not less than $_____, amortizable monthly for not less than _____ years,

☐ 1. with interest at maximum rate allowable at time of loan funding if such loan is a fixed rate loan or

☐ 2. with interest not to exceed _____% per annum and for the first _____year(s) of the loan if such loan is not fixed rate.

VA NOTICE TO BUYER: "It is expressly agreed that, notwithstanding any other provisions of this contract, the Buyer shall not incur any penalty by forfeiture of earnest money or otherwise or be obligated to complete the purchase of the Property described herein, if the contract purchase price or cost exceeds the reasonable value of the Property established by the Veterans Administration. The Buyer shall, however, have the privilege and option of proceeding with the consummation of this contract without regard to the amount of the reasonable value established by the Veterans Administration."

If Buyer elects to complete the purchase at an amount in excess of the reasonable value established by VA, Buyer shall pay such excess amount in cash from a source which Buyer agrees to disclose to the VA and which Buyer represents will not be from borrowed funds except as approved by VA. If VA reasonable value of the Property is less than the Sales Price (3C above). Seller may reduce the Sales Price to an amount equal to the VA reasonable value and the parties to the sale shall close at such lower Sales Price with appropriate adjustments to 3A and 3B above.

☐ C.   TEXAS VETERANS' HOUSING ASSISTANCE PROGRAM LOAN:

This contract is also subject to approval for Buyer of a Texas Veterans' Housing Assistance Program Loan (the Program Loan) in an amount of $_____ for a period of at least _____ years at the interest rate established by the Texas Veterans Land Board at the time of closing.

Buyer shall apply for all loan(s) within _____ days from the effective date of this contract and shall make every reasonable effort to obtain approval. Such financing shall have been approved when Buyer has satisfied all of lender's financial requirements, e.g., sale of other property, requirements of a co-signer or financial verification. If such loan approval has not been secured by the Closing Date, this contract shall terminate and Earnest Money shall be refunded to Buyer.

5.   EARNEST MONEY: $_____ is herewith tendered by Buyer and is to be deposited as Earnest Money with _____ _____ at _____ (Address) as Escrow Agent, upon execution of the contract by both parties. ☐ Additional Earnest Money of $_____ shall be deposited by Buyer with the Escrow Agent on or before _____, 19_____.

6.   TITLE: Seller at Seller's expense shall furnish to Buyer an Owner's Policy of Title Insurance (the Title Policy) issued by _____ _____in the amount of the Sales Price and dated at or after closing. NOTICE TO SELLER AND BUYER: AS REQUIRED BY LAW, Broker advises Buyer that Buyer should have the Abstract covering the Property examined by an attorney of Buyer's selection, or Buyer should be furnished with or obtain a Title Policy. If a Title Policy is to be obtained, Buyer should obtain a Commitment for Title Insurance (the Commitment) which should be examined by an attorney of Buyer's choice at or prior to closing. If the Property is situated in a Utility District, Section 50.301 Texas Water Code requires the Buyer to sign and acknowledge the statutory notice from Seller relating to the tax rate and bonded indebtedness of the District.

7.   PROPERTY CONDITION: (Check A or B)

☐ A.   Buyer accepts the Property in its present condition, subject only to FHA or VA required repairs and _____.

☐ B.   Buyer requires inspections and repairs required by the FHA or VA and the Property Condition Addendum attached hereto.

On Seller's receipt of all loan approvals and inspection reports, Seller shall commence repairs and termite treatment required of Seller by the contract, any lender and the Property Condition Addendum, if any, and complete such repairs prior to closing. Seller's obligation to make repairs required by this contract and Property Condition Addendum shall be limited to those items which Seller has the sole obligation to maintain and repair under the terms of the Declaration. Seller's responsibility for the repairs, termite treatment and repairs to termite damage shall not exceed $_____. If Seller fails to commence or complete such repairs, Buyer may do so and Seller shall be liable up to the amount specified and the same paid from the proceeds of the sale. If the repair costs will exceed the stated amount and Seller refuses to pay such excess, Buyer may (1) pay the additional cost or (2) accept the Property with the limited repairs unless such repairs are required by FHA/VA or (3) Buyer may terminate this contract and the Earnest Money shall be refunded to Buyer. Buyer shall make his election within three (3) days after Seller notifies Buyer of Seller's refusal to pay such excess. Failure of Buyer to make such election within the time provided shall be deemed to be Buyer's election to accept the Property with the limited repairs as permitted by FHA/VA, and the sale shall be closed as scheduled. (NOTE: If VA Buyer pays additional costs of repairs, Buyer may be paying in excess of the VA Certificate of Reasonable Value.)

If the repair costs will exceed five (5) percent of the Sales Price of the Property and Seller agrees to pay the cost of such repairs, Buyer shall have the option of closing the sale with the completed repairs, or terminating the sale and the Earnest Money shall be refunded to Buyer. Buyer shall make this election within three (3) days after the Seller notifies Buyer of Seller's willingness to pay the cost of such repairs that exceed five (5) percent of the Sales Price. Failure of Buyer to make such election within the time provided shall be deemed to be Buyer's election to close the sale with the completed repairs. After buyer receives reports of any needed common element repairs that are not the responsibility of Seller, Buyer shall have five (5) days to give written notice to Seller that Buyer will terminate this contract unless Buyer receives a written commitment from the Association that such repairs will be made in a reasonable time without any special assessment for the cost thereof. If Buyer does not give such notice to Seller, Buyer will be deemed to have accepted the Property without such repairs. If Buyer gives such notice, Seller shall have five (5) days to cause the Association's written commitment to be delivered to Buyer. If such commitment is not delivered within the time specified, Buyer may terminate this contract and the Earnest Money shall be refunded to Buyer.

Broker(s) and sales associates have no responsibility or liability for inspections or repairs made pursuant to this contract.

105

FHA or VA Financed Residential Condominium Earnest Money Contract concerning _____ Page Three   02-08-85
(Address of Property)

8. BROKER'S FEE: _____, Listing Broker, and any Co-Broker represent
Seller unless otherwise specified herein. Seller agrees to pay Listing Broker the fee specified by separate agreement between Listing Broker and Seller. Escrow
Agent is authorized and directed to pay Listing Broker's fee from the sale proceeds at closing.

9. CLOSING: The closing of the sale shall be on or before _____, 19_____, or within seven (7) days after objections to title
have been cured, whichever date is later (the Closing Date); however, if financing approval has been obtained pursuant to Paragraph 4, the Closing Date shall be
extended daily up to fifteen (15) days if necessary to complete loan requirements. If either party fails to close this sale by the Closing Date, the non-defaulting
party shall be entitled to exercise the remedies contained in Paragraph 16 immediately and without notice.

10. POSSESSION: The possession of the Property shall be delivered to Buyer on _____
in its present or required improved condition, ordinary wear and tear excepted. Any possession by Buyer prior to or Seller after closing that is not authorized by
the Buyer's Temporary Residential Lease or Seller's Temporary Residential Lease forms promulgated by the Texas Real Estate Commission shall establish a landlord-
tenant at sufferance relationship between the parties.

11. SPECIAL PROVISIONS: (Insert factual statements and business details applicable to this sale.)

12. SALES EXPENSES TO BE PAID AT OR PRIOR TO CLOSING:
    A. Loan appraisal fees shall be paid by _____.
    B. (1) FHA Sale: The total of the loan discount and buydown fees shall not exceed $_____ of which Buyer shall pay the first
        $_____ and Seller shall pay the remainder.
        (2) VA Sale: The total of the loan discount and buydown fees shall not exceed $_____ which shall be paid by Seller.
    C. Seller's Expenses: (1) FHA or VA required repairs and any other inspections, reports or repairs required of Seller and in the Property Condition Addendum
        (2) releases of existing loans, including prepayment penalties and recordation; tax statements; preparation of deed; ½ of escrow fee (3) expenses VA prohibits
        Buyer to pay (e.g., preparation of loan documents, copies of restrictions, photos, excess cost of survey, remaining ½ of escrow fee) (4) any Texas Veterans'
        Housing Assistance Program Participation Fee (5) other expenses stipulated to be paid by Seller under other provisions of this contract.
    D. Buyer's Expenses: Interest on the note(s) from date of disbursement to one (1) month prior to date of first monthly payment, expenses stipulated to be paid
        by Buyer under other provisions of this contract and any customary Texas Veterans' Housing Assistance Program Loan costs for Buyer.
        (1) FHA Buyer: (a) All prepaid items required by applicable HUD-FHA or other regulations (e.g., required premiums for flood and hazard insurance, reserve
            deposits for other insurance, ad valorem taxes and special governmental assessments) (b) expenses incident to any loan (e.g., ½ of escrow fee, preparation
            of loan documents, survey, recording fees, copies of restrictions and easements, amortization schedule, Mortgagee's Title Policy, loan origination fee,
            credit reports, photos) (c) loan related inspection fees.
        (2) VA Buyer: (a) All prepaid items (e.g., required premiums for flood and hazard insurance, reserve deposits for other insurance, ad valorem taxes and
            special governmental assessments) (b) expenses incident to any loan (e.g., credit reports, recording fees, Mortgagee's Title Policy, loan origination fee,
            that portion of survey cost VA Buyer may pay by VA Regulation) (c) loan related inspection fees.
    E. The VA Loan Funding Fee or FHA Mortgage Insurance Premium (MIP) in the amount of $_____ is to be paid by _____.
        If paid by Buyer, it is to be [   ] paid in cash at closing [   ] added to the amount of the loan to the extent permitted by lender. If financed, the amount is
        to be added to the loan amount in Paragraph 3-B by lender but is not part of the Contract Sales Price.
    F. If any sales expenses exceed the maximum amount herein stipulated to be paid by either party, either party may terminate this contract unless the other party
        agrees to pay such excess. In no event shall Buyer pay charges and fees expressly prohibited by FHA/VA Regulations.

13. PRORATIONS: Ad valorem taxes, rents, flood and hazard insurance premiums, interest and any current regular condominium assessments shall be prorated through
    the Closing Date. Cash reserves from regular condominium assessments for deferred maintenance or capital improvements established by the Association shall not
    be credited to Seller except as otherwise provided by the Declaration. Any unpaid special assessments due the Association shall be the obligation of Seller except
    as otherwise provided by the Condominium Documents.

14. TITLE APPROVAL: The Title Policy shall guarantee Buyer's title to be good and indefeasible subject only to (1) restrictive covenants affecting the Property (2)
    any discrepancies, conflicts or shortages in area or boundary lines, or any encroachments, or any overlapping of improvements (3) taxes for the current and
    subsequent years, and subsequent assessments for prior years due to change in land usage or ownership (4) existing building and zoning ordinances (5) rights of
    parties in possession (6) liens created as security for the sale consideration (7) terms and provisions of the Condominium Documents including the platted easements
    and assessments set out therein and (8) other exceptions permitted by the terms of this contract. Exceptions permitted in the deed and zoning ordinances shall not
    be valid objections to title. If the Title Policy will be subject to exceptions other than those recited above in sub-paragraphs (1) through (7) inclusive, Seller shall
    deliver to Buyer the Commitment and legible copies of any documents creating such exceptions that are not recited in sub-paragraphs (1) through (7) above at least
    five (5) days prior to closing. If Buyer has objection to any such previously undisclosed exceptions, Buyer shall have five (5) days after receipt of such Commitment
    and copies to make written objections to Seller. If no Title Commitment is provided to Buyer at or prior to closing, it will be conclusively presumed that Seller
    represented at closing that the Title Policy would not be subject to exceptions other than those recited above in sub-paragraphs (1) through (7). If Buyer makes such
    objections, Seller shall have fifteen (15) days from the date such objections are disclosed to cure the same, and the Closing Date shall be extended accordingly. If
    the objections are not satisfied by the extended closing date, this contract shall terminate and the Earnest Money shall be refunded to Buyer, unless Buyer elects to
    waive the unsatisfied objections and complete the purchase. Seller shall furnish tax statements showing no delinquent taxes and a General Warranty Deed conveying

title subject only to liens securing payment of debt created or assumed as part of the consideration, taxes for the current year and easements, and restrictions, reservations and conditions permitted by this contract or otherwise acceptable to Buyer. Each note herein provided shall be secured by vendor's and deed of trust liens. In case of dispute as to the form of the deed, note(s) or deed of trust, forms prepared by the State Bar of Texas shall be used.

15. CASUALTY LOSS: If any part of the Unit is damaged or destroyed by fire or other casualty loss, Seller shall restore the same to its previous condition as soon as reasonably possible, but in any event by Closing Date. If Seller is unable to do so without fault, Buyer may terminate this contract and the Earnest Money shall be refunded to Buyer. If any part of the Common Elements or any Unit adjoining the Unit described in Paragraph 2A is damaged or destroyed by fire or other casualty loss, Buyer shall have five (5) days from receipt of notice of such casualty loss within which to notify Seller in writing that the contract will be terminated unless Buyer receives written confirmation from the Association that the damaged condition will be restored to its previous condition within a reasonable time at no cost to Buyer. Unless Buyer gives such notice within such time, Buyer will be deemed to have accepted the Property without confirmation of such restoration. Seller shall have five (5) days from the date of receipt of Buyer's notice within which to cause to be delivered to Buyer such confirmation. If required by Buyer and written confirmation is not delivered to Buyer as required above, Buyer may terminate this contract and the Earnest Money will be refunded to Buyer. NOTICE TO BUYER: CONSULT YOUR INSURANCE AGENT PRIOR TO THE CLOSING DATE DUE TO THE UNIQUE REQUIREMENTS OF THIS TYPE OF PROPERTY.

16. DEFAULT: If Buyer fails to comply herewith, Seller may either (a) enforce specific performance and seek such other relief as may be provided by law or (b) terminate this contract and receive the Earnest Money as liquidated damages. If Seller is unable without fault to deliver the Commitment required herein, Buyer may either terminate this contract and receive the Earnest Money as the sole remedy or extend the Closing Date up to fifteen (15) days. If Seller is unable without fault to deliver the Certificate described in Paragraph 20 within the time herein specified, Buyer may either terminate this contract and receive the Earnest Money as the sole remedy or extend the time for delivery up to fifteen (15) days. If Seller fails to comply herewith for any other reason, Buyer may either (a) enforce specific performance hereof and seek such other relief as may be provided by law or (b) terminate this contract and receive the Earnest Money, thereby releasing Seller from this contract.

17. ATTORNEY'S FEES: Any signatory of this contract, Broker or Escrow Agent who is the prevailing party in any legal proceeding brought under or with relation to this contract or transaction shall be additionally entitled to recover costs and reasonable attorney fees from the nonprevailing party.

18. ESCROW: The Earnest Money is deposited with Escrow Agent with the understanding that Escrow Agent (a) is not a party to this contract and does not assume or have any liability for performance or non-performance of any party or other signatory (b) has the right to require from all signatories a written release of liability of the Escrow Agent which authorizes the disbursement of the Earnest Money (c) is not liable for interest or other charge on the funds held and (d) is not liable for any losses of escrow funds caused by the failure of any banking institution in which such funds have been deposited, unless such banking institution is acting as Escrow Agent. If any signatory unreasonably fails to deliver promptly the document described in (b) above, then such signatory shall be liable to the other signatories as provided in Paragraph 17. At closing, the Earnest Money shall be applied first to any cash down payment required, then to Buyer's closing costs and any excess refunded to Buyer. Any refund or payment of the Earnest Money under this contract shall be reduced by the amount of any actual expenses incurred on behalf of the party receiving the Earnest Money, and Escrow Agent will pay the same to the creditors entitled thereto.

19. REPRESENTATIONS: Seller represents that as of the Closing Date (a) there will be no unrecorded liens, assessments or Uniform Commercial Code Liens against any of the Property which will not be satisfied out of the Sales Price, unless securing payment of any deferred consideration (b) the present amount of the regular condominium assessment is $_____ which will be current and (c) Seller has no knowledge of any misrepresentation or errors in the Condominium Certificate or any material changes in the information contained therein. If any representation in this contract or the Certificate is untrue on the Closing Date, this contract may be terminated by Buyer and the Earnest Money shall be refunded to Buyer. All representations contained in this contract shall survive closing.

20. CERTIFICATE BY THE ASSOCIATION: The Certificate shall state or have attached thereto:
    A. Any right of first refusal held by the Association on the Unit;
    B. The amount of the monthly common expense assessment and the amount and effective date of any increase in such assessment;
    C. Any unpaid common expense or special assessment due and unpaid by the Seller to the Association;
    D. Any other unpaid amounts payable by Seller to the Association;
    E. Future capital expenditures approved by the Association;
    F. The amount of reserves for capital expenditures and any portion of those reserves allocated by the Association for specified projects;
    G. The most recent regularly prepared balance sheet and income and expense statement;
    H. The current operating budget of the Association;
    I. Any judgments against the Association and the nature of pending suits to which the Association is a party;
    J. A description of any insurance coverage provided for the benefit of Unit owners;
    K. The remaining term of any leasehold estate on which the condominium project is situated;
    L. Any knowledge by the governing body of the Association (the Board) of alterations or improvements to the Unit or to any other portions of the project which violate any provision of the Declaration;
    M. Any knowledge by the Board of violations of the Health or Building Codes with respect to the Unit or any other portion of the project; and
    N. Any knowledge of a condition which, in the good faith opinion of the Board, is a material physical defect in the Unit or in the common elements of the project.
    The Certificate may be in a form approved by the Texas Real Estate Commission for use with this contract.

21. AGREEMENT OF PARTIES: This contract contains the entire agreement of the parties and cannot be changed except by their written agreement. Texas Real Estate Commission promulgated addenda which are a part of this contract are: (list) _____
_____
_____

22. NOTICES: All notices shall be in writing and effective when delivered at the addresses shown below.

23. CONSULT YOUR ATTORNEY: The Broker cannot give you legal advice. This is intended to be a legally binding contract. READ IT CAREFULLY. Federal law may impose certain duties upon Brokers or Signatories to this contract when any of the signatories is a foreign party, or when any of the signatories receives certain amounts of U.S. currency in connection with a real estate closing. If you do not understand the effect of any part of this contract, consult your attorney BEFORE signing.

FHA or VA Financed Residential Condominium Earnest Money Contract — Page Five   02-08-85

Seller's Attorney: _____   Buyer's Attorney: _____

EXECUTED in multiple originals effective the _____ day of _____, 19_____. **(BROKER: FILL IN THE DATE OF FINAL ACCEPTANCE.)**

_____   _____
Buyer   Seller

_____   _____
Buyer   Seller

_____   _____
Buyer's Address   Phone No.   Seller's Address   Phone No.

AGREEMENT BETWEEN BROKERS

Listing Broker agrees to pay _____, Co-Broker.
a fee of _____ of the total sales price when the Broker's fee described in Paragraph 8 is received. Escrow Agent is authorized and directed to pay Co-Broker from Listing Broker's fee at closing.

_____   _____
Co-Broker   License No.   Listing Broker   License No.

By: _____   By: _____

_____   _____
Co-Broker's Address   Phone No.   Listing Broker's Address   Phone No.

EARNEST MONEY RECEIPT

Receipt of $_____ Earnest Money is acknowledged in the form of _____

_____

Escrow Agent: _____   By: _____

Date: _____, 19_____.

Canons / Texas Real Estate Commission

CANONS OF PROFESSIONAL ETHICS
AND
CONDUCT FOR BROKERS AND SALESMEN

A real estate broker or salesman, while acting as an agent for another, is a fiduciary. Special obligations are imposed when such fiduciary relationships are created. They demand:

ARTICLE 1: Fidelity

  (a) That the primary duty of the real estate agent is to represent the interests of his client, and his position, in this respect, should be clear to all parties concerned in a real estate transaction; that, however, the agent, in performing his duties to his client, shall treat other parties to a transaction fairly;

  (b) that the real estate agent be faithful and observant to trust placed in him, and be scrupulous and meticulous in performing his functions;

  (c) that the real estate agent place no personal interest above that of his client.

A real estate broker or salesman has a special obligation to exercise integrity in the discharge of his responsibilities, including employment of prudence and caution so as to avoid misrepresentation, in any wise, by acts of commission or omission.

ARTICLE 2: Integrity

It is the obligation of a real estate agent to be knowledgeable as a real estate brokerage practitioner. He should

ARTICLE 3: Competency

  (a) be informed on market conditions affecting the real estate business and pledged to continuing education in the intricacies involved in marketing real estate for others;

  (b) be informed on national, state and local issues and developments in the real estate industry;

  (c) exercise judgment and skill in the performance of his work.

Real Estate Math Review

PERCENT   Percent (%) means parts per hundred. For example, 25% means 25 parts per hundred; 10% means 10 parts per hundred. Percentages are related to common and decimal fractions as follows:

$$5\% = .05 = 1/20$$
$$10\% = .10 = 1/10$$
$$25\% = .25 = 1/4$$
$$75\% = .75 = 3/4$$
$$99\% = .99 = 99/100$$

A percentage greater than 100% is greater than 1. For example:

$$110\% = 1.10 = 1\text{-}1/10$$
$$150\% = 1.50 = 1\text{-}1/2$$
$$200\% = 2.00 = 2$$
$$1,000\% = 10.0 = 10$$

To change a decimal fraction to a percentage, move the decimal point two places to the right and add the % sign. For example:

$$.0001 = .01\%$$
$$.01 = 1\%$$
$$.06 = 6\%$$
$$.35 = 35\%$$
$$.356 = 35.6\%$$
$$1.15 = 115\%$$

A percentage can be changed to a common fraction by writing it as hundredths and then reducing it to its lowest common denominator. For example:

$$20\% = 20/100 = 1/5$$
$$90\% = 90/100 = 9/10$$
$$225\% = 2\text{-}25/100 = 2\text{-}1/4$$

ADDING AND   To add decimals, place the decimal points directly over one another.
SUBTRACTING DECIMALS   Then place the decimal point for the solutions in the same column and add. For example:

```
 6.25
 1.10
10.277
17.627
```

If you are working with percentages, there is no need to convert to decimal fractions; just line up the decimal points and add. For example:

```
 68.8%
  6.0%
 25.2%
100.0%
```

When subtracting, the same methods apply. For example:

1.00	100%
− .80	− 80%
.20	20%

When there is a mixture of decimal fractions and percentages, first convert them all either to percentage or to decimal fractions.

Multiplying decimals is like multiplying whole numbers except that the decimal point must be correctly placed. This is done by counting the total number of places to the right of the decimal point in the numbers to be multiplied. Then count off the same number of places in the answer. The following examples illustrate this:

.6	.2	1.01	6	6	.03
×.3	×.2	× 2	×.1	×.11	× .02
.18	.04	2.02	.6	.66	.0006

When dividing, the process starts with properly placing the decimal point. A normal division then follows. When a decimal number is divided by a whole number, place the decimal point in the answer directly above the decimal point in the problem. For example:

$$\begin{array}{r} 1.03 \\ 3\,)\overline{3.09} \end{array} \qquad \begin{array}{r} .033 \\ 3\,)\overline{.099} \end{array}$$

To divide by a decimal number, you must first change the divisor to a whole number. Then you must make a corresponding change in the dividend. This is done by simply moving both decimal points the same number of places to the right. For example, to divide .06 by .02, move the decimal point of each to the right two places.

$.02\,)\overline{.06}$ becomes $2\,)\overline{6}$

$.5\,)\overline{3}$ becomes $5\,)\overline{30}$

$.05\,)\overline{30}$ becomes $5\,)\overline{3,000}$

When multiplying or dividing with percentages, first convert them to decimal form. Thus 6% of 200 is

200
× .06
12.00

The basic equation for solving rate problems is:
Percent times **Base amount** equals **Result**
$$P \times B = R$$

If you know the result and the percent and you want the base amount, then divide both sides of the equation by P to get:

$$B = \frac{R}{P}$$

If you know the result and the base amount and you want to know the percentage, divide both sides of the equation by B to get:

$$P = \frac{R}{B}$$

> **Note:** An equation will remain an equation as long as you make the same change on both sides of the equal sign. If you add the same number to both sides, it is still an equation. If you subtract the same amount from each side, it is still equal. If you multiply both sides by the same thing, it remains equal. If you divide both sides by the same thing, it remains equal.

One way to remember the basic equation for solving rate problems is to think of a campaign button that looks like this:

$$R = P \times B \qquad P = \frac{R}{B} \qquad B = \frac{R}{P}$$

Another useful tool in solving rate problems is to think of
the word **is** as = (an equal sign).
the word **of** as × (a multiplication sign).
the word **per** as ÷ (a division sign).
for example:
"7% of $50,000 is $3,500"
translates:
7% × $50,000 = $3,500

Problem 1
Beverly Broker sells a house for $60,000. Her share of the commission is to be 2.5% of the sales price. How much does she earn?
Her commission is 2.5% of $60,000
Her commission = .025 × $60,000
Her commission = $1,500
This is an example of Result = Percent × Base.

Problem 2
Sam Salesman works in an office which will pay him 70% of the commission on each home he lists and sells. With a 6% commission, how much would he earn on a $50,000 sale?
His commission is 70% of 6% of $50,000
His commission = .70 × .06 × $50,000
His commission = $2,100
This is an example of Result = Percent × Base

Problem 3

Newt Newcommer wants to earn $21,000 during his first 12 months as a salesman. He feels he can average 3% on each sale. How much property must he sell?

3% of sales is $21,000

.03 × sales = $21,000

sales = $21,000 ÷ .03

sales = $700,000

This is an example of Base = Result ÷ Percent

Problem 4

An apartment building nets the owners $12,000 per year on their investment of $100,000. What percent return are they receiving on their investment?

$12,000 is __ % of $100,000

$12,000 = __ % × $100,000

$$\frac{\$12,000}{\$100,000} = 12\%$$

This is an example of Percent = Result ÷ Base

Problem 5

Smith wants to sell his property and have $47,000 after paying a 6% brokerage commission on the sales price. What price must Smith get?

$47,000 is 94% of selling price

$47,000 = .94 × selling price

$$\frac{\$47,000}{.94} = \text{selling price}$$

$50,000 = selling price

Problem 6

Miller sold his home for $75,000, paid off an existing loan of $35,000 and paid closing costs of $500. The brokerage commission was 6% of the sales price. How much money did Miller receive? The amount he received is 94% of $75,000 less $35,500

amount = .94 × $75,000 − $35,500

amount = $70,500 − $35,500

amount = $35,000

Problem 7

The assessed valuation of the Kelly home is $10,000. If the property tax rate is $12.50 per $100 of assessed valuation, what is the tax?

$$\text{The tax is } \frac{\$12.50}{100} \text{ of } \$10,000$$

$$\text{tax} = \frac{\$12.50}{100} \times \$10,000$$

tax = $1,250

Problem 8

Property in Clark County is assessed at 75% of market value. What should the assessed valuation of a $40,000 property be?

Assessed valuation is 75% of market value

Assessed valuation = .75 × $40,000

Assessed valuation = $30,000

Problem 9

An insurance company charges $.24 per $100 of coverage for a one-year fire insurance policy. How much would a $40,000 policy cost?

Cost is $\dfrac{\$.24}{\$100}$ of $40,000

Cost = $\dfrac{\$.24}{\$100}$ × $40,000

Cost = $96

AREA MEASUREMENT

The measurement of the distance from one point to another is called *linear* measurement. Usually this is along a straight line, but it can also be along a curved line. Distance is measured in inches, feet, yards, and miles. Less commonly used are chains (66 feet) and rods (16½ feet). Surface areas are measured in square feet, square yards, acres (43,560 square feet), and square miles. In the metric system, the standard unit of linear measurement is the meter (39.37 inches). Land area is measured in square meters and hectares. A hectare contains 10,000 square meters or 2.471 acres.

To determine the area of a square or rectangle, multiply its length times its width. The formula is:

Area = Length × Width

A = L × W

Problem 10

A parcel of land measures 660 feet by 330 feet. How many square feet is this?

Area = 660 feet × 330 feet

Area = 217,800 square feet

How many acres does this parcel contain?

Acres = 217,800 ÷ 43,560

Acres = 5

If a buyer offers $42,500 for this parcel, how much is the offering per acre?

$42,500 ÷ 5 = $8,500

To determine the area of a right triangle, multiply one-half of the base times the height:

A = 1/2 × B × H
A = 1/2 × 25 × 50
A = 625 square feet

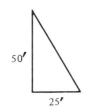

A = 1/2 × B × H
A = 1/2 × 40 × 20
A = 400 square feet

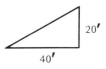

To determine the area of a circle, multiply 3.14 (π) times the square of the radius:

A = π × r²
A = 3.14 × 40²
A = 3.14 × 1,600
A = 5,024 sq ft

Note: where the diameter of a circle is given, divide by two to get the radius.

To determine the area of composite figures, separate them into their various components. Thus:

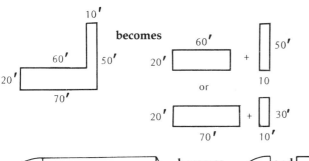

20′ × 60′ = 1,200 sq ft
10′ × 50′ =   500 sq ft
           1,700 sq ft

20′ × 70′ = 1,400 sq ft
10′ × 30′ =   300 sq ft
           1,700 sq ft

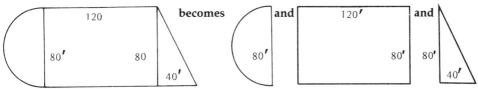

$(3.14 × 40′^2 × \frac{1}{2}) + (80′ × 120′) + (\frac{1}{2} × 40′ × 80′) = 13,712$ sq ft

Volume is measured in cubic units. The formula is:
Volume = Length × Width × Height
     V = L × W × H
For example, what is the volume of a room that is 10 ft by 15 ft with an 8 ft ceiling?
    V = 10′ × 15′ × 8′
    V = 1,200 cu ft

VOLUME MEASUREMENT

Caution: When solving area and volume problems, make certain that all the units are the same. For example, if a parcel of land is one-half mile long and 200 ft wide, convert one measurement so that both are expressed in the same unit; thus the answer will be either in square feet or in square miles. There is no such area measurement as a mile-foot. If a building is 100 yards long by 100 feet wide by 16' 6" high, convert to 300 ft by 100 ft by 16.5 ft before multiplying.

RATIOS & PROPORTIONS

If the label on a five-gallon can of paint says it will cover 2,000 square feet, how many gallons are necessary to cover 3,600 sq ft?

A problem like this can be solved two ways:

One way is to find out what area one gallon will cover. In this case 2,000 sq ft ÷ 5 gallons = 400 sq ft per gallon. Then divide 400 sq ft/gal into 3,600 sq ft and the result is 9 gallons.

The other method is to set up a proportion:

$$\frac{5 \text{ gal}}{2{,}000 \text{ sq ft}} = \frac{Y \text{ gal}}{3{,}600 \text{ sq ft}}$$

This reads, "5 gallons is to 2,000 sq ft as 'Y' gallons is to 3,600 sq ft." To solve for "Y," multiply both sides of the proportion by 3,600 sq ft. Thus:

$$\frac{5 \text{ gal} \times 3{,}600 \text{ sq ft}}{2{,}000 \text{ sq ft}} = Y \text{ gal}$$

Divide 2,000 sq ft into 3,600 sq ft and multiply the result by 5 gallons to get the answer.

FRONT-FOOT CALCULATIONS

When land is sold on a front-foot basis, the price is the number of feet fronting on the street times the price per front foot.

Price = front footage × rate per front foot

Thus a 50 ft × 150 ft lot priced at $1,000 per front foot would sell for $50,000. Note that in giving the dimensions of a lot, the first dimension given is the street frontage. The second dimension is the depth of the lot.

Measurement Conversion Table

Mile =
  5,280 feet
  1,760 yards
  320 rods
  80 chains
  = 1.609 kilometers

Square mile =
  640 acres
  = 2.590 sq kilometers

Acre =
  43,560 sq ft
  4,840 sq yds
  160 sq rods
  = 4,047 sq meters

Rod =
  16.5 feet
  = 5.029 meters

Chain =
  66 feet
  4 rods
  100 links
  = 20.117 meters

Meter =
  39.37 inches
  = 1,000 millimeters
  3.281 feet
  = 100 centimeters
  1.094 yards
  = 10 decimeters

Kilometer =
  0.6214 mile
  3,281 feet
  1,094 yards
  = 1,000 meters

Square meter =
  10.765 sq ft
  1.196 sq yds
  = 10,000 sq centimeters

Hectare =
  2.47 acres
  107,600 sq ft
  11,960 sq yds
  = 10,000 sq meters

Square kilometer =
  .3861 sq mile
  247 acres
  = 1,000,000 sq meters

Kilogram =
  2.205 pounds
  = 1,000 grams

Liter =
  1.053 quarts
  .263 gallon
  = 1,000 milliliters

Metric ton =
  (tonne)
  2,205 pounds
  1.102 tons
  = 1,000 kilograms

Answers to Chapter Questions and Problems

VOCABULARY REVIEW

a. 17	**e.** 9	**i.** 16	**l.** 7	**o.** 5
b. 4	**f.** 11	**j.** 8	**m.** 18	**p.** 14
c. 15	**g.** 1	**k.** 12	**n.** 6	**q.** 2
d. 10	**h.** 13			**r.** 3

QUESTIONS AND PROBLEMS

1. Lot, block, tract. (Metes and bounds if acreage.)

2.

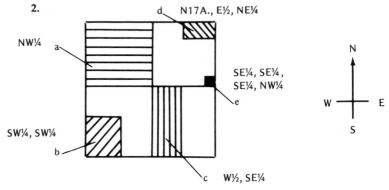

3. (a) 160 acres   (c) 80 acres   (e) 2½ acres
   (b) 40 acres   (d) 17 acres

4. (a) NE¼   (d) W½ of the SE¼ of the NW¼

   (b) E½ of the SE¼   (e) NE¼ of the SE¼ of the NW¼

   (c) SW¼ of the NW¼

5.

6. No. In the general public interest, laws have been passed that give aircraft the right to pass over land provided they fly above certain altitudes.

7. The key to a door, although highly portable, is adapted to the door and as such is real property.

8. Requires individualized answer. However, as a general rule, anything that is permanently attached is real property and anything that is not attached is personal property.

9. Prior appropriation.

10. Unless corrections are made (and they usually are) survey inaccuracies would result.

VOCABULARY REVIEW

a. 8	e. 17	i. 13	m. 10	q. 3
b. 12	f. 19	j. 14	n. 16	r. 9
c. 4	g. 7	k. 1	o. 15	s. 20
d. 18	h. 5	l. 6	p. 2	t. 11

CHAPTER 3
Rights and Interests in Land

QUESTIONS AND PROBLEMS

1. For a freehold estate to exist, there must be actual possession of the land (that is, ownership) and the estate must be of unpredictable duration. Leasehold estates do not involve ownership of the land and are of determinate length. Freehold estate cases are tried under real property laws. Leasehold cases are tried under personal property laws.

2. An easement is created when a landowner fronting on a public byway deeds or leases a landlocked portion of his land to another person. This would be an easement by necessity. A second method is by prolonged use and is called an easement by prescription.

3. Passed Equal Rights Amendment.

4. Dower, curtesy and homestead are referred to as statutory estates because they are created by state laws and not by the landowner.

5. The holder of an easement coexists side-by-side with the landowner; that is, both have a shared use of the land in question. The holder of a lease obtains exclusive right of occupancy and the landowner is excluded during the term of the lease.

6. An encumbrance is any impediment to clear title. Examples are: lien, lease, easement, deed restriction, and encroachment.

7. Requires local answer. (Answers will likely center around zoning, building codes, general land planning, rent control, property taxation, eminent domain, and escheat.)

8. Total protection is provided if property is within homestead limits and the debt is for purposes other than purchase money, ad valorem taxes, or home improvements.

9. A lease, being both a contract and a conveyance in Texas. is subject to laws concerning both types of instruments.

CHAPTER 4
Holding Title

VOCABULARY REVIEW

a. 8	**e.** 5	**h.** 17	**k.** 13	**n.** 3
b. 1	**f.** 12	**i.** 14	**l.** 15	**o.** 2
c. 16	**g.** 11	**j.** 4	**m.** 9	**p.** 6
d. 10				**q.** 7

QUESTIONS AND PROBLEMS

1. The key advantage of sole ownership is flexibility—the owner can make all decisions without approval of co-owners. The key disadvantages are responsibility and the high entry cost.
2. Undivided interest means that each co-owner has a right to use the entire property.
3. The four unities are—
   Time: each joint tenant must acquire his or her ownership at the same moment.
   Title: all joint tenants acquire their interests from the same source.
   Interest: each joint tenant owns an undivided whole of the property.
   Possession: all joint tenants have the right to use the whole property.
4. Right of survivorship means that upon the death of a joint tenant, his interest in the property is extinguished and the remaining joint tenants are automatically left as the owners.
5. Community property.
6. Yes.
7. The three women would be considered to be tenants in common with each owning an undivided one-third interest.
8. No assumption can safely be made based on name only. Inquiry must be made into whether the land in question was separate or community property.
9. The key differences are in the financial liability of the limited partners, the limited management role of the limited partners, and the fact that limited partners are not found in a general partnership.
10. REITs offer investors single taxation, built-in management, small minimum investment, and liquidity.

CHAPTER 5
Transferring Title

VOCABULARY REVIEW

a. 15	**e.** 14	**i.** 20	**m.** 3	**q.** 13
b. 18	**f.** 16	**j.** 1	**n.** 12	**r.** 10
c. 9	**g.** 5	**k.** 17	**o.** 11	**s.** 2
d. 7	**h.** 6	**l.** 4	**p.** 19	**t.** 8

QUESTIONS AND PROBLEMS

1. Yes. The fact that a document is a deed depends on the wording it contains, not what it is labeled or not labeled.

2. Title passes upon delivery of the deed by the grantor to the grantee and its willing acceptance by the grantee.

3. The full covenant and warranty deed offers the grantee protection in the form of the grantor's assurances that he is the owner and possessor, that the grantee will not be disturbed after taking possession by someone else claiming ownership, that the title is not encumbered except as stated in the deed, and that the grantor will procure and deliver to the grantee any subsequent documents necessary to make good the title being conveyed.

4. Warranty deed. It provides the grantee with the maximum title protection available from a deed.

5. No.

6. The hazards of preparing one's own deeds are that any errors made will cause confusion and may make the deed legally invalid. Pre-printed deeds may not be suitable for the state where the land is located or for the grantor's purpose. An improperly prepared deed, once recorded, creates errors in the public records.

7. Dower right, curtesy right, community property right, mortgage right of redemption, tax lien, judgment lien, mechanic's lien, undivided interest held by another, inheritance rights, and easements are all examples of title clouds.

8. When a person dies without leaving a will, state law directs how his assets are to be distributed.

9. An executor is named by the deceased in his will to carry out its terms. In the absence of a will, the state appoints an administrator to settle the deceased's estate.

10. Yes, two.

11. No. Occupancy on a rental basis is not hostile to the property owner, but rather is by his permission.

12. Galveston Island, Padre Island, Rio Grande River.

VOCABULARY REVIEW

a. 10	**e.** 2	**h.** 14	**k.** 13	**n.** 5
b. 3	**f.** 6	**i.** 16	**l.** 4	**o.** 15
c. 1	**g.** 8	**j.** 9	**m.** 11	**p.** 12
d. 7				**q.** 17

CHAPTER 6
Recordation, Abstracts, and Title Insurance

QUESTIONS AND PROBLEMS

1. By visibly occupying a parcel of land or by recording a document in the public records a person gives constructive notice that he is claiming a right or interest in that parcel of land. Actual notice is knowledge that one has actually gained, based on what he has seen, heard, read, or observed.

2. County Clerk's Office.

3. Depends on County Clerk. Needs acknowledgment or proper witnessing to be recorded.
4. The grantor and grantee indexes are used to locate documents filed in the public recorder's office.
5. Although the bulk of the information necessary to conduct a title search can be found in the public recorder's office, it may also be necessary to inspect documents not kept there, for example, marriage records, judgment lien files, probate records, and the U.S. Tax Court.
6. A certificate of title issued by an attorney is his opinion of ownership, whereas a Torrens certificate of title shows ownership as determined by a court of law.
7. A title report shows the condition of title at a specific moment in time. An abstract provides a complete historical summary of all recorded documents affecting title. From this an attorney renders an opinion as to the current condition of title.
8. The purpose of title insurance is to protect owners and lenders from monetary loss due to errors in title report preparation and inaccuracies in the public records.
9. Although Williams did not record his deed, his occupancy of the house constitutes legal notice. The out-of-state investor who probably felt safe because he bought a title insurance policy apparently did not read the fine print which, in most owner's policies, does not insure against facts, rights, interests or claims that could be ascertained by an on-site inspection or by making inquiry of persons in possession. The out-of-state investor is the loser unless he can recover his money from Thorsen.
10. Requires local answer.

CHAPTER 7
Contract Law

VOCABULARY REVIEW

a. 12	e. 8	h. 3	k. 13	n. 15
b. 14	f. 10	i. 16	l. 7	o. 17
c. 4	g. 11	j. 5	m. 9	p. 2
d. 1				q. 6

QUESTIONS AND PROBLEMS

1. An expressed contract is the result of a written or oral agreement. An implied contract is one that is apparent from the actions of the parties involved. (Examples will vary with personal experiences.)
2. A legally valid contract requires: (a) legally competent parties, (b) mutual agreement, (c) lawful objective, (d) sufficient consideration or cause, and (e) a writing when required by law.
3. A void contract has no legal effect on any party to the contract and may be ignored at the pleasure of any party to it. A voidable contract binds one party but gives the other the right to withdraw.

4. Examples of legal incompetents include: minors, insane persons, drunks, and felons. (Exceptions are possible in the latter two.)

5. An offer can be terminated by the passage of time and by withdrawal prior to its acceptance. Passage of time can be in the form of a fixed termination date for the offer or, lacking that, a reasonable amount of time to accept, as fixed by a court of law.

6. Mistake as applied to contract law arises from ambiguity in negotiations and mistake of material fact.

7. Consideration is one of the legal requirements of a binding contract. The concept of one party doing something and receiving nothing in return is foreign to contract law. Examples generally fall into four categories: money, goods, services, and forebearance.

8. The parties to a legally unenforceable contract can still voluntarily carry out its terms. However, compliance could not be enforced by a court of law.

9. Alternatives include: mutual rescission, assignment, novation, partial performance, money damages, unilateral rescission, specific performance suit, or liquidated damages.

10. His primary concern would be whether money damages would suitably restore his position or whether actual performance is necessary.

VOCABULARY REVIEW

a. 4	**d.** 3	**f.** 9	**h.** 12	**j.** 8
b. 7	**e.** 5	**g.** 10	**i.** 1	**k.** 11
c. 6				

CHAPTER 8
Real Estate Sales Contracts

QUESTIONS AND PROBLEMS

1. The purchase contract provides time to ascertain that the seller is capable of conveying title, time to arrange financing, and time to carry out the various terms and conditions of the contract.

2. Anything left to be "ironed out" later is an area for potential disagreement and possibly a lost deal. Moreover, the basic contract requirement of a meeting of the minds may be missing.

3. The advantages are convenience (the bulk of the contract is already written) and time (it is faster to fill out a form than construct a contract from scratch). The disadvantages are that a preprinted contract may not adequately fit a given transaction and the blank spaces still leave room for errors.

4. A seller can accept an offer with or without a deposit. (An exception is that some court-ordered sales require a specified deposit.)

5. Most fixtures are considered by law to be a part of the land and therefore do not need separate mention. However, mention is made of any fixture that might be open to differences of opinion.

6. If a seller is not under pressure to sell quickly and/or there are plenty of buyers in the marketplace, he can hold out for price and

terms to his liking. If a buyer is aware of other buyers competing for the same property, he will act quickly and meet (or offer close to) the seller's price and terms. If the seller is in a rush to sell or is afraid that there are few buyers for his property in the market, he will negotiate terms more to the buyer's liking rather than risk not making the sale. If the buyer is aware of this he can hold out for price and terms to his liking.

7. The advantages to the seller of holding title in an installment contract sale are that the seller already has title in the event of the buyer's default and where nonrecording provisions are valid and used, the seller can pledge the property as collateral for a loan.

8. Requires statutory redemption period for forfeiture. No special provisions for non-recording.

9. The key advantages of trading are the tax-free exchange possibility and the need for little or no cash to complete the transaction. The disadvantages are in finding suitable trade property for all parties involved and in the fact that there are more transaction details in a trade (compared to a cash sale) that can go awry and ruin the trade.

CHAPTER 9
Mortgage Theory and Law

VOCABULARY REVIEW

a. 9	**e.** 2	**i.** 4	**m.** 16	**q.** 11
b. 13	**f.** 18	**j.** 15	**n.** 12	**r.** 19
c. 6	**g.** 5	**k.** 1	**o.** 17	**s.** 14
d. 10	**h.** 3	**l.** 8	**p.** 7	**t.** 20

QUESTIONS AND PROBLEMS

1. A prepayment privilege is to the advantage of the borrower. Without it he cannot repay his debt ahead of schedule.

2. Lien theory sees a mortgage as creating only a lien against a property whereas title theory sees a mortgage as conveying title to the lender subject to defeat by the borrower.

3. Strict foreclosure gives title to the lender whereas foreclosure by sale requires that the foreclosed property be sold at public auction and the proceeds used to repay the lender. Texas requires foreclosure by sale.

4. The first mortgage is the senior mortgage while the second and third mortgages are classed as junior mortgages.

5. Posting at courthouse door. Public sale on first Tuesday of the month.

6. Nothing. No provisions.

7. Requires personal answer.

8. The obligor is the party making the obligation, that is, the borrower. The obligee is the party to whom the obligation is owed, that is, the lender.

9. The lender includes mortgage covenants pertaining to insurance,

property taxes, and removal in order to protect the value of the collateral pledged under the mortgage.

10. A certificate of reduction is prepared by the lender and shows how much remains to be paid on the loan. An estoppel certificate provides for a borrower's verification of the amount still owed and the rate of interest.

VOCABULARY REVIEW

CHAPTER 10
Deed of Trust

a. 3   **b.** 1   **c.** 2   **d.** 4

QUESTIONS AND PROBLEMS

1. Under a deed of trust the borrower gives the trustee title and the lender a promissory note. When the debt is paid, the lender instructs the trustee to reconvey title back to the borrower. With a mortgage, the lender acquires both the note and title (or lien rights) under the mortgage. Upon repayment the lender releases the mortgage directly. In the event of default under a deed of trust, the trustee conducts the sale and delivers title to the buyer. With a mortgage, the lender is responsible for conducting the sale (if power of sale is present) or carrying out foreclosure proceedings.

2. The trustee's title lies dormant and there is no right of entry or use as long as the promissory note secured by the trust deed is not in default.

3. A release of lien is notification from the beneficiary to the trustee to reconvey (release) the trustee's title to the grantor.

4. The power of sale clause gives the trustee the right to foreclose the borrower's rights, sell the property and convey title to a purchaser without having to go to court.

5. An assignment of rents clause gives the lender the right to operate the property and collect any rents or income generated by it if the borrower is delinquent.

6. The deed of trust is the most common mortgage in Texas.

VOCABULARY REVIEW

CHAPTER 11
Lending Practices

a. 10	**e.** 6	**i.** 4	**m.** 15	**q.** 3	**u.** 19
b. 9	**f.** 12	**j.** 24	**n.** 18	**r.** 7	**v.** 2
c. 11	**g.** 23	**k.** 17	**o.** 20	**s.** 1	**w.** 13
d. 8	**h.** 14	**l.** 5	**p.** 16	**t.** 22	**x.** 21

QUESTIONS AND PROBLEMS

1. The major risk is that when the balloon payment is due, the borrower will not have the cash to pay it, and will not be able to find a lender to refinance it.

2. An amortized loan requires equal, periodic payments of principal and interest such that the loan balance owing will be zero at maturity. During the life of the loan, payments are first applied to interest owing and then to principal. As the balance owed is reduced, less of each monthly payment is taken for interest and more applied to principal reduction until finally the loan is repaid.

3. $65 \times \$9.91 = \$644.15$ per month

4. $\$800 \div \$9.53 \times \$1,000 + \$10,000 = \$93,945$

5. $\$800 \div \$8.05 \times \$1,000 + \$10,000 = \$109,379$

6. $\$902 \times 90 = \$81,180$

7. The purpose of Section 203b insurance is to qualify buyers of modest-priced homes for low down-payment loans. This is done by insuring lenders against loan default and charging borrowers an insurance premium for this.

8. The VA offers a qualified veteran the opportunity of purchasing a home with no cash down payment.

9. A point is one percent. It is a method of expressing loan origination fees and discounts in connection with lending. Discount points are used to increase the effective rate of interest (yield) to the lender without changing the quoted interest rate.

10. The basic purpose of the Truth in Lending Act is to show the borrower how much he will be paying for credit in percentage terms and in total dollars.

11. As a rule, it is from the borrower's monthly income that monthly loan payments will be made. The assets, although substantial in size may not be available for monthly payments.

CHAPTER 12
Sources of Financing

VOCABULARY REVIEW

a. 1	e. 10	i. 9	m. 12	q. 18	u. 11	y. 23
b. 24	f. 16	j. 17	n. 13	r. 5	v. 6	z. 26
c. 2	g. 21	k. 22	o. 20	s. 3	w. 19	
d. 8	h. 15	l. 25	p. 7	t. 14	x. 4	

QUESTIONS AND PROBLEMS

1. A mortgage broker brings borrowers and lenders together. A mortgage banker makes loans and then resells them.

2. The main source is investors who buy mortgage-backed securities.

3. Loan servicing refers to the care and upkeep of a loan once it is made. This includes payment collection and accounting, handling defaults, borrower questions, loan payoff processing and mortgage releasing.

4. An adjustable rate mortgage is a loan on which the interest rate can be adjusted up or down as current interest rates change.

5. Both the *de la Cuesta* case and the Garn Act allow due-on-sale clauses to be enforced.

6. FNMA buys, by auction, mortgage loans. These purchases are financed by the sale of FNMA stock and bonds as well as the sale of these loans to investors. GNMA guarantees timely repayment of privately issued securities backed by pools of federally insured mortgages.

7. A loan dollar that is the result of real savings won't cause inflation. That is because the borrower is using goods and services the saver has foregone. But a fiat money dollar does not represent available goods and services; instead it competes with real savings dollars and pushes prices up.

8. Adjustable rate loans share the risk of changing interest rates between the borrower and the lender. The lender feels more comfortable knowing the interest rate charged will change with the cost of money to the lender.

9. Rentals and leases are considered financing forms as they allow a person the use of something without having to first pay the full purchase price.

10. Above all, the investor should make certain that the realistic market value of the property is well in excess of the loans against it.

VOCABULARY REVIEW

CHAPTER 13
Taxes and Assessments

a. 8	d. 5	f. 9	h. 10
b. 2	e. 4	g. 7	i. 1
c. 3			j. 6

QUESTIONS AND PROBLEMS

1. Sources of funds other than property taxes are subtracted from the district budget. The remainder is then divided by the total assessed valuation of property in the district to obtain the tax rate.

2. $960,000 divided by $120,000,000 equals 8 mills.

3. $40,000 times $.008 equals $320.

4. $10,000 times $0.05 divided by $100 equals $5.

5. Requires local answer.

6. Appeal to Board of Equalization. However, the point is that the assessor does not set the tax rate. He only applies it. If the complaint regards assessment procedures, the assessment appeal process is taken. If it regards the tax rate, the city, county, or state budget makers are responsible.

7. The greater the amount of tax-exempt property in a taxation district, the less taxable property is available to bear the burden of taxation.

8. Current appraisals plus real estate sales.

9. $68,000 − $5,000 − ($21,000 + $2,000 + $5,000) = $35,000

10. $68,000 − $5,000 − $58,000 = $5,000
    It will be a long-term capital gain.

11. There are none in Texas.

CHAPTER 14
Title Closing and Escrow

VOCABULARY REVIEW

a. 1	**c.** 3	**d.** 2	**e.** 6	**f.** 4
b. 5				**g.** 7

QUESTIONS AND PROBLEMS

1. Escrow agent duties include preparation of escrow instructions, holding buyer's earnest money, ordering a title search, obtaining title insurance, making prorations, loan payoffs, loan disbursement, deed and mortgage delivery, and handling papers and paperwork relative to the transaction.

2. The key difference is that an escrow holder is a common agent of the parties to the transaction. This eliminates the need for each party to attend the closing and personally represent himself.

3. The escrow agent is an agent of the buyer with respect to the buyer's role in the transaction and an agent of the seller with respect to the seller's role. The same holds true for the lender, title company, etc.

4. $180 divided by 12 equals $15 per month or 50¢ per day. Using standard 30-day months and presuming the buyer is the owner commencing with the settlement date, there are one month and 26 days used and 10 months and 4 days remaining. For this remaining coverage, the buyer pays the seller 10 times $15 plus 4 times $.50 equals $152.00.

5. Daily rate equals $45,000 times 8% divided by 360 equals $10. The buyer is credited 11 days times $10 equals $110. The seller is debited the same amount.

6. **Buyer:**
   lender's title policy
   loan appraisal fee
   mortgage recording

   Seller:
   deed stamps
   deed preparation
   mortgage release

CHAPTER 15
Real Estate Leases

VOCABULARY REVIEW

a. 4	**d.** 2	**f.** 6	**h.** 10	**j.** 7
b. 8	**e.** 1	**g.** 11	**i.** 12	**k.** 9
c. 5				**l.** 3

QUESTIONS AND PROBLEMS

1. From the tenant's standpoint, the lease assures him of space and the rent stated in the lease. But it also requires him to pay for it. The month-to-month arrangement commits him to a maximum of one month at a time; however, it also commits the landlord for only one month at a time.

2. Forcible entry and detainer proceedings.

3. 30 days.

4. Contract rent is the amount of rent the tenant must pay the landlord. Economic rent is market value rent.

5. The tenant's basis would be that the premises is unfit to occupy as intended in the lease. The tenant's purpose is to terminate the lease and be relieved of liability to pay rent.

6. An option to renew is to the advantage of the lessee.

7. Real estate licensees are not to accept sole or rental listings where they are asked to discriminate, nor are they permitted to make, print, or publish any statement or advertisement with respect to a sale or rental of a dwelling which suggests discrimination because of race, color, religion, or national origin.

8. No. None.

9. 30 days.

VOCABULARY REVIEW

CHAPTER 16
Real Estate Appraisal

a. 7	**e.** 1	**i.** 25	**m.** 17	**q.** 13	**u.** 2	**y.** 6
b. 16	**f.** 8	**j.** 10	**n.** 21	**r.** 14	**v.** 3	**z.** 23
c. 22	**g.** 5	**k.** 18	**o.** 4	**s.** 9	**w.** 11	
d. 12	**h.** 20	**l.** 24	**p.** 26	**t.** 15	**x.** 19	

QUESTIONS AND PROBLEMS

1. Enough comparables should be used to reasonably estimate market value but not so many as to involve more time and expense than is gained in added information. For a single-family house, 3 to 5 good comparables are usually adequate, but not excessive.

2. Asking prices are useful in that they set an upper limit on value. Offering prices are useful in that they set a lower limit on value.

3. Adjustments are made to the comparable properties. This is because it is impossible to adjust the value of something for which one does not yet know the value.

4. Using comparables that are not similar to the subject property with respect to zoning, neighborhood characteristics, size or usefulness, requires adjustments that are likely to be very inaccurate or impossible to make.

5. Gross rent times gross rent multiplier equals indicated property value. The strength of this approach is in its simplicity. Its weakness is also in its simplicity as it overlooks anything other than gross rents.

6. The five steps are (1) estimate land value as though vacant, (2) estimate new construction cost of a similar building, (3) subtract estimated depreciation from construction cost to obtain, (4) the indicated value of the structure, and (5) add this to the land value.

7. The income approach values a property based on its expected monetary returns in light of current rates of return being demanded by investors.

8. In the standard market comparison approach, a specific dollar adjustment is made for each item of difference between the comparables and the subject property. With competitive market analysis, adjustments are made in a generalized fashion in the minds of the agent and the seller. The CMA approach is usually preferred for listing homes for sale because there is less room for disagreement. The standard market approach is preferred for appraisal reports as it shows exactly how the appraiser valued the adjustments.

9. The principle of diminishing marginal returns warns against investing more than the capitalized value of the anticipated net returns.

10. **Lender:** form report.
    Buyer: oral or letter report.
    Executor: letter or narrative report.
    Highway department: narrative report.

CHAPTER 17
The Owner-Broker Relationship

VOCABULARY REVIEW

a. 8	**e.** 6	**g.** 10	**i.** 2	**k.** 13
b. 12	**f.** 5	**h.** 9	**j.** 1	**l.** 14
c. 11				**m.** 4
d. 7				**n.** 3

QUESTIONS AND PROBLEMS

1. An agency is created when one person (called the principal) empowers another (the agent) to act as his representative.

2. A universal agency is very broad in scope in that the principal gives his agent the legal power to transact matters of all types for him. A general agency gives the agent the power to transact the principal's affairs in a particular trade or business.

3. Broker cooperation refers to the sharing of a single commission fee among the various brokers who brought about a sale. It is achieved by an agreement between the listing broker and the cooperating brokers.

4. An exclusive right-to-sell listing protects the broker by entitling him to a commission no matter who sells the property. The exclusive agency listing puts the broker in competition with the owner by allowing the owner to find a buyer and owe no commission. The open listing adds other brokers to the competition as any number of brokers can have the listing simultaneously and the owner can still sell it himself and pay no commission.

5. The open listing allows the owner to employ any number of brokers simultaneously and to sell the property himself and owe no commission. However, this arrangement usually results in no broker being

willing to put much effort into finding a buyer—which is presumably why the property was listed in the first place.

6. **Faithful:** the broker must perform as promised in the listing contract and not depart from the principal's instructions.

   Loyal: the broker owes his allegiance to the principal and as such works for the benefit of the principal. This means promoting and protecting the principal's best interests and keeping him informed of all matters that might affect the sale of the listed property.

7. "Ready, willing, and able buyer" means a buyer who is ready to buy now, with no further coaxing, and who has the financial capacity to do so.

8. Yes.

9. Listings are usually terminated with the completion of the agency objective, namely finding a buyer or a tenant. Lacking a buyer, termination usually results when the listing period expires. A listing can also be terminated if the broker fails to perform as agreed in the listing.

10. The purpose of the HUD property disclosure statement is to require that sellers of subdivisions of 50 or more lots sold across state lines provide prospective purchasers a standardized property report with information regarding the property they are being asked to buy.

11. Steering means to guide a client away from one neighborhood and/ or to another based on the client's race, color, religion, sex, or national origin. Blockbusting is the illegal practice of inducing panic selling in a neighborhood for financial gain.

12. The case of *Jones* v. *Mayer* nullified the exemptions for race discrimination allowed to owners of small income properties by the 1968 Civil Rights Act.

VOCABULARY REVIEW

a. 6	**d.** 4	**g.** 3	**i.** 5	**k.** 11
b. 7	**e.** 8	**h.** 12	**j.** 13	**l.** 10
c. 1	**f.** 2			**m.** 9

CHAPTER 18
*Licensing Laws and
Professional Affiliation*

QUESTIONS AND PROBLEMS

1. Early license laws were primarily aimed at protecting the public by qualifying license applicants based on their honesty, truthfulness and good reputation. Real estate examinations and education requirements were added later.

2. Generally speaking, a real estate license is required when a person, who for compensation or the promise of compensation, lists or offers to list, sells or offers to sell, buys or offers to buy, negotiates or offers to negotiate, either directly or indirectly, for the purpose of bringing about a sale, purchase, option to purchase, exchange, auction, lease or rental of real estate. Some states also require that

real estate appraisers, property managers, mortgage bankers and rent collectors hold real estate licenses.

3. In deciding on a compensation schedule for his salespersons, a broker must consider office overhead, employee retention, and the emphasis he wishes to place on listing versus selling.

4. 21 semester hours or 315 classroom hours.

5. The trend is to much higher educational standards.

6. Take and pass GRI course.

7. Andy James. Oversees the activities of TREC and has complete authority to exercise powers and duties of TREC.

8. Appointed by the Governor. Administration of the provisions of the Act. Passes rules to provide guidelines and facilitate enforcement and clarify procedures.

9. Section 15 of Texas Real Estate License Act.

10. The purpose of a bond requirement or a recovery fund is to have funds available that can be drawn upon in the event a court judgment against a licensee, resulting from a license-related wrongdoing, is uncollectible. Recovery fund.

11. The purpose of the National Association of Realtors is to promote the general welfare of the real estate industry by encouraging fair dealing among Realtors and the public, supporting legislation to protect property rights, offering education for members, and in general doing whatever is necessary to build the dignity, stability and professionalization of the industry.

12. An employment contract will cover such matters as compensation, training, hours of work, company identification, fees and dues, expenses, use of automobile, fringe benefits, withholding of taxes, termination of employment, and general office policies and procedures.

13. You would want to consider location, compensation, broker's reputation, working hours, broker support, training opportunities, advertising policy, expense reimbursement, and fringe benefits.

CHAPTER 19
Condominiums, Cooperatives,
and Planned Unit Developments

VOCABULARY REVIEW

a. 16	**e.** 3	**i.** 2	**m.** 17	**q.** 20
b. 15	**f.** 1	**j.** 8	**n.** 4	**r.** 19
c. 7	**g.** 11	**k.** 14	**o.** 5	**s.** 12
d. 13	**h.** 6	**l.** 9	**p.** 10	**t.** 18

QUESTIONS AND PROBLEMS

1. Condominiums are often cheaper to buy than single-family houses, are often better located, may offer better security and maintenance and can be individually financed.

2. Each condominium unit owner holds an undivided interest in the

land in a fee simple condominium project. The corporation owns the land in a cooperative.

3. A proprietary lease is a lease issued by a corporation to its stockholders. The lease "rent" is actually the stockholder's share of the cost of operating the building and repaying the debt against it. In a residential lease, the tenant pays for use of the premises, is not responsible for operating expenses nor debt repayment and does not have an ownership interest in the premises.

4. The master deed converts a given parcel of land into a condominium subdivision.

5. The wall between two condominium apartments belongs to the condominium owners as a group.

6. CC&Rs are the covenants, conditions and restrictions by which a property owner agrees to abide. They are established for the harmony and well-being of the owners as a group.

7. Maintenance fees (association dues) pay for common operating costs and are spread among the unit owners. Failure to pay creates a lien against the delinquent owner's unit.

8. The owners' association hazard and liability policy covers only the common elements. To be protected against property loss and accident liability within a dwelling unit, the owner must have his own hazard and liability policy.

9. Right-to-use is a contractual right whereas fee simple is ownership of real estate.

10. In a PUD each owner holds title to the land occupied by his unit and is a member of an owners' association which holds title to the common areas.

VOCABULARY REVIEW

CHAPTER 20
Property Insurance

a. 7	**d.** 2	**f.** 10	**h.** 11	**j.** 6
b. 1	**e.** 3	**g.** 4	**i.** 8	**k.** 5
c. 9				

QUESTIONS AND PROBLEMS

1. Fire policies cover losses resulting from negligence but not damage intentionally caused by the insured.

2. An endorsement or rider is an agreement by the insurer and the insured to modify the coverage in the basic policy.

3. Public liability insurance is concerned with insuring against financial losses resulting from the responsibility of one person to another with regard to one's actions or failure to take action.

4. Section I in a homeowner's policy covers loss of and damage to the insured's property. Section II deals with the public liability of the insured.

5. All-risk insurance policies cover loss or damage resulting from any

cause not excluded by the policy. A broad-form policy is one that covers a large number of perils that are specifically named in the policy.
6. "New for old" means that the insurer will pay for replacement at today's costs. Thus, although the property lost by the insured was used; that is, old; he will receive a new replacement from the insurer.
7. Coverage is suspended on vacant buildings because they are more attractive to thieves, vandals, and arsonists than are occupied buildings.

CHAPTER 21
Land-Use Control

VOCABULARY REVIEW

a. 4	**c.** 7	**e.** 3	**g.** 8
b. 6	**d.** 1	**f.** 5	**h.** 2

QUESTIONS AND PROBLEMS

1. The individual property owner does not consider his property to be a community resource. Thus, any substantial progress in land planning and control in the future must also consider the right of the individual to develop his land.
2. The authority of government to control land use is derived from the state's right of police power. Through enabling acts, this authority is passed on to the counties, cities, and towns in the state.
3. A variance allows an individual landowner to deviate slightly from strict compliance with zoning requirements for his land. A variance must be consistent with the character of the neighborhood and general objectives of zoning as they apply to that neighborhood.
4. Requires local answer.
5. Deed restrictions and building permits.

CHAPTER 22
Real Estate and The Economy

VOCABULARY REVIEW

a. 1	**c.** 4	**e.** 8	**g.** 10	**i.** 5
b. 6	**d.** 3	**f.** 7	**h.** 9	**j.** 2

QUESTIONS AND PROBLEMS

1. Requires local answer.
2. Requires local answer.
3. Requires local answer.
4. $15\% \times (100\% - 28\%) = 10.8\%$; $10\% \times (28\%) = 7.2\%$; $5\% \times (100\% - 28\%) = 3.6\%$.
5. The purpose of the Equal Credit Opportunity Act is to require lenders to make credit available without regard to sex or marital status.
6. Requires local answer.

7. Large federal deficits compete against home buyers for available loan funds and in the process push up interest rates.
8. The economic goals of the Federal Reserve Board are high employment, stable prices, steady growth and a stable foreign exchange value for the dollar.
9. The advantage is that in the short-run interest rates can be pushed down which gives the economy a boost. The disadvantage is that inflation will result.
10. Falling prices.

VOCABULARY REVIEW

a. 7	c. 12	e. 1	g. 9	i. 5	k. 2	m. 6
b. 14	d. 8	f. 11	h. 4	j. 13	l. 10	n. 3

QUESTIONS AND PROBLEMS

1. A tax-sheltered investment is one where part or all of the return from a property is not subject to income taxes. The primary source is depreciation, which, although shown as an expense for calculating income taxes, is not an out-of-pocket (cash) expense.
2. Investors in real estate look for cash flow, tax shelter, mortgage reduction and appreciation.
3. The major risk of owning vacant land is having to wait too long for an increase in value.
4. The advantages of duplexes and triplexes are that, compared to larger buildings, the investor's capital, management and risk are on a smaller scale. These buildings are not, however, as efficient to manage and rents are often relatively low per dollar of purchase price.
5. "Better off" must be considered in light of the investor's objectives and ability to take risks. The earlier one invests, the bigger the risks and potential rewards. By waiting, one can lower the risks and the rewards.
6. Higher returns are necessary in an older building to compensate for major replacement, repair and refurbishing costs; for increasing maintenance expenses; for the risk that the neighborhood may decline in popularity; and that the building itself may have limited remaining economic usefulness.
7. A person who has a number of high-income years remaining in life can more comfortably take risks as there is time to recover financially if losses should result. An older person without the time and energy to recover financially would seek to avoid risky investments.
8. $22,000 ÷ .10756 = $204,537. Round to $205,000.
9. $22,000 ÷ .11819 = $186,141. Round to $186,000.
10. Limited partnerships offer the investor the advantages of relatively small minimum investment, built-in property management, limited

financial liability, the opportunity to diversify and the same tax benefits as sole owners.

11. A careful investor will check out both the properties and the general partners. Do the general partners have a good record in selecting, organizing and managing real estate investments? Are they honest and creditworthy? Are there lawsuits or other legal complaints against them? Regarding the properties, are the income and expense projections accurate and reasonable? Are the properties in sound physical and financial condition? Are they well located? Are they priced right? Are the tax benefits realistic? Is there financial responsibility or liability for the limited partner in the future? Is the limited partner willing and able to stay in the partnership for its full lifespan?

debt but without giving up possession of it, 188

Illiquid asset: an asset that may be difficult to sell on short notice, 266

Illiquidity: the possibility that it may be very difficult to sell on short notice, 83

Immobility of land, 35–36

Implied authority: agency authority that arises from custom rather than expressed agreement, 427

Implied contract: a contract created by the actions of the parties involved, 140

Impound or Reserve account: an account into which the lender places monthly tax and insurance payments, 237

Improvement district: an area that receives the benefits of a special public improvement which is paid for by its residents, 304

Improvements: any form of land development, such as buildings, roads, fences, pipelines, etc., 14–15

Inchoate: inchoate dower interest, 59

Income approach: a method of valuing property based on the monetary returns that a property can be expected to produce, 382, 400–405

Income taxes, 325–29; basis calculation, 326–27; capital gain, 329–30; deductions, 330–31, 562–63; gain on sale calculation, 327; installment sale, 330; investment property, 580–85; lifetime exemption, 329; postponement, 327–29

Incurable depreciation: depreciation that cannot be fixed and simply must be lived with, 399

Independent contractor: one who contracts to do work according to his own methods and is responsible to his employer only as to the results of that work, 481–82

Indestructibility of land, 36

Index rate: the interest rate to which an adjustable mortgage is tied, 295

Indicated value: the worth of the subject property as shown by recent sales of comparable properties, 389

Individuals as lenders, 278–79

Industrial brokerage, 7

Inflation, 557, 566–71; cost-push, 566; demand-pull, 566; monetary, 566–67; real-cost, 567

Inflation guard: an insurance policy endorsement that automatically increases coverage during the life of a policy, 528

Informal reference: to identify a parcel of land by its street address or common name, 21

Innocent misrepresentation: wrong information but without the intent to deceive, 146

Installment contract: a method of selling and financing property whereby the seller retains title but the buyer takes possession while he makes his payments, 172–78, 306–7; financing tool, 206–7; *illustrated contract*, 174–77

Installment sale: the selling of an appreciated property on terms rather than for cash so as to spread out the payment of income taxes on the gain, 330, 584

Insulation *illustrated,* Appendix A

Insulation disclosure, 169

Insurable interest: the insured's financial interest in a property, 532

Insurance, mortgage, 244–51, 254–55; (*see also* **Property insurance; Title insurance**)

Insurance premium: the amount of money one must pay for insurance coverage, 524

Insurance value: value concerned with the cost of replacing damaged property, 411

Interest: compensation allowed by law for the use or forbearance or detention of money, 290; deduction, 330–31, 562; proration, 345–46

Interest rate cap: the maximum interest rate charge allowed on an adjustable loan, 296

Interest rates, effect on loan repayment, 234–36; below-market, 331; factors in determining, 290–91; FHA loan, 247–48; VA loan, 254; (*see also* **Financing methods**)

Interests in land, 43–69; overview *illustrated,* 66

Interim loan: a loan that is to be replaced by a permanent loan, a construction loan, 301–2

Intermediate theory: the legal position that a mortgage is a lien until default at which time title passes to the lender, 189

Internal Revenue Code of 1986, 330–31, 580–85

Internal Revenue Service, 326

Inter vivos trust: a trust that takes effect during the life of its creator, 88